Quality Lesson Plans for Secondary Physical Education

Second Edition

Dorothy B. Zakrajsek, PhD
Ohio State University
Columbus, Ohio

Lois A. Carnes, MEd
Solon City Schools
Solon, Ohio

Frank E. Pettigrew Jr., PhD
Ashland University
Ashland, Ohio

Human Kinetics

Library of Congress Cataloging-in-Publication Data

Zakrajsek, Dorothy.
  Quality lesson plans for secondary physical education / Dorothy B.
Zakrajsek, Lois A. Carnes, Frank E. Pettigrew Jr.—2nd Ed.
      p. cm.
Includes bibliographical references (p.   ).
  ISBN 0-7360-4485-X (Soft Cover)
  1. Physical education and training—Study and teaching (Secondary) 2.
Physical education and training—Curricula. 3. Lesson planning. I.
Carnes, Lois. II. Pettigrew, Frank E., 1950- III. Title.
  GV363 .Z27 2003
  613.7'071'2—dc21   2002013862

ISBN-10: 0-7360-4485-X
ISBN-13: 978-0-7360-4485-1

The Web addresses cited in this text were current as of February 2003, unless otherwise noted.

Acquisitions Editor: Scott Wikgren; **Developmental Editor:** DK Bihler; **Assistant Editor:** Amanda Gunn; **Copyeditor:** DK Bihler; **Proofreader:** Jim Burns; **Permission Manager:** Dalene Reeder; **Graphic Designer:** Robert Reuther; **Graphic Artist:** Yvonne Griffith; **Photo Manager:** Leslie A. Woodrum; **Cover Designer:** Andrea Souflee; **Photographer (cover):** Kevin Fleming/CORBIS; **Art Manager:** Kelly Hendren; **Illustrators:** Gretchen Walters, Tim Offenstein, and Argosy; **Printer:** Total Printing Systems

Human Kinetics books are available at special discounts for bulk purchase. Special editions or book excerpts can also be created to specification. For details, contact the Special Sales Manager at Human Kinetics.

Printed in the United States of America   20   19   18   17   16   15   14   13   12

The paper in this book is certified under a sustainable forestry program.

Human Kinetics
Website: www.HumanKinetics.com

United States: Human Kinetics, P.O. Box 5076, Champaign, IL 61825-5076
800-747-4457
email: humank@hkusa.com

Canada: Human Kinetics, 475 Devonshire Road Unit 100, Windsor, ON N8Y 2L5
800-465-7301 (in Canada only)
email: info@hkcanada.com

Europe: Human Kinetics, 107 Bradford Road, Stanningley, Leeds LS28 6 AT, United Kingdom
+44 (0) 113 255 5665
email: hk@hkeurope.com

Australia: Human Kinetics, 57A Price Avenue, Lower Mitcham, South Australia 5062
08 8372 0999
e-mail: info@hkaustralia.com

New Zealand: Human Kinetics, P.O. Box 80, Torrens Park, South Australia 5062
0800 222 062
e-mail: info@hknewzealand.com

We dedicate this book to our professors at Central Michigan, Kent State, and Ashland Universities, who gave us our foundation in physical education; our colleagues, who enriched our professional lives; and our students, who gave us a reason to learn and write.

—Dorothy Zakrajsek, Lois Carnes, Frank Pettigrew Jr.

Contents

Section IV   Minor Units 401

Section V   **Single-Day Lessons** **599**

Preface

For years secondary physical education teachers sought a serviceable book that communicated fundamental physical education principles in complete and usable units and lesson plans. *Quality Lesson Plans for Secondary Physical Education* was the first book of its kind to respond to that need. This book, the second edition, goes a step further, offering updated and expanded lesson plans, new units, and a greater variety of single-day lessons. In addition, this edition focuses on assessment, offering a new chapter titled "From Grading and Testing to Alternative Assessment" as well as assessment chapters for each physical education unit. Also new to this edition is a CD-ROM, which contains an individualized learning unit for students as well as performance standards and checklists, fitness guidelines, and advocacy materials.

Quality Lesson Plans for Secondary Physical Education, Second Edition will serve as both a resource and an assistant. Primarily designed for physical education teachers in middle schools, junior high schools, and senior high schools, the units and lesson plans provided were created to assist in the development and delivery of high-quality secondary physical education programs.

This book will also be of use to undergraduate students and recreational leaders. Its prepared lessons can serve as instructional models, allowing undergraduates to concentrate on refining teaching and management skills without having to formulate specific physical education content. The organization of units into individual lessons will also help undergraduates, student teachers, and recreation professionals study various aspects of pedagogy (e.g., how to develop sport and other skills, how to break down games and activities into teachable segments, how to incorporate fun and variety in the classroom or recreational setting).

In short, this text systematizes accurate and detailed physical education instruction—including comprehensive sets of skills, practice activities, and games—into complete, sequential daily lessons in both traditional and innovative physical education activities. Such a pedagogical structure greatly simplifies the lesson- and unit-planning process.

How This Book Is Organized

Section I outlines the framework of this book. The first chapter, titled "Introduction to Units and Lessons," outlines the structure of each unit and lesson. The other chapter in section I, new to this edition and titled "From Grading and Testing to Alternative Assessment," focuses on moving teachers from the traditional practice of summative grading and testing to an alternative approach of incorporating ongoing (formative) assessment into the learning experience. This shift leads to better skill development and improved performance in students. After reading this chapter, teachers will also come to understand the importance of authentic outcomes, which encourage students to demonstrate performance in the real-life context of "the game."

Applying the principles of alternative assessment, assessment and resources chapters are included throughout the book—one assessment chapter at the end of section II, and a separate assessment chapter at the end of every unit in sections III and IV. These chapters will solidify teachers' understanding of the assessment process by suggesting ways to incorporate assessment into unit and lesson instruction. Ongoing assessment is much more effective in skill development and performance improvement because it ensures that students learn skills and strategies correctly. It also enables teachers to identify those students who may need more help, or may be more responsive to a different teaching style. Early identification tends to result in improved self-esteem and self-confidence in students, and perhaps more enthusiasm for an activity. In the resources section of these chapters, other sources of activity information (e.g., rules, game variations) as well as suppliers of equipment or other items needed for the activities described in the unit are provided.

The units and lessons in this book are divided into four sections:

- Section II: Fitness Units
- Section III: Major Units
- Section IV: Minor Units
- Section V: Single-Day Lessons

Sections II through IV comprise 2 to 11 units (alphabetized for easy location), each containing 4 to 12 sequential lessons and an assessment and resources chapter. Each lesson teaches students a particular skill, strategy, or movement—or combinations thereof—specific to that unit. Section V comprises 30 lessons that can be taught in a single class period.

Two units are in section II: an aerobic conditioning unit and a weight training and conditioning unit. Lessons in "Aerobic Conditioning" address various aspects of cardiovascular performance, including fitness preassessment, cardiovascular monitoring, aerobics, interval training, and fitness postassessment. Lessons in "Weight Training and Conditioning" cover weight training with handheld and machine weights, conditioning activities using exercise bands and exercise balls, and methods for improving flexibility and building muscular strength and endurance. Many of these lessons are new to this edition and are not found in other secondary physical education books.

Section III includes the more traditional (hence the "major" designation) units of physical education curricula: badminton, basketball, flag football, line dancing (new to this edition), soccer, social and square dancing, softball, tennis, and volleyball. Each unit comprises 10 to 12 lessons. Section IV, "Minor Units," includes 4 to 6 lessons on the less traditional activities such as bowling, disc golf (new to this edition), floor hockey, golf, in-line skating (new to this edition), jumping rope, lacrosse (new to this edition), orienteering, pickleball, team handball, and ultimate Frisbee. Section III and IV units that are new to this edition reflect the current trends in physical education and, thus, will surely be popular with students.

Section V, "Single-Day Lessons," features a wide variety of activities perfect for rainy days or breaks between major or minor unit lessons. Thirty lessons are in this section (many of them new to this edition), each providing an array of activities geared toward skill development, variety, and maximum enjoyment for students. For example, kickball golf (new to this edition), a combination of golf and kickball that develops kicking skills and accuracy, is a highly active game that is played outdoors—a definite perk for students. Climbing wall, also new to this edition and another lesson in section V that can be taught outdoors, offers basic instruction in an increasingly popular sport and reinforces this learning with a variety of challenges—at the same time improving students' muscular strength, balance, coordination, flexibility, and problem-solving skills. These challenges include one-arm climbing, speed climbing, and a combination climb–scavenger hunt.

The appendix contains the warm-up activities suggested in each lesson throughout the book. These warm-ups, selected because they are well-suited for each lesson, are more than conventional calisthenics. Activities such as the crab walk, grapevine step, high jumper, and lateral hops are mixed with traditional stretches, squats, flexibility movements, and strength-building exercises to provide some variety in a comprehensive and varied warm-up regimen for every class period.

Finally, a CD-ROM is included with this edition. Yet another new feature of *Quality Lesson Plans for Secondary Physical Education, Second Edition,* the CD-ROM contains standards and forms for assessing students' performance, fitness charts and guidelines on interpreting these charts, and advocacy materials for promoting physical education to parents, administrators, boards of education, and the community. The CD-ROM also features an individualized learning unit, a credit-based, independent study program that enables students to use community agencies to enrich their secondary physical education experience. Under the direction of a physical education teacher, students using the individualized learning unit will have an opportunity to participate in instructional programs not usually available in a traditional school curriculum, thus increasing student interest and motivation. The principles outlined in the individualized learning unit can be adapted to any of the units in this book. A model based on beginning golf is provided to illustrate the application of individualized learning.

How to Use This Book

Like the first edition of *Quality Lesson Plans for Secondary Physical Education,* this second edition has been designed with practicality and flexibility in mind. The sequential structure of lessons enable quick and simple organization of a physical education unit suitable for any class situation or recreational setting. For example, breaking a unit into separate lessons is especially useful for inexperienced middle and high school students who will need more time to develop sport-specific skills and strategies. To accommodate experienced students, or longer class periods, individual lessons can be combined.

Each unit and lesson can be adapted to augment teaching repertoires, expand the traditional physical education curriculum, and provide a varied and exciting year-long curriculum, thus avoiding having to repeat the same activities year after year. Such flexibility enables the teacher to spend time teaching, not creating lesson plans. For those instructors and recreational leaders who have already amassed myriad lesson- and activity-programming resources, *Quality Lesson Plans for Secondary Physical Edition, Second Edition* can be an excellent library supplement. For those professionals just starting out, this book can be an invaluable guide to creating exciting and interesting lesson plans for students, and can point the way to finding other useful resources.

The lessons and format of this text can be adjusted—both in content and time—to fit any situation. The units, lessons, activities, and skills presented can help to broaden any physical education curriculum and enhance day-to-day lesson planning and delivery. In short, this book is a much-needed resource for secondary physical education teachers, one that the authors hope will enrich the overall quality of secondary physical education.

Effective teaching results from creatively modifying learning conditions for students. We encourage you to use this book in whatever manner is most beneficial.

Credits

Triceps skinfold measurement (pp. 22 and 81)

Adapted, by permission, from The Cooper Institute for Aerobic Research, 1999, *FITNESSGRAM* (Champaign, IL: Human Kinetics).

Shoulder stretch, right side (pp. 24 and 91)

Adapted, by permission, from The Cooper Institute for Aerobic Research, 1999, *FITNESSGRAM* (Champaign, IL: Human Kinetics).

Standards for Healthy Fitness Zone, Boys (p. 77)

Reprinted, by permission, from The Cooper Institute for Aerobic Research, 1999, *FITNESSGRAM* (Champaign, IL: Human Kinetics), 38, 39. © 1992, 1999, The Cooper Institute for Aerobics Research, Dallas, Texas.

Standards for Healthy Fitness Zone, Girls (p. 77)

Reprinted, by permission, from The Cooper Institute for Aerobic Research, 1999, *FITNESSGRAM* (Champaign, IL: Human Kinetics), 38, 39. © 1992, 1999, The Cooper Institute for Aerobics Research, Dallas, Texas.

Trunk Extension (p. 70)

Adapted, by permission, from The Cooper Institute for Aerobic Research, 1999, *FITNESSGRAM* (Champaign, IL: Human Kinetics).

Personal Fitness Record (p. 75)

Adapted, by permission, from The Cooper Institute for Aerobic Research, 1999, *FITNESSGRAM* (Champaign, IL: Human Kinetics).

Class Score Sheet (p. 76)

Reprinted, by permission, from The Cooper Institute for Aerobic Research, 1999, *FITNESSGRAM* (Champaign, IL: Human Kinetics).

Flexed Arm Hang (p. 88)

Adapted, by permission, from The Cooper Institute for Aerobic Research, 1999, *FITNESSGRAM* (Champaign, IL: Human Kinetics).

Shoulder stretch, left side (p. 91)

Adapted, by permission, from The Cooper Institute for Aerobic Research, 1999, *FITNESSGRAM* (Champaign, IL: Human Kinetics).

Pinch grip (p. 622)

Adapted, by permission, from G. Hittingh, 1988, *The climber's handbook*, (Cape Town, South Africa: New Holland Publishers (Pty) Ltd.).

Foot positions (p. 623)

Adapted, by permission, from G. Hittingh, 1988, *The climber's handbook*, (Cape Town, South Africa: New Holland Publishers (Pty) Ltd.).

Cascading (p. 649)

Adapted, by permission, from P. Dauer and R. Pangrazi, 1979, *Dynamics for physical education for elementary school children* (Minneapolis, MN: Burgess Publishing).

Showering (p. 650)

Adapted, by permission, from P. Dauer and R. Pangrazi, 1979, *Dynamics for physical education for elementary school children* (Minneapolis, MN: Burgess Publishing).

Acknowledgments

Our appreciation goes to the following people who assisted us in the preparation of this second edition:

- Sally Helms, line dance instructor and performer, for music and dance suggestions
- David Fitz-Gerald, Tony DiGiovanni, Mark Osgood, and Janice Kampf, high school teachers, for sharing in-line skating ideas
- Amy Pettigrew, Frank Pettigrew's wife, and Ashland University colleagues and students for their support of and contributions to this text
- Dr. Ernest Carnes, Lois Carnes' husband, and Sam and Pam Silva for computer and software assistance

We are also grateful to the Human Kinetics staff, especially Scott Wikgren, DK Bihler, and Amanda Gunn for their guidance in the development of this new edition.

Framework

The first part of any journey is knowing where you're going and how you will get there. The two chapters in this section—"Introduction to Units and Lessons" and "From Grading and Testing to Alternative Assessment"—provide that knowledge, outlining the format, structure, and methodology used in developing this book.

The first chapter outlines the basic structure of the units and lessons found in sections II through V: "Fitness Units," "Major Units," "Minor Units," and "Single-Day Lessons." The second chapter explains the current shift in student evaluation from summative assessment to formative assessment. It also provides suggestions for incorporating formative, alternative assessment into the physical education classroom.

These chapters should be read carefully. With a solid understanding of the structure and premise of this book, you will be better able to use it as a resource when planning your physical education curriculum.

Introduction
to Units and Lessons

This text was developed to provide a comprehensive physical education curriculum for middle and secondary school teachers. Like the first edition of *Quality Lesson Plans for Secondary Physical Edition*, this second edition is structured for practicality in the teaching environment, providing sequential lesson plans that enable efficient organization of physical education units. Sections II through IV—"Fitness Units," "Major Units," and "Minor Units"—contain these lesson plans. Each lesson in the unit sequence teaches a new or more advanced skill or activity. In other words, each subsequent lesson in a unit builds on the previous lesson(s). Lessons are also found in section V, but these are single-day lessons for use as fillers, at the end of a term, or simply some variety amid a long unit.

Each section provides a distinct element of middle and secondary school physical education curriculum. A brief summary of each section follows.

▶ Section II, titled "Fitness Units," contains two units—"Aerobic Conditioning" and "Weight Training and Conditioning"—as well as a separate assessment and resources chapter. When combined, the 6 to 10 lessons in these units offer a well-rounded fitness curriculum with training and conditioning exercises to improve cardiovascular performance and flexibility, and build muscular strength and endurance. Fitness lessons can be taught in sequence as a complete instructional unit or, preferably, interspersed throughout the year (e.g., one lesson taught every few weeks) for an ongoing emphasis on fitness training and conditioning.

Note: The assessment and resources chapter in this section, which is the foundation of lessons 1, 2, 9, and 10 of the aerobic conditioning unit, contains the FITNESSGRAM assessment tools. (A complete description of the FITNESSGRAM can be found in the assessment and resources chapter of section II and on the CD-ROM accompanying this book.)

▶ Section III, "Major Units," contains 9 units, each with 10 to 12 lessons, on traditional physical education activities. These units require fairly elaborate systems for learning individual and team skills, complex playing strategies, and rules. Thus, it is preferable to teach these units in sequence as a complete instructional unit. Once students have mastered the skills and strategies, the final lessons in many of these units can be used throughout the year for review. Each unit in this section concludes with an assessment and resources chapter.

▶ Section IV, "Minor Units," contains 11 units, each with 4 to 6 lessons, on activities not traditionally found in high school physical education curricula. Most of these units do not require proficiency in multiple skills, and the games presented are fairly simple. Because they are shorter in duration, these units are ideal for times throughout the year when class schedules, term breaks, or other activities hinder starting a major unit. As in section III, each unit in this section concludes with an assessment and resources chapter.

▶ Section V, "Single-Day Lessons," contains 30 lessons, each presenting one or more activities that generally can be mastered in a single day. Most of the skills required in these activities use or build on basic movements and fundamental sport skills learned in earlier school years.

To help you navigate each unit and lesson quickly and easily, a consistent format has been used to organize units and lessons. These formats are explained in the rest of this chapter, first the units and then the lessons.

The Units

The units, found in sections II through IV, start with a unit description, or unit opener, which begins with a general description of the sport or activity, including information about its history or development. The following information is also presented:

▶ Equipment—A description of necessary equipment

▶ Unit Organization—Suggestions for teaching the unit as well as an outline of the lessons therein

▶ Social Skills and Etiquette—Conduct and behavior to emphasize or discuss with students as well as suggestions for enforcing proper etiquette

▶ Lesson Modifications—Ways to adapt certain lessons and activities to help students with special needs (e.g., changing the size of the playing area, substituting larger or different types of equipment, eliminating or altering some of the rules, modifying expectations of performance)

▶ Safety—Potential hazards and risks of injury inherent in the unit activities

▶ Rules—The rules and sequence of the game

▶ Terms—Definitions and descriptions of terminology used throughout the unit

▶ General Teaching Cues—Teaching suggestions and cues that apply to all lessons in the unit

Terms and general teaching cues are provided only when necessary. When appropriate, field or court dimensions and figures unique to the sport are also provided in the unit opener.

Section V, "Single-Day Lessons," opens with a modified version of this format. Because these lessons are mini units in and of themselves, no historical or organizational information is presented. Rather, you'll find the following information, relevant to all activities in this section.

▶ Social Skills and Etiquette

▶ Rules

▶ Lesson Modifications

Assessment and Resources Chapters

As introduced in the preface, assessment and resources chapters apply the principles of alternative assessment to teaching a physical education unit. (This is the topic of the next chapter, titled "From Grading and Testing to Alternative Assessment.") The assessments suggested in these chapters provide methods and tools for evaluating students, both during and after the unit. There is one assessment and resources chapter at the end of section II and a separate assessment and resources chapter at the end of every unit in sections III and IV.

Resource listings provide other references on the subject, should more information be needed or desired, including books and articles. In some cases, Web sites and equipment suppliers are also listed when relevant to the unit and an important resource on a particular unit topic. Because the single-day lessons (section V) were designed for a single class period, ongoing assessment is not necessary and, thus, assessment suggestions are not provided in these lessons. When available, resources are listed at the end of each lesson in section V.

The Lessons

After each unit description in sections II through IV is a sequential lesson plan, including 4 to 12 lessons for instruction and review. These lessons as well as the single-day lessons in section V follow the same easy-to-understand, ready-to-use format. Most lessons are intended for between 30 and 60 minutes of class time. Because class periods vary from school to school, however, lessons may have to be modified to fit the time available. Students' skill levels may also vary and, thus, necessitate time adjustments to develop skill proficiency.

Each lesson includes the following information.

▶ Lesson number and title. In most cases, the lesson title also serves as an at-a-glance reference of the skills and topics taught in each lesson.

▶ Purpose. This is a short listing of the lesson's primary objectives—in other words, what students are expected to master.

▶ Facility and Equipment. The first element in this listing is the facility or type of area best suited to the activities in each lesson. The rest of this listing specifies the materials and equipment needed for each lesson activity. Because class size will vary, ratios (e.g., 1 ball per 4 students) are often used. If fewer pieces of equipment are available, adjust the lesson accordingly. For example, increase the number of students per group or team, or use alternate equipment. It is best to use the maximum amount of equipment per activity to maximize student participation. Note: Certain activities in each lesson require preparation before class. When this is the case, an asterisk (*) follows the equipment listing.

▶ Warm-Ups. The warm-ups found in each lesson are related to the lesson activities and are both general and specific. Specific warm-ups prepare the muscles that will be used most frequently during the lesson (e.g., arm circles as a warm-up for a throwing activity). General warm-ups engage the entire body (e.g., jogging, fast walking, jumping rope, jumping jacks) and are important before stretching. (Recent research demonstrates that if muscles are not warmed up before they are stretched, the risk of muscle tears or other injuries is higher. Elevating body or muscle temperature protects muscles and tendons from injuries.) When the lesson does not involve significant cardiovascular activity, the suggested warm-ups are geared toward vigorous aerobic conditioning. Note: Warm-ups may be expanded (see the appendix for other warm-ups) or modified to suit students' or instructional needs.

▶ Skill Cues. This section lists the critical psychomotor elements of each skill involved in the lesson activities. These elements should be presented at the beginning of the lesson, generally in the first activity preceding skill practice, and then used as reminders on proper form, technique, or focus. Note: All lessons do not present skill cues (e.g., when a lesson is offered as a review); they are provided only when appropriate.

▶ Teaching Cues. These are suggestions and explanations teachers may find useful, both in understanding the skills or activities of each lesson and in setting up the learning environment to accommodate the instructional process more effectively. Note: All lessons do not present teaching cues; they are provided only when appropriate.

▶ Safety Tips. These are found only in section V lessons and take the place of the "Safety" heading used on unit openers in sections II through IV.

▶ Activities. The activities are the main part of each lesson, most requiring 30 to 40 minutes of the allotted class time. A series of developmental tasks progressing from the simplest to the most complex, the activities usually begin with some sort of instruction or explanation of the game or basic skills. Each activity can stand alone. Because the component tasks build in complexity as the lesson progresses, however, it is recommended that activities be used in sequence. If class time permits, try to incorporate every activity into a single class period. If student skill levels or class times prohibit completing every activity in one class session, consider spreading the lesson over two or more periods. Note: The time allotment for each activity is a guide; more or less time may be needed to develop an appropriate skill level.

▶ Optional Activities. Some lessons include optional activities. These may be used if more practice is needed before moving to the next activity, while students are waiting for classmates to finish a previous activity, or as substitutes for one or more of the activities. For example, an optional activity may be better suited to younger students or those with different skill levels than the preceding activity. In this case, replace the activity with an optional activity. Because optional activities are just that—optional—the allotted time for optional activities is not included in the 30 to 40 minutes allocated to lesson activities. Likewise, when more optional activities than can be utilized in a single class session are provided, choose among them or carry some over to the next lesson.

▶ Closure. This part of the lesson serves as a review, offering questions for class discussion and teachers' observations about students' understanding, progress, or performance. This type of learning reinforcement is an important part of the teaching process.

Another dimension of closure is a cool-down period. Except in some of the lessons in "Fitness Units," specific cool-down activities are not provided. Nevertheless, allowing the muscles to cool down is important, particularly after strenuous activity. Appropriate cool-down returns blood circulation and breathing rates to normal and decreases the risk of muscle tightness and injury.

Allow time for cooling down when appropriate, either at the end of the lesson or during the lesson closure. For example, while discussing the closure topics and questions, have students sit or stand and slowly stretch the muscles used during the lesson activities (e.g., the arms after throwing activities, the legs after running activities). Students could also lie down after completing the last activity, pulling the knees up to the chest, and hold that position for 1 or 2 minutes. In the case of a heavy exercise session or strenuous activity, slow walking using long steps and dangling the arms freely is one of the simplest ways to cool down. Slow walking can be performed while assembling into a class circle for the lesson closure, or students can simply walk around the gym or playing area a few times. Finally, the slow, stretching activities listed in the appendix may also serve as cool-downs.

▶ Variations. These are found only in section V lessons. Variations can greatly improve a game or activity by increasing challenge and participation or responding to different skill levels.

▶ Resources. These are found only in section V lessons and take the place of the assessment and resources chapters after each unit in sections II through IV.

From Grading and Testing to Alternative Assessment

The purpose of this chapter is to move teachers from the traditional practice of grading and testing students, which typically emphasizes a formal summative evaluation, to an alternative system of integrating various assessment techniques into the learning process. Grading implies the level of student performance by attaching a determinate indicator of what has already been achieved, a summary report. This, in turn, may serve as a motivator for future effort. Alternative assessment, on the other hand, encompasses a variety of evaluation techniques to demonstrate understanding, knowledge, and skill in a context that allows for continued learning and growth. Such alternative assessment techniques should be part of students' everyday learning experiences, with the goal of promoting increased understanding and improvement.

Grading and alternative assessment are linked, particularly at the high school level, but they are also different. Grades are a report of performance level; as such, they usually serve as documentation of learning. Class or overall grades are frequently calculated by averaging a number of different assessment measurements collected throughout the grading period. In the physical education arena, grades are not usually based on a series of performance measures that extends throughout the curriculum. Rather, they reflect one-shot (i.e., overall, comprehensive) assessments that occur at the end of an instructional unit, as shown in the figure. In this model, program effectiveness is determined solely by course expectations developed by the instructor prior to instruction. These usually become inaccurate as unit instruction progresses and do not take into consideration actual student or program outcomes. Course expectations are predictions, whereas outcomes are what actually occurred.

Alternative assessment is an ongoing process of gathering information from multiple sources (e.g., teacher and peer observation, student portfolios and journals) about a

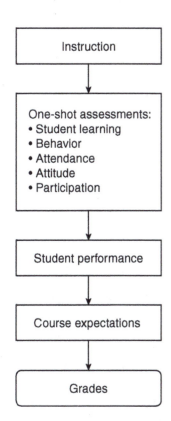

Typical performance-grade exchange system

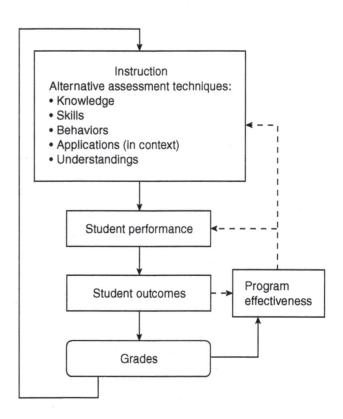

Refocused performance-grade exchange system

student's level of achievement, which is then used by teachers, students, and parents to make educational decisions. The frequent and systematic nature of alternative assessment provides students with continual feedback about their progress, strengths, and weaknesses. Alternative assessment also provides a more comprehensive vehicle for judging the effectiveness of the curriculum, program, and student outcomes as shown in the figure.

The current shift from a traditional emphasis on participation to an emphasis on achievement and accountability has forced teachers and administrators to reexamine their grading policies and practices. Educational reform and performance have come to stress the importance of authentic student outcomes. An outcome is authentic if it requires students to perform in a contextual environment, which necessitates the use of previously learned skills and knowledge. Authentic outcomes are measured through authentic assessment—in other words, allowing students to demonstrate performance in the real-life context of "the game."

Student performance can be assessed in numerous ways, including both formal and informal procedures. Typically, formal assessments are highly structured and do not represent an authentic environment. They measure student performance, but the results cannot be generalized to other environments. Take, for example, the standard badminton skill test of having students serve a badminton shuttlecock into a square for a certain point value. While it does measure a student's mastery of the serve, this measurement lacks context. In other words, without the pressure and excitement of a competitive game, a serving test conducted in isolation is not a genuine measure of how that student will serve during an actual game.

Standards-based educational reform is founded on a curriculum-instruction-evaluation/grading model in which curricular evaluation drives the instructional process, as shown in the common model in the figure. A better process is shown in the suggested model, which reflects an expanded paradigm of curriculum-instruction-assessment-instruction-assessment-evaluation model.

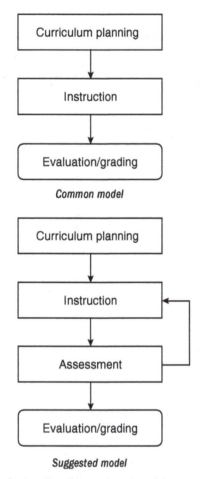

Curriculum planning

↓

Instruction

↓

Evaluation/grading

Common model

Curriculum planning

↓

Instruction

↓

Assessment

↓

Evaluation/grading

Suggested model

Instructional assessment models

This model suggests adaptations in instruction based on assessments conducted formatively throughout the instructional process.

Schools and teachers are also being held more accountable for ensuring that students achieve specified outcomes and for providing evidence of that achievement. Standards-based education demands that teachers choose achievable outcomes, communicate those outcomes, and hold students accountable for their achievement. Thus, teachers are being called on to produce assessment and accountability systems that are aligned with curricular standards and are contextually practical. *Quality Lesson Plans for Secondary Physical Education, Second Edition* offers such a system. The assessments suggested at the end of each unit reflect the shift from summative grading and formal testing to a formative system of alternative assessment. These alternative assessment activities, which reflect the expanded paradigm mentioned earlier, are meant to be conducted throughout each instructional unit, focusing on either authentic or performance outcomes.

To help summarize and to help clarify the assessment techniques described in the next section of this chapter, some terms are presented and defined here:

assessment—The systematic process of gathering and organizing information from multiple sources about student achievement. This information is used by teachers, students, and parents to make educational decisions; to provide feedback about student progress, strengths, and weaknesses; and to judge the effectiveness of the curriculum and instruction.

formative assessment—Assessment that occurs throughout the instructional unit, the intent being that work on the same skill or topic will continue, and thus lead to improvement. Because formative assessment is continual, it allows students to receive information about their ongoing progress and allows teachers to assess the effectiveness of their instruction.

summative assessment—Assessment that takes place at the end of instruction and measures the degree to which instructional objectives have been achieved. Information collected compares student performance to predetermined standards or class performance and is usually used for assigning student grades, but it is also used to evaluate the instructional process itself.

formal assessment—Assessment that is standardized and conducted in isolation. Typically summative, formal assessment often involves the use of the following tools: skill tests, written tests, fitness tests, win-loss records, performance records, and so on.

informal assessment—Assessment used as a learning experience to promote student progress and measure the effectiveness of both instruction and teachers.

alternative assessment—Assessment that involves formative techniques and incorporates assessment into the learning experience. In other words, alternative assessment is part of the instructional process rather than a final evaluative procedure (summative).

authentic assessment—An informal assessment in which students apply previously learned skills and knowledge in context. Assessing student strategies and problem solving during a game and having students plan a fitness program or choreograph a line dance are examples of authentic assessment.

performance assessment—An informal assessment that focuses on performance. This type of assessment usually involves the use of a checklist or rating scale to measure the presence, degree, or quality of critical elements in a motor skill.

The Assessment Process

Essentially, the assessment process consists of gathering and then interpreting information. This information, which relates to the instructional process as well as student performance, can be collected using both formal and informal techniques, as outlined in the figure.

Formal assessment can be both formative and summative, although formal assessments are typically conducted as a summative culmination to an instructional unit. Formal assessment usually involves standardized tests with norm-referenced or criterion-referenced evaluation that enables teachers to interpret and compare student scores. Formal assessment tools, which are usually contrived skill tests performed in isolation and without the context of the game or other genuine settings, measure student performance but cannot be generalized to authentic situations. A putting test at the end of a golf unit (e.g., students are required to putt from varying distances to a predetermined target) is an example of a formal summative assessment to measure putting ability but does not address all the skills necessary in becoming a successful putter (e.g., reading the green, seeing the slope, understanding the contextual environment for each putt).

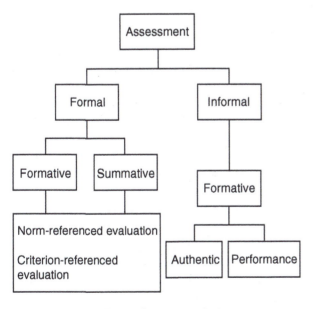

Types of assessment

Formal assessment is used primarily when comprehensive and reliable information is needed. Formal assessment techniques, which supply normative data and standards, are particularly helpful when teachers want to compare students' performances. Formal assessment can also be used periodically throughout an instructional unit to measure student understanding of skill and technique, game rules and strategies, and so on. Formal evaluation can include skill and fitness tests, written tests, performance records, and win-loss records.

Informal assessment incorporates ongoing, formative evaluation into the learning experience with a primary goal of promoting student improvement. This type of assessment is becoming increasingly popular because it focuses on more meaningful, real-life learning and is suitable for all learning environments. Because it is ongoing, informal assessment tends to be more helpful than formal assessment in evaluating the instructional process and curriculum. For example, observing students driving a golf ball and noting aspects of their performance to provide feedback later is an informal means of assessment.

Alternative assessment reflects a shift from the use of traditional, formal, summative evaluation and grading to the use of both: traditional and nontraditional, summative and formative, formal and informal evaluation. It is an ongoing process of gathering information about students' skills, understanding, and performance to promote individual progress and improve instruction.

Authentic assessment, a form of alternative assessment, is usually conducted in real-life, or authentic, situations—for example, the real-life context of a game. Using a checklist to evaluate students' basketball-playing ability, including dribbling, strategizing, teamwork (i.e., passing and blocking), and shooting, is an example of authentic assessment. The other type of informal assessment is performance assessment. A peer-assessment checklist is an example of a performance assessment tool, as is having students assess their progress at free-throwing by shooting on a daily basis and recording their scores in a journal. When used periodically throughout a curriculum, informal evaluation can also include the formal assessment instruments—skill and fitness tests, written tests, performance records, and win-loss records—but it can also include more informal techniques such as observation, student journals and portfolios, and event tasks.

The remainder of this chapter describes various formal and informal, formative and summative assessment techniques and instruments for gathering information about student performance. These tools and techniques can be used in any physical education setting. Ideally, alternative assessment should be used to evaluate students in all areas of physical education. That is, formal and informal assessment techniques should be conducted formatively (i.e., on an ongoing basis) to provide students with feedback on their own performance and to help teachers assess student understanding and progress as well as evaluate the instructional process and curriculum.

The problem with formal grading and testing is that it tends to be summative and provides the student with no opportunity to practice or improve after testing. Usually, the unit is complete. Many of the formal tests (e.g., skill tests) currently used in physical education curricula have a strong relationship to the context of an authentic setting and, thus, can be used in the suggested, alternative assessment model. For example, the putting test described earlier can be incorporated into a putting lesson as a legitimate learning experience, first allowing students to practice their putts and then administering a putting test from predetermined distances. Students then have "real" feedback about their performance and are able to practice on skills to improve.

Assessment Instruments

Before examining each assessment technique in detail, it will be helpful to explore the different types of assessment tools available to the physical education teacher. These instruments can be used in conjunction with many of the assessment techniques explained later in this chapter (e.g., observation, event tasks, self-assessment). The most common assessment instruments include the following:

▶ Checklists
▶ Rating scales
▶ Evaluation forms

In developing and using these tools, teachers should identify critical elements of each skill and watch for those elements, keeping in mind that including too many elements will lead to an inaccurate assessment. Decide how much information can be assessed reliably. Likewise, the assessment criteria should not be so complex that specific elements cannot be isolated and observed.

Checklists

Checklists are used to identify specific behaviors or characteristics of performance, most often to assess motor performance. The elements to be checked off should include all necessary components of a particular skill (e.g., was the student's shooting elbow aligned correctly?). Checklists may also be used as a result measure (i.e., did the student make the free throw?). The disadvantage of using checklists lies in the type of information gathered: a checklist provides only limited information on whether a specific element was demonstrated and often ignores the quality of the performance.

Rating Scales

Rating scales are a step above checklists, identifying specific behaviors and performance characteristics as well as indicating the degree or quality of a selected criterion. Degrees may be assessed numerically (e.g., 1-5), descriptively (e.g., always, sometimes, or never), or by level (e.g., beginning, intermediate, or advanced). A sample rating scale, this one for slow-pitch softball, is shown in the figure.

Completing a rating scale is more complex than checking off criteria on a checklist because it requires both observing the skill and assessing the quality of performance. Thus, the two key advantages of using rating scales are (1) the information gathered is more complete and (2) students are encouraged to focus on the quality of their performance. Rating scales can be used by students and teachers alike.

Rating Scale (Slow-Pitch Softball)				
Skills	Beginning	Intermediate	Advanced	Comments
Throwing				
Catching				
Fielding grounders				
Fielding fly balls				
Batting				
Bunting				
Base running				
Pitching				

Evaluation Forms

An evaluation form is the most complex of the three assessment instruments commonly used. Essentially a multidimensional rating scale used to judge performance or the result of a performance, an evaluation form consists of performance criteria divided into different categories. Evaluation forms can range from simple to complex, the latter including multiple playing levels, multilayered rating scales, and so on. A simple, or general, evaluation form for basketball is shown in the figure. Similar and more complex forms can be developed for different sport activities.

Creating such a multidimensional assessment instrument is often helpful for teachers because it necessitates identifying and isolating different skill components as well as determining an appropriate rating scale for each. When criteria are shared with students before the actual assessment, evaluation forms can also promote good performance.

Assessment Techniques

Following are practical examples and suggestions for incorporating both informal and formal testing into the formative alternative assessment paradigm. These ideas can be used to supplement the formative assessment methods suggested in the assessment and resources chapters in sections II through IV, or to create new formative assessment methods for every instructional unit of a comprehensive physical education curriculum.

Observation

Observation simply involves watching students perform various skills and assessing their performance. The student being assessed can be observed by the teacher, his or her classmates, or both. As such, other assessment techniques described in this section—namely, peer assessment and event tasks—also involve observation.

Evaluation Form (Basketball)

Basketball

Setting: This assessment should be made throughout the entire basketball unit, using a formative assessment process. The criteria included should be observed during game play but can also be used whenever basketball skills are being performed.

Scoring: Rate each criterion using the following scale of 1 to 4. Once all criteria have been rated, total and average the scores if desired.

1 = Always demonstrates consistently	2 = Demonstrates consistently but not always	3 = Demonstrates on occasion	4 = Never demonstrates

Rules, Safety, and Etiquette

❑ Displays good etiquette

❑ Praises teammates and opponents on good play and doesn't get too upset at his or her own performance

❑ Follows the rules of the game

❑ Interprets the rules of basketball accurately

❑ Appropriately selects and uses equipment

❑ Follows safety procedures and does not put players at risk

Basketball Skills

❑ Shoots the ball using the correct stance, movement, technique, and follow-through

❑ Dribbles the ball with control

❑ Can perform a variety of passes and uses them appropriately in a game

❑ Gets into proper rebound position when the ball is shot at the basket

❑ Makes no errors in scoring

Offensive and Defensive Team Play

❑ Demonstrates understanding of and the ability to play zone and person-to-person defense

❑ Knows how to play his or her position offensively on an out-of-bounds play

❑ Knows how to play his or her position defensively on an out-of-bounds play

❑ Understands the basic offensive plays

In addition to on-the-spot feedback (e.g., skill cues), the following tools are generally used in conjunction with teacher observation:

- Checklists
- Rating scales
- Evaluation forms

Peer Assessment

Peer observation and assessment can be a good learning experience for students. Both the performer and the observer learn from the process. To be effective, of course, peer assessment requires that students know what to observe, the correct technique or movement, and

Peer Assessment Form (Basketball)

Student name	# of shots attempted	# of shots completed	# of turnovers	# of rebounds	# of assists
Player 1					
Player 2					
Player 3					
Player 4					
Player 5					

the criteria for assessment. Students should also be taught how to observe, evaluate, record results, and provide feedback.

In addition to on-the-spot feedback, peer observation can also use checklists and rating scales. An example of a peer assessment form for basketball is shown in the figure.

There are no set criteria; students are simply assessed for their performance and given this important feedback. This determines the status of their activity performance and could be done several times to compare performances.

Student Journals

Student journals are like diaries, except they are focused on the physical education setting and are handed in to the teacher. The process of journalizing allows students to record their thoughts, feelings, impressions, perceptions, and attitudes about their physical education experiences on a regular basis. This information enables teachers to personalize physical education and possibly adjust the instructional process if necessary.

Because journals reflect personal feelings, thoughts and impressions, they are not typically graded for content. They can, however, be evaluated with the following criteria:

- Quantity and completeness of entries
- Focus (if designated beforehand)
- Quality and quantity of thought (e.g., responses to questions asked in class)
- Neatness (if desired)

- Ideas or suggestions offered (e.g., extra points or recognition given to students who come up with a usable instructional format or activity)

Teachers should not only collect and review journals on a regular basis but also respond to students' comments. Student journals can be an excellent way to establish a personal dialogue with students and to get an understanding of how students are feeling about the class, the teacher, and their peers.

Portfolios

A portfolio is a collection of student work that documents the student's effort, progress, and achievement of program goals. Before portfolios can be used for assessment, however, criteria and scoring protocols should be developed. For example, a physical education student portfolio might include checklists and rating scales for predetermined program standards, such as fitness scores, skill test results, written projects, and outside or after-school participation in physical activity. Portfolios can be used to record students' work throughout an instructional unit, a term, the full school year, or even several years.

Students should be involved in developing the format of their portfolios. Allowing students to customize their portfolios, or simply be involved in determining the format or structure, produces a feeling of ownership that will induce excitement about the project and produce high-quality work. The types of portfolio formats are numerous. Among the most recent is an electronic portfolio that includes video clips, text, graphics, and scanned photographs. Many computer graphics and word-processing programs on the market can be used to develop student portfolios (e.g., ProSight portfolio software [www.prosight.com], Aurbach and Associates, Inc. portfolio software [www.aurbach.com]).

Event Tasks

Event tasks are informal assessments representing what the student has learned throughout an instructional unit. Providing opportunities for students to use what they have learned is easy to do in the physical education setting; hence, event tasks are a common assessment tool. The key component of event tasks is that students be given the opportunity to use what they have learned in meaningful ways. That means the event tasks should be instruction specific and allow students to demonstrate ability as well as improvement. Building authentic assessment into the mix, event tasks should be performed in the real-life context of a game or other authentic setting whenever possible. After an instructional unit on tennis, for example, authentic assessment would involve skill evaluation (e.g., serving) during a competitive game.

Event tasks are usually assessed using an evaluation form, similar to the basketball form shown earlier, and can be administered by the teacher or students (e.g., one group of students watches while other students play a game). Some examples of events in which this type of assessment can be implemented include games and tournaments, self-choreographed dance and fitness routines, group activities, and fitness and wellness challenges.

Self-Assessment

Assessment can become an educational process in itself when students document their own performance or progress. Self-assessment is important because students should learn to assess and modify their own performance if necessary. Specific to the physical education setting, self-assessment is useful for comparison with program goals or predetermined standards. In general, self-assessment can help students develop the self-discipline that will carry them through a lifetime of setting and achieving personal fitness (or other) goals.

Self-assessment requires students to

- reflect upon their performance,
- learn to compare good against bad performances,
- develop kinesthetic awareness, and
- be able to analyze and correct incorrect technique.

The primary goal of self-assessment is that students learn to monitor their own progress toward achieving identified (program or personal best) goals.

Following are some specific ideas for self-assessment activities using the assessment tools and assessment techniques explained in this chapter:

- Completing a checklist
- Conducting a self-evaluation using a rating scale
- Ranking progress and improvement as they relate to program goals
- Keeping a student log or journal that identifies personal progress and improvement
- Maintaining personal (or class) performance records
- Completing an activity or unit portfolio

Psychomotor Skill Tests

The use of psychomotor skill tests as a means to conducting alternative formative assessment has many possibilities. The best skill tests are those that produce valid and reliable results measurements. For example, many skill tests can be used for formative peer or self-assessment. Used in this way, skill tests such as the putting test mentioned earlier allow students to see and chart their progress over time.

Teachers often cite administration difficulties as one of the main reasons for not administering periodic skill tests. If, however, skill tests are conducted as a formative alternative assessment—for example, if they are built into some of the unit lessons and students are taught how to administer and score the tests for one another or for themselves—numerous skill tests could be given to the entire class in a very short period of time.

Written Tests

Written tests are typically used as a summative assessment technique in all school curricula. This is appropriate in the physical education arena as well. Indeed, the formal, summative written test is still one of the best ways for teachers to assess student understanding of cognitive concepts and general knowledge. Unfortunately, traditional written physical education tests are problematic. True-false, multiple-choice, matching, and short-answer formats are typically used, which often necessitates limiting the testing topics to game or activity rules, procedures, history, and etiquette.

Ideally, written tests could also focus on other, and sometimes more important, information. For example, written tests could be devised that examine whether students understand critical elements of a psychomotor skill. Likewise, students could be asked to identify critical cues for improving performance, or to identify safety issues or explain game tactics and strategies that could improve their team's success.

Although written tests are often daunting for students and teachers alike, they don't have to be. Properly administered written tests do not have to be formal, intimidating, and time consuming. Rather, they can be as simple as a 2- to 5-minute, informal question-and-answer period at the beginning or end of class. Many of the lesson closures in sections II through V of this book include class discussion questions that could be adapted into written tests. Simply read these questions aloud and have students write their answers on paper.

Conclusion

Alternative assessment improves student learning. Because it is formative, students get periodic feedback about their skills, progress, and understanding—assessment that is not possible through strictly summative evaluation methods. Alternative assessment also leaves room for students to develop self-assessment skills, which improve and often augment their own learning process. Formative assessment is also important for the teacher. It identifies and documents student learning and achievement, which can lead to greater accountability in evidencing program goals. Indeed, as standards-based educational reform continues to make accountability a critical factor in schools today, it is becoming imperative that teachers be able to assess and document student learning.

Alternative assessment is an ongoing process, one that differs dramatically from the traditional, one-shot, summative grading techniques. Ideally it is authentic, meaning students actively apply what they've learned to the real-life context of a game or activity. Authentic assessment techniques and ideas are suggested in the unit assessment and resources chapters (sections II through IV) throughout this book. The assessment instruments suggested should be administered formatively—that is, throughout the teaching or learning process as the unit progresses. However, these assessment techniques are merely suggestions; they may be used as they are written, they may be expanded, or they may simply serve as ideas for developing other assessment instruments and protocols.

References

Doolittle, S., and T. Fay. 2002. *Authentic assessment of physical activity for high school students*. Oxon Hill, MD: American Alliance for Health, Physical Education, Recreation and Dance Publications.

Rink, J. 2002. *Teaching physical education for learning*, 4th ed. New York: McGraw-Hill.

Siedentop, D., and D. Tannehill. 2000. *Developing teaching skills in physical education*. 4th ed. Mountain View, CA: Mayfield.

Section II

Fitness Units

Physical fitness is an important element in every physical education curriculum. In light of the contemporary emphasis on promoting a lifetime of wellness, physical fitness should become a priority for every middle and high school student. In *Promoting Better Health for Young People Through Physical Activity and Sports* (2000), the secretaries of the U.S. Health and Human Services and Education departments identify some of the health benefits of exercise. These include increased longevity, reduced heart disease and stress, stronger bones, increased muscular strength and flexibility, and reduced obesity. Fitness has also been linked to positive changes in learning capacity—for example, faster cognitive responses and enhanced retention and memory retrieval.

Physical fitness comprises various components, all of which must be addressed to promote total fitness. The key components are improving cardiovascular endurance and building muscular strength, muscular endurance, and flexibility. These are accomplished through aerobic conditioning and weight training conditioning, the two units in this section.

Section Structure

This section contains two units—"Aerobic Conditioning" and "Weight Training and Conditioning"—as well as an assessment and resources chapter. The lessons in these two units encompass the primary foci of total fitness: improving cardiovascular endurance and building muscular strength, muscular endurance, and flexibility. They can be used over a 2- to 3-week period of instruction or, preferably, stretched out over the school year to facilitate an emphasis on fitness across the curriculum.

The aerobic conditioning unit begins and ends with fitness assessment. Lessons in between concentrate on measuring and improving cardiovascular capacity and performance, including such activities as monitoring heart rate, interval training, pace running, aerobic movement, fitness walking, and circuit training. Lessons in the weight training and conditioning unit concentrate on building muscular strength and endurance as well as flexibility. For example, specific muscle-toning exercises, weight training with handheld weights and weight machines, stretching, and activities using elastic bands and exercise balls are presented.

Each unit is introduced with a brief history of the sport or activity, safety considerations, rules governing game play, suggestions for etiquette, terminology (if relevant), and methods for modifying the lessons. The focus of the lessons in each unit is also explained in the unit introduction. (See "Introduction to Units and Lessons" [page 2] for more information about the structure of units and lessons.)

Only one assessment and resources chapter is included in this section, located after the weight training and conditioning unit. It applies to both the aerobic conditioning and weight training and conditioning units. Featuring the FITNESSGRAM battery of tests, the assessment and resources chapter also provides the FITNESSGRAM healthy fitness zone tables and contains 2 score recording sheets (1 for teachers and 1 for students). The FITNESSGRAM, developed by The Cooper Institute for Aerobics Research in Dallas, Texas, is a widely acclaimed test of health-related fitness that includes a computerized reporting system.

Aerobic Conditioning

Aerobic training activities increase the heart's ability to pump oxygen throughout the body. Oxygen intake, transport, and utilization are all improved through aerobic training. Historically, the terms *cardiovascular* or *cardiorespiratory fitness* were used to describe a physically fit person. Although these terms are synonymous with the word *aerobics,* more recent research has demonstrated that assessing the heart's ability to use oxygen during exercise was the most accurate measurement of fitness. Thus the term *aerobic fitness* has become more widely used.

Unit Organization

This unit consists of 10 lessons that address ways to build and increase cardiovascular health. Following is a brief description of each lesson.

- Lessons 1 and 2 present several options for physical fitness preassessment, using the FITNESSGRAM battery of tests.

- Lesson 3 outlines a means of measuring cardiovascular performance with a step test and a 20-minute walk or run to monitor target heart rate.

- Lesson 4 focuses on monitoring cardiovascular recovery with use of a heart monitor or by taking a pulse.

- Lesson 5 focuses on increasing cardiovascular performance through interval training and pace running.

- Lesson 6 presents another means of increasing cardiovascular performance: aerobic movement.

- Various running activities as well as fitness walking are presented in lesson 7.

- Lesson 8 features the use of obstacle courses, circuit training, and agility runs to build overall physical fitness.

- Lessons 9 and 10 present the same battery of FITNESSGRAM tests as a postassessment measure for determining improvement in physical fitness.

Assessment is the basis of lessons 1, 2, 9, and 10 in this unit because it is important, and thus recommended, to establish baseline fitness scores for each student and then measure improvement in those scores. Accurate baseline scores also enable teachers to identify common areas for improvement among the class, and they enable students to establish personal fitness goals. As noted, the FITNESSGRAM is used for this assessment.

Social Skills and Etiquette

Before starting the lessons in this unit, students should be oriented in class rules and procedures. One reason for setting class ground rules is that fitness assessment can create apprehension in some students. For example, students should be discouraged from comparing fitness scores and performance. Such comparison sets up a competitive dynamic, which can make some students feel deficient, weak, or, worse, inferior. Some of the assessment measures, in particular, can be intimidating for some students. Overweight students, for example, may feel insecure about others seeing their weight or body mass index scores. In these cases, it may be advisable to have students fill out their own personal fitness records or for teachers to record these highly personal measurements privately.

In addition, students should be encouraged to motivate one other. It is best to reinforce this instruction when introducing the fitness lessons. During partner or group activities, for example, encourage students to motivate their partners and group members by providing positive feedback and urging them to achieve more. Fitness goals will differ from individual to individual, but creating a class atmosphere that instills self-confidence and the desire to achieve will enhance individual performance.

Lesson Modifications

It may be necessary to modify certain lesson activities. For example, consider slowing the pace (intensity) or shortening the exercise session (duration) for less-fit students. If certain exercises or tests are too difficult for some students, consider modifying the activity itself. In the preassessment and postassessment lessons, for example, a modified push-up can be substituted for a push-up, a partial curl-up for a curl-up, and so on.

Safety

To prevent injury, several safety factors should be observed in class organization and instruction. Because this unit makes great physical demands on students, be aware of any physical conditions or limitations that may prohibit students' involvement in certain activities. For example, tasks that require near-maximal cardiovascular output (e.g., distance running and aerobics) could be dangerous for students with asthma, cystic fibrosis, or congenital coronary conditions.

Emphasizing the importance of warming up before and cooling down after exercise is also important. Make sure to allow enough time in class. Before doing stretches, students should warm up for a few minutes by jogging or fast walking. (Recent research demonstrates that muscles should be warmed up *before* they are stretched.) Warming up properly helps to protect muscles and tendons from tears and injury, and cooling down helps to reduce muscle soreness and prevent lightheadedness after exercise.

Terms

aerobic—Literally, "living or occurring in the presence of oxygen." Aerobic movement or exercise is an activity or a series of activities performed strenuously enough to increase heart rate and respiration but not so strenuously that it results in an oxygen debt (called *anaerobic*).

aerobic fitness—An indication of the heart's ability to recover from vigorous exercise. Aerobic fitness is a component of overall (physical) fitness and is sometimes called *cardiovascular fitness*.

aerobics—A system of physical conditioning that involves aerobic exercise (e.g., running, walking, swimming).

caliper—An instrument used to measure the thickness of an area of skin and subcutaneous fat by gently pinching a portion of the skinfold.

duration—The amount of time spent exercising, usually defined by the total time per session.

fitness walking—A style of fast walking in which the arms are swinging vigorously up and down while the body keeps a good posture.

frequency—The number of exercise or activity sessions, usually defined by the number per week.

heart rate recovery—The amount of time it takes the heart to return to a nonexercising heart rate. This is contingent on the heart's ability to intake, transport, and utilize oxygen efficiently, which is also a measure of aerobic fitness.

heart zone—A target range of heart rates that approximate 70 to 85 percent of a person's average maximum heart rate.

intensity—The amount of exercise completed in a specific period of time or how "hard" a person exercises.

maximum heart rate—Calculated as 220 minus a person's age, the maximum heart rate is theoretically the highest heart rate of 100% capacity.

overload—A way to improve the capacity of the muscles, heart, or lungs by increasing frequency, duration, or intensity of exercise.

skinfold—A portion of skin and subcutaneous fat that can be gently pinched for caliper measurement. Typical measurement sites include under the triceps, the calf, the abdomen, and so on.

Lesson 1

Physical Fitness Preassessment I

Purpose

This lesson is the first day of physical fitness preassessment. It uses three batteries of FITNESSGRAM tests: (1) skinfold measurements or body mass index; (2) the curl-up; and (3) the push-up, pull-up, modified pull-up, or flexed-arm hang. (For a detailed description of each test, see the assessment and resources chapter at the end of this section as well as the CD-ROM accompanying this book.)

Facility and Equipment

- Gym or outdoor area with a smooth surface
- See pages 79-91 for testing equipment
- 1 personal fitness record (see page 75) per student
- 1 pencil per group

Warm-Ups (6-8 Minutes)

1. Running in place
2. Imaginary jump rope
3. Leg lifts
4. Achilles tendon stretch
5. Arm rotators

Skill Cues

1. Grasp the skinfold between the thumb and index finger before using the calipers to measure it.
2. For the curl-up, keep the feet flat on the floor with the knees slightly bent.
3. For the push-up, keep the back and legs straight.
4. In the modified pull-up, use only the arms to pull the body up.
5. For the pull-up and flexed-arm hang, be sure the palms are away from the body.

Teaching Cues

1. This first day of preassessment measures body composition as well as upper body and abdominal strength. Lesson 2, "Physical Fitness Preassessment II," measures flexibility, muscular and aerobic endurance, and musculoskeletal strength. If desired, the order of lessons 1 and 2 can be reversed.
2. The FITNESSGRAM tests presented in this lesson measure the following components of physical fitness:
   - ▸ Body composition: skinfold measurements or body mass index
   - ▸ Abdominal strength: curl-up
   - ▸ Upper body strength: push-up, modified pull-up, pull-up, or flexed-arm hang
3. Skinfold measurements will likely require supervision.

4. Mass testing can be used for the curl-up. Pair up students or have them choose partners. One partner performs the test while the other records scores; then partners switch roles.

5. Preassessment is recommended to ascertain students' baseline scores. Participation in the aerobic conditioning unit should improve postassessment scores (see lessons 9 and 10).

6. The FITNESSGRAM suggests testing modification for special-needs students (see the CD-ROM accompanying this book).

7. A detailed description of all FITNESSGRAM tests, as well as the equipment needed for each, can be found in the assessment and resources chapter at the end of this section.

8. To keep students active while they wait to be tested, create practice stations for other preassessment tests. For example, you could set up pull-up bars and back-saver sit and reach boxes (see lesson 2). Practice will help some students perform better on certain tests.

Activities (30-40 Minutes)

1. Set up three testing stations, one for each test battery. Present the components of each test chosen for this lesson, emphasizing the proper skill cues. Explain the FITNESSGRAM healthy fitness zones (see the tables in the assessment and resources chapter, pages 77-78). (6-8 minutes)

2. Divide the class into three groups. Assign or have students elect a leader for each group to record student names, ages, and test scores using the personal fitness record (see page 75). Administer the following three preassessment test batteries. After each group has completed the first test, students rotate to a different testing station. (24-32 minutes)

   ▸ Skinfold measurements or body mass index

   ▸ Curl-up

   ▸ Push-up, pull-up, modified pull-up, or flexed-arm hang

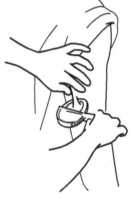

Triceps skinfold measurement

Closure (3-5 Minutes)

Review and discuss the lesson with students. Use the following ideas to reinforce learning, check understanding, and provide feedback.

1. Discuss how students can use their results from today's tests (e.g., to determine what areas of fitness they most need to work on).

2. Ask students to set and then write down personal goals for fitness achievement throughout the unit.

Physical Fitness Preassessment II

Purpose

This lesson is a second day of physical fitness preassessment. As in lesson 1, FITNESSGRAM tests are used, but on this day three different test batteries are offered: (1) the trunk lift; (2) the back-saver sit and reach or shoulder stretch; and (3) the 1-mile (1.6-kilometer) walk or run or PACER. (For a detailed description of each test, see the assessment and resources chapter at the end of this section as well as the CD-ROM accompanying this book.)

Facility and Equipment

◆ Gym or outdoor area with a smooth surface
◆ See pages 79-91 for testing equipment
◆ 1 personal fitness record (see page 75) per student
◆ 1 pencil per group

Warm-Ups (6-8 Minutes)

1. Slapping jacks
2. Side pattern jumps
3. Waist twists
4. Leg stretch
5. Seated hamstring stretch

Skill Cues

1. For the trunk lift, keep the toes pointed, the hands under the thighs, and the body in a prone position.
2. For the back-saver sit and reach, keep the foot flat against the end of the box.
3. When doing the 1-mile (1.6-kilometer) walk or run, keep a steady pace to conserve energy for a faster final lap.
4. During the PACER, run the early laps slowly, thus conserving energy for the faster pace to come in later laps.

Teaching Cues

1. This second day of preassessment measures flexibility, muscular and aerobic endurance, and muscular strength. If desired, the order of lessons 1 and 2 can be reversed. (Lesson 1, "Physical Fitness Preassessment I," measures body composition as well as upper body and abdominal strength.)
2. The FITNESSGRAM tests presented in this lesson measure the following components of physical fitness:
   ▶ Aerobic capacity and endurance: 1-mile (1.6-kilometer) walk or run or PACER
   ▶ Trunk extensor strength and flexibility: trunk lift
   ▶ Flexibility: back-saver sit and reach or shoulder stretch

3. Preassessment is recommended to ascertain students' baseline scores. Participation in the aerobic conditioning unit should improve postassessment scores (see lessons 9 and 10).

4. The FITNESSGRAM suggests test modification for special-needs students (see the CD-ROM accompanying this book).

5. A detailed description of all FITNESSGRAM tests, as well as the equipment needed for each, can be found in the assessment and resources chapter at the end of this section.

Activities (30-40 Minutes)

1. Set up three testing stations, one for each test battery. Present the components of each test chosen for this lesson, emphasizing the proper skill cues. Explain the FITNESSGRAM healthy fitness zones (see the tables in the assessment and resources chapter, pages 77-78). (6-8 minutes)

2. Divide the class into three groups. Assign or have students elect a leader for each group to record student names, ages, and test scores using the personal fitness record (see page 75). Administer the following three preassessment test batteries. After each group has completed the first test, students rotate to a different testing station. (24-32 minutes)

   ▶ Back-saver sit and reach or shoulder stretch

   ▶ 1-mile (1.6-kilometer) walk or run or PACER

   ▶ Trunk lift

**Shoulder stretch,
right side**

Closure (3-5 Minutes)

Review the lesson with students. Use the following ideas to reinforce learning, check understanding, and provide feedback.

1. Discuss how students can use their results from today's tests (e.g., to determine what areas of fitness they most need to work on).

2. Ask students to set and then write down personal goals for fitness achievement throughout the unit.

Measuring Cardiovascular Performance

Purpose

In this lesson students measure cardiovascular performance by monitoring their heart rates during a step test and a 20-minute walk or run.

Warm-Ups (6-8 Minutes)

1. Running in place
2. Quadriceps stretch
3. Hamstring straight-leg stretch
4. Shoulder pushes
5. Achilles tendon stretch

Facility and Equipment

- Gym or outdoor running track
- Stopwatch
- 1 12-inch (30.5-centimeter) step, bench, or stool per 2 students
- 1 Heart Rates Following the Step Test table per 2 students (or 1 posted prominently)
- 1 Target Heart Rates table per 2 students (or 1 posted prominently)
- 1 heart rate monitor per 2 students (if available)
- Music or metronome (if desired)

Skill Cues

1. Measure the radial artery pulse at the wrist using the index and middle fingers.
2. For the best step test performance, firmly plant the foot flat on the step, bench, or stool.
3. To maximize energy during the 20-minute walk or run, keep a steady pace.

Teaching Cues

1. Explain to students that the step test is used to determine aerobic fitness, which indicates the heart's ability to recover from vigorous exercise and is a sign of fitness. The step test is based on the premise that recovery time from vigorous exercise is a valid measure of cardiovascular condition.
2. Have students warm up for 6 to 8 minutes to reduce stiffness, improve cardiovascular performance, and reduce the risk of injury.
3. It may be helpful to use music or a metronome to set the pace of the step test. Select music with a cadence of (or set the metronome to) 96 beats per minute.
4. Use the 20-minute walk or run to introduce fitness training. Explain that the results of exercise are maximized by following these guidelines:
   - Frequency: 3 to 5 times per week
   - Intensity: in the target zone (see Target Heart Rates table)
   - Duration: 20 or more minutes per exercise session

Explain that training at an intensity below the target zone will not produce as great an effect as training at an intensity within the target zone.

4. Be sure to allow enough time to cool down; 3 to 5 minutes is recommended. Adequate cool-down promotes faster recovery from fatigue, keeps blood flowing through working muscles, stabilizes blood pressure, reduces the possibility of dizziness, and allows the heart rate to decrease slowly.

5. For special-needs students who cannot complete the step test, modify the height of the step, slow the tempo, or shorten the duration of the test.

Activities (38-45 Minutes)

1. Present the methods of measuring cardiovascular performance, emphasizing the appropriate skill and teaching cues. (1-5 minutes)

2. Pair up students or have them select partners. One student takes the step test while his or her partner counts step cycles. Then the other student takes the step test. (6 minutes)

Step Test

The step test lasts 3 minutes. (Be sure to keep the time accurately.) Students should perform 24 4-step cycles (i.e., up, up; down, down = 1 cycle) in 1 minute. If music or a metronome is used, a step should be taken on every beat.

Step test sequence

3. After completing the test, students should immediately count their pulse rates for 1 minute (use heart monitors if available) and then compare their results to the table shown here. (3-4 minutes)

4. Explain the following Target Heart Rates table and have students calculate their average maximum heart rates and their target zones. (Average maximum heart rate = 220 – age. Target zone = average maximum heart rate × 70 to 85%; use 85% for high-intensity exercise such as interval training, 70% for low-intensity exercise such as slow walking.) If heart monitors are not available, teach students to measure pulse (i.e., count it for 10 seconds and multiply by 6). (5 minutes)

5. Have students walk or run for 20 minutes, maintaining a heart rate within the target zone (see the Target Heart Rates table). Be sure to have them pause briefly every several minutes to monitor their heart rates (if using heart monitors) or take a pulse. (20 minutes)

HEART RATES FOLLOWING THE STEP TEST

Subject	Excellent	Good	Above average	Average	Below average	Fair	Poor
Male	81	99	103	120	123	127	136
Female	79	94	109	118	122	129	137

Data from *Y's Way to Physical Fitness: Fitness Specialist Training Notebook* by L. Golding, C. Meyers, and W. Sinning, 1989, Chicago: YMCA of the USA.

TARGET HEART RATES

Age	Target zone*	Average maximum heart rate**
10	147-178	210
11	146-177	209
12	145-176	208
13	144-175	207
14	144-175	206
15	143-174	205
16	142-173	204
17	142-172	203
18	141-171	202
19	140-170	201

*Target zone = 70 to 85% of average maximum heart rate

**Average maximum heart rate = 220 – student age

6. Have students walk for 3 to 5 minutes as a cool-down. After the 20-minute walk or run, it is best not to sit down immediately. The cool-down period is also a good indicator of exertion level. If breathing and heart rates have not returned to normal within 5 minutes, the exercise session required too much exertion. For most students, normal breathing rates are between 12 and 16 breaths per minute; normal heart rates are below 120 beats per minute. These ranges can differ by individual, however. (3-5 minutes)

Closure (3-5 Minutes)

Review the lesson with students. Use the following ideas to reinforce learning, check understanding, and provide feedback.

1. Discuss the importance of warming up and cooling down. (Warm-up prevents muscle pulls and gives the cardiovascular system a chance to increase performance gradually. Cool-down reduces muscle soreness and prevents light-headedness.)

2. Discuss students' step test scores and encourage students to use their test results as a motivator for starting a cardiovascular conditioning program.

Lesson 4

Cardiovascular Monitoring of Recovery Time

Purpose

In this lesson students learn how to measure heart rate recovery time after an activity, and how to record and graph the results.

Warm-Ups (6-8 Minutes)

1. Agility run
2. Hamstring conditioners
3. Forward lunges
4. High jumper
5. Toe lifts

Facility and Equipment

◆ Gym or outdoor running track; indoor or stadium stairs
◆ 1 sheet of graph paper and pencil per student
◆ Stopwatch
◆ 1 jump rope per student
◆ 1 heart rate monitor per student (if available)

Skill Cues

1. Measure the radial artery pulse at the wrist using the index and middle fingers (if heart monitors are not available).
2. Training at an intensity below the target zone will not produce as great a training effect as training within the target zone.

Teaching Cues

1. Explain to students the importance of heart recovery rate as a measure of fitness.
2. If no heart monitors are available, show students how to measure their heart rates manually: count the pulse at the radial artery for 10 seconds and multiply it by 6.
3. Be sure to allow enough time for warm-ups because the activities in this lesson require a lot of ballistic stretching.
4. This lesson can be repeated at the end of the school year to determine if cardiovascular recovery time has improved.

Activities (30-40 Minutes)

1. Present the appropriate skill and teaching cues to record and monitor heart rate recovery time. (3-4 minutes)
2. Have students put on heart monitors and record the resting heart rate. If heart monitors are not available, take pulse at the radial artery. (3-4 minutes)
3. Start the clock and have students jump rope for 5 minutes. They should record their heart rates immediately after jumping, then at 1-minute intervals until heart rate drops 40 beats. Call out 10-second increments so that students can record their heart rate recovery times. (7-8 minutes)

4. Have students run four 100-meter sprints. They should record their heart rates immediately after sprinting, then at 1-minute intervals until heart rate drops 40 beats to determine heart rate recovery time. (6-8 minutes)

5. Have students climb stairs for 5 minutes. They should record their heart rates immediately after climbing, then at 1-minute intervals until heart rate drops 40 beats to determine heart rate recovery time. (6-8 minutes)

6. Have students chart their heartbeat patterns, including

   ▸ resting heart rate;

   ▸ maximum heart rates after jumping rope, sprinting, and stair climbing; and

   ▸ heart rate recovery times. (5-8 minutes)

Closure (3-5 Minutes)

Review the lesson with students. Use the following ideas to reinforce learning, check understanding, and provide feedback.

1. Discuss the physiological reasons for faster heart rate recovery in physically fit students (i.e., the heart's ability to intake, transport, and utilize oxygen increases with fitness. Exercise lowers blood pressure, which results in a more efficient vascular system).

2. Have students identify which activity most increased heart rate. Why?

Lesson 5

Interval Training

Purpose

In this lesson students will increase cardiovascular performance with interval training.

Warm-Ups (6-8 Minutes)

1. Reverse run
2. Step and calf taps
3. Curl and stretch
4. Waist twists
5. Inverted hurdler's stretch

Facility and Equipment

◆ Gym or outdoor area with a smooth surface
◆ Stopwatch
◆ 1 jump rope per student

Note: A 400-meter track is preferable for this lesson; use cones if no track is available.

Skill Cues

Running

1. Do not move the head up and down during the stride.
2. To improve form, pump the arms (as though punching).
3. Push off with the rear leg.
4. For efficiency, "float" after the push-off (i.e., the body becomes airborne) and then touch down on the outside of the rear foot.

Walking

1. Contact the surface with the heel first, then roll to the toe.
2. Push off with the toes.
3. Point the feet forward.
4. Rotate the hips to increase stride length.
5. Straighten the support leg.
6. Keep one foot in contact with the ground (i.e., no floating).

Jumping Rope

1. For maximum aerobic conditioning results, take 70 to 80 steps per minute.
2. Land on the balls of the feet with the knees slightly bent.

Teaching Cues

When introducing this lesson's activities, explain the following to students:

1. Interval training can build cardiovascular endurance.
2. Exercising with short recovery periods between builds stamina because the intensity of the overall workout can be greater.

3. Endurance can be further improved by maintaining (or increasing) the duration of the work interval while shortening the rest interval.

Activities (30-40 Minutes)

1. Present the interval training method of increasing cardiovascular performance, emphasizing the skill and teaching cues. (2-5 minutes)

2. Have students run 400 meters, walk 200-meters as a recovery, and then run 400 meters followed by a 200-meter walk again. Repeat for four cycles. The runs (400 meters) should take approximately 1.5 minutes and the recovery period (200-meter walking) should take approximately 2.5 minutes. (16-20 minutes)

3. Have students jump rope to reach their target heart zone (80-85% of maximum heart rate). This should take approximately 2 minutes. When they reach their target zone, students should begin a rest interval of walking to reach a heart rate of 120 beats per minute. Recovery should not take more than 2 minutes. Continue the interval training for two cycles. (8-11 minutes)

4. After the interval training, bring students together to cool down (e.g., walking or mild stretching). (4 minutes)

Jumping rope

Closure (3-5 Minutes)

Review the lesson with students. Use the following ideas to reinforce learning, check understanding, and provide feedback.

1. Discuss the advantages of interval running (e.g., it builds cardiovascular fitness and endurance because the recovery periods enable a greater workout intensity).

2. Give students an assignment to write a journal entry describing the lesson and the types of aerobic activities they participated in during class. If they do not have journals, this would be an opportunity to begin them.

Lesson 6

Aerobic Movement

Purpose

In this lesson students will increase cardiovascular performance with aerobic exercise.

Warm-Up (0 Minutes)

The warm-ups for this lesson are included in the aerobics routine.

Skill Cues

1. To reduce impact when jumping, land on the balls of the feet and bend the knees slightly.
2. Keep aerobic movements smooth; avoid jerky motions.
3. Gently extend the neck and back during motion, avoiding hyperextension.

Facility and Equipment

◆ Gym or outdoor area with a smooth surface
◆ Music and player (CD or audiocassette)
◆ 3 aerobics videotapes, VCRs, and monitors

Note: Choose music with a steady beat, preferably a 4-count rhythm. (Moving to irregular beats is too difficult.) Ideally, compile a CD with music of varying tempos: slow tempos for the warm-up, fast tempos for the aerobic phase, and slow tempos for the cool-down.

Aerobics videotapes are available through most physical education equipment vendors.

Teaching Cues

1. To keep students motivated about fitness, and to emphasize the purpose of this lesson, choreograph an aerobics routine that involves more than just dance activities. The routine should utilize all components of fitness (see the suggested routine in "Activities"):
   - Muscle endurance
   - Muscular strength
   - Flexibility
   - Cardiovascular conditioning

   The aerobics routine should also include the following phases:
   - Warm-up phase (6-8 minutes) to reach a target heart rate (i.e., target zone)
   - Aerobic phase (15-20 minutes) to sustain a target heart rate
   - Cool-down phase (5 minutes) to recover

   Extend or reduce the length of the routine based on students' cardiovascular fitness levels.
2. Beginners and less-fit students should sustain the aerobic phase for as long as they can, rest, and then continue after recovery.
3. If you decide to extend this lesson to another class period—you may want to involve students in choreographing an aerobics routine, for example—activity 4 can be amended. Expand the activity to have each group rotate to a different aerobics video after performing the routine.

Activities (35-55 Minutes)

1. Show students how to increase cardiovascular performance and maximize the results of aerobic movement, emphasizing the skill and teaching cues. Scatter students around the gym so that everyone can see the aerobics leader and have enough room to move. (2-6 minutes)

2. Begin the warm-up phase of the routine. (6-8 minutes)

   The suggested warm-up phase includes the following warm-ups from the appendix:

   ▸ Scissors (1-2 minutes)
   ▸ Triceps stretch (1 minute)
   ▸ Arm pumps (1.5 minutes)
   ▸ Side stretch (1.5 minutes)
   ▸ Mad cat (1-2 minutes)

3. Begin the aerobic phase of the routine. (15-20 minutes)

   The following exercises, most of which are warm-ups from the appendix, are suggested:

   ▸ Scissors (1 minute)
   ▸ Running in place while doing shoulder shrugs (1.5 minutes)
   ▸ Single-leg curls (1.5 minutes)
   ▸ Hopping on each foot two times (1-2 minutes)
   ▸ Floor touches (1 minute)
   ▸ Sit and curl (1 minute)
   ▸ Alternate leg raises (1-2 minutes)
   ▸ Side slides (1 minute)
   ▸ Step touches (1.5-2 minutes)
   ▸ Elbow-knee touches (standing) (1-2 minutes)
   ▸ Step and calf taps (1.5-2 minutes)
   ▸ High jumper (1-2 minutes)
   ▸ Waist twists (1 minute)

4. Begin the cool-down phase of the aerobics routine. (5 minutes)

   A suggested cool-down could include the following movements, all found in the appendix:

   ▸ Hamstring straight-leg stretch (1 minute)
   ▸ Upper body rotations (1 minute)
   ▸ Sit and stretch (1.5 minutes)
   ▸ Hamstring curls (1.5 minutes)

5. Set up three aerobics stations (one station for each VCR, monitor, and aerobics videotape). Divide the class into three groups, and scatter each group around a monitor (at least 10 feet [3.05 meters] away). Have each group perform an aerobics routine. (7-16 minutes)

Closure (3-5 Minutes)

Review the lesson with students. Use the following ideas to reinforce learning, check understanding, and provide feedback.

1. Give students the written assignment of choreographing an aerobics routine. Review the three phases of an aerobics routine: the warm-up, aerobic, and cool-down phases.

2. Discuss the goals of executing an aerobics routine (i.e., cardiovascular conditioning is most important, followed by flexibility and strengthening).

Lesson 7

Fitness Walking and Running

Purpose

In this lesson students will increase their cardiovascular performance with running and fitness walking.

Warm-Ups (6-8 Minutes)

1. Horizontal run
2. Russian floor kicks
3. Upper body rotations
4. Abdominal curls

Skill Cues

Running

1. Do not move the head up and down during the stride.
2. To improve form, pump the arms (as though punching).
3. Push off with the rear leg.
4. For efficiency, float after the push-off (i.e., the body becomes airborne) and then touch down on the outside of the rear foot.

Fitness Walking

1. Contact the surface with the heel first, then roll to the toe.
2. Push off with the toes.
3. Point the feet forward.
4. Rotate the hips to increase stride length.
5. Straighten the support leg.
6. Keep one foot in contact with the ground (i.e., no floating).
7. Swing the arms up and down vigorously.
8. Use good posture when fitness walking.

Teaching Cues

1. Have students warm up and cool down after running and fitness walking.
2. Make sure students avoid the following running mistakes:
   ▶ Wide arm swings
   ▶ Hunched shoulders
   ▶ Striding too far apart
   ▶ Landing on the heels

▸ Running on the toes

3. To achieve a target heart rate, increase the intensity of fitness walking by having students swing the arms vigorously and carry handheld weights or wear wrist weights. (Beginners should achieve 70 to 75% of maximum heart rate, advanced fitness walkers should achieve 80 to 85% of maximum heart rate; see lesson 3 for more information on determining target heart rate.)

4. If available, students should wear pedometers to measure the distance of their walk. Pedometers are worn on the waist and count steps by sensing the vertical motion within each step.

5. Watch for and correct the following fitness walking mistakes:

   ▸ Swinging arms to the side

   ▸ Watching the feet

   ▸ Slumping

   ▸ Clenching the hands and teeth

   ▸ Overreaching the step

Activities (30-40 Minutes)

1. Pair up students or have them choose partners. (Be sure paired students have similar cardiovascular fitness levels.) Present the methods of increasing cardiovascular performance, emphasizing the skill and teaching cues (also see lesson 5). (5-8 minutes)

2. Have students line up at the starting cone. One partner begins in the lead and sets the pace for the other partner who runs behind. When lead partners reach the first cone, their partners sprint past to assume the lead position. At the next cone, partners reverse positions again, and so on. (5-7 minutes)

   Optional Activity: Running Catch or *Optional Activity: Sprint-to-Lead Drill*

3. Have student partners fitness walk, preferably on an outdoor path. To have a positive impact on cardiovascular fitness, students should walk at least 15 minutes. (15-20 minutes)

4. Have student partners take an easy walk for 5 minutes to cool down. (5 minutes)

Optional Activities

Running Catch (0-10 Minutes)

Pair up students or have them choose a partner (of similar running ability). Partners run beside each other along a quarter-mile (.4-kilometer) running course, tossing a tennis ball back and forth. (To keep in stride and catch the ball, students receiving the ball should remain slightly ahead of students throwing the ball. Thus, students should sprint ahead after throwing to be ready for the catch.)

Sprint-to-Lead Drill (0-10 Minutes)

Divide the class into four groups according to cardiovascular fitness levels and have each group line up at the start of a quarter-mile (.4-kilometer) course. (Use a shorter course for less-fit students and a longer course for fit students.) Space the groups far enough apart that students can run beside the line as they move forward. Students begin running in line. The last student sprints to the front of the line to become the leader. After the new leader is in place, the student who is now at the end of the line sprints to the front to become the next leader. This pattern continues until each student group completes the course.

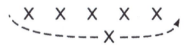

Sprint-to-lead drill

Closure (3-5 Minutes)

Review the lesson with students. Use the following ideas to reinforce learning, check understanding, and provide feedback.

1. Discuss the mistakes to avoid when running and fitness walking (e.g., landing on the heels, running on the toes, watching the feet, slumping and hunching).

2. Assign 20 minutes of fitness walking, either outdoors or indoors, before the next class session.

Lesson 8

Fitness Activities

Purpose

This lesson teaches students to build muscular strength, muscular endurance, flexibility, agility, and cardiovascular endurance with fitness activities, including circuit training and an agility run.

Warm-Ups (6-8 Minutes)

1. Running in place
2. Side lunges
3. Mule leg pushes
4. Hip rolls
5. Side slides

Skill Cues

1. In the obstacle course and the agility run, change direction quickly and smoothly.
2. When sprinting, raise the knees high and land on the balls of the feet.
3. When running, lean forward slightly and use opposition (i.e., swing the arms so that the right arm swings forward as the left leg strides and the left arm swings forward as the right leg strides).
4. For chin-ups, the palms should be toward the body.

Facility and Equipment

- Gym or outdoor area with a smooth surface
- 15 to 20 cones
- 4 chairs
- 8 tires
- 2 benches
- 6 hoops
- 2 large gymnastics mats
- 1 chin-up bar
- 5 or 6 jump ropes
- Music and player (CD or audiocassette)
- 1 aerobics videotape, VCR, and monitor
- Stopwatch
- Whistle

Note: This equipment list will provide for 1 obstacle course, 1 agility course, and 1 circuit-training course. More courses will require more equipment.

Teaching Cues

1. Have students warm up and cool down before and after all fitness activities.
2. Point out the following fitness principles to students:
   - ▷ Overload the muscles to build muscular strength and endurance.
   - ▷ Overload the muscles by increasing frequency, intensity, duration, or a combination of these.

      Reach a target heart rate between 70 and 85% of the maximum heart rate (see lesson 3 for information about determining maximum heart rate).
   - ▷ Recovery from vigorous exercise should be evident within 5 minutes (see lessons 3 and 4 for information about recovery).
   - ▷ Improve flexibility through muscle stretching that increases the range of motion.
   - ▷ Hold a stretch 15 to 30 seconds to effectively lengthen a muscle.
   - ▷ Cross-training will increase muscular strength, muscular endurance, flexibility, and cardiovascular endurance more evenly.

3. Use the equipment suggested to set up an obstacle course and an agility course before class. For more variety, use different equipment (e.g., hurdles, balance beams).

4. Use music during circuit training to keep students motivated.

Activities (30-40 Minutes)

1. Present ways to improve total fitness, emphasizing the skill and teaching cues. These components are muscular strength, muscular endurance, flexibility, agility, and cardiovascular endurance. (3-5 minutes)

2. Divide the class in half. Each half should line up behind the start of either the obstacle course or the agility course. After completing one course, student groups change places and complete the other course, spending 3 to 7 minutes on each. (7-15 minutes)

Obstacle Course

The focus of the obstacle course is to improve flexibility and cardiovascular endurance. Students form a line and begin staggered starts through the course. When they complete the course, students automatically begin again, thus keeping their cardiovascular rates elevated. Students must run as they move to each obstacle. For more variety and challenge, have them move backward through various parts of the course.

A suggested obstacle course could contain benches for hurdling, chairs to run around, tires to crawl through and jump in, cones to jump over, and hoops for running in and out.

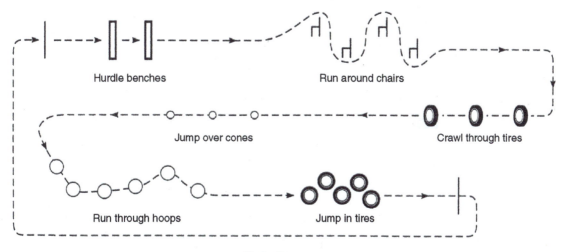

Hurdle benches Run around chairs

Jump over cones Crawl through tires

Run through hoops Jump in tires

Obstacle course

Agility Course

The focus of the agility course is to increase cardiovascular endurance and to be able to change direction quickly and easily. Students form a line and begin staggered starts through cones set up in a zigzag pattern. When they complete the run, students automatically begin again, thus keeping their cardiovascular rates elevated.

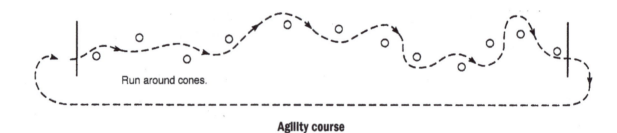

Agility course

The course illustrated here contains only cones, but hoops, chairs, or benches can also be used.

3. Set up a six-station circuit-training course. Divide students into six groups and have each group line up at a different station. Students remain at the station and continue the activity there until the signal. Students then rotate to the next station, complete the training, and then rotate to the next (approximately 2.5 minutes per station). Circuit training ends when students have completed all the stations. (15 minutes)

The goal of circuit training is to promote muscular strength, muscular endurance, flexibility, agility, and cardiovascular endurance. A suggested circuit-training course might include the following activities:

- ▶ Station 1: Aerobics routine (videotape)
- ▶ Station 2: Sit-ups on mats
- ▶ Station 3: Reverse runs using cones
- ▶ Station 4: Push-ups on mats
- ▶ Station 5: Jumping rope
- ▶ Station 6: Chin-ups on chin-up bar

4. Have students walk around the perimeter of the gym to cool down. (5 minutes)

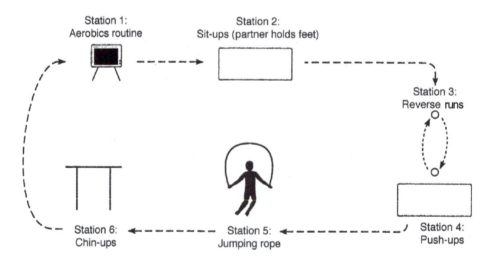

Circuit-training course

Closure (3-5 Minutes)

Review the lesson with students. Use the following questions and ideas to reinforce learning, check understanding, and provide feedback.

1. Ask students to identify the fitness components of each circuit-training station. The components are as follows:
   - Aerobics: cardiovascular endurance and flexibility
   - Sit-ups: abdominal strength and endurance
   - Reverse runs: agility
   - Push-ups: upper arm and shoulder strength
   - Jumping rope: cardiovascular endurance
   - Chin-ups: upper arm and shoulder strength
2. Give students the written assignment of designing their own obstacle course, using a variety of equipment to enhance flexibility and cardiovascular endurance.

Lesson 9

Physical Fitness Postassessment I

Purpose

This lesson presents the first day of physical fitness postassessment to determine improvements in physical fitness performance after participation in the aerobic conditioning unit. The FITNESSGRAM test batteries used in this lesson are the same as those used in lesson 1 (see page 21): (1) skinfold measurements or body mass index; (2) curl-up; and (3) push-up, pull-up, modified pull-up, or flexed-arm hang.

Facility and Equipment

◆ Gym or outdoor area with a smooth surface
◆ See pages 79-91 for testing equipment
◆ 1 personal fitness record (see page 75) per student
◆ 1 pencil per group

Warm-Ups (6-8 Minutes)

1. Reverse runs
2. Sit and stretch
3. Waist twists
4. Leg lifts

Skill Cues

1. Grasp the skinfold between the thumb and index finger before using the calipers to measure it.
2. For the curl-up, keep the feet flat on the floor with the knees slightly bent.
3. For the push-up, keep the back and legs straight.
4. In the modified pull-up, use only the arms to pull the body up.
5. For the pull-up and flexed-arm hang, be sure the palms are away from the body.

Teaching Cues

1. As in lessons 1 and 2, the order of lessons 9 and 10 can be reversed.
2. Compare postassessment with preassessment physical fitness scores to determine students' progress after completing the fitness units. Analyze the test results to assess the effectiveness of the fitness units and to prescribe continued fitness development.
3. The FITNESSGRAM tests presented in this lesson measure the following components of physical fitness:
   ▶ Body composition: skinfold measurements or body mass index
   ▶ Abdominal strength: curl-up
   ▶ Upper body strength: push-up, modified pull-up, pull-up, or flexed-arm hang

4. Skinfold measurements will likely require supervision.

5. Mass testing can be used for the curl-up. Pair up students or have them choose partners. One partner performs the test while the other records scores; then partners switch roles.

6. The FITNESSGRAM suggests testing modification for special-needs students (see the CD-ROM accompanying this book).

7. A detailed description of all FITNESSGRAM tests, as well as the equipment needed for each, can be found in the assessment and resources chapter at the end of this section.

8. To keep students active while they wait to be tested, create practice stations for other postassessment tests. For example, you could set up pull-up bars and back-saver sit and reach boxes (see lesson 2). Practice will help some students perform better on certain tests.

9. If possible, provide a computer printout of the preassessment and postassessment results. You might also send the results to parents.

Activities (30-40 Minutes)

1. Set up three testing stations, one for each test battery. Present the components of each test chosen for this lesson, emphasizing the skill and teaching cues. Explain that the results will measure improvement in fitness levels and performance. (3-5 minutes)

2. Divide the class into three groups. Assign or have students elect a leader for each group to record student names, ages, and test scores using the personal fitness record (see page 75). (Use the same record used for the preassessment tests in lesson 1.) Administer the following three postassessment test batteries. After each group has completed the first test, students rotate to a different testing station. (27-35 minutes)

   ▸ Skinfold measurements or body mass index

   ▸ Curl-up

   ▸ Push-up, pull-up, modified pull-up, or flexed-arm hang

Closure (3-5 Minutes)

Review the lesson with students. Use the following ideas to reinforce learning, check understanding, and provide feedback.

1. Have students compare their test results from lesson 1 and analyze their progress. If students did not make progress in a certain area, determine whether or not the principles of fitness (e.g., duration, intensity) were applied.

2. Discuss the importance of continuing a lifelong fitness program and prescribe methods students can use to continue their quest for physical fitness.

Lesson 10

Physical Fitness Postassessment II

Purpose

This lesson presents the final day of physical fitness postassessment to measure improvement in physical fitness after participation in the aerobic conditioning unit. The FITNESSGRAM test batteries used in this lesson are the same as those used in lesson 2 (see page 23): (1) trunk lift; (2) back-saver sit and reach or shoulder stretch; and (3) 1-mile (1.6-kilometer) walk or run or PACER.

Facility and Equipment

- ◆ Gym or outdoor area with a smooth surface
- ◆ See pages 79-91 for testing equipment
- ◆ 1 personal fitness record (see page 75) per student
- ◆ 1 pencil per group

Warm-Ups (6-8 Minutes)

1. Scissors
2. Quadriceps stretch
3. Shoulder pushes
4. Triceps stretch

Skill Cues

1. For the trunk lift, keep the toes pointed, the hands under the thighs, and the body in a prone position.
2. For the back-saver sit and reach, keep the foot flat against the end of the box.
3. When doing the 1-mile (1.6-kilometer) walk or run, keep a steady pace to conserve energy for a faster final lap.
4. During the PACER, run the early laps slowly, thus conserving energy for the faster pace to come in later laps.

Teaching Cues

1. As in lessons 1 and 2, the order of lessons 9 and 10 can be reversed.
2. Compare postassessment scores with preassessment scores to determine students' progress after completing the fitness units. Analyze test results to assess the effectiveness of the fitness units and to prescribe continued fitness development.
3. The FITNESSGRAM test batteries presented in this lesson measure the following components of physical fitness:
   - ▶ Aerobic capacity and endurance: 1-mile (1.6-kilometer) walk or run or PACER
   - ▶ Trunk extensor strength and flexibility: trunk lift
   - ▶ Flexibility: back-saver sit and reach or shoulder stretch

4. The FITNESSGRAM suggests test modification for special-needs students (see the CD-ROM accompanying this book).

5. A detailed description of the FITNESSGRAM as well as equipment needed can be found in the assessment and resources chapter at the end of this section.

6. If possible, provide a computer printout of the preassessment and post-assessment results. You might also send the results to parents.

Activities (30-40 Minutes)

1. Set up three testing stations, one for each test battery. Present the components of each test chosen for this lesson, emphasizing the skill cues. Explain that the results will measure improvement in fitness levels and performance. (3-5 minutes)

2. Divide the class into three groups. Assign or have students elect a leader for each group to record student names, ages, and test scores using the personal fitness record (see page 75). (Use the same record used for the preassessment tests in lesson 2.) Administer the following three postassessment test batteries. After each group has completed the first test, students rotate to a different testing station. (27-35 minutes)

   ▸ Back-saver sit and reach or shoulder stretch

   ▸ 1-mile (1.6-kilometer) walk or run or PACER

   ▸ Trunk lift

Closure (3-5 Minutes)

Review the lesson with students. Use the following ideas to reinforce learning, check understanding, and provide feedback

1. Have students compare their test results from lesson 2 and analyze their progress. If students did not make progress in a certain area, have them set goals for developing their difficult area(s).

2. Discuss the importance of continuing a lifelong fitness program and prescribe methods students can use to continue their quest for physical fitness.

Weight Training and Conditioning

It was in the early 1800s that Alan Calvert developed a weightlifting system using weighted plates attached to bars. Barbells consisted of a long bar held by both hands with the weight on each end, while dumbbells were two shorter bars with weights for use in each hand. In the 1930s, DeLorme and Wadkins, two physical therapists, were successful in using weight training to rehabilitate military personal for arm and leg injuries. As weight training grew in popularity, researchers began studying its effects and developed sound information about how to build strength, power, and muscle mass. Many weight training myths were dispelled with the research. With the increased interest and information about weight training came the development of weight machines. These machines provided more safety, more controlled motion, and less opportunity for lifting and lowering incorrectly. Handheld as well as machine weights continue to be an excellent way to improve sport performance and build strength, power, and muscle mass.

Equipment

Basic equipment for weight training and conditioning includes gymnastics mats and weights, either handheld or machine weights. Because this equipment can be expensive, it is recommended that a weight room be used if available. For serious weight trainers or experienced students, a good set of weights is recommended. For beginning or younger students, basic weights can be used. Handheld weights can vary greatly in cost and quality. Basic weights usually consist of a steel bar with round end weights. Higher quality sets may be made of chrome, have hexagonal end weights that do not roll, be coated with rubber, have additional holes in the end for easy carrying, or have contoured handles for more comfort to the hands.

Unit Organization

This unit consists of six lessons addressing ways to build muscular strength and endurance as well as flexibility.

- ▶ Improving muscle tone through specific exercises that build muscular strength and endurance is the focus of lesson 1.
- ▶ Lessons 2 and 3 offer other means of developing muscular strength: weight training with handheld weights and weight machines.
- ▶ Lessons 4 and 5 feature the alternative conditioning methods of using exercise bands and exercise balls.
- ▶ Lesson 6 addresses developing flexibility through muscular stretching.

Social Skills and Etiquette

Before starting the lessons in this unit, students should be oriented in class rules and procedures. One reason for setting class ground rules is that weight training and conditioning can cause apprehension in some students. For example, students should be discouraged from comparing performance. Such comparison sets up a competitive dynamic, which can make some students feel deficient, weak, or, worse, inferior.

Students should also be encouraged to motivate one other. During partner or group activities, for example, encourage students to motivate their partners and group members by providing positive feedback and urging them to achieve more. Weight training and conditioning goals will differ from individual to individual, but creating a class atmosphere that instills self-confidence and the desire to achieve will enhance individual performance.

Lesson Modifications

It may be necessary to modify certain activities in these unit lessons. Potential modifications for less-fit students include reducing repetitions (frequency), slowing down the pace or reducing the load (intensity), and shortening the exercise session (duration). Likewise, consider increasing the frequency, intensity, or duration for fit students. Activities that are simply too difficult for less-fit and younger students should be eliminated.

Safety

To prevent injury, several safety factors should be observed in class organization and instruction. Because this unit makes great physical demands on students, be aware of any physical conditions or limitations that may prohibit students' involvement in some activities. Likewise, certain movements can be dangerous and should be avoided. For example, arching the neck or flexing a joint excessively can result in injury. When students are using weights, be sure to explain proper technique and form beforehand.

The following safety precautions are recommended:

▷ Students should train gradually—that is, they should build on the various fitness components by incorporating them slowly. This can be accomplished by progressively increasing the frequency, intensity, and duration of exercise sessions.

▷ Be sure to emphasize the importance of warming up before and cooling down after exercise, and make sure you allow enough time in class. Before doing warm-up stretches, students should jog or walk quickly. (Recent research demonstrates that muscles should be warmed up *before* they are stretched.) Warming up properly helps to protect muscles and tendons from tears and injury, and cooling down helps to reduce muscle soreness and prevent lightheadedness after exercise.

▷ When possible, attend sports medicine workshops and read the trade literature to stay current on trends and medical discoveries, including contraindicated exercises.

▷ Post safety rules and proper techniques around the gym or facility.

Terms

barbell—A long bar with weights on the ends that is grasped by both hands.

bilateral flexibility—Equal flexibility on both sides of the body.

contraction—Tightening a muscle either to shorten (isotonic), or tense it (without any movement of the muscle [isometric]).

duration—The amount of time spent exercising, usually defined by the total time per session.

exercise ball—A sphere used for building muscle groups such as triceps, biceps, abdominals.

exercise band—Elastic ropes that are used to provide resistance to the targeted muscles. They are available in different thicknesses, which increase or decrease the resistance.

frequency—The number of exercise or activity sessions, usually defined by the number per week. *Frequency also refers to the number of repetitions.*

handheld weights or dumbbells—Small bars with weights on each end that can be used in pairs (one in each hand).

hyperextension—Overextending a joint or body part beyond its normal extension point.

hypertrophy—An increase in the size of muscle fiber.

intensity—The amount of work completed in a specific period of time or how "hard" the person exercises.

overload—Improving the capacity of the muscle by increasing the frequency, duration, or intensity with which a person exercises with weights.

repetitions—The number of times an exercise or activity is repeated. For example, performing a dead lift 10 times in succession would constitute 10 repetitions, also called *reps*.

session—One workout period.

set—One string of reps followed by a rest interval.

static stretch—A slow stretch followed by a hold.

wrist weights—Weights worn on the wrist. Wrist weights are typically light, ranging from 1 to 3 pounds (.45 to 1.36 kilograms) and are fastened to the wrists by a Velcro or other strap.

Lesson 1

Building Muscular Strength and Endurance

Purpose

In this lesson students will improve muscle tone with specific exercises that build muscular strength and endurance.

Facility and Equipment

◆ Gym
◆ 1 gymnastics mat per student
◆ 1 record (sheet) per student
◆ 1 pencil per 2 students
◆ Poster board and markers
◆ Stopwatch

Warm-Ups (6-8 Minutes)

1. Running in place
2. Shoulder stretch
3. Side stretch
4. Step and calf taps
5. Gluteal stretch

Skill Cues

1. For the sit and hold, lean against the wall while bending the legs at a 90-degree angle.
2. For the curl and hold, sustain the body at a 45-degree angle, like a sit-up position.
3. For the wall push-away, keep the body straight and bend from the elbows.

Teaching Cues

1. Explain that body tone results from overloading the muscles. Increasing frequency (how often), intensity (load and resistance), and duration (length of workout) strengthens the muscle targeted by the exercise.
2. Point out the distinction between building muscular endurance and muscular strength: performing more repetitions with less resistance builds muscular endurance; performing fewer repetitions with more resistance builds muscular strength.
3. Have students work the large muscles first. If the smaller muscles are exercised first and the body begins to fatigue, the student may not be able to handle the heavier load required of larger muscles. Smaller muscles are easier to exercise when tired.
4. Students should work opposite muscles in sequence. For example, they should work the quadriceps with the hamstring muscles, or biceps with triceps. This approach produces muscle balance and reduces the risk of injury.
5. Students should move slowly and steadily during static stretching, avoiding quick, explosive movements.
6. Be sure students use a full range of motion so that the muscles being worked do not lose flexibility.

7. Allow enough time for warm-up and cool-down.

8. The tests in this lesson measure muscular strength in the lower, middle, and upper body.

9. Before class, construct three large charts using poster board and post these charts around the gym. Each chart should describe specific exercises for developing muscle tone in the upper body, the middle body, and the lower body. Suggested exercises for each body area include the following (see the appendix for a description of each exercise):

   ▶ Upper body (chest, shoulder, biceps, and triceps): push-ups, triceps stretch, arm isometrics, crab walk, arm rotators

   ▶ Middle body (waist, abdominals, and back): curl-ups, leg lifts, elbow-knee touches (supine), mad cat, hip lifts

   ▶ Lower body (hips, thighs, buttocks, and calves): slapping jacks, step touches, high jumper, running in place, quadriceps stretch, mule leg pushes

Activities (30-40 Minutes)

1. Explain the importance and requirements of achieving body tone, emphasizing the skill and teaching cues. (5-8 minutes)

2. Pair up students or have them choose partners. One partner takes the following series of challenges while the other keeps track of time (or repetitions) for each task and records the results. After one partner completes the entire series of challenges, partners switch roles and the other repeats the tasks. (8-11 minutes)

Curl and Hold

Lie down with the knees bent at a 90-degree angle (feet are *not* held by the partner) and the wrists crossed over the chest. Raise the head, shoulders, and upper body to a 45-degree angle; then hold. Partners record the length of time the curl position is held; a good score is 25 seconds or more.

Curl and hold

Wall Push-Away

Stand at arm's length from the wall. Place the hands on the wall with fingers pointing up. Take two steps away from the wall to reach the starting position. Bend the arms to bring the chest near the wall, keeping the body straight. Quickly push away from the wall, returning to the starting position. Partners record the number of wall push-aways performed in 1 minute; a good score is 40 or more.

Wall push-away

Sit and Hold

Lean against a wall with the back straight and the knees bent 90 degrees (like a sitting position). Hold this position. Partners record the length of time this position can be held; a good score is 1 minute or more.

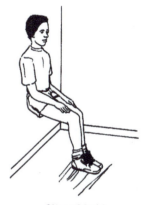

Sit and hold

3. Divide the class into three groups and have each group line up at a different chart. Each student should work through the chart exercises. After 4 or 5 minutes, the groups rotate to another chart. After students have completed each chart, they may move to another chart of their choosing for an additional workout. (12-16 minutes)

4. Have students walk around the gym to cool down. (5 minutes)

Closure (3-5 Minutes)

Review the lesson with students. Use the following ideas to reinforce learning, check understanding, and provide feedback.

1. Ask a few students to explain to the rest of the class what activities they could use to build weak abdominals, improve poor upper arm strength, or increase flexibility.

2. Give students a written assignment to list which muscle groups they need to tone and what methods they will use to do so. Encourage creativity in designing these exercise programs.

Lesson 2

Weight Training With Handheld Weights

Purpose

In this lesson students will increase muscular strength with weight training using handheld weights.

Warm-Ups (6-8 Minutes)

1. Jump rope or jump rope laps
2. Quadriceps stretch
3. Single-leg crossovers
4. Side stretch
5. Shoulder pushes

Facility and Equipment

- Indoor or outdoor area with a smooth surface
- 1 set of 3-pound (1.36-kilogram) handheld weights per student
- 1 jump rope per student
- Poster board and markers
- Stopwatch

Skill Cues

1. Keep the back straight when using weights.
2. Move the weights through a full range of motion.
3. Move slowly and gently when using weights.
4. Minimize momentum. Make the muscle work; do not allow the weight to travel on its own.
5. Hold at full muscle contraction.
6. Pay attention to the lowering phase of the movement.
7. Maximize the workout by varying the order, number of sets, and combination of repetitions and sets.

Teaching Cues

1. To reduce the risk of injury, be sure students warm up the muscles by running or jumping rope before weight training.
2. Explain how to build muscular strength (i.e., more weight and fewer repetitions). This also results in hypertrophy, or an increase in muscle size.
3. Explain how to develop muscular endurance (i.e., less resistance and more repetitions).
4. Tell students that they should work out with weights at least 3 to 4 times per week to produce a measurable change in body tone, strength, or endurance.
5. Explain the differences between the various resistance exercises in activity 2 (e.g., presses, curls, rows).
6. Consider making a wall chart that lists relevant skill and teaching cues. In addition, make separate wall charts that list safety protocol as well as the mechanics of each exercise explained in activity 2.

Activities (30-40 Minutes)

1. Present the methods of increasing muscular strength with handheld weights, emphasizing the skill and teaching cues. Be sure to go over any safety precautions that should be observed when using weights. (3-5 minutes)

2. Provide each student with a set of handheld weights. Demonstrate and then have students execute the following resistance exercises. Provide a 2-minute rest between exercises. (27-35 minutes)

Back Lateral Raise

Stand with the feet shoulder-width apart. Hold the weights in each hand with the palms at the thighs and lean forward. Slowly lift the weights straight up (i.e., behind the back) to shoulder level; then lower them slowly.

Side Lateral Raise

Stand with the feet shoulder-width apart and the weights held down at the sides, palms down. Lift the weights out and up, and hold; then lower them slowly.

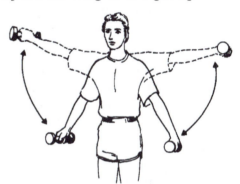

Side lateral raise

Military Press

Stand with the feet shoulder-width apart and the weights held above the shoulders (i.e., on either side of the head), palms away from the body. Without locking the elbows or arching the back, raise the weights straight up; then lower them slowly.

Shoulder Press

Stand with the feet shoulder-width apart and the weights held above the shoulders (i.e., on either side of the head), palms toward the head. Without locking the elbows or arching the back, raise the weights straight up; then lower them slowly.

Military press

Chest Press

Lie face up with the knees bent, holding the weights just above the chest, palms up (i.e., away from the body). Extend the arms straight up, pushing the shoulders up to follow the direction of the hands; then slowly return the weights to the chest.

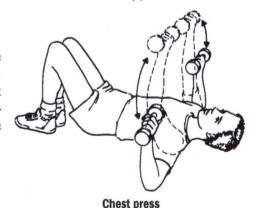

Chest press

Pull-Over

Lie face up with the knees bent, holding the weights on the thighs, palms down. Bring the weights up and overhead until they almost touch the floor above the head; then slowly return the weights to the thighs.

Chest Fly

Lie face up with the knees bent. Hold the weights out to each side, palms up. Raise the arms overhead, keeping them straight; then lower them slowly.

Swim With Weights

Standing with a weight in each hand, palms toward the body, imitate a front crawl stroke.

Weighted Arm Rotators

Standing with a weight in each hand, palms toward the body, rotate the arms in forward circles at either side of the body; then reverse the motion, rotating in the opposite direction.

Double Biceps Curls

Stand with the shoulders down and hold the weights at the sides, palms away from the body. Flex the arms, bringing both weights up to the shoulders; then lower them slowly.

Single Biceps Curls

Stand with the shoulders down and hold the weights at the sides, palms away from the body. Flex the arms and bring one hand up to the chest and then down; then lift the other hand.

Triceps Curls

Stand holding one weight in both hands. Raise the weight overhead and lower it slowly behind the head and upper back. Raise the weight to just above (but in back of) the head; then lower it slowly.

Single biceps curl

Lateral Dumbbell Row

Standing with a weight in each hand, bend at the waist and keep the arms straight (the weights should almost touch the floor). One arm at a time, lift the weight up, toward the biceps, while bending at the elbow; then lower it slowly.

3. Bring the class together for an easy jog to cool down. (5 minutes)

Closure (3-5 Minutes)

Review the lesson with students. Use the following questions and ideas to reinforce learning, check understanding, and provide feedback.

1. Ask students to explain how weight training to build muscular strength would differ from weight training to improve muscular endurance (i.e., use more weight and fewer repetitions to develop strength, less weight and more repetitions to develop endurance).

2. Discuss the mechanical elements of building muscle with handheld weights. (Examples of mechanical principles used in handheld weights include third-class levers [biceps curl], the law of inertia [encompasses all handheld weight skills], and Newton's second law [encompasses all handheld weight skills].)

Lesson 3

Weight Training With Machines

Purpose

In this lesson students will increase muscular strength with machine weight training.

Facility and Equipment

◆ Weight room or gym with weight machines
◆ Variable resistance or weight training equipment (e.g., Nautilus, Hammer Strength, Cybex)

Warm-Up (6-8 Minutes)

Run or jump rope for 6 to 8 minutes to warm up the muscles before using the weight equipment.

Skill Cues

1. Work the large muscles first, then the smaller muscles.
2. The lowering phase should be slower than the lifting phase of the lift.
3. Pause between the lowering and lifting phases, and between lifts.
4. Exhale while lifting; inhale while lowering.
5. Set the machine for enough weight to perform 2 or 3 sets each of 8 to 12 repetitions.
6. Keep the body aligned; do not twist.
7. Rest 48 hours between training sessions. This gives the small muscle fibers time to heal after each session.

Teaching Cues

1. Students should work the large muscles (e.g., quadriceps, hamstrings) first, then the smaller muscles (e.g., wrist flexors, gastrocnemius).
2. Have students rest a few minutes between each machine.
3. Remind students not to tense the face, hands, or other muscles when exercising a particular muscle group. Only that one group should be tensed.
4. If safety rules are not posted in the facility, explain these precautions to students before starting the activities.
   ▶ Perform exercises on resistance machines slowly and controlled to prevent injury to muscles, tendons, and joints.
   ▶ Check machine for frayed cables, worn pulleys, or broken welded areas.
   ▶ Adjust levers and seats for the body size.
   ▶ Never place hands between weight stacks or by belts or pulleys.
   ▶ Fasten seat belt.

Activities (30-40 Minutes)

1. Present the skill and teaching cues needed at each weight machine. (3-5 minutes)

2. Demonstrate each weight machine. Students should execute a complete set of resistance exercises at the following machines. Allow for several minutes of rest between each machine. (27-35 minutes)

Leg Extension Machine

Targeted muscles: quadriceps. Sitting at the machine, with the back against the machine base, place the feet behind the rollers and extend one leg. Hold; then return the leg to the starting position. Do 8 to 12 repetitions; then repeat with the other leg.

Leg Curl Machine

Targeted muscles: hamstrings. Lying face down on the machine, place both feet under the rollers and grasp the handles. Bring the rollers up toward the buttocks, allowing the hips to raise only 2 inches (5.1 centimeters). Hold; then return to the starting position. Do 8 to 12 repetitions.

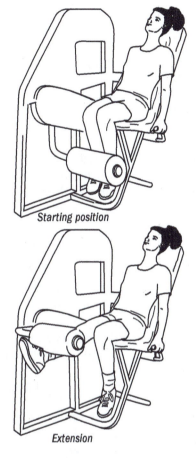

Starting position

Extension

Leg extension

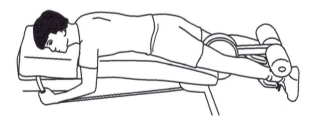

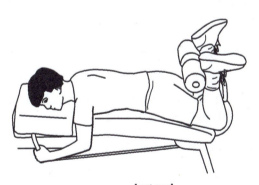

Leg curl

Abductor Machine

Targeted muscles: gluteus maximus. Sit at the machine and grasp the handles. Using the force of the thighs, press outward against the machine. Hold; then return to the starting position. Do 8 to 12 repetitions.

Adductor Machine

Targeted muscles: adductors. Sit at the machine and grasp the handles. Push inward, using the thighs, to resist the force of the machine. Hold; then return to the starting position. Do 8 to 12 repetitions.

Lateral Pull-Over Machine

Targeted muscles: latissimus dorsi. Sitting at the machine, bring the arms overhead and place the fingers on the crossbar and the elbows in the pads. Release the foot plate and bring the crossbar down. (Use the elbows, not the hands, to draw the crossbar down.) Hold; then return to the starting position. Do 8 to 12 repetitions.

Lateral Pull-Down Machine

Targeted muscles: trapezius. Sitting at the machine, reach up and pull the bar down. Hold the handles and lean forward, keeping the elbows straight. Pull the crossbar behind the neck. Hold; then return to the starting position. Do 8 to 12 repetitions.

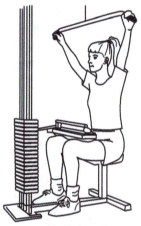

Starting position

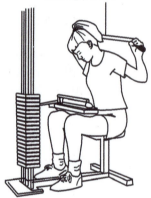

Pull-down

**Lateral
pull-down**

Rowing Torso Machine

Targeted muscles: trapezius and deltoids. Sitting at the machine, place the arms through the rollers and cross the forearms. Push the rollers back as far as possible, bringing the shoulder blades together. Hold; then return to the starting position. Do 8 to 12 repetitions.

Lateral Raise Machine

Targeted muscles: deltoids. Sitting at the machine, grasp the handles and push out and up with the elbows so the arms are parallel to the floor. Hold; then return to the starting position. Do 8 to 12 repetitions.

Arm Cross Machine

Targeted muscles: trapezius and pectorals. Sitting at the machine, place the forearms against the pads and hold the handles. With the forearms, press toward the center of the chest. Hold; then return to the starting position. Do 8 to 12 repetitions.

Bench Press Machine

Targeted muscles: pectorals, deltoids, and triceps. Lie down on the bench with the knees bent and the feet flat. Placing pressure on the handles, begin to lift the weights off the stack. Press the handles up and extend the arms without locking the elbows. Hold; then return to the starting position. Do 8 to 12 repetitions.

Military Press Machine

Targeted muscles: biceps and triceps. Sitting at the machine, place the hands on the handles, palms up. Press the handles up and extend the arms without locking the elbows. Hold; then return to the starting position. Do 8 to 12 repetitions.

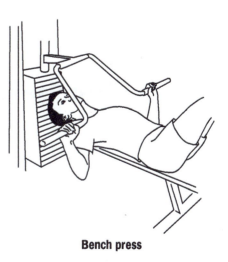

Bench press

Triceps Machine

Targeted muscles: triceps. Sitting at the machine, place the elbows on the pad and the hands in the grip, palms facing each other. (The shoulders will be lower than the elbows.) Extend both arms at the same time, without locking the elbows. Hold; then return to the starting position. Do 8 to 12 repetitions.

Biceps Machine

Targeted muscles: biceps. Sitting at the machine, place the elbows on the pad and the hands in the grip, palms up. Pull the hands up halfway to the shoulders. Lower the handles, keeping the elbows slightly bent; then curl the handles back until the hands almost touch the ears. Hold; then return to the starting position. Do 8 to 12 repetitions.

Closure (3-5 Minutes)

Review the lesson with students. Use the following ideas to reinforce learning, check understanding, and provide feedback.

1. Discuss the mechanics of using machines to develop muscular strength (e.g., variable resistance, levers).
2. Have students identify a "problem area" they'd like to target. Then ask them to set a goal for building muscular strength and endurance using machine weights.

Lesson 4

Exercise Bands

Purpose

In this lesson students learn how to use exercise bands, considered an alternative piece of exercise equipment, by performing various exercises that promote cardiovascular fitness, flexibility, and muscular strength.

Warm-Ups (6-8 Minutes)

1. Scissors
2. Upper body rotations
3. Waist twists
4. Quadriceps stretch

Skill Cues

1. Perform one set (10-15 repetitions) of each exercise.
2. Begin with the lowest resistance until proper form has been achieved. Then select a resistance that allows 10 to 15 repetitions in a smooth, steady motion.
3. Wrap the bands loosely. Tying a band too tight can elevate blood pressure.
4. Move through the full range of motion during each repetition. Ensure flexibility by slowly stretching during the first 3 or 4 repetitions.
5. Do not hyperextend or lock the joints while performing the exercises.
6. Keep the body straight and aligned; avoid twisting or shifting during movement.

Facility and Equipment

◆ Gym, exercise room, or multipurpose room
◆ 1 exercise band per student

Note: Exercise bands come in different resistances. The degree of resistance should be appropriate for each student's level of fitness and strength. Resistance is measured by color. The typical color code is as follows:

▶ Red = light resistance
▶ Blue = medium resistance
▶ Yellow = heavy resistance
▶ Silver = extra-heavy resistance.

This color code is not universal, however. Different brands use different colors. With the Dyna-Band, for example, pink = low resistance; green = medium resistance; and purple = high resistance.

Teaching Cues

1. Explain the different resistance levels and colors of the exercise bands.
2. Emphasize the following safety rules:
   ▶ Snapping the bands is not allowed.
   ▶ Do not place the bands near or in the mouth.
   ▶ Do not tie the band tightly around the body.
3. Make sure students maintain proper body alignment when completing each exercise.
4. Students may work in partners during this lesson. Pairing students of similar size is recommended.
5. Encourage students to take between 4 and 6 seconds to complete each repetition.

Activities (30-40 Minutes)

1. Introduce the use of the exercise bands as an alternative way to achieve fitness goals. Exercise bands provide a unique way to build muscle because they deliver progressive resistive exercise without using bulky weights or machines. Discuss the safety rules and explain the color-coding system before distributing and using the exercise bands. (3-5 minutes)

2. Demonstrate and then have students execute the following exercises. (27-35 minutes)

Abdominal Curl

Targeted muscles: abdominals. Lie supine with the knees bent and the arms cradled behind the head. Grip the band with both hands behind the head and have a partner hold the other end of the band behind the feet on the floor. Contract the abdominal muscles while curling the shoulders up toward the knees. Release the abdominals and slowly curl downward, but do not allow the shoulders to touch the ground. Do 10 to 15 repetitions; then partners switch roles.

Dead Lift

Targeted muscles: hamstrings and gluteus maximus. Place the band on the floor. With the feet shoulder-width apart, stand on the band; then bend and grasp the ends of the bands with both hands outside of the legs. The knees should be bent about 45 degrees. Using only the back muscles, stand erect. Then slowly lower the band back toward the floor. Do 10 to 15 repetitions.

Dead lift

Biceps Curl

Targeted muscles: biceps. Stand in a staggered up and back stance. With the right foot forward, place the right foot on one end of the band while grasping the other end with the right hand. Flex the arm at a 90-degree angle (at the elbow) close to the body. Raise the arm straight up toward the shoulder while keeping the wrists firm. Do 10 to 15 repetitions; then switch hands and repeat the exercise.

Leg Extension

Targeted muscles: hamstrings. Lie supine with the knees bent. Tie the ends of the band together and place it around the instep of the left foot and right ankle. Extend the lower right leg upward to the point of resistance. Hold momentarily; then release to the starting position. Do 10 to 15 repetitions; then switch legs.

Bench Press

Targeted muscles: pectorals, deltoids, and triceps. Lie supine on the floor with the legs bent. (This exercise may also be done standing.) Place the band under the armpits and across the back. Grasp the ends of the band with the arms flexed and the hands shoulder-width apart. Press the arms straight out to full extension; then release slowly. Do 10 to 15 repetitions.

Leg Press

Targeted muscles: quadriceps and glutei. Sit on the floor with the knees bent, the bottom of the feet flat on the floor. Place the band around the instep of the right foot, keeping the left foot flat on the floor. Hold the ends of the band with palms down. From a bent-knee position, extend the right leg straight out. (Use the left leg for balance.) Slowly release to the starting position. Do 10 to 15 repetitions; then switch legs.

Shoulder Press

Targeted muscles: trapezius and latissimus dorsi. Place the right hand on the left shoulder while holding one end of the band. Hold the opposite end of the band in the left hand. With palms in, extend the left arm straight up without locking the elbows. Slowly release to the starting position. Do 10 to 15 repetitions; then switch arms.

Closure (3-5 Minutes)

Review the lesson with students. Use the following ideas to reinforce learning, check understanding, and provide feedback.

1. Discuss the use of exercise bands as an acceptable alternative to standard exercise routines.

2. Encourage students to share their ideas for additional exercises using the exercise bands.

Lesson 5

Exercise Balls

Purpose

In this lesson students learn to use the exercise ball, another alternative piece of exercise equipment. The ball exercises in this chapter help to improve fitness by increasing flexibility around the midsection (i.e., abdominals and lower back) and improving muscular strength.

Warm-Ups (6-8 Minutes)

1. Side stretch
2. Single-leg crossovers
3. Curl and stretch
4. Waist twists
5. Seated hamstring stretch

Facility and Equipment

- Indoor gym or multipurpose room with a smooth floor
- 1 exercise ball per student
  Note: Exercise balls should be the appropriate size according to students' height:
  - For students between 5 feet (152.4 centimeters) and 5 feet 5 inches (165.1 centimeters), use a small ball measuring 22 inches (55.9 centimeters) in diameter.
  - For students between 5 feet 6 inches (167.6 centimeters) and 5 feet 11 inches (180.3 centimeters), use a medium ball measuring 26 inches (66 centimeters) in diameter.
  - For students between 6 feet (182.9 centimeters) and 6 feet 3 inches (190.5 centimeters), use a large ball measuring 30 inches (76.2 centimeters) in diameter.

Skill Cues

1. Perform one set (8-12 repetitions) of each exercise.
2. A comprehensive training program can be developed and implemented using the exercise balls. Such a program, however, will focus primarily on training in functional movement.

Teaching Cues

1. Explain to students that most of the ball activities are modified versions of common exercise and weight training activities. The exercise balls assist in completing some complex or challenging exercises.
2. Exercise balls are inexpensive, ranging from $18.00 to $35.00.
3. The following safety precautions should be explained and enforced while using the exercise balls:
   - Do not bounce on the balls.
   - Do not roll around on the balls.
   - Do not throw the balls or handle them in an otherwise rough manner.
   - Do not push others when they are using the ball.
   - Do not use an underinflated ball.

Activities (30-40 Minutes)

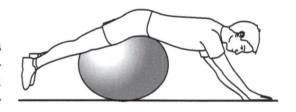

1. Introduce the use of the exercise balls as an alternative way to achieve health-related fitness goals. Discuss exercise ball safety and explain how to select an appropriate-sized exercise ball. Then distribute the exercise balls. (3-5 minutes)

2. Demonstrate and then have students execute the following ball exercises. (27-35 minutes)

Biceps Push

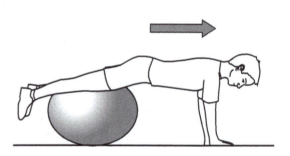

Targeted muscles: biceps. Lie on the ball with the hips supported on top of the ball and the arms reaching forward on the floor, shoulder-width apart. Lift the legs off the floor and use the arms to pull the body forward until the hands are under the shoulders. Hold; then slowly push the body back to the starting position, trying to keep the spine straight during the entire movement. Do 8 to 12 repetitions.

Biceps push

Triceps Lift

Targeted muscles: triceps. Kneel on the floor in front of the ball. Keeping the back straight, reach behind and lift the ball for 10 seconds. Hold; then lower the ball to the floor. Do 8 to 12 repetitions.

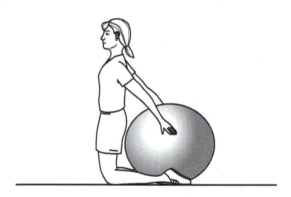

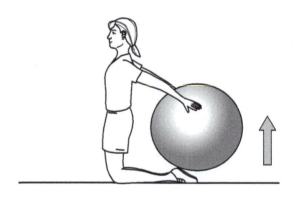

Triceps lift

Abdominal Curl

Targeted muscles: abdominals. Lie on the ball with the arch of the back supported, the arms crossed behind the head, and the feet on the floor. Curl the upper body, squeezing the abdominals and lifting the shoulders and upper back. (Do not pull on the head and neck.) Return to the starting position. Do 8 to 12 repetitions.

Abdominal Extension

Targeted muscles: abdominals and oblique muscles. Lie on the side with the waist and hips on the ball. Bend the inside leg and stretch the outside leg. For stability, rest the top arm on the front of the ball and place the hand of the other arm to the head. Lift the upper body using the oblique muscles while squeezing the rib cage. (Do not let the top hip roll forward or backward.) Hold; then return to the starting position. Do 8 to 12 repetitions; then switch sides.

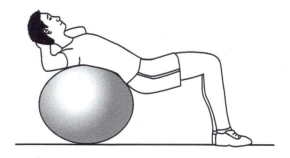

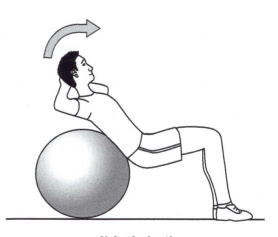

Abdominal curl

Abdominal extension

Pelvic Tilt

Targeted muscles: gluteus maximus. Lean with the back and waist on the ball, the hands on the thighs. The feet should be flat on the floor, shoulder-width apart. Lift the pelvis, raising the hips a few inches; then return to the starting position. (Focus on using the abdominals to lift the hips.) Do 8 to 12 repetitions.

Hip Extension

Targeted muscles: gluteus maximus and abdominals. Lie face up on the floor, the arms by the sides and the knees bent and on top of the ball. Lift the hips off the floor until the back is straight. (If necessary, use the arms to assist the back.) Hold; then return to the starting position. Do 8 to 12 repetitions.

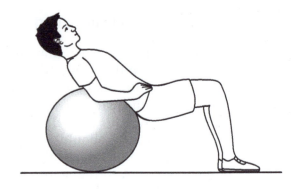

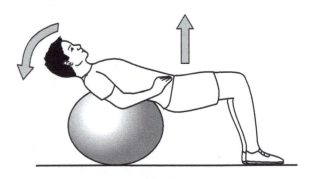

Pelvic tilt

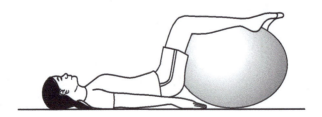

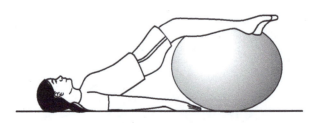

Hip extension

Leg Curl

Targeted muscles: gastrocnemii and glutei. Lie face up on the floor with the legs outstretched and the heels and calves on the ball. Place the hands on the floor by the sides. Press the heels down firmly into the ball, bending the knees and rolling the ball toward the body until the feet are flat on the ball. Hold; then return to the starting position. Do 8 to 12 repetitions.

Upper Thigh Flex

Targeted muscles: glutei, gastrocnemii, and hamstrings. Stand with the ball pressed between the lower back and a wall. Take two steps away from the wall, positioning the feet shoulder-width apart, and reach the arms straight out for balance. Bend the knees and squat, allowing the ball to roll up the back. Hold when the thighs are parallel to the floor. (Keep the knees over the feet.) Do 8 to 12 repetitions.

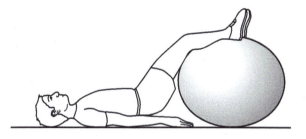

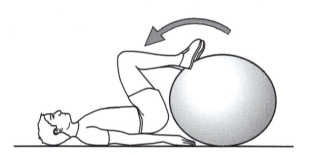

Leg curl

Upper thigh flex

Inner Thigh Flex

Targeted muscles: adductors and gastrocnemii. Lie face up on the floor with the feet flat on the floor with the arms extended by the side, palms down. Grip the middle of the ball between the knees, using the knees, inner thighs, and inside calves. Squeeze the knees together, pressing into the ball. Hold for 5 to 10 seconds; then release. Do 8 to 12 repetitions.

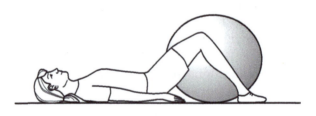

Inner thigh flex

Closure (3-5 Minutes)

Review the lesson with students. Use the following ideas to reinforce learning, check understanding, and provide feedback.

1. Discuss the advantages of exercising with balls (e.g., little space is required, they're inexpensive, they provide a comprehensive workout).
2. Have students share their ideas about additional ball exercises.

Lesson 6

Improving Flexibility

Purpose

In this lesson students will improve flexibility with muscle-stretching that increases the range of joint motion.

Warm-Ups (6-8 Minutes)

1. Scissors
2. Quadriceps stretch
3. Shoulder pushes
4. Achilles tendon stretch

Skill Cues

1. Hold a stretch 15 to 30 seconds to effectively lengthen a muscle.
2. Stretch at least three days a week to maintain flexibility.
3. Stretch gently; never push to the point of pain.

Teaching Cues

1. Explain that students can improve flexibility by using muscle stretches that increase the range of joint motion. Static stretching—slow stretching followed by a hold—is the preferred method of increasing flexibility.

2. After completing the stretches, have students set goals to work on their least-flexible areas.

3. Encourage students to work for bilateral flexibility—equal flexibility on both sides of the body.

4. If you or your students want to keep track of the stretching measurements, which may be a good idea for ongoing assessment as well as personal motivation, use the personal fitness record (see page 75) as a template to create a stretch scoring sheet. Or, simply have students record their scores in their notebooks or on a blank sheet of paper.

5. Before class, or before activity 3, construct three large charts using poster board and post these charts around the gym. Each chart should describe specific exercises for developing flexibility in the upper body (see the sample chart), the middle body, and the lower body. Suggested exercises for each area include the following (see the appendix for a description of each exercise):

   ▶ Upper body (shoulders and arms): Arm rotators, shoulder pushes, shoulder shrugs, triceps stretch, wrist rotation and flexion, phalange flings

   ▶ Middle body (waist and back): Mad cat, curl and stretch, elbow-knee touches (supine), side stretch, waist twists

▶ Lower body (thighs, buttocks, hamstrings, quadriceps, and calves): Quadriceps stretch, hamstring straight-leg stretch, Achilles tendon stretch, sit and stretch, inverted hurdler's stretch

---

Upper Body Flexibility

Arm rotators

Shoulder pushes

Shoulder shrugs

Triceps stretch

Wrist rotation and flexion

Phalange flings

Sample flexibility exercise chart

Activities (30-40 Minutes)

1. Present the flexibility stretches in this lesson, emphasizing the skill and teaching cues. (3-5 minutes)

2. Pair up students or have them choose partners. One partner takes the following flexibility tests to measure flexibility while the other partner assists when necessary and measures the stretch using the yardstick. After one partner has completed all of the tests, the other partner takes them. (10-12 minutes)

Shoulder Lift

Lie face down and extend both arms forward while holding a stick with both hands, palms down. Keeping the chin on the floor and the elbows straight, use the arms to lift the stick as high as possible.

Measurement. A good flexibility score is 23 to 25 inches (58.4-63.5 centimeters) for males and 21 to 24 inches (53.3-61 centimeters) for females.

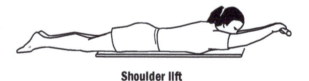

Shoulder lift

Trunk Extension

Lie face down with the fingers clasped behind the neck. While partners stabilize the legs on the ground, raise the head and chest as high as possible.

Measurement. A good flexibility score is 20 to 22 inches (50.8-55.9 centimeters) for males and 17 to 19 inches (43.2-48.3 centimeters) for females.

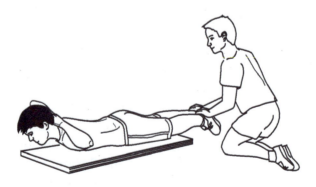

Trunk extension

Hamstring Stretch

Sit on a straight chair, bench, or box with the back straight and one leg resting on the floor. Extend the other leg out as far as possible. Repeat with the opposite leg.

Measurement. Being able to extend the leg fully without moving the other leg shows good flexibility.

Hamstring stretch

Shoulder Stretch

Reach behind the neck and down the back with the right hand while sliding the left hand upward from the small of the back.

Measurement. Being able to touch hands on the back and overlap the fingers shows good flexibility in the arms and shoulders.

Achilles Tendon Stretch

Stand at a wall. Place the palms of the hands on the wall and bend forward until the chin touches the wall.

Measurement. Keeping the body straight and the feet flat on the floor shows good flexibility in the calves.

Shoulder stretch

Achilles tendon stretch

3. Divide the class into three groups and position each group at one of the wall charts. Have students perform each exercise on the chart, holding each stretch from 15 to 30 seconds to maximize results. Then each group rotates to a different chart. (12-18 minutes)

4. Have students walk around the gym to cool down. (5 minutes)

Closure (3-5 Minutes)

Review and discuss the lesson with students. Use the following ideas to reinforce learning, check understanding, and provide feedback.

1. Discuss the principles of increasing flexibility (e.g., holding a stretch 15 to 30 seconds, working toward bilateral flexibility, stretching at least 3 days a week).

2. Have students list their least-flexible body areas on a sheet of paper, noting the appropriate stretches and exercises for improvement. Have them continue to work on developing flexibility in those areas outside of class. In one month, repeat the flexibility tests in this lesson to measure improvement.

Assessment and Resources

Countless guidelines and resources are available for assessing overall fitness levels (e.g., Council for Physical Education for Children 1998; National Association for Sport and Physical Education 1995; Centers for Disease Control and Prevention 1997; *Physical Best Activity Guide*, Human Kinetics 1999; *Fitness for Life*, Human Kinetics 2002). In *Quality Lesson Plans for Secondary Physical Education, Second Edition*, the FITNESSGRAM (Human Kinetics 1999; also available on CD-ROM [version 6.0] and the World Wide Web) assessment protocol is used. FITNESSGRAM is a comprehensive fitness and activity assessment system designed to assist teachers in achieving the primary goal of youth fitness programs—namely, helping students to incorporate physical activity into their lives.

Although FITNESSGRAM tests form the basis of lessons 1, 2, 9, and 10 (preassessment and postassessment lessons) in the aerobic conditioning unit, some of these tests also apply to the weight training and conditioning lessons. These include the following:

- ▶ Curl-up
- ▶ Trunk lift
- ▶ Push-up
- ▶ Pull-up
- ▶ Modified pull-up
- ▶ Flexed-arm hang
- ▶ Back-saver sit and reach
- ▶ Shoulder stretch

Other suggestions for alternative tests, from lessons 1 and 6 of the weight training and conditioning unit, are provided at the end of this chapter.

In the test listings throughout this chapter, the protocol for each FITNESSGRAM test is explained step by step. Before getting into testing specifics, however, a brief introduction to FITNESSGRAM scoring and analysis follows. (More detailed testing standards and data for evaluating FITNESSGRAM test results are provided on the CD-ROM included with this book.)

Note: The most recent versions of the FITNESSGRAM are available on CD-ROM (6.0) and the World Wide Web (7.0), both available from Human Kinetics. The *FITNESSGRAM Test Administration Manual, Second Edition* is also available from Human Kinetics. Computer software (both for PC and Macintosh platforms) included with this manual enables students and teachers to print out reports on individual and class test scores, test results summaries, and statistical data sorted by student data or test date. This software also enables students and teachers to compare current test scores to previous test results and to the FITNESSGRAM healthy fitness zones. Student certificates and individualized recommendations for improving or maintaining fitness levels can also be printed with this software.

FITNESSGRAM Scoring

Two test score recording sheets are included in this book. The first is a personal fitness record, which students can use to record their test results. These recording sheets should be collected at the end of each testing period and the results compiled on the second recording sheet provided, the class score sheet. The personal fitness records may be used for the next testing session.

Both recording sheets list the standard FITNESSGRAM test batteries. When more than one FITNESSGRAM test can be used (e.g., the 1-mile [1.6-kilometer] walk or run or the PACER can be used to measure aerobic capacity), or to record alternative testing protocols, blank lines are provided. Columns on the personal fitness record are provided for students to record their healthy fitness zones (HFZ) and see how their scores compare to FITNESSGRAM standards (see the FITNESSGRAM healthy fitness zone tables for boys and girls on pages 77-78. Improvement columns are provided on the class score sheet to record students' progress from one test date to the next.

In addition to its reporting and self-assessment features, the FITNESSGRAM also provides national fitness standards for boys and girls. These standards, titled "FITNESSGRAM Standards for Healthy Fitness Zone," are shown here and are found on the CD-ROM accompanying this book. Post or distribute copies of these standards for students to use when filling out their personal fitness records.

Personal Fitness Record

Name_____ School_____

Grade _____ Age _____ Height _____ Weight _____

	Date:		Date:	
	Score	HFZ	Score	HFZ
Aerobic capacity: _____				
Curl-up				
Trunk lift				
Upper body strength: _____				
Flexibility: _____				
Skinfolds:				
Triceps				
Calf				
Other:				
Total score				

HFZ = healthy fitness zone.

I understand that my fitness record is personal. I do not have to share my results. My fitness record is important because it allows me to check my fitness level. If it is low, I will need to do more activity. If it is acceptable, I need to continue my current activity level. I know that I can ask my teacher for ideas on improving my fitness level.

Adapted, by permission, from The Cooper Institute for Aerobics Research, 1999, *FITNESSGRAM Test Administration Manual,* 2nd ed. (Champaign, IL: Human Kinetics), 91.

From *Quality Lesson Plans for Secondary Physical Education,* 2nd ed., by Dorothy B. Zakrajsek, Lois A. Carnes, and Frank E. Pettigrew Jr., 2003, Champaign, IL: Human Kinetics.

Class Score Sheet

Teacher _____ Class _____ Grade _____ Test date _____

Student ID#	Student name	Birth date	Gender	Height	Weight	Aerobic capacity	Curl-up	Upper body strength	Trunk lift	Flexibility L/R	Skinfolds Triceps	Calf
										/		
										/		
										/		
										/		
										/		
										/		
										/		
										/		
										/		
										/		
										/		
										/		
										/		
										/		
										/		
										/		
										/		
										/		

Adapted, by permission, from The Cooper Institute for Aerobics Research, 1999, *FITNESSGRAM Test Administration Manual*, 2nd ed. (Champaign, IL: Human Kinetics), 90.

From *Quality Lesson Plans for Secondary Physical Education*, 2nd ed., by Dorothy B. Zakrajsek, Lois A. Carnes, and Frank E. Pettigrew Jr., 2003, Champaign, IL: Human Kinetics.

Age	1-mile run* minutes:seconds		PACER* # laps		Walk test and $\dot{V}O_2$max *ml/kg/minute		Percent body fat*		Body mass index*		Curl-up* # completed	
5	Completion of		Participate in				25	10	20	14.7	2	10
6	distance. Time		run. Lap count				25	10	20	14.7	2	10
7	standards not		standards not				25	10	20	14.9	4	14
8	recommended.		recommended.				25	10	20	15.1	6	20
9							25	10	20	15.2	9	24
10	11:30	9:00	23	61	42	52	25	10	21	15.3	12	24
11	11:00	8:30	23	72	42	52	25	10	21	15.8	15	28
12	10:30	8:00	32	72	42	52	25	10	22	16.0	18	36
13	10:00	7:30	41	72	42	52	25	10	23	16.6	21	40
14	9:30	7:00	41	83	42	52	25	10	24.5	17.5	24	45
15	9:00	7:00	51	94	42	52	25	10	25	18.1	24	47
16	8:30	7:00	61	94	42	52	25	10	26.5	18.5	24	47
17	8:30	7:00	61	94	42	52	25	10	27	18.8	24	47
17+	8:30	7:00	61	94	42	52	25	10	27.8	19.0	24	47

Age	Trunk lift* inches		Push-up* # completed		Modified pull-up* # completed		Pull-up* # completed		Flexed-arm hang* seconds		Back-saver sit and reach** inches	Shoulder stretch
5	6	12	3	8	2	7	1	2	2	8	8	Passing =
6	6	12	3	8	2	7	1	2	2	8	8	touching
7	6	12	4	10	3	9	1	2	3	8	8	fingertips
8	6	12	5	13	4	11	1	2	3	8	8	together
9	6	12	6	15	5	11	1	2	4	10	8	behind the
10	9	12	7	20	5	15	1	2	4	10	8	back.
11	9	12	8	20	6	17	1	3	6	13	8	
12	9	12	10	20	7	20	1	3	6	13	8	
13	9	12	12	25	8	22	1	4	12	17	8	
14	9	12	14	30	9	25	2	5	15	20	8	
15	9	12	16	35	10	27	3	7	15	20	8	
16	9	12	18	35	12	30	5	8	15	20	8	
17	9	12	18	35	14	30	5	8	15	20	8	
17+	9	12	18	35	14	30	5	8	15	20	8	

*The number on the left is the lower end of the HFZ; the number on the right is the upper end.

**Test is scored pass or fail; must reach this distance to pass.

STANDARDS FOR HEALTHY FITNESS ZONE—GIRLS

Age	1-mile run* minutes:seconds		PACER* # laps		Walk test and V̇O₂max *ml/kg/minute		Percent body fat*		Body mass index*		Curl-up* # completed	
5	Completion of		Participation in				32	17	21	16.2	2	10
6	distance. Time		run. Lap				32	17	21	16.2	2	10
7	standards not		count not				32	17	22	16.2	4	14
8	recommended.		recommended.				32	17	22	16.2	6	20
9							32	17	23	16.2	9	22
10	12:30	9:30	15	41	40	48	32	17	23.5	16.6	12	26
11	12:00	9:00	15	41	39	47	32	17	24	16.9	15	29
12	12:00	9:00	23	41	38	46	32	17	24.5	16.9	18	32
13	11:30	9:00	23	51	37	45	32	17	24.5	17.5	18	32
14	11:00	8:30	23	51	36	44	32	17	25	17.5	18	32
15	10:30	8:00	23	51	35	43	32	17	25	17.5	18	35
16	10:00	8:00	32	61	35	43	32	17	25	17.5	18	35
17	10:00	8:00	41	61	35	43	32	17	26	17.5	18	35
17+	10:00	8:00	41	61	35	43	32	17	27.3	18.0	18	35

Age	Trunk lift* inches		Push-up* # completed		Modified pull-up* # completed		Pull-up* # completed		Flexed-arm hang* seconds		Back-saver sit and reach** inches	Shoulder stretch
5	6	12	3	8	2	7	1	2	2	8	9	Passing =
6	6	12	3	8	2	7	1	2	2	8	9	touching
7	6	12	4	10	3	9	1	2	3	8	9	fingertips
8	6	12	5	13	4	11	1	2	3	10	9	together
9	6	12	6	15	4	11	1	2	4	10	9	behind the
10	9	12	7	15	4	13	1	2	4	10	9	back.
11	9	12	7	15	4	13	1	2	6	12	10	
12	9	12	7	15	4	13	1	2	7	12	10	
13	9	12	7	15	4	13	1	2	8	12	10	
14	9	12	7	15	4	13	1	2	8	12	10	
15	9	12	7	15	4	13	1	2	8	12	12	
16	9	12	7	15	4	13	1	2	8	12	12	
17	9	12	7	15	4	13	1	2	8	12	12	
17+	9	12	7	15	4	13	1	2	8	12	12	

*The number on the left is the lower end of the HFZ; the number on the right is the upper end.

**Test is scored pass or fail; must reach this distance to pass.

Reprinted, by permission, from The Cooper Institute for Aerobics Research, 1999, FITNESSGRAM Test Administration Manual, 2nd ed. (Champaign, IL: Human Kinetics), 38.

FITNESSGRAM Tests

The FITNESSGRAM tests discussed in this chapter (and used in lessons 1, 2, 9, and 10 of the aerobic conditioning unit) measure aerobic capacity, body composition, muscular strength, endurance, and flexibility. These are the major components of the aerobic conditioning and weight training and conditioning units in this section of the book. The following tests apply to these measurements.

Aerobic capacity	1-mile (1.6-kilometer) walk or run
	PACER
Body composition	Body mass index
	Skinfold measurements
Muscular strength	Curl-up
	Flexed-arm hang
	Modified pull-up
	Pull-up
	Push-up
	Trunk lift
Endurance	1-mile (1.6-kilometer) walk or run
	Curl-up
	Flexed-arm hang
	Modified pull-up
	PACER
	Pull-up
	Push-up
Flexibility	Back-saver sit and reach
	Shoulder stretch
	Trunk lift

One-Mile (1.6-Kilometer) Walk or Run

This test measures aerobic capacity. The object is to run for 1 mile (1.6 kilometers) in as short a time as possible. Walking is permitted if students cannot run the entire distance. (See the CD-ROM accompanying this book for further information on test administration and assessment.)

Note: Mass testing can be used for the 1-mile (1.6-kilometer) walk or run. Pair up students or have them choose partners. One partner performs the test while the other records scores; then partners switch roles.

Protocol

1. Students should warm up before taking the test.
2. At the signal to start, students begin to run.
3. When they cross the finish line, elapsed time is called out and recorded. Future test times should show progress after participation in the fitness units.

Facility and Equipment

◆ 1-mile (1.6-kilometer) running course
◆ Stopwatch
◆ 1 personal fitness record (see page 75) and pencil per student

4. Students should cool down by continuing to walk for several minutes after completing the test.

PACER

The PACER (Progressive Aerobic Cardiovascular Endurance Run), a multistage shuttle run, also measures aerobic capacity. The object is to run back and forth across a 21.9-yard (20-meter) distance at a specified pace for as long a time as possible. (See the CD-ROM accompanying this book for further information on test administration and assessment.)

Future test scores should show progress after participation in the fitness units.

1-mile (1.6-kilometer) walk or run

Protocol

1. Mark two course lines 21.9 yards (20 meters) apart using cones or tape. Have students warm up before taking the test.

2. Students line up along one of the course lines. At the signal (whistle or beep), they run from one line to the other, attempting to reach the opposite line before the next signal. At the next signal, they turn around and run back to the other line.

3. Students who reach the line before the signal must wait for the next signal before running to the other line. Students who do not reach the line before the signal must immediately turn around and return to the closest starting line to wait for the next lap (2 segments = 1 lap). Students proceed in this manner until they fail to reach the line before the signal for the second time.

4. Students tally their scores by counting the total segments completed. Partial segments are not counted.

5. Students should cool down by continuing to walk for several minutes after completing the test.

Facility and Equipment

- Flat, nonslippery surface at least 21.9 yards (20 meters) long
- 1 tape measure
- 4 cones or tape
- PACER music and player (CD or audiocassette) or whistle
- 1 personal fitness record (see page 75) and pencil per student

Note: Prerecorded PACER music CDs and audiocassettes (available from the American Fitness Alliance; see the resources section at the end of this chapter) cue students through the PACER with progressively faster music or beeps for each segment of the test.

Skinfold Measurements

This test is a measure of body composition, taken at the triceps and calf skinfolds, to determine the percentage of body fat. (See the CD-ROM accompanying this book for further information on test administration and assessment.)

Protocol

1. Pair up students or have them select partners. One partner takes the test while the other assists with the skin caliper and records the scores; then partners switch roles.

2. Students should relax the arm or leg being measured, then grasp the skinfold between the thumb and forefinger before using the caliper.

   ▸ The triceps skinfold is measured at the back of the right arm, over the triceps muscle.

   ▸ The calf skinfold is measured on the inside of the right calf.

3. Students should take three sets of measurements (one at each site before taking the second set) and then record the median (middle) score.

Triceps skinfold measurement

Body Mass Index

The body mass index (BMI) is also a measure of body composition, the objective being to determine the appropriateness of weight according to height by calculating BMI and then comparing it to the FITNESSGRAM healthy fitness zones (see the tables on pages 77-78). Because the BMI formula is metric, weight and height measured in pounds and inches must be converted. (See the CD-ROM accompanying this book for further information on test administration and assessment.)

Protocol

1. Students should remove their shoes.

2. One at a time, students step on the scale and record their own weight. If weight is measured in pounds, convert it to kilograms using the following formula:

   Kilograms = Pounds × 0.453592

   For example, if a student weighed 120 pounds, weight in kilograms would be 54.43 (120 × 0.453592).

3. Pair up students or have them select partners. One partner should measure and record the other partner's height using the tape measure or yardstick; then students should switch roles. If meters are not shown on the measuring device, convert inches to meters using the following formulas:

   Centimeters = Inches × 2.540005

   Meters = Centimeters + 100

For example, if a student were 5 feet, 6 inches tall (66 inches), height in meters would be calculated thus:

$$66 \times 2.540005 = 167.64 \text{ centimeters}$$

$$167.64 \div 100 = 1.68 \text{ meters (rounded up)}$$

4. Using the height and weight measurements from activities 2 and 3, students calculate their own body mass index (BMI) using the following formula:

$$\text{BMI} = \text{Weight (kilograms)} \div \text{Height}^2 \text{ (meters)}$$

To complete the earlier example, the student would have a BMI of 19.57 (54.43 ÷ 2.78 [1.67^2]), which is in the healthy fitness zone for both boys and girls (see the tables on pages 77-78).

Curl-Up

The curl-up is primarily a measure of abdominal strength and endurance. The object is to complete as many curl-ups as possible at a specified pace (i.e., approximately 20 curl-ups per minute, to a maximum of 75 curl-ups per minute). (See the CD-ROM accompanying this book for further information on test administration and assessment.)

Protocol

1. Pair up students or have them choose partners. One partner takes the test while the other records the score; then partners switch roles.

2. Students start by lying on their backs, the knees slightly bent over the measuring strip. At the signal to start (teachers should call a cadence), students curl up slowly, sliding the fingers across the width of the measuring strip. When the fingertips reach the other side, students curl back down to the starting position.

3. Students proceed until they complete 75 curl-ups or make two form corrections. Form corrections include the following:

   ▸ Raising the heels from the mat

   ▸ Not returning the head to the mat

Facility and Equipment

◆ Gym or other area with a flat surface
◆ 1 gymnastics or tumbling mat per 2 students
◆ 1 measuring strip per 2 students
◆ 1 personal fitness record (see page 75) per student
◆ 1 pencil per 2 students

Make a measuring strip out of cardboard. It should be 30 inches (76.2 centimeters) long and 4.5 inches (11.4 centimeters) wide. (Ready-made strips can be purchased from the American Fitness Alliance; see the resources section at the end of this chapter.)

▸ Pausing or resting between curl-ups
▸ Not touching the other side of the measuring strip

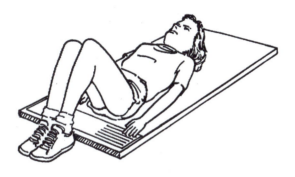

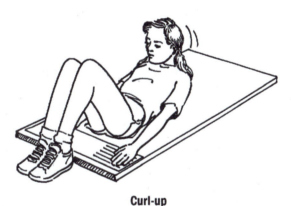

Curl-up

Trunk Lift

The trunk lift is a measurement of trunk extensor strength and flexibility. The object is to lift the upper body as high as possible, to a maximum of 12 inches (30.5 centimeters), and then hold the position. (See the CD-ROM accompanying this book for further information on test administration and assessment.)

Protocol

1. Pair up students or have them select partners. One partner measures while the other performs the test; then they switch roles.

2. Students taking the test begin by lying face down on the mat, the hands under the thighs.

3. Using the back muscles, students lift the upper body to a maximum of 12 inches (30.5 centimeters) off the mat and then hold the position for measurement. The toes should be pointed, the hands should remain under the thighs, and the body should be held in a prone position.

Facility and Equipment

◆ Gym or other area with a flat surface
◆ 1 gymnastics or tumbling mat per 2 students
◆ 1 yardstick or ruler per 2 students
◆ 1 personal fitness record (see page 75) per student
◆ 1 pencil per 2 students

Note: Use tape to mark the 6- and 12-inch (15.2- and 30.5-centimeter) points on the yardsticks or rulers.

Trunk lift

Push-Up

The push-up is a measure of upper body strength. The object is to complete as many push-ups as possible at a rhythmic pace. (See the CD-ROM accompanying this book for further information on test administration and assessment.)

Protocol

1. Pair up students or have them select partners. One partner performs the test while the other counts push-ups and checks for correct form; then students switch roles.

2. Students start in a prone position on the mat with the hands placed under the shoulders, the fingers outstretched, the legs straight and slightly apart, and the toes tucked under. Keeping the back and legs straight, students use the arms to push up off the mat until the arms are straight.

3. In a complete push-up, students use the arms to lower the body until the elbows bend 90 degrees (i.e., the upper arms should be parallel to the floor). The chin should not touch the mat.

Facility and Equipment

◆ Gym or other area with a flat surface
◆ 1 gymnastics or tumbling mat per 2 students
◆ Recorded cadence (audiocassette or CD) and player
◆ 1 personal fitness record (see page 75) per student
◆ 1 pencil per 2 students
Note: PACER CDs and tapes contain a recorded push-up cadence. (See the PACER test on page 80 for purchase information.)

"Down" position   *"Up" position*

Push-up sequence

4. Using a cadence of 20 push-ups per minute, or 1 push-up every 3 seconds, students try to complete as many push-ups as possible until they make the second form correction. Form corrections include the following:

   ▸ Stopping to rest

   ▸ Not maintaining a rhythmic pace

   ▸ Not achieving a 90-degree angle with the elbow

   ▸ Not extending the arms fully on each push-up

   ▸ Bending the legs or back

Pull-Up

The pull-up measures upper body strength. The object is to complete as many pull-ups as possible. Students who cannot perform at least one pull-up should not attempt this test. (See the CD-ROM accompanying this book for further information on test administration and assessment.)

Protocol

1. Pair up students or have them select partners. One partner takes the test while the other checks form and counts pull-ups; then partners switch roles.

2. Students taking the test start by hanging from the bar with an overhand grip (i.e., the palms away from the body). Using the arms, students pull the body up until the chin is above the bar and then lower the body back to the starting hanging position.

3. Students complete as many pull-ups as possible until two form corrections are made. Form corrections include the following:

   ▸ Swinging the body (partners can help prevent swinging by bracing their partners' legs)

   ▸ Kicking or jerking

   ▸ Not raising the chin above the bar

   ▸ Not returning to the full hanging position between pull-ups

Facility and Equipment

◆ Gym

◆ Horizontal bar

◆ 1 personal fitness record (see page 75) per student

◆ 1 pencil per 2 students

Note: The horizontal bar should be positioned high enough that students' feet clear the floor or ground when hanging with the arms extended.

Pull-up

Modified Pull-Up

The modified pull-up measures upper body strength and can be used as a substitute for the pull-up. The object is to complete as many modified pull-ups as possible. (See the CD-ROM accompanying this book for further information on test administration and assessment.)

Protocol

1. Pair up students or have them select partners. One partner takes the test while the other assumes the role of assistant, setting the bar position, checking form, and counting modified pull-ups; then partners switch roles.

2. Students taking the test start by lying on their backs with the shoulders directly under the bar. Assistants set the bar 1 to 2 inches (2.5-5.1 centimeters) above their partner's reach and then place an elastic band 7 to 8 inches (17.8-20.3 centimeters) below and parallel to the bar.

3. Students start by hanging from the bar, using an overhand grip (i.e., the palms facing away from the body), the arms and legs straight and the buttocks off the floor. Only the heels should be touching the floor. Using the arms, students pull up until the chin is above the elastic band and then lower to the starting (hanging) position.

Modified pull-up

4. Students complete as many modified pull-ups as possible until two form corrections are made. Form corrections include the following:
   ▸ Stopping to rest between modified pull-ups
   ▸ Not raising the chin above the elastic band
   ▸ Not returning to the full hanging position between modified pull-ups
   ▸ Touching the buttocks to the floor

Modified Pull-Up Stand Construction

Materials

- ▶ 1 .75-inch (1.9-centimeter) plywood 24 by 39 inches (61 by 99 centimeters) for support platform
- ▶ 2 48-inch (121.9-centimeter) 2 x 4s for uprights
- ▶ 2 24-inch (61-centimeter) 2 x 8s for upright bases
- ▶ 1 steel pipe (diameter: 1.12 inches [2.8 centimeters]; length: 43 inches [109.2 centimeters]) for chinning bar
- ▶ 1 dowel (diameter: 1.25 inches [3.2 centimeters]; length 39 inches [99 centimeters]) for top support
- ▶ 1 elastic band (should stretch to 39 inches [99 centimeters])
- ▶ 24 dowel pieces (1.37-inches [3.5-centimeter] diameter) cut 3.5 inches (8.9 centimeters) long for the elastic band holders
- ▶ Nails, wood screws, and wood glue for construction
- ▶ Polyurethane or shellac

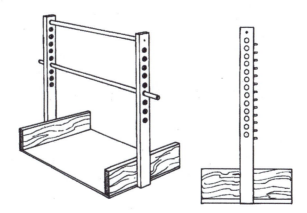

Modified pull-up stand construction

Assembly

1. Beginning 2.5 inches (6.3 centimeters) from the top end of each 2 × 4 (uprights), drill a 1.25-inch (3.2-centimeter) hole through the wide (i.e., 4-inch) width for the top support.

2. Starting below the 1.25-inch (3.2-centimeter) hole for the top support, drill 11 more 1.12-inch (2.8-centimeter) holes through the wide width of each 2 × 4 (uprights). Space the holes 2.5 inches (6.3 centimeters) from center to center. These are the holes for the steel pipe (chinning bar).

3. Beginning 3.75 inches (9.5 centimeters) from the top of each 2 × 4 (uprights), drill 12 1.37-inch (3.5-centimeter) holes into the narrow (i.e., 2-inch) width of each 2 × 4. Drill approximately 2 inches (5.1 centimeters) deep. Center these holes, which will hold the 3.5-inch (8.9-centimeter) dowel pieces, between the holes for the steel pipe (chinning bar).

4. Attach the upright bases to the uprights and assemble the rest of the pieces. Finish the stand with polyurethane or shellac.

Adapted, by permission, from The Cooper Institute for Aerobics Research, 1999, *FITNESSGRAM Test Administration Manual*, 2nd ed. (Champaign, IL: Human Kinetics), 73.

Flexed-Arm Hang

The flexed-arm hang test measures upper body strength. The object is for students to keep their chins above the bar as long as possible. (See the CD-ROM accompanying this book for further information on test administration and assessment.)

Protocol

1. Pair up students or have them select partners. One student performs the test while the other serves as a spotter and records the time; then partners switch roles.

2. Students taking the test start by grasping the bar with an overhand grip (i.e., the palms facing away from the body). Using the arms and with assistance of one or more spotters, students pull the body up until the chin is above the bar, the elbows flexed and the chest close to the bar. Once this position is reached, the spotter should start the stopwatch.

3. The stopwatch is stopped, and total time is recorded, when the student's chin drops below the level of the bar or after the second form correction. Form corrections include the following:

   ▸ Touching the chin to the bar
   ▸ Tilting the head backward (to keep the chin off the bar)

If the student's body starts to swing during the test, the spotter may stop the swinging motion by holding an extended arm across the front of the thighs.

Facility and Equipment

◆ Gym
◆ Horizontal bar
◆ Chair
◆ Stopwatch
◆ 1 personal fitness record (see page 75) per student
◆ 1 pencil per 2 students

Note: The horizontal bar should be positioned high enough that students' feet clear the floor or ground when hanging with the arms extended.

Starting position   *"Up" position*

Flexed-arm hang

Back-Saver Sit and Reach

This test is a measure of flexibility, predominantly of the hamstring muscles. The test is performed on one side at a time so that students will not have to hyperextend. The object of the back-saver sit and reach is to be able to reach forward a specified distance, first on the right side of the body and then on the left. (See the CD-ROM accompanying this book for further information on test administration and assessment.)

Protocol

1. Divide the class into three groups, each group lined up behind a back-saver sit and reach box. The first student in line should take the test, then go to the back of the line. The next student in line should record the score for the student taking the test. Students should remove their shoes before taking the test.

Facility and Equipment

◆ Gym or other area with a flat surface
◆ 3 back-saver sit and reach boxes
◆ 1 personal fitness record (see page 75) per student
◆ 1 pencil per group

2. Students start the test by sitting at a back-saver sit and reach box, the hips square to the box. The left leg should be fully extended, the left foot flat against the face of the box; the right knee is bent, with the sole of the right foot flat on the floor and beside the left (extended leg) knee. The arms should be extended slightly forward over the measuring scale on the top of the box, palms down and one hand on top of the other.

3. Students perform the test by reaching both hands forward four times along the measuring scale. If necessary, students may move the bent knee to the side as they reach forward, but the extended leg must remain straight. On the fourth reach, the position is held and the measurement is recorded.

4. Then students switch sides and repeat the test with the right leg fully extended and the left knee bent. Record the number of inches on each side to the nearest half inch or centimeter. The maximum score is 12 inches (30.5 centimeters).

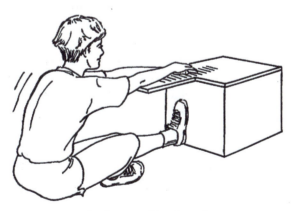

Back-saver sit and reach

Back-Saver Sit and Reach Box Construction

Materials

- ▶ 1 .75-inch (1.9-centimeter) plywood or comparable material 24 by 35 inches (61 by 88.9 centimeters) for the box
- ▶ Nails or screws
- ▶ Wood glue
- ▶ Measuring tape
- ▶ Polyurethane or shellac

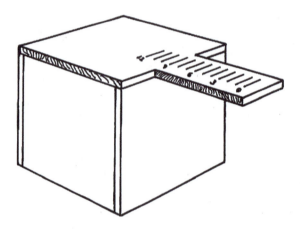

Back-saver sit and reach box construction

Assembly

1. Cut the following box pieces from the plywood:
   - ▶ 2 12-inch (30.5-centimeter) squares for the front and back
   - ▶ 2 small rectangles 12 by 10.5 inches (30.5 by 26.7 centimeters) for the sides
   - ▶ 1 large rectangle 12 by 22 inches (30.5 by 55.9 centimeters) for the top

2. Shape the top of the box by cutting a small rectangle 10 by 4 inches (25.4 by 10.2 centimeters) on each side of one end. This will create the overhang used for measuring. Beginning at the end of the overhang, use a measuring tape to mark every inch or centimeter, up to 12 inches (30.5 centimeters). The 9-inch (22.9-centimeter) mark must be exactly in line with the front of the box (i.e., the side against which students will place their feet). The 0 mark will be at the end nearest the students.

3. Construct the front, back, and sides of a box using the remaining 4 pieces, nails or screws, and wood glue.

4. Attach the top of the box by aligning the sides with the long edges of the top (both should be 10.5 inches [26.7 centimeters]).

5. Finish the box with polyurethane or shellac.

Adapted, by permission, from The Cooper Institute for Aerobics Research, 1999, *FITNESSGRAM Test Administration Manual*, 2nd ed. (Champaign, IL: Human Kinetics), 29, 74.

Shoulder Stretch

The shoulder stretch is a measure of upper body flexibility. The object is to touch the fingertips together behind the back by reaching over the shoulder and under the elbow. (See the CD-ROM accompanying this book for further information on test administration and assessment.)

Protocol

1. Pair up students or have them select a partner. One student performs the test while the other judges the stretch (e.g., complete, partial, how close, and so on); then partners switch roles.

2. The student taking the test starts the right shoulder stretch by reaching the right hand over the right shoulder and down the back while reaching with the left hand up the back.

> ### Facility and Equipment
> ◆ Gym or other area with a flat surface
> ◆ 1 personal fitness record (see page 75) per student
> ◆ 1 pencil per 2 students

3. If students are able to touch their fingers, "yes" should be recorded on the personal fitness record. If students are not able to touch their fingers, "no" should be recorded.

4. The same student repeats the test, this time performing the left shoulder stretch (i.e., reaching the left hand over the left shoulder and down the back while reaching with the right hand up the back), and the partner records the score.

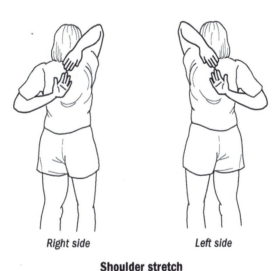

Right side   **Left side**

Shoulder stretch

Alternative Assessment

The following activities could also be adapted for assessment purposes during and after the fitness units. Use the blanks provided on the personal fitness record and class score sheet (see pages 75 and 76) to record the results of the tests you choose.

▶ Monitoring heart rate recovery time after sprinting, jumping rope, and stair climbing (see Aerobic Conditioning lesson 4, activities 3, 4, and 5; this lesson can also be repeated at the end of the school year to determine if cardiovascular recovery time has improved)

▶ Muscular strength test (see Weight Training and Conditioning lesson 1, activity 2)

▶ Flexibility test (see Weight Training and Conditioning lesson 6, activity 2)

▶ Using pedometers on 10 consecutive days, chart on graph walking dstances each day. Set a goal of 10,000 per day.

▶ Keep a journal for one month of changes perceived in body tone, energy levels, and moods experienced through the progress of a fitness program.

Resources

American Alliance for Health, Physical Education, Recreation, and Dance. 1999. *Physical best activity guide: Secondary level.* Champaign, IL: Human Kinetics.

American Alliance for Health, Physical Education, Recreation, and Dance. 1999. *Physical education for lifelong fitness.* Champaign, IL: Human Kinetics.

American College of Sports Medicine. 1998. *Fitness book.* 2nd ed. Champaign, IL: Human Kinetics.

Beighle, A., R. Pangrazi, and S. Vincent. 2001. Pedometer, physical activity, and accountability. *Journal of Physical Education, Recreation and Dance* 72 (9): 16-19.

Bompa, T. 2000. *Total training for young champions.* Champaign, IL: Human Kinetics.

Brzycki, M., ed. 1999. *Maximize your training.* Chicago: Master Press.

Cooper Institute for Aerobics Research. 1999. *FITNESSGRAM Test Administration Manual.* Champaign, IL: Human Kinetics. (Note: A CD-ROM version [6.0] and a Web-based version [7.0] of the FITNESSGRAM are also available from Human Kinetics.)

Cooper, K. 1991. *Kid fitness: A complete shapeup program from birth through high school.* New York: Bantam Books.

Corbin, C. and R. Lindsey. 2002. *Fitness for life.* Champaign, IL: Human Kinetics.

Department of Health and Human Services and Department of Education. 2000. *Promoting better health for young people through physical activity and sports: A report to the president from the secretary of health and human services and the secretary of education.* Washington, DC: U.S. department of Health and Human Services, Government Printing Office.

Fronske, H. 2001. *Teaching cues for sport skills.* 2nd ed. Needham Heights, MA: Allyn & Bacon.

Golding, L., C. Myers, and W. Sinning. 1989. *Y's way to physical fitness: The complete guide to fitness testing and instruction.* 3rd ed. Champaign, IL: Human Kinetics.

Iknoian, T. 1998. *Walking fast.* Champaign, IL: Human Kinetics.

Jensen, E. 2000. *Learning with the body in mind.* San Diego, CA: The Brain Store.

Landis, T. 1991. *Exercise for life.* Dubuque, IA: Kendall/Hunt.

Nieman, D. 1990. *Fitness and sports medicine: An introduction.* Palo Alto, CA: Bull Publishing.

Pangrazi, R., and P. Darst. 1997. *Dynamic physical education for secondary school students: Curriculum and instruction.* Needham Heights, MA: Allyn & Bacon.

Prevention Institute. 2001. *Promoting physical activity among youth: It's everyone's business.* Columbus, OH: Prevention Institute.

Williams, M. 1990. *Lifetime fitness and wellness.* Dubuque, IA: Brown.

Additional Resources

American Fitness Alliance
P.O. Box 5076
Champaign, IL 61825-5076
Phone 800-747-4457
   Sells prerecorded PACER music CDs.

Major Units

This section contains nine major physical education units, each covering a different sport, game, or activity. The term *major* is an indication of the number of lessons dedicated to the activity, not its importance in the physical education curriculum. In other words, some activities require more skills, and thus require more time to teach, than others.

The units in this section were chosen because

▶ they represent units of instruction typically found in most secondary school curriculums,

▶ the facilities and equipment required are usually available at most secondary schools, and

▶ the complex nature of the activity may require more learning time.

While the same characteristics may be applied to a few of the units found in section IV, "Minor Units," the general availability of facilities and equipment overruled their inclusion.

Section Structure

The units in this section are arranged alphabetically. They include some traditional team sports (i.e., basketball, flag football, softball, soccer, and volleyball), court games (i.e., bad-minton and tennis), and dance (i.e., social and square dancing and line dancing). Each unit contains 10 to 12 lessons that progress from basic to more advanced levels of motor skills, cognitive concepts, and performance. Within each lesson the sequence of activities is designed to move students toward greater skill achievement.

These units are designed to be taught over a 3- or 4-week period, depending on the number of days and minutes per class session. The amount of time allotted to each lesson as well as the suggested time for each activity may need to be modified. For example, seventh-graders may need more time to complete a full lesson than sophomores. These lesson plans may be further amended as necessary—for example, by incorporating other delivery activities that promote successful skill building and game play.

Each unit is introduced with a brief history of the sport or activity, safety considerations, rules governing game play, suggestions for etiquette, terminology (if relevant), and methods for modifying the lessons. The focus of the lessons in each unit is also explained in the unit introduction. Chapters offering assessment ideas for evaluating learner outcomes and guides to resources are located at the end of each unit. (See "Introduction to Units and Lessons" on page 2 for more information about the structure of units and lessons.)

Badminton

The origins of badminton have been traced to India, China, and even Poland, but these historical tracings suggest only general similarities. Badminton got its name from England's duke of Beaufort, whose English country estate, named Badminton, was the site of a lawn party in 1873. Guests played the game and afterward referred to it as *the Badminton game.* Badminton was introduced in the United States by two British players in 1878. Shortly thereafter the New York Badminton Club, the oldest existing club in the world, was formed. Today the game is played around the world, and badminton organizations are found in more than 90 countries.

Badminton did not become popular in the United States until the 1930s. The American Badminton Association (ABA) was founded in 1935 (and renamed the U.S. Badminton Association in 1978), and it conducted the first national tournament in April 1937. Other competitions have developed over the years, including the Thomas Cup for men in 1948, and the Uber Cup for women in 1957. Both competitions are held every three years and represent the best in badminton play. Badminton became an official medal sport during the 1992 Olympic Games in Barcelona, after its introduction as an exhibition game in Munich in 1972 and Seoul in 1988.

Badminton is a great game for everyone, regardless of age, gender, or strength. Unlike many sports, badminton is a game in which new players can achieve success quickly. The lightness of the racket, the floating speed of the shuttlecock, and a relatively small court allow learners of all ages to experience game satisfaction early on. Although learning the essential skills of the game is relatively easy, mastering the strokes and strategies can be quite challenging.

Because badminton is dominated not by strength but by skill and finesse, students need not be grouped by gender or size. Instead, complementary skills should be emphasized; in badminton, quickness, finesse, and accuracy are more valuable than power and strength. Indeed, perhaps more than any sport, badminton offers a game where females and males can compete on an equal footing.

Equipment

Basic badminton equipment is relatively inexpensive for recreational players. Backyard sets, although not very durable, afford many hours of fun for a small investment. For the more serious player, even a high-quality racket, shuttlecocks, and court shoes are still quite inexpensive when compared with the cost of playing gear for most other sports.

For school use, the following equipment is recommended:

- Badminton net, as shown in the diagram on page 96.
- Rackets. Metal (rather than wooden) rackets have an advantage because they can be strung tighter, can be stored without fear of warping, and are more durable.

- Shuttlecocks, also called *shuttles*. Goose feather shuttlecocks are the top of the line, but because they are expensive and wear out quickly, they are impractical for school use. Rather, good-quality nylon shuttles with cork bases will endure several hours of game play, have a good flight trajectory, and thus are recommended. Plastic shuttles with rubber tips, although quite inexpensive, should be avoided; the trajectory and flight distances are faulty, and the shuttles tend to break easily.

To keep the equipment in good repair, encourage students to adhere to the following rules:

- Lay the rackets down; do not drop or throw them.
- If shuttles are caught in the net, carefully remove them by pushing them through from the direction of entry.
- Do not lean or pull on the net. Badminton nets are lightweight and can be ripped or damaged easily.

Unit Organization

Because students are able to gain some measure of success quickly in badminton, there is a tendency to move into the game before students develop good game-playing skills. The lessons in this unit are designed not only to progress through the skills but also to promote skill proficiency.

Following is a description of each lesson in this unit.

- Lesson 1 emphasizes the need to develop powerful shots. A player who cannot clear a shot from one end of the court to the other will never experience the thrill of game play.
- The serve is presented in lesson 2 through a series of individualized tasks that move students from mere execution toward greater accuracy. This lesson can be followed as it is presented or it may be taught with an alternative, preferred methodology.
- Stroking, including the smash, drop, and drive shots are covered in lessons 3 and 4.
- In lesson 5, students learn to develop net shots.
- The doubles game is introduced in lesson 6 with a side-by-side partner formation.
- In lesson 7 students practice more game strategies, including the up-and-back partner system.
- After the rotation system is introduced in lesson 8, a two-flight round-robin tournament begins in lesson 9 and continues in lesson 10.

Selected resources as well as assessment ideas and activities follow the unit lessons.

If you want to teach more advanced skills and techniques (e.g., more backhand shots, the round-the-head clear, the drive-and-flick serve, and so on), you will need to make time adjustments and amend the drills. The lessons in this unit are organized to accommodate 30 students on 4 to 6 courts. If enough courts are available or if other activities are scheduled simultaneously, singles play is encouraged.

Note: An asterisk (*) following a facility or equipment listing indicates that preparation is required before the lesson.

Social Skills and Etiquette

Several courtesies should be observed during the game of badminton, including the following:

- Compliment an opponent's good shots.
- Call faults immediately.
- Return the shuttle to the server after each point.
- Avoid talking or distracting opponents or a partner during play.
- Do not make excuses for poor shots.
- Offer to replay a point if interference or a dispute occurred.
- Do not enter someone's court unless play has stopped.

Lesson Modifications

Badminton calls for few modifications. For nonambulatory students, a small space can be set up outside the regular court area with a lower net for "chair badminton." For visually impaired students, substituting brightly colored fleece balls for the shuttles may enable them to track the ball more easily and, thus, develop better game skills.

Safety

Badminton is a relatively safe activity. To avoid accidental collisions and hits with the racket, the following safety procedures should be implemented:

- ▶ Students should maintain an adequate distance when swinging rackets.
- ▶ When performing shuttle-hitting drills, students should face the same direction.
- ▶ In doubles play, partners should call shots that could be taken by either player.

Rules

The basic game involves serving, stroking, footwork, and speed along with mentally keeping the opponent off balance (e.g., anticipating the opponent's shots, disguising one's shots, ferreting out the opponent's weaknesses, and staying alert).

With the exception of boundaries and serving order, the singles and doubles rules for badminton are essentially the same. The following rules and game details apply to both singles and doubles unless otherwise noted.

Boundaries

In singles play, the inner sidelines and back boundary lines delimit the court. The singles service court (narrow and long) extends from the short service line to the singles long service line. In doubles play, the outer sidelines and back boundary lines delimit the court. The doubles service court (wide and short) extends

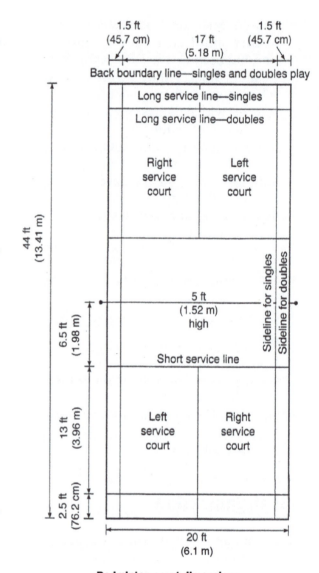

Badminton court dimensions

from the short service line to the doubles long service line.

Play

The server stands behind the service line and strikes the base of the shuttle in an underhand motion. The receiver must then return the shuttle before it hits the floor; then the players hit the shuttle back and forth (i.e., rallying) until one side fails to return it legally over the net.

Play ends when the shuttle hits the floor on one side of the court or when one player makes a fault. If the serving side commits the fault, the opposing side gets the serve. If the receiving side commits the fault, the serving side earns a point.

The following rules govern game play:

▶ A shuttle landing on a line is in play.

▶ When following through after a shot, a player's racket may cross but may not touch the net.

▶ The shuttle may touch the net during a rally. If it falls inbounds, it is in play.

▶ If on the serve or during a rally the shuttle goes out-of-bounds but the receiver makes contact, the shuttle is in play. If, on the other hand, the receiver swings and misses it completely (i.e., no contact), it is ruled out-of-bounds.

Scoring

Badminton games are played to 15 or 11 points; doubles and men's singles game are played to 15, and women's singles games are played to 11. The first team or player to reach the winning point total wins.

In the event of a tie score, the following apply:

▶ If a game is tied at 13 points, the team reaching 13 first can set the game at 5 more points or just play to 15.

▶ If a game is tied at 14 points, the team reaching 14 first can set the game at 3 more points or just play to 15.

▶ For an 11-point game, the option is 3 or 0 points at 9-all, and 2 or 0 at 10-all, with the first player reaching either 9 or 10 calling the option or set.

Only the serving team or player scores points. Points are scored when the opponent

▶ fails to return the shuttle,

▶ hits it out-of-bounds, or

▶ faults.

Serving

The game begins with the server serving from the right service court to the receiver in the diagonally opposite service court. The service procedure and rules governing serving are as follows:

▶ In singles the server always serves from the right service court when the server's score is even (i.e., 0, 2, 4, and so on) and from the left service court when the score is odd (i.e., 1, 3, 5, and so on).

▶ In doubles the server alternates service courts until the serve is lost. Receiving partners alternate receiving the serve. No receiver may receive two consecutive serves.

▶ Only one partner on the team with the first serve to start the doubles games may serve in that team's half of the inning. After a fault by the serving team, both opponent partners get to serve in their half of the inning. Thereafter, both partners serve in their respective half-innings.

▶ If the shuttle touches the net on the serve but still falls into the proper service court, called a *let* serve, the shuttle is served again.

Faults

Two types of faults can occur in badminton: serving faults and playing faults. During the serve, faults include the server

▶ striking the skirt of the shuttle first,

▶ contacting the shuttle above the waist,

▶ stepping outside of the correct service court,

▶ not keeping the feet stationary at the time of contact, and

▶ failing to hit the shuttle to the proper opposing service court.

The receiver can be faulted for

▶ not being within the service court,

▶ not having both feet on the floor at serve delivery, and

▶ moving before the serve is made.

During play, faults include

▶ hitting the shuttle out-of-bounds;

▶ hitting the shuttle into the ceiling, wall, lights, or standards;

- hitting the shuttle through or under the net (i.e., not hitting it over the net);
- double-hitting a shot (i.e., hitting the shuttle more than once on a side);
- touching the net or standards (with a racket or the body);
- hitting the shuttle before it crosses the net;
- contacting the shuttle with any part of the body;
- "carrying" the shuttle on the racket; and
- demonstrating nonsporting behavior (e.g., intentionally distracting or obstructing an opponent).

Lesson 1

Clear Shots

Purpose

In this lesson students develop the forehand and backhand clear shot using overhead and underhand strokes.

Warm-Ups (6-8 Minutes)

1. Arm pumps
2. Body circles
3. Wrist rotation and flexion
4. Push-ups
5. Running in place

Skill Cues

Facility and Equipment

◆ Gym or outdoor area with walls and floor lines
◆ 1 racket per student
◆ 2 to 3 shuttles per student
◆ Tape or cord

Forehand Grip

1. "Shake hands" with the racket handle so that the butt of the handle rests against the base of the hand.
2. Form a **V** with the thumb and forefinger on the top of the handle.
3. Spread the forefinger and middle finger slightly apart and wrap the thumb around the handle.

Backhand Grip

1. Rotate the racket a quarter-turn clockwise so that the **V** is over the top left bevel (diagonal side of handle).
2. Extend the thumb along the back bevel of the handle for more power.

Overhead Clear Shot

1. Drop the racket arm down behind the shoulder (forehand or backhand), cock the wrist, and keep the weight over the back foot.
2. Lead with the elbow on the forward motion of the racket, and shift weight to the forward foot.
3. Contact the shuttle slightly in front of the body with the racket face slightly open (i.e., tilted toward the ceiling, as shown in the figure on the following page).

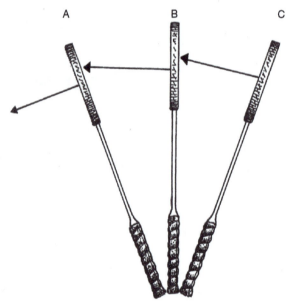

A = Closed, smash
B = Square, drop
C = Open, clear

Contact points

4. Follow through forcefully (up and down) using forearm power and a wrist snap.

Underhand Clear Shot

1. Use the same mechanics as for the overhead clear, except that the shuttle is contacted from below, driving the shuttle upward and deep.
2. Make a wide semicircular pattern with the racket arm, contacting the shuttle with an open racket face.
3. Rotate the body into the shot, and follow through forcefully and high.

Teaching Cues

1. Explain the five elements that create a powerful, forceful swing:
   - ▶ Long backswing
   - ▶ Rotation of the total body into the shot
   - ▶ Contacting the shuttle with full extension of the racket arm
   - ▶ Gripping the fingers firmly on contact
   - ▶ Finishing with a forceful follow-through
2. Explain that the shuttle's flight direction is determined by the angle of the racket face on contact. Distance of flight is determined by the speed of the racket on contact.

Activities (30-40 Minutes)

1. Position students in a semicircle; then explain and demonstrate the forehand grip. Students should practice the grip, using a buddy system to check one another. Have students spread out around the gym, 6 to 8 feet (1.83-2.44 meters) apart. Demonstrate the forehand overhead clear shot using the ap-

propriate skill and teaching cues. Have students take 10 to 12 swings each, trying to make a swishing sound each time. Repeat the exercise using the forehand underhand clear shot. (4-6 minutes)

2. Explain and demonstrate the backhand grip, and repeat activity 1 using the backhand overhead and backhand underhand clear shots. Emphasize pivoting on the back foot and stepping across the body with the other foot while preparing to clear. (4-6 minutes)

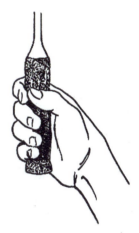

Forehand grip

3. Wall drill. Position students around the perimeter of the gym, standing 20 to 25 feet (6.1-7.62 meters) from and facing a wall (or curtain). Have students practice tossing the shuttle high and clearing it into the wall, concentrating on timing and swinging forcefully. Students who can successfully hit five consecutive forehand and backhand clears into the wall should move further back from the wall, around 30 feet (9.14 meters), and repeat. (5-6 minutes)

4. Partner toss. Have students pair up with the student to their left (still facing the wall). Have one partner toss high shuttles to the other partner, who hits clear shots (forehand and backhand overhead and underhand clear shots) into the wall from 25 feet (7.62 meters). Partners switch roles after 10 tosses. For more challenge, increase the distance to 30 or 35 feet (9.14-10.67 meters) from the wall. (6-8 minutes)

Backhand grip

5. Rally clear shot drill. Use tape or cord to mark a line 4 feet (1.22 meters) inside the back boundary line of the court. No net is used in this drill. Partners rally clear shots from behind these taped lines, trying to drive each other all the way back to or outside their back boundary lines. Partners may not step across the taped line to return a clear shot. (6-8 minutes)

6. Clear game. Have students change partners and repeat activity 5, this time adding a scoring element. Students should keep track of their own scores. (5-6 minutes)

   ▸ 1 point: clearing the shuttle across the taped line
   ▸ 2 points: clearing the shuttle beyond the back boundary line
   ▸ −1 point: failing to get the shuttle across the taped line

Closure (3-5 Minutes)

Review the lesson with students. Use the following questions and ideas to reinforce learning, check understanding, and provide feedback.

1. How many students could consistently clear a tossed shuttle 20 feet (6.1 meters)? 25 feet (7.62 meters)? 30 feet (9.14 meters)?

2. Direct students to close their eyes and visualize a powerful swing, thinking about what each body part is doing to create force and speed.

3. Discuss the five elements that create a powerful swing (i.e., long backswing, rotating body into the shot, full extension of arm at contact, firm grip on contact, and forceful follow-through).

Lesson 2

Serve

Purpose

In this lesson students develop the short, low serve and the high, deep serve.

Warm-Ups (6-8 Minutes)

1. Slapping jacks
2. Wrist rotation and flexion
3. Sit and stretch
4. Triceps dips
5. Sprint-jog intervals

Skill Cues

Use the following sequence when performing a serve:

1. Start with a forehand grip and stand in a forward stride position, knees flexed.
2. Hold the shuttle between the thumb and forefinger, either at its base (i.e., the cork end) or at the edge of the skirt, about waist high in front of the forward foot in the arc path of the swinging racket.
3. Move the racket back, about waist high; cock the wrist at the backswing.
4. Release the shuttle while starting the forward swing, allowing minimal transfer of weight.
5. Uncock the wrist on contact using the lower arm and wrist for power.
6. Contact the shuttle below the hand and waist level, ahead and away from the body.
7. Follow through slightly on the short serve and more on the deep serve.

Teaching Cues

1. Make sure that students contact the shuttle below waist height, with the racket head lower than the hand (see the figure). They should also keep the feet stationary until after contact (see the rules of badminton on page 96 and 97).

Facility and Equipment

- Gym with line markings[†]
- 4 badminton courts (2 without nets and 2 or more with nets and standards)
- 1 racket per student
- 3 shuttles per student
- 1 badminton serve task sheet (see page 104) and pencil per student
- 1 quiz sheet per student
- 2 wall charts*

[†]Mark the gym with the following taped lines:

- Wall: 5 feet (1.52 meters) up the wall
- Floor: 7 and 25 feet (2.13 and 7.62 meters) away from the wall

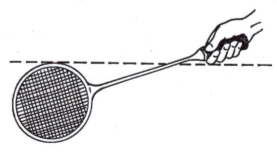

Hand-racket relationship for legal serve

2. Remind students to adjust the angle of the racket face for short and deep serves.

3. The tasks on the badminton task serve sheet use courts with and without nets. As open courts become available, set up more nets.

4. Reproduce and enlarge the placement areas diagram for wall charts.

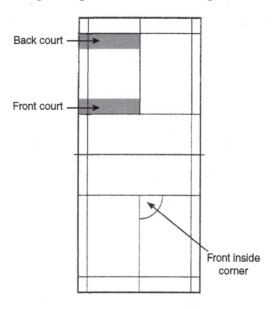

Placement areas chart

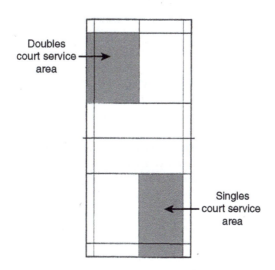

Singles and doubles service courts

Activities (30-40 Minutes)

1. Explain and demonstrate the short, low serve and the high, deep serve using the skill cues. (3-5 minutes)

2. Distribute the student task sheets and pencils, and explain how the gym has been arranged. Remind students that these tasks are not races. The goal is mastery, not how many tasks are completed or how quickly. (2-5 minutes)

3. Students should spend the rest of the period performing the tasks on the badminton serve task sheet located on the following page. (25-30 minutes)

Badminton Serve Task Sheet

Student name _____

Instructions: Tasks 3 and 6 must be checked and initialed by the teacher. Tasks 2, 7, 8, and 9 must be checked and initialed by a classmate. Check the rest of the tasks yourself. Do not move to the next task until you have been checked and passed according to the task conditions.

Tasks check-off (✓)

❏ 1. Stand behind a line anywhere in the gym and serve 10 times, concentrating on timing the drop and swing.

❏ 2. Repeat task 1 concentrating on the rules. Get a classmate to check your serve according to the rules.

❏ 3. Move to a wall area and stand behind the first taped line (7 feet [2.13 meters]) and serve into the wall, trying to contact the wall just above the 5-foot (1.52-meter) line. After five consecutive good serves, move back to the second taped line (25 feet [7.62 meters]) and repeat. Ask your teacher to check you on each task.

❏ 4. Stand in the front inside corner area of a court with no net and serve 10 times into the front area of the opposite diagonal court. (Check the wall chart for placement areas.) Four students can serve at the same time on the same court. After serving at least five times into the placement area, check the task sheet to show that you have completed the task.

❏ 5. Repeat task 4, serving into the backcourt area.

❏ 6. Move to a court with a net. Continue to serve short and low to the front doubles court (see the chart). When you have served five consecutive good serves, ask your teacher to check you. Four can practice at one time.

❏ 7. Repeat task 6, this time serving to the doubles backcourt (see the chart for singles and doubles court lines). When you have served five consecutive good serves, ask a classmate to check you.

❏ 8. In partners and in diagonal courts (four to a court), one student serves short and low and the other underhand clears to the deep area of the court. After every five serves, reverse roles. When you think that you are good at both skills, ask a classmate to check you and your partner. You need at least 3 (out of 5) good serves and good clears to pass. ❏ Pass

❏ 9. Change partners and repeat task 8, this time using high and deep serves and an overhead clear return. Use the same standards for passing: 3 out of 5 good serves and clears. ❏ Pass

❏ 10. Serve and clear game. Change partners and take turns serving five shuttles. Mix your serves, trying to deceive your partner. Score 1 point if your partner is unable to return a legal serve. Score 1 point for each clear that lands between the singles and doubles backcourt lines. Play 4 rounds of 5 serves each. Enter your scores for serves and clears. Serves _____ Clears _____

Closure (3-5 Minutes)

Review the lesson with students. Use the following questions and ideas to reinforce learning, check understanding, and provide feedback.

1. Collect the task sheets and explain that students will have the first 10 minutes of the next lesson to work on unfinished tasks, if necessary.

2. To make sure that students have a solid grasp of the court service areas and the serving sequence, prepare and give a quiz. Following are quiz suggestions:

   ▶ Name three rules governing the serve.

   ▶ Shade in a service court and receiving court for doubles play.

   ▶ Shade in a service court and receiving court for singles play.

Lesson 3

Smash

Purpose

In this lesson students learn about the smash shot, including its offensive advantage, how to perform it, and how to avoid an opponent's smash.

Warm-Ups (6-8 Minutes)

1. Arm rotators
2. Elbow-knee touches (supine)
3. Grapevine step
4. Shoulder shrugs
5. Horizontal run

Facility and Equipment

◆ Gym with court markings or outdoor area with walls
◆ Nets and standards for 2 or more courts
◆ 1 racket per student
◆ 2 to 3 shuttles per student
◆ 30 to 35 hula hoops or other targets
◆ 1 unfinished badminton serve task sheet per student (see lesson 2, page 104)

Targets can also be made from ropes shaped in a circle, drawn with white shoe polish, or taped.

Skill Cues

1. The stroke preparation for the smash is the same as that for the overhead clear: Use a tight grip and reach high to contact the shuttle slightly in front of the forward foot.
2. Shift weight to the back foot as the shuttle approaches; take the racket back, letting the racket head drop behind.
3. Shift weight forward into the stroke and whip the racket head upward and into the descending shuttle.
4. Contact the shuttle with a closed racket face (i.e., angled slightly downward; see contact points diagram on page 100). The distance from the net determines the angle of the racket face; the shorter the distance, the more closed the angle.
5. Rotate the arm and wrist fully on contact and follow through with speed and power.

Teaching Cues

1. Instruct students to use the smash whenever the shuttle is high in the front court near the net.
2. Instruct students to aim for open spaces on the court or the racket shoulder of the opponent.
3. Advise students not to use a backhand smash if they have enough time to move into a forehand position. The backhand smash is more effective when performed close to the net.

Activities (30-40 Minutes)

1. Clear rally. Organize students in partners and assign two sets to each court. With both partners deep in the backcourt, have them begin a rally with a high, deep serve and practice clear shots, trying to place the shot near the back boundary area. If courts are limited, students can practice their shots between courts.(4-6 minutes)

2. Return the badminton serve task sheets and allow students to complete unfinished tasks. Students who finished the task sheet can check serving skills, assist others, practice their own skills, or move on to the optional activity. (8-10 minutes)

Optional Activity: Flying Shuttles

3. Introduce the smash shot, explaining that this is an offensive shot meant to end the rally (and get the point). Explain that the best defense against a smash shot is to direct returns either deep in the opponent's court or downward close to the net so a smash can't be returned. Demonstrate the difference between an overhead clear and a smash shot in terms of racket face angle and contact point (see contact points diagram on page 100). (2-3 minutes)

4. Shadow drill. Position students in a scatter formation around the gym 6 to 8 feet (1.83-2.44 meters) apart. Have them practice the smash shot without shuttles, concentrating on a powerful swing, driving sharply downward, and rotating the wrist fully. Remind students to produce a strong swishing sound. (3 minutes)

Optional Activity: Self-Toss Smash drill

5. Smash drill. Position partner groups four to a court. One partner sets up the shuttle and the other practices smashes from the front court area. After five smashes, students switch roles. If enough courts aren't available, pairs can alternate turns. (4-6 minutes)

6. Target smash drill. Place the targets on the court and have students change partners. Repeat activity 5. Each time the shot lands inside the target or hits the rim, students get a point. (5-6 minutes).

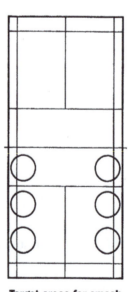

Target areas for smash

7. Smash and return drill. Have students change partners. The first partner sets up the shuttle, the second partner smashes, and the first partner tries to return the smash. (4-6 minutes)

Optional Activities

Flying Shuttles (0-10 Minutes)

Arrange 2 teams of 4 students on a badminton court; 2 players per team are confined to the service courts (1 to each service court), and the other 2 players are confined to the area between the net and the front service line. Give 2 shuttles to each team. The object of the game is to keep the shuttles on the opposing team's side of the net. Shuttles are always started with a serve. At a designated time period, play stops and the team with the fewest shuttles on its side wins. Rotate front and back court players and begin a new game.

Self-Toss Smash Drill (0-4 Minutes)

Position students 10 (3.05 meters) feet from a wall. Students should toss the shuttle high and slightly forward to hit smashes, aiming for the point where the wall and floor meet.

Closure (3-5 Minutes)

Review the lesson with students. Use the following questions and ideas to reinforce learning, check understanding, and provide feedback.

1. Ask students to demonstrate the racket face angles for contact on the smash and clear shots.
2. Review the body mechanics for generating force during the smash.
3. Ask students when the smash advantage is the greatest (i.e., anytime the shuttle is high in the front court).
4. Discuss the best defense against a smash (i.e., do not return a high shot to the front court).
5. How many students were able to execute the smash successfully? How many were successful in directing the smash toward the targets?

Lesson 4

Drop and Drive Shots

Purpose

In this lesson students develop the overhand drop and drive shots while incorporating previously learned skills.

Warm-Ups (6-8 Minutes)

1. Facedown flank
2. Sit and curl
3. Side slides
4. Upper body rotations
5. Reverse run

Skill Cues

Drop Shot

1. Begin the drop stroke with the same body mechanics used in the clear and smash shots.
2. Contact the shuttle with a square racket face slightly in front of the body (this is also the same as the clear and smash).
3. Slow the racket speed considerably just before contact.
4. Follow through slightly (i.e., with minimal force) so that the shuttle barely clears the net and drops into the front court.

Drive Shot

1. Generate force by rotating the body away from the net on the backswing, shifting the weight from the rear foot to the front foot on the forward swing, fully extending the arm, and uncocking the wrist at contact.
2. Contact the shuttle above shoulder height and follow through somewhat parallel to the floor in a slightly downward motion.

Teaching Cues

Drop Shot

1. Be sure students understand to use minimal force on the contact and follow-through.
2. Explain that this is a deceptive shot meant to confuse an opponent.
3. This shot should be used when an opponent is in midcourt to backcourt.

Drive Shot

1. The path of the shuttle is somewhat flat.
2. Explain to students that this shot should be used to pass an opponent or for quick changes crosscourt or down the line.

Activities (30-40 Minutes)

Optional Activity: Controlled Rally

1. Present the drop shot, stressing its mechanics and deceptive value. (2-4 minutes)
2. Overhand drop drill. Pair up students or have them select partners and position them two sets to a court. One partner serves and the other receives. The receiver practices the overhand drop shot, concentrating on the proper mechanics of the swing (i.e., the same as those for the clear and smash shots) and adjusting racket speed just before contact. Students switch roles after 6 to 8 trials. (5-6 minutes)
3. Clear, smash, and drop drill. Students change partners. One serves high to the other, who returns the shot and tries to mask whether the return will be a clear, smash, or drop shot. After 6 to 8 trials, students switch roles. (5-6 minutes)
4. Present the skill and teaching cues for the drive shot, stressing the importance of power, a flat trajectory, and directing the drive crosscourt and down the line. (2-3 minutes)
5. Partner fast exchange drill. Position two pairs of students on each court. Students practice a rapid exchange of forehand and backhand drives, making every shot forceful. If not enough courts are available, use the space between courts and perimeter zones if safe distance can be maintained. (4-5 minutes)
6. Doubles fast exchange drill. Divide students into groups of four and assign each group to a court. Player 1 hits the shuttle straight across the net to player 2, who drives it diagonally across to player 3, who drives it straight across to player 4, who returns it diagonally back to player 1. This drill promotes crosscourt and down-the-line drives. After 4 to 5 exchange cycles, have students rotate so that all get a chance to drive from each court position. (5-6 minutes)
7. Skill game. Pair up students and position two teams to a court. Start with a serve and continue play until the shuttle is out of play (e.g., the shuttle hits the net or goes out-of-bounds). The team that did not commit an error scores 1 point. After each point, rotate the serve to the opponents (each player serves every fourth serve). Stress the following game skills: mixing shots; aiming for corners, open spaces, and opponent's backhand side; and deceiving opponents. (7-10 minutes)

Optional Activity

Controlled Rally (0-6 minutes)

Pair up students and assign two pairs to a court, with partners standing on opposite sides of the net near the front service line. Students start the rally with light underhand shots to the front court area, concentrating on controlling the shuttle's flight pattern. After 2 minutes, students move back to middle court, maintaining shuttle control by returning it with both underhand and overhand shots. After another 2 minutes, students move to the backcourt and exchange powerful clears.

Closure (3-5 Minutes)

Review the lesson with students. Use the following topics and questions to reinforce learning, check understanding, and provide feedback:

1. Using the palm of the hand, show the contact point for an overhead clear, smash, and overhand drop.
2. Review the flight pattern of the shuttle for each of the three shots.
3. Discuss the advantage of using a drop shot.
4. Discuss the advantages of using a drive shot.
5. In the last game, how many teams scored 5 or more points? 7 or more? 8 or more? 10 or more?

Lesson 5

Net Shots

Purpose

In this lesson students learn the underhand net shots: the hairpin, the crosscourt, and the underhand drop.

Warm-Ups (6-8 Minutes)

1. Step and calf taps
2. Wrist rotation and flexion
3. Waist twists
4. Push-ups
5. Imaginary jump rope

Skill Cues

1. Net shots can be played forehand and backhand, although forehand shots are generally easier and more successful.
2. Hold the racket less firmly and shorten the grip.
3. When making the shot, get under the shuttle and try to guide it over the net. The lower the shuttle descends before contact, the less chance for success.
4. Return the shuttle as close to the net as possible, trying to drop it just over the top. If the shuttle is too far above the net, an opponent can block it, sending it back (an offensive move). If the shuttle is just over the net, however, an opponent must tap the shuttle up and over the net (a defensive move).

Facility and Equipment

- Gym with court markings or outdoor area with a wall
- Nets and standards for 3 courts
- 1 racket per student
- 1 shuttle per student
- 1 rules handout* per student
- 1 pencil per student
- 12 hula hoops
- 1 rope (25 feet [7.62 meters] long)
- Tape
- Station wall charts*
  Mark the gym with the following taped lines:
  - Wall: 5 and 7 feet (1.52 and 2.13 meters) up the wall
  - Floor: 2 and 4 feet (.61 and 1.22 meters) away from the wall

Teaching Cues

1. If time permits, have students shorten their grip for better control.
2. Explain that net shots should be used both to deceive the opponent and when the opponent is away from the net area.
3. The underhand drop shot can be played as far back as the short service line; the hairpin and crosscourt shots should be played at the net.
4. Create five wall charts, each explaining one of the station drills.
5. Create a handout of the rules for doubles badminton and make a copy for each student.

Activities (30-40 Minutes)

1. Introduce net shots by stressing the importance of good net play. Explain and demonstrate the hairpin, crosscourt, and underhand drop net shots using the skill and teaching cues. Explain the following stations, telling students that various net shots will be practiced at five stations. Divide students into five groups, each starting at a different station. Students should rotate stations every 6 to 8 minutes. Students will find a chart that explains the drill at each station. (30-40 minutes)

   ▶ Station 1: Wall Drill

   Align students along the wall, standing behind the 4-foot (1.22-meter) floor line. Students drop a shuttle from above the 5-foot (1.52-meter) wall line and aim the shot between the 5- and 7-foot (1.52- and 2.13-meter) wall lines. If the shuttle bounces (off the wall) further back than the 2-foot (.61-meter) floor line, the shot was hit too hard. Students continue to drop hit the shuttle 15 times, counting the number of good hits (i.e., shuttles that hit the wall between the 5- and 7-foot [1.52- and 2.13-meter] wall lines and fall between the wall and the 2-foot [.61-meter] floor line).

   ▶ Station 2: Hoop Rally Drill

   Place two hoops per set of partners end to end under a net extending an equal distance into each court (each court can accommodate three sets of partners). Partners take positions opposite each other and one step behind their hoops, and facing each other. Students rally back and forth using underhand hits so that the shuttle falls over the hoop area closest to their partners. Students should not reach outside their hoop areas to return a shuttle—to do so is a fault and does not count. After partners practice a few minutes, have them start counting consecutive good hits.

   ▶ Station 3: Cross-Hoop Drill Rally

   Arrange two hoops per set of partners about 10 feet (3.05 meters) apart diagonally with the top of each hoop touching a floor line. Each partner stands behind and to the outside of a hoop and hits underhand shots (alternating forehand and backhand) to one another, trying to direct the shuttle above and into the hoop area. After a few practice minutes, students change positions and continue practicing. During the final 2 minutes, students count the number of good shots (e.g., shuttles hit into and returned within the hoop area). Start the count over if the shuttle goes outside the hoop rim.

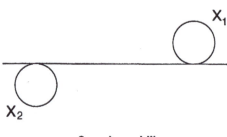

   Cross-hoop drill

   ▶ Station 4: Court Drill

   Position partners (up to three partner sets per court) on either side of the net, 1 to 2 feet (.3-.61 meters) inside the short service line. Partners hit hairpin net shots back and forth, trying to keep the shuttle crossing within 1 foot (.3 meters) of the top of the net and falling within 3 feet (.91 meters) of the net. After a few minutes of practice, students count the number of consecutive good shots.

▶ Station 5: Court Rope Drill

Extend a rope 2 feet (.61 meters) above and parallel to the net. Position groups of three students on each side of the court with each about 3 feet (.91 meters) from the net. Use one shuttle. Students hit crosscourt net shots to their right or left, trying to get the shuttle between the net and the rope. Rotate positions every few minutes.

Closure (3-5 Minutes)

Review the lesson with students. Use the following questions and ideas to reinforce learning, check understanding, and provide feedback.

1. Ask students which station they found the most difficult. The easiest?
2. Discuss why net shots are so difficult.
3. Discuss why shortening the grip gives more control.
4. Distribute the rules for doubles badminton and have students read them before the next lesson.

Lesson 6

Doubles Game

Purpose

In this lesson students learn side-by-side formation and will apply the rules for playing doubles badminton.

Warm-Ups (6-8 Minutes)

1. Alternate leg raises
2. Mad cat
3. Russian floor kicks
4. Push-ups
5. Agility run

Skill Cues

1. When playing side by side, each partner covers half of the court, extending from the net to the back boundary line and from the centerline to the doubles sideline.
2. Call out shots in the center. Usually the player with the forehand shot takes the center returns.
3. Mix various shots to deceive opponents.

Teaching Cues

1. See the rules of doubles badminton on pages 96-98.
2. The player with the strongest backhand should start in the left court.
3. Make sure servers (S), receivers (R), and serving and receiving partners (SP and RP) are in the proper formation before starting the game.

S = Server
R = Receiver
SP = Serving partner
RP = Receiving partner

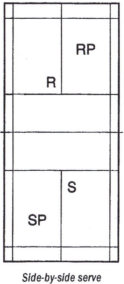

Side-by-side serve

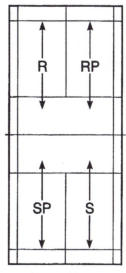

Side-by-side play

Side-by-side doubles formations

4. The side-by-side doubles formation is useful because it is easy to understand and it enables complete court coverage if both partners are strong players. The disadvantages of this formation include the following:

   ▸ Opponents can attack with a combination of clear and drop shots.

   ▸ If one player is weak, opponents can continuously return shots to that side of the court to force faults.

5. Before class, prepare a list of quiz questions for the end of class. A 10-item written quiz about the major rules (e.g., lines, scoring, and side-by-side formation) is suggested.

Activities (30-40 Minutes)

1. Mixed shot rally. Position four students on a court. (If court space is limited, 6 students can play on a court; 1 plays up and 2 play back). Have students rally, practicing all the different shots. (8 minutes)

2. Demonstration game. Select four students to demonstrate the doubles game. Position them on the court and have other students sit down around the court perimeter. Explain side-by-side formation using the skill and teaching cues. Explain the rules and scoring while four players demonstrate positions and game play. (12 minutes)

3. Practice doubles play. Divide students into doubles teams and position them on each court. Have students practice the game using a side-by-side team formation. Rotate one set of partners every 5 minutes. If available courts are insufficient for the number of courts, assign one team per court to act as referees and rotate them into the game every 5 minutes, or let them practice in other gym areas. (10-20 minutes)

Closure (3-5 Minutes)

Review the lesson with students. To make sure they have the necessary information to play and referee on their own, present one of the following testing ideas:

1. Position students in groups of three around the gym and give each group a written quiz about the major badminton rules. Allow students to discuss answers within their groups.

2. In place of a written quiz, give the group a verbal quiz and discuss their answers in class.

Lesson 7

Doubles Play I

Purpose

In this lesson students apply doubles rules, practice doubles play, learn the up-and-back formation, and review the side-by-side formation.

Facility and Equipment

◆ Gym with court markings or outdoor area
◆ Nets and standards for all courts
◆ 1 racket per student
◆ 1 shuttle per student

Warm-Ups (6-8 Minutes)

1. Shoulder shrugs
2. Wrist rotation and flexion
3. Scissors
4. Arm circles
5. Running in place

Skill Cues

1. Play up and back with one partner covering the net area and the other covering the backcourt area.
2. Because partners tend to stay in center court, the side areas are most vulnerable to attack.
3. Mix shots to deceive opponents.

Teaching Cues

1. Make sure servers (S), receivers (R), and serving and receiving partners (SP and RP) are in the proper formation before starting the game. The partner who serves or receives takes the net area.

S = Server
R = Receiver
SP = Serving partner
RP = Receiving partner

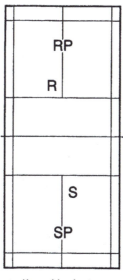

Up-and-back serve   Up-and-back play

Up-and-back doubles formations

2. Give students a chance to practice both up-and-back positions by rotating positions after each serve. Then, if one partner is stronger on clears or faster in shifting positions, or if one partner is a better net player, permanent court areas can be assigned.

Activities (30-40 Minutes)

1. Have students sit around a court and review the rules quiz from lesson 6. Explain rules that are unclear or misunderstood. (5-6 minutes)

2. Demonstration game. Select four students to demonstrate the game. Position them on the court and have other students sit down around the court perimeter. Explain up-and-back formation using the skill and teaching cues. Explain the rules and scoring while four players demonstrate up-and-back positions and game play. (3-4 minutes)

3. Practice doubles play. Pair students with different partners and have them practice the doubles game using the up-and-back formation. Rotate teams every 5 minutes. If courts are limited, use extra teams to referee or rotate a doubles team in after 5 points. (12-15 minutes)

4. Doubles play. Pair students with different partners and have them play an actual doubles game using the side-by-side formation. Rotate teams after 5 minutes. (10-15 minutes)

Closure (3-5 Minutes)

Review the lesson with students. Use the following questions and ideas to reinforce learning, check understanding, and provide feedback.

1. Have students describe which formation they liked best and why.

2. Ask students to note weaknesses in their play as well as in their opponents'.

3. Explain any rules students are still unsure about.

4. Share your observations about good positioning, accurate use of rules, effective use of strategies, and so on.

Lesson 8

Doubles Play II

Purpose

In this lesson students continue to apply doubles-playing skills, learn the rotation formation, and select partners for a round-robin tournament.

Facility and Equipment

◆ Gym with court markings or outdoor area
◆ Nets and standards for all courts
◆ 1 racket per student
◆ 1 shuttle per student
◆ Player roster

Warm-Ups (6-8 Minutes)

1. High jumper
2. Body circles
3. Single-leg curls
4. Back stretch
5. Reverse run

Skill Cues

1. Stay alert; pay attention to quick formation changes.
2. Players should cover the backcourt when their partners are in front court, and cover the front court when their partners are back.

Teaching Cues

1. Explain that the rotation system is a combination of the up-and-back and the side-by-side formations. In general, when the team is on the offense the up-and-back formation is used; the side-by-side formation is used when the team is on the defense.
2. Explain that partners should constantly change formation, which requires that students have good coordination and know their partners. When the serve is short, the receiver plays the net and the receiving partner is back. If the serve is deep, the receiver plays back and the receiving partner plays the net.

Activities (30-40 Minutes)

1. All-shot rally. In partners or in groups of four, students should rally using all shots. Each player must use each shot—clears, net shots, drives, smashes, and overhand drops—at least twice, one backhand and one forehand. (7-8 minutes)
2. Seat students around a court and present the rotation system for doubles. Have four students demonstrate on the court while explaining the rotation formation. (4-5 minutes)
3. Rotation system drill. Have students practice rotation in teams by alternating the serve to the next player at the end of each rally. This will give students many chances to learn and adjust to the rotation system. (5-7 minutes)

4. Announce that a two-flight round-robin tournament will start the next class. Based on skill level, assign students to flight X (higher skill level) or flight Z (lower skill level). Students may select their partners from within their flight group. Record the tournament teams on the player roster. (4-5 minutes)

5. Team practice. In the teams designated in activity 4, students should play 5-minute doubles games against different teams. Be sure to have teams practice different formations and familiarize themselves with other teams' strengths and weaknesses. (10-15 minutes)

Closure (3-5 Minutes)

Review the lesson with students. Use the following ideas to reinforce learning, check understanding, and provide feedback.

1. Discuss any problems students had with the rotation formation.

2. Answer any questions students have about rules or formation systems.

3. Announce that the round-robin tournament schedule will be posted at the start of the next class.

Lesson 9

Round-Robin Tournament I

Purpose

In this lesson students apply their skills, knowledge, and strategies in the game.

Warm-Ups (6-8 Minutes)

1. Grapevine step
2. Arm rotators
3. Abdominal crunches
4. Mule leg pushes
5. Side slides

Skill Cues

1. Call out the score before each serve.
2. Call out team faults.
3. Replay a point if students have a difference of opinion.
4. Be alert, be ready, and move quickly.
5. Disguise shots to deceive opponents, and aim for open spaces.
6. Whenever possible, direct the shuttle flight downward.

Teaching Cues

1. Keep students on task.
2. Encourage students to play fairly, using good sporting behavior. Remind them that the lesson's emphasis is on demonstrating game rules and skills, not just competition.
3. If courts are limited, students can practice serves and net shots in other gym areas, officiate games, observe line violations, watch videotapes of skill development and game strategies, or chart a court player's shot placement.
4. Before class, create a tournament schedule listing partner teams by number or letter and the sequence of game play.

Activities (30-40 Minutes)

1. Show students the tournament schedule and adjust it for any absent students. Announce that games will be 7 minutes or 11 points, whichever comes first, and that the winning team should mark their win on the tournament schedule. (2-5 minutes)
2. Play four to five rounds of the tournament. (28-35 minutes)

Facility and Equipment

◆ Gym with court markings or outdoor area
◆ Nets and standards for all courts
◆ 1 racket per student
◆ 1 shuttle per student
◆ Tournament schedule and marker*

Closure (3-5 Minutes)

Review the lesson with students. Use the following topics and questions to reinforce learning, check understanding, and provide feedback.

1. Share your observations of effective strategic play. Explain that "reading" the other team can help determine the next shot, and review how to use body language to disguise shots.

2. Share your observations of good teamwork, etiquette, and sporting behavior during tournament play.

3. Ask students to name the toughest opponent in flight X. Flight Z?

4. Ask student team how many won at least 1 game. 2 games? 3 or more? Did any teams win all of their games?

Lesson 10

Round-Robin Tournament II

Purpose

This lesson is a continuation of lesson 9, giving students a second day to apply the skills, knowledge, and strategies of badminton through game play.

Facility and Equipment

- Gym with court markings or outdoor area
- Nets and standards for all courts
- 1 racket per student
- 1 shuttle per student
- Tournament schedule and marker (see lesson 9)*

Warm-Ups (6-8 Minutes)

1. Agility run
2. Arm circles
3. Gluteal stretch
4. Faceup flank
5. Running in place

Skill Cues

1. Call out the score before each serve.
2. Call out team faults.
3. Replay a point if students have a difference of opinion.
4. Be alert, be ready, and move quickly.
5. Disguise shots to deceive opponents, and aim for open spaces.
6. Whenever possible, direct the shuttle flight downward.

Teaching Cues

1. Refer to the tournament schedule for team pairings.
2. Keep students on task.
3. Encourage students to play fairly, using good sporting behavior. Remind them that the lesson's emphasis is on demonstrating game rules and skills, not competition.
4. If courts are limited or when teams are not playing, have students practice serves and net shots in other gym areas or help officiate games by observing line violations.

Activities (30-40 Minutes)

1. Show students the tournament schedule and adjust it for any absent students. Remind students that games will be played to 11 points or for 7 minutes, whichever comes first. The team that wins should update the tournament schedule.

Answer any questions students have based on their experiences on the first day of tournament play. (2-5 minutes)

2. Proceed with tournament play. (28-35 minutes)

Closure (3-5 Minutes)

Review the lesson with students. Use the following topics and questions to reinforce learning, check understanding, and provide feedback.

1. Share your observations of effective strategic play, emphasizing the discussion points of the previous lesson's closure (e.g., "reading" the other team to determine the next shot, using body language to disguise shots).

2. Share your observations of good teamwork, etiquette, and sporting behavior during tournament play.

Assessment and Resources

Two quizzes should be given early in the badminton unit (these are suggested in lessons 2 and 6) to check for basic understanding before starting game play. Too often such testing is given at the conclusion of a unit, which can lessen skill understanding and development as well as reduce the effectiveness of game play.

Skill tests and game play assessment can be formal or informal. You can use many of the lesson drills for testing or give separate skill tests. In general, testing the short and deep serves, and the clear and smash shots is sufficient.

▶ Serve testing. Mark target areas on both courts of the same side, giving higher values to the most desirable targets. In groups of 4, 2 students should serve at the same time, 1 should record and 1 should retrieve shuttles. Students serve 6 (or any even number) shuttles, half from the right court and half from the left. Scores are totalled and scaled to a grade.

▶ Clear and smash shots testing. Students will need an accurate and consistent shuttle setup for these tests. (For consistency, you may want to provide the setup yourself or have class assistants do so.) As in serve testing, mark target court areas, assigning higher values to the most desirable targets. Assessing the smash requires a judgment of speed and the downward angle of the shuttle. Assessing the clear requires a judgment of height and distance.

▶ Playing skills can also be evaluated. A subjective assessment could be made during game play (e.g., looking for effective rotation, shots, and so on). For a more objective assessment, total the number of team points scored in all tournament games (lessons 9 and 10) and then convert those points into a grading scale for the unit. (This method encourages students to keep trying even when they are losing.) However, assessment should focus on skill development, not just competition. By organizing tournaments into two flights of skill level (flights X and Z), extreme differences in student ability won't be as apparent.

Resources

Chafin, M.B., and M.M. Turner. 1988. *Badminton everyone.* Winston-Salem, NC: Hunter Textbooks.

Mood, D., F. Musker, and J. Rink. 1991. *Sports and recreational activities for men and women.* 10th ed. St. Louis: Mosby.

White, J.R., ed. 1990. *Sports rules encyclopedia.* Champaign, IL: Leisure Press.

Zakrajsek, D., and L. Carnes. 1986. *Individualizing physical education: Criterion materials.* 2nd ed. Champaign, IL: Human Kinetics.

Basketball

The game of basketball was actually developed to help condition football players during the winter months. In 1891 Dr. James Naismith, the physical education director at the YMCA College in Springfield, Massachusetts, introduced the game. The first basketball games were played with a soccer-style ball and with peach baskets as the goals. The number of players on a team and the number of balls in play were unlimited in these games. In fact, it was not uncommon to have as many as 50 players on the floor using 4 or 5 balls at a time. The first official game of basketball was not played until 1892, when Naismith developed 13 basic rules, some of which are still in use today. The game and the rules were published in a YMCA magazine and distributed throughout the country. The game quickly became popular at other YMCAs, playgrounds, schools, colleges, and community centers.

By 1897 players were starting to be called by their positions, but there was still no limit to the number who could play at one time. The decision to limit players to five was not made until 1899. From 1910 to 1923, each team had a standing guard, a running guard, two forwards, and a center. The standing guard was used for defense, like a soccer goalie. The running guard helped on defense and traveled into the offensive territory to assist the forwards in scoring. The standing forward was used primarily for offense and generally stayed on the offensive end of the court. The running forward often moved the length of the floor, helping not only in scoring but also in passing the ball to the standing forward.

The first intercollegiate basketball game was played in 1896 (i.e., Yale vs. Connecticut Wesleyan), and in 1899 women formulated their own rules. The National Basketball Association and the National Collegiate Athletic Association now govern the rules of basketball.

Equipment

The basketball playing court is a rectangular surface, usually a hardwood floor, measuring 94 by 50 feet (28.65 by 15.24 meters) for college teams and 84 by 50 feet (25.6 by 15.24 meters) for high school teams. A backboard, 4 feet (1.22 meters) high by 6 feet (1.83 meters) wide, is located in the center of each end of the court. The basket is an open hammock net, suspended from the backboard by a metal rim 18 inches (45.7 centimeters) in diameter. The rim must be 6 inches (15.2 centimeters) from the backboard and 10 feet (3.05 meters) from the ground.

The only piece of equipment used in basketball is the ball. In men's basketball, the ball weighs 20 to 22 ounces (567-623.7 grams) and has a circumference of 30 inches (76.2 centimeters). The basketball used by women has a circumference of 28.5 inches (72.4 centimeters) and weighs 18 to 20 ounces (510.3-567 grams). Although official basketballs are usually covered with leather, basketballs used in other games can also be covered with rubber or a synthetic material.

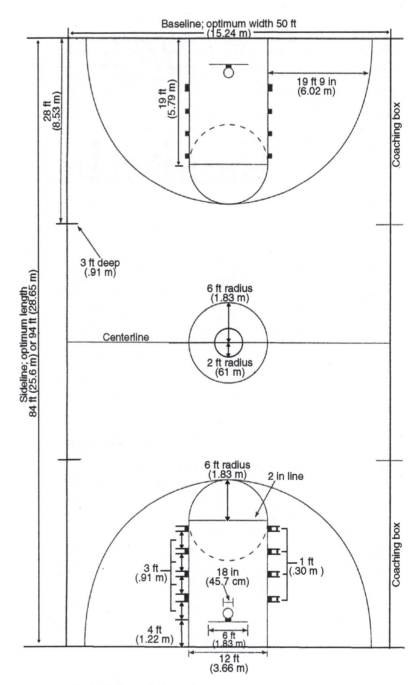

All lines are 2 in (5.01 cm) wide (neutral zones excluded).

Baseline; optimum width 50 ft (15.24 m)

28 ft (8.53 m)

19 ft (5.79 m)

19 ft 9 in (6.02 m)

Coaching box

3 ft deep (.91 m)

Sideline: optimum length 84 ft (25.6 m) or 94 ft (28.65 m)

6 ft radius (1.83 m)

Centerline

2 ft radius (61 m)

6 ft radius (1.83 m)

2 in line

3 ft (.91 m)

18 in (45.7 cm)

1 ft (.30 m)

4 ft (1.22 m)

6 ft (1.83 m)

12 ft (3.66 m)

Coaching box

Basketball court dimensions

Unit Organization

Some of the lessons in this unit may present more instruction than can be offered in a single class period. Although time specifications fit within the usual parameters (i.e., 6-8 minutes for warm-ups), many of the lessons recommend ball-handling skills during the warm-up period. Such review is crucial in this unit, particularly early on, offering continued reinforcement of skills and technique, and may require more class time. Observe students closely to make sure they understand the various passes used in basketball. If necessary, select the most appropriate activities for your students or expand certain lessons to allow for a full review of ball-handling skills as well as all recommended activities.

Following is an overview of each lesson in this unit.

- Lesson 1 starts the unit by teaching basic ball-handling skills. These skills lead up to the various passes and ball techniques used throughout the unit.
- Passing, dribbling, shooting, guarding, and rebounding are presented in lessons 2 through 6.
- Lessons 7 and 8 focus on offensive and defensive strategies.
- Students get to play modified games and are introduced to the official rules of basketball in lesson 9.
- In lesson 10 students solidify their understanding of the rules and play a game of regulation basketball.

Selected resources and assessment ideas are found in the assessment and resources chapter at the end of the unit.

Note: An asterisk (*) following a facility or equipment listing indicates that preparation is required before the lesson.

Social Skills and Etiquette

Because basketball is a team game, requiring teamwork and cooperation for success, social skills and etiquette are important during play. Discussions on teamwork and fair play are essential at the beginning of and throughout this unit. Instruct students in supporting and encouraging one another, including their teammates as well as players on the opposing team. Recognizing and complimenting good shots, nice plays, and so on can go a long way in nurturing a class atmosphere of collaboration and rapport among students. The activities in this unit will also help in this regard. Many require students to work in small groups, thus providing excellent opportunities for students to interact socially, emotionally, and cognitively as well as physically.

Lesson Modifications

Basketball can be strenuous for students, particularly those on the lower end of fitness levels and those with less cardiovascular stamina. To accommodate these students, suggested modifications include reducing the size of the playing court and restricting the length of playing time. For students who may have difficulty handling and shooting the ball, a smaller, lighter basketball can be used and the basket can be lowered.

Changing the rules slightly may make the game easier to play for beginning or less-advanced students. For example, allowing unlimited dribbling as well as removing restrictions on moving with the ball (traveling) and time in certain court locations would alter the game significantly.

Safety

The primary safety concern in basketball is the ball; players must pay constant attention to its location and movement. Other safety considerations include the following:

- Obstructions outside the court, such as benches, walls, and equipment could be hazardous. Make sure students are aware of their proximity to the court, and alert students if they are approaching these or other obstructions.
- In the game itself, all fouls should be called immediately to safeguard players from personal injuries and to instill the importance of playing fairly and playing by the rules.
- Aggressive players should be held to the rules of the game; no exceptions.

Rules

Basketball is played by 2 teams of 5 players: 2 guards, 2 forwards, and 1 center. Players attempt to outscore their opponents by passing, bouncing, handing off, or dribbling the basketball into position to then shoot it into their offensive basket. The game is monitored by a scorer, a timer, and 2 or 3 floor officials.

At the end of the game, the team with the most points wins. Regulation basketball games consist of either 8-minute quarters (high school), 20-minute halves (college), or 12-minute quarters (professional).

Following are the rules and sequence of play in basketball:

- ▶ An official puts the ball into play at the beginning of the game by tossing the ball in the air at midcourt while two players from opposing teams attempt to tip the ball to their respective teammates. Play continues until the designated time expires.

- ▶ A team scores a field goal (a basket worth 2 or 3 points, depending on the distance from which the ball was shot) when one of its players shoots the ball from the field into its offensive basket. A free throw (worth 1 point) is scored similarly, although play is stopped for the free throw shot.

- ▶ After each field goal, the team scored against puts the ball into play from out-of-bounds behind the baseline near its own defensive basket.

- ▶ Offensive players get into position to shoot the ball by passing, dribbling, handing off, or bouncing the ball. At the same time, defensive players block and guard offensive players, attempting to prevent the offensive team from scoring.

Play continues until either team commits a violation or foul, at which time the fouled player gets a free throw or possession of the ball changes. A change of possession follows a violation, and the opposing team takes the ball out-of-bounds. When a foul is committed, the opponents may either be given the opportunity to shoot 1 or 2 free throws or get to take the ball in from out-of-bounds.

Ball-Handling Skills

Purpose

Ball-handling skills are the precursor to specific basketball skills. In this lesson students learn the basics of handling a basketball.

Facility and Equipment

◆ Gym or outdoor area with a smooth surface
◆ 1 basketball per student

Warm-Ups (6-8 Minutes)

1. Lateral hops
2. Waist twists
3. Abdominal crunches
4. Side slides
5. Arm rotators

Skill Cues

Pops

A pop is performed by slapping at the ball (alternating hands) to keep it bouncing low to the ground.

1. Use the full hand to slap the ball.
2. Control the ball.
3. Keep the ball bouncing.

Fingertips

To handle the ball using the fingertips, sit on the floor with the legs extended straight out and dribble the ball with the fingertips. Lift the legs to dribble the ball beneath them and alternate dribbling hands.

1. Keep the ball close to the side of the body.
2. Keep the head up.
3. Spread the fingers wide.
4. Use only the tips of the fingers to bounce the ball.

Funnel

In the funnel, the ball is passed quickly back and forth between the hands, starting at head level and going down the body to the chest, waist, knees, and ankles.

1. Keep the head up.
2. Pass the ball from hand to hand.
3. Start with the head high and move down the body.
4. Use only the fingertips to touch the ball.

Body Circles

This is a skill that involves circling the ball around various parts of the body while passing the ball from hand to hand. Start at the head, then go to the chest, then the waist, then the knees, and finally the ankles.

1. Keep the head up.
2. Keep the body still.
3. Keep the ball under control.

Figure 8s

To perform a figure 8, move the ball from hand to hand through the legs.

1. The feet should be shoulder-width apart.
2. Keep the ball close to the legs.
3. Keep both hands on the ball when it is going through the legs.
4. Keep one hand on the ball when it is going around the legs.

Pretzels

The pretzel involves holding the ball between the legs, with one hand in front and the other in back of the ball, then quickly switching hands and catching the ball before it hits the floor.

1. Watch the ball.
2. Switch hands quickly.
3. Keep the ball between the legs.

Windmill

Perform a windmill by bouncing the ball with one hand behind the back and then between the legs to catch it in front of the body with the other hand. With the front hand, circle the ball around to the back of the body and repeat the sequence.

1. Make good bounces. The ball should bounce low and diagonally for best results.
2. Keep the head up.
3. Make good circles around the body. The circles should be tight to the body, made as rapidly as possible.

Teaching Cues

1. When presenting the skills used in this lesson, demonstrate two at a time, allowing students to practice them before introducing the next two skills.
2. In subsequent lessons in this unit, students should practice these skills as part of the warm-up activities.

Activities (30-40 Minutes)

1. Introduce the different ball-handling methods in this lesson using the skill cues. Then scatter students around the gym and give each student a basketball. Demonstrate two skills at a time and allow students to practice. (9-12 minutes)

2. Working in their own space around the gym floor, students should practice each ball-handling skill for 3 or 4 minutes. (21-28 minutes)

Closure (3-5 Minutes)

Review the lesson with students. Use the following ideas to reinforce learning, check understanding, and provide feedback.

1. Discuss the importance of being able to handle the ball when playing a game.

2. Have two students perform selected skills in front of the class. Discuss their technique, having the class identify skill cues when they see them (e.g., Is the student's head up? Is he watching the ball? Is she keeping the ball close to her legs?).

Lesson 2

Passing and Catching

Purpose

In this lesson students develop passing and catching skills, two fundamental skills in basketball.

Warm-Ups (6-8 Minutes)

1. Side pattern jumps
2. Heel lifts
3. Arm support lifts
4. Lateral hops
5. Selected ball-handling skills (see lesson 1)

Skill Cues

Facility and Equipment

◆ Gym or outdoor area with a smooth surface and wall space
◆ 1 basketball per student
◆ 20 wall targets

Chest Pass

1. Stand with the feet shoulder-width apart and the knees slightly bent.
2. Hold the ball with the fingers, not the palms. The fingers should be on the sides of the ball and the thumbs should be on the back of the ball.
3. Hold the ball at chest level, the elbows out to the sides.
4. Step forward when passing.
5. Extend the arms outward and flip the thumbs downward, putting a backspin on the ball.
6. Focus the eyes on the target, trying to pass to the partner's chest.

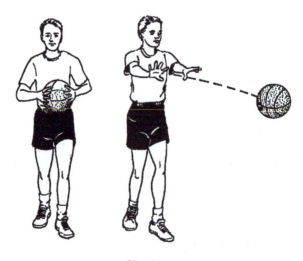

Chest pass

Two-Handed Overhead Pass

1. Hold the ball with both hands above the head, the elbows out to the sides.
2. Extend the arms and flick the wrists, pointing the fingers downward.
3. Focus on the partner's shoulders.
4. Release the ball at the forehead.

Two-handed overhead pass

Two-Handed Bounce Pass

The bounce pass is much the same as the chest pass.

1. Keep the elbows at the sides.
2. Rather than focus on the partner's chest, focus on a point two-thirds of the way to the target.
3. Extend the arms toward the target (two-thirds of the way).
4. Bounce the ball up to the partner's waist.

Two-handed bounce pass

One-Handed Bounce Pass

1. Begin the pass between the shoulders and the waist.
2. Balance the ball with the free (i.e., nonpassing) hand.
3. Place the passing hand behind and toward the top of the ball with the fingers extending upward.
4. Keep the passing elbow flexed and close to the body.
5. Push the ball downward to a spot on the floor so that it quickly bounces up to thigh level of the receiver. Usually this is around two-thirds of the way toward the receiver.

Shoulder (or One-Arm) Push Pass

1. Hold the ball with both hands, the pushing hand behind the ball.
2. Bring the ball above and in front of the throwing shoulder.
3. Extend the arm and push the ball away from the shoulder toward the target.
4. Just before release, snap the wrist.

Catch

1. Step out toward the ball.
2. Catch the ball with both hands, grasping it with the fingers.
3. Pull the ball into the chest.
4. Keep the eyes focused on the ball.

Teaching Cues

1. Students should get past the fundamentals and into the application of each pass. Spend more class time on fundamentals if students are having difficulty performing any of these passes.
2. Demonstrate each pass as you explain it.

Activities (30-40 Minutes)

1. Introduce and demonstrate the chest pass, the two-handed bounce pass, and the two-handed overhead pass, and show students how to catch each pass from the wall rebound, emphasizing the skill cues. (5-7 minutes)
2. Pair up students or have them select partners and position partners 10 feet (3.05 meters) from a wall target. Students should perform the 3 passes (5 trials each) introduced in activity 1, concentrating on form and accuracy when passing the ball. Each student will catch their partner's ball as it rebounds off the wall. (3-5 minutes)
3. Introduce and demonstrate the remaining two passes (i.e., the one-handed bounce pass and the shoulder push pass) using the skill cues. (3-4 minutes)
4. Have partners pass to the wall target (from 10 feet [3.05 meters] away) using these two new passes. After 1 partner tries each pass 5 times, the other partner should try both passes. (3-4 minutes)
5. Divide students into groups of 3. Two group members stand 15 feet (4.57 meters) apart, passing back and forth to each other. The third group member, standing

anywhere between the passing partners, acts as a defender and tries to intercept the passes. Students should use all passes, periodically switch roles, and vary their passing distances. (4-6 minutes)

6. Continuing in groups of 3, 2 group members pass to one another from 10 to 15 feet (3.05-4.57 meters) away and the third member acts as a defensive player, defending the passer and then the receiver. This time, however, receivers should move in various directions. Students should take turns passing, receiving, and defending. (6-7 minutes)

7. Divide the class into three groups and have each group line up at one end of the court (about 10 feet [3.05 meters] apart). Explain and have students perform the three-person weave. (6-7 minutes)

Three-Person Weave

Three students run down the court at the same time. The middle student starts the weave by passing the ball to the student on the right, then cuts behind and continues to run beside that student down the court while the student on the left advances down the court. The receiving student (i.e., the one on the right) then passes the ball to and moves behind the student on the left. This pattern continues all the way down the court. Students should use a variety of passes as they weave down the court. After the first 3 students complete three passes, the next group of 3 starts. This will keep the students moving and decrease waiting time.

Solid lines = players' travel paths

Dotted lines = passes

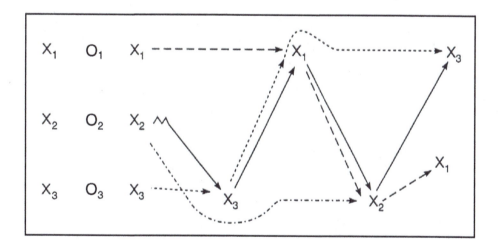

Weave drill

Closure (3-5 Minutes)

Review the lesson with students. Use the following ideas to reinforce learning, check understanding, and provide feedback.

1. Discuss the importance of passing in the game of basketball.

2. Have two students identify the major differences between the push pass and the two-handed chest pass.

3. Discuss the difference between passing to a moving target and passing to a stationary target.

Lesson 3

Dribbling

Purpose

In this lesson students focus on the skill of dribbling, learning to apply control and speed.

Facility and Equipment

◆ Gym or large outdoor area with a smooth surface
◆ 1 basketball per student
◆ 20 cones

Warm-Ups (6-8 Minutes)

1. Leg stretch
2. Arm rotators
3. Upper body rotations
4. Grapevine step
5. Selected ball-handling skills (see lesson 1)

Skill Cues

Dribbling

1. Flex at the knees.
2. Keep weight on the balls of the feet in the forward stride position.
3. Bend forward at the waist in a crouch.
4. Keep the head up; don't look at the ball.
5. Keep the wrist limp and cup the hand slightly.
6. Dribble with the finger pads, not the palm.
7. Never bounce the ball higher than the waist.
8. Use the free (i.e., nondribbling) arm and hand to protect against defenders while dribbling.

Speed Dribbling

1. Use the arm and wrist to push the ball forward, out in front of the body.
2. Push the ball farther out in front of the body when running faster.
3. Keep the body in an upright position, leaning slightly forward with the upper torso.

Teaching Cues

1. Have students use both hands when learning to control the ball.
2. It may be helpful to have them close their eyes while dribbling to get a feel for the ball and the rhythm of dribbling.
3. Explain the dynamics of control: the lower the dribble, the more control students will have.
4. For all dribbling activities, require students to dribble with the right hand, then the left. They should alternate hands when crouching down.

Activities (30-40 Minutes)

1. Introduce dribbling using the skill cues. Explain that dribbling is the only way a player can independently move the ball down the court. (3-5 minutes)

2. Scatter students around the gym to work on dribbling. Students should concentrate on controlling the ball. (3-5 minutes)

3. Once proficient at basic dribbling, have students practice in their own space while changing speeds, hands, and directions. If desired, have students travel in a larger area around the gym while dribbling. (5-7 minutes)

4. Introduce speed dribbling using the skill cues. Then have students practice speed dribbling down the length of the court, encouraging them to progressively run faster while maintaining control of the ball. (5-7 minutes)

Dribbling position

5. Pair up students or have them select partners: one partner dribbles while the other acts as a passive defender (i.e., the defender should guard the dribbler by backpedaling, moving backward down the court, but should not try to steal the ball). After advancing up and down the entire length of the court, partners should switch roles. (7-8 minutes)

6. Give each student a ball and use cones to mark a space in which they can dribble. (The space should be one-third of the court or smaller). Explain the rules of and have students play hit away. (7-8 minutes)

Hit Away

While dribbling, players attempt to knock other players' basketballs away from them. When players' basketballs are knocked outside the restricted area, they are eliminated from the game and must go to the other half of the court and practice dribbling individually. The game continues until only one dribbler is left in the restricted area. For more challenge, reduce the size of the restricted area as the game progresses.

Closure (3-5 Minutes)

Review the lesson with students. Use the following questions and ideas to reinforce learning, check understanding, and provide feedback.

1. Ask students to explain how to protect the ball from a defender.

2. Discuss the importance of keeping the head up while dribbling, particularly in activity 6.

Lesson 4

Lay-Up and Push Shots

Purpose

This lesson is the first of two lessons on shooting. In it students develop the fundamental shooting skills of the one-handed push shot and the lay-up.

Warm-Ups (6-8 Minutes)

1. Arm support lifts
2. Side stretch
3. Arm circles
4. Sprint-jog intervals
5. Selected ball-handling skills (see lesson 1)

Facility and Equipment

◆ Gym
◆ 6 baskets (2 lower than regulation height if possible)
◆ 1 basketball per student
◆ 1 hula hoop per 2 students

Skill Cues

One-Handed Push Shot (Foul Shot)

This sequence is for a right-handed push (foul) shot; in step 3, the hands are reversed for left-handed players.

1. Distribute weight evenly over the balls of the feet with the shooting-side leg and foot slightly forward in the stance.
2. Hold the ball about level with the shooting shoulder.
3. Place the left hand under and to the left of the ball while the right hand is behind and slightly under the ball; cock the right wrist.
4. Extend the body and push the ball upward, using the legs to produce most of the force.
5. Follow through with a gentle wrist snap in the direction of intended flight.

Lay-Up Shot

This sequence is for a right-handed lay-up; hands and directions are reversed for left-handed players.

1. Approach the basket at a 45-degree angle.
2. Carry the ball with the left hand in front and under the ball.
3. Place the right hand on top and slightly behind the ball.
4. Carry the ball to shoulder and head height as the left (inside) foot pushes off the floor.
5. Lift the body with the right (outside) knee.

6. Direct the ball to the backboard with the right (outside) hand.

7. Follow through with the palm of the right (outside) hand high in the direction of the backboard.

Teaching Cue

When introducing the shots in this lesson, demonstrate the technique without a basket first so that students can concentrate on proper form.

Activities (30-40 Minutes)

1. Introduce the one-handed push (foul) shot, emphasizing the skill cues. (3-5 minutes)

2. Scatter students around the gym and have them practice their shooting form individually, shooting into the air or against a wall but not at the basket. (3-5 minutes)

3. Pair up students or have them select partners. One student holds a hula hoop parallel to the floor at shoulder level on either side of the body with the arm extended. The other student shoots the ball through the hula hoop from distances ranging from 10 to 15 feet (3.05-4.57 meters). After five trials, partners should switch roles. (3-4 minutes)

4. Position partners at a basket (try to assign an equal number of pairs to each basket). One partner shoots at the basket from designated spots on the floor, varying the distance and angles of each shot, while the other partner rebounds and passes the ball back to the shooter. Partners should switch roles after 10 shots. (7-8 minutes)

5. Using the same student arrangement, one student dribbles into position and then shoots for a basket. Partners should switch roles after five shots. After both students have taken five shots, one partner acts as a passive defender, guarding the shooter but not blocking the shot or trying to steal the ball. After a few trials, partners should switch roles. (7-8 minutes)

6. Have students gather around and introduce the lay-up shot using the skill cues. (2-4 minutes)

Lay-up shot

7. Tell students to go back to their partner positions at each basket (see activity 4) and practice the lay-up shot. Students should stand close to the basket on the right side (left side for left-handed players), hold the ball properly, lift the right (left for left-handed players) leg, and shoot the ball using the backboard. (5-6 minutes)

Closure (3-5 Minutes)

Review the lesson with students. Use the following ideas to reinforce learning, check understanding, and provide feedback.

1. Review the fundamentals of the one-handed push shot.
2. Select a student to demonstrate the lay-up shot in front of the class and have students look for proper technique during the demonstration. (If you have both right- and left-handed students in class, have one of each demonstrate the lay-up.)
3. Inform students that they will continue to work on the lay-up and will also learn the jump shot during the next class period.

Lesson 5

Lay-Up and Jump Shots

Purpose

In this lesson students continue to develop lay-up skills and learn the jump shot.

Facility and Equipment

◆ Gym
◆ 6 baskets (2 lower than regulation height if possible)
◆ 1 basketball per student

Warm-Ups (6-8 Minutes)

1. Lateral hops
2. Waist twists
3. Push-ups
4. Arm rotators
5. Selected ball-handling skills (see lesson 1)

Skill Cues

Lay-Up

The following sequence is for right-handed players; reverse hands for left-handed players.

1. Approach the basket at an angle.
2. Carry the ball with the left hand in front and under the ball.
3. Place the right hand on top and slightly behind the ball.
4. Carry the ball to shoulder and head height as the left (inside) foot pushes off the floor.
5. Lift the body with the right (outside) knee.
6. *Place* the ball, rather than throw it, against the backboard.
7. Follow through with the palm of the right (outside) hand high in the direction of intended flight.

Jump Shot

The following sequence is for right-handed players; reverse hands for left-handed players.

1. Square the body toward the basket.
2. Place the left hand on the side of the ball for balance and the right hand behind the ball.
3. Jump upward, bringing the ball slightly above and in front of the head.
4. Cock the wrist and point the elbow toward the basket.
5. Shoot at the top of the jump while focusing on the basket.
6. Follow through in the direction of the basket and snap the wrist downward in the follow-through to develop backspin on the ball.

Teaching Cue

When introducing the shots in this lesson, demonstrate the technique without a basket first so that students can concentrate on proper form.

Activities (30-40 Minutes)

1. Demonstrate and review the lay-up using the skill cues. (3-5 minutes)

2. Pair up students or have them select partners. Assign partners to a basket and give a ball to each pair. One partner approaches the basket, carrying the ball at a slow jog, from a distance of 5 to 8 feet (1.52-2.44 meters) and then shoots for a lay-up. Remind right-handed students to stride left and leap off the left foot, bringing the right knee up while pushing the ball with the right hand toward the spot on the backboard for banking the shot into the basket (left-handed students use the opposite hands, knees, and feet). Partners rebound the shot. After shooters attempt three lay-ups, partners should switch roles. (6-7 minutes)

3. Using the same partner arrangement, one partner dribbles half-speed to the basket from 15 to 20 feet (4.57-6.1 meters) away, concentrating on the elements and technique of the lay-up and focusing on the target spot (i.e., the backboard). After five trials, students should switch roles. Then one partner acts as a passive defender (i.e., guards but does not block the shot or try to steal the ball) while the other partner dribbles and shoots lay-ups from both the left and right sides. After five trials, students should switch roles. (6-8 minutes)

4. Have students gather around and introduce the jump shot using the skill cues. (2-4 minutes)

Jump shot

5. Have students get back into their partner positions at a basket (see activity 2). One partner should pass to the other, who shoots from designated spots on the floor. Passers should also retrieve the ball. After five attempts, partners switch roles. Then both partners practice shooting off the dribble from the designated spots. Finally, one partner should act as a passive defender while the other shoots. (6-8 minutes)

6. Mark 2 designated spots on the floor approximately 15 feet (4.57 meters) from the basket. Divide students into teams of 4 and assign 2 teams to each basket. Explain the rules and play a game of twenty-one. If time allows, teams may play another game. (7-8 minutes)

Twenty-One

Each team member shoots 2 shots at the basket, 1 shot from either 15-foot (4.57-meter) marking (i.e., the long shot) and 1 lay-up. Students score 2 points for making the long shot and 1 point for making the lay-up shot. Each player should shoot the long shot first, then retrieve the ball, shoot the lay-up, and return the ball to the next team player. Players continue to shoot until their team scores exactly 21 points.

Closure (3-5 Minutes)

Review the lesson with students. Use the following ideas to reinforce learning, check understanding, and provide feedback.

1. Discuss the advantages of a jump shot over a one-handed push shot (i.e., players are higher when shooting, enabling them to shoot over taller defensive players; the jump shot also provides for a quicker shot).

2. Have students identify why it is important to bank lay-ups off the backboard regardless of the angle from which the shot was attempted (i.e., angled shots off the backboard are easier to make because the ball doesn't hit the rim, which sometimes causes the ball to bounce out of the basket).

Lesson 6

Defensive Guarding and Rebounding

Purpose

In this lesson students learn basketball guarding and rebounding skills, including 1-on-1 (i.e., person-to-person) guarding.

Facility and Equipment

- Gym or outdoor basketball courts with a smooth surface
- 6 or more baskets
- 1 basketball per student

Warm-Ups (6-8 Minutes)

1. Inverted hurdler's stretch
2. Side slides
3. Arm rotators
4. Forward lunges
5. Selected ball-handling skills (see lesson 1)

Skill Cues

Guarding

1. The primary purpose of guarding is to keep an opponent from scoring.
2. The cardinal rule of guarding is to stay between the person being guarded and the basket.
3. The proper defensive stance is a forward stride position (i.e., the dominant foot forward and the other foot backward), while bending forward at the waist with the knees slightly flexed. One arm is high and forward, toward the opponent, and the other arm is low and to the side of the body.
4. Once an opponent is moving, the defensive guard must move to maintain the position between the opponent and the basket.
5. The defensive guard must be moving continuously.
6. Guards should focus on the opponent's waist (center of gravity) so as not to be faked out. Do not focus on the opponent's head, or on the ball.
7. Keep a distance of 3 feet (.91 meters) away from the opponent.
8. Try to avoid crossing the feet; instead, use the shuffle step.

Rebounding

1. Keep the body in a low, crouched position.
2. Distribute weight on the balls of the feet.
3. Extend the arms overhead.
4. Spread the legs for a wide base of support.
5. Take a wide stance with the arms out and the feet apart.

6. Face the basket to block the opponent from getting the rebound.

7. Box out opponents by pivoting in front of them, blocking their path to the ball.

8. Pull down the ball with both hands.

Activities (30-40 Minutes)

1. Introduce guarding using the skill cues. Emphasize the cardinal rule of staying between an opponent and the basket. Demonstrate the proper guarding position and shuffling motion. (2-4 minutes)

2. Scatter students around the gym and have them assume the proper guarding position. Give hand signals to direct students to shuffle in various directions: forward, backward, sideways, and diagonally. (4-5 minutes)

3. Pair up students or have them select partners. One partner dribbles forward down the court while the other partner faces the first and moves backward in the guarding position. Guards should concentrate on moving backward, avoiding body contact, and staying between the dribbler and the basket. Partners should switch roles and then repeat the activity; this time guards should try to deflect the ball away from the dribbler. (4-5 minutes)

4. Divide students into groups of 3 to 6 and play keep-away using 1-on-1 (i.e., person-to-person) defense. (Playing 3-on-3 is ideal.) Restrict the space in which each group can move, and limit offensive players to passing and dribbling. Guards should concentrate on guarding their opponents by playing the ball or potential receiver closely, which will make it easier to intercept or force bad passes. (5-6 minutes)

5. Have students gather around and introduce rebounding using the skill cues. Specifically describe the rebounding sequence. (2-4 minutes)

6. Divide students into groups of 5 or 6 and have them stand in front of a backboard.

Rebounding sequence

Students should toss the ball off the backboard while timing the jump to reach the ball at the highest point of the jump. (3-4 minutes)

7. Pair up students or have them select partners. Starting 15 feet (4.57 meters) away from the basket, the first partner fakes, drives, and shoots at the basket while the other partner concentrates on defending and getting the rebound. After three trials, partners switch roles. (4-5 minutes)

8. Divide students into groups of 4: 2 offensive players and 2 defensive players. The offensive players shoot from 10 to 18 feet (3.05-5.49 meters) away and then quickly move toward the basket. The defensive players box out the offensive players and rebound the ball, trying to keep themselves between the opponent and the basket. After three trials, offense and defense switch roles. (6-7 minutes)

Closure (3-5 Minutes)

Review the lesson with students. Use the following questions and ideas to reinforce learning, check understanding, and provide feedback.

1. Have students identify why it is important to box out an opponent on defense and explain how this is done.

2. Ask students to name the cardinal rule of playing defense (i.e., staying between the opponent and the basket) and explain why it is so important.

3. Select two students to demonstrate the proper defensive guarding position.

Lesson 7

Offensive Strategy

Purpose

In this lesson students learn offensive strategies in basketball, including the pick and roll, screening, cutting, and the give and go.

Facility and Equipment

◆ Gym or outdoor basketball courts
◆ 6 or more baskets
◆ 1 basketball per student

Warm-Ups (6-8 Minutes)

1. Waist twists
2. Sit and curl
3. Side slides
4. Elbow squeezes
5. Selected ball-handling skills (see lesson 1)

Skill Cues

Cutting

A cut is an explosive movement toward the basket used when trying to elude a defender.

1. A player can cut with or without the ball.
2. Usually a cut starts with a feint of the head or arms.
3. A front-door cut is made by cutting between the defensive player and the passer.
4. A back-door cut is made by cutting behind the defensive player and toward the basket.

Screening

Screening involves blocking a defender from guarding or staying close to a teammate.

1. Screens are most effective against 1-on-1 (i.e., person-to-person) defense.
2. Players set a screen by positioning themselves in the path of the defensive player to be screened. Stop in position (get set), take a wide stance, and plant both feet.
3. A screen is illegal if the screening player is moving.

Pick and Roll

The pick and roll is performed after the picker sets the screen on the defensive player. The picker pivots and rolls toward the basket to receive a pass from the dribbler.

Give and Go

The give and go is a variation of the cut.

1. The ball handler passes to a teammate, then feints the defender with the head and breaks for the basket.
2. The teammate with the ball passes back to the ball handler (cutter), who receives this quick pass and advances the ball down the court or shoots for the basket.

Teaching Cues

1. Make sure students realize that the primary function of any offensive movement is to get a good shot at the basket.
2. For the most effective instruction, demonstrate each move while explaining it.

Activities (30-40 Minutes)

1. Introduce the cut and the give and go using the skill and teaching cues. (3-5 minutes)
2. Divide the class into 5 or 6 groups of at least 4 players and assign each group to a basket. Have students play 2-on-2, starting 15 feet (4.57 meters) from the basket. An offensive player with the ball tries to pass to the other offensive player as that player fakes and cuts toward the basket. The two defensive players try to intercept or stop the pass. Have extra students rotate into a different position after each attempt (i.e., rotate offensive players to defense and vice versa). Make sure students vary their cuts to the basket. While waiting to rotate in, extra students can practice passing or dribbling skills. (5-6 minutes)
3. Have students repeat activity 2, this time adding the give and go offensive technique. The offensive ball handler passes to the teammate and then feints and breaks toward the basket. (5-6 minutes)
4. Have students gather around and then introduce the screen and the pick and roll using the skill and teaching cues. (5-7 minutes)
5. Assign 6 students to a basket and have them assume a 3-on-3 position. Offensive players set screens for their teammates to shoot over. Defensive players box out the offensive players and try to get the rebound. After three shots, players should switch roles. (6-8 minutes)
6. Repeat activity 5, this time having offensive players set picks for their teammates and then use the pick and roll. The defensive team should call out picks, then box out and rebound. After three trials, students should switch roles. (6-8 minutes)

Closure (3-5 Minutes)

Review the lesson with students. Use the following ideas to reinforce learning, check understanding, and provide feedback.

1. Discuss the necessity of teamwork on both offense and defense.
2. Have two students demonstrate the pick and roll, and explain when it is most effective (i.e., when driving [dribbling toward the basket]) and why (i.e., it keeps the defender from guarding the offensive player).

Lesson 8

Defensive Strategy

Purpose

In this lesson students learn the basic defenses used in basketball: the 1-on-1 (i.e., person-on-person) defense and the 1-2-2 zone defense.

Warm-Ups (6-8 Minutes)

1. Leg stretch
2. Curl-ups
3. Arm rotators
4. Push-ups
5. Selected ball-handling skills (see lesson 1)

Skill Cues

One-on-One Defense

1. Defensive players must guard an assigned offensive player, no matter where that player goes on the court.
2. Try to guard the assigned opponent on defense and evade that player on offense.
3. Positions do change on the playing court, and it is sometimes advantageous for defensive players to switch assignments (e.g., in the case of being screened or picked).
4. Stay with the assigned opponent.
5. Defensive players must communicate with each other during a game, especially on picks and screens.
6. Be ready at all times to switch from a defensive to an offensive role, which will become necessary the moment the defensive team gains possession of the ball.

Zone Defense

In zone defense, defensive players are assigned to an area instead of a person. Zones are numerically named and identified by the arrangement of the defensive players (i.e., the 1-2-2, 2-3, 3-2, or 2-1-2 defense).

1. A defensive player is responsible for any player in the assigned zone.
2. Keep the arms and hands up in the air on a zone defense to restrict passes across the court.
3. A player's defensive position remains relatively constant, regardless of the ball position.

4. If a zone is overloaded, guard the nearest player to the basket or the one with the ball.

5. On the change of possession from offense to defense, get back to the assigned zone quickly and set up.

Teaching Cues

1. Stress that defensive strategy is based on individual defensive fundamentals and teamwork.

2. The only zone defense presented in this lesson is the 1-2-2; other defenses (i.e., 2-3, 3-2, and 2-1-2) can be demonstrated or practiced as you deem appropriate.

Activities (30-40 Minutes)

1. Introduce the 1-on-1 (i.e., person-to-person) defense using the appropriate skill and teaching cues. Give examples of when players switch defensive assignments (e.g., pick and roll) and when to switch back. (3-5 minutes)

2. Divide the class into groups of 6 (3 offense and 3 defense), 1 group at each basket and using half the court. The offensive players pass the ball to one another, attempting to complete 10 consecutive passes without allowing the defense to deflect or intercept the ball. (Shooting at the basket is prohibited.) Defensive students play strict 1-on-1 defense, trying to deflect or intercept the ball (no picks, screens, or pick and rolls are allowed) before the offense completes its 10 passes. After 10 consecutive passes or at an interception, students switch roles. (5-7 minutes)

3. Repeat activity 2, this time allowing offensive players to use all techniques (including screens, cuts, and picks and rolls) to complete the 10 passes. Defensive players must call out picks and switches, and should practice guarding different players (i.e., switching). Students are still not allowed to shoot at the basket. (6-7 minutes)

4. Introduce playing a zone defense using the appropriate skill and teaching cues. Demonstrate the court positions for the basic 1-2-2 defense. (6-7 minutes)

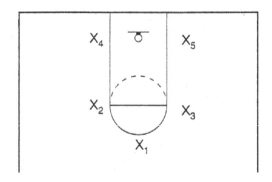

1-2-2 zone defense positions

5. Divide students into teams of five and assign each student a defensive position within the 1-2-2 zone. Two teams spread out at midcourt and, on command, quickly drop back into their zone positions. Rotate all teams and repeat three times. (5-7 minutes)

6. Divide the class into groups of 8 and designate 5 players to be the zone defense and 3 to be the offense. The offensive players pass, dribble, and move around the court while the defensive players guard them by adjusting to their position and location as well as the movement of the ball. Rotate students into all positions. (5-7 minutes)

Closure (3-5 Minutes)

Review the lesson with students. Use the following ideas to reinforce learning, check understanding, and provide feedback.

1. Discuss the major differences between the 1-on-1 defense and the zone defense (i.e., zone defenses are used to better cover spaces and 1-on-1 defenses to cover players).

2. Have students identify the location of each of the five positions in the 1-2-2 zone defense; then discuss possible ways to develop teamwork while playing defense.

3. If desired, have students identify the positions used in other zone defenses (e.g., 2-3, 3-2).

Lesson 9

Modified Game Play

Purpose

In this lesson students learn in-bounding and jump ball procedures, and they play modified games of basketball.

Warm-Ups (6-8 Minutes)

1. Leg stretch
2. Body circles
3. Arm pumps
4. Push-offs
5. Selected ball-handling skills (see lesson 1)

Facility and Equipment

◆ Indoor or outdoor basketball courts
◆ 6 or more baskets
◆ 1 basketball per student
◆ 1 handout of official basketball rules per student
◆ 1 pinnie per 2 students

Skill Cues

Jump Ball

1. A jump ball at midcourt starts the game.
2. The player on the team who has the best (i.e., highest) vertical jump should be the designated jumper.
3. The jumper faces the offensive basket.
4. The official tosses the ball straight up in the air between the two jumpers and they attempt to tip it to one of their teammates.
5. Jumpers are not allowed to grab the ball; they must tip it.

In-Bounding

1. When in-bounding from underneath the defensive basket, try to get the ball to a guard (who has the best ball-handling skills).
2. A team has 10 seconds to move the ball across the midcourt line (from backcourt to front court).
3. When in-bounding from underneath the offensive basket, try to pass the ball in close to the goal (i.e., basket) for an easy shot, but also have a player stand away from the goal as a safety precaution.
4. A team has 5 seconds to in-bound the ball.

Teaching Cues

1. Most class periods will not be long enough to play every modified game in this lesson. Select the most appropriate games for your students or extend the lesson over several class periods.

2. With exception of the 1-on-1 modified game, all students should be actively involved in the game. If you choose the 1-on-1 modified game, leave at least two baskets open for other students to practice their shooting and dribbling skills.

3. Sideline basketball involves more players; use it for maximum participation.

4. The 3-on-3 game can be modified as follows to speed up the pace and allow more player rotations:

   ▸ Do not allow foul shots.

   ▸ Do not permit in-bounding the ball.

   ▸ Do not allow jump balls.

   ▸ Impose passing, dribbling, or shooting restrictions, such as requiring a specified number of passes before shooting.

5. The basic game in this lesson is 1-on-1 modified basketball; it should be explained or played to understand the rules and play of other modified games.

Activities (30-40 Minutes)

1. Select students to demonstrate the jump ball and in-bounding process, emphasizing the skill cues. (8-10 minutes)

2. Choose two of the following modified games. Spend 11 to 15 minutes playing each game. (22-30 minutes)

One-on-One Modified Basketball

This game is played on half of a regulation court and pits one player against one player. Offensive players take the ball at the top of the key, then shoot or dribble and shoot to make a basket. If the shot is successful, offensive and defensive players switch roles. If the shot is missed,

   ▸ the defensive player may rebound the ball and take it back above the key to become the offensive player; or

   ▸ the offensive player may rebound the ball and play continues.

Three-on-Three Modified Basketball

An expansion of the 1-on-1 game, 3-on-3 modified basketball is also played on half the regulation court and uses the same rules as 1-on-1. The only difference is that players play 3-on-3 with 3 players on each team.

Sideline Basketball

This is a common modification of basketball. Divide the class into 2 teams and position 5 players from each team on the court (other players line up on their respective sidelines just out-of-bounds). The same rules in 1-on-1 modified basketball apply, with one exception: court players may pass to a teammate on the sidelines to advance the ball up and down the court. After a designated period of time, or a certain number of baskets, sideline players should rotate on and court players should rotate off (i.e., to the sidelines) the court.

Closure (3-5 Minutes)

Review the lesson with students. Use the following ideas and questions to reinforce learning, check understanding, and provide feedback.

1. Discuss offensive and defensive strategies when a team in-bounds the ball underneath its own basket.

2. Discuss the modified games played in this lesson, asking the following questions:
   - ▸ Which did students like best?
   - ▸ How do the rules relate to specific basketball game play?

3. Give each student a handout of official basketball rules to study before the next class period (see the unit introduction on page 127 and various skill cues throughout this unit to compile a complete listing of basketball rules).

Lesson 10

Regulation Game

Purpose

In this lesson students learn the rules and play a game of regulation basketball.

Facility and Equipment

◆ Indoor or outdoor basketball courts
◆ 1 basketball per student
◆ 1 pinnie per 2 students

Warm-Ups (6-8 Minutes)

1. Sit and curl
2. Push-ups
3. Lateral hops
4. Waist twists
5. Selected ball-handling skills (see lesson 1)

Skill Cues

1. Use teamwork on both offense and defense.
2. Communicate to teammates throughout the game.
3. Defensive players should box out on rebounds.
4. Offensive players should try to get the best percentage shot at the goal.

Teaching Cues

1. Review all of the skill cues taught throughout this unit.
2. Ensure that all players have equal playing time by rotating them every few minutes or after a certain number of baskets are made.
3. If class size is large, keep at least two baskets open for extra students to either play a modified game (see lesson 9, activity 2) or practice their shooting and dribbling skills individually.

Activities (30-40 Minutes)

1. Review the rules of basketball and instruct students on the game using the skill cues. (3-5 minutes)
2. Divide the class into teams, assign two teams per court, and have teams put on pinnies. Play a regulation game of basketball. (27-35 minutes)

Closure (3-5 Minutes)

Review the lesson with students. Use the following questions and ideas to reinforce learning, check understanding, and provide feedback.

1. Ask students to describe which offensive and defensive strategies were most effective during game play.
2. Have students identify aspects of the game or skills they need to improve.

Assessment and Resources

Informal assessment techniques can be used throughout this unit. As students play modified and regulation games (see lessons 9 and 10), check for skill development and cognitive understanding of the game. Self-assessments, peer evaluations, and student portfolios could also be easily implemented in this unit. For example, selected checklists identifying skill components for dribbling could be used.

Following are formal and summative techniques for assessment in basketball. Evaluate such elements as form and technique for each of these skills.

▶ Foul shot testing. Have students shoot 10 free throws. Score 1 point for hitting the rim and 2 points for making a basket.

▶ Pass testing. Have students pass to a wall target 20 times, using a variety of passes, from 15 feet (4.57 meters) away from the wall. More formative passing evaluation can be conducted during game situations. (You may want to develop a skills checklist to observe students' techniques.)

▶ Lay-up shot testing. Have students dribble in and shoot five lay-ups from each side of the basket. Score 1 point for each successful lay-up. For more formative testing, record how many lay-ups they make and miss in a game situation.

▶ Dribbling evaluation. Have students dribble through an obstacle course made of cones spread at least 4 feet (1.22 meters) apart. For more formative testing, determine a maximum course time. Students get points for completing the course in less time, 1 point for every second under the maximum set time.

You can also modify lesson activities throughout this unit for testing purposes, including the following:

▶ Twenty-one (see lesson 5, activity 6)

▶ Lesson 6, activity 6

Resources

Griffin, L., S. Mitchell, and J. Oslin. 1997. *Teaching sport concepts and skills.* Champaign, IL: Human Kinetics.

Mood, D., F. Musker, J. Rink. 1999. *Sports and recreational activities.* 12th ed. New York: McGraw-Hill.

Philipp, J., and J. Wilkerson. 1990. *Teaching team sports: A coeducational approach.* Champaign, IL: Human Kinetics.

Schmottlach, N., and J. McManama. 1997. *The physical education handbook.* 9th ed. Needham Heights, MA: Allyn & Bacon.

Flag Football

Although team games using a kicked ball date back to the beginning of the Christian era, American football as we know it today originated in the late 19th century. It was developed from two English sports: soccer and rugby.

Some colleges in the United States—namely, Yale, Columbia, and Princeton—began to compete against one another in football following the soccer-based London Football Association rules in 1860. Under those rules, teams could kick and butt but not carry the ball. The Harvard team, however, favored rugby rules and soon learned of an egg-shaped ball and kicking returns when it accepted a challenge from McGill University in Canada. The next year, Harvard challenged Yale to a game played primarily using rugby rules but with certain modifications. These modifications started a move toward the more liberal game of football we know today. Walter Camp, later known as the father of football, was a freshman on this team. In 1876 the Intercollegiate Football Association was formed, and this organization developed many uniform rules of the game, including setting the scrimmage line, the system of downs, and the scoring system.

Touch and flag football, modifications of football that can be played safely without the use of pads, grew out of the interest in American football. Flag football eliminated the controversy inherent in the touch football game; when a defender could snatch a flag, it clearly was a successful tackle. The skill to grab or protect the flag also made flag football more interesting than touch football.

Equipment

The equipment used in flag football is few. It consists of the football, made of regulation leather or rubber, and waist belts with short plastic flags (usually attached with Velcro fastenings) on each side. For high school instruction, junior footballs can also be used. These footballs, which are slightly smaller and lighter than regulation footballs are typically easier for students to throw and catch.

Unit Organization

Following is a description of each lesson in this unit.

- ▶ Lessons 1 and 2 present the skills of passing, catching, and receiving a football.
- ▶ Lesson 3 focuses on pass patterns and how to defend a receiver.
- ▶ In lesson 4 students learn how receive a handoff and carry the ball.
- ▶ Lesson 5 focuses on blocking and tackling.
- ▶ Lesson 6 covers punting and placekicking.
- ▶ In lessons 7, 8, 9, and 10, students learn about team play, including offensive and defensive tactics as well as game rules and strategies.

Selected resources and assessment ideas are found in the assessment and resources chapter at the end of the unit.

Note: An asterisk (*) following a facility or equipment listing indicates that preparation is required before the lesson.

Social Skills and Etiquette

Flag football has great potential for the development of coed social skills. Success in the game demands the use of teamwork, and the unit includes numerous partner and group activities that emphasize communication and interaction between students. Discussions about teamwork, including sharing the responsibilities of playing positions, can set the proper tone for flag football instruction and are thus recommended early on in the unit.

The game itself is a gentler form of football, replacing tackling and other body contact with stealing flags. As such, it discourages inappropriate touching and rough play. Emphasis on proper etiquette should go further, however. Encourage students to demonstrate fair play and sporting behavior throughout each activity. This includes acknowledging good play and technique, encouraging teammates and others in class, and so on.

Lesson Modifications

Flag football is a fairly strenuous activity and may be difficult for some students with disabilities. This unit requires minimal competency in psychomotor skill. To accommodate students with limited mobility, lessons in this unit may be modified using the following methods:

▷ Use smaller playing fields.

▷ Have disabled students play positions that do not require a great deal of movement, such as linemen.

Other suggested modifications include the following.

▷ Designate fewer players per team.

▷ Use smaller or lighter footballs.

▷ Change the rules as necessary (e.g., allow only 3 attempts for a first down, instead of 4).

▷ Use a rotation system to select teams, coupling advanced students with those of limited ability.

Safety

Several safety factors should be observed in this unit. For starters, before each game or activity, make sure the playing field is free from obstacles that might cause injuries. In addition, the following restrictions and enforcement are recommended:

▷ To prevent player collisions, strictly enforce the no-contact rule for screen blocking.

● Do not permit blocking below the waist.

▷ Do not allow blockers to jump in the air on a block.

▷ Make sure blockers keep their elbows in (i.e., touching the torso rather than extending them away from the body).

▷ Do not allow ball carriers to elbow or otherwise contact defenders who are attempting to pull their flags (i.e., tackle).

Rules

The objectives of the game are to carry or pass the football over the defense's goal line (i.e., score) while preventing the opposition from advancing the ball into its own offensive end zone. Playing time consists of two 20-minute halves, but other time limits may be used to accommodate the class schedule.

A team usually comprises 8 players; however, 9 players may be used when class sizes are large, designating the ninth player as an extra running back. The basic 8-player offensive lineup consists of the following positions:

▷ 1 center (snaps the ball to the quarterback)

▷ 2 tackles (protect the quarterback from a defensive rush)

▷ 2 ends or flankers (receive passes, protect the quarterback, block for running backs)

- 2 running backs (receive passes and handoffs to advance ball downfield)
- 1 quarterback (receives passes)

When the offense consists of 8 players, so does the defensive lineup. Defensive teams usually have 3 linemen and 5 backs, although the defense is free to develop any alignment they want (e.g., 5 linemen and 3 backs) to handle an offensive formation. If a ninth player is added, usually it is as a lineman. The basic position breakdown is as follows:

- 3 defensive linemen (rush the quarterback and tackle ball carriers)
- 2 safeties (lineman; cover offensive receivers, try to intercept passes)
- 3 linebackers (stop the sweep run, prevent pass receptions)

Scoring

The team scoring the most points wins the game. Two types of scores are possible in flag football: the touchdown and the conversion.

- Touchdowns count 6 points and occur when the offensive team passes or carries the ball over the opponent's goal line.
- The offense can also score a 2-point conversion immediately after a touchdown by moving the ball over the opponent's goal line from 3 yards (2.74 meters) away.

The defense scores a safety by tackling the offensive ball carrier behind the offensive goal line (i.e., within the end zone). A safety is worth 0 points, but it results in the defense getting possession of the ball.

Play

The ball is put into play by a placekick from the kicking team's 20-yard (18.28-meter) line at the beginning of the game, the beginning of the second half, and after each score. From the placekick, the receiving team becomes the offense and tries to advance the ball according to regular play rules.

Numerous and diverse rules govern such things as passing, blocking, tackling, and so on. Thus, these rules are explained when each

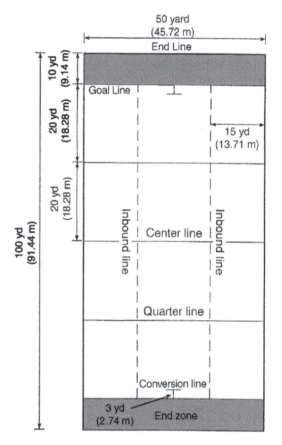

Flag football field dimensions

skill is introduced, in the skill cues and activities lesson sections. Following are the general rules and basic game sequences for flag football:

- The offense has 4 consecutive attempts (called *downs*) to advance the ball to the next zone, which is 10 yards (9.74 meters) away. If successful, the team gets 4 more downs (i.e., getting a first down) to advance the ball into the next zone or the opponents' end zone. If unsuccessful, the defense takes possession of the ball at that point on the field (i.e., the line of scrimmage), becoming the offense.

- Offensive players may advance the ball by running with it (i.e., carrying) or passing it.

- Defensive players stop (i.e., down) ball carriers or receivers by stealing one of the flags from their belts (i.e., tackling). On the down, the ball is placed at the point on the field where the flag was taken, called the *line of scrimmage*, and play continues.

▶ Defenders may not physically contact a receiver before the receiver touches the football.

▶ A team may punt the ball to the opposition any time during the four-down sequence. Usually a team punts only when making a first down seems out of reach.

Blocking and Tackling

Because the types of blocks and tackles are numerous in flag football, specific rules governing each are listed where each skill (e.g., specific blocking technique) is introduced. The rules listed here are more general in nature.

▶ The tackle is performed by pulling one flag off the offensive ball carrier.

▶ Tacklers may not push blockers out of the way but instead must try to go around them.

▶ The block is performed by placing the body between the ball carrier and the tackler.

▶ No body contact is allowed during blocking, except in the shoulder block.

▶ Blockers and tacklers may never leave their feet (e.g., leap, jump) to block an opponent or grab a flag.

Passing and Catching

Purpose

In this lesson students develop passing (throwing) and catching (receiving) skills, including the football passing stance, grip, motion, and catching positions.

Facility and Equipment

- Large outdoor playing area or gym
- 1 football per 2 students
- 1 wall target per 2 students

Warm-Ups (6-8 Minutes)

1. Leg stretch
2. Push-ups
3. Arm circles
4. Toe lifts
5. Reverse run

Skill Cues

Passing

1. Grip the ball by placing the thumb and index finger on the back of the ball; spread the other fingers across the laces (seam) of the football.
2. Stabilize the ball by placing the free (i.e., nonthrowing) hand on the front of the ball.
3. Move the foot of the nonthrowing side forward.
4. Start the throwing motion with the throwing arm and hand cocked slightly behind the head.
5. Begin the throw by flexing the elbow and moving it forward while focusing on the target.
6. At the point of release, snap the wrist downward, giving the ball the required spin to develop a spiral motion.

Catching (Receiving)

1. To catch the ball above the waist, form a triangle with the hands, spreading the fingers wide and pointing the thumbs inward, toward the body. To catch the ball below the waist, keep the little fingers together.
2. Create a target with the hands.
3. Stretch the arms out to meet the ball; do not lock the elbows.
4. Watch the ball as it approaches, and try to catch the ball with both hands.
5. At contact, absorb the force of the throw by bringing the ball, hands, and arms into the body.

6. Continue to focus on the ball while bringing it tight to the body.

7. Switch the ball to one arm, using the hand to cover the forward tip of the ball.

Teaching Cue

For better student understanding, demonstrate each skill while explaining it.

Activities (30-40 Minutes)

1. Introduce the pass and the catch using the skill cues. (5-7 minutes)

2. Pair up students or have them select partners and position them approximately 5 yards (4.57 meters) apart, kneeling with the throwing-side knee on the ground and the opposite knee bent at a 90-degree angle with the foot flat on the ground. Have students practice throwing back and forth to each other, concentrating on developing a spiral motion in the throw and proper receiving techniques. Emphasize snapping the wrist on release and following through on the throw. As students become proficient, increase the distance between them. (6-8 minutes)

3. Have student partners stand 10 feet (3.05 meters) from a wall target. One partner throws at the target and the other partner retrieves the footballs. After five throws, students should switch roles. Eventually increase the distance from the target to 5, 10, and 15 yards (4.57, 9.14, and 13.71 meters). (6-8 minutes)

4. Have student partners stand 5 yards (4.57 meters) apart, facing each other, and pass back and forth. Receivers should give passers a good target by placing their hands in the proper triangle position. (6-8 minutes)

5. Have students select new partners. One partner throws to the receiver who is moving forward, backward, and sideways to the left or right. The thrower should concentrate on throwing the ball far enough ahead of the receiver (in the direction he or she is traveling) so that the receiver doesn't have to stop to catch the ball. (This is called *leading* the receiver.) Limit the distance between partners to 10 yards (9.14 meters). (7-9 minutes)

Closure (3-5 Minutes)

Review the lesson with students. Use the following ideas to reinforce learning, check understanding, and provide feedback.

1. Discuss proper throwing technique and explain the importance of developing a tight spiral on the ball (i.e., allows better accuracy and distance).

2. Identify the key components of receiving a football. Ask students to explain the difference between catching a football and catching a baseball.

Lesson 2

Center Snap, Receiving, and Passing

Purpose

In this lesson students solidify their passing and receiving skills, and learn the center snap (hiking) and lateral passing.

Facility and Equipment

◆ Large outdoor playing area or gym
◆ 1 football per 2 students

Warm-Ups (6-8 Minutes)

1. Triceps dips
2. Arm pumps
3. Lateral hops
4. Waist twists
5. Reverse run

Skill Cues

Center Snap

The quarterback should be 5 yards (4.57 meters) behind the center.

1. Grip the ball the same way as in passing.
2. Spread the feet slightly more than shoulder-width apart.
3. Place the nonsnapping hand on the same knee, and extend the snapping hand and arm back through the legs.
4. Snap the wrist as the ball is released, pointing the hand toward the quarterback.
5. The ball should have a spiral on it and should be received by the quarterback at about chest height.
6. The snapper should look back through the legs to find the quarterback before the snap. When snapping, however, the head should be up, facing the opponents.

Lateral (One-Handed Underhand) Pass

1. Pass underhand.
2. Pass to the side or behind the passer.
3. Grasp the ball with the dominant hand.
4. Place the palm of the throwing hand under the ball and spread the fingers.
5. Snap the wrist back to put spin on the ball and produce a spiral motion.
6. The passer must pass laterally or backward to the receiver.

Teaching Cue

Review proper catching and passing techniques before teaching this lesson.

Activities (30-40 Minutes)

1. Review passing and receiving using the skill cues in lesson 1. Emphasize the importance of developing spin on the ball as it is being thrown. (3-5 minutes)

2. Pair up students or have them select partners and position them 5 yards (4.57 meters) apart, facing each other. Partners pass back and forth from various distances (5, 10, 15, and 20 yards [4.57, 9.14, 13.71, and 18.28 meters). Then have students pass to a moving (forward, backward, and sideways) receiver, limiting the distance between partners to 15 yards (13.71 meters). (7-8 minutes)

3. Have students gather around; then introduce and demonstrate the center snap using the skill cues. Emphasize that the ball is snapped with one hand, with a snap of the wrist, to put a spin on the ball as it is released. (3-5 minutes)

Center snap position

4. Pair up students or have them select partners. Students should practice snapping back and forth to each other from 5 yards (4.57 meters) until they are proficient at this distance; then should increase the distance to 10 yards (9.14 meters). (5-6 minutes)

5. Introduce the lateral pass using the skill cues. Emphasize that the pass must be made laterally or backward to a player (a forward lateral pass beyond the line of scrimmage is illegal). (3-5 minutes)

6. Have student partners practice lateral passing back and forth to each other from 5 yards (4.57 meters). Emphasize using one hand and trying to develop spin on the ball. At first the receiver should remain stationary, but eventually both the passer and receiver should be moving when the lateral pass is made. (4-5 minutes)

7. Divide students into groups of 3: 1 snapper, 1 quarterback, and 1 running back. Have the snapper hike the ball to the quarterback, who runs with the ball a short distance to the side and then laterals the ball to the trailing running back. After three trials, students should switch roles. (5-6 minutes)

Closure (3-5 Minutes)

Review the lesson with students. Use the following ideas to reinforce learning, check understanding, and provide feedback.

1. Have students identify the similarities between the forward, lateral, and center snap pass.

2. Discuss the regulations for using the lateral pass in flag football.

Lesson 3

Running Pass Patterns and Defensive Guarding

Purpose

In this lesson students learn running pass patterns and how to defend (i.e., guard) against them. Students also practice passing, receiving, pattern running, and defensive guarding skills.

Facility and Equipment

◆ Outdoor playing area or gym
◆ 1 football per 3 students
◆ 1 handout of passing patterns per student*

Warm-Ups (6-8 Minutes)

1. Leg stretch
2. Lateral hops
3. Upper body rotations
4. Arm pumps
5. Arm and leg lifts

Skill Cues

Running Pass Patterns

1. Before catching a ball, get into an open area by running a predetermined pattern.
2. The purpose of running patterns is to elude a defender.
3. Patterns consist of running and making at least one cut or quick movement involving a change of direction.
4. A cut is made by pushing off from the inside of the foot opposite to the intended direction of the cut. For example, a cut to the right requires pushing off from the inside of the left foot. The sequence of a cut is as follows:
   ▶ Run at a controlled speed using small steps.
   ▶ Lower the body by slightly bending the knees.
   ▶ Feint a head or body movement (fake) to elude the defender and increase the chance of getting open.
   ▶ Push off from the inside of the proper foot.
   ▶ Turn the head to watch the quarterback and focus on the flight of the ball as it approaches.

Defending a Receiver

Any defensive player is allowed to defend a receiver, but it is the primary job of defensive backs—namely safeties and cornerbacks.

1. The first move should be backward.
2. Defenders should never allow a receiver to get behind them.
3. Watch the quarterback to anticipate where the ball will be thrown.
4. React quickly to a receiver's cut, always staying 5 yards (4.57 meters) away from the receiver before the cut.
5. Try to intercept or knock down any balls thrown to a receiver.
6. Defenders may not physically contact a receiver before the receiver touches the football.

Activities (30-40 Minutes)

1. Introduce the various running pass patterns using the skill cues. Distribute handouts or diagrams of the basic patterns to optimize student understanding. (4-6 minutes)
2. Divide students into groups of 5 or 6 and have them practice all 11 running pass patterns. Emphasize making quick, sharp cuts and looking at the quarterback to anticipate the flight of the ball. (6-8 minutes)

The 11 running pass patterns are as follows:

- Down and in
- Down and out
- Hook in
- Hook out
- Hook and go
- Z in
- Z out
- Quick in
- Fly
- Post
- Corner

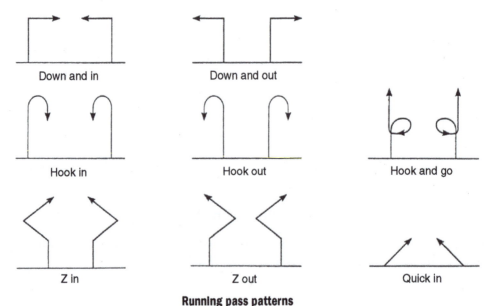

Running pass patterns

3. Divide students into groups of 3: 1 receiver, 1 center snapper, and 1 quarterback. The snapper hikes the ball to the quarterback, who throws it to the receiver, who runs a predetermined pattern. Repeat three times; then have students switch positions. (It may be necessary to keep the same group of quarterbacks during early activities to make sure students learn and understand the pass patterns.) (5-8 minutes)

4. Introduce guarding a receiver using the skill cues. (4-6 minutes)

5. Divide students into groups of 4: 1 center, 1 quarterback, 1 receiver, and 1 defender (guard). The center snaps the ball to the quarterback, who in turn throws it to the receiver. The receiver should run a predetermined pattern while the defender passively (i.e., without trying to intercept the ball) tries to prevent the completion of the pass. Repeat three times; then have students switch positions. (11-12 minutes)

Closure (3-5 Minutes)

Review the lesson with students. Use the following ideas to reinforce learning, check understanding, and provide feedback.

1. Have students identify selected running pass patterns.

2. Ask one student to describe how to cover a receiver.

3. Discuss the importance of sticking to a selected pass pattern instead of changing it as the play develops (i.e., quarterback cannot guess where the receivers might be; the patterns must stay consistent).

Lesson 4

Handing Off and Carrying the Ball

Purpose

In this lesson students focus on ball-handling (i.e., taking the handoff) and carrying skills, including learning to carry the ball and make open field moves (i.e., cuts) to avoid defenders.

Facility and Equipment

◆ Large outdoor playing field or gym
◆ 1 football per 3 students
◆ 5 cones per group

Warm-Ups (6-8 Minutes)

1. Leg stretch
2. Upper body rotations
3. Hip extenders
4. Arm pumps
5. Abdominal crunches

Skill Cues

Carrying the Ball

1. Always cover the tip of the ball with the hand; the remainder of the forearm should cover the ball.
2. When numerous players are in the area, cover the ball with both hands.
3. When running in a stretch of open field, carry the ball on the open field side (i.e., away from the defenders).

Taking a Handoff

1. Raise the arm on the side of the quarterback to have the elbow at shoulder level. Keep the forearm directly in front of the body with the palm facing down. This position requires a 90-degree bend at the elbow.
2. Keep the other arm (i.e., away from the quarterback) below the waist with the palm facing up and directly in front of the body, also requiring a 90-degree bend at the elbow.
3. Do not reach out for the ball; players should wait until the quarterback places it at his or her midsection between the hands.
4. Grasp the ball with both hands until getting into an open stretch of field.

Running With the Ball

1. Lean slightly forward.
2. Run with the head up; always scan the field for an open area.
3. Hold the ball tightly and cover its front point with the hand.

4. When making a cut, plant the foot opposite the direction of the cut. For example, if cutting to the right, plant the left foot and push off.

5. Change speeds and make cuts while running, yet still maintain balance.

Activities (30-40 Minutes)

1. Introduce and demonstrate the elements of carrying the ball and taking the handoff using the skill cues. (4-6 minutes)

Ball-carrying position

2. Divide students into groups of 10 and have each group form two lines, 10 yards (9.14 meters) apart, and face each other. The first student in one line runs toward the first student in the other line, 1 with a ball and 1 without a ball. As they pass each other, the runner with the ball hands it off to the runner without the ball. Then the second students go, continuing the process of handing off the ball back and forth. After each handoff, students go to the back of the opposite line and await their next turn. (7-9 minutes)

3. Divide students into groups of 3: 1 quarterback, 1 center, and 1 running back. The center snaps the ball to the quarterback, who in turn hands it off to the running back (going forward toward the opponent's goal). The running back should alternate running to different sides of the quarterback, taking the handoff from both the right and left sides. Repeat three times; then students should switch roles. (7-9 minutes)

4. Using the same arrangement, have the running back take the handoff from the quarterback and weave in and out of five cones (placed every 5 yards [4.57 meters]) down the field. Repeat three times; then have students switch positions. (7-9 minutes)

5. Repeat activity 3, but this time the center is a defender after he or she snaps the ball. The center starts out 10 yards (9.14 meters) away from the running back. The running back takes the handoff from the quarterback and tries to avoid the defender for 15 yards (13.71 meters), who tries to stop the running back. Repeat three times; then have students switch roles. (Be sure to stress no-contact safety during this activity by using flag football belts, or enforce appropriate touches.) (5-7 minutes)

Closure (3-5 Minutes)

Review the lesson with students. Use the following ideas to reinforce learning, check understanding, and provide feedback.

1. Discuss the proper way to take a handoff from a quarterback, emphasizing proper arm and hand position.

2. Have three students demonstrate a cut that could be used to avoid a defender. Analyze the moves with the rest of the class.

Lesson 5

Screen and Shoulder Blocking and Tackling

Purpose

In this lesson students learn blocking and tackling skills.

Warm-Ups (6-8 Minutes)

1. Lateral hops
2. Arm circles
3. Waist twists
4. Abdominal tighteners
5. Scissors

Facility and Equipment

- Outdoor field or large gym
- 1 football per 3 students
- 1 set of flag football belts and flags per 3 students

Skill Cues

Screen Blocking

1. Start with a three-point stance: both feet and one hand on the ground.
2. Keep the feet in a side-straddle position, shoulder-width apart with weight evenly distributed on the balls of the feet.
3. Slightly flex the knees and place the upper arm (i.e., the arm not touching the ground) across the thigh once in the set position.
4. Keep the buttocks low and lean forward on the hand resting on the ground.
5. The screen block does not allow for any body contact; blockers simply place the body between the ball carrier and the tackler.
6. Tacklers may not push blockers out of the way but instead must try to go around them.

Shoulder Block

1. The shoulder block is the only body blocking allowed in flag football.
2. Blockers may never block below the knees or on the back of an opponent and may never use their hands to grab an opponent.
3. Blockers may never leave their feet (e.g., leap, jump) to block an opponent.
4. Place the shoulder against the opponent's shoulder, chest, or midsection.
5. Be sure to have a stable base of support.
6. Put one foot forward and slightly flex the knees to take a crouched, forward stride position; keep the head up.
7. Once making contact with an opponent, keep moving the feet and drive the opponent downfield.

Tackling

In flag football, the tackle is performed by pulling one flag off the offensive ball carrier.

1. As the ball carrier is approaching, the tackler must be in good body position, the weight evenly distributed on the balls of the feet, to move in any direction.
2. Focus on the flags of the runner so that the runner cannot feint effectively.
3. As the ball carrier approaches, move in quickly and grab the flag.
4. Tacklers may not leave their feet (e.g., leap, jump) to grab a flag.

Teaching Cues

1. Exercise caution when having students practice shoulder blocking. Emphasize the skill cues and make it clear that students should not try to push one another to the ground.
2. This lesson must be closely supervised.

Activities (30-40 Minutes)

1. Introduce the skills of shoulder blocking, screen blocking, and tackling, emphasizing the skill and teaching cues. Explain that blocking is the only way to protect a teammate (most often the ball carrier) from a defender. (4-6 minutes)
2. Pair up students of similar height and weight, and have them stand 3 feet (.91 meters) apart. Designate 1 student as the blocker and the other as the defender. On the signal, partners step toward each other. The blocker then attempts to control the defender for 5 seconds using the shoulder block. Have students stand 5 feet (1.52 meters) apart, then move forward and make contact. Again the blocker tries to control the defender for 5 seconds. (Make sure students understand not to knock one another down.) (5-7 minutes)
3. Using the same partners, have the blockers (offensive) screen block the defenders, who are trying to evade the blockers and get to a designated spot on the field. Remind the blockers to keep their bodies between the designated spot and the defenders. Repeat three times; then have partners switch roles. (7-9 minutes)
4. Divide students into groups of 3: 1 blocker, 1 ball carrier, and 1 defender. The ball carrier tries to run 15 yards (13.71 meters) in an area no more than 10 yards (9.14 meters) wide without being touched by the defender. The offensive blocker attempts to block the defender using a screen or shoulder block. Repeat three times; then have students switch roles. Repeat the activity, this time having the ball carrier wear a flag belt. The defender tries to tackle the ball carrier by grabbing either flag. (7-9 minutes)
5. Divide students into groups of 6. Designate 3 offensive players and 3 defensive players in each group: a center, quarterback, and running back (offense); and a defender for each offensive position. Offensive players run the ball four times while the defenders try to tackle them. The quarterback may hand off to the ball runner or keep the ball and run it, but no passing is allowed. Have players switch positions every four downs. (7-9 minutes)

Closure (3-5 Minutes)

Review the lesson with students. Use the following ideas to reinforce learning, check understanding, and provide feedback.

1. Review the differences between screen blocking and shoulder blocking.
2. Have one student demonstrate the proper procedure for tackling a ball carrier. Have students watch and analyze the skills.

Lesson 6

Punting and Placekicking

Purpose

In this lesson students develop punting and placekicking skills.

Facility and Equipment

◆ Large outdoor play area
◆ 1 football per 3 students
◆ 1 kicking tee per 2 students

Warm-Ups (6-8 Minutes)

1. Arm circles
2. Hip stretch
3. Reverse run
4. Push-offs
5. Grapevine step

Skill Cues

Punting

Punting is used to move the ball the farthest distance from a team's goal before giving it up to the opponents.

1. Grip the ball with the laces up.
2. Place one hand on the rear of the ball and the other hand on the front of the ball.
3. Take a step and a half on the approach—a short step with the kicking leg, then a full step with the nonkicking leg—and then kick.
4. Drop the ball onto the top instep of the kicking foot. Angle the ball slightly to point it inward on the instep. Point the toes of the kicking foot downward when kicking the ball.
5. Keep the hands out for balance after the kick, and follow through with the leg in the direction of intended flight.
6. Focus on the ball while kicking.
7. Use the foot to give the ball a spiral spin, which adds significantly to the distance the ball will travel.

Placekicking

Placekicking is used to start play. The following sequence describes the straight-on placekicking style.

1. Slowly approach the ball from a distance of 7 to 10 yards (6.4-9.14 meters).
2. Plant the nonkicking foot approximately 12 inches (30.5 centimeters) behind and to the side of the ball.
3. Flex the kicking leg at the knee and straighten it as the foot contacts the ball.

4. Lock the ankle at contact; the foot and leg should form a 90-degree angle.

5. Focus on the ball, trying to contact it just below the midline.

6. Follow through in the direction of intended flight, letting the kicking leg carry the body off the ground.

Activities (30-40 Minutes)

1. Introduce and demonstrate the elements of punting, emphasizing the skill cues. (3-5 minutes)

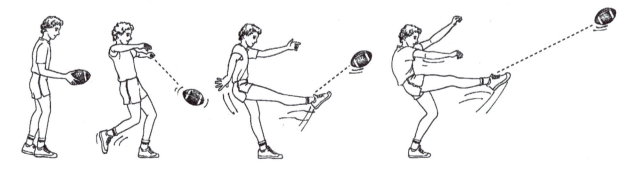

Punting sequence

2. Have student partners stand 20 to 30 yards (18.28-27.43 meters) apart and punt back and forth from a stationary position. Players should not take approach steps. (5-6 minutes)

3. Have students punt back and forth to each other, this time adding the approach steps before kicking the ball. Be sure they concentrate on technique rather than result (e.g., distance). (4-6 minutes)

4. Divide students into groups of 3: 1 snaps the ball to the punter, who punts the ball downfield to a receiver. Repeat five times; then have partners switch roles. (5-6 minutes)

5. Introduce and demonstrate placekicking using the skill cues. Emphasize that the ball must be contacted below center to get it airborne. (3-5 minutes)

6. Pair up students; 1 kicker and 1 retriever. Kickers kick 5 times using a 1-step approach and concentrating on technique. (Students should use kicking tees to hold the ball in place. If no tees are available, add a third student to serve as a holder.) After five kicks, have students switch roles. (5-6 minutes)

7. Repeat activity 6, but this time have students take a full run at the ball and kick for distance. Emphasize the importance of planting the foot and focusing on the ball as it is being kicked. (5-6 minutes)

Closure (3-5 Minutes)

Review the lesson with students. Use the following ideas to reinforce learning, check understanding, and provide feedback.

1. Review the times during a game when the punt and placekick are used.
2. Discuss strategies that might be useful when punting or placekicking, those that give the kicking team an advantage and those that give the receiving team an advantage.

   ▶ Kicking team advantages: Place the football in the corners of the field, or where there are not waiting receivers; kick it very high to allow good pursuit downfield.

   ▶ Receiving team advantages: organize a wall for a good return; have fastest students as receivers; catch the ball on the run if possible.

Lesson 7

Offensive Game Play and Strategy

Purpose

In this lesson students learn general offensive game strategies, including team positions, offensive formations, and play development.

Warm-Ups (6-8 Minutes)

1. Leg stretch
2. Sit and curl
3. Lateral hops
4. Arm rotators
5. Sprint-jog intervals

Skill Cues

Position and Play Development

1. The basic 8-player offensive set consists of the following positions:
   ▸ 1 center
   ▸ 2 tackles
   ▸ 2 ends (flankers)
   ▸ 2 running backs (flankers; halfback)
   ▸ 1 quarterback
2. Ends and all three backs are eligible to catch a pass.
3. The offensive team should develop a variety of both passing and running plays that can be executed from different formations.

General Offensive Strategy

1. Learn to vary the offensive plays to avoid detectable patterns.
2. Save special plays for crucial situations.
3. Keep plays simple, but be creative.
4. Try to move the ball forward on each down.
5. It is generally easier to gain a small amount of ground each down than to make a big gain with a long pass.

Teaching Cues

1. The most essential offensive skills are passing, catching, and open field running. Because the offensive game is mostly a passing game, however, most practice time should be devoted to developing the passing skills.

2. Try to assign teams according to ability in this lesson so that teams are as evenly matched as possible.

3. If the number of students is not equally divisible by 8, assign extra students to different teams and have students rotate after each play or assign some 9-player teams (the ninth player is an extra lineman).

Activities (30-40 Minutes)

1. Introduce flag football play development and strategy using the skill cues. (2-3 minutes)

2. Introduce the basic formations shown in the diagram and explain each offensive position. Have teams get into the basic offensive formations, identifying the positions in each. (5-7 minutes)

   Following are the basic offensive and defensive positions:

   ▸ Quarterback

   ▸ Center

   ▸ Linemen (tackles, ends)

   ▸ Halfbacks (running backs)

   ▸ Flanker (shown in the second formation only)

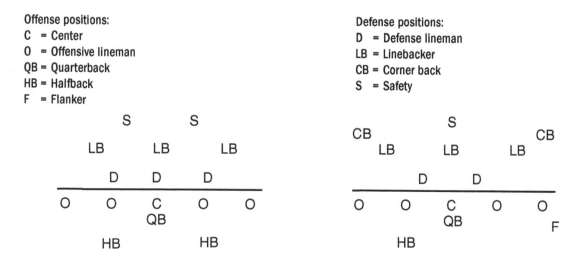

Offense positions:
C = Center
O = Offensive lineman
QB = Quarterback
HB = Halfback
F = Flanker

Defense positions:
D = Defense lineman
LB = Linebacker
CB = Corner back
S = Safety

Basic offense and defense positions and alignment

3. Once students understand the basic formations, have them develop at least three different formations. They will simply vary where the quarterback, running backs, and receivers stand in terms of spacing from line of scrimmage and each other (9-12 minutes)

4. Divide students into teams of 8 or 9. Have teams develop and run at least 4 running plays and 4 passing plays using different formations. Teams should name or number the plays to be identified in the huddle without much explanation. (14-18 minutes)

   Common running plays in flag football include the following:

   ▸ Pitch-outs: the quarterback tosses the ball underhand to a running back.

▸ Sweeps: the quarterback hands the ball off to a running back, who follows teammates (usually down a sideline).

▸ Reverses: the quarterback runs one way and hands off to a running back traveling in the opposite direction.

Closure (3-5 Minutes)

Review the lesson with students. Use the following ideas to reinforce learning, check understanding, and provide feedback.

1. Discuss different formations and have students identify advantages and disadvantages of each (e.g., if a team has speed, align the flanker and tight end on the same side to confuse the defense).

2. Make sure students can identify all playing positions and the major responsibilities of each.

3. Choose a team to demonstrate 1 running play and 1 passing play from among those they developed. The rest of the class can analyze the play.

Lesson 8

Defensive Game Play and Strategy

Purpose

In this lesson students learn defensive game play and strategy, including defensive positions, formations, types of coverage for receivers, and general defensive strategy.

Warm-Ups (6-8 Minutes)

1. Inverted hurdler's stretch
2. Arm pumps
3. Upper body rotations
4. Sit-ups
5. Reverse run

Skill Cues

Facility and Equipment

◆ Large outdoor field
◆ 4 cones per field
◆ 1 football per team
◆ 1 set of flag football belts and flags per student
◆ 1 handout of defensive player responsibilities per student*

Note: the field should be large enough that it can be divided into four 20-yard (18.28-meter) playing areas.

Formations and Positioning

1. An 8-player team usually consists of 3 defensive linemen and 5 defensive backs.
2. The defense is free to develop any alignment they want (3 linemen and 5 backs, or 5 linemen and 3 backs) to handle an offensive formation.
3. Linemen's main responsibilities are to rush the quarterback and to tackle ball carriers.
4. Defensive backs' main responsibilities are to stop the sweep run and prevent pass receptions.

General Defensive Strategy

1. The main role of the defense is to stop the ball carrier and prevent receivers from catching the ball.
2. The fastest defensive backs should defend against the long pass.
3. A defensive team can play a 1-on-1 (i.e., person-to-person) defense or a zone defense.
    ▶ The 1-on-1 defense requires a defensive back to guard a receiver no matter where the receiver runs on the field.
    ▶ In a zone defense, defensive backs guard receivers who come into their zone or area. They never leave the assigned area until the ball is thrown or run. In the typical zone defense, the 3 deep parts of the field are assigned to the deep backs and the 2 flats (the short outside areas of the field) are assigned to the linebackers.

Activities (30-40 Minutes)

1. Introduce defensive play in flag football using the skill cues. Distribute a handout of defensive player responsibilities to each student. (A diagram showing positions, formations, and alignments of defensive players will also help students understand.) (6-8 minutes)

2. Divide students into teams of 8 or 9 players. (Extra students should rotate in after each play.) Have teams develop at least three defensive alignments (formations) to be used during game play, assigning students to play linemen or defensive backs. (9-12 minutes)

3. Using the same teams, assign 2 teams to each playing field: 1 offense and 1 defense. (Both teams must wear flag belts.) The offensive team has 4 downs to advance the ball to the next zone (i.e., 20 yards [18.28 meters]) while the defensive team attempts to prevent the advance. After 4 downs; teams should switch roles regardless of whether they succeeded. (15-20 minutes)

Closure (3-5 Minutes)

Review the lesson with students. Use the following ideas to reinforce learning, check understanding, and provide feedback.

1. Discuss the strengths and weaknesses of various defensive formations.

2. Make sure students understand the differences between zone and 1-on-1 (i.e., person-to-person) defense.

Lesson 9

Modified Game Play

Purpose

In this lesson students develop their playing skills through modified flag football games that highlight defensive and offensive strategies.

Warm-Ups (6-8 Minutes)

1. Leg stretch
2. Arm rotators
3. Slapping jacks
4. Imaginary jump rope
5. Grapevine step

Facility and Equipment

- Large outdoor field
- 4 cones per field
- 1 football per team
- 1 set of belts and flags per student
- 1 handout of flag football rules per student*

  Note: The field should be large enough to accommodate 4 20-yard (18.28-meter) fields and 2 50-yard (45.72-meter) fields.

Skill Cues

General Offensive Strategies

1. The offense should develop and use set plays.
2. Mix up the play calling to include both running and passing plays.
3. Throw to different receivers.
4. It is generally more effective to advance the ball downfield a short distance each down than to try for large gains.
5. Set a goal of reaching just a first down, until a touchdown is scored.

General Defensive Strategies

1. Try both 1-on-1 (i.e., person-to-person) and zone defensive coverage.
2. Never allow a long pass to be completed.
3. Put constant pressure on the passer.

Activities (30-40 Minutes)

1. Introduce the strategies for flag football using the skill cues and explain the modified games students will be playing in this lesson. (4-6 minutes)
2. Divide the class into teams of 8 or 9 players and have 2 teams play each other in 1 of the 3 following modified flag football games. Extra players should rotate in after each play. (13-17 minutes)

20-Yard Football

The offensive team has 4 downs to score on a 20-yard (18.28-meter) field. After the team scores or completes 4 downs, teams switch roles.

Passing Football

Teams play on a 50-yard (45.72-meter) field. Only 1 running play is permitted in 4 downs; players must pass on the other 3.

No-Foot Football

Teams play on a 50-yard (45.72-meter) field. No punting or kicking is allowed. A team takes possession of the ball at its own 10-yard (9.14-meter) line after each score. If a team opts to punt, the ball is automatically moved forward 25 yards (22.86 meters), and play resumes from that spot, with the defensive team taking over possession of the ball.

3. Using the same teams or assigning new teams, have 2 teams of 8 or 9 players compete against each other using a different modified game. (13-17 minutes)

Closure (3-5 Minutes)

Review the lesson with students. Use the following questions and ideas to reinforce learning, check understanding, and provide feedback.

1. Discuss various offensive and defensive player responsibilities. For example, ask students the following:
   ▶ What position covers a running back who goes out to the side of the field for a pass (i.e., linebacker)?
   ▶ What do the defensive linemen do?
2. Distribute the flag football rules handouts and tell students to study them before the next class period.

Regulation Game

Purpose

In this lesson students use their previously learned skills in a regulation game of flag football.

Warm-Ups (6-8 Minutes)

1. Leg stretch
2. Waist twists
3. Abdominal crunch
4. Arm circles
5. Slapping jacks

Facility and Equipment

- 1 flag football field (regulation if possible) per game
- 4 cones per field
- 1 football per game
- 1 set of flag football belts and flags per player

Note: Use the cones to mark boundaries if necessary.

Teaching Cues

1. Review the following skills presented in previous lessons.
   - Passing (see lessons 1 and 2)
   - Catching (see lessons 1 and 2)
   - Taking a handoff and carrying the ball (see lesson 4)
   - Running pass patterns (see lesson 3)
   - Guarding (see lesson 3)
   - Blocking (see lesson 5)
   - Punting (see lesson 6)
   - Placekicking (see lesson 6)

2. If class size is too large or available fields are too few, develop a rotation system to allow all students to play. While waiting to rotate into the game, students may play modified games (see lesson 9) or practice their flag football skills individually.

Activities (30-40 Minutes)

1. Quickly review the relevant skill and teaching cues in this unit. (3-5 minutes)
2. Divide the class into teams of 8 or 9 to play a regulation game of flag football. Review the rules handouts from lesson 9 and ask if there are any questions. (5-7 minutes)
3. Have students play a game of flag football. (22-28 minutes)

Closure (3-5 Minutes)

Review the lesson with students. Use the following ideas to reinforce learning, check understanding, and provide feedback.

1. Discuss what students could do to improve team play (e.g., communicate when opponent's weakness is noticed; vary widely who touches the football).
2. Ask students to identify their team's strategy on offense and defense. Why was it successful or not successful?

Assessment and Resources

Formative assessment is encouraged in this unit. In modified or regulation game play (see lessons 9 and 10), individual and team performances can be assessed using checklists or self-assessment techniques. Cognitive skills (i.e., learning strategies) presented in lessons 7 and 8 can be assessed with formal classroom testing as well as on the field during play.

Following are some formal and summative forms of assessment appropriate to this unit. These may be appropriate for assessing individual skills.

▶ Pass testing. From a distance of 10 yards (9.14 meters), have students throw five balls at a stationary wall target 4 feet (1.22 meters) in diameter. Repeat from 15 yards (13.71 meters). Award 1 point each time the student hits the target.

▶ Catching evaluation. Have students run 2 running pass patterns: 1 down and in, and 1 down and out. Throw 5 passes to each student for each pattern. Award 1 point for each caught pass.

▶ Punting and placekicking evaluation. Have students punt and placekick the ball five times from one end of a line 40 yards (36.57 meters) long, trying for accuracy as well as distance. Mark where the ball hits the ground and measure the distance. Then subtract the sideways distance (i.e., how far the ball is from the line) to give an overall score.

▶ Snapping (hiking) evaluation. This is a test of accuracy. Have students snap the ball by hiking it 5 to 7 yards (4.57-6.4 meters) through a hula hoop 3 feet (.91 meters) in diameter. Score 1 point each time the student puts the ball through the hoop.

Resources

Griffin, L., S. Mitchell, and J. Oslin. 1997. *Teaching sport concepts and skills*. Champaign, IL: Human Kinetics.

Mood, D., F. Musker, and J. Rink. 1999. *Sports and recreational activities*. 12th ed. New York: McGraw-Hill.

Pangrazi, R., and P. Darst. 1997. *Dynamic physical education for secondary school students*. 3rd ed. Needham Heights, MA: Allyn & Bacon.

Sabock, R. 2000. *Coaching: a realistic perspective*. 6th ed. San Diego: College Press.

Line Dancing

Line dancing is a mixture of traditional and modern dance steps set to lively country-and-western music. Although the style may look different from other types of dance, many of the movements are taken from all forms of dance. Some claim that line dancing finds its roots in historical folk dances; others say it stemmed from contemporary disco. Whatever its source, popularity and growth of line dancing has been inextricably tied to country-and-western music. As this style of music swept across America, the need for complementary physical expression gave birth to the line dancing movement. Today, line dancing reflects the dance tastes of modern society. But line dancing is more than a craze; indications are that it is here to stay.

One of the major attractions to line dancing is that no partner is needed, thereby removing the ballroom stigmas of intimidation and insecurity. Everyone dances alone, side by side, facing the same direction in lines or rows. Even if one gets mixed up or off-step, it is easy to catch up without feeling silly or apologetic. Each dance consists of a sequence of steps that are repeated throughout the music. Although a variety of music may be used, the major emphasis is on country-and-western music.

Line dance names and step sequences may differ regionally and within regions, as may terminology for the same steps (e,g., buttermilk, pigeon toes, heel clicks, heel splits). As new music hits the charts, choreography becomes a typical activity among instructors giving vent to variations of the same tunes.

However, this usually doesn't pose problems for the dancer once basic steps and patterns are learned.

Dance steps are usually done to a set number of counts per sequence with repetitions of the sequence throughout the music. Almost all steps are danced to 4 counts or combinations of 4 counts. Generally, 2 beats are put with 2 beats (e.g., step right, left, right, kick). If only 2 beats are used, then the other 2 beats are made up elsewhere in the sequence.

Equipment

The equipment required to teach line dancing is minimal. Because most schools have some sort of music player and speakers, the major outlay is the cost of tapes or CDs. A wireless microphone helps but is not mandatory. Instructional videotapes can be helpful when teaching a line dancing unit, allowing for a larger inventory of dances along with visual performances of various styles and techniques. Videotapes are usually available at public libraries and commercial outlets.

Although not a cost for schools, shoes become a consideration for most activities performed on gym floors. Some schools may restrict or discourage certain types of footwear, which could pose a problem that will need addressing. Because line dancing patterns require some brisk changes in direction and sliding movements, smooth-soled or low-traction tennis shoes are recommended.

Unit Organization

This unit comprises 11 lessons that cover 13 line dances. Each dance is a progression in difficulty in terms of both steps and the number of skills used in each dance. All lessons include a review and practice of previously learned dances to help students reinforce and expand their skill learning, gain confidence, personalize their styles, and have more fun. Such review and practice is necessary regardless of grade level.

Following is a description of each lesson in this unit. In lesson 1 students are introduced to line dancing and its music, and given an overview of the unit. They will learn some terms, a few basic steps, a warm-up activity, and a beginning line dance. In lesson 2 more steps and two dances are added. In each of the following lessons, with the exception of lessons 8 and 11, previously learned dances are repeated and new steps and dances are added. In lesson 8 students choreograph their own sequence of steps and perform their dances for the class. Lesson 11 serves as a final review of line dancing. Assessment suggestions are provided in the assessment and resources chapter at the end of the unit, as are resources for more information about line dancing and music suppliers.

Where appropriate, dance skills and suggested music are listed at the beginning of each dance. Knowing which steps are involved without having to read through the entire dance should aid in lesson planning. Although each dance is set to the suggested music, other favorite tunes may be substituted; however, you will need to make sure that the step sequences used in the dance fit the alternate music.

A few illustrations are provided for some of the more complicated dance steps. For better comprehension of foot patterns, many illustrations show a back view. This should also make it easier to model the steps.

You will note that the warm-ups in these lessons are not taken from the appendix. Instead, the warm-up dance, gettin' ready, and previously learned dances are used. These warm-up dance steps mentally prepare students for the lesson ahead, loosen the muscles, and reinforce dance and step instruction.

Social Skills and Etiquette

As in all dancing, sociability is part of the fun and, thus, is an important outcome. Because line dancing is an individual activity, however, students are not restricted by the same etiquette governing partner dance. It is probably sufficient to remind students that attitude and perseverance are important when learning to line dance, as they are in any other endeavor.

Lesson Modifications

Because of the nature of line dancing, a few suggestions for the physically or mentally disabled are worth noting. Shadow dancing (i.e., positioning a student who grasps the dance in front of one having difficulty) can be extremely helpful for students who have difficulty remembering step sequences. Writing a sequence on the chalkboard or providing a handout of the dance steps can be helpful. Because partners are not required in line dancing and because dance steps are performed to counts, students with limited physical mobility can be encouraged to set their own movements to the rhythm of the music, even adding hand and arm movements.

Given the different proficiency levels across grades and within classes, more or less time may be needed to develop and master line dancing skills. In some cases it may even be necessary to repeat a lesson before moving on to the next. Likewise, when two or more dances are introduced in a lesson, it may be advisable to break the lesson apart and teach only one new dance per class.

Safety

Running or traction shoes should not be worn because they constrict smooth transitions of movement and prevent sliding, which could result in tripping or falling. Stocking feet, another hazard, place too much strain on the feet and also cause slips and falls. As explained earlier, smooth-soled or low-traction tennis shoes are recommended.

Terms and Steps

The explanation for many of the steps begins with the right foot for two reasons: Although the steps could be initiated with either foot, (1) almost all dances and dance sequences start with the right foot; and (2) their use in the following dances begins with a right foot lead.

brush—A sweeping motion forward; the foot brushes against the floor (1 count).

bump—Shake the hip forward or backward (1 count).

buttermilk or **pigeon toe** or **heel click** or **heel split**—Feet together with weight on the balls of the feet, both heels rotate outward on count 1 and back on count 2 (2 counts).

circle dance—A dance in a circle formation.

clockwise—A movement in the direction that clock hands travel, circling to the left.

counterclockwise—A movement in the opposite direction that clock hands travel, circling to the right.

cowboy strut—A lively three-step forward walk with a kick (e.g., right, left, right, kick left) or three backward steps with a toe tap beside or behind (left, right, left, toe tap right) (4 counts).

dip—Move the hip downward and upward, making a circle (2 counts).

fan or **toe fan**—Rotate one foot outward on count 1 and back on count 2 while maintaining the heel in contact with the floor (2 counts).

four-step—Walk forward right, left, right, and toe touch the left foot to the right; or walk backward left, right, left, and toe touch the right foot to the left (4 counts).

heel—Touch either heel diagonally out front (1 count).

heel Charleston—Step forward right, touch the left heel forward, step backward left, tap the right toe behind (4 counts).

heel close or **heel toe**—In place, touch either heel in front and bring the foot back beside the other or tap the toe (2 counts).

heel hook—Touch the right heel out diagonally forward and cross back ankle over the left ankle (2 counts).

heel hook, heel close or **heel hook, heel tap**—Touch the right heel out diagonally forward, cross the right foot in front of the left foot, touch the heel out diagonally forward, and tap the right foot in place (or close right) (4 counts).

hitch or **hitch and quarter turn**—Lift and cross the knee over and in front of the supporting foot (like a hop). Use the momentum of crossing the foot to carry a quarter of a turn (1 count).

kick—Thrust the foot out forward (1 count).

limp—A four-count step, right or left, usually sequenced together, ending with a quarter turn right (8 counts). Brush and swing the right foot outward and cross it over the left (1 count), step down on the right foot (1 count), rock backward on the left foot (1 count), and rock forward on the right foot (1 count). Brush and swing the left foot outward and cross it over the right (1 count), step down on the left foot (1 count), rock backward on the right foot (1 count), and rock forward on the left foot (1 count).

pivot—A sharp half or quarter turn to the left or right. Step forward right, half turn left, step left (2 counts).

rock—Shift the weight forward on one foot and backward on the other or reverse (2 counts).

scuff—Strike the floor forward with the heel (1 count).

shuffle (two step)—A three-step forward right or left on 2 counts with a rhythm of quick, quick, slow, or step, close, step. Step forward right, close left (taking weight on the left), step forward right. Repeat beginning with the left.

side, back, and front toe touch—Stretch the foot out to the side, back, or front. Touch the toe to the floor, extending the knee, and return (2 counts).

squash or **squash heels** or **swivel heels**—With feet together and up on the balls of the feet, twist the body to the right while turning the heels out to the right, twist back to the center bringing the heels down; up on the balls of the feet and twist to the left while turning the heels out to the left, twist back to the center (4 counts, 2 + 2).

stamp or **dig**—A forceful slap of the foot or toes to the floor with no weight bearing (1 count).

stomp—A forceful slap of the foot or heel to the floor with weight bearing (1 count).

traveling vine—A turning vine with two half turns. Start with the first four steps of the turning vine. On step 5, cross right behind left, start a quarter turn to the left, step right to complete the turn, and close left to face the original wall (8 counts, 4 + 4).

turning vine—A continuous vine alternating crossing in front and back and facing two opposite walls (half turn on counts 3 and 4). Step right, step left behind, step right starting to turn, step left completing turn, step right behind left, step left, step right in front and close left. (8 counts, 4 + 4).

vine or **grapevine**—A four-step move to the right or left with the last step usually a toe tap, brush, or kick. For example, vine to the right is step right, step left (crossing behind the right foot), step right, toe tap left. Vine to the left is the opposite (4 counts).

wall dance—The number of walls, or directions, faced during a dance. Almost all line dances are 2-wall or 4-wall dances, meaning the dance is performed facing 2 walls (using half turns during the dance) or all 4 walls (using quarter turns). A few are 1-wall dances, meaning that the whole dance is performed facing one direction or wall.

General Teaching Cues

It is wise to be sensitive to students' attitudes about dance when introducing this unit. Not all students may be eager to participate. Gaining full cooperation may take some imagination. Because boys, more than girls, tend to need more prompting for dance instruction, having a male teacher assist or give the instruction is a plus. Introducing the unit with a demonstration dance or showing a videotape that reflects participant enjoyment and a "western" spirit can set the right tone early on.

Teaching cues specific to the lesson are provided in each lesson. Because many of the same teaching cues are applicable to all lessons in this unit, however, they are not repeated in every lesson. Instead, a general listing follows:

1. Teach new steps separately.
2. Teach each dance in segments, adding steps as previous ones are learned.
3. Practice an entire dance in sequence before adding music.
4. Repeat each new dance 2 or 3 times with the music.
5. Write the sequence of dance steps on a chalkboard.
6. Call out each step before students perform it.
7. Start each dance after calling out the last four beats of the introduction: "And 5, 6, 7, 8"; then start the dance.
8. Position skilled dancers on the perimeter of the line formation to act as models for 2- and 4-wall dances.
9. Remind students that almost all dance steps begin with a right foot lead.
10. To help students understand each dance better, distribute handouts of the dance steps and terms before each lesson, or as a packet at the beginning of the unit.

Lesson 1

Introduction: Gettin' Ready and Tulsa Time

Purpose

In this lesson students are introduced to line dancing and learn some basic steps, a warm-up dance (i.e., gettin' ready), and the Tulsa time.

Facility and Equipment

◆ Gym or multipurpose area
◆ Music (CD or audiocassette) and player
◆ Microphone
◆ Videotape and VCR (optional)

Warm-Ups (6-8 Minutes)

Position students in a scatter formation and have them move around the room using the following steps. (Playing country-and-western music in the background will add to the setting and prompt attention to the new unit.)

1. Walk forward, girls' hands clasped behind the back and boys' hands on the waistband with thumbs tucked in.
2. Walk backward.
3. Walk forward 4 steps and backward 4 steps.
4. Walk forward 3 steps and kick on the 4th step.
5. Walk backward 3 steps and toe touch in place on the 4th step.
6. Cross-step sideways to the right (step, cross-step behind; step, cross-step in front; and so on).
7. Cross-step to the left.

Skill Cues

1. Listen for the beat of the music.
2. Start together on cue.
3. Take small steps to keep the body aligned vertically.
4. Maintain an upright posture: chin up and eyes forward.
5. Clap loudly.

Teaching Cues

1. See the general teaching cues for this unit (page 191).
2. Model the dance segments in front with your back to the class (this gets harder as the lines face another wall). After a few segments, watch while calling out the steps.
3. Start and stop if more instruction is needed.

4. Explain that line dancing is performed in lines and that the lines typically change direction a quarter of a turn or a half turn, hence the terms *2-wall* and *4-wall* dances. Only a handful of dances are 1-wall, meaning the whole dance is performed facing a single wall.

5. In the warm-up, stress stretching and lifting the knee.

Activities (30-40 Minutes)

1. Introduce line dancing by setting a positive attitude, asking if students listen to country-and-western music, what their favorite tunes are, if their parents line dance, and so on. Let them know that they have already performed some line dancing steps during the warm-up. Explain that line dancing is performed in lines and that the lines for most dances change direction a quarter or a half turn, hence, the terms *one-wall, two-wall,* and *four-wall* dances. Demonstrate hand positions: girls clasp their hands behind their backs or place them on their hips, and boys tuck their thumbs in their waistbands or hook them in their front pockets. To further motivate interest in line dancing and in the unit ahead, play a videotape segment. (6-8 minutes).

2. Position students in rows, all facing the front of the gym, and explain and demonstrate the daily warm-up. Explain that unless otherwise stated, all steps begin with the right foot. (4-6 minutes)

3. Demonstrate and have students perform gettin' ready. (6-8 minutes)

Gettin' Ready (4-Wall)

Skills: toe touches, knee lifts, kick, clap, jump
Suggested music: "I've Had Enough" (The Tractors), "Fast As You," or "Pink Cadillac" (Southern Pacific, Country Line Dance)
Toe touch to the right, and then back, 2 times.
Toe touch to the left, and then back, 2 times.
Toe touch backward to the right, and then back, 2 times.
Toe touch backward to the left, and then back, 2 times.
Lift and lower the right knee 2 times.
Lift and lower the left knee 2 times.
Kick the right foot out.
Kick the left foot out.
Clap hands.
Jump a quarter turn to the right (facing a different wall).
Continue the sequence.

4. Demonstrate and have students practice the steps of the Tulsa time using the skill and teaching cues. (6-8 minutes)

Tulsa Time (4-Wall)

Skills: vine, step, quarter turn

Suggested music: "On the Road Again" (Willie Nelson), "Western Girls" (Marty Stewart, Country Line Dancing)

Vine to the right.

Vine to the left.

Walk forward right, left, right; touch the left toe beside the right foot.

Walk backward left, right; on the left foot, turn a quarter turn to the right; touch the right toe beside the left foot.

Continue the sequence.

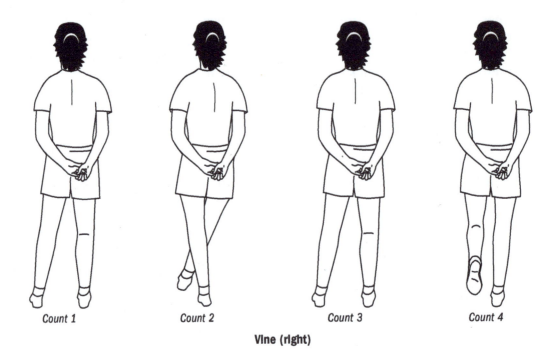

Count 1   Count 2   Count 3   Count 4

Vine (right)

5. Perform the Tulsa time to music. (8-10 minutes)

Closure (3-5 Minutes)

Review the lesson with students. Use the following questions and ideas to reinforce learning, check understanding, and provide feedback.

1. Ask students for comments and questions.

2. Share your observations, commenting on the positive aspects of students' performances as well as offering reminders about technique and posture.

Lesson 2

Elvira, and Heel and Shuffle

Purpose

In this lesson students learn the Elvira, the heel and shuffle, and more dance steps.

Facility and Equipment

- Gym or multipurpose area
- Music (CD or audiocassette) and player
- Microphone

Warm-Ups (6-8 Minutes)

1. Gettin' ready (see lesson 1)
2. Tulsa time (see lesson 1)

Skill Cues

1. Listen for the "5, 6, 7, 8"; then begin.
2. On the shuffle, the lead step should be longer. The other two steps should almost be in place.
3. Stomp to be heard.
4. For a quarter turn at the end of a left vine, step left, right behind, left and hop slightly on the left foot while turning, and kick right.

Teaching Cues

1. See the general teaching cues for this unit (page 191).
2. Review and demonstrate each warm-up before performing it.
3. Encourage students to stomp, clap, and slap loudly.
4. Separate the dances into separate segments. Add the next segment as proficiency is reached. Note: Isolate the quarter turns in both dances and practice them separately.
5. Demonstrate the shuffle by showing how 3 steps are taken in 2 counts.
6. Both dances in this lesson are four-wall dances, meaning students will use quarter turns and face all four walls when performing them.

Activities (30-40 Minutes)

1. Demonstrate the Elvira using the appropriate skill and teaching cues and have students practice the steps. (7-10 minutes)

Elvira (4-Wall)

Skills: vine, step, kick, rock, quarter turn
Suggested music: "Elvira" (Oak Ridge Boys)
Vine to the right.
Vine to the left.
Walk backward right, left, right, and kick.
Step the left foot forward and rock back on the right foot.
Rock forward on the left foot.
Raise the right knee and make a quarter turn to the left, hopping in place on the left foot.
Repeat the sequence.

2. Perform the Elvira. (8-10 minutes)
3. Demonstrate the heel and shuffle using the appropriate skill and teaching cues. Have students practice each skill separately and then in sequence. (7-10 minutes)

Heel and Shuffle

Skills: heel close, shuffle, vine, slap, quarter turn, stomp, squash
Suggested music: "Fast As You" (Country Dance Kings, Country Line Dance), "I Want You Bad & That Ain't Good" (Country Line Dance Jubilee 2)
Heel close right, left, right, left.
Shuffle forward 4 times starting with the right foot.
Vine to the right (step right, cross behind left, step right, and lift the left knee and slap it with the left hand).
Vine to the left (step left, cross behind right, step left, make a quarter turn left, hopping slightly on the left foot, and kick right).
Walk back 3 steps and stomp (right, left, right, and stomp on the left foot.
Squash (right and left).
Continue the sequence.

4. Perform the heel and shuffle to music. (8-10 minutes)

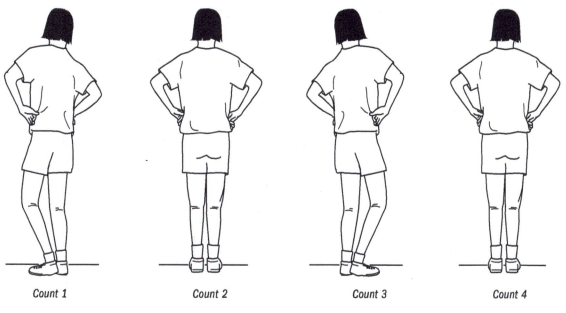

| Count 1 | Count 2 | Count 3 | Count 4 |

Squash

Closure (3-5 Minutes)

Review the lesson with students. Use the following questions and ideas to reinforce learning, check understanding, and provide feedback.

1. Discuss the parts of the dances that were difficult for students.
2. Select students with good technique and ask them to demonstrate different steps, directing others' attention to key movements.

Lesson 3

Coca-Cola Cowboy and Review

Purpose

In this lesson students learn the Coca-Cola cowboy and other dance steps, and review previous dances.

Facility and Equipment

◆ Gym or multipurpose area
◆ Music (CD or audiocassette) and player
◆ Microphone

Warm-Ups (6-8 Minutes)

1. Gettin' ready (see lesson 1)
2. Tulsa time (see lesson 1)

Skill Cues

1. Listen to the beat of the music and time steps to the rhythm.
2. Maintain an upright posture.
3. Point the toe slightly upward and outward on the cowboy strut.
4. Perform the quarter turn by turning the left foot a quarter turn to the left while stepping backward. Toe touch the right toe next to the left foot, keeping the weight on the left foot.

Teaching Cues

1. See the general teaching cues for this unit (page 191).
2. Encourage students to swagger a little when performing the cowboy strut.
3. Model each dance and call out each step the first time through.
4. Teach the Coca-Cola cowboy as a single sequence.

Activities (30-40 Minutes)

1. Review the Elvira dance sequence (see lesson 2), first without and then with music. (8-10 minutes)
2. Review the heel and shuffle dance sequence (see lesson 2), first without and then with music. (8-10 minutes)
3. Demonstrate and have students practice the cowboy strut and quarter turn using the appropriate skill and teaching cues. (5-8 minutes)
4. Perform the Coca-Cola cowboy. (9-12 minutes)

Coca-Cola Cowboy (4-Wall)

Skills: vine, kick, cowboy strut, quarter turn

Suggested music: "Rock My World" or "If Bubba Can Dance" (Country Dance Kings, Country Line Dance)

Vine to the right and kick the left foot.

Vine to the left and kick the right foot.

Vine to the right and kick the left foot.

Vine to the left and kick the right foot.

Cowboy strut forward right, left, right, and kick the left foot.

Cowboy strut backward left, right; left making a quarter turn to the left and toe touch right beside the left foot.

Continue the sequence.

Closure (3-5 Minutes)

Review the lesson with students, using the following question and topics to reinforce learning, check understanding, and provide feedback.

1. Discuss the review dances as well as the cowboy strut, encouraging students to identify steps or sequences they are finding difficult.

2. Ask the students why they think line dancing is so popular (e.g., the music, dancing alone, the freedom to add individual style without worrying about a partner, repetition of basic steps).

Lesson 4

New York, New York and Wagon Wheel

Purpose

In this lesson students learn the New York, New York; the wagon wheel; and more dance steps.

Warm-Ups (6-8 Minutes)

1. Gettin' ready (see lesson 1)
2. Elvira (see lesson 2)

Facility and Equipment

◆ Gym or multipurpose area
◆ Music (CD or audiocassette) and player
◆ Microphone

Skill Cues

1. Count out the eight steps when performing the turning vine.
2. Dip the body slightly downward on the behind crossovers on the turning vine.
3. On the buttermilk, the weight should be on the balls of the feet as the heels go out, in, out, in.
4. Flex the knees on the buttermilk and squash.

Teaching Cues

1. See the general teaching cues for this unit (page 191).
2. For New York, New York teach the turning vine in isolation before teaching the dance.
3. Teach and dance the wagon wheel in one circle first, then in smaller circles.
4. Remind students to keep the circle from closing inward.
5. Encourage students to add some spice to the buttermilk by moving their elbows in sync with their heels and twisting the body with squash movements.
6. Rotate lines and positions if needed.

Activities (30-40 Minutes)

1. Demonstrate and have students practice the eight steps of the turning vine. (4-6 minutes)
2. Review the shuffle; then demonstrate and have students practice the New York, New York using the appropriate skill and teaching cues. (13-15 minutes)

New York, New York (2-Wall)

Skills: heel close, shuffle, turning vine
Suggested music: "There's a Tear in My Beer" (Hank Williams), "Chicago" (any artist)
Heel close right.
Heel close left.
Heel close right.
Heel close left.
Shuffle forward right.
Shuffle forward left.
Shuffle forward right.
Shuffle forward left.
Turning vine right, left, right (short half turn), left (complete half turn); right, left, right, left.
Continue the sequence.

Count 1   Count 2   Count 3   Count 4

Count 5   Count 6   Count 7   Count 8

Turning vine

4. Position students in a large circle. Demonstrate and have students practice the wagon wheel using the appropriate skill and teaching cues. (5-8 minutes)

Wagon Wheel (Circle Dance)

Skills: cowboy strut, squash, heel hook, traveling vine, buttermilk
Suggested music: "Tulsa Shuffle" (The Tractors), "Pink Cadillac" (Southern Pacific, Country Line Dancing)
Cowboy strut forward (right, left, right, kick).
Cowboy strut backward (left, right, left, right toe touch behind).
Cowboy strut forward.
Cowboy strut backward.
Squash right, then center; left, then center.
Heel hook (right heel touches diagonally forward, cross right foot back over left ankle).
Traveling vine right, left, right (half turn), left; right, left, right (half turn), left.
Buttermilk (heels out, in, out, in).
Continue the sequence.

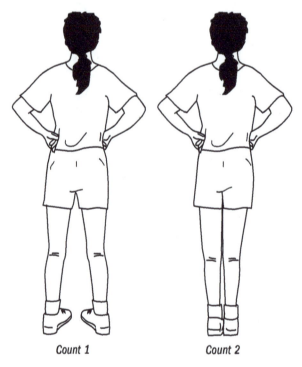

Count 1   Count 2

Buttermilk

5. Divide students into smaller groups and perform the wagon wheel. (8-11 minutes)

Closure (3-5 Minutes)

Review the lesson with students. Use the following questions and ideas to reinforce learning, check understanding, and provide feedback.

1. Have students share their observations from the lesson.
2. Discuss some of the benefits of using the wagon wheel as a closing dance (e.g., many skills are involved, the circular structure allows students to see one another).

Lesson 5

Prima and Review

Purpose

In this lesson students learn a variation of New York, New York and the prima.

Facility and Equipment

◆ Gym or multipurpose area
◆ Music (CD or audiocassette) and player
◆ Microphone

Warm-Ups (6-8 Minutes)

1. Gettin' ready (see lesson 1)
2. Heel and shuffle (see lesson 2)

Skill Cues

1. During the fan, keep the heel in contact with the floor.
2. Slap the heel against the floor on the scuff.
3. Balance on the left foot and make the heel hook, heel close flow.

Teaching Cues

1. See the general teaching cues for this unit (page 191).
2. On the turning vine, remind students that the turn starts on step 3 and is completed on step 4.
3. Teach the vines, quarter turn, scuff, and heel hook, heel close as a single sequence.

Activities (30-40 Minutes)

1. Review and perform the New York, New York (see lesson 4). (6-8 minutes)
2. Introduce and demonstrate the fan, which will be added to the New York, New York. (2-4 minutes)
3. Demonstrate and have students practice the New York, New York with the fan step. The first sequence is the same, but 4 fans replace the 4 heel closes in the second sequence. (6-8 minutes)

New York, New York (With Fan) (2-Wall)

Skills: heel close, shuffle, turning vine, fan
Suggested music: "There's a Tear in My Beer" (Hank Williams), "Chicago" (any artist)
Heel close right.
Heel close left.
Heel close right.
Heel close left.
Shuffle forward right.
Shuffle forward left.

(continued)

New York, New York (With Fan) (2-Wall) *(cont.)*

Shuffle forward right.

Shuffle forward left.

Turning vine right, left, right (start half turn), left (finish half turn); right, left, right, left.

Fan right.

Fan left.

Fan right.

Fan left.

Shuffle forward right.

Shuffle forward left.

Shuffle forward right.

Shuffle forward left.

Turning vine right, left, right (half turn), left; right, left, right (half turn), left.

Continue the sequence.

3. Demonstrate and have students practice the prima using the appropriate skill and teaching cues. (6-8 minutes)

Prima (4-Wall)

Skills: cowboy strut; vine; scuff; heel hook, heel close

Suggested music: "God Bless Texas" (Country Dance Kings, Best of Country Line Dance), "The Little Man" (The Tractors)

Cowboy strut forward right, left, right, kick left.

Cowboy strut backward left, right, left, right toe touch backward.

Cowboy strut forward.

Cowboy strut backward.

Vine right and toe touch.

Vine left, quarter turn left, and scuff the right heel (left, right, turn left, right scuff).

Heel hook, heel close (right heel touch diagonally forward, cross right over left, right heel touch diagonally forward, close right).

Continue the sequence.

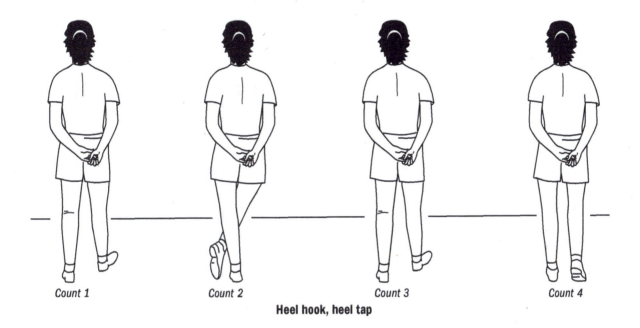

Count 1   Count 2   Count 3   Count 4

Heel hook, heel tap

4. Perform the prima. (10-12 minutes)

Closure (3-5 Minutes)

Review the lesson with students. Then ask students to select a partner. One partner should direct the other through the steps of the buttermilk; squash; heel hook; and heel hook, heel close while the other performs each step.

Lesson 6

Cowboy Boogie and Review

Purpose

In this lesson the students learn the cowboy boogie and more dance steps, and review previous dances.

Warm-Ups (6-8 Minutes)

1. Gettin' ready (see lesson 1)
2. New York, New York (either version; see lessons 4 and 5)

Facility and Equipment

- Gym or multipurpose area
- Music (CD or audiocassette) and player
- Microphone

Skill Cues

1. Perform the hitch by stepping on the left foot while turning left, then lifting the right knee up and across the left foot.
2. Think of the hitch as a hop-step.

Teaching Cues

1. See the general teaching cues for this unit (page 191).
2. Teach the quarter turn and hitch separately.
3. On the hitch, accentuate the knee lift.
4. Rotate lines after reviewing the dances.

Activities (30-40 Minutes)

1. Review and perform the prima (see lesson 5). (6-8 minutes)
2. Review and perform the Elvira (see lesson 2). (6-8 minutes)
3. Demonstrate and have students practice the dance steps using the appropriate skill and teaching cues. (6-9 minutes)

Cowboy Boogie (4-Wall)

Skills: vine, step, kick, rock, quarter turn, hitch

Suggested music: "All Shook Up" (Elvis Presley), "Setting the Woods on Fire" (The Tractors)

Vine right and kick (right, left, right, kick left).

Vine left and kick (left, right, left, kick right).

Right step forward and left kick.

Left step forward and right kick.

Right step backward, left step backward, right step backward, and left kick.

Left step, slightly forward, and rock the hips left 2 times.

Rock backward on the right foot and rock the hips right 2 times.

Rock the hips left.

Rock the hips right.

Left step a quarter turn left, hitch right.

Continue the sequence.

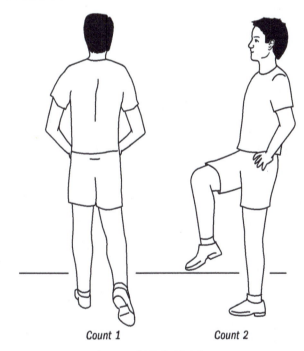

Count 1   Count 2

Step and hitch (right)

4. Perform the cowboy boogie. (12-15 minutes)

Closure (3-5 Minutes)

Review the lesson with students. Ask students which skills, if any, are giving them trouble, or mention any steps you have seen students struggling with. Announce that you will review these at the beginning of the next lesson.

Lesson 7

Chicken Four Corners and Review

Purpose

In this lesson students learn the chicken four corners and more dance steps, and review a previous dance.

Facility and Equipment

◆ Gym or multipurpose area
◆ Music (CD or audiocassette) and player
◆ Microphone

Warm-Ups (6-8 Minutes)

1. Gettin' ready (see lesson 1)
2. Coca-Cola cowboy (see lesson 3)

Skill Cues

1. The heel Charleston involves a right step forward, a left heel touch forward, a left step backward, and then a right toe tap backward behind the left foot.
2. Stomp loudly.
3. Bend backward on the heel Charleston, keeping the body aligned on the left heel forward; then lean forward on the right toe tap, keeping the body aligned.
4. Use the arms for balance and in opposition.

Teaching Cues

See the general teaching cues for this unit (page 191).

Activities (30-40 Minutes)

1. Review the cowboy boogie steps that were problematic for students in lesson 6; then perform the cowboy boogie. (7-11 minutes)
2. Demonstrate and have students practice the dance steps for the chicken four corners using the appropriate skill and teaching cues. (7-9 minutes)

Chicken Four Corners (4-Wall)

Skills: heel close; buttermilk; heel hook, heel close; heel Charleston; shuffle; stomp; quarter turn

Suggested music: "Pink Cadillac" (Southern Pacific, Country Line Dancing), "Jealous Bone" (Patty Loveless, Country Line Dancing)

Heel close right.

Heel close left.

Buttermilk 2 times (heels out, in, out, in).

Heel hook, heel close 2 times (right then left).

Heel Charleston (step forward right, heel forward left, step backward left, toe tap backward right).

Shuffle right.

Shuffle left.

Stomp right a quarter turn.

Stomp (heavily) left together.

Continue the sequence.

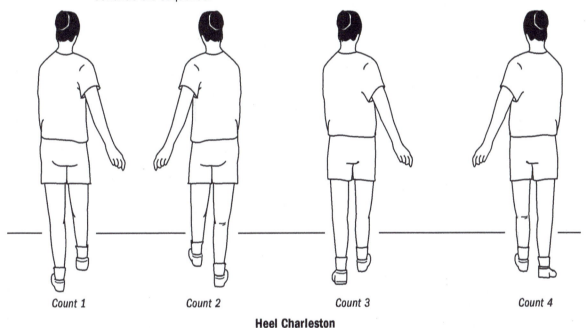

| Count 1 | Count 2 | Count 3 | Count 4 |

Heel Charleston

3. Perform the chicken four corners. (12-14 minutes)

4. Position students in 2 or 3 circles. Review the steps of and perform the wagon wheel (see lesson 4). (4-6 minutes)

Closure (3-5 Minutes)

Review the lesson with students. Use the following questions and ideas to reinforce learning, check understanding, and provide feedback.

1. Ask how many had problems with the heel Charleston. Review the sequence if necessary.

2. Announce that students will make up their own line dance in the next lesson and, if necessary, introduce the parameters of the lesson.

Lesson 8

Student Choreography

Purpose

In this lesson students will choreograph their own dance and present it to the class.

Warm-Up (3-4 Minutes)

1. Gettin' ready (see lesson 1)

Skill Cues

1. Use a variety of steps in the dance.
2. Make sure the dance steps fit into the 32 beats.

Teaching Cues

1. Preselect groups to ensure representative skill levels and equal gender distribution.
2. This lesson may be used to evaluate student performance.
3. This would be a good time to videotape each group—a good motivator, too.
4. If you can choose to use more than one selection of music, this will require using multiple music players and having to define the number of counts per sequence.
5. Allow students to create an entire dance on their own, or require a few steps within each dance.
6. Reduce the warm-up time and add the time to group work.

Activities (33-43 Minutes)

1. Divide students into 3 or 4 groups. Explain that each group will choreograph a dance using 32 beats or counts and repeat the dance to the end of the music. Play the selected music for students before they start working in their groups. (6-8 minutes)
2. Have groups work with and without music. (17-20 minutes)
3. Have groups present their dances to the rest of the class. (10-15 minutes)

Facility and Equipment

- Gym or multipurpose area
- Music (CD or audiocassette) and player
  Note: Suggested music includes "Alley Cat" (Al Hirt or any artist) and "Dumas Walker" (The Kentucky Headhunters).

Closure (3-5 Minutes)

Review the lesson with students. Use the following questions and ideas to reinforce learning, check understanding, and provide feedback.

1. Have students review and discuss the dances they choreographed. Use the following questions to stimulate discussion.
   - ▸ Which dance was the most creative?
   - ▸ Which had the most difficult steps?
   - ▸ What was the hardest part in choreographing a dance?
   - ▸ Why might dances with the same name have different step sequences?

2. Have students share their observations about creativity and performance technique with the group (encourage positive feedback).

3. If the groups were videotaped and there isn't time for playback, viewing could be at the beginning of the next lesson.

Lesson 9

Nola and Review

Purpose

In this lesson students learn the nola and more dance steps, and review previous dances.

Warm-Ups (6-8 Minutes)

1. Gettin' ready (see lesson 1)
2. Prima (see lesson 5)

Skill Cues

1. Flex the opposite knee while side toe touching.
2. Use 1 count on the brush and swing.
3. Complete a quarter turn on the second limp, using the brush and swing.

Teaching Cues

1. See the general teaching cues for this unit (page 191).
2. On the side toe touch, emphasize that students should point the toe out to the side and look at it.
3. Teach the limp in isolation.

Activities (30-40 Minutes)

1. Review and perform the New York, New York. (6-8 minutes)
2. Review and perform the chicken four corners. (8-10 minutes)
3. Demonstrate and have students practice the nola using the appropriate skill and teaching cues. (6-8 minutes)

Nola (4-Wall)

Skills: vine, shuffle, step, side toe touch, limp
Suggested music: "Nola" (any artist)
Vine right.
Vine left.
Shuffle 4 times (right, left, right, left).
Step backward 4 times (right, left, right, left).
Right toe touch to the right side.
Left toe touch to the left side.
Limp (see terms). Brush and swing right foot, step down, rock backward, rock forward, and repeat with a left foot lead, making a quarter turn right on the brush and swing.
Continue the sequence.

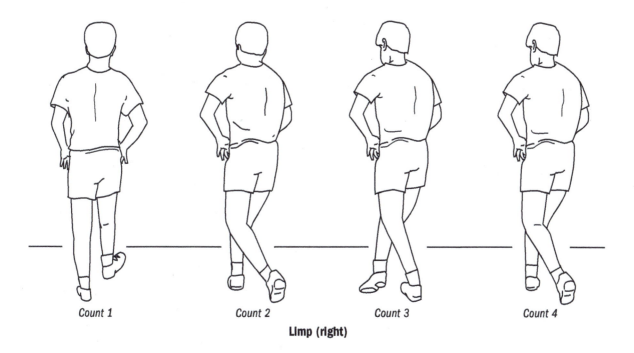

Count 1   Count 2   Count 3   Count 4

Limp (right)

First count of the limp (left)

4. Perform the nola. (10-14 minutes)

Closure (3-5 Minutes)

Review the lesson with students. Have them explain which steps they've mastered and which ones need more practice. These will be reviewed in lesson 10.

Lesson 10

Tush Push and Review

Purpose

In this lesson students learn the tush push and other dance steps, and review previous dances.

Facility and Equipment

- Gym or multipurpose area
- Music (CD or audiocassette) and player
- Microphone

Warm-Ups (6-8 Minutes)

1. Gettin' ready (see lesson 1)
2. Cowboy boogie (see lesson 6)

Skill Cues

1. On the heel, toe, heel, heel, move (or hop) quickly when changing from the right set to the left set.
2. Perform the heel with a clap by quickly thrusting each heel out (3 counts); then clap.
3. Flex the knees on the dips, moving downward and upward in a circle.
4. Stay up on the ball of the pivoting foot.
5. Think of the return after the shuffle as almost a rocking step, forward and backward or backward and forward.

Teaching Cues

1. See the general teaching cues for this unit (page 191).
2. Teach the pivot and the shuffle and return separately.
3. Stress making the pivot a "crisp" turn.
4. Tell students to make the bump "sassy."
5. Remind students that there are 2 counts to the bump, dip, turn, pivot, shuffle, and stamp and clap; there are 4 counts per shuffle and return as well as the first three sets of the heel with a clap.

Activities (30-40 Minutes)

1. Review and perform the nola (see lesson 9). (5-8 minutes)
2. Demonstrate and have students practice the steps of the tush push, using the appropriate skill and teaching cues. (10-12 minutes)

Tush Push (4-Wall)

Skills: heel toe, clap, bump, dip, shuffle and return, pivot, quarter turn, stamp, clap

Suggested music: "Boot Scootin' Boogie" (any artist), "Baby Likes to Rock It" (The Tractors), "Two of a Kind" (Garth Brooks)

Right heel toe, heel, heel (tap right heel forward, toe tap together, heel, heel).

Left heel toe, heel, heel, (tap left heel forward, toe tap together, heel, heel).

Right heel, left heel, right heel, clap.

Bump right twice (diagonally forward).

Bump left twice (diagonally backward).

Dip right (circle motion downward and upward).

Dip right again.

Right shuffle forward and return (shuffle forward, step left forward, step right backward).

Left shuffle backward and return (shuffle backward, step right backward, step left forward).

Shuffle forward right.

Pivot a half turn to the right (step forward left, make a half turn to the right, step down right).

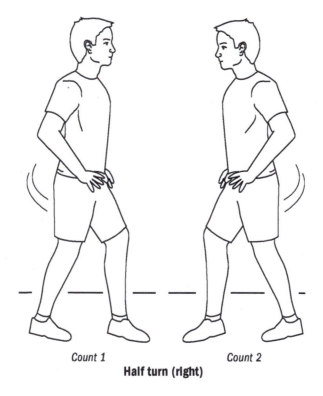

Count 1   Count 2

Half turn (right)

Shuffle forward left.

Pivot a half turn to the left (step forward right, make a half turn to the left, step down left).

Make a quarter turn to the left (step right, turning to the left; step left, feet together).

Stamp right and clap.

Continue the sequence.

3. Perform the tush push. (15-20 minutes)

Closure (3-5 Minutes)

Review the lesson with students. Use the following topics and questions to reinforce learning, check understanding, and provide feedback.

1. Share your observations and provide feedback about technique and step sequencing.
2. Remind students that the next lesson will be a review of the dances in this unit. Let them know if they will be evaluated.

Lesson 11

Line Dancing Review

Purpose

In this lesson students will perform the dances they've learned during this unit.

Facility and Equipment

◆ Gym or multipurpose area
◆ Music (CD or audiocassette) and player
◆ Microphone

Warm-up (3 Minutes)

1. Gettin' ready (see lesson 1)

Skill Cues

1. Concentrate on the music and stay with the beat.
2. Try to show some individual style within the confines of each dance.

Teaching Cues

1. Rotate lines after each dance.
2. This lesson may be used to evaluate student performance.

Activities (30-40 Minutes)

1. Review and perform the tush push (see lesson 10). (7-10 minutes)
2. Review and perform as many dances as time will allow. (20-25 minutes)
3. Position students in a large circle and perform the wagon wheel (see lesson 4). (3-5 minutes)

Closure (3-5 Minutes)

1. Review the line dancing unit with students. Use the following questions and ideas to reinforce learning, check understanding, and provide feedback.
    ▸ Which steps were the most difficult to master?
    ▸ Which dance did students like best? Why?
    ▸ Which dance was the most difficult? The easiest?

   Ask students if they would feel comfortable line dancing at a public event or party, such as a wedding reception.
2. If you will be conducting a formal assessment of this unit, let students know that their knowledge and skill will be evaluated during the next class period.

Assessment and Resources

Achievement in line dancing can be assessed using different measures of performance and knowledge, some formal and some informal. Throughout the unit, students should be periodically evaluated on social skills and attitude as evidenced by attendance, readiness, cooperation with others (e.g., in group work), and willingness to practice and participate.

Formal assessment is a bit more challenging. Because each student dances alone, evaluating skill is an individual endeavor and, therefore, subjective. Choosing an assessment tool (or tools) will largely depend on the number of students in class and how much time is available. Some testing suggestions are provided in this chapter.

Lessons

The following lessons may be used for assessment purposes. Assessment protocol is listed with each.

▶ Lessons 5 through 10. Use the review dances in these lessons as an ongoing measure of student knowledge and performance.

▶ Lesson 8. Assign points or grades for creativity and level of difficulty in student-choreographed dances. During the presentation phase, points or grades could be awarded for dance technique, individual form, and group presentation.

▶ Lesson 11. Use this lesson as the final evaluation of student knowledge and skill mastery.

▶ All lessons. Evaluate social skills and attitude as evidenced by attendance, readiness, cooperation, willingness to practice and participate.

Other Assessment

The following are suggestions for formal assessment of skill mastery and knowledge in line dancing.

1. Prepare different sequences of 4 to 5 dance steps. Divide the class into groups of 3 or 4 students and assign a sequence to each group. Allow a few minutes for practice and then rate each student on knowledge and technique.

2. Prepare a written test on the dance terms and step counts used in this unit.

3. Have student groups choreograph and perform a line dance to their own choice of country-and-western music.

Resources

Lane, C. 2000. *Christy Lane's complete book of line dancing*. 2nd ed. Champaign, IL: Human Kinetics.

Schenk, J. 1995. Dandylines. Unpublished manuscript.

Additional Resources

Line dancing audiocassettes and CDs can be obtained from the following sources:

Human Kinetics
P.O. Box 5076
Champaign, IL 61825-5076
Phone 800-747-4457
  Offers *Christy Lane's Line Dancing Music* (1998) on CD and audiocassette

Kimbo Educational Records
P.O. Box 477
N. Third Ave.
Long Branch, NJ 07740
Phone 800-631-2187
  Offers a variety of line dancing music suitable for physical education instruction

K-tel International (USA), Inc.
15535 Medina Rd.
Plymouth, MN 55447
  Offers *Country Line Dance* (1995) and *Country Line Dance Jubilee*, vol. 2 (1993)

Priority Records, Inc.
P.O. Box 2186
Los Angeles, CA 90078
  Offers *Country Line Dance, vol. 1* (1994)

Soccer

In every country except the United States, soccer is referred to as *football*. The history of soccer goes back some 2,000 years ago, evidenced by records of different types of soccer in ancient Greece and Rome. But it was in England during the Middle Ages that football began to take the shape recognized as soccer (or football) today.

Originally considered a vulgar, rowdy pastime, constant efforts were made by law-abiding mayors, sheriffs, and clerics to suppress the game. It was thought that the game kept men from their Christian duties and from "proper" occupation, and it wasted valuable time that might otherwise have been profitably spent in the practice of archery and other military skills. Despite these efforts to stamp it out, however, the people went on playing.

What came to be known as *mob football,* soccer was little more than a violent street battle in early England. The field was the length of the town, the number of players might be as many as 500, the conflict continued for an entire day, and vast numbers of windows and legs were broken. There were even some deaths. It was upon this turmoil that some order was finally imposed, and from that order the game of soccer emerged.

Formal soccer rules were first adopted by the English Football Association. As is the case with the evolution of all sports, with each passing development, rules were amended and changed to increase safety and allow for fair play. Field dimensions, starting and play positions, goal parameters, and other specifics were introduced along the way.

Soccer is much more popular in Europe and South America than in the United States. In fact, soccer is the focus of the largest sporting event in the world. The World Cup, the international professional soccer championship held every four years, draws crowds in the millions. Today soccer is gaining popularity in the United States. The game is unique among other U.S. sports because players (except for the goaltender) use only the feet, chest, and head, not the hands. With an emphasis on kicking instead of catching, soccer skills remain quite distinct from the majority of other team sports played around the world.

Equipment

Aside from the field equipment, which consists of two goals 8 yards (7.31 meters) wide and 8 feet (2.44 meters) high, the only other equipment required for game play are soccer balls. Soccer balls should be sized appropriately for players' ages. Adults or teens use a size 5 soccer ball (circumference 27-28 inches [68.6-71.1 centimeters]) and children aged 7 to 12 use a size 4 (circumference 25-26.5 inches [63.5-67.3 centimeters]).

Player equipment consists of proper shoes and padding. Soccer shoes, which are often called cleats, are rubber-bottomed (as opposed to the metal spikes used in baseball). The cleats are important for improving running traction and preventing injury. Padding consists of shin guards for all players and elbow, hip, and knee pads for goalies. Goaltenders also wear special gloves that have a rubber insert sewn on the palm, These gloves can be moistened to produce greater grip for the goaltender.

Unit Organization

Some of the lessons in this unit may present more instruction than can be offered in a single class period. In these instances, either select the most appropriate tasks for students based on their skills and knowledge of the game (this unit is based on the assumption that students have learned basic soccer skills in lower grades) or expand the lesson to fill two or more classes.

Following is an overview of each lesson in this unit.

- Lessons 1, 2, 3, and 4 present the offensive soccer skills of dribbling, passing, shooting, and heading.
- Lesson 5 introduces the trap, a skill in which both offensive and defensive players must be proficient.
- Tackling and goaltending are presented in lessons 6 and 7.
- Lesson 8 integrates the skills learned in lessons 1, 2, 3, and 4 into an offensive strategy.
- In lesson 9 tackling and goaltending are revisited as defensive strategy.
- In Lesson 10 students participate in a series of games and activities that lead up to lesson 11, in which a regulation game of soccer is played.

Selected resources as well as assessment ideas and activities follow the unit lessons.

Note: An asterisk (*) following a facility or equipment listing indicates that preparation is required before the lesson.

Social Skills and Etiquette

Social skills should be emphasized in this unit because soccer involves not only competition but also teamwork. Preliminary discussions can set the atmosphere for fair play and fun during this unit. Instruct students on the importance of being good sports, including accepting referee decisions and treating opponents and teammates with respect. One way to encourage teamwork is rotating positions frequently both in practice and in game play.

Lesson Modifications

Soccer is a strenuous activity for many students. For those of lesser ability and lower fitness levels, the following modifications can be made to accommodate the needs of students:

- Use a Nerf ball or a larger ball.
- Reduce the size of the playing area.
- Enlarge the goal area.
- Allow more players per team.
- Eliminate some of the more technical rules (e.g., indirect free kicks, offsides). For example, the teacher can give the ball to the opposite team to throw in instead of following the more technical rules when a player commits a foul (infraction). A throw-in is a ball toss from the sideline near where the foul occurred. The ball is held behind the head with both hands and tossed out onto the field.

Safety

Although the game of soccer is relatively safe, a few extra safety precautions should be observed. For indoor soccer, use a softer or slightly deflated ball for safety and control. For indoor and outdoor soccer, students should be instructed to

- avoid high kicking when close to another player,
- protect their heads from high balls by folding their arms across their faces,
- avoid tripping, body blocking, pushing, and shoving (enforce the rules pertaining to rough play), and
- kick with the instep (shoelace area) and the inside of the foot to prevent toe injuries.

In addition, girls should be permitted to cross their arms over their chests and goaltenders should be careful when picking up the ball with their hands so they are not kicked by an opposing player.

Rules

The object of the game is to score as many goals as possible. At the end of the game, the team with the most goals wins. The length of the game will be determined by the amount of class time available, but regulation games consist of two 45-minute halves. Regulation soccer teams consist of 11 players, including the goaltender. However, if necessary the game can be played with up to 15 players per team. Each team consists of 4 or 5 defensive players, 3 or 4 midfielders, 3 or 4 forwards, and 1 goaltender.

The game begins with a kickoff by one team. The player who kicks off cannot touch the ball again until another player has touched it. All players must be on their own side (i.e., their own half) of the field for the kickoff, which also occurs after halftime and after each goal.

Play

The basic skills of play includes players kicking, passing, and dribbling the ball to advance it downfield. Following is a listing of rules governing normal play. As mentioned earlier in this unit introduction, rules may be modified to accommodate the needs of students.

▸ All players except the goaltender advance the ball using the feet and head only, not the hands; goalies may use their hands to pick up and throw the ball out of the goal area.

▸ When the ball crosses over the sidelines, it is out of play. The last team to touch the ball before it went out-of-bounds loses possession and the other team gets a throw-in. For a throw-in, both feet must stay on the ground and remain outside of the sideline. The thrower must use both hands to throw the ball from behind the head, and another player must touch

the ball before the thrower can touch the ball again.

▸ A goal cannot be scored from a throw-in.

▸ When the defensive team kicks the ball out-of-bounds over the end line, a corner kick occurs. The offensive players can stand as close as they want to the kicker but the opposing team must be 10 yards (9.14 meters) away. Corner kicks are taken from the nearest corner, marked off with a 1-yard (.91-meter) radius.

▸ When the offensive team kicks the ball out-of-bounds over the end line (but not into the goal), a goal kick occurs. The defensive team places the ball within the goal area (on the same side of the goal where the ball went over the end line) and kicks it downfield. Usually the goaltender will take goal kicks.

▸ When the game is stopped because of a player injury, a drop ball occurs. The soccer ball is dropped between two opponents who try to gain possession of the ball after it touches the ground.

Fouls and Penalties

Fouls and misconduct are penalized with direct free kicks, penalty kicks, and indirect free kicks. A direct free kick is awarded when a major foul occurs. The fouled player performs the kick, shooting directly at the goal from the place where the foul occurred. The defending team must stand 10 yards (9.14 meters) away and not closer until the ball is kicked.

Major fouls include the following:

▸ Handling the ball (i.e., using the arms or hands)

▸ Kicking an opponent intentionally

▸ Striking an opponent

▸ Tripping an opponent

▸ Holding an opponent (i.e., physically grasping an opponent)

▸ Pushing an opponent

▸ Charging or jumping at an opponent

▸ Charging an opponent from behind

▸ Other nonsporting conduct

When the defensive team commits a major foul within the penalty area, a penalty kick is awarded. The offensive team member kicks the ball toward the goal from just outside the penalty area; the goaltender is the only player allowed to defend.

An indirect free kick is awarded when a minor foul occurs. In an indirect free kick, the fouled player stands at the place where the foul occurred and kicks the ball toward the goal, but the ball must be touched by another player (standing 10 yards [9.14 meters] away) before a goal can be scored. Minor fouls include the following:

▸ Dangerous play (e.g., kicking an opponent near the head)

▸ Obstruction (i.e., stopping the progress of an opponent—may not involve holding the opponent.)

▸ The goaltender taking more than four steps while holding the ball with the hands.

▸ Offsides

Offsides occurs when the ball is passed to an offensive player near the goal without at least two defensive players between the offensive player and the goal.

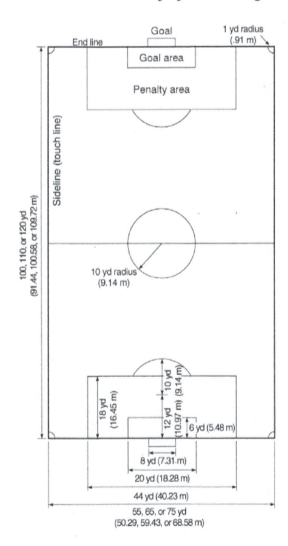

Soccer field dimensions

Lesson 1

Dribbling

Purpose

In this lesson students develop dribbling skills using the inside and outside of the foot, instep and toe.

Warm-Ups (6-8 Minutes)

1. Sprint-jog intervals
2. Waist twists
3. Elbow-knee touches (standing)
4. Inverted hurdler's stretch

Facility and Equipment

◆ Outdoor field or gym
◆ 1 soccer ball per student
◆ 3 cones per 2 students
◆ 1 pinnie per 2 students

Skill Cues

1. Tap the ball lightly below its center.
2. Use both feet for dribbling.
3. Keep the ball 12 to 24 inches (30.5-61 centimeters) in front of the feet.
4. Use the arms for balance.
5. Watch the ball, but be alert to other players' positions.
6. Use the inside of foot, outside of foot, instep, or toe to dribble the ball.

Teaching Cues

1. Explain that dribbling is used to advance the ball while maintaining control.
2. Students may have a tendency toward using only the inside of the foot when dribbling; remind them to use both the inside and the outside of the foot.

Activities (30-40 Minutes)

1. Introduce dribbling emphasizing the skill and teaching cues. (4-6 minutes)

Inside of foot   *Outside of foot*

Dribbling

2. Dribble escape. Each player has a soccer ball and on a signal begins to dribble around the field. Designate two players without soccer balls as "chasers." These players attempt to kick the ball away from the others. Any player whose ball is kicked by the chaser also becomes a chaser. (New chasers must place their soccer balls out of play before they begin to chase.) Continue until all players have become chasers. (8-10 minutes)

3. Obstacle dribble. Divide the class into groups of four and have each group line up behind a line of 6 cones; place a soccer ball in front of the first student in line. On the signal, the first student in line dribbles the ball by weaving in and out of the cones. When the student returns to the starting position by weaving back through the cones, the next student goes. (6-8 minutes)

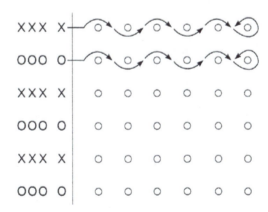

Obstacle dribble

4. Circle dribble. Divide the class into 4 teams and position them in 2 large circles on the field; each team occupies half a circle. Assign each team member a number; two students will have the same number in each circle. When their number is called out, both students in each circle begin to dribble the ball around their circle. The object is to dribble as quickly as possible and beat the opposing team member back to the starting point. To increase the action, have the 2 students from one circle race against the 2 students in the other circle. (6-8 minutes)

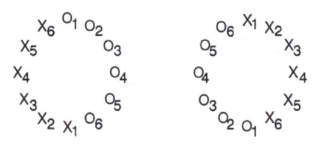

Circle dribble

5. Dribble and turn. Pair up students or have them select partners. Position 2 cones 30 yards (27.43 meters) apart and another cone 20 feet (6.1 meters) away from one end. Partners stand at the 2 outside cones and one begins to dribble toward the other. The student dribbling passes the ball to the partner upon reaching the 20-foot (6.1-meter) cone. The receiving partner runs toward the cone to receive the pass and then dribbles back to the starting cone. Partners switch roles. (6-8 minutes)

Optional Activity

Dribble Soccer (0-18 Minutes)

Divide the class into 4 teams and distribute pinnies to 2 of the teams (2 games will be played). Using cones, set up goals (8 yards [7.31 meters] wide) and goal lines (35 yards [32 meters] apart). Begin the game by throwing the ball onto the field in the center (midfield). Each team tries to take possession of the ball. The team in control of the ball then dribbles downfield, trying to score a goal (worth 1 point). The only way to advance the ball downfield is by dribbling. A player can pass the ball to a team member while dribbling downfield but may not kick it in forward direction or use any other means to advance the ball to the goal; otherwise, the opposing team gains possession. After each goal, the team that lost the previous point starts the ball.

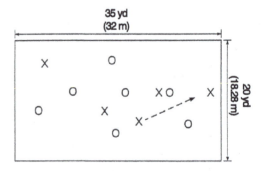

Dribble soccer

Closure (3-5 Minutes)

Review the lesson with students. Use the following ideas to reinforce learning, check understanding, and provide feedback.

1. Choose 4 students to demonstrate dribbling: 1 using the inside of the foot, 1 using the outside of the foot, 1 using the instep (shoelace area), and 1 using the toe.

2. Review the proper dribbling technique.

Lesson 2

Passing

Purpose

In this lesson students develop various passing skills, including chip and instep passing as well as passing with the inside and the outside of the foot.

Warm-Ups (6-8 Minutes)

1. Scissors
2. Side stretch
3. Leg lifts
4. Gluteal stretch

Skill Cues

1. Watch the ball and keep the arms at the sides for balance.
2. Contact the ball at its center for a push pass on the ground.
3. Contact the ball below its center for a low drive in the air.
4. Contact the ball below its center but without follow-through for a chip pass.
5. Follow through in the direction of the pass for the push pass and low drive.
6. To pass using the inside of the foot, point the toes of the kicking foot upward and outward with the ankle locked.
7. To pass using the outside of the foot, point the toes of the kicking foot downward and inward with the ankle locked.
8. To pass using the instep (shoelace area), point the toes of the kicking foot straight downward.

Teaching Cues

1. Explain that the purpose of passing is sending the ball to a teammate.
2. Throughout these activities, remind students that the inside or the outside of the foot as well as the instep (shoelace area) can be used to pass the ball.

Activities (30-40 Minutes)

1. Introduce the various soccer passes using the skill and teaching cues. Have students practice each pass using both the inside and the outside of the foot as well as the instep (shoelace area). (4-6 minutes)

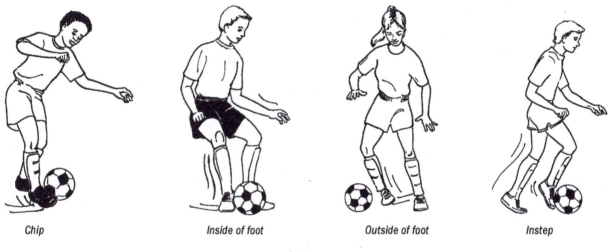

Chip   Inside of foot   Outside of foot   Instep

Passes

2. Pinball soccer. Pair up students or have them select partners. Each student pair plays in a small area of the field using a ball and a cone. The object of this activity is to pass the ball at a cone 15 feet (4.57 meters) away using either a push pass or a low drive. If the first player hits the cone, the second player must make the same type of pass using the same part of the foot. If the first player misses, the second player can challenge the first player with a different pass. (6-8 minutes)

3. Zigzag soccer pass. Position student partners on the field standing side by side 10 feet (3.05 meters) apart. Both partners run forward, partner 2 running ahead to receive the ball as partner 1 passes it. Then partner 1 runs ahead to receive a pass from partner 2. This pattern continues as both partners advance down the field. Encourage students to vary their running speed and passing technique with each pass. (8-10 minutes)

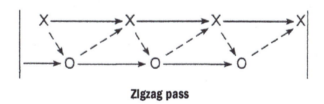

Zigzag pass

4. Bridge soccer. Divide students into six teams and have each team form a line on the field about 15 feet (4.57 meters) apart. Each student should stand with the legs apart (like a bridge) and hold a soccer ball. On the signal, the first student in line passes the soccer ball through the legs of the other teammates, then runs to the end of the line, forms a bridge, and picks up and holds the ball once the ball has been passed under the last bridge. The next team member (now in the first position in line) repeats the activity, passing another ball through

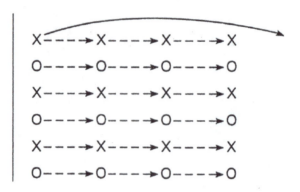

Bridge soccer

the bridges and running to the end of the line. With each pass, the team will advance downfield. (6-8 minutes)

Optional Activity: Golf Soccer

5. Chip away. Distribute a soccer ball to each student and have them stand about 20 feet (6.1 meters) from a hoop on the ground. The object is to chip the soccer ball into the hoop as many times as possible. (6-8 minutes)

Optional Activity

Golf Soccer (0-25 Minutes)

Set up six or more holes on the field, each hole represented by a cone with a flag. (Design the holes to encourage some low drives, some push passes, and possibly a chip pass.) Groups of 3 or 4 students start at different holes, about 25 to 45 yards (22.86-41.14 meters) from the hole, each student with a soccer ball. Players advance the ball toward the hole using only a soccer pass. They complete the hole when the ball hits the cone. The object of the game and the rules are the same as in golf (e.g., players try to complete each hole in the fewest number of passes; see the golf unit on page 447).

Closure (3-5 Minutes)

Review the lesson with students. Use the following ideas to reinforce learning, check understanding, and provide feedback.

1. Stress that all parts of the foot (inside, outside, and instep) should be used for passing. Ask student to demonstrate each type of passing.

2. Select a student to demonstrate using the push pass or low drive to hit a designated target.

Lesson 3

Shooting

Purpose

In this lesson students develop their shooting skills.

Warm-Ups (6-8 Minutes)

1. Running in place
2. Single-leg crossovers
3. Floor touches
4. Arm and leg lifts

Skill Cues

1. Focus on the ball and keep the arms at the sides for balance.
2. Contact the ball at its center with the inside of the foot, instep, or toe.
3. Place the stationary (i.e., nonkicking) foot beside the ball in preparation for the kick.
4. Kick with either foot.
5. Follow through in the direction of the kick.
6. Use shooting as a technique to score.

Teaching Cues

1. Explain that shooting skills are used to score a goal.
2. Students may have a tendency to use a toe kick to shoot; remind them that the inside foot kick may be more accurate once practiced and learned.

Activities (30-40 Minutes)

1. Introduce soccer shooting using the skill cues. (3-5 minutes)
2. Partner shoot. Position two students 20 feet (6.1 meters) apart. One student serves (rolls) a ball to the other, who shoots the ball back to the server. After the server rolls 10 times, partners switch roles. The object of this activity is to shoot the ball back as accurately as possible, sending it directly to the server. (4-6 minutes)
3. Target shoot. In groups of 3 students, 2 players shoot from 15 yards (13.71 meters) at a goal formed by 2 cones (8 yards [7.31 meters] apart); the third player retrieves the balls and tosses them back. The first shooter attempts 5 shots from the right, then rotates to make 5 shots from the left. After completing 10 shots, the shooter moves behind the goal to retrieve. Then the second shooter attempts 5 shots from the left, then 5 shots from the right, and then moves behind

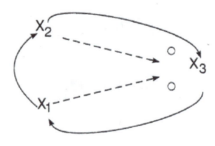

Target shoot

the goal to retrieve. This rotation continues until all players have had a chance to shoot. (9-11 minutes)

Optional Activity: Shoot the Cones

4. Pressure shooting. Divide students into new groups of 3: 1 player is the shooter, 1 is the server, and 1 retrieves the ball. The shooter stands 20 yards (18.28 meters) from the goal (formed by cones); the server stands slightly further away from the goal; and the retriever stands behind the goal. The server rolls the ball to the shooter, who must shoot for the goal immediately without controlling the ball first. As soon as the shot is made, the shooter returns to the original position to receive another ball from the server. After shooting three balls, players rotate positions. (6-8 minutes)

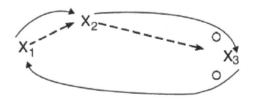

Pressure shooting

5. Line shoot. Divide the class into four teams (play two games simultaneously) and position each team on a line 15 yards (13.71 meters) from the opposite team. Assign each player a number (this number will correspond to a player on the other team) and center a ball between the two teams. To begin the game, call out a number. Players with that number run forward to gain possession of the ball, then dribble it before passing it back to their team linesmen to shoot through the opposing team. If the soccer ball passes through the opposing team's line, a point is scored, the ball is placed back in the center, and another number is called. Only the linesmen can score, and they may score only by shooting. If the soccer ball does not pass through the opposing team's line, no point is scored and the opposing team gets to take a free shot. (8-10 minutes)

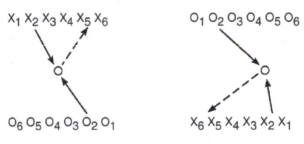

Line shoot

Optional Activities

Shoot the Cones (0-16 Minutes)

Set up two fields, each 20 by 35 yards (18.28 by 32 meters) with a safety zone at each end of the field; place 5 cones in each safety zone. Divide the class into four teams (two games are played simultaneously) and distribute a ball to each team. The object of the game is to try to knock over the opponent's cones by using soccer shooting. Players may not enter the safety zone but may retrieve balls from the other side of the zone. Once a cone is knocked over, it remains down for the rest of the game. The first team to knock down all of the opponent's cones is the winner.

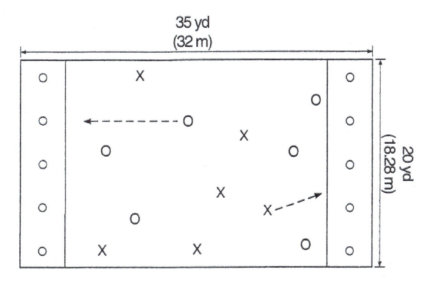

Shoot the cones

Croquet Soccer (0-20 Minutes)

Set up eight pairs of cones with enough space between them to allow a soccer ball to pass through. Spread each pair of cones around the field to form a croquet course. Divide students into two teams; players from each team alternate through the course. The object is for players to kick a soccer ball through all the cones, in order, as quickly as possible. (It may be necessary to number the cones.) Just as in croquet, players may knock other players' balls away from the cones during the game. The first player to successfully complete the course wins.

Guard Ball (0-12 Minutes)

Position students in groups of four, each at a circle with a cone in the center. One player stands in the circle and guards the cone from the other three players who attempt to hit the cone by shooting the soccer ball. Players may pass the ball across the circle, shooting at the cone when the time is right. When the cone is hit, the kicker becomes the new guard and stands in the circle. If the guard steals the ball, the last player to touch it becomes the guard.

Closure (3-5 Minutes)

Review the lesson with students. Use the following ideas to reinforce learning, check understanding, and provide feedback.

1. Discuss techniques that can be used to improve accuracy in shooting (e.g., follow through in the direction of the kick, place the nonkicking foot beside the ball before the kick).

2. Choose one student to demonstrate shooting. Describe the technique as the student shoots.

Lesson 4

Heading

Purpose

In this lesson students learn the skill of heading.

Warm-Ups (6-8 Minutes)

1. Jump rope or jump rope laps
2. Hip lifts
3. Horizontal run
4. Curl and stretch

Skill Cues

1. Focus on the ball.
2. Contact the ball at the forehead, using the legs to propel the trunk, neck, and head forward to meet the ball. The head should hit the ball; the ball should not hit the head.
3. Lean backward before contacting the ball.
4. Head upward by heading under the middle of the ball.
5. Head downward by heading above the middle of the ball.
6. Follow through with the forehead.

Teaching Cues

1. Explain that heading is used to pass, score goals, and clear the ball out of the area.
2. Emphasize that students should head in all directions: forward, to both sides, and backward.

Activities (30-40 Minutes)

1. Introduce heading using the skill and teaching cues. (4-6 minutes)
2. Distribute a ball to each student and have them toss a soccer ball in the air, head it once, and then catch it. When all students can head the ball once successfully, have them attempt to head it twice consecutively before catching it. (4-6 minutes)
3. Partner heading. Pair up students or have them select partners. One partner tosses the soccer ball underhand so that it arches and drops toward the other partner's head. This partner heads the ball forward, attempting to send it back to the first partner.

Heading

Partner heading

After four tosses, partners switch roles. Once proficient, students should try to head the soccer ball to each other rather than toss it. (6-8 minutes)

4. Circle heading. Divide the class into three circles and designate a leader for each. The leader stands in the middle of the circle and tosses the soccer ball to players, who head it back to the leader. After 1 minute (blow a whistle each minute) another student should step into the middle and be the leader. (8-10 minutes)

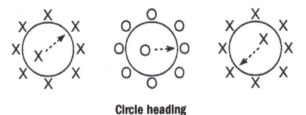

Circle heading

5. Backward heading. Divide students into groups of three. Space each player 15 feet (4.57 meters) apart in a straight line. The first player (tosser) tosses the soccer ball to the second player (header), who heads the ball backward to the third player (catcher) to catch. The catcher then tosses the ball to the header to head backward again to the tosser. Once the header heads six tosses, players should rotate one position. (8-10 minutes)

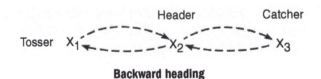

Backward heading

Optional Activity

Heading Relay (0-15 Minutes)

Using the same formation and rotation as in activity 5, players rotate one position after each toss (i.e., the tosser runs forward to become the header, the header runs forward to become the catcher, and the catcher stays in place to become the new tosser). With each rotation the team moves farther downfield. The first group to reach the end of the field wins.

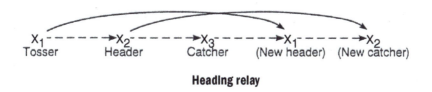

Heading relay

Closure (3-5 Minutes)

Review the lesson with students. Use the following ideas to reinforce learning, check understanding, and provide feedback.

1. Discuss the three uses of heading (i.e., to pass, score goals, or clear the ball from the area).
2. Select a student to demonstrate heading a tossed ball in an upward direction, another student to demonstrate heading backward, and another to demonstrate heading downward.

Lesson 5

Trapping

Purpose

In this lesson students develop trapping skills for air and ground balls.

Facility and Equipment

◆ Outdoor field or gym
◆ 1 soccer ball per 2 students
◆ Whistle

Warm-Ups (6-8 Minutes)

1. Reverse run
2. Curl-ups
3. Leg lifts
4. Hamstring curls

Skill Cues

1. Align the body with the oncoming ball.
2. Focus on the ball.
3. Cushion the ball to get control.
4. Wedge ground balls by lowering the foot on top of the ball, but not too hard or the ball will bounce away.
5. Trap air balls by allowing them to hit the chest or thigh and letting the body absorb the impact so the ball does not have much rebound. The ball should drop straight down to the ground after impact.

Chest trap

Thigh trap

6. Use the inside of the lower leg, the inside of both legs, the front of both legs, and the sole of the foot to execute ball traps on the ground.

Teaching Cues

1. Explain that trapping is used to stop a rolling or bouncing ball.
2. Remind students to use the inside, outside, instep, and sole of the foot when trapping along the ground; use the thigh or chest when trapping a ball in the air.
3. Remind girls to cross their arms over their chest when doing a chest trap.

Activities (30-40 Minutes)

1. Introduce the soccer trap using the appropriate skill and teaching cues. (4-6 minutes)
2. Toss and trap grounders. Pair up students or have them select partners. The first player tosses the ball along the ground for the second player to trap, calling out which foot the trapper should use. After five tosses, partners switch roles. (4-6 minutes)
3. Toss and trap air balls. Divide students into groups of three and position each group in a triangle formation. The first player tosses the ball in the air for the second player to trap using either the chest or thigh. After the trap, the second player passes the ball to the third player, who picks up the ball and tosses an air ball to the first player. The first player traps the ball and then passes the ball to the second player, and so on. (6-8 minutes)

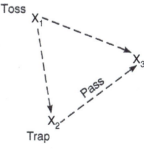

Toss and trap air balls

4. Circle trap. Divide the class into three groups and position each group in a circle. A leader for each group tosses the ball randomly to players, who use an appropriate trap. The choice of trap will depend on the type of toss (i.e., on the ground or in the air). The trapper then passes the ball back to the leader, who tosses it to another player. Execute the activity quickly to simulate trapping in a game situation. Different students should become the leader every minute (blow a whistle to indicate leader changes). (6-8 minutes)

5. Circle soccer. Divide the class into two teams and position each team around half of a circle. One player starts the ball by kicking toward the other team, aiming below shoulder level. The opposing team member tries to trap the ball using the appropriate trap for either a ground ball or an air ball. If successful, the trapper tries to send it back (below shoulder level) to an opposing team member. If unsuccessful and the ball gets past the opponent, the kicking team scores a point. No player can go inside the circle to get the ball; the ball must come to the player. If a ball lands and stays inside the circle, it is out of play. The teacher should retrieve it and put it back into play. (10-12 minutes)

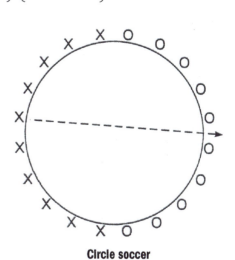

Circle soccer

Optional Activity

Net Soccer (0-15 Minutes)

Six players stand on each side of a volleyball net. One player throws (serves) the soccer ball over the net and the opposing team tries to use a chest, knee, head, or foot trap on the ball before catching it. If a player catches the ball without a trap or if the ball hits the ground, the other team gets a point. Teammates should take turns serving the ball. One team continues to serve the ball until it misses a point.

Closure (3-5 Minutes)

Review the lesson with students. Use the following ideas to reinforce learning, check understanding, and provide feedback.

1. Review the various types of ground ball traps (i.e., inside the lower leg, inside both legs, front of both legs, or sole of the foot).

2. Describe the technique used in trapping an air ball (i.e., cushion it by giving with the ball, use the thigh or chest).

Lesson 6

Tackling

Purpose

In this lesson students develop tackling skills including the front block and the side and poke tackles.

Warm-Ups (6-8 Minutes)

1. Running in place
2. Hamstring straight-leg stretch
3. Push-ups
4. Shoulder shrugs

Skill Cues

1. For the front block tackle, face the opponent.
2. For the side or poke tackle, stand to the side of the opponent.
3. Flex the knees, distribute weight evenly, incline the body forward, keep the arms free at the sides for balance, and focus on the ball.
4. Reach and place the inside of the foot against the ball for the front block tackle.
5. In a side or poke tackle, place the foot against the ball to tap the ball away.
6. Shift the weight onto the back foot.
7. Avoid body contact with the opponent.

Teaching Cues

1. Explain that the purpose of the tackle is to take the ball away from an opponent.
2. Point out the differences between the front block tackle and the side or poke tackle.
   ▶ The front block tackle approach is from the front of the opponent and the inside of the foot is used to take the ball.
   ▶ The side or poke tackle's approach is from the side of the opponent and the outside of the foot is used to tap the ball away.
3. Tell students to use both types of tackles throughout the lesson activities.

Activities (30-40 Minutes)

1. Introduce the soccer tackles using the appropriate skill and teaching cues. (4-5 minutes)

Front block tackle

Side or poke tackle

2. Mark off square 15-foot (4.57-meter) areas using four cones. Pair up students or have them select partners. Give each pair a soccer ball. The first partner in possession of the ball dribbles, trying to avoid being tackled by the partner. After tackling the first partner, the other partner dribbles and also tries to avoid being tackled. Body contact and sending the ball outside the designated play area are prohibited. Play continues for 3 minutes, after which all players find a new partner and repeat. (5-8 minutes)

3. Set up two cones 12 feet (3.66 meters) apart. Using the last partner arrangement in activity 2, the first partner tries to dribble the soccer ball through the cones without being tackled. After four attempts, partners switch roles. (5-7 minutes)

4. Win the tackle. Divide the class into four teams (play two games simultaneously) and assign a number to each player on a team (both teams will have a player with the same number). Two teams stand opposite each other in a line, 30 feet (9.14 meters) apart. Place the balls between each corresponding player (i.e., 15 feet [4.57 meters]) and instruct students to take a ready position (in case their number is called). When their number is called, both players run toward and try to take possession of the ball by using a tackle. The player who gets the ball tries to dribble to the

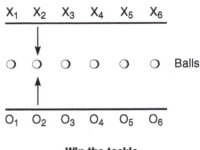
Win the tackle

opposite side as the opposing player attempts to tackle. When one player reaches the opposite side, call a new number. For more challenge, call 2 or 3 numbers at a time. (8-10 minutes)

5. Escape the tackle. Divide students into groups of 3 and give 1 student from each group a soccer ball. Students with a ball scatter around the field and begin

to dribble. On the signal, the other two students (without soccer balls) try to win possession of a soccer ball by tackling. Any player who loses possession of a ball then becomes a new defender. (8-10 minutes)

Closure (3-5 Minutes)

Review the lesson with students. Use the following ideas to reinforce learning, check understanding, and provide feedback.

1. Describe the differences between the two types of tackles (see the skill and teaching cues).
2. Give students the assignment of writing down at least three skills used by a goaltender. Goaltending will be the focus of the next class session.

Lesson 7

Goaltending

Purpose

In this lesson students develop goaltending skills.

Warm-Ups (6-8 Minutes)

1. Agility run
2. Leg lifts
3. Hamstring curls
4. Phalange flings

Facility and Equipment

- Outdoor field or gym
- 1 soccer ball per 2 students
- 1 cone per student

Skill Cues

1. Stand with the knees bent, weight forward on the balls of the feet, and hands held at chest level.
2. Move the body in line with the ball.
3. Sidestep to move sideways.
4. Collect ground shots by bending at the waist, scooping the ball into the arms (palms forward), and bringing the ball to the chest.
5. Collect air shots by pointing the hands downward when a ball is below the waist and upward when a ball is above the waist. Extend the arms toward the ball and use the fingertips to catch it.
6. Deflect shots using a punch shot with the fists and a push shot with the open hands.
7. The sequence of the punt is as follows:
   - Begin with the knee bent and the toes pointed.
   - Hold the ball with both hands in front at waist height.
   - Take three steps, straighten the knee, contact the soccer ball with the instep, and punt the ball out of the hands.
   - Rise up on the toes of the stationary foot to get effective punting action.
   - Throw with one arm (long arm the ball like a discus throw) with a slight loft to the ball. The ball can also be rolled by the goaltender.

Teaching Cues

1. Explain that goaltenders collect (catch) shots, deflect shots, and play offense by throwing and punting.
2. Emphasize the differences in collecting technique for ground shots and air shots.
3. Help students distinguish the proper hand position for air shots above and below the waist.

Activities (30-40 Minutes)

1. Introduce goaltending techniques using the skill and teaching cues. Be sure to introduce both defensive (i.e., collecting and deflecting shots) and offensive (i.e., throwing and punting) techniques. (4-6 minutes)

2. Pair up students or have them select partners. One player tries to throw the soccer ball past the other player, the goaltender, but not farther than two steps to the side or above arm's reach. As long as goaltenders catch the balls, they may continue playing the position. When they miss the ball, partners should switch roles. (5-7 minutes)

3. Goaltending relay. Set up three cones in a triangle formation, one formation per group of students. Divide students into groups of four. The goaltender stands in the center of the triangle. The other three players take turns shooting the ball at the goaltender, who attempts to either deflect or collect the ball. After each save, the goaltender throws the ball back to another player and prepares for another shot. After each player has shot the ball at the goaltender three times, players should rotate positions. (5-7 minutes)

4. Pair up students or have them select partners. The first player shoots the ball toward the second player, the goaltender, who retrieves the ball and punts it toward the first player. After eight punts, players should switch positions. (8-10 minutes)

Goaltending relay

5. Ready, set, fire. Eight students form a circle with a goaltender in the center. The players on the circle pass the ball to each other and, when the goalie is not expecting it, shoot at the goal. (Remind goalies to be ready for a shot at all times.) After fielding a shot, the goalie sends the ball back to one of the other players on the circle. After 2 minutes, a different student should be the goaltender. (8-10 minutes)

Optional Activity

Goaltending Drill (0-12 Minutes)

In partners, students practice defending a goal (cones 8 yards [7.31 meters] apart) and trying to score. One student dribbles and attempts to score on the goaltender by dribbling or shooting (no long shots are permitted). After a score or save, players switch roles. Each save is worth 1 point; the student with the most points wins.

Closure (3-5 Minutes)

Review the lesson with students. Use the following ideas to reinforce learning, check understanding, and provide feedback.

1. Discuss the defensive (i.e., collecting and deflecting shots) and offensive (i.e., throwing and punting) functions of a goaltender.

2. Choose a student to demonstrate a goaltender's ready position (i.e., knees bent, weight forward, hands at chest level, and prepared to use a sidestep to line up with the ball).

Lesson 8

Offensive Strategy

Purpose

In this lesson students learn offensive strategies in soccer, combining the skills of dribbling, passing, shooting, and heading the ball.

Warm-Ups (6-8 Minutes)

1. Jump rope or jump rope laps (hopping on one foot)
2. Step touches
3. Mad cat
4. Hip rolls

Skill Cues

1. Move quickly to create an open space for shooting.
2. Spread out the attack to make guarding difficult for the defense.
3. Use the body to shield the ball from an opponent.

Facility and Equipment

◆ Outdoor field or gym
◆ 1 soccer ball per 2 students
◆ 4 cones per 2 students
◆ 1 pinnie per 2 students
◆ 2 regulation goals per game
◆ 1 jump rope per student

Shielding

4. Keep moving, even when not in possession of the ball.
5. Keep possession and control of the ball with tight passing.
6. Move away from the teammate in possession of the ball so that defenders using 1-on-1 (i.e., person-to-person) defense are also drawn away from the player with the ball.
7. Use depth in the attack to pass the ball forward toward the goal or backward toward teammates.

Teaching Cues

1. Explain how the skills used in this lesson—dribbling, passing, shooting, and heading—form the basis of offensive strategy.

2. Before introducing each activity, students should spend some time developing offensive strategy. Have students write down where each offensive player should move to execute an effective offensive play. (The offense usually includes 4 forwards and 2 midfielders.) If they suggest an alternative way to work on offensive strategy than that provided in this lesson, adjust the activities accordingly.

Activities (30-40 Minutes)

1. Introduce offensive strategy in soccer using the appropriate skill and teaching cues. (4-6 minutes)

2. Partner offensive drill. Mark off an area 8 by 12 yards (7.31 by 10.97 meters) with four cones. Pair up students or have them select partners; 1 player defends and 1 player plays offense. The defender passes the ball to the offensive player 5 yards (4.57 meters) away, who then attempts to dribble past the defender to the end line without losing the ball or going out-of-bounds. The defender tries to intercept the ball or kick it out of the area. After four passes, players switch roles. (6-9 minutes)

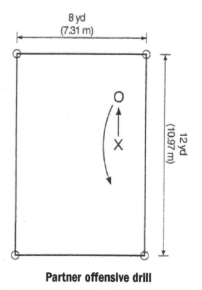

Partner offensive drill

3. Soccer circuit for offensive skills. Divide the class into three lines, each in front of a circuit marked by cones. Each circuit consists of 5 cones placed 10 feet (3.05 meters) apart and a goal formed by 2 cones 10 feet (3.05 meters) apart. Pass a ball to the first student in each line, who traps and then dribbles the ball by weaving it in and out of the cones. At the last cone, the student shoots at the goal, then retrieves the ball and passes it to the next student in line, who repeats the circuit. Students waiting in line should work on heading with a partner (i.e., one tosses the ball, the other heads). (8-10 minutes)

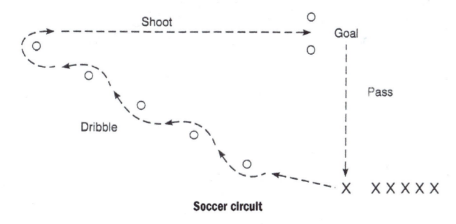

Soccer circuit

Optional Activity: Capture the Ball

4. Divide the class into teams of 6 players and position 2 teams in an area 20 by 40 yards (18.28 by 36.57 meters), divided (with cones) into two zones with a goal at each end. Position 3 attackers from team 1 and 3 defenders from team 2 in one zone, and 3 attackers from team 2 and 3 defenders from team 1 in the other zone (no goaltenders). Then have students play zone soccer. Set up two games simultaneously or add more players to each team for more participation. (12-15 minutes)

Zone Soccer

The game begins with one team in possession of the ball. Each team defends its own goal (3 defenders) and tries to score in the opposing goal (3 attackers). Players may not leave their zone. Defenders who get the ball should pass it to a teammate in the opposite zone. After a goal, the ball goes to the team that was scored against. The team with the most goals at the end of the game wins.

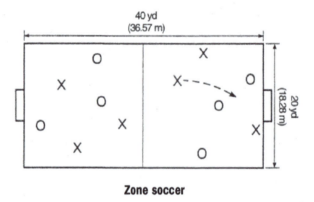

Zone soccer

Optional Activity

Capture the Ball (0-15 Minutes)

Divide students into two teams and position each team along an end line, corresponding players standing opposite each other. Place a ball halfway between each pair of opponents. On the signal, players from both teams run to the ball in front of them, and the player who gains possession attempts to dribble across the opponent's end line. (The player who loses possession of the ball becomes the defender.) For each ball dribbled or kicked over the end line, that team gets 1 point. The game continues until all balls are dribbled or kicked over the end line; the team with the most points wins. (0-15 minutes)

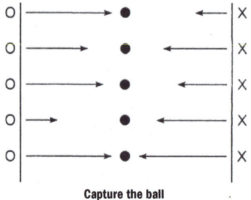

Capture the ball

Closure (3-5 Minutes)

Review the lesson with students. Use the following ideas to reinforce learning, check understanding, and provide feedback.

1. Discuss when it might be necessary to switch roles from defensive to offensive play (e.g., when a team gets possession of the ball, when a teammate has no one to pass the ball to).

2. Give students the assignment of designing one offensive play using their knowledge of offensive strategy.

Lesson 9

Defensive Strategy

Purpose

In this lesson students learn defensive strategy in soccer with the use of tackling and goal keeping.

Warm-Ups (6-8 Minutes)

1. Running in place
2. Scissors
3. Inverted hurdler's stretch
4. Triceps stretch

Facility and Equipment

◆ Outdoor field or gym
◆ 1 soccer ball per 3 students
◆ 25 to 30 cones
◆ 1 pinnie per 2 students
◆ 2 regulation goals per game

Skill Cues

1. Guard players by taking a position between the opponent and goal; cover the area in front of the goal at all times and keep team players positioned between the goal and the ball.
2. Force the opponents to play the ball away from their own goal and toward the outside of the field.
3. Reduce the opposing team's shooting angle by moving toward the ball.
4. For the best defensive strategy, use 1-on-1 (i.e., person-to-person) or zone defense, or a combination of both.
5. Move away from the opponent as the offense gets farther from the goal, but move toward the opponent as the offense moves toward the goal.

Teaching Cues

1. Explain how the skills in this lesson—tackling and goaltending—form the basis of defensive strategy.
2. Before introducing each activity, students should spend time developing a defensive strategy. Have students write down where each defensive player should move to execute an effective defensive play. (The defense usually includes 4 defenders, 2 midfielders, and 1 goaltender.) If they suggest an alternative way to work on defensive strategy than that provided in this lesson, adjust the activities accordingly.

Activities (30-40 Minutes)

1. Introduce offensive strategy in soccer using the appropriate skill and teaching cues. (4-5 minutes)

2. Pass and defend drill. Divide students into groups of 3, 2 to play offense (passer and receiver) and 1 to play defense (defender). Playing on an area 20 by 30 feet (6.1 by 9.14 meters) using 2 cones as the goals, the passer sends the ball to the receiver, who is guarded from behind by the defender. The receiver then attempts to turn and shoot at the goal while the defender tries to stop the shot. After six passes, players should switch positions. (6-8 minutes)

Pass and defend drill

3. Zone defense drill. Divide the class into groups of 6 and position 2 players in each of 3 field zones. (For maximum participation, set up 4 or more fields.) The players in the offensive zones (on either end) play offense and try to pass the ball through the middle defensive zone. Defensive players in the middle zone attempt to block passes. Players may not leave their zones, but they may move around within their zones. After 4 minutes, players should switch positions. (8-12 minutes)

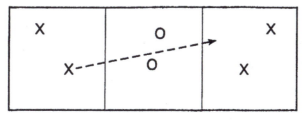

Zone defense drill

4. One-on-one soccer. Play two games simultaneously, each in an area 20 by 40 yards (18.28 by 36.57 meters) with a goal positioned on both end lines. Divide the class into 4 teams, 2 offense and 2 defense; then have players choose the opponent they will cover with 1-on-1 (i.e., person-to-person) defense. Start the game with a throw-in; then teams compete for possession of the ball, attempting to score in the opponent's goal. The lack of a goaltender in this activity forces close 1-on-1 coverage to prevent opponents from shooting at the open goal. No scoring is necessary in this game. (12-15 minutes)

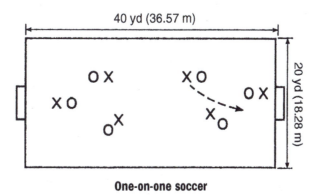

One-on-one soccer

Closure (3-5 Minutes)

Review the lesson with students, using the following ideas to reinforce learning, check understanding, and provide feedback.

1. Discuss when it is best to use 1-on-1 (i.e., person-to-person) defense and when it is best to use zone defense (i.e., 1-on-1 defense is best used when both teams are of equal ability; zone defense is best used when the opposing team is more skilled and aggressive).

2. Give students the assignment of defining the following soccer terms, which they will need to understand to play the games in the next lesson. (The definition of each term can be found in the rules section of the unit introduction on page 222.)

   ▸ Direct free kick
   ▸ Indirect free kick
   ▸ Drop ball
   ▸ Penalty kick
   ▸ Corner kick
   ▸ Goal kick

Lesson 10

Modified Game Play

Purpose

In this lesson students combine the skills they have learned to perform rudimentary games of soccer.

Warm-Ups (6-8 Minutes)

1. Sprint-jog intervals
2. Waist twists
3. Push-ups
4. Floor touches

Skill Cues

1. Use dribbling, passing, shooting, and heading skills as offensive and defensive maneuvers.
2. Use tackling and defensive strategy to prevent scoring.

Teaching Cues

1. Assign the following playing positions: defenders, midfielders, forwards, and goaltenders. Midfielders play both defense and offense.
2. Choose a playing formation before play. (The playing formation determines whether the team will be emphasizing offensive or defensive play.) For example, in a 4-2-4 formation, the team has 4 defenders, 2 midfielders, and 4 forwards. In a 3-3-4 formation the team has 3 defenders, 3 midfielders, and 4 forwards. (The goalie is an additional player.) The 3-3-4 formation might be used if the team is losing and there is an increased effort to try to score.

Activities (30-40 Minutes)

1. Introduce the activities in this lesson, emphasizing the skill cues. (3-4 minutes)
2. Explain the rules of regulation soccer (see the unit introduction on page 220). (4-6 minutes)
3. Mark the centerline on a field 30 by 60 yards (27.43 by 54.86 meters). Divide students into 2 teams and assign positions: one-third of the team should be forwards, one-third defenders, and one-third goalies. Play rotation soccer. (11-15 minutes)

Rotation Soccer

A kickoff by either team starts the game; thereafter the team that is scored against takes the kickoff. Before each kickoff, all players must be on their own half of the field. After the kickoff, forwards play on their opponent's half of the field; defenders and goalies play on their own half.

The object is to score as many goals as possible, each worth 1 point. Basic play is as follows:

▶ Forwards kick the ball (below shoulder level) over the opponent's end line to score a goal.

▶ Whenever a point is scored, team players rotate positions (i.e., forwards become defenders, then goalies; goalies become forwards, then defenders; and so on).

▶ Goalies may perform all skills allowed in a regulation soccer game (e.g., use their hands, perform goal kicks, and so on).

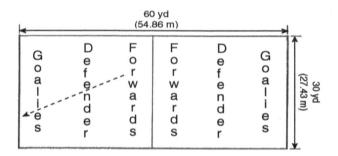

Rotation soccer field and player positions

4. Sideline soccer. Divide the class into two teams; half of each team will be on-field players and half will be sideline players. On-field players kick the ball over the opposing team's end line and into the goal (no goaltenders) using regulation positions, play, and rules. Sideline players return the ball inbounds by passing it to their on-field teammates, but they cannot score. Goals are worth 1 point; after each goal, sideline and on-field players switch positions. (12-15 minutes)

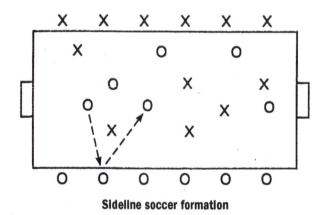

Sideline soccer formation

Optional Activities

Alley Soccer (0-15 Minutes)

Use cones to mark 5 lengthwise alleys on a field 30 by 60 yards (27.43 by 54.86 meters) and place a cone at each corner of both end lines. Divide the class into 2 teams; each team has 5 alley players (the rest are goalies). Alley players attempt to kick the ball below shoulder level over the opponent's end line to score. Players must remain in their alley, but they can travel the entire length of the alley. If a player leaves the alley, the opposing team gets a direct kick (at the spot where the foul occurred). Start the game by dropping the ball between two players. Following each score, players should switch positions.

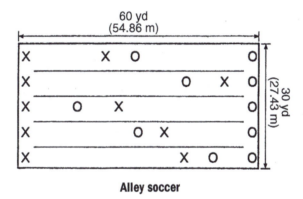

Alley soccer

Diagonal Soccer (0-15 Minutes)

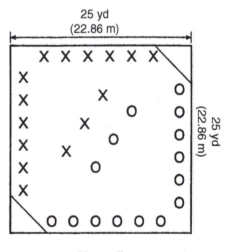

Diagonal soccer

Divide the class into two teams and position them on adjacent sides of a 25-yard (22.86-meter) square. Each team's goal line is a diagonal corner of the square marked by cones. Three players from each team are the offensive line and play in the square; the other teammates are defenders and stand along the sidelines. At the start of the game, the offensive players from each team move into the playing area. Only offensive players may score; they do so by kicking the ball (below shoulder height) through the opposing team's goal. Defenders block and keep the ball from going out-of-bounds, but they may not score. When a team scores, offensive players rotate to the sidelines and three different defenders become offensive players.

Four-Goal Soccer (0-25 Minutes)

This is just like regulation soccer, except a square field and 4 goals are used: 1 on the north end, 1 on the east end, 1 on the south end, and 1 on the west end of the field. Divide students into four teams. Each team attempts to score in their own goal while defending the other goals. For more challenge, use more than one ball. (Four-goal soccer can also be played with two teams, each team shooting at both goals.)

Closure (3-5 Minutes)

Review the lesson with students. Use the following ideas to reinforce learning, check understanding, and provide feedback.

1. Discuss the 4-2-4 formation (i.e., 4 defenders, 2 midfielders, and 4 forwards). Ask students to think of other possible formations for effective soccer play.
2. Distribute the soccer rules handouts (see the unit introduction on page 220) to each student. Tell them to be sure they understand the rules for regulation soccer, which will be played during the next class period.

Lesson 11

Regulation Game

Purpose

This lesson will help students learn the rules and play a game of regulation soccer.

Warm-Ups (6-8 Minutes)

1. Lateral hops
2. Step touches
3. Leg lifts
4. Side stretch

Skill Cues

1. Use dribbling, passing, shooting, and heading skills as offensive and defensive maneuvers.
2. Use tackling and defensive strategy to prevent scoring.

Teaching Cues

1. Assign or have teams designate the following team positions: defenders, midfielders, forwards, and goaltenders. Midfielders play both defense and offense.
2. Encourage students to choose a team playing formation before play (e.g., a 4-2-4 formation divides the team into 4 defenders, 2 midfielders, and 4 forwards) to determine offensive versus defensive play.

Activities (30-40 Minutes)

1. Review the rules and the skills needed to play soccer. (6-8 minutes)
2. Divide students into two teams and play a game of regulation soccer (see the unit introduction on page 220 for a complete description of the rules and game play). Toss a coin; the team that wins the toss can choose either to kick off or to select which end of the field they wish to defend. At halftime, the other team gets to kick off and the teams switch ends of the field. (24-32 minutes)

Closure (3-5 Minutes)

Review the lesson with students. Use the following ideas to reinforce learning, check understanding, and provide feedback.

1. Discuss ways to improve team play (e.g., pass more, pass to teammates who are in a good position to score, play more to the sides of the field than to the center).
2. Ask students to identify and then describe some effective soccer strategies (e.g., try to get the goaltender out of position by forcing him or her to block another shot, use many passes to make it difficult for the other team's defense to predict the path of the ball).

Assessment and Resources

After some of the assignments suggested in this unit (see lessons 6, 8, 9, and 10), quizzes could be given to check for basic understanding of the game. Too often such testing is given at the conclusion of a unit. Testing earlier would increase understanding of both game and skills for the student.

Skill tests and game play assessment can be formal or informal. Many of the lesson drills can be used for testing. In general, testing students' skills in passing and goaltending is sufficient. For example, the following activities could be adapted for assessment purposes:

- Chip away (see lesson 2, activity 5)
- Goaltending drill (see lesson 7, optional activity)

Playing skills can also be evaluated. A subjective assessment (e.g., looking for effective teamwork; offensive and defensive positioning; individual skills such as shots, passes, and blocks) could be made during game play (see the game activities in lessons 8 through 11).

For a more objective assessment, use point scoring for each activity. Total the number of points and then convert those points into a grading scale for the unit.

Finally, separate skill testing can be useful in this unit. Following are suggested skill tests:

- Speed dribble. Time students as they dribble from a starting line, around a cone 30 feet (9.14 meters) away, and back to the starting line. Count the best of three trials.

- Wall passing. Place a soccer ball behind a line 12 feet (3.66 meters) from a wall and count the number of passes each student can make within 1 minute. Each pass rebound should be trapped so that the ball can be quickly passed back to the wall again.

- Quick pass. In partners standing 30 feet (9.14 meters) apart, students must complete as many passes to their partner (without using the hands) as possible in 3 minutes.

- Target wall shoot. Mark a target area 2 by 3 feet (.61 by .91 meters) on a wall. Count the number of times a student hits the target from a line 20 feet (6.1 meters) away during a 1-minute period.

▶ Distance punt. From behind a line at one end of a grassy field, students get three attempts at punting the soccer ball for distance. Mark and measure the best punt from the point where it first hits the ground. (Do not count the punt if the student crosses the starting line.)

Resources

American Sport Education Program. 2001. *Coaching youth soccer.* Champaign, IL: Human Kinetics.

Bailey, G. 2000. *The ultimate sport lead-up game book.* Camas, WA: Educators Press.

International Football Association. 2000. *Official rules of soccer.* Chicago, IL: Triumph Books.

Luxbacher, J. 1991. *Teaching soccer: Steps to success.* Champaign, IL: Leisure Press.

McAvoy, N. 1998. *Teaching soccer fundamentals.* Champaign, IL: Human Kinetics.

Pangrazi, R., and P. Darst. 1997. *Dynamic physical education for secondary school students: Curriculum and instruction.* 3rd ed. Needham Heights, MA: Allyn & Bacon.

Reeves, J., and J. Simon. 1991. *Select soccer drills.* Champaign, IL: Leisure Press.

Wien, H. 2000. *Developing youth soccer players.* Champaign, IL: Human Kinetics.

Yakzan, R. 2000. *105 practical soccer drills.* Orange, CA: Oceanprises Publications.

Zakrajsek, D., and L. Carnes. 1986. *Individualizing physical education: Criterion materials.* 2nd ed. Champaign, IL: Human Kinetics.

Social and Square Dancing

Dance, an important part of every society's cultural heritage, can be traced back centuries. Indeed, during the later Paleolithic period some 30,000 years ago, before verbal language was developed, dance was a means of communication. Later dance became more symbolic, a ritualistic means for both narrative and religious expression. It included musical and rhythmic accompaniment in the form of chanting, stamping, clapping, or drumming. Through the study of primitive dance forms still in existence today, researchers have learned that ancient and contemporary cultures relied upon dance for communication, religion, courtship, celebration, and social interaction.

In the Western world, dance evolved along two principal tracks: (1) mystical and religious dance, which was performed by community leaders and special performers at ceremonial rites and various public displays, and (2) communal dance, which was performed by common people and grew into what we now know as folk dance. Emerging from those tracks, dance is now considered either a spectator or event performance, or a social activity. Although any kind of dance performed for personal interaction and enjoyment—including folk, western, square, round, contra, and mixers—can be interpreted as social, dance performed outside of a formal performance setting is usually classified as folk, western, square, social, or ballroom.

▶ Folk dance is often associated with a particular ethnic group, because it involves cultural symbolism and customs, and is performed to music with a culturally distinct rhythm or sound.

▶ Western and square dancing date back to the early settlement of the United States. Although they reflect some regional distinctions in terms of tempo and fundamental movements, these dances are generally associated with lively music, casual dress, and fun and fellowship.

▶ Social and ballroom dancing involves couples and is associated with formal dress as well as a mix of music with slow and fast tempos. Social dance, which originated in Europe as court dancing, is noted for formality as well as elaborate, precise movements. As the general population copied these dances, some of the elegance associated with them was lost. They evolved into a more comfortable style.

Whatever the form of dance or its origin, each era ushers in new dances. Some of these dances become embedded into the culture and others fade away. In general, most people find satisfaction in moving to music, whether they use sophisticated styles and fancy footwork or know only simple movements and a few steps.

Equipment

Minimal equipment is needed to teach this dance unit. An audiocassette or CD player, music, and a microphone complete the requirements. A cordless microphone is preferred because it allows freedom in moving around the gym or instructional area. Although optional, dance videotapes and VCRs may help to get students' attention and motivate them to learn and become more proficient.

Unit Organization

Because this unit includes several types of dances, only the basic skills for each dance are introduced. Thus, you can teach all of the dances in this unit consecutively, as a single instructional unit, or in segments interspersed throughout the year. (Note, however, that many of the dance steps are progressive; that is, subsequent lessons use steps learned in previous lessons.)

Following is a description of each lesson in this unit.

▶ Lessons 1 and 2 focus on mixers, which are intended to ease students into dance without requiring close proximity and partner relationships. The dances in these lessons teach some basic movements, introduce the concepts of rhythm and music in a nonthreatening environment, and promote the enjoyment of group participation. The format for lesson 1 differs from that of the others: the first activity is an introduction to dance, followed by a warm-up for movement and dance.

▶ Lessons 3, 4, and 5 focus on square dancing. These lessons draw upon some of the skills learned in the mixers in lessons 1 and 2. Square dances are usually orchestrated by calls; these are explained and listed in each dance. Use square dancing music with calls or use country-and-western and two-step music while doing your own calling.

▶ Lessons 6, 7, and 8 are devoted to the sequences of the foxtrot. This is a basic ballroom slow dance that, if learned well, forms the basis for learning other dances.

▶ The waltz is introduced in lesson 9, which could easily be expanded to include other movements (e.g., cross step, balance, twinkle, and combinations).

▶ Two forms of the polka are suggested in lesson 10. The regular polka is a highly coordinated, fast-stepping dance that many find difficult to master. The Jessie polka is easier to learn and is an acceptable substitute for the regular polka.

▶ The jitterbug, or swing, is the focus of lesson 11. This is an outgrowth of ragtime and popularized by the boogie woogie era. The livelier the music, the more open and informal the dance positions.

▶ The culminating activity for this unit is the dance demonstration in lesson 12. This lesson can also serve as an evaluation of dance skills, social skills, and dance etiquette.

The assessment and resources chapter at the end of this unit suggests some assessment ideas and activities, and lists selected resources for the type of music used throughout the unit.

Warm-up activities are somewhat different in this unit. Unlike the sport units, which use warm-ups from the appendix, this unit incorporates mixers, folk dances, and other current dances into the warm-up period. You may use these suggested dances or substitute them with your own warm-up dances and movements— for example, contemporary and low-impact aerobic dances.

Social Skills and Etiquette

The value of dance lies in its sociability. Social and square dancing is a group activity that promotes rhythmic movement, fun, and fellowship. Hence, attention to social skills and etiquette is essential. Some students will be regarded as less-desirable dance partners. Create and enforce an atmosphere of acceptance and sensitivity in the classroom. Talking about this issue during the unit introduction, dealing promptly with rude or nasty behavior as it occurs, and having a plan for changing partners and putting students into pairs can eradicate most, if not all, problems. Proper hand placement during partner dances is part of the instruction and should be enforced.

In this unit students should also learn the following courtesies:

▶ How to ask someone to dance
▶ How to accept an invitation to dance

▸ How to graciously decline an invitation (for a good reason)

▸ The proper way to leave a partner. Emphasize that students should never leave a partner on the dance floor and walk away. Instead, partners should walk off together and thank each other before separating, or they should walk to another couple and offer to exchange partners.

▸ The importance of good grooming. Because dancing with a partner involves close proximity to another person, students should be instructed on and encouraged in basic grooming habits (e.g., neat and clean appearance, fresh breath).

Lesson Modifications

The nature of this type of dancing requires maintaining couple or group cadence. Thus, few modifications can be made to accommodate the physically and mentally disabled. Teacher aides can assist disabled students, or these students could be included in the class by being instructed to clap or use rhythmic instruments to keep time with the music. You might also ask these students for suggestions. Sometimes students with physical or mental disabilities can be quite creative, often taking on the responsibility of devising ways they can participate.

Given the different proficiency levels across grades and within classes, more or less time may be needed to develop and master certain skills and sequences. In some cases it may even be necessary to repeat a lesson before moving on to the next. Likewise, when two or more dances are introduced in a lesson, it may be advisable to break the lesson apart and teach only one new dance per class.

Safety

Dance is a safe activity. Because they constrict smooth movement and prevent sliding, traction and tennis shoes should not be worn. Rather, encourage students to wear street shoes with low-traction soles. Dancing in socks could also present a problem, because students could slip, especially when traveling fast and changing directions quickly. If cornmeal is used for ease of gliding, students should be careful to avoid slipping during fast dances.

Terms and Calls

"allemande left"—Partners give left hands to their corners and make a complete circle around them. This call is usually followed by a "grand right and left" or "swing your partner."

"allemande left and grand right and left" or **"grand chain"**—Partners give left hands to their corners and walk around that person until they are facing back home with a right hand to their partner. They continue in that direction around the whole circle, giving left, then right, hands to each person they meet. They continue to chain until they are back home to their partners.

"all join hands and circle eight"—Four couples join hands and circle to the left. "Circle eight till you get straight" means circle to the left until partners return to their original position.

balance (simple)—Partners turn to face each other and join right hands, forming a star. Each partner rocks back on the left foot, lifting the other foot slightly, then rocks forward. While rocking forward, the boy lifts the couple's joined hands and the girl makes a half twirl under while both return to original position.

balance and swing—A balance followed by a swing. Use an elbow swing or take a closed dance position and swing rapidly around.

breaks, trimmings, or **fillers**—Calls that are used between the main sections of a square dance, such as "do-si-do," "allemande left and swing your partner," "grand right and left," "balance and swing," "honor your partner and corner the same," "circle left," and so on.

brush—The foot sweeps forward, brushing against the floor.

buzz-step—Partners take a closed position, place the right insides of their feet next to each other, lean backward (away from each other), and push vigorously with their left feet to pivot on their right feet in a circle.

cast-off—Partners separate; the boy turns left and the girl turns right, to lead their lines of dancers to the foot of the set.

chain—Two girls from head or side couples move across the set and chain by stepping into the circle, giving right hands to the opposite girl and left hands to the opposite boy, walking around the opposite boy and into the circle, then giving a right hand to the opposite girl and a left hand to her partner.

"circle four and leave that couple" or **"pass right through"**—In a traveling square, the traveling couple finishes dancing with another couple in the set by circling (clasping four hands) around to the left. If leaving that couple, they drop hands and go to the next couple. If passing through, or right and left through, they drop hands and pass through the couple, facing the next couple. On a pass-through, the boy passes right shoulders with the boy and the girl passes right shoulders with the girl (and left shoulders with the boy).

closed position—Couples face their partners and stand close together; the girl's right hand is in the boy's left hand at shoulder height, the boy's right hand is on the girl's left hip, and the girl's left hand is on the boy's right shoulder.

conga line—A column of dancers, one behind the other. Dancers place their hands on the hips of the person in front.

Closed position

contra set or **longway set**—A line of boys facing a line of girls, with partners opposite each other. Usually 6 to 8 couples form a contra set. Any number can be in a longway set.

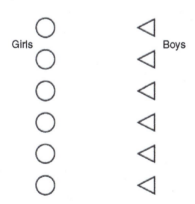

Contra (or longway) set

corner—The boy to the right of the girl and the girl to the left of the boy; in other words, the dancer on either side of a couple.

courtesy turn—From a side-by-side position, the boy takes the girl's left hand in his left hand and places his right hand on her right hip, then both turn together to the boy's left until they are facing the center.

"do-si-do" or **"do-sa-do"** or **"dos-a-dos"**—Partners face and then walk around each other, without turning their bodies. Partners pass right shoulders (going forward), pass back to back, pass left shoulders (going backward), and return to the starting position. This move is usually performed with the arms folded across the chest. The three terms are interchangeable, although in some regions they have different meanings.

"elbow swing"—Hook right elbows and swing to the right; then hook left elbows and swing to the left, taking skipping or running steps. An elbow swing with the corner involves taking a half turn and swinging with right elbows, then heading back to original partners.

ending—The last call in a square dance; an ending can be as simple as "and that's all."

facing position—Couples face their partners, standing slightly apart and clasping hands between them.

Facing position

head couple—The first couple of a set. In a square dance set, the head couple is couple 1.

heel-toe touch or **heel touch**—Stick the heel out and touch the toes.

home or **home position**—The original position of each couple.

"honor your partner"—Facing each other, the boy bows to the girl and the girl curtsies.

introductory call—The beginning call that precedes the main body or figure of a square dance. Introductory calls are often interchangeable with breaks and usually include "honor your partner," "allemande left and grand right and left," "circle eight," and "promenade."

main figure—The body of a square dance, usually named for the action (e.g., "chase that rabbit").

open position—Partners stand side by side, the boy's left and the girl's right hands clasped in front and their other hands behind their partner's waist.

Open position

promenade—Partners march around the set counterclockwise, the boy on the inside and the girl on the outside of the circle. The three promenade positions are as follows: crossed hands, western, and varsouvianna.

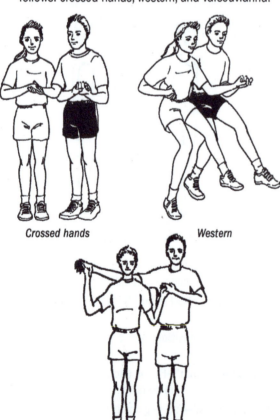

Crossed hands   Western

Varsouvianna

Promenade positions

reel—In a longway (or contra) set, the head couple meets in the middle, hooks right elbows, turns one and a half times around, and then separates, facing the next couple (opposite sex) in line. Partners then take a left elbow swing with the first person in line and go back to the center for a right elbow swing with their partner; then they take a left elbow swing with the next person in line, then a right elbow swing with their partner; and so on down the line.

running set or **traveling set**—One couple moves to another couple in the set, performs some activity, and then moves to the next couple.

set—A grouping of dancers. See also *square dance set* and *contra set.*

shuffle—Three steps forward in 2/4 time with a rhythm of quick, quick, slow or step, close, step.

side couples—Couples 2 and 4 in a square dance set.

square dance set—Four couples in a square: (1) the head couple, (2) the second couple on the right (called a *side couple*), (3) the third couple across from the head couple (this couple is often called the *foot* in a set), and (4) the fourth couple to the left of the head couple (called a *side couple*). Head and foot couples are designated 1 and 3, respectively, and side couples are designated 2 and 4. The boy stands to the left of his partner. See also *contra set.*

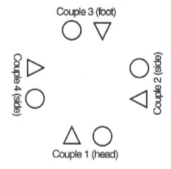

Square dance set

star position—Partners face each other and join right hands, forming a star.

Star position

shoulder-waist position—partners place the right insides of their feet near each other, lean backward (away from each other), and push vigorously with their left feet to pivot on their right feet.

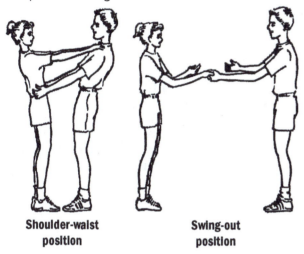

Shoulder-waist position

Swing-out position

toe tap—touch the toe to the floor in whatever direction is given.

General Teaching Cues

Students may be uncomfortable with the close contact and touching inherent in this type of dance. Hand holding and light touching (e.g., on the hips, back, shoulders) may be particularly awkward for those students who are shy. The dances in lessons 1 and 2 may help these students feel more comfortable. If, however, students are hesitant or unwilling to participate, you may want to have a class discussion about the nature of dance and some specifics of touching.

Couples dancing can sometimes become a popularity contest among high school students. Certain boys may not want to dance with certain girls, and vice versa. If these situations arise, it is best to discourage these types of comments and behaviors right away. No one should ever give the impression (verbally or nonverbally) of dissatisfaction with a partner. You may also want to hold a class discussion and emphasize that dancing with a particular partner does not mean forming a lifelong commitment to that person.

In addition, the following suggestions will help make this unit a success. Because these teaching cues are applicable to all lessons in this unit, they are not repeated in every lesson but instead are listed here.

1. Select music with a clear and definite beat. This will aid students in matching foot movements with the rhythm.
2. Increase the amount of practice and instructional time if students are not progressing as intended or when adding skills and additional dances to the unit.
3. Teach new steps separately, adding new steps once previous steps are understood.
4. To help students understand the dances and steps better, distribute handouts of the dance steps and terms before each lesson.
5. Practice an entire dance in sequence before adding music.
6. Repeat each new dance 2 or 3 times with the music.

Lesson 1

Dance Mixers

Purpose

In this lesson students learn the courtesies of dance, enjoy rhythmic movement, and develop some basic skills in group dancing.

Warm-Ups (8 Minutes)

1. Ask students to stand on any line and move according to the directions given:
   - Walking lines forward (on foot, then on toes)
   - Walking lines backward (on foot, then on toes)
   - Walking lines sidestepping (on foot, then on toes; left, right, left; and so on)
   - Walking lines sidestepping and cross-stepping (step, cross-step behind; step, cross-step in front; and so on)
2. Position students in a circle—boy, girl, boy, girl—with their arms out and their hands on the shoulders of the students next to them. Then have them perform the hora, an Israeli folk dance *(hora* means "tempo").

Hora

Skills: step, cross-step, kick
Suggested music: the hora
Move counterclockwise three steps and kick:
    Step right to the side, cross left foot behind right, step right, kick left foot across right foot while hopping on right.
Step and kick:
    Step left to the side, kick right foot across left while hopping on left.
Repeat sequence, noting that the music gets faster.

Facility and Equipment

- Gym or multipurpose area
- Music (Folk music [hora, bunny hop, chicken dance, and patty-cake polka] on CD or audiocassette) and player
- Microphone

Skill Cues

1. Take small steps.
2. Listen to the music.
3. For the hora, keep the head up and lean backward. Hold the arms up; do not press down on the shoulders of other students.
4. During the bunny hop, move both feet when hopping and toe touching at the same time.

Teaching Cues

1. Emphasize listening to the music, moving with the music, and trying to relax.
2. During the patty-cake polka, caution against widening the circle as students move forward.

Activities (30-40 Minutes)

1. Introduce the dance unit. Use the information presented in the unit introduction (see pages 260-265) and communicate the following to students to establish a positive mind-set toward dance. (8-10 minutes)

   ▷ Explain the role that dance plays in our culture. Dance is a part of every cultural heritage. It is a means of communication and in many cultures is associated with joy and celebration. In earlier societies dance reflected the customs of the people and served ceremonial, ritualistic, and religious purposes.

   ▷ Explain that the music is what gives dance its distinctive movement patterns. Discuss the necessity of listening for changes in tempo, beat, and rhythm, which alter movement sequences.

   ▷ Stress the importance of classmates' feelings and reemphasize that students should not, under any circumstances, give the impression that they are dissatisfied with a partner.

   ▷ Remind students to observe good manners and to come to class clean. Encourage them to wash their hands before class.

2. Position students in one or more conga lines. Demonstrate and have students practice the dance steps of the bunny hop using the appropriate skill and teaching cues. (6-8 minutes)

Bunny Hop

Skills: toe, heel, hop, jump
Suggested music: the bunny hop
Hop right, touch left heel out to the side.
Hop right, touch left toe near the right foot.
Repeat.
Hop left, touch right heel.
Hop left, touch right toe.
Jump forward (slow), jump backward (slow).
Jump forward 3 times (quick, quick, quick).

3. Have students take a scatter formation, either as singles or in pairs. Demonstrate and perform the chicken dance. (6-8 minutes)

Chicken Dance

Skills: hand pecking, flapping elbows, twist, elbow swing, skip

Make a beak with both hands and imitate a bird chirping (4 counts).

Flap the elbows to and fro with the hands under the armpits (4 counts).

Flex the knees and twist the body downward (4 counts) and upward (4 counts).

Hook elbows with a partner (or anyone nearby).

Elbow swing and skip clockwise around each other (8 counts).

Repeat, skipping counterclockwise (8 counts). (If dancing in partners, get a new one.)

4. Pair up students. Have them stand in a double circle, boys on the inside and girls on the outside, facing their partners with joined hands. (If boys outnumber girls, or vice versa, have "extras" play the girl or boy part.) Demonstrate and perform the patty-cake polka. (10-14 minutes)

Patty-Cake Polka

Skills: heel-toe touch, slide, walk, clap, elbow swing

Suggested music: a fast two-step, "Little Brown Jug," or polka music

Touch heel-toe twice on the same foot (boy's left, girl's right); then slide 4 times counterclockwise (boy goes left, girl goes right).

Repeat on the other foot; then slide 4 steps clockwise (back to starting position).

Clap the thighs 3 times.

Clap hands 3 times.

Clap partner's right hand 3 times.

Clap partner's left hand 3 times.

Hook right elbows and skip or walk around each other (6 counts).

Boy walks 2 steps (beats) to the left, to a new partner.

Repeat sequence.

Closure (3-5 Minutes)

Review the lesson with students. Use the following questions and ideas to reinforce learning, check understanding, and provide feedback.

1. Share your observations about students' performance, commenting on staying in step with the music, movement, dance posture, and so on. Try to be as positive as possible.

2. Ask students why they think they started with walking lines (i.e., walking in different directions in a line, especially on the toes, requires balance and fluidity of movement, similar to the skills needed in dance; walking and changing directions requires transferring weight from one foot to the other, which is a part of every dance step).

Lesson 2

Square Dance Mixer and Reel

Purpose

In this lesson students learn the circle and contra set formations.

Warm-Ups (6-8 Minutes)

1. Hora (see lesson 1)
2. Chicken dance (see lesson 1)

Facility and Equipment

◆ Gym or multipurpose area
◆ Music (CD or audiocassette) and player
◆ Square dance music, with or without calls, hora, chicken dance, Tennessee wig walker
◆ Microphone

Skill Cues

1. Listen to the calls and keep in step with the music.
2. Clap softly or tap the foot to the rhythm of the music when not involved in the dance.
3. Take short steps whether walking, skipping, or running.

Teaching Cue

1. Teach one segment at a time, first without and then with music. Then add another segment, adding music after the segment is understood.

Activities (30-40 Minutes)

1. Pair up students and position them in a single circle, boys facing counterclockwise (CCW) and girls facing clockwise (CW). Demonstrate and perform the steps of the Tennessee wig walker. (Note: the steps are the same for both girls and boys.) (12-18 minutes)

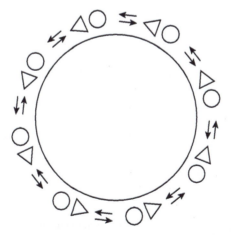

Single circle (partners facing)

Tennessee Wig Walker

Skills: Toe touch, vine, walk, brush, shuffle

Toe touch left in front of the right foot; toe touch left to the left side.

Vine right (left cross-step behind right, step right, close left to right), weight on the left foot.

Repeat with right lead (right toe touches and vine to the left, starting with the right foot).

Join right hands and make a full turn by walking left, right, left, brush the right (weight on the left foot); then right, left, right, brush the left (weight on the right foot).

Shuffle left forward and hold (1, 2, 3, hold),

Shuffle right forward and hold (boys CCW, girls shuffle CW; both meet a new partner).

Repeat the sequence.

Optional Activity: Turkey in the Straw

2. Position students in a contra or longway (i.e., 6 to 8 pairs) set, boys on one side and girls in the same pattern facing their partners. Demonstrate and perform the Virginia reel. (18-22 minutes)

Virginia Reel

Skills: walk, skip, elbow swing, reel, cast-off, do-si-do

Suggested music: square dance music (with or without the calls)

Boys and girls take 4 steps toward each other, then 4 steps back.

Repeat.

Boys and girls walk forward, join right hands, circle around their hands (to the right), and then walk back to their lines (8 counts).

Repeat with the left hand (8 counts).

Repeat with both hands (8 counts).

Do-si-do.

Do-si-do

Head couple takes 8 slides (facing each other with joined hands) down the inside of the set, then 8 slides back to the head of the line.

Head couple bows and reels (takes a right elbow swing in the center one and a half turns and reels with opposite [girl with boy, boy with girl] boy and girl, with a left elbow, back to the center with right elbow to partner, then next in line with a left elbow and partner with a right elbow, and so on down the line.

After elbow swinging with the foot couple of the set, the head couple slides back to their starting position and casts off (boys go left and follow the lead boy along the outside; girls go right and follow the lead girl) to the foot of the set.

Once in the foot position, the head couple forms an arch with their hands. Other couples join hands as they meet and go under the arch. The first couple through the arch becomes the new head couple.

Repeat entire sequence with a new head couple.

Optional Activity

Turkey in the Straw (0-18 Minutes)

Skills: slide, walk, stamp, skip, elbow swing

Suggested music: square dance or fast two-step music (4/4 time)

Students stand in a single circle with hands joined (if in couples, the girl is to the right of the boy; otherwise, girl, boy, girl, boy).

Take 8 slides to the left, then 8 slides to the right.

Walk 2 steps (left, right) to the center and stamp the feet 3 times (left, right, left).

Walk back 2 steps (right, left) and stamp the feet 3 times (right, left, right).

Hook right elbows (boys hook elbows with the girls on their right) and turn in place with 4 skipping or walking steps.

Drop elbows and boys take 4 skipping or walking steps to the right (to the next girl or partner); girls take 4 steps in place.

Repeat.

Closure (3-5 Minutes)

Review the lesson with students. Use the following questions and ideas to reinforce learning, check understanding, and provide feedback.

1. Share your observations about students' performances, being as positive as possible.

2. Ask students what they can do to make the dance appear more attractive (e.g., keep steps small, glide on the slides, extend joined hands out to the sides when sliding).

Lesson 3

Square Dance: Circle and Swing, and Split the Ring

Purpose

This lesson develops square dance skills and cultivates an appreciation for early American dance.

Warm-Up (6-8 Minutes)

1. Turkey in the straw or Tennessee wig walker (see lesson 2)

Facility and Equipment

◆ Gym or multipurpose area
◆ Music (CD or audiocassette) and player
◆ Square dance music with or without calls, turkey in the straw, Tennessee wig walker, and march
◆ Microphone

Skill Cues

1. Listen for the calls; do not move before each call.
2. Keep the feet directly under the body on all steps.

Teaching Cues

1. Assign some students to make up one set; then have them demonstrate while the rest of the class observes.
2. Check understanding throughout the lesson by asking questions or stopping to monitor students' progress at each sequence.
3. Practice the calls to music before class. Time calls to the rhythm and phrasing of the music. Allow about 12 beats before starting the first call.
4. Emphasize the first word or syllable of a call to change direction or movement (e.g., "*Alle*-mande left with your left hand . . . and a *right* to your partner . . . and a *right and left* grand . . . *honor* your partner . . . and *corner* the same").
5. Time calls so that all students are ready for the next movement or direction. (This is the primary advantage of doing your own calls: you can wait for dancers to untangle themselves or catch up.) It is best to use one dance set to pace your calls (i.e., keep the call in rhythm with the dancers).

Activities (30-45 Minutes)

1. Position students in a large, single circle for a grand march. (3-10 minutes)

Grand March

Skills: walk

Suggested music: marching music or none

Break the circle and have either a boy or girl lead the group around the perimeter of the gym in single file.

At a certain point, direct girls to go right and boys to go left (girls follow the head girl and boys follow the head boy) around perimeter.

When they meet, boy and girl march side by side to the other end.

The first couple goes right; the second goes left. (Every other couple follows right and left.)

When couples come together, two couples merge into a foursome, then march side by side to the other end.

One foursome goes right, the next goes left, and so on.

When foursomes meet, two foursomes become a group of eight.

2. Once students are in their new groups of eight (a square dance set), direct each group to a specific area of the gym. All head couples should face one wall, the foot couple should face the head couple, and the side couples should face each other. (If students are left over, have them form their own group to practice the introductory calls and breaks; then switch groups part way through the next activity.) With students in position, explain the following parts of a square dance set (see the unit introduction on pages 263-264 for definitions). (3-5 minutes)

   ▶ Head couple

   ▶ Side couples

   ▶ Couple 1 (i.e., head couple)

   ▶ Couple 2 (i.e., to the right of couple 1)

   ▶ Couple 3 (i.e., opposite couple 1; foot couple)

   ▶ Couple 4 (i.e., to the left of couple 1)

   ▶ Corner (i.e., person to the girl's right, boy's left)

   ▶ Home (starting position)

   ▶ Partner position (i.e., boy on the left)

   Check for understanding by having students raise their hands when they hear their position name and number called.

3. Explain and demonstrate the following skills (for definitions and sequences, see the unit introduction on pages 262-264). Practice calling each skill, mixing the order until students are able to respond quickly. (6-8 minutes)

   ▶ Honor your partner (or corner)

   ▶ Swing your partner (or corner) (The elbow swing is suggested for junior high; the buzz step swing for senior high.)

   ▶ Allemande left and swing your partner

   ▶ Do-si-do your partner (or corner)

   ▶ Promenade (The crossed-hands position is suggested for junior high; the varsouvianna position for senior high.)

   ▶ Circle eight left and right (do not circle past home)

4. Have all girls move one place to the right (to get a new partner) for the circle and swing. If the selected music does not include calls, use those listed here. (8-10 minutes)

Circle and Swing

Skills: see activity 3

"Honor your partner and corner the same. All join hands, circle left, and swing your own when you get home.

Head ladies to the center and circle two.

Then swing her gent behind you.

Now skip on home and swing your own.

Allemande left with your left hand [corner] and swing your partner.

Side ladies to the center and circle two.

Then swing her gent behind you.

Now skip on home and swing your own.

Promenade your partner around the ring [counterclockwise].

Head gents to the center and stamp your feet.

Then follow your eyes and swing his sweet [opposite lady].

Now skip on home and swing your own.

Do-si-do your corner and do-si-do your partner.

Side gents to the center and stamp your feet.

Then follow your eyes and swing his sweet.

Now skip on home and swing your own.

Allemande left with your left hand and honor your partner."

5. Rotate boys one place to left and explain *balance*. If the selected music does not include calls, use those listed here. (10-12 minutes)

Split the Ring

Skills: honor, promenade, balance, swing

"Honor your partner and the one on the side [corner].

All join hands and circle wide.

Take your own and promenade [counterclockwise] back home.

Head couple balance and swing.

Down the center and split the ring [go between couple 3].

Lady go right and gent go left [go back home on the outside of the ring].

Swing when you meet, swing at the head and swing at the feet.

Now down the center as you did before.

Down the center and cut off four [split, around couples 2 and 4].

Lady go right and gent go left [go back home on the outside of the ring].

Swing when you meet, swing at the head and swing at the feet.

Down the center as you used to do.

Down the center and cut off two [split, between couples 2 and 4].

And it's swing, swing, everybody swing.

Then all promenade the outside ring."

Repeat with couples 2, 3, and 4 acting as head couples.

Closure (3-5 Minutes)

Review the lesson with students. Use the following ideas to reinforce learning, check understanding, and provide feedback.

1. Share your observations of students' performances and correct small errors that detract from the appearance of the dance.
2. Discuss the aerobic benefits of square dancing.
3. Explain some of the history of square dance (i.e., it is an American dance that originated with the early settlers; its vigorous movement and hardy spirit were characteristics of frontier life).

Lesson 4

Square Dance: Chase That Rabbit and Dip for the Oyster

Purpose

In this lesson students build on previous square dance skills and learn to do traveling or running sets.

Warm-Up (6-8 Minutes)

Today's warm-up will be a familiar dance to most students. Position the entire class into one large circle, all students facing the center. If your selected music does not include calls, use those listed here.

Facility and Equipment

◆ Gym or multipurpose area
◆ Music (CD or audiocassette) and player
◆ Hokey pokey, square dance with or without calls
◆ Microphone

Hokey Pokey

Skills: shaking body parts, turning
Suggested music: hokey pokey
"You put your right foot in [into the circle],
You put your right foot out [back and away from the circle],
You put your right foot in and you shake it all about [in the circle and shake].
You do the hokey pokey and you turn yourself around [shake hands overhead while turning once around in place],
That's what it's all about" [clap hands 4 times].
Repeat the call, using the left foot, right arm, left arm, right elbow, left elbow, right hip, left hip, head, backside, and entire body.
"You do the hokey pokey, you do the hokey pokey, you do the hokey pokey [raise arms above head; lower arms and head in a bowing motion];
That's what it's all about" [clap 6 times].

Skill Cues

1. In a running or traveling set, one couple moves to another couple in the set, performs some activity, and then moves to the next couple.
2. Listen for the calls; do not move before each call.
3. Keep the feet directly under the body by taking small steps.

Teaching Cues

1. Explain that a grand right and left usually begins with an allemande left and that it ends with another call (e.g., swing your partner, balance and swing your own).

2. Start with an allemande left and back to your partner with a right hand and stop. Check the direction (boys are facing counterclockwise [CCW] and girls are facing clockwise [CW]) pass your partner (dropping right hands), give left hands to the person coming toward you, right hands to the next, and continue around the circle. Partners will pass each other opposite the home position.

3. Be sure to allow plenty of time to teach the grand right and left, first without music.

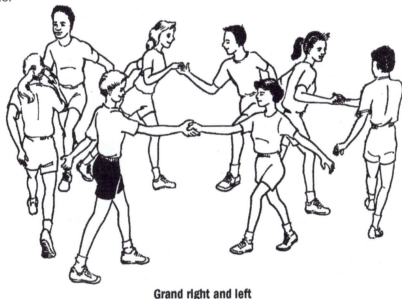

Grand right and left

4. For the circle four and the right and left through, see the term *circle four and leave that couple.*

5. Walk through the first part of the square dance before putting it to music.

Activities (30-40 Minutes)

1. Students will already be in a circle after finishing the hokey pokey. Have them perform the grand march (see lesson 3), ending in groups (sets) of eight. (4-6 minutes)

2. Introduce and demonstrate the grand right and left using the skill and teaching cues. (4-6 minutes)

3. Demonstrate and perform the chase that rabbit. If the selected music does not include calls, use the following. (12-14 minutes)

Chase That Rabbit

Skills: Allemande left, grand right and left, honor, swing
Suggested music: square dance with or without calls
"Honor your partner, corner the same.
Allemande left and a grand right and left, all the way round;
Swing your own when you get home.
Head couple out to the right [couple 1 goes to couple 2].

(continued)

Chase That Rabbit *(cont.)*

Chase that rabbit, chase that squirrel [girl 1 goes between couple 2 and around the girl; boy 1 follows];

Chase that pretty girl around the world [out to the center of the ring].

Chase that possum, chase raccoon [boy 1 now leads between couple 2 (going around boy 2); girl follows him];

Chase that big boy around the moon [out to the center of the ring].

Swing your opposites [girl 1 and boy 2 swing; girl 2 and boy 1 swing] and now your own.

Lead to the next."

Repeat with couples 3 and 4.

"Allemande left and a grand right and left. Swing when you get home."

Rotate "extras" in and repeat with couple 2 leading.

4. Have girls rotate one position to the right and the boys one position to the left. Demonstrate and perform dip for the oyster. If the selected music does not include calls, use those listed here. (10-14 minutes)

Dip for the Oyster

Skills: Allemande, swing, arches, promenade

Suggested music: square dance with or without calls

"Honor your partner and honor your corner.

Allemande left and swing your partner.

Head couple out to the right and dip for the oyster, dip [couples 1 and 2 join hands; couple 2 raises inside hands to form an arch while couple 1 steps and ducks under their raised hands and then backs out].

Dive for the clam, dive [couple 1 raises inside hands and forms an arch as they back out; couple 2 steps and ducks under].

Dip for the oyster, get a whole can [couple 2 raises inside hands to form an arch again; couple 1 goes underneath, dropping outside hands with couple 2 and inside partner's hands; girl 1 goes around boy 2 and boy 1 around girl 2, then back to the center; all join hands].

Dip for the oyster

Circle four and pass right through [couple 1 circles halfway around until facing couple 3, then passes through couple 2]."

Repeat with couple 3 and then couple 4.

Repeat the entire dance with couple 2, couple 3, and couple 4, leading out to the right.

"Honor your partner and promenade, take her over there and give her some air."

Closure (3-5 Minutes)

Review the lesson with students. Use the following questions and ideas to reinforce learning, check understanding, and provide feedback.

1. Discuss the different parts of a square dance using examples from the dances in this lesson.
   - Introductory call: start the square dance (e.g., honor your partner, allemande left)
   - Main figure: body of the dance (e.g., chase that rabbit, dip for the oyster)
   - Breaks, trimmings, or fillers: calls between sections of the main dance (e.g., do-si-do, swing your corner, circle left and back)
   - Ending: finish the dance (e.g., honor your partner and promenade, take her over there and give her some air)

2. Share your observations of students' performances, calling attention to what was good.

3. Ask why it is important to listen closely to the words of the caller (i.e., most callers will mix different breaks and endings, and sometimes change the main figure for different couples).

4. Ask students why they think square dancing was popular among rural settlers in America (e.g., informality, they didn't need fancy clothes or a large band, the dances were simple and easy to learn, dancing with everyone builds feelings of community).

Lesson 5

Square Dance: Texas Star, and Inside Arch and Outside Under

Purpose

In this lesson students build on previous skills and learn more intricate square dance movements.

Facility and Equipment

◆ Gym or multipurpose area
◆ Music (CD or audiocassette) and player
◆ Square dance with or without calls, hora, march
◆ Microphone

Warm-Ups (6-8 minutes)

1. Hora (see lesson 1)
2. Grand march (see lesson 3)

Skill Cues

1. Listen and wait for the call.
2. In the Texas star, take short running steps forward into the ring and back.
3. Form a solid arch by clasping inside hands and holding them high.
4. Keep moving, whether forming or going under an arch.

Teaching Cues

1. For the Texas star, use the elbow swing for junior high students and the shoulder-waist swing for senior high students.
2. If students are left over after the grand march (i.e., less than eight), have them form an "extras" group and rotate them into each dance before the repeat(s).
3. Use a demonstration set to teach Inside Arch and Outside Under.
4. Substitute "extras" before each repeat of the main figure.

Activities (30-40 Minutes)

1. Students will be in a square dance set after completing the warm-ups. Review and perform the allemande left and grand right and left, the balance and swing, and the promenade. (4-7 minutes)
2. Introduce the Texas star and have each set walk through the patterns once. Then perform the dance. If the selected music does not include calls, use those listed here. (10-13 minutes)

Texas Star

Skills: Allemande left, grand right and left, elbow hook, swing, honor your partner

Suggested music: square dance music (with or without calls)

"Honor your partners, corners the same.

Allemande left with your left hand, and a right to your partner;

And a right and left grand.

Meet your partner and pass her by.

Swing your own when you get home.

Ladies to the center [4 girls walk into the center].

And back to the bar [girls walk back to home].

Gents to the center and form a star [boys walk to center and take the opposite's hand (boy 1 takes boy 3's hand; boys 2 and 4 take hands)].

Right hands crossed [all four hands are touching while boys move CW around the inside ring].

Texas star hand position, boys

Back with a left hand and don't get lost [boys turn, cross left hands, and move CCW].

Meet your partner and pass her by [boys keep moving CCW to next girl].

Hook the next one on the fly [right elbow hook or hand around waist].

Gents swing out and ladies swing in [couples turn left, go back CW].

And form that Texas star again [girls form the right hand star].

Break that star with a do-si-do [drop hands and all do a do-si-do with new partner].

A little more dough.

Take your partner and promenade home" [all couples promenade CCW until boys reach home (with a new partner)].

Repeat the entire sequence three times to get back to original partners.

3. Ask all girls to move to the next set; boys remain. Once in their new sets, have girls rotate one place to the right. Explain and demonstrate a courtesy turn. Then introduce and perform the inside arch and outside under. If the selected music does not include calls, use those listed here. (16-20 minutes)

Inside Arch and Outside Under

Skills: moving arches, courtesy turn, balance and swing
Suggested music: square dance music (with or without calls)
"All jump up and never come down;
Swing [elbow or buzz] your partner round and round.
Head couple balance and swing.
Lead out to the right of the ring.
Circle four go halfway around [couple 1 faces couple 4].
Inside arch and outside under [couple 2 arches; couple 1 goes under; couple 2 does a courtesy turn home].
Inside arch and outside under [couple 1 arches; couple 4 goes under; couple 1 does a courtesy turn at couple 4's home].
Inside arch and outside under [couple 4 arches; couple 2 goes under; couple 4 does courtesy turn at couple 2's home].
Inside arch and outside under [couple 2 arches; couple 1 goes under; couple 2 does a courtesy turn at couple 4's home].
Lead to the next [couple 1 to couple 3].
Circle four; go halfway around [couple 1 faces home].
Inside arch and outside under [couple 3 arches; couple 1 goes under].
Lead to the next and go like thunder [couple 1 goes to couple 2 at couple 4's home].
Circle half; go halfway around [couple 1 faces couple 4 in couple 2's home].
Inside arch and outside under [couple 2 arches; couple 1 goes under; couple 2 does a courtesy turn].
Inside arch and outside under [couple 1 arches; couple 4 goes under; couple 1 does a courtesy turn].
Inside arch and outside under [couple 4 arches; couple 2 goes under; couple 4 does a courtesy turn home].
Inside arch and outside under [couple 2 arches; couple 1 goes under; couple 2 does a courtesy turn home].
Home you go and everybody swing" [all couples back to home positions].
Repeat for couples 2, 3, and 4.

Closure (3-5 Minutes)

Review the lesson with students. Use the following questions and ideas to reinforce learning, check understanding, and provide feedback.

1. Which dance did you like better and why? What was the hardest part of each dance?

2. Select a few couples to demonstrate the courtesy turn, balance and swing, do-si-do, and promenade.

Social Dance: Foxtrot Box Step

Purpose

This is the first of three foxtrot lessons. In it students learn the box step, learn to recognize the rhythm of a foxtrot, and begin to move with confidence.

Facility and Equipment

◆ Gym or multipurpose area
◆ Music (CD or audiocassette) and player
◆ 4/4 rhythm, hora
◆ Microphone

Warm-Up (6-8 Minutes)

1. Hora (see lesson 1)

Skill Cues

1. The sequence of the box step is as follows (boys, girls opposite):
   ▸ Step left forward
   ▸ Step right to the side
   ▸ Step left (close) to the right foot (step, side, together)
   ▸ Step right backward
   ▸ Step left to the side
   ▸ Step right (close) to the left foot (step, side, together)
2. For the boy's closed position, his right hand goes in the small of the girl's back. The boy signals movement with pressure (moving forward = light pressure; moving backward = heavy pressure). As a secondary signal for movement direction, keep the left hand up and hold the girl's right hand.
3. Girls in the closed position place their left arms on the boy's shoulder and face that shoulder.
4. Listen to the music.
5. Keep steps short and smooth; slide rather than walk.
6. Keep a tall posture; glide on the balls of the feet.
7. Avoid bouncing movements and arm pumping.

Teaching Cues

1. Use a drum or clap to demonstrate the concept of 4/4 time: there are 4 beats to a measure; the accent is on beats 1 and 3. Combinations of 4/4 dance rhythms include the following:
   ▸ One-step rhythm: quick (1 count), quick (1 count), quick (1 count), quick (1 count)
   ▸ Two-step rhythm: slow (2 counts), quick (1 count), quick (1 count)
   ▸ Promenade step: slow (2 counts), slow (2 counts).

2. Have students practice each dance step alone before attempting it in couples.

3. Separate girls and boys by arranging boys side-by-side on one side of the gym facing the center and girls likewise on the other side. Teach boy's part first. Boys should continue to do the box step while the girls are learning.

4. When demonstrating the closed position, take the boy's position and use a girl student partner.

5. Be sure to emphasize signals when teaching partners to dance together. The boy signals direction (forward or backward) with his right hand in the small of the girl's back, slightly pulling his hand just before stepping backward and keeping it loose when stepping forward. The boy can give secondary signals with his left hand, which is raised and holding the girl's right hand.

6. During the box turn (i.e., the box step with a turn), dancers make a quarter turn on each slow step. Rather than align the foot straight forward or backward, the boy toes out a quarter turn on the forward step and toes in a quarter turn on the backward step. The girl does the opposite. The boy's left hand and upper torso should guide the turn.

Activities (30-40 Minutes)

1. Introduce social dance with a brief explanation of its history as well as some of the social skills and etiquette (see the unit introduction on page 260). (3-4 minutes)

2. Explain 4/4 time (see teaching cue 1). (2 minutes)

Optional Activity: 4/4 Rhythm

3. Position students in a longway set (i.e., boys in a line on one side of the gym and girls in another line opposite the boys). Explain and demonstrate the basic box step (boys first, then the girls) using the skill and teaching cues. (It may be especially helpful to demonstrate this dance with your back to students.) Have boys and girls practice their parts separately, checking that they maintain good posture, take small steps, and stay on the balls of the feet. Continue to call "step, side, together; step, side, together," and so on; students should practice until the rhythm and steps seem comfortable. (6-8 minutes)

Basic Box Step

BOYS
Left step forward, slide the right foot forward and sidestep to the right, shifting weight to the right foot.
Close the left foot to the right, shifting weight to the left foot.
Right step backward, slide the left foot backward and sidestep to the left, shifting weight to the left foot.
Close the right foot to the left, shifting weight to the right foot.

GIRLS
Right step backward, slide the left foot backward and sidestep to the left, shifting weight to the left foot.
Close the right foot to the left, shifting weight to the right foot.
Left step forward, slide the right foot forward and sidestep to the right, shifting weight to the right foot.
Close the left foot to the right, shifting weight to the left foot.

4. Keeping the same formation, add music and have students continue to perform the basic box step. Check students for correct form and offer instruction when needed. Then have students move to a scatter formation and practice the basic box step to music. Continue to work with individual students who are having difficulty. (7-9 minutes)

5. Get a partner nearby and face each other with hands joined. Practice the basic box step to music. Anyone without a partner can practice alone. Stop the music and have students switch partners every 2 minutes. (4-5 minutes)

6. Have students switch partners and get into a closed position: Boys and girls face each other, the boy slightly to the left of the girl. The boy puts his right hand around the girl's waist in the small of her back and takes her right hand in his left, keeping both hands at about shoulder height and the elbows flexed. The girl rests her left arm on the boy's right shoulder.

   Demonstrate and have students practice the basic box step in the closed position. Practice the basic box step without music first, being sure to give the proper signals. Alert girls to tell their partners if signals are too late or not strong enough. (Have students switch partners after a few minutes.) (3-5 minutes)

7. Introduce the box turn, explaining that it is a box step with a turn. Have students try to turn their box (see teaching cue 6) as they dance the basic box step in a closed position. The boy's left hand and upper torso should signal and guide the turn. If some couples catch on quickly, have them demonstrate the move to the class and tell students what they are doing. When most couples are proficient, add music and have all couples continue to practice. (5-7 minutes)

Box Turn

BOYS

Left step forward and toe out, slide the right foot forward and sidestep to the right, shifting weight to the right foot.

Close the left foot to the right, shifting weight to the left foot.

Right step backward and toe in, slide the left foot backward and sidestep to the left, shifting weight to the left foot.

Close the right foot to the left, shifting weight to the right foot.

GIRLS

Right step backward and toe in, slide the left foot backward and sidestep to the left, shifting weight to the left foot.

Close the right foot to the left, shifting weight to the right foot.

Left step forward and toe out slide the right foot forward and sidestep to the right, shifting weight to the right foot.

Close the left foot to the right, shifting weight to the left foot.

Optional Activity: Partner Box Step and Turn

Optional Activities

4/4 Rhythm (0-5 Minutes)

This activity is more appropriate for younger middle school students. Play foxtrot music and have students clap a hand with the student closest to them; then have students walk to the beat, taking four steps per measure. Teach the accent by having students walk only on beats 1 and 3. Finally, have students change directions when walking to the beat: backward, to the sides, and diagonally.

Partner Box Step and Turn (0-5 Minutes)

Once partners are proficient at turning the box, have couples try to make their box step turns so they are not in the exact same place. Pick out 2 or 3 couples who catch on quickly and have the class watch them as you point out how the couples are moving their squares.

Closure (3-5 Minutes)

Review the lesson with students. Use the following questions and ideas to reinforce learning, check understanding, and provide feedback.

1. Ask students the following questions:
    - ▶ Which techniques make the box step graceful and attractive to watch (e.g., holding the body tall and keeping it balanced, keeping weight over the balls of the feet, gliding rather than walking, not letting the arms sag, not pumping the arms)?
    - ▶ Why are short steps necessary (e.g., to keep good balance, move in harmony, make fewer mistakes, etc.)?
2. Review the importance of the boy's signals and how girls should read them (e.g., the girl knows when the boy is going to step backward when she feels him pull on her back).
3. Review the box turn.
4. Encourage students about dance by telling them that even if they can only do the box step and turn—but do it well—they can dance for hours and look good.

Social Dance: Foxtrot Steps and Transitions

Purpose

In this second foxtrot lesson, students learn the progressive step and dip, and put their newly acquired box step skills together in a foxtrot dance sequence.

Facility and Equipment

- Gym or multipurpose area
- Music (CD or audiocassette) and player
- 4/4 rhythm
- Microphone

Warm-Ups (6-8 Minutes)

1. Arrange boys and girls in a longway set. Review the box step (see lesson 6, activity 6), having students follow your lead without music: "step, side, together" (or "step, side, close"; or "slow, quick, quick"). Add the turn (see lesson 6, activity 7) and practice.

2. Have the girls turn their backs to the boys. Now ask the boys to walk across the gym and gently tap a girl on the shoulder and ask her to dance. Make sure all students are paired up; then practice with music.

Skill Cues

1. For the progressive step, boys should loosen the right hand on the girl's back when walking forward.

2. Boys should tighten the hand and add pressure just before stepping back on the last half of the box step.

3. For the dip, keep the body's weight and alignment over the bending knee; do not bend at the waist.

Teaching Cues

1. Teach the progressive step, dip, and a sequence of foxtrot routines separately without music. Then have students practice in couples without music first, then with music.

2. Teach the boy's part first. Boys should practice while the girls learn their parts.

3. Watch the practice sessions carefully. If many students are having difficulty, stop and repeat class instruction.

4. Have students switch partners often.

Activities (30-40 Minutes)

1. Position students in a longway set, boys on one side of the gym and girls opposite them in the center of the gym. Introduce the progressive step by explaining that the progressive step is the same as the first half of the box step: boys

move forward and the girls move backward. Have students practice individually. When the girls are out of space, direct the class to turn around and practice the progressive step until they are back in their original positions. Once all students seem proficient, move to activity 2. (5-8 minutes)

Progressive Step

BOYS
Left step forward, sidestep right and close the left foot to the right.
Right step forward, sidestep left and close the right foot to the left.
Repeat.

GIRLS
Right step backward, sidestep left and close the right foot to the left.
Left step backward, sidestep right and close the left foot to the right.
Repeat.

2. Have the girls face the wall and ask the boys to tap a girl on the shoulder and ask her to dance. Pairs should scatter around the gym and assume the closed position. Explain that the box step will be added to the sequence, 1 box step after every 2 progressive steps. Remind boys about signaling forward and backward directions. Every 2 to 3 minutes, stop the music and have students switch partners. When all couples seem proficient, challenge students to add the box turn and add music. (10-12 minutes)

Progressive Step–Box Step Sequence

Skills: progressive step, box step

BOYS
Left step forward, sidestep right and close the left foot to the right.
Right step forward, sidestep left and close the right foot to the left.
Repeat.
Left step forward, sidestep right and close the left foot to the right.
Right step backward, sidestep left and close the right foot to the left.
Repeat sequence.

GIRLS
Right step backward, sidestep left and close the right foot to the left.
Left step backward, sidestep right and close the left foot to the right.
Repeat.
Right step backward, sidestep left and close the right foot to the left.
Left step forward, sidestep right and close the left foot to the right.
Repeat sequence.

3. Reposition students into a longway set. Explain and demonstrate the dip (4 counts) using the teaching and skill cues. The boy should guide his partner by firmly pulling her (on her back) toward him and then down just before stepping back on his left foot. Have students practice the dip alone and then with a partner (no music). (8-10 minutes)

Dip

Skill: dip
Suggested music: any music with 4/4 rhythm

BOYS
Left step backward, toes slightly pointing out; flex the left knee and lower the weight over the knee (1 beat).
Stretch the right leg diagonally forward, heel on the floor (hold for 2 beats).
Step up on the right foot (1 beat).

GIRLS
Right step forward, flexing and lowering over the right knee (1 beat).
Stretch the left leg diagonally backward, toes on the floor (hold 2 beats).
Step down on the left foot (1 beat).

4. Have students switch partners and create their own dance sequence that includes all of the foxtrot steps: box step, progressive step, box turn, and dip. If time is sufficient, have half of the class perform their sequences twice in front of the class; then have the other half perform. (7-10 minutes)

Closure (3-5 Minutes)

Review the lesson with students. Use the following questions and ideas to reinforce learning, check understanding, and provide feedback.

1. Share your observations about students' performances, emphasizing the positive.

2. Discuss students' willingness to dance with different partners. Also explain that dancing with different partners builds more confidence and increases skills because movement and style differ from person to person.

3. Have students identify on which foot all foxtrot changes occur (i.e., the left for boys, the right for girls). Ask them to describe proper body alignment for the dip as well as the boy's signal for a dip.

Lesson 8

Social Dance: Foxtrot Combinations

Purpose

In this lesson students will learn the side progressive open position and rock step, and then put these and other learned foxtrot skills in a dance sequence.

Warm-Up (6-8 Minutes)

Virginia reel

Skill Cues

Facility and Equipment

◆ Gym or multipurpose area
◆ Music (CD or audiocassette) and player
◆ 4/4 rhythm and Virginia reel
◆ Microphone

Rock Step

1. Think of a rocking motion when executing this step.
2. Stay on the balls of the feet and slide into steps.
3. Flex the knees slightly and put a little sway in the hips.

Side Progressive Step/Open

1. Keep steps short, especially the first one. Avoid the tendency to open with a long step.
2. Maintain a side-by-side position.
3. Signal the girl early of your intention to go into the side step by dropping your clasped hands and dropping your right elbow at the same time.

Closed position

Open position

Side progressive step (moving from closed to open)

Teaching Cues

1. Teach the rock step first without partners. Add partners when students seem proficient. The rhythm "slow, slow" may be less confusing than "quick, quick, quick, quick."

2. Teach the side progressive step/open in couples. Emphasize the boys dropping their clasped hands and right elbows a second before turning the girl.

3. List dance sequence (Activity 2) on chalkboard for easy reference.

Activities (30-40 Minutes)

1. Keep students in the Virginia reel formation and explain and demonstrate the rock step. The steps follow a quick, quick, quick, quick (4 beats) pattern or a slow, slow (4 beats) pattern instead of slow, quick, quick (4 beats). This step produces a rocking motion almost in place, hence the name. Direct all to follow your steps in unison. (5-7 minutes)

Rock Step

Skill: rock step

BOYS
Step L sideward (quick);
Slide right foot to the left, weight still on the left foot (quick).
Step right sideward (quick).
Slide left foot to right, weight still on right (quick).
Or
Step left sideward and drag right foot to left (slow, 2 beats).
Step right sideward and drag left foot to right (slow, 2 beats).

GIRLS
Same as boy only opposite feet

2. Couples for the Virginia reel move to another couple. Boys introduce the girls and ask to exchange partners. Couples move to an area and dance the following sequence. After the music is over, change partners and repeat the sequence. (8-10 minutes)

Foxtrot Combination

Skills: rock step, progressive step, box step, box turn
Two rock steps (8 beats).
Two progressive steps (8 beats).
One box step (8 beats).
One box turn (8 beats).

3. With new partners, have students take a closed position and take two forward progressive steps and stop. Boy's weight is on his right foot, and the girl's weight is on her left foot. Explain and demonstrate the open position and side progressive step. Complete a sequence of four forward progressive steps (closed position and four side progressive steps (open position). Add

music. Change partners and repeat the sequence to another musical selection. (8-11 minutes)

Side-by-Side Foxtrot

Skill: side progressive step (open position).

FROM CLOSED POSITION TO OPEN POSITION (NO BEATS)

Boy drops clasped hands to waist height.

At the same time drops right elbow, turns girl with his right hand.

Both turn to a side-by-side position.

Side progressive step (4 beats).

On the turn, the boy steps out left on the left foot, girl right on right foot (slow).

Both do a side close (quick, quick).

Repeat three side progressive steps, alternating lead foot.

Return to a closed position, dance two forward progressive steps.

Repeat.

Repeat entire sequence.

FROM OPEN POSITION TO CLOSED POSITION

Boy lifts clasped hands and elbow as boy's weight shifts to his right foot at the end of the side progressive step and girl's to her left foot.

Boy steps forward on left foot and girl steps back on right foot into a forward progressive step.

4. Boys thank and bow to their partners, girls curtsy, and both find new partners. Partners create a sequence that uses at least five steps. (9-12 minutes)

Closure (3-5 Minutes)

Review and discuss with students the content of the lesson. Use the following ideas to reinforce learning, check understanding, and give feedback.

1. Pick out 4 or 5 couples to demonstrate their dance sequences to the class. Comment on their smooth transitions and good dance techniques.

2. Give a homework assignment to write a foxtrot sequence using three or more different steps and then to teach it to a parent, other family member, or friend. At the start of the next class, have students return the assignment with the signature of the person who received the instruction.

Lesson 9

Social Dance: Waltz

Purpose

In this lesson students learn the basic waltz step and its rhythm.

Warm-Up (6-8 Minutes)

Foxtrot

Facility and Equipment

◆ Gym or multipurpose area
◆ CD or tape player, speaker, drum, music (3/4 and 4/4 time)

Skill Cues

1. Keep the weight forward over the balls of the feet.
2. Move with gliding, floating movements.

Teaching Cues

1. Explain 3/4 rhythm: 3 beats to a measure with an accent on the first beat. The step rhythm is slow, slow, slow.
2. Use a clap or a drum to demonstrate the rhythm while counting it aloud: *1,* 2, 3; *1,* 2, 3; and so on.
3. Teach steps individually and then in couples, without music and then adding music.
4. Emphasize gliding, swinging, and turning movements.

Activities (30-40 Minutes)

1. Waltz rhythm. Introduce the waltz by having the students listen to a few measures of a foxtrot and then a few measures of waltz music to get the "feel" of different sounds, tempo, and rhythm. (3-4 minutes)
2. Basic Waltz step. Arrange students in one large circle facing counterclockwise and have them count 1, 2, 3 and walk to each count while you beat a drum. All start forward on the left foot and walk to each beat. Stop the class and announce that on count 1 you will give a loud beat and on counts 2 and 3 a soft beat. They can count louder on 1 and softer on 2 and 3 while stepping forward on count 1 and in place beside the first step on 2 and 3. After all have mastered the movement, ask them to glide up on their toes on count 1, take a slight sideward step on count 2, and go up on their toes for steps 2 and 3. Continue to practice. Stop and ask them to move different directions on count 1 only—backwards, diagonally forward and backwards. Stop and announce that they are doing the basic waltz step. Demonstrate the flowing movement to the rhythm counting 1, 2, 3.

Arrange students in a scatter formation and let them practice individually to waltz music. When they feel comfortable join hands with another and continue. (8-10 minutes)

Waltz

Suggested music: any music with 3/4 time, or a drum

Arrange boys on one side and girls in the middle facing them. Tell students that the step patterns for the forward waltz and the box step are the same as the foxtrot, but the rhythm is slow, slow, slow. Have the boys take two forward waltz steps starting forward on their left foot and girls take two waltz steps starting backward on their right foot. At the end of two waltz steps, add two box steps. Practice several times without music. Add music. (8-10 minutes)

BOYS

Step forward left, side right, close left to right (forward step).

Step forward right, side left, close right to left (forward step).

Step forward left, side right, close left to right (box step).

Step backward right, side left, right to left.

Step forward left, side right close left to R (box step).

Right step backward right, side left, close right to left.

GIRLS

Same as boy only opposite feet

Procedure: Change partners and take a closed position. Partners dance farther apart than in the foxtrot, keep their weight forward on the balls of their feet, stand tall, and look elegant. Boys give the same hand signals when stepping back in the box. (3-5 minutes)

Skill: hesitation step

Change partners by having the girls say thank you and go get a new partner. Practice the hesitation step in couples without music. Boy must be strong on holding steps 2 and 3. Add music, and out into same sequence of two waltz steps, two box turns, and add two hesitation steps. (4-6 minutes)

BOYS

Step forward left and keep weight on left foot.

Bring right foot up, touch the floor beside left foot and hold for counts 2 and 3.

Step backward right and keep weight on right foot.

Bring left foot back, touch the floor beside right foot and hold for counts 2 and 3.

GIRLS

Same as boy only opposite feet

Skill: dip

Boys thank their partner and get a new one. Keep the same sequence, but add the dip at the end of the first box turn. The dip is the same as the foxtrot. Dip on count 1, hold on count 2, up on count 3, and step into the second box waltz on count 1. (4-5 minutes)

Closure (3-5 Minutes)

Review and discuss with students the content of the lesson. Use the following questions and ideas to reinforce learning, check understanding, and give feedback.

1. Ask students to listen to excerpts of music and determine if they are 4/4 or 3/4 time (foxtrot or waltz).

2. Ask students to describe the basic difference between the foxtrot and the waltz.

3. Have students explain why the waltz would be more preferred than the foxtrot or square dance for social balls and dances of the court.

Lesson 10

Social Dance: Polka

Purpose

In this lesson students learn to dance the polka.

Warm-Up (6-8 Minutes)

1. Patty-cake polka (see lesson 1)

Facility and Equipment

◆ Gym or multipurpose area
◆ Music (CD or audiocassette) and player
◆ Polka music with 4/4 syncopated rhythm

Skill Cues

1. Do a hop, step, step; or a side two-step (polka step).
2. Take small steps.
3. Keep the body balanced, the feet directly underneath.
4. Exaggerate the rhythm in the beginning by leaning down with the shoulder on the side on which the hop or step is taken.

Teaching Cues

1. Say the steps aloud: "hop, step, step; hop, step, step" and so on.
2. Use slower polka music to begin. Increase the speed when students have mastered the skills.
3. Have students with a good sense of polka rhythm dance with those who are having trouble.
4. For the regular polka, the shoulder-waist position may be used instead of the closed position (if students prefer this option).
5. Because the regular polka is tiring, particularly if fast music is used, students may revert to the Jessie polka or to the open position to catch their breath.

Activities (30-40 Minutes)

1. Introduce the lesson. The class will learn two polkas: one is slower and more relaxed; the other is the basic (fast) polka. Explain that the polka is from Eastern Europe, that it is a happy dance, and that it requires high levels of energy. If an Octoberfest is held in your area, you might relate the polka to that festival and what is known as German "oompah" music. (3-5 minutes)
2. Position students in conga lines of 5 or 6, one behind the other, with their hands on the waist of the person in front (the leader with hands on hips). Demonstrate and have students practice the Jessie polka, first without and then with music. Once students have the steps down, repeat the same sequence in groups of three, students standing side by side with their arms around waists and outside hands on hips. The steps are the same for boys and girls, and all students should begin with left foot. (10-15 minutes)

Jessie Polka

Skills: forward two-step, heel touch, toe tap

PART 1 (IN PLACE)
Left heel touch forward.

Step backward in place.

Right toe tap backward.

Right toe tap in place.

Right heel touch forward.

Step backward in place.

Left heel touch forward.

Left cross backward over right lower leg

PART 2 (FORWARD TWO-STEP)
Left step, close, step.

Right step, close, step.

Left step, close, step.

Right step, close, step.

Repeat parts 1 and 2 until the end of the music.

Optional Activity: Polka Two-Step

3. Pair up students or have them select partners. Repeat activity 2 using any of the following couple positions—open, conversation, promenade, or varsouvianna (couples may choose). (5 minutes)

4. Position students in a scatter formation. Have them practice the two-step (part 2) of the Jessie polka, this time transferring the forward motion to the side: sidestep left, close right, sidestep left; and then to the other side. (Step 1 is to the side and steps 2 and 3 are in place). Practice with music using a slow tempo and then a fast tempo. Once students are proficient at sidestepping, substitute a hop for the step. Tell them to keep the hop short and to turn as they move. (4-5 minutes)

5. Explain and demonstrate the regular polka. It might help to call out "hop, step, step" or "hop, close, step." Have students practice alone and then with a partner. Allow some time to rest and switch partners between sequences. (8-10 minutes)

Regular Polka

Skills: hop, step, step

BOYS
Hop left.

Step right close to the left and step left.

Hop right.

Step left close to the right and step right.

GIRLS
Hop right.

Step left close to the right and step right.

Hop left.

Step right close to the left and step left.

Optional Activity

Polka Two-Step (0-12 minutes)

Use this activity with beginners. Divide students into groups of 5 or 6 and position them in circles, holding hands. Have them perform the following sequence:

Slide left 4 times, then right 4 times.

Repeat 4 times.

Slide left 2 times, then right 2 times.

Repeat sequence, shortening the distance of the slides.

Slide left, slide right; this time the first step is out and the second and third steps are in place. (This sequence—a step, close, step to each side—is the same as the forward two-step in the Jessie polka.)

Repeat 2 times.

Position students in a scatter and practice the following sequence alone, taking short steps and trying to keep their feet directly beneath them. Then try the same sequence with partners, either holding hands or in a closed position. Leaning toward the side during the sidestep will help students establish the rhythm. Calling out the steps—"step, 2, 3; step, 2, 3" and so on—will assist students who may be having trouble. Once students are proficient at the polka two-step, call for a partner switch and add turning steps.

Polka Two-Step

Skills: slide, polka two-step

BOYS
Left sidestep, right close to the left (weight change), left step (weight change).
Right sidestep, left close to the right, right step.

GIRLS
Right sidestep, left close to the right, right step.
Left sidestep, right close to the left, left step.

Closure (3-5 Minutes)

Review the lesson with students. Use the following discussion topics to reinforce learning, check understanding, and provide feedback.

1. Discuss the aerobic benefits of the polka.
2. Discuss the many variations and sequences that can be added to the polka, as long as the same rhythm is maintained (e.g., open to closed positions, twirling the girl under raised hand in the star position).

Lesson 11

Jitterbug (Swing)

Purpose

In this lesson students learn the basic steps of the jitterbug.

Facility and Equipment

◆ Gym or multipurpose area
◆ Music (CD or audiocassette) and player
◆ Syncopated music in 4/4 meter or rhythm, polka music

Warm-Up (6-8 Minutes)

1. Jessie or regular polka, danced alone (see lesson 10)

Skill Cues

1. The basic step is as follows: toe, heel, step, step.
2. For the swing-out, swing girls out and under the arm by pulling and lifting one hand and pushing on the girl's lower back to push the girl away.
3. Listen to the beat and try to rock the body to the rhythm.
4. Keep the knees flexed most of the time.
5. Take small steps, maintaining a narrow moving base and keeping the feet beneath the body.

Teaching Cues

1. Say the steps aloud initially: "toe, heel, step, step."
2. Remind students to keep their weight low by flexing their knees.
3. The jitterbug dance can be done slower to foxtrot music, but generally it is danced to a syncopated or rock-and-roll beat.
4. Unlike other dances in which dancers move freely around the floor, the jitterbug is danced in a small area.

Activities (30-40 Minutes)

1. Play some jitterbug music so students get the feel of the rhythm and introduce the jitterbug by commenting on the following. (4-5 minutes)
   ▶ Liveliness of the music
   ▶ Informality of the dance
   ▶ Open dance position
   ▶ Minor leading demands for boys
2. Position students in a scatter formation, facing the front of the gym. Explain and demonstrate the basic jitterbug (i.e., toe, heel, step, step) and have students practice it alone. The toe and heel steps are performed in place. Continue to practice without music until the steps become somewhat automatic; then add music. (8-10 minutes)

Basic Jitterbug

Skill: basic jitterbug step

BOYS
Toe (left toe touch, heel up, weight on the right foot).
Heel (heel touch: drop the left heel to the floor).
Step (right step).
Step (left step).
Toe (right toe touch, heel up, weight on the left foot).
Heel (heel touch: drop the right heel to the floor).
Step (left step).
Step (right step).
Repeat sequence.

GIRLS
Toe (right toe touch, heel up, weight on the left foot).
Heel (heel touch: drop the right heel to the floor).
Step (left step).
Step (right step).
Toe (left toe touch, heel up, weight on the right foot).
Heel (heel touch; drop the left heel to the floor).
Step (right step).
Step (left step).
Repeat sequence.

3. Demonstrate how to add a side turn-out to the basic jitterbug. Have students dance alone without music first; then add music. Once proficient, students should try it with a partner, clasping hands and facing each other. On the side turn-out they may drop outside hands, but it is not necessary. (6-8 minutes)

Basic Jitterbug With a Side Turn-Out

Skills: basic jitterbug step, side turn-out, quarter turn

BOYS
Basic jitterbug steps (toe, heel, step, step).
Repeat.
Left toe touch, turning a quarter turn to the right on the heel.
Right step backward, slightly lifting the left foot off the floor.
Left step and swing back to starting position.
Right toe touch, turning a quarter turn to the left on the heel.
Left step backward, slightly lifting the right foot off the floor.
Right step and swing back to starting position.

GIRLS
Basic jitterbug steps (toe, heel, step, step).
Repeat.
Right toe touch, turning a quarter turn to the left on the heel.
Left step backward, slightly lifting the right foot off the floor.
Right step and swing back to starting position.

Side turn-out sequence (partial)

Left toe touch, turning a quarter turn to the right on the heel.

Right step backward, slightly lifting the left foot off the floor.

Left step and swing back to starting position.

4. Demonstrate the swing-out, which occurs on the last step of the side turn-out. As the boy starts the second step, he lifts his arm and pushes the girl with his other hand so that she goes out and under his arm. He keeps hold of her hand, doing 2 basic steps in place while she does 2 basic steps, 1 going out and 1 coming back. Have students practice the side turn-out, first without and then with music. (6-8 minutes)

Basic Jitterbug With a Side Turn-Out and a Swing-Out

Skills: basic jitterbug step, side turn-out, swing-out
Suggested music: 4/4 syncopated rhythm

BOYS
Basic jitterbug step (i.e., left toe, left heel, right step, left step).
Side turn-out (i.e., right toe, right heel, left step backward).
Lift the left arm, drop the right hand behind the girl's back, right step.
Basic step in place while the girl turns away.
Basic step in place while the girl comes back and join hands.
Repeat sequence.

GIRLS
Basic jitterbug step (i.e., right toe, right heel, left step, right step).
Side turn-out (i.e., left toe, left heel, right step backward).
Lift the right arm, drop the left hand, go under the boy's arm, left step.
Basic step (right toe and heel while going away; step, step while turning back).
Basic step while coming back (to facing position) and join hands.
Repeat sequence.

Swing-out sequence

5. Have students switch partners and dance the jitterbug to music. Use the following sequence (6-9 minutes)

Jitterbug Sequence

Skills: basic jitterbug step, side turn-out, swing-out
Basic jitterbug step (i.e., toe, heel, step, step).
Repeat
Side turn-out (i.e., toe, heel, step backward).
Repeat.
Swing-out.
Repeat sequence.

Closure (3-5 Minutes)

Review the lesson with students. Use the following questions and ideas to reinforce learning, check understanding, and provide feedback.

1. Discuss some of the dance names that are synonymous with the jitterbug (e.g., the lindy, double lindy, swing, shag, boogie woogie, and others) by tracing the origins of the dance to ragtime.

2. The jitterbug is sometimes described as an earthy dance. Ask students why they think it was characterized as such—that is, what about the dance suggests earthiness (e.g., ragtime involved dancing "down" by lowering the center of gravity).

3. Discuss why it is important to flex the knees and lower the center of gravity in the jitterbug (i.e., this position provides stability while dancers are moving quickly and gives a "swing" appearance).

4. Remind the class that the next session will be a review of many dances in this unit. If you will be incorporating assessment into the unit, let them know what they will be evaluated on (e.g., social skills, performance technique).

Dance Review

Purpose

In this lesson students get the opportunity to demonstrate their knowledge, social skills, and dance skills by performing a square dance as well as the foxtrot, waltz, polka, jitterbug, and hora.

Facility and Equipment

◆ Gym or multipurpose area
◆ Music (CD or audiocassette) and player
◆ All music that was used in this unit

Warm-Up (0 Minutes)

The activities provide sufficient warm-up.

Skill Cues

1. Use good dance etiquette.
2. Maintain good posture and balance.
3. Listen to the music and stay with the beat.

Teaching Cues

1. Have boys choose partners for one dance and girls the next. Continue to alternate.
2. Remind students of the need for good dance posture and positioning.
3. The last activity in this lesson is a circle dance to bring unity and remind students that they are part of a whole.

Activities (35-42 Minutes)

1. Perform split the ring. (6 minutes)
2. Perform the foxtrot. (4-5 minutes)
3. Perform the regular polka. (4-5 minutes)
4. Perform the waltz. (4-5 minutes)
5. Perform the jitterbug. (4-5 minutes)
6. Perform the Jessie polka. (4-5 minutes)
7. Perform the foxtrot again. (4-5 minutes)
8. Perform the hora (see lesson 1). (5-6 minutes)

Note: The foxtrot appears twice because it is a foundational dance, i.e., the most used and the dance in which students had the most instruction.

Closure (3-5 Minutes)

Review and discuss with students the content of the dance unit. Use the following ideas to reinforce learning, check understanding, and provide feedback.

1. Play a few measures of the different types of music used for the dances and have students identify the type of dance.

2. Demonstrate different dance steps and have students name the dance or step.

3. Demonstrate different dance positions and have students identify them by name.

4. Ask students which dances they liked best, which they thought were easiest to learn, and which they thought were difficult.

5. Share your assessment of the unit, being as positive as possible. Remind students that knowing even the basic steps of a dance can mean hours of enjoyment on the dance floor. Also remind them that many variations can be created using the basic step.

Assessment and Resources

Testing skills involved in couples dancing presents a problem because the performance of one partner depends on the performance of the other. Of course, dancing with each student is probably not a good use of time. General evaluation can and should be conducted throughout the unit on such things as social skills and attitude as evidenced by attendance, readiness, cooperation with others (e.g., different partners), and willingness to practice and participate.

The following suggestions offer some options for specific skill assessment.

▶ Use the final day of the unit (lesson 12) to evaluate student proficiency in a square dance (i.e., split the ring) as well as the foxtrot, waltz, polka, jitterbug, and hora. You may want to devise a rating system to assess specific steps and skills.

▶ Administer a written test requiring students to identify excerpts of music and various dance steps, movements, and positions.

▶ Have pairs of students select one of the social dances and create their own sequence for presentation in front of the class. To save time, have pairs who choose the same dance demonstrate their sequences at the same time.

Resources

Harris, J.A., A. Pittman, and M.S. Waller. 1969. *Dance a while.* 4th ed. Minneapolis: Burgess.

Landy, J.M., and M.J. Landy. 1993. *Ready-to-use p.e. activities for grades 7-9.* West Nyack, NY: Parker.

Stephenson, R.M., and J. Iaccarino. 1980. *Complete book of ballroom dancing.* New York: Doubleday.

Wright, J.P. 1992. *Social dance: Steps to success.* Champaign, IL: Leisure Press.

Additional Resources

Most record stores have polka, waltz, jitterbug, and foxtrot music. Many also carry Arthur Murray and Guy Lombardo music. The following organizations also offer the music suggested in this unit:

American Alliance of Health, Physical Education, Recreation and Dance (AAHPERD)
1900 Association Dr.
Reston, VA 22091
Phone 703-476-3400
    Offers instructional videotapes for folk, waltz, polka, and East and West coast swing dances

Kimbo Educational Records
P.O. Box 477
N. Third Ave.
Long Branch, NJ 07740
Phone 800-631-2187
    Offers music (audiocassette and CD) for the polka, schottische, foxtrot, square dance, mixers, Tennessee wig walker, chicken dance

Melody House
819 N.W. 92nd St.
Oklahoma City, OK 73114
Phone 800-234-9228
    Offers reel, square, folk, and polka music as well as hokey pokey and bunny hop recordings (audiocassette and CD)

Snitz Manufacturing Co. & S.S. Worldwide
75 Mill St.
P.O. Box 513
Colchester, CN 06415
    Offers music (audiocassette and CD) for folk and square dancing, mixers, the bunny hop, and the hokey pokey

Softball

The game of softball is more than 100 years old. George Hancock is credited with developing both the game and its first set of rules in Chicago in 1887. Softball was first called *inside baseball* because it was played indoors. This early version of the game was quite different from today's game, however. For starters, it was originally played with a boxing glove and a broom. Eventually the official game used a softer ball, a smaller bat, and shorter base distances than are used today. The pitcher threw the ball underhand.

The game quickly moved outdoors and was referred to by such names as kitten ball, mush ball, big ball, recreational ball, and diamond ball. The National Recreation and Park Association (NRPA) used the game extensively in its recreational programs. In 1933 the Amateur Softball Association (ASA) was formed. It gave softball its official name and developed a formal set of rules. A national tournament was held that year at the World's Fair in Chicago. Public interest in softball continued to grow before World War II; the game became even more popular after the war.

By the 1950s leagues had been established all over the country, and by the middle of that decade the 12-inch (30.5-centimeter) slow-pitch softball game had emerged. Today softball is one of the most popular games played in the United States, with more than 35 million Americans participating every year.

Equipment

Basic softball equipment includes a regulation softball bat, softball, fielding gloves, and a set of four bases. It is also recommended that, for game play, a chest protector and protective mask be provided for the catcher.

▶ Regulation softballs are 11 or 12 inches (27.9 or 30.5 centimeters) in circumference. For this unit, regulation softballs, mush balls (rag balls), softball-size Wiffle balls, and rubber softballs could be used.

▶ Bats should weigh between 28 and 38 ounces (.79 and 1.08 kilograms); bat length should range from 28 to 35 inches (71.1-88.9 centimeters). A number of softball bats, of varying weight and length, should be used when teaching this unit.

▶ Fielding gloves should be made available for students.

▶ Bases are standard in softball. The three field bases are typically 15 by 15 inches (38.1 by 38.1 centimeters). Home plate is a polygon 17 by 17 inches (43.2 by 43.2 centimeters).

The pitcher's plate, although not necessary for the game, is 6 by 24 inches (15.2 by 61 centimeters) and is positioned in the center of the diamond, 46 feet (14.02 meters) from home plate. The four bases—first base, second base, third base, and home plate—are 60 feet (18.29

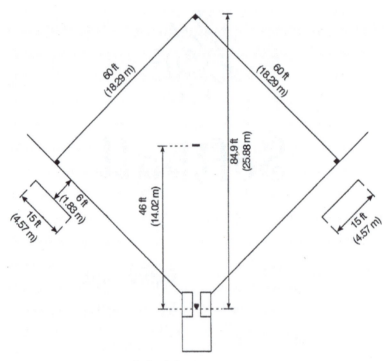

Softball field dimensions

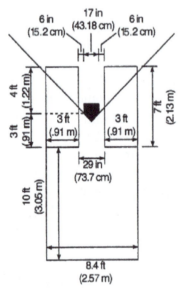

Home plate detail

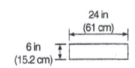

Pitcher's plate detail

meters) apart and the distance from home plate to the end of the outfield should be 250 feet (76.20 meters).

Unit Organization

Because many students will be familiar with the game of softball and will likely be able to gain some measure of success quickly, there may be a tendency to move into the game before students develop good game-playing skills. The lessons in this unit are designed not only to progress through the skills but also to promote skill proficiency.

Following is a description of each lesson in this unit.

▶ Lesson 1 serves as an introduction (or review, if students are familiar with softball) of throwing and catching skills.

- Because fielding is a major component of the game and because it involves distinct skills—fielding a fly ball differs significantly from fielding a ground ball—both lessons 2 and 3 present fielding.

- Pitching is the focus of lesson 4. It addresses basic pitching technique and sequence (i.e., windmill delivery), and then presents the slow pitch while introducing a batter.

- In lesson 5 batting is covered. (In fielding lessons 2 and 3, batting is substituted by throwing or batting off a tee.)

- Lesson 6 presents base running.

- Lessons 7 and 8 introduce offensive and defensive position play.

- Lessons 9 and 10 present modified and regulation game play.

Selected resources and assessment ideas are found in the assessment and resources chapter at the end of the unit.

Note: An asterisk (*) following a facility or equipment listing indicates that preparation is required before the lesson.

Social Skills and Etiquette

Because softball is a team sport, social skills can and should be developed throughout this unit. The game demands teamwork to be successful. Many of the activities in these lessons are designed for small groups, providing ample opportunities for social interaction.

In addition, address the need for fair play, good sporting behavior, and respect for opponents in class discussions throughout the unit. The regulation game is a competitive situation, and students should learn to handle the competition in a positive manner.

Lesson Modifications

As mentioned earlier, softer and larger balls may be used in this unit. For example, Wiffle balls may be easier to hit and catch, enabling special-needs students or those of lower ability to experience success and satisfaction with the game. Bats that are bigger than regulation-sized bats may also be used to modify the game for disabled or less-skilled students.

Other possible modifications to the lessons in this unit include the following:

- Reduce the size of the field for those with mobility problems.

- Allow more players per team to maximize participation and provide more field coverage for immobile students.

- Change the rules as appropriate to increase the enjoyment of the game for all. For example, use a tennis racket instead of a bat, allow more than 3 strikes for each player, or allow only 1 or 2 strikes if the game needs to be sped up.

Safety

Several safety factors should be observed when teaching this unit.

- For throwing or fielding practice, position the class so that all students throw in the same direction to make it less likely that students will be hit by balls.

- Batting stations should be large enough that students will not carelessly walk by and be hit with a bat or batted ball.

- All students should be required to wear fielding gloves when catching thrown or batted balls.

- As noted earlier, the catcher should wear the proper protective gear (i.e., mask and chest protector).

- When playing a modified or regulation game, make sure students who are not in the game are away from the playing area.

Rules

A variation of baseball, softball uses a softer and larger ball, a smaller and lighter bat, and a smaller playing field. Softball does not demand a fast-pitch strikeout pitcher; instead it requires the pitcher to pitch the ball with a slow arc and travel from the pitcher to just behind home plate.

A team consists of 10 players. When on offense, all players bat in a predetermined batting order. When on defense, players play their field positions:

▶ First baseman
▶ Second baseman
▶ Third baseman
▶ Shortstop
▶ Left fielder
▶ Left center fielder
▶ Right center fielder
▶ Right fielder
▶ Pitcher
▶ Catcher

Play

Basic play is as follows: The pitcher (defense) starts the game by pitching the ball to the bat-ter (offense), who attempts to hit the ball. If the batter hits the ball, she or he attempts to reach first base before the ball. If the ball is caught on the fly (i.e., in the air) or if the ball beats the batter to first base, the batter is out. If the batter reaches the base first and the ball is not caught in the air, the batter is safe and the next team member bats. The player on first becomes a base runner and attempts to run around all the bases to score a run.

This process continues until the offensive team gets three outs. Then teams switch (i.e., the fielding team [defense] becomes the batting team [offense] and vice versa). When both teams have received three outs, it makes up an inning. The game continues in this manner for seven innings, at which time the team with the most runs wins. If the score is tied after seven innings, teams play extra innings if time allows.

Offense

Following are the basic offensive rules of softball:

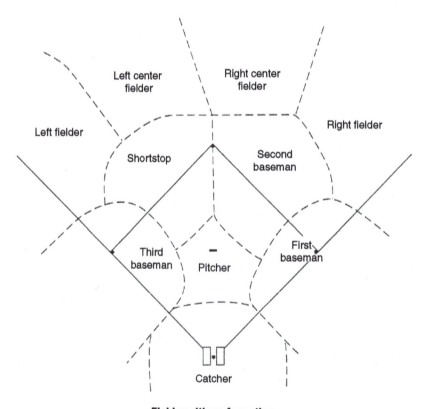

Field positions formation

▶ Each time a batter goes to the plate, the following three situations may occur:

Strikes—legal pitches (i.e., crossing home plate between the bottom of the batter's armpits to the top of the batter's knees). If the batter swings and misses the ball, it is also a strike. Three strikes equal an out.

Balls—illegal pitches (i.e., crossing home plate above the batter's shoulders or below the batter's knees, and outside or inside the width of the plate). Four balls equal a walk for the batter to first base.

Fouls—a struck ball that does not stay in the playing field. A foul ball will be counted as a strike against the batter, but will never count as the third or final strike. There are unlimited foul balls allowed once a batter has two strikes.

▶ The ball must be hit inside the third and first base lines to be considered in play. A ball hit outside the base lines is a foul ball and is out of play; a ball hit between the two base lines is a fair ball and must be played by the defensive team.

▶ Offensive players (i.e., batters, then runners) must advance the bases consecutively (i.e., from home to first, then to second, then to third, and then back to home) and must touch each base along the way.

▶ First and home bases may be overrun; runners must stop on second and third bases or risk being tagged out.

▶ No stealing or leading off base is allowed in physical education softball; runners are not permitted to leave a base until the batter swings at the ball.

Defense

Fielders play their positions while the offensive players bat and run, trying to get them out. Defensive players (defense) get batters (offense) out by

- catching a batted fly ball,
- tagging the batter (runner) with the ball before he or she gets to first base,
- striking the batter out, or
- having possession of the ball and touching a base ahead of a runner who must advance to that base.

Lesson 1

Throwing and Catching

Purpose

In this lesson students develop throwing and catching skills used in softball, emphasizing grip, stance, force absorption, and tracking.

Warm-Ups

1. Slapping jacks
2. Arm circles
3. Arm rotators
4. Waist twists
5. Spinal curls

Facility and Equipment

◆ Large, open outdoor area with a softball diamond (preferably regulation) and a large stationary wall, or gym
◆ 1 fielding glove per student
◆ 3 softballs per student
◆ 3 rag (or yarn) balls per student
◆ 10 wall targets

Skill Cues

Grip

1. Hold the ball with the fingers (i.e., off the palm).
2. Grip the ball tightly across the seams.
   ▶ For the 2-finger grip, place the index and middle fingers across the seams and rest the little finger on the side of the ball.
   ▶ Students with smaller hands should use the 3-finger grip, which requires placing 3 fingers (i.e., the index, middle, and ring fingers) across the seams.
3. Place the thumb under the ball and on the side opposite the little finger.

Throwing

1. Use a forward stride position (i.e., one foot in front of the other) with the dominant leg back. Right-handed throwers will have the right leg back; left-handed throwers will have the left leg back.
2. Throw from a stable base.
3. Face the target.
4. Increase the speed of movements.
5. Shift the center of gravity from backward to forward.
6. Rotate the throwing side forward and transfer weight to the front leg.
7. Lead the arm motion with the elbow.
8. Release with a wrist snap.
9. Follow through in the intended direction of flight.

Catching

1. Maintain stability by using a forward stride position.

2. Focus on and track the oncoming ball; align the body squarely behind the ball as it comes toward the catcher.

3. Use a large surface (i.e., the glove) to catch the ball, and on contact give with the arms and hands to absorb the force of the ball. Transfer weight backward to help absorb the force of the ball.

4. If the ball is above waist level, turn the glove so that the fingers are pointing upward; if the ball is below the waist, point the fingers downward.

5. Use the glove hand for initial contact, then use the other (i.e., bare) hand to immediately stabilize (trap) the ball.

Activities (30-40 Minutes)

1. Introduce the two-finger and three-finger grips as well as throwing, emphasizing the skill cues. You may want to give students balls to try out each grip. (7-8 minutes)

2. Have students practice their grip and throw with a rag ball. Students throw at a large target without stepping to throw. Emphasize starting in a forward stride position as well as the trunk rotation and arm motion of the throw. (5-7 minutes)

3. Repeat activity 2, this time having students use the entire throwing motion, including the step and follow-through, while throwing the rag balls at the targets. Remind students to focus on the targets and require them to vary their throws by changing the speed and distance. (5-7 minutes)

4. Introduce catching using the skill cues. Then have students select a partner to play catch. Partners stand about 10 feet (3.05 meters) apart and toss a rag ball back and forth. Instruct students to focus on aligning the body with the oncoming ball, giving with the ball as it is received, shifting their weight backward as the ball is being caught, and using both hands to catch the ball. (6-8 minutes)

5. Distribute softballs to each set of partners and gloves to each student. Have partners play catch starting 10 feet (3.05 meters) apart and then moving farther back, to a maximum of 60 feet (18.29 meters) apart. Throwers should vary their throws above and below the waist and focus on the target (i.e., the receiver's glove). The receiver should vary the target by shifting glove position every other throw and concentrate on correct glove placement (i.e., fingers up or down). As partners spread farther apart, they should take a few steps before throwing. Have partners try to catch 10, then 20, and then 25 catches consecutively. (7-10 minutes)

Closure (3-5 Minutes)

Review the lesson with students. Use the following ideas to reinforce learning, check understanding, and provide feedback.

1. Review the proper throwing technique.

2. Ask two students to demonstrate the proper catching technique, emphasizing giving with the ball on contact.

3. Discuss the two-finger and three-finger grips. Explain the importance of a good grip in throwing the ball accurately (e.g., a good grip across the seams creates spin).

Lesson 2

Fielding Ground Balls

Purpose

In this lesson students learn to field ground balls, including taking the ready position, handling the ball, and throwing.

Warm-Ups (6-8 Minutes)

1. Leg stretch
2. Waist twists
3. Arm rotators
4. Squat holds
5. Sprint-jog intervals

Facility and Equipment

◆ Outdoor softball field or gym
◆ 1 fielding glove and softball per student
◆ 1 bat per 3 students
◆ 3 sets of bases

Skill Cues

Ready Position and Alignment

1. Bend the knees and flex at the trunk so that the glove and bare hand can touch the ground.
2. Keep weight on the balls of the feet and the buttocks low to the ground.
3. Keep the feet in a forward stride position with the dominant leg back.
4. Bend the elbows and relax the arms and hands (i.e., keep the hands "soft").
5. Keep the hands in the open position, with the bare hand ready to trap the ball into the glove.
6. Use the shuffle step (avoid crossing feet whenever possible) when getting into a direct line with the path of the oncoming ball.

Handling the Ball

1. Align the body with the ball, shuffle the feet whenever possible, and charge forward on slowly hit balls.
2. Have a firm base of support (use a forward stride stance).
3. Tuck the chin as the eyes follow the ball.
4. Keep the arms and hands relaxed.
5. Hold the palms perpendicular to the path of the oncoming ball, out in front of the body.
6. Give with the ball on contact.
7. In one motion, field the ball and bring it up to the dominant hip in preparation for the throw.

Transition From Fielding to Throwing

1. Make the transition between fielding and throwing clean, smooth, and fast, in one motion.
2. Before fielding the ball, know where to throw it.
3. Find the target before releasing the ball.
4. Stabilize the base of support before releasing the ball.
5. Keep a relaxed and flexed body position.

Teaching Cue

Have students work individually at the beginning of class, but eventually team them up with other students to combine throwing and catching with fielding.

Activities (30-40 Minutes)

1. Introduce and demonstrate the ready position, proper alignment, and how to handle the ball using the skill cues. When demonstrating the ready position, shuffle [without crossing the feet] when aligning the body with the ball. (6-7 minutes)
2. Have students spread out within the infield and get into the ready position. Send a ball either to the left or right of players to have them move sideways. Make sure students use the shuffle step and remind them to watch the ball as they move. (3-4 minutes)
3. Have students work individually on fielding a softball (grounder) thrown against a wall. Students should vary their distance from the wall, starting just 5 feet (1.52 meters) away and progressively moving back to a distance of 20 feet (6.1 meters). Have students throw at various angles so they practice moving both left and right. (4-5 minutes)

Fielding a grounder

4. Pair up students or have them select partners and have them stand 15 feet (4.57 meters) apart. Partners roll the ball back and forth to each other, progressively increasing the distance between them to a maximum of 35 feet (10.67 meters). Emphasize getting into a good fielding position before the ball arrives. (7-8 minutes)

5. Have students gather around and introduce the proper transition from fielding to throwing using the skill cues. (2-4 minutes)

6. Pair up students or have them select partners and distribute a softball to each pair. Have partners stand about 20 feet (6.1 meters) apart and take turns fielding thrown ground balls (i.e., one student throws; then the other fields the ball and throws it back to the other student, who fields and throws it back, and so on). Players should throw the ball to either side so that each fielder must move left or right to field it. Remind throwers to locate their target and get set before throwing the ball. (3-5 minutes)

7. Divide students into groups of 3: 1 batter, 1 fielder, and 1 baseman. Have the batter self-toss then hit (or roll) ground balls to the fielder at a distance of about 30 feet (9.14 meters). (Proper batting form is not essential; students simply need contact the ball.) The fielder then throws the ball to the baseman standing on the base. After five fielding sequences, students should switch roles. (5-7 minutes)

Closure (3-5 Minutes)

Review the lesson with students. Use the following ideas to reinforce learning, check understanding, and provide feedback.

1. Stress the importance of taking the ready position before each pitch to field the ball effectively.

2. Discuss the importance of keeping the arms and hands relaxed throughout the fielding process (i.e., "soft" hands allow the fielder to absorb the force of the ball, which leads to fewer fielding errors).

3. Select a student to demonstrate the transition from fielding to throwing. Discuss the important elements of the transition (e.g., one motion).

Lesson 3

Fielding Fly Balls

Purpose

In this lesson students learn to field fly balls using their previously learned fielding skills and the transition from fielding to throwing.

Warm-Ups (6-8 Minutes)

1. Leg stretch
2. Arm circles
3. Sprint-jog intervals
4. Waist twists
5. Push-up hold

Facility and Equipment

- Outdoor softball field or gym
- 1 fielding glove per student
- 1 yarn (or rag) ball per student
- 1 soft ball (softer than a softball) per student
- 1 regulation softball ball per student
- 1 bat per 3 students

Skill Cues

Ready Position

1. Use a forward stride stance.
2. Face and focus on the ball as it approaches.
3. Move toward the ball if necessary.
4. Keep the body relaxed and in line with the oncoming ball.
5. Keep the glove pocket open and in front of the throwing shoulder.
6. Hold the throwing hand up by the glove, ready to grab and throw the ball.

Catching a Fly Ball

1. Keep the eyes focused on the ball when running to catch it.
2. When the ball is falling short, extend the glove toward the oncoming ball while running. Keep the glove open with the fingers down. Experienced players may even slide to get under and catch a ball that is falling short.
3. Get to the ball quickly, trying to get in front of it.
4. If the ball comes down, try to catch the ball above eye level on the throwing side of the body, holding the glove with the fingers up.
5. Place the throwing hand over the ball as it goes into the glove to trap the ball in the glove.
6. Flex the elbows to absorb the force of the ball.

Transition From Catching to Throwing

1. Smoothly and quickly transition from catching a fly ball to throwing it.
2. Before fielding the ball, know where to throw it.
3. Find the target before releasing the ball.
4. Catch the ball on the throwing side of the body and take a crossover step to plant the rear foot. This step, commonly referred to as the "crow hop," helps to produce more force and stabilize the base of support.
5. Stabilize the base of support before releasing the ball.

Activities (30-40 Minutes)

1. Introduce the ready position for fielding fly balls using the skill cues. (You may want to have skilled students demonstrate the position so that everyone will understand the detailed sequence.) (3-4 minutes)
2. Have students spread out and simulate catching a fly ball using a glove. Have them show catches with both fingers up (in the air) and fingers down (falling short). Check students for proper ready position. (3-4 minutes)
3. Introduce catching and throwing a fly ball highlighting the skill cues for catching as well as the transition from fielding to throwing. A demonstration, particularly of the crow hop, may be particularly helpful. (4-6 minutes)
4. Pair up students or have them select partners. Pairs throw high pop-ups to each other using yarn balls from various distances, such as 10, 20, and 30 feet (3.05, 6.1, and 9.14 meters). Students should practice tracking the ball from these distances and getting the body in front of and under the ball. (6-8 minutes)
5. Repeat activity 4, this time using a soft ball (i.e., softer than a softball). Students should throw from varying distances, fielders moving left, right, backward, and forward to catch the ball. When students are ready, substitute the softer balls with regulation softballs. (6-8 minutes)
6. Divide students into groups of 3: 1 hitter, 1 fielder, and 1 baseman. The hitter hits short fly balls with a bat (if possible; otherwise the student throws) to a fielder 30 to 50 feet (9.14-15.24 meters) away. The fielder, in turn, throws the ball to the baseman (using the crow hop when throwing). After five flies (or throws), students should switch roles. (8-10 minutes)

Fielding a fly ball

Closure (3-5 Minutes)

Review the lesson with students. Use the following ideas to reinforce learning, check understanding, and provide feedback.

1. Discuss the importance of tracking fly balls (i.e., if a fly ball is not caught, the batter usually gets extra bases).
2. Ask students to identify important skills required to catch a fly ball (i.e., predicting the flight of the ball, having a stable base of support, positioning in front of the ball, and using two hands to catch and trap the ball).

Lesson 4

Pitching Skills and Activities

Purpose

This lesson on pitching addresses the mechanics of the slow pitch and provides an opportunity for students to pitch against a batter.

Warm-Ups (6-8 Minutes)

1. Arm circles
2. Arm pumps
3. Curl and stretch
4. Upper body rotations
5. Lateral hops

Facility and Equipment

◆ Outdoor softball diamond or gym
◆ 1 pitching plate per 2 students
◆ 1 home plate per 2 students
◆ 1 regulation softball per student
◆ 1 Wiffle ball per 3 students
◆ 1 bat per 3 students

Skill Cues

Pitching Stance

1. Use a forward stride position.
2. Hold the ball in the glove or bare hand.
3. Bend the trunk slightly forward at waist level.
4. Keep both feet on the ground and in contact with the pitching plate. (The rear foot can be off the rubber.)
5. Square the shoulders to the target, and maintain a solid base of support.
6. Hold the ball and pitching hand in the glove at waist level.

Pitching Motion

1. The slow pitch involves a clockwise three-quarter circular motion backward to full extension and then forward.
2. The ball must arc higher than the batter's head as it approaches the plate.
3. Grip the ball across the seams for better control.
4. Cock the wrists at the top of the backswing.
5. Keep the shoulders square to the target (i.e., across home plate).
6. Observe the strike zone for a batter: from the bottom of the armpits to the top of the knees, as well as the width of homeplate.
7. Step with the leg opposite the pitching arm when beginning the downward motion of the pitch.
8. Snap the wrist and release the ball between the waist and knee level.
9. Extend the arm upward in the follow-through and step forward on the trailing leg to take a fielding position.

Teaching Cue

Use pitching and home plates for the activities in this lesson; the plates give students a visual sense of a proper pitch.

Pitching sequence

Activities (30-40 Minutes)

1. Introduce and demonstrate the basic mechanics of the slow pitch using the skill cues. (5-6 minutes)

2. Pair up students or have them select partners: one partner will pitch and the other will catch. Give a fielding glove and two regulation softballs to each pair. Have students practice the slow pitch from 30, 40, and 45 feet (9.14, 12.19, and 13.72 meters), concentrating on developing an arc when delivering the ball over the plate. After 10 pitches, partners switch roles. (5-6 minutes)

3. Repeat activity 2, this time adding the strike zone and having catchers call balls and strikes. After pitching 10 strikes, pitchers catch and catchers pitch. (6-8 minutes)

4. Divide students into groups of 3: 1 pitcher, 1 batter, and 1 catcher. The pitcher pitches to the batter from 35 feet (10.67 meters). The batter, standing at home plate, passively watches the pitched balls (i.e., batters do not swing at the pitches). The catcher calls balls and strikes. After either 3 strike-outs (i.e., 9 strikes) or 4 walks (i.e., 16 illegal pitches), students should switch roles. (7-10 minutes)

5. Using the same student groups, move the catcher to a fielding position and have the batters try to tap the ball to the fielders. (Batters should only hit balls that are strikes.) Start this activity with Wiffle balls; then switch to regulation balls. (7-10 minutes)

Closure (3-5 Minutes)

Review the lesson with students. Use the following ideas to reinforce learning, check understanding, and provide feedback.

1. Ask students to identify the strike zone and discuss why it is important for a pitcher to be able to throw strikes.

2. Ask students why an arched pitch is harder to hit than a flat-line pitch.

Lesson 5

Batting

Purpose

In this lesson students develop batting skills, including the proper stance and swing.

Warm-Ups (6-8 Minutes)

1. Leg stretch
2. Heel lifts
3. Arm rotators
4. Upper body rotations
5. Sprint-jog intervals

Facility and Equipment

◆ Large outdoor area with a softball diamond, or gym
◆ 2 Wiffle balls per 3 students
◆ 1 bat and batting tee per 3 students
◆ 1 fielding glove per student
◆ 2 regulation softballs per 3 students

Skill Cues

1. Select a bat of proper length and weight.
    ▶ The bat should be long enough to reach across the plate.
    ▶ The bat should be light enough to control on a forceful swing but not feel too heavy.
2. Take a firm grip on the bat by placing the front hand (i.e., closest to the pitcher) on the bottom of the bat and the rear hand on top of the bottom hand. The hands should be together and the knuckles aligned.
3. Face home plate with the feet parallel and shoulder-width apart. Slightly bend the knees, keeping the weight on the back foot. Stand about 6 to 8 inches (15.2-20.3 centimeters) away from the plate, the front foot aligned with the middle of the plate.
4. Lift the rear elbow away from the body and hold the bat off the shoulder in a vertical position perpendicular to the ground.
5. Focus on the ball as it is released; do not watch the pitcher's arm motion.
6. With the eyes focused on the ball, step forward with the front foot about 12 inches (30.5 centimeters) while starting to swing the bat with both arms. The bat should cover the entire surface of the plate during the swing.
7. Keep the rear foot planted while shifting weight forward.
8. Keep the hips and shoulders level.
9. Make contact with the ball in front of the plate, not over it.
10. Swing the bat as quickly as possible to produce power.
11. Roll the top hand over the bottom hand when contacting the ball.
12. Keep both hands on the bat at all times.
13. Swing the bat all the way around to the front shoulder during the follow-through.

Batting stance

Teaching Cue

In activity 4, save ball-retrieving and maximize hitting time by having batters hit the balls into a backstop, fence, or other solid surface.

Activities (30-40 Minutes)

1. Introduce the elements of batting using the skill cues. Explain bat selection, and demonstrate grip, stance, and swing. Stress the importance of developing bat speed; it is the main factor in producing power. (6-8 minutes)

2. Have students select a bat and assume a proper but comfortable batting stance at a plate. Explain the following dynamics of stride while students practice swinging the bat. (6-8 minutes)
   - ▸ Stride forward with the front foot when swinging.
   - ▸ A left- or right-handed batter who strides straight toward the pitcher when swinging has a square stride.
   - ▸ A right-handed batter who steps toward third base has an open stride.
   - ▸ A left-handed batter who steps toward third base has a closed stride.
   - ▸ A right-handed batter who steps toward first base has a closed stride.
   - ▸ A left-handed batter who steps toward first base has an open stride.

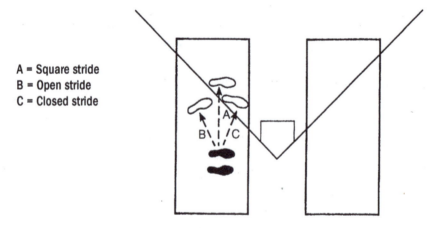

A = Square stride
B = Open stride
C = Closed stride

Batting strides (right-handed batter)

3. Divide students into groups of 5 or 6 and assign 1 batter per group. The batter hits Wiffle balls off the batting tee and the other group members (the fielders) retrieve the balls. After 10 hits, a new batter should be assigned and the activity repeated. (9-12 minutes)

4. Practice batting. Divide students into groups of 3: 1 batter, 1 pitcher, and 1 fielder. The pitcher, standing about 15 feet (4.57 meters) away from and in front of the plate, tosses a Wiffle ball to the batter, standing at a 45-degree angle to the plate. (Use two balls to keep the activity moving.) The fielder retrieves the balls. After 10 pitches, students switch positions. If space is available, you may use regulation balls instead of Wiffle balls, but will need 2 to 3 fielders per group. (9-12 minutes)

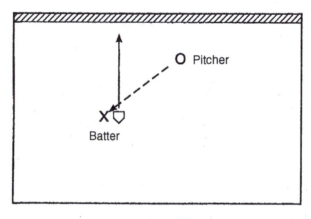

Practice batting

Closure (3-5 Minutes)

Review the lesson with students. Use the following ideas to reinforce learning, check understanding, and provide feedback.

1. Discuss the proper procedure for selecting a bat.
2. Make sure students understand the importance of contacting the ball out in front of the plate (i.e., it allows full arm extension at contact).
3. Have students explain the importance of developing bat speed (i.e., it leads to powerful hitting).

Lesson 6

Base Running

Purpose

In this lesson students learn how to run the bases in softball, specifically the various techniques for running from home to first, first to third, second to home, and home to second.

Warm-Ups (6-8 Minutes)

1. Inverted hurdler's stretch
2. Single-leg crossovers
3. Upper body rotations
4. Triceps dips
5. Abdominal tighteners

Facility and Equipment

- 1 softball diamond per 12 students
- 3 or 4 sets of bases
- 3 or more bats
- 5 or more regulation softballs
- 3 or 4 batting tees
- 1 fielding glove per student

Note: A large gym could also be used with the appropriate indoor bases, but ideally there should be a large enough space to fit three full softball diamonds.

Skill Cues

1. When running from home to first base, take the first step out of the batter's box with the rear foot.
2. Run in a straight path on the right side of the foul line. (Runners are assigned the right half of the base.)
3. Keep a constant stride, running through (i.e., running over and past, or overrunning) first base.
4. Run as quickly as possible.
5. Focus on the base when running; do not watch the ball.
6. Always turn to the right when overrunning first base.
7. Do not overrun second or third base; runners must stop on these bases, or may be put out by the defense.
8. When taking two bases in succession, curve outward slightly when approaching the first base to straighten the path to the final base. Stride to touch the first base with the left foot on the inside corner of the bag.
9. When running to home plate, focus on the plate, maintain a consistent stride, and run over and through the plate, being sure to touch (i.e., step on) it.
10. No stealing or leading off base is allowed; runners are not permitted to leave a base until the batter swings at the ball.

Activities (30-40 Minutes)

1. Introduce base running using the skill cues. Emphasize pathways and which bases may be overrun. (4-6 minutes)

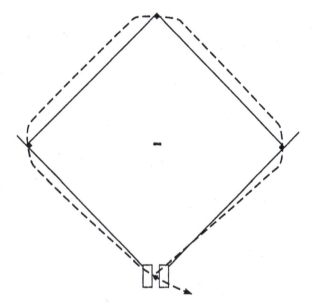

Path of a base runner

2. Scatter students around the diamond and have them simulate standing in a batter's box, performing an imaginary swing, and then taking the first five steps out of the box toward first base. Emphasize taking the first step with the rear foot and focusing the eyes on first base. (3-5 minutes)

3. Place five sets of home plate to first base, 60 feet (18.29 meters) apart and divide students into groups of 4 or 5. Assign each group to a set of bases. Have students swing a bat and run to first base. Remind them to run through the base and turn to the right after they pass it. They should be touching the right side of the base in full stride. (6-8 minutes)

4. Set up 3 or 4 softball diamonds and lay out all the bases in order. Using the same small groups as activity 3, have runners practice running from home to second and from first to third. Emphasize hitting the intermediate base (i.e., first base when running from home to second; second base when running from first to third) on the inside corner with the left foot and remind students that they must stop on their destination base. Remind runners that they cannot lead off base until the batter swings at the ball. (7-8 minutes)

5. Continuing in the same groups, have students start at second base and run home, emphasizing contacting the intermediate base properly (i.e., on its inside corner with the left foot) and running through home in full stride. To add some incentive and challenge to the activity, time the runners. (3-5 minutes)

6. Divide students into groups of 12 and position each group on a softball diamond. Assign 3 or 4 batters; the rest will field the ball. Batters hit a ball from a batting tee and run the bases, stopping when appropriate (e.g., when the ball has been caught). Fielders can rotate positions every 2 or 3 batters, and students should switch roles so that everyone gets the chance to bat. (7-8 minutes)

Closure (3-5 Minutes)

Review the lesson with students. Use the following ideas to reinforce learning, check understanding, and provide feedback.

1. Have students identify which bases they can and cannot overrun.
2. Review how to run bases when there is an intermediate base involved, checking for student understanding.
3. Have students describe the difference between running from home to first and running from first to second (e.g., paths and overrunning).

Offensive and Defensive Position Play

Purpose

In this lesson students learn offensive strategies and defensive position play.

Warm-Ups (6-8 Minutes)

1. Leg stretch
2. Arm pumps
3. V-sit toe taps
4. Run the bases twice.
5. Play catch with a partner.

Skill Cues

Batters

1. Watch the pitched ball carefully.
2. Avoid swinging at pitches outside the strike zone.
3. Hold the bat firmly but avoid tensing the entire body.
4. Be ready to hit every pitch.
5. Run on each batted ball; fielders do make errors.
6. Hit to the opposite field and behind runners.

Base Runners

Once arriving on first base, the batter becomes and stays a base runner until reaching home plate. Base runners

1. must be ready to run on each pitch;
2. should know how many outs there are;
3. should try to advance far enough to leave an empty base behind them (e.g., running to second to leave first base open);
4. should move to the next base when the ball is hit behind them;
5. should not run on fly balls with less than two outs (rather, they should go halfway to the next base on short flies to the outfield and tag up to move on to the next base on long flies to the outfield); and
6. should take a leadoff on every pitch as it passes over the plate.

First Baseman

As its name implies, the first baseman covers first base. Because all batters must touch first base before moving on to other bases and scoring runs, first base is an active position. First basemen

1. must have good catching skills and be able to handle high and low throws;
2. should cover the base, but should not interfere with the runner;
3. should play the inside of the base on throws from the infield; and
4. should play about 6 feet (1.83 meters) to the right and behind the base when no runners are on base.

Second Baseman

This player covers second base but also is responsible for the majority of the infield between first and second bases. Second basemen

1. must be agile to move both left and right to catch ground balls;
2. must be able to relay (i.e., throw or toss) the ball to the shortstop and first baseman, but a strong throwing arm is not required; and
3. should play about 10 to 12 feet (3.05-3.66 meters) to the left of and behind the base.

Shortstop

The most agile of the infielders, the shortstop is responsible for covering the majority of the infield between second and third bases. Because most right-handed batters hit line drives to this area of the field, playing shortstop is a fast-action position requiring speed, coordination, and quick judgment. Shortstops

1. must be quick and able to move both ways very well;
2. should be skilled at fielding ground balls;
3. must have a strong throwing arm;
4. must be able to make highly skilled plays with the second baseman, particularly in turning a double play; and
5. should play between second and third base about 10 to 12 feet (3.05-3.66 meters) behind the base line.

Third Baseman

This position is less demanding than first base simply because fewer runners reach this base. Third basemen

1. must have quick reactions and be very agile;
2. must have a strong throwing arm;
3. must be able to move to the left well and quickly field sharply hit ground balls; and
4. should play 6 to 10 feet (1.83-3.05 meters) left of the base and even with or slightly behind it.

Outfielders

Outfielders see action when batters hit fly balls and long drives, and when ground balls are missed by an infielder. Because they cover the largest area of any defensive player, outfielders must have good running speed. In addition, they must

1. be able to accurately judge the flight of fly balls;
2. have strong throwing arms;
3. be able to block and catch ground balls; and
4. be extremely accurate in their throws.

Teaching Cue

The activities in this lesson simulate game play, but no catcher or pitcher is used by the defense. This lesson is focused toward base running and fielding balls.

Activities (30-40 Minutes)

1. Introduce the various offensive play and defensive play positions using the skill cues. To improve students' understanding, it might be desirable to distribute copies of the field positions formation figure (see the unit introduction on page 310). (7-10 minutes)
2. Divide students into 2 teams and have players from both teams get into defensive positions on a softball diamond. Review the responsibilities of each position. Toss a coin to determine which team will bat first. Rather than bat, however, have students practice various offensive situations by placing some runners on base and hitting the ball from self-tossed balls randomly to different spots on the field. Runners should run after each hit, and infielders and outfielders should play their positions. After three outs, teams switch roles. Continue for several innings. When teams return to the field, have each player play a different position than the inning before. (12-15 minutes)
3. Repeat activity 2, this time allowing offensive players to bat from a batting tee. Runners and fielders should play as the batted balls require. (11-15 minutes)

Closure (3-5 Minutes)

Review the lesson with students. Use the following questions and ideas to reinforce learning, check understanding, and provide feedback.

1. Discuss the offensive strategy of base running.
2. Ask students to describe how to play various infield positions.
3. Ask students to describe the requirements for playing various outfield positions.

Lesson 8

General Defensive Strategy

Purpose

In this lesson students learn general defensive strategies involved in the game of softball. Students will have the opportunity to practice defensive and offensive skills during selected modified game situations.

Facility and Equipment

◆ 1 regulation softball diamond or a large outdoor area
◆ 1 set of bases
◆ 1 fielding glove per student
◆ 1 bat per 5 students
◆ 3 regulation (or softer rubberized) softballs per 5 students

Warm-Ups (6-8 Minutes)

1. Arm pumps
2. Leg stretch
3. Waist twists
4. Upper body rotations
5. Play catch with a partner.

Skill Cues

1. The primary task of a fielder is to field the ball and then to make an accurate throw to a base.
2. Before the ball is pitched, be mentally prepared. Know
   ▶ how many outs there are and what hitting skills the next batter possesses,
   ▶ what play to make if the ball approaches,
   ▶ where to throw (i.e., which base) on every play, and
   ▶ when to cover the base for a force or tag play.
3. Always play for the sure out.
4. Back up the adjacent outfielders.
5. When balls are hit past the outfielders, either the second baseman or the shortstop must go out for a relay throw.
6. Anticipate and react to each move by the offensive team.
7. Communicate with one another to determine who will catch the ball and where it will be thrown.
8. Good judgment about when and where to throw the ball is essential.

Activities (30-40 Minutes)

1. Introduce defensive strategy using the skill cues. (6-8 minutes)
2. Have students work in groups of 5: 2 outfielders, 2 infielders, and 1 batter. Outfielders should practice backing each other up and throwing to selected

bases while infielders alternate turns covering the base or going into the out-field for the relay throw if the outfielders miss the ball. (10-15 minutes)

3. Continuing with the same setup, the batter hits ground balls to the infielders, who in turn field the ball and throw to a selected base. Outfielders should practice backing up the throws by running toward the bases in case of overthrows (5-7 minutes).

4. Divide the class into 2 teams, 1 team in the field and 1 at bat. Have the defensive team practice fielding and throwing balls to the correct base after identifying how many outs there are and how many runners are on base. Set up various scenarios and game situations to test defensive players' skills and judgment about what to do with the ball when it is hit to them. Offensive players should run the bases. Play until three outs; then switch teams. (9-10 minutes)

Closure (3-5 Minutes)

Review the lesson with students. Use the following ideas to reinforce learning, check understanding, and provide feedback.

1. Have students identify three important defensive points that infielders should know (i.e., number of outs, hitters' strengths and weaknesses; and where to throw the ball).

2. Review outfielders' responsibility in backing up one another.

3. Discuss the importance of communication between players (i.e., it improves the effectiveness of the defense).

Lesson 9

Modified Game Play

Purpose

In this lesson students practice their softball skills in modified games that lead up to a regulation game of softball.

Warm-Ups (6-8 Minutes)

1. Push-offs
2. Upper body rotations
3. Back stretch
4. Arm circles
5. Play catch with a partner.

Teaching Cues

1. Decide on a rotation system before game play.
2. Assign students to the following positions for each team:
   - ▶ First base
   - ▶ Second base
   - ▶ Shortstop
   - ▶ Third base
   - ▶ Left fielder
   - ▶ Left center fielder
   - ▶ Right center fielder
   - ▶ Right fielder
   - ▶ Pitcher
   - ▶ Catcher
3. Require students to switch positions each inning.
4. You may want to add additional players to each team.

Activities (30-40 Minutes)

1. Review the various skill cues needed to play the game of softball. (6-8 minutes)
2. Divide students into teams of 15 (the extra 5 players are batters), explain the rules, and play a game of lineup softball. (12-17 minutes)

Lineup Softball

This game requires every student on the offensive team's lineup to bat once each inning. The team keeps track of the number of runs scored each inning. (An inning ends when all players from both teams have batted once.) After everyone on the team has batted once, the teams switch position.

3. Divide the class into two teams and play one-pitch rotation softball. (12-15 minutes)

One-Pitch Rotation Softball

This variation speeds up the game of softball tremendously. Things happen quickly and the game is well-liked by students. Once the defensive team gets the rotation down pat, it goes very smoothly.

In this game each batter comes to the plate with a count of 2 strikes and 3 balls for each turn at bat. Batters will either get a hit, a walk, or a strike-out on the first pitch. Any foul balls are automatic outs. Those who get a hit run the bases as they would in softball, trying to stay safe and eventually score.

At each out, the following rotation occurs (encourage students to hustle during rotation):

▸ The student making the out rotates to right field.
▸ The right fielder goes to right center field.
▸ The right center fielder rotates to left center field.
▸ The left center fielder rotates to left field.
▸ The left fielder rotates to third base.
▸ The third baseman rotates to shortstop.
▸ The shortstop goes to second base.
▸ The second baseman goes to first base.
▸ The first baseman becomes the pitcher.
▸ The pitcher becomes the catcher.
▸ The catcher goes to the end of the batting line.

When students score, the offense continues to bat.

Closure (3-5 Minutes)

Review the lesson with students. Use the following ideas to reinforce learning, check understanding, and provide feedback.

1. Review general defensive strategies utilized by different playing positions.
2. Distribute handouts of regulation softball rules. Tell students to study and be sure they know all the rules before the next class period, when a regulation softball game will be played.

Lesson 10

Regulation Game

Purpose

In this lesson students play a regulation game of softball.

Facility and Equipment

◆ 2 outdoor softball diamonds
◆ 2 sets of bases per diamond
◆ 2 sets of catcher's equipment per diamond
◆ 1 fielding glove per student
◆ 1 regulation softball per diamond

Warm-Ups (6-8 Minutes)

1. Slapping jacks
2. Upper body rotations
3. Grapevine step
4. Play catch with a partner.
5. Arm circles

Teaching Cues

1. Try to have enough games going that all students are active. If space is limited or class size makes this impossible, choose a rotation system that will enable equal playing time for students. Extra students should practice their softball skills in an assigned area while waiting to be rotated into the game.
2. Assign teams and positions before the start of the game.
3. Require all players to switch positions at the end of each inning.

Activities (30-40 Minutes)

1. Review the various skill cues for softball and go over the rules. Ask if students have any questions. (5-10 minutes)
2. Divide students into four teams and explain the rotation system (if needed) that will allow everyone to play. Start both games of regulation softball. (25-30 minutes)

Closure (3-5 Minutes)

Review the lesson with students. Use the following questions and ideas to reinforce learning, check understanding, and provide feedback.

1. Discuss ways to improve team play (e.g., better communication).
2. Ask students to identify offensive and defensive strategies that were effective during game play.

Assessment and Resources

As with most team-oriented sports, formative, authentic assessment is preferred. Checklists, self-assessments, and peer evaluations are excellent tools for assessing students' performances and knowledge of the game in this unit. Formative assessment during the earlier lessons, which stress psychomotor skill development, is recommended. This provides students with feedback and, if necessary, refocuses their learning to improve their skills.

More traditional forms of skill testing are suggested here to complete the assessment process.

▶ Throwing evaluation. Have students throw for accuracy at a target. Give 10 trials and count points based on the size of the target.

▶ Fielding evaluation. Hit 5 ground balls and 5 fly balls to students. Award points for successful fielding.

▶ Batting evaluation. Have students bat five balls from a batting tee, awarding points for each ball solidly struck.

▶ Pitching evaluation. Require students to pitch five balls to a target from a distance of 40 feet (12.19 meters). Award points for hitting the target.

Resources

Griffin, L., S. Mitchell, and J. Oslin. 1997. *Teaching sport concepts and skills*. Champaign, IL: Human Kinetics.

Mood, D., F. Musker, and J. Rink. 1999. *Sports and recreational activities*. 12th ed. New York: McGraw-Hill.

Philipp, J., and J. Wilkerson. 1990. *Teaching team sports: A coeducational approach*. Champaign, IL: Human Kinetics.

Sabock, R. 2000. *Coaching: A realistic perspective*. 6th ed. San Diego: Collegiate Press.

Schmottlach, N., and J. McManama. 1997. *The physical education handbook*. 9th ed. Needham Heights, MA: Allyn & Bacon.

Tennis

Historical evidence indicates that a game similar to tennis was played in the ancient civilizations of the Orient, Rome, Greece, Egypt, and Persia hundreds of years before Christ. Modern-day tennis developed in England and France, where it was popular in the 16th and 17th centuries, but wars and the resulting economic and social conditions virtually eradicated the sport in Europe after that.

Mary Outerbridge is credited with bringing tennis to the United States in the mid-1870s by introducing it to the Staten Island Cricket and Baseball Club. The popularity of the sport and increasing numbers of players led in 1880 to the establishment of the U.S. Lawn Tennis Association (USLTA), which still governs the game today. (Lawn was officially dropped from its name in the 1970s; it is now the USTA). Tennis began as a lawn sport, but clay, asphalt, and concrete later became the standard surfaces because they could be maintained economically despite heavy public use.

Tennis enjoyed its greatest surge of interest in the U.S. during the 1970s. Once tournaments were routinely aired on television, requests for tennis club memberships, indoor courts, and tennis lessons skyrocketed. Touring tennis tournaments and expanded media coverage raised public interest even further. Today, most people are familiar with the most prestigious tennis tournaments, among them the U.S. Open, the Australian Open, the French Open, and Wimbledon. At the 1998 Olympic Games in Seoul, Korea, tennis attained full status as an official medal sport.

Tennis is a sport that appeals to many, whether old or young, experienced or novice. It is relatively inexpensive, as far as sports go, and in most states it can be played year 'round. Tennis is also accessible. Most cities and townships, not to mention schools and community parks, have courts available for public use. Unlike many other sports, particularly the team sports, tennis requires only 2 or 4 players for an actual game. Although proficiency will dictate the level of competition, tennis can be played by both genders and all age groups. Indeed, an estimated 15 million Americans of all ages play tennis regularly.

Equipment

A tennis racket, tennis balls, court shoes, and comfortable clothing are all that is required for tennis. The price of this equipment and gear varies widely, and is often a function of brand name and performance characteristics. Rackets, for example, range in price from $25 to $400. In general, the higher the cost, the lighter and more balanced the racket. For players new to the sport, however, the single most important factor in purchasing a racket is the grip. (Players can ask a local pro to recommend a grip size. Many pros today recommend that a player use the largest grip size that he or she feels comfortable with. Typical grips on adult rackets range from 4 3/8 to 4 5/8 with 4 1/2 being the most common.)

Good assistance in sizing the grip to the hand is usually found in most sporting goods stores. Grip size should be based mainly on how the grip feels. A serve and volley player will choose a larger grip than a baseline or all-around player. New players to the sport are usually more interested in a lightweight racket because it places less stress on the elbow.

Of course, the court itself is necessary for tennis. A regulation tennis court is 78 feet (23.77 meters) long and is bisected by a net that is 3 feet, 6 inches (1.07 meters) high at each post and 36 inches (91.4 centimeters) high at the center. Court width differs for singles and doubles (see the figure on page 340). Almost all public courts are concrete or asphalt. Concrete courts are more costly to install but less costly to maintain. Concrete courts usually "play faster," meaning the ball bounces more quickly However, balls and shoes wear out faster on concrete courts, and players' feet and legs tend to tire more easily.

Unit Organization

Because the skill level of students will vary greatly, depending on their ability to learn the skills as well as their previous experience, this unit stresses ground stroke development and the serve. If learned correctly and mastered, these skills will give students a good measure of playing success. If students are more advanced, alternate tennis skills (e.g., half lob, slice serve, ball spin) and higher standards (e.g., accuracy, successful completion) may be emphasized.

Following is a brief summary of the lessons in this unit.

▶ Lessons 1, 2, and 3 address the forehand and backhand ground strokes as well as the footwork required to hit successful ground strokes.

▶ In lesson 4 students learn the basic or flat serve.

▶ Lesson 5 provides more practice on ground strokes and serves.

▶ The lob and doubles play are introduced in lesson 6.

▶ Lesson 7 presents the volley and continues instruction on developing doubles play.

▶ The smash is introduced in lesson 8.

▶ Lessons 9 and 10 offer a two-flight round-robin tournament.

Selected resources and assessment ideas are found in the assessment and resources section at the end of the unit.

The lessons in this unit are organized to accommodate 30 students on 4 to 6 courts. Singles play has been omitted from this unit because court space is usually insufficient to accommodate most class enrollments.

As with every lesson in this book, class periods may be added to cover certain topics and allow for extra practice on certain skills. Lessons may also be split to accommodate extended game play or testing.

Note: An asterisk (*) following a facility or equipment listing indicates that preparation is required before the lesson.

Social Skills and Etiquette

Basic courtesies of the court include the following:

▶ Do not interrupt play on other courts by retrieving balls or walking behind players while play is in progress.

▶ Make sure that the receiver is ready before serving.

▶ Replay points if questions or interruptions occur.

▶ Allow the receiver to call illegal serves.

Because differences in skill development will be apparent among students, tolerance and patience should be stressed in class, especially to those students who have attained higher levels of skill. Along the same lines, understand that tennis is not much fun—nor are playing skills strengthened—when opponents are unevenly matched. Students who are outmatched experience little success and can quickly become discouraged or feel intimidated by better players. Skilled players experience too little challenge and can quickly become bored when matched with less-skilled players. While it is important to encourage students of all levels of ability, it is advisable to group students of similar skill levels during games and rallying drills. To promote class unity, however, you may also want to ask skilled players to assist their less-skilled classmates during drills.

Lesson Modifications

Students experiencing extreme difficulty with ball control or those with mobility problems can use Wiffle or Nerf balls early in skill development. To accommodate students having difficulty getting to the ball, you may also

modify the rules to allow the ball to bounce more than once on each side of the court (e.g., after the serve, during the rally).

Serving and playing techniques can also be modified to accommodate students who are having difficulty. For example, they can serve closer to the net (i.e., between the baseline and the service line) or start the serve with the racket behind the back (i.e., in the back-scratching position). Students with inadequate arm strength to maintain a firm racket throughout the stroke may choke up on the racket (i.e., grip the racket toward the throat).

If court space is very limited, or if class enrollment is larger than 30, drill formations can be modified to accommodate larger numbers of students. The following figures show drill formations that allow 12, 16, and 18 students to be on the same court.

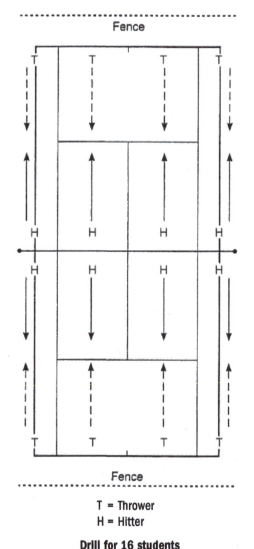

T = Thrower
H = Hitter

Drill for 12 students

T = Thrower
H = Hitter

Drill for 16 students

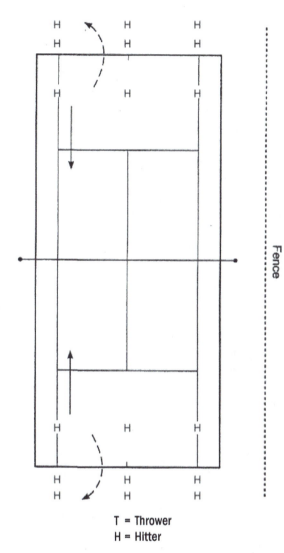

H   H   H
H   H   H

H   H   H

H   H   H

H   H   H
H   H   H

Fence

T = Thrower
H = Hitter

Drill for 18 students

Safety

Tennis is a relatively safe activity. Students should of course be discouraged from swinging rackets in close proximity to others, hitting others with the racket, and hitting or throwing balls at other students. To avoid accidental collisions and hits with the racket or balls, the following safety procedures should be implemented:

▶ For drills that involve swinging a racket, maintain adequate distance between students.

▶ For hitting drills, have students face the same direction. Hitting toward fences works quite well.

▶ In doubles play, partners should call shots that could be taken by either player.

▶ Smooth-soled tennis shoes, rather than running or traction shoes, are a must to keep from turning over ankles on fast changes in direction and stopping.

Rules

The basic game involves serving, stroking, footwork, and endurance which are enhanced with mental planning, concentration, and ferreting out the opponent's weaknesses. Although singles play is not taught in this unit, singles and doubles tennis rules are essentially the same, with the exception of sideline boundaries.

Boundaries

In doubles play, the outer sidelines (see "doubles sideline" on the figure located on the following page) and baseline delimit the court. In singles play, the inner sidelines (see "singles sideline" on the figure) and baseline delimit the court. On the serve or in play, when a ball lands on or touches a line, it is good.

Scoring

Scoring in tennis is made up of points, games, sets, and matches. It takes 4 points to win a game, 6 games to win a set, and either 2 out of 3 or 3 out of 5 sets to win the match. Each game must be won by a margin of 2 points and each set by 2 games unless the games are tied at 6-all. Then a tiebreaker occurs whereby a number of points are set (7, 9, or 12) and opponents rotate service after each point until the agreed-upon point is reached with a 2-point margin.

The following terms are used to designate points and advantages.

▶ Love = 0 points

▶ 15 = 1 point

▶ 30 = 2 points

▶ 40 = 3 points

▶ Game = 4 points

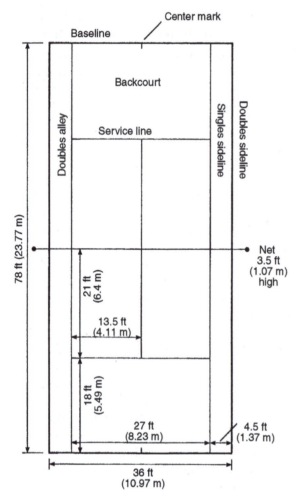

Tennis court dimensions

▶ Deuce = tie at 30-all or 40-all

Advantage in (ad-in) = server's point

▶ Advantage out (ad-out) = opponent's point

When a deuce score is reached, play continues until one team scores two consecutive points (i.e., two ad-ins or two ad-outs)

Serving

The service areas are delimited by the baseline, center mark, and singles or doubles sidelines. Servers must stand behind the baseline and between the center mark and either the right or left singles sideline (for singles) or doubles sideline (for doubles). The first serve of each game is from the right side, and all serves are crosscourt (diagonally) to the receiver).

The server has two chances to serve legally into the opponent's service court. If both serves do not land within the receiver's service court or if the server double faults, the receiver wins the point (see lesson 5). If the ball hits the net on the serve and falls into the correct service court, it is a "let" and is served again; it is a fault if it lands anywhere else.

After each point, the server alternates service courts until the game is over and then the opponent serves the next game. In doubles, one player serves every fourth game, rotating serving sides after each game.

The game starts with one player serving from the right side. If the serve is legal, the receiver must let the ball bounce once before returning it. If the serve is not returned legally, the server gets the point. If the serve is legally returned, game play continues until the ball is hit out-of-bounds, into the net, or missed. The team not making the error scores the point. Then the sequence starts again with the server serving from the other side. The server scores an "ace" (still one point) whenever the receiver is unable to touch the ball with the racket.

During the rally, players hit the ball back and forth trying to place the ball so that the opponent cannot reach it on one bounce. Mixing shots, ball spin, and playing to the opponent's weak side are basic strategies in game play.

A player (or team) wins a point if the opponent(s)

▶ double faults on the serve,

▶ does not return a ball before a second bounce,

▶ does not return the ball inbounds,

▶ touches the net or post (e.g., with the racket, clothing, or any part of the body)

▶ reaches across the net to return a ball (follow-through may carry across the net), or

▶ plays the ball more than once on a side.

Other rules include the following:

▶ In doubles, once a serving and receiving rotation is decided, it must be followed throughout the set.

▶ Players change sides of the net after all even-numbered games.

▶ A ball that touches the net during play before falling into the opponent's court is good and play continues.

▶ A "let" can be called for a dispute over a call or distraction. The point is replayed.

▶ Balls landing on lines are good and in play. The ball must be entirely outside the line to fault.

Lesson 1

Ground Stroke—Forehand Drive

Purpose

In this lesson students learn to prepare for and execute a forehand drive.

Warm-Ups (6-8 Minutes)

1. Side slides
2. Forward lunges
3. Waist twists
4. Arm rotators
5. Reverse run

Skill Cues

1. For the Eastern forehand grip, "shake hands" with the racket; form a V with the thumb and forefinger, centered on the top of the grip. The forefinger should be slightly separated from the rest of the hand.
2. Get into the ready position by facing the net with the feet shoulder-width apart, knees flexed, and weight slightly forward on the balls of the feet. Grip with the dominant hand and hold the racket throat lightly with the other hand.

Eastern forehand grip

Forehand Drive

1. Draw the racket back behind the shoulder, turning the nonracket side toward the net and planting the weight over the back foot.
2. Swing the racket forward by stepping into the ball, shifting weight forward, locking the wrist, and gripping firmly.
3. Keep the stroke flat, contacting the ball just ahead of the torso.
4. Stroke through the ball as long as possible, finishing (i.e., following through) with the racket head high and over the opposite shoulder.

Teaching Cues

1. Remind students of the following throughout this lesson:
   ▶ Watch the oncoming ball and move into position quickly.
   ▶ Start drawing the racket back before turning and planting the back foot.
   ▶ Do not move the wrist during the swing.
   ▶ Rotate the shoulders into the striking zone.
   ▶ Keep the eyes on the contact point a second after contact.
2. Be aware of differences in skill levels and group students accordingly.
3. Introduce footwork and stroking first without and then with equipment.

Activities (32-40 Minutes)

Ready position

1. Position students in a scatter formation facing you (position left-handed students on the left). Have them take a ready position and assume the hand positions for holding a racket. Demonstrate the motion of the forehand drive, calling attention to each part of the stroke. Then use a shadow drill, calling out the parts of the stroke: ready position, stroke sequence (see skill cues), and back to ready position. All students should move in unison during the drill. Make general corrections as necessary and ask students to think about their movements. When most students seem proficient, ask them to close their eyes and repeat the same exercise. (3-5 minutes)

2. Position students in a semicircle facing you. Explain and demonstrate the forehand grip (see skill cue 1). Have students use a buddy system to check one another while you walk around the class and check grips. (3-4 minutes)

3. Using the same formation as in activity 1, repeat the drill with rackets, emphasizing the skill and teaching cues. (3 minutes)

Optional Activity: Self-Dropped Hand-Hitting Drill

4. Have students stand sideways near a wall (or fence) and hit dropped balls 10 times with a racket. Remind them to keep their eyes on the point of contact and hit through the ball. (5-6 minutes)

5. Tossed ball drill. Divide the class into groups of 3 with all hitters facing the same direction. In each group, 1 student will toss the ball to the hitter's forehand side, 1 student will practice the forehand drive, and 1 student will retrieve balls. Hitters should assume a ready position before each tossed ball and try to hit each ball straight forward. After 8 to 10 hits, students should switch roles. (10-12 minutes)

6. Footwork drill. Position students in a scatter formation around the gym, facing the same direction. They should assume a ready position, but without rackets. Call out the following commands, instructing students to move accordingly:

   ▸ Slide to the left
   ▸ Slide to the right
   ▸ Slide forward (i.e., gallop)
   ▸ Slide backward
   ▸ Slide diagonally forward and backward
   ▸ Crossover (right over left, then left over right)
   ▸ Cross-behind (right behind left, then left behind right)

   Now combine callouts (specify the number) with turning to the dominant hand side, and performing an imaginary forehand drive. (5 minutes)

7. Repeat activity 6, this time using a racket. Spread students 8 to 10 feet (2.44-3.05 meters) apart (left-handed students on the left) and direct them to concentrate on moving smoothly, getting into position to hit a forehand drive, watching for the oncoming (imaginary) ball, stroking through it, and then resuming a ready position. (3-5 minutes)

Optional Activity

Self-Dropped Hand-Hitting Drill (0-3 Minutes)

Students stand sideways to a wall (or fence) and hit dropped balls 10 times with the open palm of the hand. On the backswing, they should concentrate on transferring their weight over the back foot; on the forward swing, weight should be forward and into the ball.

Closure (3-5 Minutes)

Review the lesson with students. Use the following questions and ideas to reinforce learning, check understanding, and provide feedback.

1. Have students close their eyes and think through each phase of hitting a forehand drive. Then have them visualize performing each phase.

2. Discuss why a firm grip is so important when contacting the ball (i.e., the racket will "stutter" on contact, hence the loss of ball control), also where the ball should be in relation to the body at contact.

3. Ask students how much control they had in hitting straight balls during the tossed ball drill.

Ground Stroke—Backhand Drive

Purpose

In this lesson students will become more proficient with the forehand drive and develop basic skills for the backhand drive.

Warm-Ups (6-8 Minutes)

1. Arm rotators
2. Shoulder pushes
3. Footwork drill (see lesson 1, activity 6)
4. Push-ups
5. Lateral hops

Facility and Equipment

◆ Tennis court (with a fence) or gym
◆ 1 racket per student
◆ 3 balls per student

Skill Cues

1. Take an Eastern forehand grip, rotate the hand slightly inward so that the **V** is on the left top bevel (diagonal side) of the racket handle, and spread the thumb across the back of the grip.
2. Focus on the oncoming ball and get into position quickly.
3. For a two-handed backhand drive, use a backhand grip with the dominant hand and a forehand grip with the other hand on top and touching the dominant hand.
4. For more power, take a small step on the forward foot toward the net just before contact.
5. Focus on the contact point until just after contact.

Two-handed backhand grip (right-handed)

Backhand Drive

1. During the backhand drive, flex the knees; backswing straight, taking the racket across the body; step on the back foot; and carry the free (i.e., nonracket) hand into the backswing before releasing.
2. Rotate the shoulders so that the racket side of the back is facing the net and the weight is over the back foot.
3. Shift the weight forward and swing the racket parallel to the court surface, lock the wrist and hold the racket with a firm grip, contacting the ball ahead of the forward foot.
4. Swing through, toward the net, across the front of the body, letting the racket rise slightly.

Teaching Cues

1. Remind students to keep their shoulders perpendicular to the target.
2. On the toss and hit drill, students should begin and end in a ready position.

Activities (30-40 Minutes)

1. Review the forehand grip and drive from lesson 1. Then repeat the tossed ball drill (see lesson 1, activity 5). (4-6 minutes)

2. Explain and demonstrate the Eastern backhand grip. Have students practice while you check for correctness. Present the backhand drive according to the skill cues. Emphasize each element of the backhand drive, stepping into the shot, and carrying the ball on the strings as long as possible. (4-6 minutes)

3. Foot shadow drill. Have students scatter around the court or gym, about 8 to 10 feet (2.44-3.05 meters) apart (left-handed players on the left or forming a single row), facing you and in a ready position. Call out the following commands and have students move accordingly (opposite directions for left-handed students). Continue the drill until students can smoothly execute the swing and footwork. (4-6 minutes)

Eastern backhand grip

   ▸ Pivot and turn on the left foot (left-handed students: on the right foot).
   ▸ Step across with the right foot (left-handed students: with the left foot).
   ▸ Look at the approaching ball over the right shoulder (left-handed students: over the left shoulder).
   ▸ Accelerate the racket toward contact while shifting weight to the forward foot.
   ▸ Follow through toward the net, letting the racket head rise in a perpendicular plane.
   ▸ Finish the swing just above shoulder height, the racket turning slightly downward.
   ▸ Bring the trailing leg forward, ending in a ready position.

4. Toss and hit drill. Pair up students. One partner tosses balls to the other partner's backhand side and the other practices the backhand drive. Hitters should begin and end in the ready position. For safety, all hitters should be hitting in the same direction on courts or into the perimeter fence. After 5 or 6 backhands, partners switch roles. (5-6 minutes)

Optional Activity: Baseline Backhand Drill

5. Forehand and backhand tossed ball drill. Position students in groups of 4: 1 hits from midcourt or deeper, 1 tosses from across the net, and 2 retrieve. Tossers should throw 10 balls, mixing forehand and backhand and making hitters move forward and backward to reach the ball. Rotate players until all have had a chance to hit. (7-8 minutes)

6. Rally drill. Pair up students; then position partners on a court and let them rally the ball back and forth using forehand and backhand ground strokes. Remind students that when rallying or playing, the ball never comes to an ideal

spot. They should start to move as soon as the ball leaves the opponent's racket, keeping the racket face above the wrist and both hands on the racket while moving toward the ball. (6-8 minutes)

Optional Activity

Baseline Backhand Drill (0-6 Minutes)

This drill should be done outdoors. Position students in groups of 4: 1 hitting, 1 drop tossing, and 2 retrieving (1 on each side of the net). Hitters should be in the baseline area in a ready position, and tossers should stand slightly ahead and 4 or 5 feet (1.22-1.52 meters) to the backhand side of the hitters. Tossers drop the ball and move out of the way; then hitters move into position and stroke the ball after the bounce. After each hitter gets to hit six balls, students should switch roles.

Closure (3-5 Minutes)

Review the lesson with students. Use the following questions and ideas to reinforce learning, check understanding, and provide feedback.

1. Have students close their eyes and visualize each phase of a backhand drive, talking themselves through the entire sequence.
2. Ask students to identify the most troublesome aspect of the backhand drive. How many tried to use a two-handed backhand? Did they find it easier, and if so, what made it easier?
3. Ask students to identify where most of the breakdowns in performing successful ground strokes occurred (e.g., timing? getting in position? loose grip on contact? open or closed racket face on contact? follow-through?).

Lesson 3

Ground Stroke Control

Purpose

In this lesson students continue to increase their proficiency on forehand and backhand ground strokes.

Warm-Ups (6-8 Minutes)

1. Shoulder shrugs
2. Footwork drill (see lesson 1, activity 6)
3. Waist twists
4. Imaginary jump rope
5. Sprint-jog intervals

Skill Cues

1. Assume a ready position with a relaxed grip.
2. Track the oncoming ball and move into a ready position with the knees flexed.
3. Draw the racket back early, turn sideways to the net, and shift weight forward and upward into the ball with a firm wrist grip.
4. Follow through with the racket face perpendicular to the court surface and raising and slightly rotating the arm at the completion of the swing. Quickly resume a ready position.
5. Don't crowd the ball. Learn to control it at arm's length.
6. Try to contact the ball in the center of the racket face, watching the ball hit the racket (contact point).

Teaching Cues

1. Tell students to swing through the ball as if there were three balls coming in succession. (Most beginners have a tendency to stop most of their forward momentum on contact.)
2. Remind students to drive the ball as long as possible toward the net.

Activities (30-40 Minutes)

1. Ball control drill. Pair up students. Position partners deep in the service courts on opposite sides of the net. Partners rally the ball gently back and forth, coming through with the racket head slowly and clearing the net by 3 to 5 feet (.91-1.52 meters). They should hit the ball 10 consecutive times, counting each time the ball is hit in front of the service court line. If either player goes outside the service court area to return the ball, or if either player is unable to return the ball properly, they should restart the rally. After reaching 10 consecutive re-

turns, students should move to midcourt and rally 10 consecutive times at that distance. If students are successful, they should move behind the baseline and use all ground strokes from that distance (even if they have to wait for the ball to bounce several times). If there are not enough courts for 2 sets of players on each court, arrange 3 or 4 players on each side of the net and have the closest player take the shot. (10-12 minutes)

2. Position four players on a court to rally using both forehand and backhand ground strokes. Encourage students to take different places on the court so that each gets to take shots from all positions (i.e., both sides, midcourt, and deep court). Remind students to watch the ball at all times and carry their rackets in a ready position when waiting for a return ball. (10-14 minutes)

Optional Activity: Forehand and Backhand Drill

3. Ground stroke game. Position 2 teams of 3 players on each court. (If courts are limited, have extra students wait at the sides and rotate in every 3 minutes. They can also hit drop shots into the fence or rally against a wall.) A player from the first team puts the ball in play from the baseline with a drop hit, getting two chances to hit it into the opposite court. Then teams rally back and forth, hitting the ball regardless of the number of bounces to return it over the net. (Add a one-bounce rule for skilled players.) Any player may hit the ball until it is hit out-of-bounds (lines are in play) or hits the net. The team not making an error scores a point. The game continues until one team scores 5 points. (10-14 minutes)

Optional Activity

Forehand and Backhand Drill (0-10 Minutes)

Divide the class into groups of 8 students per court—4 hitters and 4 retrievers (see the figure). The most skilled drop hitter in the retriever group (X_1 in the figure) drop hits consecutive balls, sending the ball to the first hitter in line (O_1 in the figure), who returns it using either a forehand or backhand ground stroke and then goes quickly to the end of the line. Retrievers feed balls to drop hitter. Continue until all hitters have had 4 or 5 turns; then groups should rotate (hitters become retrievers) so that all students get the chance to hit.

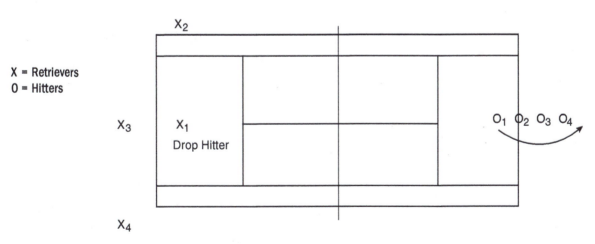

Forehand and backhand drill

Closure (3-5 Minutes)

Review the lesson with students. Use the following ideas to reinforce learning, check understanding, and provide feedback.

1. Share your observations about how successfully students executed forehand and backhand shots. Point out problems (e.g., weak shots, trouble hitting from midcourt to baseline or baseline to baseline, high and out-of-control shots).

2. Discuss whether students are moving to meet the ball, carrying their racket head up with both hands, and getting into good position.

3. Share other observations about students' strengths and weaknesses in executing good ground strokes.

Lesson 4

Serve

Purpose

In this lesson students learn to execute the basic tennis serve.

Facility and Equipment

◆ Tennis court (with a fence) or gym
◆ 1 racket per student
◆ 3 balls per student

Warm-Ups (6-8 Minutes)

1. Upper body rotations
2. Elbow-knee touches (standing)
3. Slapping jacks
4. Elbow squeezes
5. Jog around the perimeter of the court

Skill Cues

The following series of movements is for the right-handed overhand serve.

1. Take a forehand or continental grip (i.e., halfway between forehand and backhand). Stand with the left hip and shoulder sideways to the net and the left foot pointing to the right net post.
2. Hold the ball lightly in the fingers of the left hand and gently rest that hand against the racket throat. Hold the racket head up and point it toward the opponent's service court.
3. Coordinate the following movements into one sequential movement:
   ▶ Start the ball hand and racket downward together (take away), swinging the racket hand away from the body and flexing the knees.
   ▶ Toss the ball upward, extending the knees and leaning slightly forward while starting the racket upward behind the back.
   ▶ Lead with the elbow, swinging the racket upward and forward. Extend the body upward over the balls of the feet.
   ▶ With full arm extension, contact the ball ahead of the forward (left) foot, the racket face slightly closed over the descending ball. Shift weight forward and downward on contacting the ball.
   ▶ Follow through by swinging outward, across, and downward, and then step forward with the back (right) foot.
4. Visualize the total serve sequence.

Overhand serve sequence

Teaching Cues

1. Teach the ball toss separately.
2. Be sure students toss the ball up with a straight arm.
3. Have students be purposeful in executing the serve. Tell them not just to take swings but to think about their actions.

Activities (30-40 Minutes)

1. Explain and demonstrate the ball toss (without contacting the ball with the racket) using the appropriate skill and teaching cues. Position students behind a line, standing sideways, the feet shoulder-width apart, the trailing foot parallel to the line, and the forward foot pointing diagonally forward. Students should hold the ball between the thumb and the pointer and middle fingers. Instruct them to extend the tossing arm forward, flex the knees, raise the arm and body, keep a firm wrist, and toss the ball, releasing it when the arm is fully extended. (Remind them to follow the ball with their eyes.) The toss should not put any spin on the ball, and the ball should reach a little higher than the reach of the racket. The ball should drop about 12 inches (30.5 centimeters) in front of the forward foot. Have students practice tossing the ball 12 to 15 times, checking the landing spot after each toss. (4-6 minutes)

Optional Activity: Partner Check

2. Shadow serve drill. Explain and demonstrate the phases of the serve (using the continental grip) without the ball using the skill and teaching cues. If students are beginners, you may want to use the back-scratching position to start the serve instead of the full swing. After a few demonstrations, have students perform the sequence. (3-5 minutes)

3. Position students behind the baseline facing the fence to practice the overhand serve. Emphasize the following:

    ▷ tossing the ball without putting a spin on it,

    ▷ reaching high to hit,

    ▷ shifting weight upward when tossing and then downward when hitting the ball, and

    ▷ following through outward, across, and downward. (3-5 minutes)

Continental grip

4. Position 2 groups of 3 students on each court: 1 serves from behind the service line and 2 retrieve balls on the other side of the net. (All servers are on the same side of the net.) Servers should serve 6 to 8 balls, aiming into the diagonally opposite service court, and then switch service areas. After students have served from both service sides, they should switch roles so that all students get to practice their serves. (10-12 minutes)

5. Practice activity 4 from midcourt. Experienced players can practice from behind the baseline. When students are serving successfully 50 percent of the time, have them move behind the baseline and practice their serves. (10-12 minutes)

Optional Activity

Partner Check (0-3 Minutes)

Pair up students. One partner should practice the ball toss while the other partner checks for proper form and movement (e.g., flexing the knees, keeping the wrist straight, releasing the ball when the arm is fully extended, watching the ball, tossing the ball high enough that it reaches the top of the racket head, and so on).

Closure (3-5 Minutes)

Review the lesson with students. Use the following ideas to reinforce learning, check understanding, and provide feedback.

1. Discuss the elements of a good ball toss, the serving stance, and the sequence of the overhand serve.

2. Ask students to share their success rates on the serve practice (e.g., 1 out of 3, 1 out of 2).

3. Share your observations about students' serves, including form and coordination of the overall sequence.

Lesson 5

Serve and Ground Strokes

Purpose

In this lesson students learn serving rules and continue to refine their serving and ground stroke skills.

Facility and Equipment

◆ Tennis court
◆ 1 racket per student
◆ 3 balls per student

Warm-Ups (6-8 Minutes)

1. Side slides
2. Upper body rotations
3. Arm pumps
4. Side stretch
5. Jog around the perimeter of the court

Teaching Cues

1. Review the skill cues for ground strokes (see lessons 1, 2, and 3).
2. Review the skill cues for the serve (see lesson 4).
3. Explain the following serving rules. The server
   ▶ may stand anywhere between the center mark and the singles sideline (for singles) or doubles sideline (for doubles) but must remain stationary during the serve.
   ▶ may not step on the baseline or into the court until the ball is contacted.
   ▶ may use an overhand, sidearm, or underhand serve as long as the ball is struck before hitting the court.
   ▶ may catch the toss or let the ball hit the court. If a server makes no attempt to swing the racket, it is not a fault; if the server swings and misses, it is a fault.
   ▶ has two attempts to put the ball properly into play (i.e., making it fall into the diagonally opposite service court).
   ▶ should call the score before the serve, giving the server's score first.
4. Explain a let serve (see the unit introduction rules section on page 339).
5. Explain the following rules governing receivers of the serve. Receivers
   ▶ may stand anywhere but must let the ball bounce once before returning it.
   ▶ lose the point if they contact the ball before it lands in the service court.

Activities (30-40 Minutes)

1. Ball control drill. Two sets to a court and standing on opposite sides of the net, partners practice forehand and backhand ground strokes, starting in the ser-

vice court area, then the midcourt, and then the baseline. Have them count out each hit, trying for many consecutive hits in each area. (6 minutes)

2. Crosscourt drill. Join two sets of partners on each court. Students practice diagonal crosscourt ground strokes, first on one side of the court and then the other. (4 minutes, 2 minutes on each side of the court)

3. Present and demonstrate the rules of serving using the teaching cues. (3-5 minutes)

4. Serve drill. Position four students on a court: 2 students on each side of the net standing behind either the service line or the baseline. Two students serve and the others retrieve. Then retrievers serve the ball back. (7-10 minutes)

5. Serve and rally game. Position 4 or 6 players on a court. The server gets two chances to make a good serve (i.e., the ball must bounce in the proper service court area) from behind the baseline, service line, or midcourt. When the ball bounces, receivers return the serve, starting a rally. The rally continues until the ball goes out-of-bounds or hits the net; the team that does not commit a serving or playing fault gets 1 point. Rotate servers after each point so that all players on one side serve before the other side serves. The first team to score 10 points wins; winners rotate to another court. (10-15 minutes)

Closure (3-5 Minutes)

1. Review the lesson with students. Use the following questions and ideas to reinforce learning, check understanding, and provide feedback.

   ▸ Share your observations about students' ground strokes and serves.

   ▸ Discuss students' consistency in hitting good ground strokes. Are they getting into position quickly? Are they stroking through the ball? Are they gripping firmly before contact? Are they consciously trying to contact the ball in the middle of the racket face? Do they return to a ready position?

   ▸ Discuss students' consistency in serving. Are they tossing the ball too high or too far out? Are they keeping the racket arm straight at contact? Do they contact the ball in front of the forward foot?

2. Quiz students verbally about serving rules.

3. Assign students to watch a televised tennis match (or a tennis videotape in the media center) and note scoring, court positions, rules governing play, footwork, and mechanics for executing all strokes. Ask them to prepare 3 to 5 written comments about their observations and any questions they have about the tennis play. Have students complete the assignment before lesson 7.

Lesson 6

Lob and Demonstration Doubles Game

Purpose

In this lesson students learn the lob and doubles game play.

Facility and Equipment

◆ Tennis court
◆ 1 racket per student
◆ 3 balls per student

Warm-Ups (6-8 Minutes)

1. Step and calf taps
2. Push-ups
3. Grapevine step
4. Body circles
5. Reverse runs

Skill Cues

1. Use the same grip and beginning body mechanics used in the forehand and backhand drives (see lessons 1 and 2).
2. Shorten the backswing, open the racket face, and loft the ball in a high arc.
3. Carry the forward swing in an upward plane and use less force than that used in a drive.
4. Follow through upward and outward.

Teaching Cues

1. Instruct students to prepare for the lob as they do for any other ground stroke to deceive their opponents.
2. Describe the difference between offensive and defensive lobs: use a lifting motion on offensive lobs and a blocking motion on defensive lobs.
3. For safety during the serve and lob drill, students on one side of the net should serve while the other lobs, and vice versa.

Activities (30-40 Minutes)

1. Explain that the lob is a high arching shot intended to clear an opponent's outstretched racket and fall into the backcourt. It is used offensively when opponents are in front court (i.e., near the net), and it is used defensively when a player is out of position and needs time to recover (i.e., get back into position). Demonstrate the mechanics of the forehand and backhand lobs using the appropriate skill and teaching cues. (3-4 minutes)

Forehand lob

Backhand lob

2. Drop and lob drill. Position three sets of partners on a court, partners on opposite sides of the net and in the backcourt area. Students on one side drop the ball and lob it to their partners on other side, concentrating on the amount of force needed to reach the backcourt, the angle of the racket face angle (the angle will vary with the distance), and the trajectory of the ball after contact. Each student hits five lobs; partners retrieve and drop lob them back. (6-8 minutes)

3. Serve and lob drill. In partners with 2 or 4 sets to a court, 1 partner serves and the other lobs the return. After 5 or 6 serves and lobs, students switch roles. (5-8 minutes)

Optional Activity: Rally

Optional Activity: Tennis Keep-Away

4. Present the basic rules (see the unit introduction) and playing positions for doubles play. Have four skilled players demonstrate the positions and game play while you explain scoring and identify serving and playing faults as well as other fundamentals of the game. (Position the rest of the class around the perimeter of the court.) Continue play for a few minutes, asking students to call out faults as they see them, determine the scoring of the demonstration game, and specify serving rotation before players rotate. (8-10 minutes)

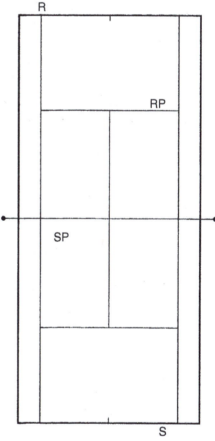

S = Server
R = Receiver
SP = Serving partner
RP = Receiving partner

Doubles serve and receive positions

5. Doubles game. Students practice playing a doubles game, concentrating on game rules and positions. (For beginners, one student should play in front court and the other in backcourt, or both should play in backcourt, covering the right or left side of the court.) If courts are limited, extra students can rally against the backboards or practice serving; then rotate teams in after two games and have the new team serve. (8-10 minutes)

Optional Activities

Rally (0-6 Minutes)

Have students (four to a court) rally, mixing lobs and drives. If courts are limited, rotate 2 or 4 players whenever play stops.

Tennis Keep-Away (0-10 Minutes)

Position students in 2 teams of 6 players, 1 offensive team and 1 defensive team. Offensive players are positioned in the backcourt areas (3 on each side), and defensive players are positioned in the front court (3 on each side). The offensive team starts the game with a drop hit to their opposite backcourt teammates who drive or lob the ball back. Defensive players try to knock down the return. Offensive players count the number of consecutive successful hits. After 5 minutes, teams rotate. The team with the most consecutive hits wins.

Closure (3-5 Minutes)

1. Review the lesson with students. Use the following questions and ideas to reinforce learning, check understanding, and provide feedback.
   ▶ Ask students to use their hands to show the racket face position on contact for a forehand drive, lob, and serve.
   ▶ Question students about serving, receiving, scoring, and general playing rules.
2. Remind students to complete the video or television tennis match assignment before the next lesson.

Lesson 7

Volley and Game Play

Purpose

In this lesson students learn the volley and increase their doubles playing skills.

Facility and Equipment

◆ Tennis court
◆ 1 racket per student
◆ 3 balls per student

Warm-Ups (6-8 Minutes)

1. Sprint-jog intervals
2. Arm circles
3. High jumper
4. Hamstring conditioners
5. Footwork drill (see lesson 1, activity 6)

Skill Cues

1. Choke up on the racket (i.e., grip it slightly higher on the handle, toward the throat); keep the knees flexed throughout the volley, and use a short backswing.
2. Step into the shot and punch the ball, keeping the wrist and grip firm, and the racket in front.
3. Stop the racket head just after it strikes the ball; use very little follow-through.
4. Keep the racket in front with the arms extended.

Teaching Cues

1. The volley is an offensive stroke taken close to the net. It is a short stroke that resembles a punch, or block, of the ball.
2. Tell students to move forward to take a volley and contact the ball early.
3. The racket should be driven into the ball, and angled downward and away from the opponent.

Activities (30-40 Minutes)

1. Ball control drill. Student partners hit 10 consecutive balls from the service court, midcourt, and baseline. (5-6 minutes)
2. Explain the mechanics and strategy of the volley and demonstrate the volley using the skill and teaching cues. (4-5 minutes)

3. Position students in partners on each side of the net. Have one student toss balls from midcourt and the other volley from a position near the net. After 5 to 6 balls, students should switch positions. (6-8 minutes)

4. Hit and volley drill. Have students switch partners and position themselves on each side of the net. One player drop hits from the baseline and rushes to the net area. The other partner returns the shot, and the first player volleys back. After a few volleys, partners switch roles and repeat. (5-6 minutes)

Optional Activity: Volley and Lob Drill

5. Doubles game. Position doubles teams on a court and have them play a practice doubles game. Encourage students to use different strokes in the practice. Play a set of three games and then rotate the winning teams. If players outnumber the courts available, assign a doubles team to each court to help retrieve balls and rotate the extra team in (as the serving team) after each game. (10-15 minutes)

Optional Activity

Volley and Lob Drill (0-5 Minutes)

Position student partners on either side of the court, one at the baseline and the other near the net. The baseline partner hits a forehand drive, the net partner returns a volley, and the baseline partner returns a lob. Score a point each time the volley goes into the backcourt and each time the lob goes into the backcourt. Switch roles after one player scores 3 points.

Closure (3-5 Minutes)

Review the lesson with students. Use the following ideas to reinforce learning, check understanding, and provide feedback.

1. Discuss when the volley should be used and when it is an effective offensive stroke.

2. Review the correct body position for the volley.

3. Share your observations of game play, concentrating on rules and playing skills.

4. Ask for students' written assignments (see lesson 5) and if time permits, discuss some of their observations and questions.

Smash and Game Play

Purpose

In this lesson students learn the fundamentals of the smash while continuing to refine their playing skills and knowledge of the doubles game.

Facility and Equipment

◆ Tennis court
◆ 1 racket per student
◆ 3 balls per student
◆ 1 quiz sheet per student*

Warm-Ups (6-8 Minutes)

1. Side slides
2. Upper body rotations
3. Elbow-knee touches (standing)
4. Shoulder shrugs
5. Run around the perimeter of the court

Skill Cues

1. Use a continental grip (i.e., halfway between the forehand and backhand grips), flex the knees, and take the racket head down behind the head. Point the free hand at the ball as it descends.
2. Shift weight forward, rotating the shoulders and hips, reach for the ball, fully extend the racket arm, throw the racket strings up and over the ball, and snap the racket head powerfully through the ball.
3. Rotate the wrist outward before contact.
4. Contact the ball just ahead of the forward foot, let the racket swing quickly downward, and step forward on the follow-through.
5. Use less windup in the backswing than in the serve.

Teaching Cues

1. The smash is an offensive shot executed to win the point. It is similar to the serve, except the potential for error is less because the full backswing is somewhat reduced on the smash.
2. The feet should stay active while preparing to smash; tell students not to plant their feet and wait for the oncoming ball.
3. Stress angling the overhead smash rather than trying to overpower the ball with speed.
4. Remind students to turn sideways to the net and snap their wrists on contact to propel the ball downward.

Activities (30-40 Minutes)

1. Explain and demonstrate the smash using the skill and teaching cues. (2-4 minutes)

2. Shadow smash drill. Have students spread out and practice hitting imaginary overhead smashes, concentrating on footwork, rotating the shoulders and hips forward and the wrist slightly outward, and contacting the ball with the arm and racket fully extended. (3-4 minutes)

3. Smash drill. In groups of 3, 1 player tosses or hits high, arcing balls across the net to a player standing in the service court who smashes the ball. The third player retrieves balls. After 8 to 10 attempts, students should rotate positions. On the second round, have students put more emphasis on angling the smash to the outer or deeper court areas. (10-12 minutes)

Smash sequence

Optional Activity: Lob-Smash Drill

4. Position student doubles teams on a court and have them practice playing a doubles game. Encourage teams to try different positions: both teammates deep (i.e., in backcourt), both up (i.e., in front court), and 1 up and 1 back. Switch partners and teams after 8 to 10 minutes. (15-20 minutes)

Optional Activity

Lob-Smash Drill (0-5 Minutes)

Position student partners on a court: 1 in the backcourt (deep court) who lobs and 1 across and near the net (front court) who returns the lob with a smash. Switch positions after 5 to 6 balls.

Closure (3-5 Minutes)

Review the lesson with students. Use the following questions and ideas to reinforce learning, check understanding, and provide feedback.

1. Discuss when to use the smash (i.e., to win the point) and in which areas of the court it is most successful (i.e., front court and sideline).

2. Ask students the following questions:

   ▶ What doubles positions worked best?

   ▶ How many were able to use all the strokes (i.e., forehand, backhand, volley, lob, smash, and serve) at least once in the doubles game?

3. Discuss the advantages and disadvantages of both playing close to the net after the serve is returned.

4. Hand out a 10-question quiz on scoring and the basic rules of doubles play. Students may work independently or in partners. This quiz can also be given as a homework assignment.

Lesson 9

Round-Robin Tournament I

Purpose

In this lesson students get to apply their playing skills and knowledge of doubles play in a tournament.

Facility and Equipment

◆ Tennis court
◆ 1 racket per student
◆ 2 balls per student
◆ 1 tournament schedule*

Warm-Ups (6-8 Minutes)

1. Side slides
2. Inverted hurdler's stretch
3. Waist twists
4. Side arm push-ups
5. Sprint-jog intervals

Skill Cues

1. Call out the score before each serve.
2. Move quickly into position to return the ball.
3. Call out shots that are close to both partners.
4. Use the entire body, not just the arm, to hit the ball.
5. Stay focused on the ball, not on the opposing team.

Teaching Cues

1. Create a tournament schedule using divisions (the divisions should be based on ability). For team pairings, assign teams or allow students to select their own partners within the same division.
2. If a difference of opinion occurs during tournament play, replay the point.
3. Ask students to concentrate more on returning a successful shot than on placement.
4. Remind students that the lesson's emphasis is on skill development, not just competition.

Activities (30-40 Minutes)

1. Assign students to two divisions, or flights, and present the tournament schedule to the class. Remind students about game strategy and conduct (see the unit description). (5-10 minutes)
2. Doubles tournament play. Teams should play a full set (6 games) or for 8 to 10 minutes, and then rotate to the next round of the tournament. If courts are limited, teams can practice against a backboard, serve into the perimeter fence, retrieve balls for other teams, or call lines. (25-30 minutes)

Closure (3-5 Minutes)

Review the lesson with students. Use the following ideas to reinforce learning, check understanding, and provide feedback.

1. Discuss your observations about how well students followed the rules, their playing strategy, and their game skills.

2. Call attention to good conduct and etiquette throughout tournament play.

3. Go over the quiz and discuss questions that were most troubling. Clarify unclear rules and stroke analysis.

Lesson 10

Round-Robin Tournament II

Purpose

In this lesson students continue to apply their tennis skills and knowledge in tournament play.

Warm-Ups (6-8 Minutes)

1. Horizontal run
2. Arm and leg lifts
3. Upper body rotations
4. Arm circles
5. Running in place

Facility and Equipment

◆ Tennis court
◆ 1 racket per student
◆ 2 balls per student
◆ 1 tournament schedule

Skill Cues

1. Call out the score before each serve.
2. Move quickly into position to return the ball.
3. Call out shots that are close to both partners.
4. Use the entire body, not just the arm, to hit the ball.
5. Stay focused on the ball, not on the opposing team.

Teaching Cues

1. Refer to the tournament schedule for team pairings.
2. If a difference of opinion occurs during tournament play, it is best to replay the point.
3. Ask students to concentrate more on returning a successful shot than on placement.
4. Remind students that the lesson's emphasis is on skill development, not competition.
5. Go over the tournament schedule before class, making sure that every team will have played every other team in the division by the end of the tournament.

Activities (30-40 Minutes)

1. Remind students about playing tactics and etiquette. Answer any questions about game play after the first day of the tournament. (5-10 minutes)
2. Doubles tournament play. Teams should play a full set (6 games) or for 8 to 10 minutes, and then rotate to the next round of the tournament. If courts are limited, teams can practice against a backboard, serve into the perimeter fence, retrieve balls for other teams, or call lines. (25-30 minutes)

Closure (3-5 Minutes)

Review the lesson with students. Use the following ideas to reinforce learning, check understanding, and provide feedback.

1. Discuss your observations about how well students followed the rules, their playing strategy, and their game skills.

2. Call attention to good conduct and etiquette.

3. Ask students how many teams won most of the games and to name some of the skills and strategies that contributed to winning.

4. A homemade trophy or certificate could be awarded to the teams with the most wins in each division.

Assessment and Resources

Assessment of the tennis unit can include testing students on specific skills, their knowledge of the rules and strategies, and effectiveness during game play. The quiz suggested in lesson 8 is an excellent tool for assessing students' understanding of scoring and the basic rules of doubles play. Suggestions for skill and game play assessment are provided in this chapter.

Skill Assessment

Skill testing can be formal or informal. In general, testing the serve (forehand or continental grip) and the ground strokes (forehand and backhand drives) is sufficient.

▶ Serve testing. Test for proper form by using the skill and teaching cues listed in lesson 4. Test the serve for accuracy using the larger target of the service court. For more advanced students, reduce the size of the target to a specific area of the service court. Allow each server a specific number of trials from each service side (e.g., 10 serves), and tally the number of successful serves.

▶ Ground stroke testing. Draw a net line 3 feet (.91 meters) high across the backboard or wall, and draw a restraining line on the floor 20 feet (6.1 meters) from the wall. Students stand behind the restraining line and rally the ball against the wall, trying to hit it above the line (over the net) as many consecutive times as possible while staying behind the restraining line. Count either the number of successful shots or the number of consecutive successful shots hit in 1 minute. Give 2 or 3 trials, counting either the best trial or the total number of successful hits. If the ball bounces away, drop another one. This test will need a counter, a ball feeder, and a timer.

Lessons

Many of the lesson drills in this unit can be used for assessment, or you can modify them to create separate skill tests. The following lessons may be used for assessment purposes. Assessment protocol is listed with each.

The ball control drill in lesson 3 makes a good test. Conduct two trials, each with a different partner from each of the three court areas. Record only the highest number of consecutive hits of the two trials from the service court, midcourt, and baseline. In other words, partner rally in each court area twice and record one score: the highest number of consecutive hits for each area. Then students get new partners and repeat. Add the two sets of scores for each student and convert to a grading scale.

Game Play Assessment

Playing skills can also be evaluated. A subjective assessment could be made during game play (e.g., looking for effective rotation, shots, hustle, and so on). For a more objective assessment, total the number of team points scored in the tournament games (lessons 9 and 10) and then convert those points into a grading scale for the unit. (This method encourages students to keep trying even when they are losing.) However, assessment should focus on skill development, not just competition. By organizing tournaments into two divisions, based on skill level, extreme differences in student ability will not be as apparent.

Resources

Bailey, G. 2000. *The ultimate sport lead-up game book.* Rev. ed. Camas, WA: Educators Press.

Brown, J. 1989. *Tennis: Steps to success.* Champaign, IL: Leisure Press.

Helfrich, J.S. 1976. *Tennis made easy through individualized program instruction.* Dubuque, IA: Kendall/Hunt.

Mood, D., F.F. Musker, and J.E. Rink. 1991. *Sports and recreational activities for men and women.* 10th ed. St. Louis: Mosby.

Pangrazi, R.P., and P.W. Darst. 1985. *Dynamic physical education curriculum and instruction for secondary school students.* Minneapolis: Burgess.

U.S. Tennis Association. 1996. *Tennis tactics: Winning patterns of play.* Champaign, IL: Human Kinetics.

White, J.R., ed. 1990. *Sports rules encyclopedia.* Champaign, IL: Leisure Press.

Zakrajsek, D., and L. Carnes. 1986. *Individualizing physical education: Criterion materials.* 2nd ed. Champaign, IL: Human Kinetics.

Volleyball

The game of volleyball was invented in 1895 by William Morgan of Holyoke, Massachusetts, as an alternative to the popular game of basketball. Morgan borrowed the idea of hitting a ball back and forth over the net from the game of tennis and other techniques from the game of handball. The YMCA promoted volleyball over the next 30 years, and in 1928 the United States Volleyball Association was formed. In recent years, the game has evolved to include more action and force through the use of power volleyball skills. The best world teams compete for the Triple Crown, which entails winning the Olympic Games, the World Cup, and the World Championship in succession.

Equipment

The equipment used in volleyball consists of the ball and the net. The volleyball should have a circumference of 25 to 27 inches (63.5-68.6 centimeters) and must weigh between 9 and 10 ounces (255.1-283.5 grams). It can be made of rubber, leather, or simulation leather.

The volleyball net should be set at a height of 7.96 feet (2.43 meters) for high school players and 7.34 feet (2.24 meters) for junior high school players.

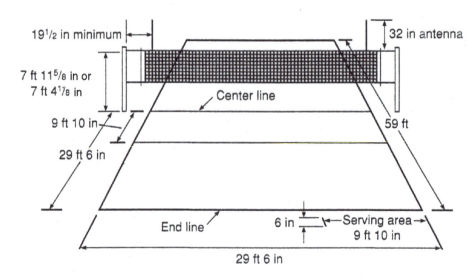

Volleyball court dimensions

Unit Organization

Some of the lessons in this unit may present more instruction than can be offered in a single class period. In these instances, either select the most appropriate tasks for students based on their skills and knowledge of the game (this unit is based on the assumption that students have learned basic volleyball skills in lower grades) or expand the lesson to fill two or more classes.

Following is an overview of each lesson in this unit.

- Lesson 1 presents some activities for developing the serve.
- Lessons 2, 3, and 4 encompass the offensive skills in volleyball, including the forearm pass, set pass, tip, and spike. These skills are later integrated in lesson 7 in a lesson on offensive strategy.
- The block and the dig are presented in lessons 5 and 6, and are reexamined in lesson 8, which focuses on defensive strategy.
- Lesson 9 provides a series of games and activities that lead up to lesson 10, which defines the rules and format for a game of regulation volleyball.

Selected resources as well as assessment ideas and activities follow the unit lessons.

Note: An asterisk (*) following a facility or equipment listing indicates that preparation is required before the lesson.

Social Skills and Etiquette

Basic courtesy and other social skills are necessary in the game of volleyball. Although competition is an integral part of the game, cooperation is just as important. For example, setting up the ball for another player is integral to effective team play. Encouraging and offering support to teammates are also key to team success.

Some rules of etiquette that should be observed include the following:

- Servers should announce the score before each serve.
- Players should return the ball to the server by rolling it under the net.
- Students should play the ball only when it is near them to allow other teammates a fair chance to participate in the game.

Lesson Modifications

Although not a particularly strenuous game, volleyball can be challenging for students of lesser ability and lower fitness levels. The following modifications can be made to accommodate the needs of students:

- Lower the net.
- Shorten the service distance (i.e., allow players to stand in the court while serving).
- Use an oversized or lighter ball.

Game rules may also be changed to accommodate less-fit or physically challenged players. For example,

- allow more than one hit per person or more hits per side,
- permit 1 or 2 bounces per side, or
- allow 2 or 3 serving attempts.

Safety

Several safety factors should be observed in class organization and instruction.

- Instruction in the proper hand and finger position is important to avoid injury.
- When spiking, students must take care to avoid injuring other players by directing the ball properly.
- Teammates must be alert during service in case the ball does not clear the net.
- Before play, inspect volleyball standards to make sure they are stable.

Rules

The object of the game of volleyball is to score as many points as possible. A game is played to 15 points and the winning team must lead by 2 points. Players send the ball back and forth over the net, trying to prevent the opposing team from returning it.

The game begins with one team serving from behind the end line in the back right corner. Service faults occur when

- the server contacts the end line,
- the ball touches or passes under the net,
- the ball touches a serving team member before going over the net, and
- the ball lands outside the court.

The same player serves until committing a fault.

After a legal serve, teams volley back and forth, hitting the ball up to three times on each side of the court before sending it to the other side. Volleying continues until one of the following occurs:

- The ball hits the floor.
- The ball is hit by a team more than three times in a row.
- The ball is hit consecutively by the same player.
- The ball touches a player below the waist.
- The ball is touched by an opponent reaching under the net.
- The net or standards are touched by a player.

- A player completely crosses the center line to play the ball.
- The ball is hit out-of-bounds or hits the ceiling.
- A team is out of position during service.

These are called *team faults* and result in a point for the opposite team or loss of the serve (called a *side-out*).

When the receiving team commits a team fault, the serving team gets the point. If the serving team commits the team fault, no point is scored and the other team gets the serve (side-out). The server on the serving team rotates (see the following figure) at the beginning of his or her service (i.e., after receiving the ball following a side-out).

General Teaching Cues

Regulation volleyball teams are comprised of 6 players. To ensure maximum class participation, however, students can be divided into 4 teams and assigned to 2 courts. Position teams in 2 or 3 lines and vary rotation patterns according to the number of lines.

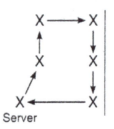

Rotation for two lines

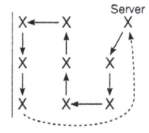

Rotation for three lines

Server rotation patterns

Serve

Purpose

In this lesson students develop serving skills, including the underhand and overhand volleyball serves.

Warm-Ups (6-8 Minutes)

1. Jump rope or jump rope laps
2. Side stretch
3. Floor touches
4. Arm rotators

Facility and Equipment

- 2 volleyball courts (indoor or outdoor)
- 1 volleyball per student
- 2 nets
- 1 balloon per student
- 1 jump rope per student

Skill Cues

Underhand Serve

1. Use a forward stride position, keeping the knees bent.
2. Hold the ball in the nondominant hand, across and in front of the body.
3. Hold the striking (dominant) hand beneath the ball, swing downward and backward, then upward and forward to hit the ball off the hand.
4. Transfer weight from the rear foot to the front foot and contact the ball with the heel of the hand.
5. Follow through in the direction of intended flight.

Overhand Serve

1. Use a forward stride position with the knees slightly flexed.
2. Toss the ball about 3 feet (.91 meters) above the shoulder so that the hand can meet the ball just above the head.
3. Transfer weight from the rear foot to the front foot when contacting the ball.
4. Contact the ball with the heel of the hand above the head; hold the hand in a fist and extend the elbow and flex the wrist forward to make contact with the ball.
5. Follow through in the direction of intended flight and then swing downward.

Teaching Cues

1. For activity 2, mark an 8-foot (2.44-meter) line on the wall.
2. Court markings are needed for activity 4: divide half of each court into nine rectangles and write the serving scores (i.e., 1, 3, 5, or 10) with chalk or tape cards to each rectangle.

Activities (30-40 Minutes)

1. Introduce the two types of volleyball serves—underhand and overhand—using the skill cues. (6-8 minutes)

2. Have students stand 12 feet (3.66 meters) from a wall and serve a volleyball, aiming above the 8-foot (2.44-meter) line. Students should try 5 underhand and 5 overhand serves to determine their most accurate serving method. Then have students repeat 10 more serves using the preferred method. (4-6 minutes)

Underhand serve   **Overhand serve**

3. Pair up students or have them select partners. Partners stand 15 feet (4.57 meters) from the net on opposite sides of the court. (Five pairs can work at each net.) Students serve the ball over the net to their partners, who should be able to catch it without moving more than 3 feet (.91 meters) from the original position. Then the receiving partners serve it back. The object of this activity is to improve serving aim. (6-8 minutes)

4. Divide the class into two groups and assign each group to a volleyball court marked with the grid shown in the figure. From the proper serving position, each student serves, attempting to make the ball land in a high scoring zone (i.e., the 10- and 5-point rectangles). After three serves, the student goes to the receiving side of the net to return the next student's serves. While awaiting their turn to serve, students can practice the underhand and overhand serves using a balloon. (14-18 minutes)

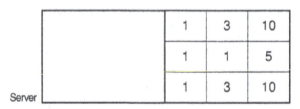

Serving score grid

Optional Activities

Serving Around the World (0-12 Minutes)

Use the same court markings as in activity 4. A server attempts to serve into every scoring zone in order (i.e., moving from left to right across row 1, row 2, and row 3). If at any time a zone is missed, the server's turn ends and the next server begins.

H-O-R-S-E (0-15 Minutes)

Use the same court markings as in activity 4. Pair up students or have them select partners. Both partners stand on the same side of the net in the serving area. Player 1 tells player 2 which zone he or she will attempt to hit while serving. If successful, player 2 must also serve to the same zone or get the letter H. If player 1 misses the zone, player 2 chooses a zone and attempts to hit it while serving. If successful, player 1 must hit the same zone or get a letter; and so on until one player accumulates the letters (by missing) H, O, R, S, and E.

Serve and Catch (0-18 Minutes)

Divide the class into 4 teams and assign 2 teams to opposite sides of a court (2 games are played simultaneously). To begin, the serving team serves the ball over the net quickly, trying to prevent the receiving team from catching it. If the ball is caught, it is immediately served from the receiving team's serving area. If the ball is not caught, the serving team scores a point. Increase the action and challenge of the game by using more than one ball in each game. Play continues until one team scores 21 points.

Closure (3-5 Minutes)

Review the lesson with students. Use the following ideas to reinforce learning, check understanding, and provide feedback.

1. Discuss the important components of a good underhand or overhand serve (see the skill cues).
2. Ask students to explain why a serve might not move in the intended direction (e.g., hitting the ball off the side of the hand, not following through in the intended direction of flight, failing to toss the ball high enough, tossing it too high on the overhand serve).

Lesson 2

Forearm Pass (Bump)

Purpose

In this lesson students develop the volleyball forearm pass (bump).

Facility and Equipment

◆ 2 volleyball courts (indoor or outdoor)
◆ 1 volleyball per student

Note: Mark an 8-foot (2.44-meter) line on the wall.

Warm-Ups (6-8 Minutes)

1. Running in place
2. Seated hamstring stretch
3. Elbow-knee touches (standing)
4. Triceps stretch

Skill Cues

1. Use a forward stride position, bending at the knees and waist.
2. Interlock or cup the fingers and turn the palms upward. (Finger position is a matter of preference.)

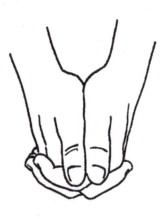

Interlocked hand position

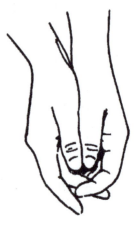

Cupped hand position

3. Keep the forearms, wrists, and elbows straight.
4. Contact the ball with the forearms, using an upward motion.
5. Extend the body when contacting the ball.
6. Follow through in the direction of intended flight.

Teaching Cues

1. Explain that the bump is used to return a ball received at or below the waist.
2. When used to return a serve, the bump is also considered an offensive technique.

Activities (30-40 Minutes)

1. Introduce the forearm pass (bump), including the interlocked and cupped hand positions, using the skill and teaching cues. (3-5 minutes)

2. Have students stand 12 feet (3.66 meters) from a wall and bump a volleyball using the forearm pass. Students should toss the ball into the air and then bump it, aiming above the 8-foot (2.44-meter) line on the wall. (4-6 minutes)

3. Pair up students or have them select partners. Partner 1 tosses the volleyball to partner 2 (the ball should drop below the waist), who then bumps the volleyball using a forearm pass at an 8-foot (2.44-meter) line on the wall. After 10 tosses and bumps, partners should switch roles. (4-6 minutes)

4. Divide students into groups of three. Player A tosses the volleyball (so it drops below the waist) to player B, who then bumps the volleyball to player C using a forearm pass. Player C catches the ball and throws it back to player A. After five bumps, students should rotate positions. (5-7 minutes)

5. Bump ball relay. Divide the class into six teams and have each form a line. One player from each team stands opposite the line and, at the signal, bump passes the volleyball to the first player in line. That player quickly bump passes the ball back and runs to the end of the line so that the next player in line can get ready to receive the next pass. (7-8 minutes)

6. Keep it up. Divide the class into team circles of eight players, each team with a volleyball. At the signal, teammates use bump passes to send the volleyball to one another, keeping the ball in the air without touching the ground. The team that keeps the ball up the longest wins. If necessary, this game can be simplified by allowing the ball to bounce once between passes. (7-8 minutes)

Bump ball relay

Closure (3-5 Minutes)

Review the lesson with students. Use the following ideas to reinforce learning, check understanding, and provide feedback.

1. Choose two students to demonstrate the forearm bump. Have students observe and analyze each phase of the pass.

2. Ask students when the bump should be used during a game (i.e., as an offensive technique, when receiving a serve, to send the ball back over the net).

Lesson 3

Set Pass

Purpose

In this lesson students learn how to perform the set pass.

Warm-Ups (6-8 Minutes)

1. Reverse run
2. Triceps stretch
3. Step touches
4. Single-leg curls

Facility and Equipment

◆ 2 volleyball courts (indoor or outdoor) with walls
◆ 1 volleyball per student
◆ 2 nets
◆ 1 or more basketball backboards

Skill Cues

The following skill cues are for a set pass executed while facing a target. If the back is to the target, the ball would be hit in an upward and backward direction by tilting the head backward and arching the body.

1. Use a forward stride position and keep the knees bent.
2. Flex the knees and elbows before the hit.
3. Tilt the head backward, form a window with the hands above the face, and watch the ball closely.
4. Hit the ball with the fingertips in an upward and forward direction.
5. Extend the body upward on contact.
6. Follow through in the direction of intended flight.

Teaching Cues

1. Explain that the set pass is used to position the ball for another player to spike.
2. Be sure to introduce both types of set passes (i.e., facing toward and away from a target).

Activities (30-40 Minutes)

1. Introduce the set pass using the skill and teaching cues. (3-5 minutes)
2. Have students toss a volleyball against a wall and set pass the ball on the rebound as many times as possible in 30 seconds (signal the start and stop of each time period). (4-6 minutes)

Set pass position

3. Pair up students or have them select partners. Partner 1 tosses the volleyball to partner 2, who then set passes it against a wall. After 12 set passes, partners should switch roles. (4-6 minutes)

4. Divide students into groups of 3 and position up to 4 groups on a court. Player 1 tosses the volleyball (in a high arc) to player 2, who then set passes it from a front position (facing the target) over the net. Player 3 retrieves the ball and rolls it back to player 1. After player 2 has performed three set passes, students should rotate positions. (4-6 minutes)

5. Use the same groups and court assignment as in activity 4. Player 1 tosses the volleyball (in a high arc) to player 2, who then set passes it from a back position (facing away from the target) over the net. Player 3 attempts to return the ball over the net. After player 2 has performed three set passes, students should rotate positions. (5-7 minutes)

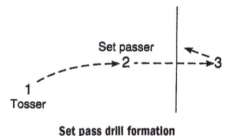

Set pass drill formation

6. Backboard set pass drill. Divide the class into teams of six players and have each team line up in front of a backboard (the more backboards, the greater the participation). The first player in line moves forward to stand under the basketball backboard, then turns and tosses the volleyball to the next player in line (now in the first position), who set passes the volleyball and attempts to hit the backboard. That player then moves forward to stand under the backboard (the first player goes to the back of the line in front of the backboard), turns and tosses the volleyball to the next player in line, who set passes the volleyball to hit the backboard, and so on. Team members waiting for their turn should form a circle and set pass to one another as many consecutive times as possible without letting the volleyball touch the floor. (If only 2 backboards are available, each team should perform the drill for 2 minutes, at which point 2 new teams should take their places by the backboards.) (10 minutes)

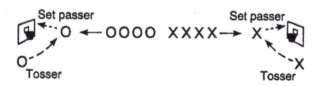

Backboard set pass drill formation

Optional Activity

Pickle in the Middle (0-12 Minutes)

Two players bump and set pass the ball back and forth while the player in the middle attempts to intercept the ball. When successful, the middle player takes the place of the player who last contacted the ball.

Closure (3-5 Minutes)

Review the lesson with students. Use the following ideas to reinforce learning, check understanding, and provide feedback.

1. Discuss what students must do to get height on the set pass (e.g., tilt the head backward, flex the knees and elbows before hitting, hit in an upward and forward direction, extend the body upward on contact, and so on).

2. Select a student to demonstrate a forward set pass and another student to demonstrate a backward set pass in front of the class.

Lesson 4

Spike and Tip

Purpose

In this lesson students develop spiking and tipping skills.

Warm-Ups (6-8 Minutes)

1. Jump rope or jump rope laps (on one foot)
2. Alternate leg raises
3. Leg lifts
4. Curl-ups

Skill Cues

1. Get ready for the spike or tip by facing the direction of the ball, shifting weight forward, and preparing to jump.
2. Take off on the jump from one foot, turn the body to the side in midair, and contact the ball at the highest possible point with a stiff arm and quick flex of the wrist.
3. Strike the ball on its top so that its flight is straight downward for a spike, slightly upward and then downward for the tip.
4. Use the heel of the hand and a wrist snap to contact the ball for a spike.
5. Use the upper two finger joints to contact the ball for a tip.
6. Follow through toward the target, and land on both feet with knees bent.

Teaching Cues

1. Explain that spiking and tipping are offensive techniques used to direct the ball downward across the net (like a tennis smash shot).
2. Point out the differences in execution between the tip and the spike:
   ▶ The tip is similar to a one-handed set. The ball is directed to go over the net and drop behind or to the side of the blocker.
   ▶ The ball is contacted with the upper two finger joints in a tip.

Tip

▷ The spike puts a forceful downward motion on the ball.

▷ The ball is contacted with the heel of the hand in a spike.

3. Activity 3 demonstrates the on-hand and off-hand positions in volleyball.

▷ The on-hand position is used when the ball approaches a player's dominant hand before it crosses in front of the body.

▷ The off-hand position is used when the ball approaches from the side opposite the player's dominant hand (i.e., the ball must cross in front of the body before contact is made).

Spike

Activities (30-40 Minutes)

1. Introduce the spike and tip using the appropriate skill and teaching cues. (4-6 minutes)

2. Pair up students or have them select partners. Partner 1 tosses the volleyball (high) to partner 2, who tips 5 balls toward the base of the wall and then spikes 5 balls straight down to the base of the wall. After 10 tosses, partners switch roles. (4-6 minutes)

3. Tipping and spiking drill. Divide students into groups of 3 and position up to 4 groups on a court, 2 players from each group on one side of the net and the other player from each group on the other side. Player 1 tosses the volleyball (high) 6 times from the left side to player 2, who tips 3 balls and then spikes 3 balls over the net. Player 3 retrieves the ball and rolls it back after each tip or spike. Then students switch positions. When every player has spiked and tipped three times from the left side, repeat the activity tossing the ball from the right side. (6-8 minutes)

4. Tip the hoop drill. Divide the class into 4 groups and position 2 groups in a line on the same side of a court. Designate or have students select a leader and a retriever to start. The retriever goes to the other side of the net. The leader of each group tosses the ball (high) to the first player in line, who then tips the ball and aims at a hoop on the other side and then goes to the other side of the court to become the retriever. The retriever goes to the back of the line and waits to tip the ball into a hoop. (8-10 minutes)

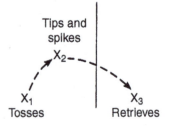

Tipping and spiking drill formation

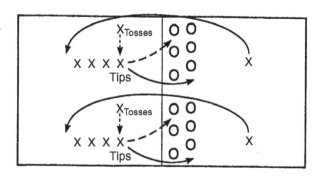

Tip the hoop drill formation

5. One-on-one spiking. Divide the class into groups of 6 and position 3 students on each side of the net. One side tosses the volleyball over the net and the other side spikes the ball back over the net. Students practice spiking until successful, at which point they switch roles. After 3 minutes, 6 different students take their positions on the court and practice spiking. Students awaiting their turns can practice spiking into the wall after their partners toss the ball to them. (8-10 minutes)

Closure (3-5 Minutes)

Review the lesson with students. Use the following ideas to reinforce learning, check understanding, and provide feedback.

1. Discuss some ways that students can increase accuracy when tipping and spiking (e.g., contacting the ball at the highest point, hitting the top of the ball for downward flight in a spike and slightly upward and then down for a tip, making sure the body is turned to the side during the jump).

2. Have a student demonstrate the tip and spike from the right side and then from the left. Review proper technique on each side.

Lesson 5

Block

Purpose

In this lesson students develop blocking skills.

Warm-Ups (6-8 Minutes)

1. Agility run
2. Shoulder shrugs
3. Push-ups
4. Elbow-knee touches (supine)

Skill Cues

1. Stand close to the net.
2. Jump up to meet the ball as the spiker jumps.
3. Keep the fingers extended and straight as they contact the ball.
4. Thrust the arms forward and upward.
5. Do not swing the arms forward as the body lands (to prevent a net foul).
6. When deflecting the ball to a teammate, instead of rebounding it over the net, the sequence is the same except the arm is thrust backward—not forward—and the hand is turned in the direction of intended flight.

Teaching Cues

1. Explain that the block is a defensive technique used to make the ball rebound over the net or to deflect the ball to a teammate.
2. Point out that the block is usually used as a defensive technique against the spike.
3. Before class, mark an 8-foot (2.44-meter) line on the wall.

Activities (30-40 Minutes)

1. Introduce the block using the appropriate skill and teaching cues. (4-6 minutes)
2. Pair up students or have them select partners. One student throws the volleyball at the 8-foot (2.44-meter) wall line and the other student attempts to block the rebound. After 10 tosses, partners switch roles. (6-8 minutes)

Facility and Equipment

- 2 volleyball courts (indoor or outdoor) with wall space
- 1 volleyball per 2 students
- 2 nets
- 24 cones

Block

3. Divide the class into 6 groups and position them in a straight line on one side of the court, 3 groups to a court. One player from each group stands on the opposite side of the net and then jumps and throws the volleyball over the net, toward the floor. The first student in line attempts to block the ball and then runs to the end of the line as the next student in line prepares to block another ball. After the entire line has had a turn at blocking, each group should select a new player to throw the volleyball. (8-10 minutes)

4. Blocking drill. Divide students into groups of 3, and position 2 students (i.e., players 2 and 3, the deflector and the catcher) on one side of the net and 1 student (i.e., player 1, the thrower) on the other. (Up to 3 groups can play on 1 court.) Player 1 jumps and throws the volleyball down and over the net. Player 2 attempts to deflect the ball backward (rather than rebound it over the net). Player 3 catches the ball and rolls it back to player 1 to toss again. Each player makes six attempts at deflecting the ball backward; then students rotate positions. Students awaiting their turns can practice blocking rebounded balls thrown by a partner against a wall. (12-16 minutes)

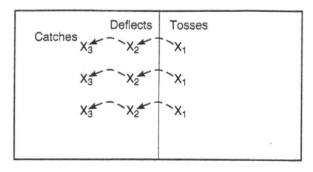

Blocking drill formation

Closure (3-5 Minutes)

Review the lesson with students. Use the following questions and ideas to reinforce learning, check understanding, and provide feedback.

1. Discuss the proper arm motion for the block (i.e., the arm is thrust forward and upward, the fingers are extended and straight for rebounding).

2. Ask students how to prevent a net foul while blocking a ball (i.e., avoid swinging the arms forward as the body comes down).

Lesson 6

•

Dig

Purpose

In this lesson students develop the digging skill.

Warm-Ups (6-8 Minutes)

1. Jump rope or jump rope laps (alternate jumping forward and backward)
2. Scissors
3. Side stretch
4. Wrist rotation and flexion

Facility and Equipment

◆ 2 volleyball courts (indoor or outdoor)
◆ 1 volleyball per 2 students
◆ 2 nets
◆ 6 chairs
◆ 1 jump rope per student

Skill Cues

1. Keep weight forward, with one foot slightly ahead of the other.
2. Bend the knees and keep the hips low to get under the ball.

Digging stance

3. Hold the hands in an interlocked or cupped position and keep the arms in front of the body at waist height.
4. Keep the forearms, wrists, and elbows straight.
5. Contact the ball with both arms parallel to the floor.
6. Move the body forward in a thrusting motion, keeping the arms steady, and follow through in the direction of intended flight.

Teaching Cues

1. Explain that the dig is a defensive technique used to receive a spike and send a pass to a teammate; it is not used to return the ball over the net.
2. Demonstrate the proper hand position for the dig so that students will be able to execute it properly.

Activities (30-40 Minutes)

1. Introduce the dig using the skill and teaching cues. (4-6 minutes)
2. Pair up students or have them select partners. One student throws the volleyball downward from an overhead position and the other attempts the dig. After eight digs, students switch roles. (6-10 minutes)
3. Divide the class into six groups and have each group line up on one side of the net (up to three groups per net). A student from each group, standing on a chair on the opposite side of the net, throws the volleyball forcefully over the net toward the back of the court. The first student in line attempts the dig, then retrieves the ball, tosses it to the thrower on the other side of the net, and runs to the end of the line. Then the next student in line attempts the dig. After everyone has had a turn at digging, repeat the activity, this time having a different student throw the ball. (10-12 minutes)
4. Digging and receiving drill. Have students form 4 lines, 2 on the same side of a court (2 lines work together as 1 team at each net). A student from each team stands on a chair on the other side of the net to toss the ball. The first student in the first line moves into the court, then digs the ball thrown (forcefully) by the tosser. The first student in the second line moves into the court, receives the dig by catching the volleyball, and then returns it to the tosser. After each student in line has had a chance to dig or receive the dig, students rotate positions: a new student tosses, diggers become receivers, and receivers become diggers. (10-12 minutes)

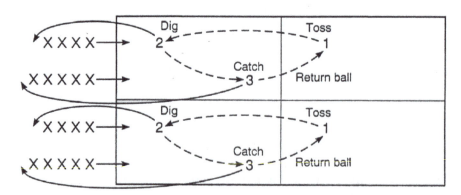

Digging and receiving drill formation

Optional Activity

Shuffle Dig (0-12 Minutes)

Use the same formation and lines as in activity 4. The tosser stands on a chair on the other side of the net and throws the volleyball forcefully toward the backcourt. The first player in either line shuffles across the court, attempts to dig the ball without sending it over the net, then retrieves the ball, returns it to the tosser, and runs to the end of the line. Then the first player in the other line shuffles, digs, retrieves, and returns.

Closure (3-5 Minutes)

Review the lesson with students. Use the following ideas to reinforce learning, check understanding, and provide feedback.

1. Discuss the differences between the forearm pass (bump; see lesson 2) and the dig (i.e., the dig is a defensive skill used to receive spikes or send the ball to a teammate; the bump is an offensive technique used to receive a serve and return it over the net).

2. Give students the assignment of defining the five offensive skills that will be the focus of the next lesson:
   - Serve
   - Forearm pass (bump)
   - Set pass
   - Tip
   - Spike

Lesson 7

Offensive Strategy

Purpose

In this lesson students learn about offensive strategy in volleyball. Offensive skills include the serve, forearm pass (bump), set pass, tip, and spike.

Facility and Equipment

◆ 2 volleyball courts (indoor or outdoor)
◆ 1 volleyball per 4 students
◆ 2 nets

Warm-Ups (6-8 Minutes)

1. Sprint-jog intervals
2. High jumper
3. Sit and curl
4. Mad cat

Skill Cues

1. An effective offensive pattern is as follows: the bump to the set and then to the tip or spike.
2. Use the tip or spike whenever possible; it is the best offensive technique.
3. Pass the ball to the setter, in the middle front position, to set up the ball for a spike.
4. Serve to those court areas that the other team has trouble covering, or to a poor passer.
5. Designate players to spike or set.

Teaching Cues

1. Explain how the skills used in this lesson—the serve, forearm pass (bump), set pass, tip, and spike—form the basis of offensive strategy.
2. Before introducing each activity, have students spend some time developing an offensive strategy. If they suggest an alternative way to work on offensive strategy than that provided in this lesson, adjust the activities accordingly.

Activities (30-40 Minutes)

1. Introduce offensive strategy using the appropriate skill and teaching cues. (8-10 minutes)
2. Offensive pattern drill. Divide the class into teams of 4 players and have 1 team work at each net for 2 to 3 minutes, then another team. Player 1 serves the ball over the net to backcourt. Player 2 bumps the ball to the setter (player 3), who

sets the ball for a spike (by player 4). The spiker then sends the ball back over the net, toward the server (player 1), using either the tip or spike. Player 1 repeats four serves; then students rotate to another position. While teams are awaiting their turns, have them form a small circle and set pass the ball to one another. (10-15 minutes)

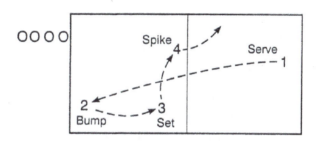

Offensive pattern drill formation

3. Receiving a serve drill. Position a team on each side of the court in the offensive ready position (see the figure). A server from one team serves to the receiving team. The receiving team then passes the ball to the setter, who sets the ball (either forward or backward) to a spiking teammate. After the ball is spiked over the net, the other team rotates and serves. Teams should alternate serving so that the opposite team can practice offensive play. Continue the drill until all players have rotated back to their starting position. (12-15 minutes)

The player at the net (the spiker) faces the team to receive the ball once it is bumped to him.

Offensive ready position

Optional Activity

Three Hits (0-15 Minutes)

This is like a regulation volleyball game, but the scoring is different. A point is scored only if the team sets the ball up and it is contacted by three players of the offensive team before it is hit over the net. Encourage students to use bumps, sets, and spikes during the game.

Closure (3-5 Minutes)

Review the lesson with students. Use the following ideas to reinforce learning, check understanding, and provide feedback.

1. Discuss some of the elements of good offensive strategy (e.g., sending the serve to the other team's weak areas or to a poor passer, using the spike frequently, setting up the ball to middle front players, and so on).

2. Ask students to define the two most common defensive skills (i.e., blocking and digging). These will be discussed further in the next lesson.

Lesson 8

Defensive Strategy

Purpose

In this lesson students learn defensive strategy in playing volleyball. Defensive skills include the block and the dig.

Warm-Ups (6-8 Minutes)

1. Jump rope or jump rope laps (skip while jumping)
2. Single-leg crossovers
3. Hamstring curls
4. Hip lifts

Facility and Equipment

- 2 volleyball courts (indoor or outdoor)
- 1 volleyball per 4 students
- 2 nets
- 2 net covers (flat sheets, queen or king size, work best)
- 1 jump rope per student

Skill Cues

1. Net players should use the block.
2. Backcourt players should dig the ball.
3. Designate players as either blockers or diggers.
4. Position at least one player near the end line for balls that are served deep in the backcourt.
5. Play all balls that are close to the end line so that a legal serve is not missed.

Teaching Cues

1. Explain how the skills used in this lesson—the block and the dig—form the basis of an effective defensive strategy.
2. Before introducing each activity, have students spend some time developing a defensive strategy. If they suggest an alternative way to work on defensive strategy than that provided in this lesson, adjust the activities accordingly.
3. Make sure all players can see the server and the ball.
4. Before class, mark an 8-foot (2.44-meter) line on the wall.

Activities (30-40 Minutes)

1. Introduce defensive strategy in volleyball, reviewing the block and dig and emphasizing the appropriate skill and teaching cues. (8-10 minutes)
2. Two-ball spike, block, and dig. Divide the class into teams of eight. Assign the first team to a volleyball court with a net. Two spikers (offense) stand on one side of the court and the remaining six team players stand on the opposite side to perform blocks and digs (defense). The offensive players jump and spike the

ball over the net as the defensive players try to either block or, if the ball gets past the blockers, dig the ball. Spikers may fire balls at the same time. This requires constant attention by the defense. After 4 minutes of play, rotate a new team into the activity. As teams await their turns on the court, teammates should pair off on the side and practice digging (one player tosses and the other digs; then they switch). (12-16 minutes)

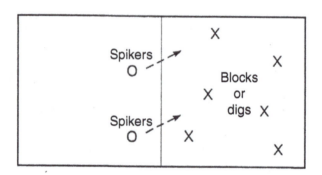

Two-ball, spike, block, and dig drill formation

3. Dig in the dark. Cover the volleyball net with a sheet or other cover so that players on one side of the court cannot see the players on the other side preparing to spike. Divide the class into teams of 7; then position 1 player on one side of the net and the other 6 players on the other side (1 team to a court). The single player spikes the ball over the net toward the back of the opposite court. Any of the six players can attempt to receive the spike with a dig. Play continues for 4 minutes, at which point a new team rotates in. Students awaiting their turns can pair off and practice digging a tossed ball toward an 8-foot (2.44-meter) line on the wall: one player tosses the ball while the other digs and then they switch roles. (10-14 minutes)

Optional Activity

Block in the Dark (0-14 minutes)

Keep the net covered from activity 3. Divide students into teams of 4; then position 1 lead player on one side of the court and the other 3 players on the other side at the net ready to block (1 team to a court). The lead player spikes the ball over the net and the other players try to block the spike. After 3 minutes of play, a new team rotates in. Teams awaiting their turns can practice blocking with a partner: one student throws the volleyball against a wall (approximately 8 feet [2.44 meters] high) and the other attempts to block the rebound. After five blocks, partners switch roles.

Closure (3-5 Minutes)

Review the lesson with students. Use the following questions and ideas to reinforce learning, check understanding, and provide feedback.

1. Ask students which is a more effective defensive technique, a dig or a block. (Blocking should be a team's first line of defense because it provides a quicker reaction than a dig. A dig should be used when the ball gets past the blockers.)

2. Discuss ways to improve defensive strategies in a game (i.e., designate players as either blockers or diggers and position diggers near the end line).

Lesson 9

Modified Game Play

Purpose

In this lesson students practice their volleyball skills with activities that lead up to an actual game.

Facility and Equipment

◆ 2 volleyball courts (indoor or outdoor)
◆ 1 volleyball per game
◆ 2 nets
◆ 2 net covers
◆ 1 volleyball rules handout per student*

Warm-Ups (6-8 Minutes)

1. Sprint-jog intervals
2. Waist twists
3. Floor touches
4. Extended body leg drops

Skill Cues

1. Serve the volleyball with the most accurate serve, either underhand or overhand.
2. Use the forearm pass (bump) when receiving a serve.
3. Set up the ball for the spike.
4. Spike the ball whenever possible; spiking is the most powerful offensive technique.
5. Rebound the spike with the defensive block.
6. Use the dig whenever the ball gets past the blockers at the net.

Activities (30-40 Minutes)

1. Introduce the activities in this lesson and present the skill cues. (3-5 minutes)
2. Explain the rules of regulation volleyball (see the unit introduction on page 370). (3-5 minutes)
3. Unlimited hits. This is like regulation volleyball except each team gets as many hits as it takes to return the ball over the net. (A player may not hit the ball more than once in a row, however.) For more practice setting up shots and bumping, add another rule to this game: each team must hit the ball three times before returning it over the net. If a team returns the ball over the net with less than three hits, it loses the serve or the opposing team gets a point. (12-15 minutes)
4. Four-player volleyball. This game also follows regulation volleyball rules but only allows four players per team. (Playing with smaller teams places greater demands on the players and helps them develop their playing skills.) If courts are limited, rotate a new team in after 4 minutes of play using a challenge method: the team that is ahead remains on the court and a new team rotates in

to challenge. If 1 team remains on the court for 3 or more games, however, declare that team the champion and begin a new round of games with 2 new teams. Teams awaiting their turns can form a circle and practice setting up the ball to one another, trying to keep it aloft as long as possible without allowing it to hit the ground. (12-15 minutes)

Optional Activities

Mystery Volleyball (0-15 Minutes)

This game follows regulation volleyball rules, but a cover is placed over the net so that the other team's action and strategy cannot be seen or anticipated. Playing in this way develops quick reactions among players.

Three-Net Volleyball (0-15 Minutes)

Set up a volleyball net and attach two other nets to the center; the nets should divide the court into quadrants. Divide the class into four teams and position each team in a quadrant. One team starts by serving into one of the other quadrants. Other regulation volleyball rules apply with the following exceptions:

- Players should rotate after every serve.
- Teams must hit the ball three times before hitting it over the net into another quadrant (this encourages setting up the volleyball).
- An additional ball can be added to make the game more challenging.

Closure (3-5 Minutes)

Review the lesson with students. Use the following ideas to reinforce learning, check understanding, and provide feedback.

1. Ask students to name the faults that constitute a side-out in volleyball (e.g., the ball hits the floor, is hit more than once in a row by one player, is hit more than three times by a team before going over the net, touches a player below the waist).
2. Distribute volleyball rules handouts and ask students to study them before the next class period.

Lesson 10

Regulation Game

Purpose

In this lesson students learn the rules and play a regulation game of volleyball.

Warm-Ups (6-8 Minutes)

1. Running in place
2. Side lunges
3. Step touches
4. Leg lifts

Facility and Equipment

◆ 2 volleyball courts (indoor or outdoor)
◆ 1 volleyball per game
◆ 1 net per court

Skill Cues

1. Serve the volleyball with the most accurate serve, either underhand or overhand
2. Use the forearm pass (bump) when receiving a serve.
3. Set up the ball for the spike.
4. Spike the ball whenever possible; it is the most effective offensive technique.
5. Rebound the spike with the defensive technique of blocking.
6. Use the dig whenever the ball gets past the blockers at the net.

Activities (30-40 Minutes)

1. Review the skill cues needed to play volleyball. (3-5 minutes)
2. Divide students into 2 or 4 teams and review the rules of regulation volleyball. Ask if students have any questions after studying their rules handouts. (5-7 minutes)
3. Play a regulation game of volleyball. If two games are being played simultaneously, the winners can play each other in a second game. (22-28 minutes)

Closure (3-5 Minutes)

Review the lesson with students. Use the following questions and ideas to reinforce learning, check understanding, and provide feedback.

1. Discuss what students could do to improve their team play (e.g., set the ball up higher, set pass to other teammates rather than send the ball right back over the net, aim for the opponent's areas of weakness, be ready to block spikes).
2. Ask students to describe some good strategic techniques for volleyball (e.g., serve for accuracy, set up the ball for the spike, use spiking whenever possible).

Assessment and Resources

After some of the assignments suggested in this unit (see lessons 6 and 9), quizzes could be given to check for basic understanding of the game. Too often such testing is given at the conclusion of a unit. Testing earlier in the unit would increase understanding of both game play and skills.

Skill tests and game play assessment can be formal or informal. Many of the lesson drills can be used for testing. In general, testing students' skills in serving as well as defensive and offensive techniques (e.g., digging, spiking, and so on) is sufficient. For example, the following activities could be adapted for assessment purposes:

▶ Lesson 1, activity 3
▶ Lesson 1, activity 4
▶ Lesson 2, activity 2
▶ Lesson 2, activity 3
▶ Lesson 3, activity 2
▶ Lesson 3, activity 3
▶ Lesson 4, activity 4
▶ Lesson 5, activity 2

Playing skills can also be evaluated. A subjective assessment (e.g., looking for effective teamwork; player positioning and rotation; individual skills such as passes, blocks, and spikes) could be made during game play (see lessons 9 and 10). For a more objective assessment, use point scoring for each activity. Total the number of points each student scores and then convert those points into a grading scale for the unit.

Finally, separate skill testing can be useful in this unit. Following are suggested skill tests:

▶ Service test. Stretch a rope 6 feet (1.83 meters) above and parallel to the top of the volleyball net. Each server gets five attempts at serving between the rope and the net. Score 1 point for each legal serve (i.e., it lands inbounds) that goes over the rope and 2 points for each legal serve that goes between the rope and the net.

▶ Set pass test. Stretch a rope 6 feet (1.83 meters) above and parallel to the top of the net. Toss the ball high from the side of the court to a student, who gets five attempts to set pass (forward) the ball over the rope into the opposite court. Score 1 point for each set pass that clears the rope and lands inbounds. Repeat the test for a backward set pass.

▶ Forearm pass (bump) test. Mark a 4-foot (1.22-meter) zone along the end line of the court. A student stands in the opposite court and tosses the ball over the net to another student, who bumps the ball toward the zone. Students get five attempts at bumping the ball and score 1 point for each successful bump.

Resources

American Sport Education. 2001. *Coaching youth volleyball.* Champaign, IL: Human Kinetics.

Asher, K., ed. 1997. *Coaching volleyball.* Champaign, IL: Human Kinetics.

Bartlett, J., L. Smith, K. Davis, and J. Peel. 1991. Development of a valid volleyball skills test battery. *Journal of Physical Education, Recreation and Dance* 62 (2): 19-21.

Kiraly, K. 1990. *Championship volleyball.* New York: Simon & Schuster.

Pangrazi, R., and P. Darst. 1997. *Dynamic physical education for secondary school students: Curriculum and instruction.* 3rd ed. Needham Heights, MA: Allyn & Bacon.

Viera, B., and B. Ferguson. 1996. *Volleyball: Steps to success.* 2nd ed. Champaign, IL: Human Kinetics.

Wise, M., ed. 1999. *Volleyball drills for champions.* Champaign, IL: Human Kinetics.

Zakrajsek, D., and L. Carnes. 1986. *Individualizing physical education: Criterion materials.* 2nd ed. Champaign, IL: Human Kinetics.

Zartman, S., and P. Zartman. 1997. *Youth volleyball: The guide for coaches and parents.* Cincinnati, OH: Betterway Books.

Minor Units

This section contains 11 minor physical education units, each covering a different sport, game, or activity. The term *minor* is an indication of the number of lessons dedicated to the activity, not its importance in the physical education curriculum. Fewer lessons, and thus less time, are required to teach a minor unit—as opposed to the major units in section III that demanded a somewhat lengthy progression of skill development. Some of the units in this section were given the "minor" designation because, although popular, they are nontraditional and require special equipment (e.g., lacrosse, orienteering). Most of the units in this section were selected for their value as lifetime recreational pursuits (e.g., golf, bowling) and their popularity as new and exciting sports (e.g., disc golf, in-line skating).

Section Structure

The units in this section are arranged alphabetically. They include team games (i.e., floor hockey, lacrosse, and team handball) as well as individual and partner sports and activities (i.e., bowling, disc golf, golf, in-line skating, jumping rope, orienteering, pickleball, and ultimate Frisbee). Each unit consists of 4 to 6 lessons that progress from basic to more advanced levels of motor skills, cognitive concepts, and performance. As with the major units in section III, the sequence of skill and game activities within each lesson is designed to move students toward greater skill achievement.

These units have been designed to be taught over a 1- or 2-week period, depending on the number of days and minutes per class session. The amount of time allotted to each lesson as well as the suggested time for each activity may need to be modified. Middle school students, for example, may need more time to complete a full lesson than senior high school students. Like the major units, every lesson in these units may be amended in whatever manner is appropriate—for example, using different teaching techniques, or substituting the suggested drills with other skill instruction.

Each unit is introduced with a brief history of the sport or activity, safety considerations, rules governing game play, suggestions for etiquette, terminology (if relevant), and methods for modifying the lessons. The focus of the lessons in each unit is also summarized in the unit introduction. Assessment and resources chapters, located at the end of each unit, suggest measures for evaluation and provide resources for additional information about the sport or activity as well as suppliers of specific equipment needed. (See "Introduction to Units and Lessons" [page 2] for more information about the structure of units and lessons.)

Bowling

Modern bowling began in northern Italy as a game called *bowls*. The game later spread to Germany, Holland, and England, where it was played on grass (the bowling green) and was known as nine pins. In the early 1600s, the Dutch brought the game to America, where it was played on grass or clay and later on a single board.

The game was very popular in America, especially among people who liked to wager on the outcome. Indeed, nine pins was so closely linked to gambling that several states banned it in the 1840s. In response to the pre-scribed law forbidding *9 pins*, players added a pin and called the game *10 pins* so they could continue to bowl and gamble.

Near the late 1800s, the game became known as bowling. In 1895 the American Bowling Congress, which continues to govern all the rules of bowling, was organized. Bowling hit its pinnacle of popularity when it became an official Olympic event during the summer games in 1992.

Equipment

The typical bowling facility is a bowling alley. Each game is played on a bowling lane, which includes the ball return, setup pit, and lane. Bowling lanes are constructed of hard maple or laminate. The bowling lane is 63 feet (19.2 meters) long and 42 inches (106.7 centimeters) wide. Range finders (or spots) are engraved 10 to 15 feet (3.05-4.57 meters) down the lane and are used to help the bowler aim the ball toward the pins. Attached to both sides of the lane are channels, or gutters, 9 inches (22.9

centimeters) wide to catch errantly thrown balls. Additionally, a 15-foot (4.57-meter) approach, or runway, provides a lane entry and delivery area for the bowler.

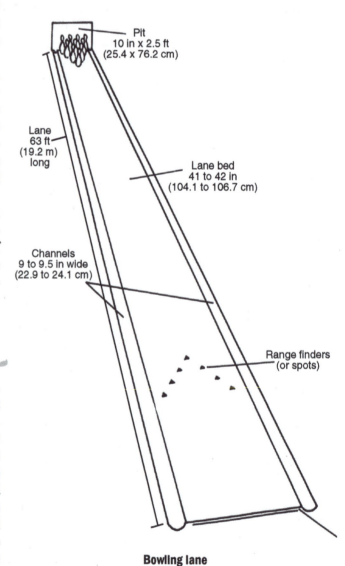

Bowling lane

Bowling equipment consists of 10 bowling pins, a bowling ball, and bowling shoes. Bowling balls are constructed of synthetic plastic or hardened rubber and have a circumference not more than 27 inches (68.6 centimeters). The official 260 ball weighs between 8 and 16 pounds (3.62-7.26 kilograms) and usually has three bored finger holes to assist the bowler in controlling the path of the ball. For beginning bowlers, the balls should weigh 9 to 11 pounds (4.08-4.99 kilograms) for girls and 11 to 15 pounds (4.98-6.8 kilograms) for boys.

The bowling pins are 15 inches (38.1 centimeters) high with a 2.25-inch (5.7-centimeter) base. They are placed at the end of the bowling lane in an equilateral triangular design, the center of each pin 12 inches (30.5 centimeters) from the next. Each pin has a number for identification purposes.

Pin positions and numbers

Unit Organization

The basic skills and strategies of bowling are relatively simple (e.g., throwing and walking into the delivery; trying to knock down as many pins as possible), but technique and form will likely require practice. Therefore, isolated skills may need further development, necessitating unit expansion.

Following is a description of each lesson in this unit.

- Lesson 1 emphasizes ball selection and the introductory delivery skills.

- Lesson 2 offers further instruction on delivery skills, including the four-step approach and throwing a hook ball.

- In lesson 3 students learn to develop a strike and spare system, including picking up spares.

- Lesson 4 presents scoring and continued practice.

- In lesson 5, students bowl an actual game.

Selected resources and assessment ideas are found in the assessment and resources chapter at the end of the unit.

Note: An asterisk (*) following a facility or equipment listing indicates that preparation is required before the lesson.

Social Skills and Etiquette

Social skills are easily incorporated into bowling. The nature of the game allows for social interaction to occur during the match. Students may work alone, with partners, or in small groups.

Bowling etiquette is relatively straightforward, including the following rules:

- The bowler should not be interrupted.

- Only one person should be on each lane's approach area at any given time. If two bowlers happen to be on the approach area at the same time, the person to the right should bowl first.

Lesson Modifications

Few modifications are required for this unit, other than individualizing equipment. Bowlers should choose the proper size shoes, and a bowling ball that fits properly and is the right weight. For students with physical disabilities, special bowling ramps are available and air-filled bumpers can fill in the gutters to allow errantly thrown balls to bounce into the pins.

This unit is designed to be taught at a bowling alley. However, it can be taught in a gym by using special rubber balls and plastic pins or 2-liter empty soda bottles (e.g., use smaller Indian clubs and soft balls).

Safety

Safety factors to consider in bowling concern the delivery and the release of the ball. Students should develop the skills of the delivery sequence without using a ball before attempting to bowl the ball. Instruct students how to retrieve the ball from the ball return so they will not pinch or otherwise injure their fingers.

Rules

Each bowler gets two chances to bowl from behind the foul line in an attempt to knock down all 10 pins. Each round of two chances is called a *frame*. A game consists of 10 frames. Basic play is as follows:

1. Bowlers, one at a time, step up to the approach area, retrieve the ball from the ball return, and prepare to bowl.

2. They bowl their first ball of the frame, trying to knock down all 10 pins. If successful, they have bowled a strike.

3. After bowling the first ball, bowlers wait for the ball to be returned and then bowl a second ball.

4. On the second ball, bowlers try to knock down the remaining pins. If successful, they have bowled a spare.

5. Bowlers count the total number of pins knocked down in two balls and record their scores.

6. All 10 pins are reset and the next bowler bowls.

After 10 frames, the bowler with the highest score wins the game.

The following rules apply to the game of bowling:

▶ If bowlers knock down all 10 pins with the first ball (a strike), they do not bowl the second ball of the frame.

▶ If a bowler crosses the foul line with the foot, hand, or arm while delivering the ball, the ball is considered foul. Any pins knocked down with a foul ball are reset, but the ball counts as a bowled ball by the player.

Note: Scoring as well as other rules and techniques of play are explained in the unit lessons.

Terms

1-3 pocket—The strike pocket for right-handers; left-handers use the 1-2 pocket.

2 o'clock-8 o'clock position— A hand position for left-handed bowlers. The thumb points at 2 o'clock, the pointer finger at 9 o'clock, and the pinky between 6 and 7 o'clock.

10 o'clock-4 o'clock position—A hand position for right-handed bowlers. The thumb points at 10 o'clock, the pointer finger points at 3 o'clock, and the pinky finger points between the 5 and 6 o'clock positions.

approach—The area where bowlers start the bowling action.

arrow or **range finder** or **spot**—A visual target for bowlers that is displayed on the lane.

foul ball—A ball that was delivered after the bowler crossed the foul line with the foot, hand, or arm.

four-step delivery approach—The basic beginning approach to bowling, consisting of the stance, push-away, approach, swing, and follow-through.

frame—Each bowler's individual turn, consisting of 2 balls, or 1 ball in the case of a strike; 10 frames constitute a game.

hook—A spin on rolling on the ball that curves it into the strike pocket.

key pin—The pin for which bowlers aim; on spares, usually the front pin (i.e., the pin closest to the bowler).

pin combination—A combination of pins hit or aimed for. Pin combinations are stated by pin numbers (e.g., a 1-2-3 pin combination comprises pins 1, 2, and 3; see the figure detailing pin positions and numbers on page 403).

point of origin—Where a bowler stands on approach for first ball delivery.

span—The distance between the thumbhole and finger holes on a bowling ball.

spare— Knocking down all 10 pins using both balls in a frame.

spin—The rotation put on the bowling ball upon release.

spot bowling—Using the arrows (or spots) as an intermediate target to aim the ball at the key pin(s).

strike—Knocking down all 10 pins with the first ball of the frame.

Ball Selection and Delivery

Purpose

In this lesson students focus on ball selection skills—analyzing fit, weight, and span—and begin to develop the four-step approach delivery, focusing on stance, grip, and point of origin.

Facility and Equipment

◆ Bowling alley (1 lane per 4 students)
◆ 1 bowling ball per student
◆ 1 pair of bowling shoes per student

Warm-Ups (6-8 Minutes)

1. Arm rotators
2. Arm pumps
3. Waist twists
4. Arm circles
5. Heel lifts

Skill Cues

Choosing a Ball

1. The weight of the ball is important. Choose one that does not feel too heavy.
2. The size of thumb and finger holes is also important when selecting a ball. The holes should fit snugly, but the fingers should come out of the ball without sticking or popping.
3. The span (i.e., the distance between the thumbhole and the finger holes) of the ball is another important aspect of a good fit. Slide the thumb comfortably in the thumbhole and stretch the hand across the other two holes, fingers flat out. The lines on the second knuckles (i.e., closest to the fingernails) of the middle and ring fingers should fall approximately .25 inches (.6 centimeters) beyond the edge of the finger holes.

Grip and Stance

1. Hold the hand position constant throughout the stance, swing, and delivery.
2. Hold the ball in the free (i.e., nonbowling) hand while getting into the proper stance.
3. Grip the ball by spreading the two outside fingers apart and pressing downward against the surface of the ball with the fingertips. Insert the two middle fingers into the finger holes. The thumb points at 10 o'clock, the pointer finger points at 3 o'clock, and the pinky finger points between the 5 and 6 o'clock positions. This is the 10 o'clock-4 o'clock

10 o'clock-4 o'clock position

position. (For left-handed bowlers use the 2 o'clock-8 o'clock position: the thumb points at 2 o'clock, the pointer finger at 9 o'clock, and the pinky between 6 and 7 o'clock.)

4. Develop a point of origin for consistently beginning the approach to the lane.

5. Coordinate lateral placement with the point of origin to begin the approach to the lane. Right-handed students identify lateral placement to the lane by standing far enough left on the approach so that the right arm is in a direct line with the second arrow (range finder) from the right. For left-handers, the left arm must be in line with the second arrow from the left.

6. In the right-handed stance, the left foot is slightly in front of the right foot and the knees are flexed. Hold the ball at waist level on the right side of the body with the forearm resting on the hip. (Left-handed bowlers do the opposite.) Square the shoulders and hips to the target.

Activities (30-40 Minutes)

1. Explain how to select a ball using the skill cues. Focus on weight and span of the ball. Allow students to try to fit a variety of bowling balls. (7-10 minutes)

2. Have students practice their grip as described in the skill cues. They should put the ball down, pick it up, and grip it several times to get the proper feeling of grip and control. (5-7 minutes)

3. Have students develop a point of origin from which to start their approach. While facing away from the bowling lane, students should stand with their heels just off the foul line and take four and a half steps toward the end of the approach area. The spot where the last foot lands will be the correct starting distance to the foul line. Students should do this several times to find a consistent beginning position, including both the point of origin and lateral placement. (7-8 minutes)

4. Present the stance to the students, emphasizing the appropriate skill cues. Allow students to practice their stance in reference to their derived point of origin. (5-7 minutes)

5. Have students start from their point of origin and move forward toward the bowling lane without using the ball. (This serves as a good practice for the four-step delivery.) Students should start with the dominant foot (i.e., the foot on the side of the bowling hand) and practice taking four steps and then sliding toward the lane. They should adjust their points of origin if they slide over the foul line. (6-8 minutes)

Closure (3-5 Minutes)

Review the lesson with students. Use the following questions and ideas to reinforce learning, check understanding, and provide feedback.

1. Review and discuss the proper method for ball selection and grip.

2. Ask students to explain how to find their point of origin and lateral alignment.

3. Discuss the importance of developing a consistent stance (i.e., so one does not cross over the foul line).

Four-Step Approach

Purpose

This lesson focuses on the development of the four-step delivery approach, recognized as the basic beginning approach to bowling, as well as the release necessary for a hook ball.

Warm-Ups (6-8 Minutes)

1. Shoulder shrugs
2. Quadriceps stretch
3. Side stretch
4. Arm pumps
5. Arm rotators

Facility and Equipment

◆ Bowling alley (1 lane per 4 students)
◆ 1 bowling ball per student
◆ 1 pair of bowling shoes per student
◆ 1 approach checklist per 2 students*

Skill Cues

1. During the approach, take three steps and then slide.
2. Step in a straight line, focusing on the target.
3. Straighten the elbow with the weight of the ball on the push-away, which is the start of the swing. The push-away pushes the ball away from the body straight out, toward the lane, which causes the bowling arm elbow to extend.
4. Keep the wrist firm during the swing and use the proper hand (i.e., 10 o'clock-4 o'clock for right-handers; 2 o'clock-8 o'clock for left-handers) position to develop a hook ball spin.
5. Keep the shoulders and hips square to the target during the swing.
6. During the delivery, release the ball over the foul line as it starts upward on the swing.
7. During release, maintain the 10-4 position; don't twist the hand.
8. First release the thumb from the ball, then release the fingers in an upward motion. This off-center release will give the ball a counterclockwise rotation (spin), which results in a slight hook when the ball reaches the pins.
9. During the follow-through, keep the eyes focused on the target and move the arm forward in line with the target arrow (range finder).

Teaching Cues

1. Review the proper stance (see lesson 1).
2. Emphasize that the push-away is a crucial part of the approach and should straighten the bowling arm. The push-away gets the body in motion.

3. The approach consists of the following elements:
   ▸ Stance
   ▸ Push-away
   ▸ Approach
   ▸ Swing
   ▸ Delivery
   ▸ Follow-through

   Be sure students understand the proper components of each. If necessary, have students practice each element separately.

4. Students should bowl on open lanes without pins first; then add the ball.

5. Before class, develop an approach checklist (using the teaching and skill cues) for students to use in activity 4.

Activities (30-40 Minutes)

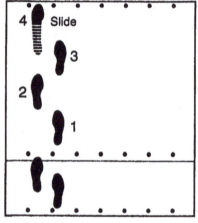

Four-step delivery approach

1. Present the four-step delivery approach, emphasizing the stance, push-away, approach, swing, and follow-through. Have students practice without using the ball and, if possible, on the approach area of a bowling lane. Have them practice several times so they can develop a rhythm to their approach. They should start slowly but accelerate through the motion. (8-10 minutes)

2. Add a ball to activity 1, this time having students practice the push-away and swing motion of the approach. They must understand that this has to be a coordinated motion. (7-9 minutes)

The proper sequence is as follows:

First step:	Push-away
Second step:	Bring the ball to the side
Third step:	Extend the ball backward
Fourth step:	Slide the front foot and bring the ball forward and release it toward the target.

3. Have students practice the delivery, slide, and release components of the approach, actually taking the last step and slide and releasing the ball. Check each student's grip and remind students that if the grip is correct, the ball will have a spin that causes it to hook. Check that each student releases the thumb first and then the fingers. Students should keep their grip position constant throughout the delivery, not letting their hands twist (If possible, do not use pins during this activity.) (7-9 minutes)

4. Pair up students or have them select partners and distribute an approach checklist to each pair. Partners should check each other's approach using the checklist. (4-6 minutes)

5. Have students begin practicing the entire motion, from the stance to the follow-through, without pins and disregarding foul lines. Emphasize the importance of developing rhythm and smoothness. Students should concentrate on rolling, not throwing, the ball down the lane. (4-6 minutes)

Closure (3-5 Minutes)

Review the lesson with students. Use the following ideas to reinforce learning, check understanding, and provide feedback.

1. Review each specific element of the four-step approach.
2. Ask if students understand the need for rhythm and acceleration in the four-step approach.
3. Discuss the importance of developing spin on the ball to make it hook into the pins.
4. Be sure students understand the relationship between grip, release, and spin.

Lesson 3

Developing a Strike and Spare System

Purpose

In this lesson students learn a strike and spare technique to become more successful in bowling.

Warm-Ups (6-8 Minutes)

1. Arm pumps
2. Arm rotators
3. Arm circles
4. Body circles
5. Waist twists

Facility and Equipment

Bowling alley (1 lane per 4 students)
1 bowling ball per student
1 pair of bowling shoes per student

Skill Cues

1. Use the second arrow (range finder) as the constant point of aim.
2. Move the point of origin in the direction of the error or mistake.
3. Face and approach the arrow; approach the lane at a slight angle.
4. Strike the 1-3 pocket at the appropriate angle by hooking the ball into the pocket.
5. Identify a key pin—usually the front pin—in all spare conversions.
6. To pick up a spare, move to the side of the approach area opposite the side of the lane where the pins are standing.
7. Always walk toward the key pin, delivering the ball in the same way a strike ball is delivered.
8. Square the shoulders to the target, not to the foul line.
9. Use the arrows, or spots, as intermediate targets to aim the ball at the key bowling pin(s). This is called *spot bowling*.

Teaching Cues

1. In developing a strike system, encourage students to hit the 1-3 pocket (1-2 for left-handers).
2. To develop a spare system, help students evaluate where to start their approach based on the pins left standing after they have thrown their first ball.

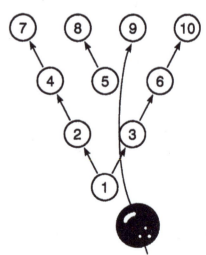

Strike pin action

Activities (30-40 Minutes)

1. Explain to the students the rationale of hooking the ball into the 1-3 pocket (i.e., increasing the probability of getting a strike). Inform students that they should move in the direction of the error in throwing the ball. That is, if the ball goes too far to the right, the bowler should move the lateral point of origin to the right while continuing to use the second arrow in from the gutter as the aiming point. (6-8 minutes)

2. Have students practice throwing strikes. (Ideally, automatic pin setters will be able to place only the 1-2-3 pin combination [i.e., set only the first three pins]). Check students' strike adjustments as they practice. (8-10 minutes)

3. Explain the spare conversion system, emphasizing the appropriate skill cues. Pay particular attention to spot bowling techniques, which involve aiming at a spot (or arrow), not a pin. (Points of aim and release for spot bowling are shown in the figure.) (7-10 minutes)

4. Have students practice picking up spares by making the necessary adjustments to their lateral points of origin. Check to be sure students are squarely facing the intended target, not the foul line. (9-12 minutes)

Points of aim

Closure (3-5 Minutes)

Review the lesson with students. Use the following ideas to reinforce learning, check understanding, and provide feedback.

1. Make sure students understand how to move in relation to the lanes to throw a strike.

2. Discuss the spare conversion process, making sure students understand how to identify the key pin in relation to converting the spare.

3. Check for students' understanding of how to adjust the point of origin in relation to converting a spare.

Lesson 4

Scoring

Purpose

In this lesson students learn how to keep score in bowling and develop practical applications of scoring through actual game play, including the 10th frame.

Warm-Ups (6-8 Minutes)

1. Shoulder shrugs
2. Waist twists
3. Quadriceps stretch
4. Arm circles
5. Shoulder pushes

Facility and Equipment

◆ Bowling alley (1 lane per 4 students)
◆ 1 bowling ball per student
◆ 2 to 3 score sheets per student*
◆ 1 pencil per student

Skill Cues

1. A bowling game consists of 10 frames; up to 2 balls are allowed per frame.
2. The bowling score is cumulative: add each frame's score to the running total.
3. If neither a spare nor strike is bowled in a frame, the actual pin count is added to the running total.
4. Knocking down all 10 pins on the first ball of a frame is a strike.
5. Knocking down all 10 pins by the second ball of a frame is a spare.
6. Spares and strikes involve a bonus system.
   ▶ The bonus for a strike is the number of pins knocked down on the next two thrown balls.
   ▶ The bonus for a spare is the number of pins knocked down on the next ball.
   ▶ For the 10th frame, a strike earns 2 extra balls and a spare earns 2 extra balls.
7. The maximum possible score per frame is 30, the score of 3 strikes in a row.
8. The maximum possible score in a game is 300, the cumulative total of 12 consecutive strikes (10 frames of strikes with 2 bonus strikes).
9. Scoring symbols in bowling are as follows:

   X   Strike
   /   Spare
   –   Miss (no pins knocked down)
   0   Split
   F   Foul (stepping over the line)

Teaching Cue

Before class, create a few different game scenarios for students to score in activity 1 using sample score sheets.

Activities (30-40 Minutes)

1. Present the scoring system to students, emphasizing the skill cues. Have students answer questions about different scoring scenarios (e.g., a spare followed by a strike, a strike followed by 3 pins and then a miss, and so on). Present some different scenarios and have students practice scoring on sample score sheets. (12-15 minutes)

1	2	3	4	5	6	7	8	9	10
1 2	1 2	1 2	1 2	1 2	1 2	1 2	1 2	1 2	1 2 3
☒	☒	☒	7 2	8 /	9 9	☒	7 /	9 –	☒ ☒ 8
30	57	76	85	95	104	124	143	152	180

☒	9 /	9 –	8 /	9 7
Strike	Spare	Miss	Split	Foul

Sample game scoring

2. Pair up students or have them select partners. Then have them bowl a half game, starting with the 5th frame and finishing with the 10th frame. Have students score their own games or their partner's games. (18-25 minutes)

Closure (3-5 Minutes)

Review the lesson with students. Use the following ideas to reinforce learning, check understanding, and provide feedback.

1. Review the scoring procedure to confirm that students understand it.
2. Determine whether students understand what each scoring symbol means.

Lesson 5

Regulation Game

Purpose

In this lesson students bowl a regulation game, enabling them to use all previously learned skills and scoring procedures.

Facility and Equipment

Bowling alley (1 lane per 4 students)
1 bowling ball per student
1 pair of bowling shoes per student
1 pencil and score sheet per lane

Warm-Ups (6-8 Minutes)

1. Arm rotators
2. Shoulder shrugs
3. Arm pumps
4. Arm circles
5. Waist twists

Teaching Cue

Assign no more than four students to a lane.

Activities (30-40 Minutes)

1. Review all the bowling skill cues, including how to find the point of origin, the four-step approach, and scoring. (8-10 minutes)
2. Divide students into groups of 4, assign each group to a lane, and assign a bowling rotation. Then have students bowl a regulation game. Students should be responsible for their own scoring (using a group score sheet) and be instructed to turn in the score sheets after the game. If time permits, assign students to new groups and bowl another game. (22-30 minutes)

Closure (3-5 Minutes)

Review the lesson with students. Use the following ideas to reinforce learning, check understanding, and provide feedback.

1. Discuss the critical points necessary for a high score in bowling (e.g., scoring strikes and spares consecutively).
2. Ask how many students bowled at least an 80-point game.
3. Share your observations about bowling etiquette during play.

Assessment and Resources

Skill and performance can be assessed throughout the unit. Following are some evaluation suggestions:

▶ Four-step delivery. Assess each student's four-step delivery formatively and frequently as students progress in their learning.

▶ Scoring. A cognitive understanding of the strike and spare system should be checked formatively after lesson 4 and again in lesson 5.

▶ Approach and points of aim. Have students demonstrate physically where to stand for picking up selected spare combinations.

▶ Technique. Various evaluations can be conducted throughout this unit. For example, check for the type of spin developed by students as they release the ball. Likewise, make sure the ball is rolling forward (or sideways for a hook ball), not sliding down the alley. If students do not have a good release, the ball will slide rather than roll during the first part of the throw.

▶ Skill. Use the actual bowling scores from lesson 5, or conduct a pretest and posttest and then average the scores to assess student ability.

Resources

Grinfelds, V., and B. Hultstrand. 1985. *Right down your alley.* 2nd ed. Champaign, IL: Leisure Press.

Mood, D., F. Musker, and J. Rink. 1999. *Sports and recreational activities.* 12th ed. New York: McGraw-Hill.

Schmottlach, N., and J. McManama. 1997. *The physical education handbook.* 9th ed. Needham Heights, MA: Allyn & Bacon.

Disc Golf

Disc golf is a relatively new sport. First played in California in the late 1960s, it evolved from recreational Frisbee throwing into a competitive sport that has attracted worldwide interest and enthusiasm. Indeed, in the United States more than a half million players participate in the sport today on over 1,000 disc golf courses, and both numbers are increasing every year. Because *Frisbee* is a registered trademark, the sport was named *disc golf* (sometimes spelled *disk golf*). Along with the name came a distinctive set of rules and equipment. In 1976 the Professional Disc Golf Association (PDGA) was established to promote the sport, govern rules, and sanction competitive events at all levels.

Until recently, young men dominated the sport. Today, however, men and women, and girls and boys of all ages enjoy the game, making it a lifetime fitness activity. Some of the characteristics that make disc golf popular among so many include the following:

- No special clothing is required.
- The cost of playing is nominal (and often free).
- The game offers year-round play, even in snow.

Disc golf is similar to traditional golf.

- Courses generally comprise 18 holes.
- Fairways average 200 to 500 feet (60.96-152.4 meters).
- The object of the game is to complete each hole in the fewest throws.

- After the tee-off, each throw is made from the previous landing spot on the fairway, the challenge being to accurately propel the disc from various distances toward the intended target.
- Like the avid ball golfer, disc golfers carry several discs, each having a specific purpose.
- Score cards often list both amateur and professional par scores for each hole.

Both games benefit from beautiful landscapes, but disc golf typically is played on more rugged terrain, land that is maintained in its natural state.

Equipment

Disc golf can be played with a single disc—although most beginners start with two: a driver and a putt and approach disc. In general, discs fall into 1 of 3 classifications: driver, mid-range driver, and putter. Within each category are several discs, allowing for every possible situation (e.g., terrain, wind conditions). As experience and skill increase, it is not uncommon for amateurs to carry six or more discs, and professionals tote even more.

When compared to Frisbees, discs are smaller in diameter and weigh more, typically between 5 and 6 ounces (142-170 grams) per disc. They are made of harder plastic and have sharper edges that make for greater aerodynamic performance. Top-quality discs cost about $10 each. To keep costs down, and because this unit aims to teach basic disc golf skills, only 2 discs are required per 2 students: 1 driver and 1 putt (or approach) disc.

The target is called a *basket,* or is referred to by its trade name (e.g., Chainstar, DISCatcher, or Pole Hole; the latter, called simply *pole hole,* is most prevalent). Targets made of galvanized steel cost about $375, but schools on a tight budget may improvise by using a round, plastic laundry basket (20-24 inches [50.8-61 centimeters] in diameter) or square box anchored on the seat of a folding chair or resting on the ground. Another option is to purchase one regulation target on wheels (these cost about $300), the instructional advantages being (1) that students would get to use at least one realistic target, and (2) easy mobility and storage.

Disc golf target

As noted earlier, the typical disc golf course is a rugged terrain. That means open fields and the like can serve as disc golf courses. For more realism in the game, consider moving the class to an actual disc golf course, which can be found in many public and municipal parks. Michigan leads the nation in the number of public disc golf courses, with over 48 courses, including a few that are among the finest in the country. To find the course locations in your state, consult the online directory hosted by the Professional Disc Golf Association (www.pdga.com/dgc-online.php).

Unit Organization

Following is a brief description of the lessons in this unit. With the exception of lesson 1, all lessons should be taught outdoors.

▶ In lesson 1 students are given an overview of the sport and then practice with the backhand throw and putt. This lesson can be conducted indoors if a curtain or netting is available, which could save valuable time normally spent chasing discs.

▶ The focus of lesson 2 is teaching the sidearm, or forehand, throw and refining the backhand throw.

▶ The tomahawk or overhand throw is introduced in lesson 3 and a modified game is played.

▶ In lesson 4 students apply their throwing skills and rules knowledge to a game on a simulated course.

Selected resources and assessment ideas are found in the assessment and resources chapter at the end of the unit.

The unit may be expanded to provide more opportunities for practice. Because distance and throwing accuracy will vary (sometimes widely) among students, expanding the unit or extending individual lessons may be advisable to build students' self-confidence. Note: All skill cues are written for right-handed students.

Note: An asterisk (*) following a facility or equipment listing indicates that preparation is required before the lesson.

Social Skills and Etiquette

As is always the case, good sporting etiquette demands positive reinforcement and encouragement between players. Students' social skills can be enhanced through partner and group activities, which promote sharing equipment, taking turns, acknowledging good performance, and helping less-skilled classmates.

In addition, certain rules of etiquette should be followed on the disc golf course, including the following:

- Ask that players respect the landscape and plant life by not littering or cutting any natural vegetation that impedes their play.
- If playing at a park or other public course, remind students to respect other park users.
- Do not divert the attention of throwers with noise or visual distractions.
- Assist, whenever possible, in the search for lost discs.

Lesson Modifications

Like traditional or ball golf, disc golf is essentially an individual activity. The game is easy to learn, and players throw their own discs and challenge themselves to achieve more (e.g., accuracy, longer distances). Because players are able to pace themselves according to their individual capabilities, few adjustments are necessary for special-needs students. Nonambulatory students will need assistance in retrieving discs, of course. When appropriate, these students can be given shorter tee-off distances during game play.

Safety

Disc golf is a relatively safe activity. Because beginners may have difficulty controlling their throws, however, remind students to stay alert and watch out for flying discs. In addition, the following rules should be explained and enforced during class:

- Make sure that the field or fairway is clear before throwing.
- Do not throw discs close to other students.
- If a throw goes further than intended or off course, call out to students in the disc's path.

- To accommodate different strength and skill levels, be sure to allow plenty of space for throwing and playing (e.g., use a large field and scatter students far enough apart).

Terms

Following is a listing of common disc golf terminology. Not all terms are included, only those necessary for beginners and recreational players.

ace—A hole-in-one.

anhyzer—A disc's flight arc that fades to the right for a right-handed backhand throw.

birdie—Completing a hole one stroke under par.

driver—A disc designed for fast, long-distance flight. The driver is the most difficult to control.

hyzer—A disc's flight arc that fades to the left for a right-handed backhand throw.

lie—The spot where a disc lands and from where the next throw is taken.

mid-range driver—A driver disc designed for slower and more stable flight.

mini—A small disc used to mark a player's lie.

par—The average number of throws for an experienced player to complete a hole.

pole hole or **basket**—The receptacle for catching the disc.

putter or **putt disc** or **putt and approach disc**—A disc designed for short-distance and stable flight.

roller—A rolling disc advance (e.g., the disc rolls along the ground).

stable—Flying straight; when released flat, a disc has a tendency to fly straight.

tee pad—The designated tee-off area.

tomahawk—An overhand throw at a vertical angle.

Rules

The game of disc golf is played somewhat like traditional golf. Each hole starts with a tee-off, followed by subsequent throws until players reach the basket. Scoring is the same as ball golf. A stroke is counted each time the disc is thrown and when a penalty is imposed (see the following listing for these penalties). Strokes are totaled to arrive at the game score. If competing in groups, the player with the fewest strokes wins.

Following is a listing of the basic play, including the rules, for disc golf. The rules listed are for recreational disc golf only; they do not include those used in competition.

▸ Tee-offs, or tee throws, must be thrown from within the designated area. Taking a few steps or running on the tee pad before throwing is permissible but neither foot can carry forward outside the tee pad. If violated, a warning is issued which, if repeated, may result in a 1-throw penalty.

▸ After teeing off, players walk down the fairway to the spots where their discs landed. The player farthest from the pole hole throws first.

▸ Players continue down the fairway toward the pole hole. At each tee-off, the player with the lowest score for the previous hole is the first to tee off.

▸ Fairway throws must be made with one foot on the spot where the disc came to rest and the other foot behind or to the side; players may not step closer to the pole hole.

▸ A disc that comes to rest more than 6.56 feet (2 meters) above the ground is considered unplayable and is played from the ground at that spot (and a 1-throw penalty is imposed). Discs that land and rest lower are considered playable.

▸ If a disc is lost or considered unsafe to play, another is played from the closest area (and a 1-throw penalty is imposed).

▸ Along the fairway and until players are 32.8 feet (10 meters) from the pole hole, stepping forward on the follow-through (after release) is acceptable. Stepping forward closer to the pole hole before the disc lands constitutes a falling putt (a 1-throw penalty) and must be thrown again.

▸ To complete the hole, or hole out, the disc must rest either within the chains or in the basket. A disc that rests on top of the hole apparatus does not constitute a hole out.

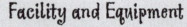

Lesson 1

Introduction to Disc Golf and the Backhand Throw

Purpose

In this lesson students learn about the game of disc golf, including the equipment used, and start to develop their grip and backhand throwing techniques.

Warm-Ups (6-8 Minutes)

1. Side pattern jumps
2. Floor touches
3. Wrist rotation and flexion
4. Heel lifts
5. Sprint-jog intervals

Skill Cues

1. For the backhand throw, use either a three-finger grip or a four-finger grip.
   - ▸ The four-finger grip is as follows: grip the disc with four fingers curled under the rim and the thumb on top.
   - ▸ The three-finger grip is as follows: grip the disc by holding three fingers curled under the rim, the thumb on top, and the index finger along the side of the disc.
2. Take a stable stance, keeping the knees flexed, with the right side toward the intended target.

Facility and Equipment

- ◆ Large outdoor area or gym with a curtain or netting
- ◆ 1 driver per student
- ◆ 1 putt and approach per student
- ◆ 1 cone per 4 or 5 students

Four-finger grip

Three-finger grip

3. Swing the disc backward, crossing the chest to the left side, and cock the wrist on the backswing.

4. Let the disc rest on the left hand to ensure a level start; then unwind the arm, keeping the disc flat.

5. Snap the wrist on release.

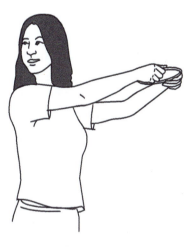

Backhand swing

Backhand release (flat)

6. Use an open body stance on the putt and do not carry either foot forward.

Teaching Cues

1. Explain that successful throwing performance is as much a matter of individual style as individual skill. Therefore, stance, grip, swing, release, and overall form show wide variations.

2. Encourage students to use a four-finger grip, but if the three-finger grip works better for certain students, do not discourage it.

3. Tell students that cocking the wrist and snapping the wrist on release provide much of the speed and, therefore, distance.

4. Remind students that good form necessitates balance, weight distribution, and using the center of gravity to increase force.

5. Concentrate initially on form and trajectory.

6. Encourage students to analyze their release, noting that the tilt of the disc produces different flight patterns.

7. Allow plenty of space between students when practicing their throws. It may be advisable to move stronger throwers to one end of the area.

8. Remind students to watch out for flying discs.

Activities (30-40 Minutes)

1. Present some information about the growing popularity of disc golf. Introduce the equipment, terms, and some basic rules of the game; then discuss where there are courses in your area. Encourage students who have played disc golf to share their experiences, likes and dislikes, and other information. (3-5 minutes)

2. Explain and demonstrate the three- and four-finger grips, including proper stance and release, for the backhand throw using the appropriate skill and teaching cues. (3-5 minutes)

3. Practice drill. Position students in partners about 75 feet (22.86 meters) apart and have them practice the backhand throw. One partner throws; the other retrieves and throws back. Start with the putt discs because control will be easier. Remind students to concentrate on form and flat release. (10-14 minutes)

4. When students are comfortable with the putters, increase the distance between students and distribute drivers. Have students perform the practice drill, concentrating on form and release in putter throws. Assist students who are having difficulty. (6-8 minutes)

5. Putting drill. Position students in groups of 4 or 5 and place a cone 25 to 30 feet (7.62-9.14 meters) in front of them. Students practice putting at the target (cone), trying to hit it or land the disc as close as possible. Once every student in the group has thrown, all should retrieve their discs. (8 minutes)

Closure (3-5 Minutes)

Review the lesson with students. Use the following ideas to reinforce learning, check understanding, and provide feedback.

1. Share your observations of students' performances, including form, release, and distance.

2. Review the major elements of the backhand throw.

Lesson 2

Sidearm Throw

Purpose

In this lesson students refine the backhand throw, work on distance and accuracy, and develop the sidearm throw.

Facility and Equipment

- ◆ Large outdoor field
  1 driver per 2 students
- ◆ 1 putt and approach disc per 2 students
- ◆ 1 cone per 4 students

Warm-Ups (6-8 Minutes)

1. Step touches
2. Side holds
3. Arm pumps
4. Lateral hops
5. Running in place

Skill Cues

1. For a sidearm throw, grip the disc using either a three- or two-finger grip. The disc rests against the little finger (three-finger) or ring finger (two-finger) and the thumb is on top.
2. Take a stable stance, keeping the knees flexed, with the left side toward the intended target.
3. Draw the throwing arm backward, across the same side of the body, cocking the wrist at the end of the backswing, and whipping the disc forward into a flat forward thrust.
4. Snap the wrist on release.

Two-finger sidearm throw

Teaching Cues

1. Let students know that it is permissible to run a few steps on teeing-off before releasing the disc on the tee pad.
2. Point out that the sidearm throw is more difficult to control.
3. Tell students to think of the sidearm movement as similar to a sidearm ball throw.
4. Explain that the sidearm throw may be the only throw possible from some lies.

Activities (30-40 minutes)

1. Review the backhand throw and the four-finger grip. Have them perform the practice drill in lesson 1 (see activity 3) with a driver. (8-10 minutes)
2. Explain and demonstrate the sidearm, or forehand, throw using the skill and teaching cues. Have the students practice the proper form without discs. (4-6 minutes)
3. Sidearm practice drill. Keeping the same partners and drill formation, have students practice the sidearm throw using drivers. (8-10 minutes)
4. Accuracy drill. Divide the class into two groups: those with longer and those with shorter throwing distance. Then divide students into groups of 4; distribute 2 drivers and 1 cone to each group. Have each student take a practice throw and then place each group's cone at the average throwing distance down the field. In the drill, 2 students throw and 2 retrieve. Throwers take 4 throws at the cone, alternating backhand and sidearm; then students switch positions. (10-14 minutes)

Closure (3-5 Minutes)

Review the lesson with students. Use the following ideas and questions to reinforce learning, check understanding, and provide feedback.

1. Ask students to consider and respond to the following questions:
   ▸ Which throw, the backhand or the sidearm, gave the most control? The most distance?
   ▸ Which was more difficult? Why?
2. Ask how many students were able to increase their distance on the backhand throw. Discuss the results of running a few steps before release (e.g., did distance and accuracy increase or decrease?).
3. Discuss left and right flight fades. Introduce the terms *hyzer* and *anhyzer* (see the terms listing in the unit introduction). Talk about possible causes such as wind conditions, release trajectory, stance, and wrist snap. Some discs are purposely designed to provide more left or right fade.

Overhand Throw

Purpose

In this lesson students learn the overhand, or tomahawk, throw and put their learned skills into a modified game.

Warm-Ups (6-8 Minutes)

1. Slapping jacks
2. Phalange flings
3. Side pattern jumps
4. Arm circles
5. Scissors

Facility and Equipment

- Large outdoor field
- 1 driver per 2 students
- 1 putt and approach disc per 2 students
- 9 hoops
- 9 numbered cones*
- 9 numbered jump ropes*
- Rules and terms handouts*

Skill Cues

1. Use a three- or two-finger tomahawk grip for the overhand throw.

Three-finger tomahawk grip

2. Take a forward stride position.
3. Draw the disc backward, over the shoulder, and keep it vertical to the ground.
4. Cock the wrist and bring the arm forward for the release.

Two-finger tomahawk release

Teaching Cues

1. Explain that the movements of the tomahawk, or overhand throw, are similar to an overhand baseball throw.

2. Point out that the tomahawk is used mainly when the opening (e.g., trees) to throw through is narrow.

3. Try different release points for distance and accuracy.

4. Remind students to be alert and watch for flying discs.

5. Before class, set up the disc golf course for activity 3. Place the hoops at various distances on the field and place a cone in the center of each hoop. (Allow plenty of space between holes and far enough apart for safety.) These represent the pole holes; you can paint hole numbers on the cones or affix signs to each. Use the jump ropes to delimit the tee-off areas (tee pads) for each hole. (Locate them at a distance away from each hole that will be challenging for students, but not so far away that students will not be able to reach them in three throws—using a driver and a putter for each hole.) Mark the tee pads with numbers that correspond with the hole numbers, or place large number signs near each tee pad.

Activities (30-40 Minutes)

1. Explain and demonstrate the tomahawk, or overhand throw, using the appropriate skill and teaching cues. (3-5 minutes)

2. Tomahawk drill. Arrange groups of three students in a triangle formation about 50 feet (15.24 meters) apart. Give each group a driver or putter. Students throw the disc overhand to one another, throwing it randomly or in a triangle pattern. Shorten or lengthen the distance according to skill. (7-9 minutes)

3. Three-throw game. Explain the disc golf course: there are 9 holes (cones and hoops) and 9 tee pads (jump ropes). Remind students that they must stay within the tee pad area during tee-off. Divide the class into teams of 3; distribute 2 discs (a driver and a putter) and assign a different tee pad to each. Each team gets 3 throws per hole, 1 throw per student. (Students should take turns teeing off and putting at different holes.) Each player must use at least 1 sidearm and 1 overhand throw during the game. Teams earn 1 point for each completed hole (i.e., getting the disc into the basket). After all teams have completed 9 holes, the team with the most baskets wins. (20-26 minutes)

Closure (3-5 Minutes)

Review the lesson with students. Use the following ideas and questions to reinforce learning, check understanding, and provide feedback.

1. Ask students the following questions about the three-throw game:
   - How many times did each team either hit the target cone or land within the hoop?
   - What were some of the problems encountered using the overhand throw? The sidearm throw? The putt?

2. Tell students that they will play a modified game of disc golf during the next lesson. Provide a handout of basic terms and rules to be studied before the next class.

Lesson 4

Modified Disc Golf Game

Purpose

In this lesson students will play a modified game of disc golf, applying the rules and strategies of the game.

Warm-Ups (6-8 Minutes)

1. Push-ups or step and calf taps
2. Arm circles or wrist rotation and flexion
3. Grapevine step or elbow-knee touches (standing)
4. Forward lunges or faceup flank
5. Sprint-jog intervals or imaginary jump rope

Skill Cues

1. Record the number of throws at the end of each hole.
2. Use the grips and throws that are most developed (and most comfortable) at this point in the unit.
3. Stay alert; watch for flying discs.

Teaching Cues

1. Check if there are rule questions before starting play.
2. Keep this lesson moving; be sure students do not waste time because others will be waiting to play.
3. If there is enough space and class size merits it, add more course holes.
4. If student pairs outnumber holes, double up the skilled playing pairs at the same tee pad.
5. Before class, set up the disc golf course. If regulation baskets are not available, make your own using cones and hoops (see lesson 3, teaching cue 5) or laundry baskets (see "Equipment" in the unit introduction).
6. For more authenticity, make up score cards before class.
7. It may be advisable to make up a player or pair roster before class. If skill levels vary widely among students, try to pair up similarly skilled players to play together.
8. If desired, add a second or third class session to give students more time to understand the game and refine their playing skills.

Facility and Equipment

- Large outdoor field with a course* or disc golf course
- 2 discs per 2 students
- 9 numbered baskets*
- 9 numbered tee pads*
- Pairs tee-off schedule*
- Score cards*

Activities (30-40 Minutes)

1. Explain the game and course layout. Use the following modified rules and suggestions if appropriate. (5-7 minutes)
   - ▶ Skill and accuracy: For the hole-out to count, the disc must either land in the basket or be over halfway inside the hoop.
   - ▶ Time: Players must move to the next tee pad after eight throws, even if they have not holed out.
   - ▶ Disc availability: With limited discs (two per pair of students), two playing and scoring options are suggested: (1) Pairs can alternate throws per hole and score each hole as one score and then total all 9 holes for a pair score, following the same procedure for the next class session. (2) Each plays every other hole for an individual score and alternates the holes the next class session, totaling individual scores for all 9 holes.

2. Assign pairs to tee-off areas and begin play. Pairs will play all 9 holes progressing to the next numbered hole with #9 going to #1. (25-33 minutes)

Closure (3-5 Minutes)

Review the lesson with students. Use the following ideas and questions to reinforce learning, check understanding, and provide feedback.

1. Ask students to share their hole-out strokes. How many were able to hole out in 8 or fewer throws? on 6 holes? 5 holes? at least 1 hole? Did anyone hole out in 5 or fewer throws? on any holes? How many?

2. Question students about their understanding of game rules and clear up any misunderstandings and confusion.

3. Share your observations of students' playing techniques and rules application.

4. If more class sessions will be devoted to this unit, announce that the next class will be a continuation of today's nine-hole game.

Assessment and Resources

Students' knowledge of and skill in disc golf can be judged formally or informally. Observe students during the nine-hole game in lesson 4, or conduct written testing at the end of the unit. Skill tests can also be given after every lesson; however, because distance and accuracy of throwing determine success in playing disc golf, the following two skill tests are suggested.

▶ Distance throwing. Mark distances of 50, 75, 100, 125, and 150 feet (15.24, 22.86, 30.48, 38.1, and 45.72 meters) using cones arranged in a straight line. From behind a starting line, students get three chances to throw a driver (using whichever grip they prefer), trying for the greatest distance possible. Total the score for three throws. Use the following scoring system:

Over 50 feet (15.24 meters)	1 point
Over 75 feet (22.86 meters)	2 points
Over 100 feet (30.48 meters)	3 points
Over 125 feet (38.1 meters)	4 points
Over 150 feet (45.72 meters)	5 points

You may want to adjust distances and scoring according to physical size and gender.

▶ Putting accuracy. Set up two concentric circles (use ropes, washable spray paint, and so on): a circle 5 feet (1.52 meters) in diameter inside a circle 10 feet (3.05 meters) in diameter. Place a basket in the center of the inner (5-foot [1.52-meter]) circle. Draw a tee-off line 25 feet (7.62 meters) away from the basket. Students get three chances to throw for a putt from the line, trying to get the disc as close to the basket as possible. Total the score for three throws. Use the following scoring system:

Inside the outer circle	1 point
Inside the inner circle	2 points
In the basket	3 points

Resources

Professional Disc Golf Association (PDGA). 1997. *Rules of play.* Toronto, ON, Canada: PDGA.

Sullivan, B. 2001. The disk golf sensation. *The Park & Recreation Trades* 8 (5): 4-6.

Additional Resources

Disc Golf Industries
www.discgolf.com
> Offers suggestions for designing disc golf courses and sells disc golf apparel, equipment, and merchandise.

Everything Disc Golf
Phone 888-818-DISC (3472)
www.everythingdiscgolf.com
> Offers disc golf apparel and equipment, articles about the sport, and an online directory of disc golf courses.

Professional Disc Golf Association
115 Front St. East, Suite 485
Toronto, Ontario, Canada M5A-4S6
Phone 416-203-9628
www.pdga.com
> Offers rules listings, professional tour statistics and schedules, and an online directory of disc golf courses.

Floor Hockey

Floor hockey originally evolved as an adaptation of ice hockey for play on the streets. Called *street hockey,* this game was played on pavement using modified ice hockey equipment. Unfortunately, this equipment did not hold up to street use. In 1963 a few sport equipment companies began developing plastic sticks and pucks suitable for indoor and outdoor use (on smooth surfaces). It was then that the game of floor hockey emerged.

The original floor hockey rules were adapted from National Hockey League rules. The National Hockey League was founded in 1917 in Montreal, Canada. Many of the penalties (minor, major, and misconduct) and infractions in ice hockey have been adopted as

floor hockey rules. High sticking, hooking, checking, and charging are examples of offenses that apply to both sports. Both games also have three periods of play time.

Floor hockey is an excellent addition to a secondary physical education curriculum because it is easily taught, the skills are not very specialized, and the rules are simple.

Equipment

Floor hockey can be played on any area, but a basketball court with a centerline is ideal. This line and goal lines are required for a floor hockey court. The goal is an area 2 by 6 feet

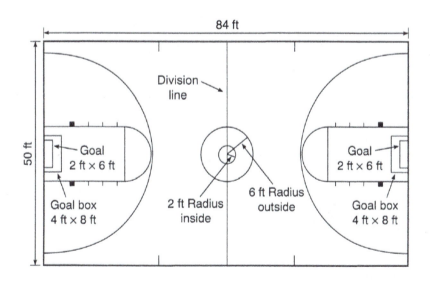

Floor hockey court dimensions

(.61 by 1.83 meters) centered at each end of the playing area. The goal box is a rectangle 4 by 8 feet (1.22 by 2.44 meters) around the goal.

Game equipment consists of goals, plastic hockey sticks, and plastic goalie sticks. Balls or plastic pucks may be used. The end of the goalie stick is wider and more square than the end of other players' sticks. It is also recommended that gloves be worn by the goalie for protection when stopping the puck with the hands.

Unit Organization

Lessons in this unit have been created based on the assumption that students have had previous experience with floor hockey during the lower grades. If necessary, devote more class time to review basic floor hockey skills at the beginning of the unit.

Following is a brief description of each lesson in this unit.

▶ Lesson 1 offers instruction in dribbling and passing, and teaches students how to grip and handle the stick.

▶ Shooting and goaltending skills are developed in lesson 2.

▶ Lesson 3 introduces the various player positions in floor hockey and presents strategy for each position. It also provides lead-up activities to sharpen students' playing skills.

▶ In lesson 4 students get the opportunity to play a regulation game of floor hockey.

Selected resources and assessment ideas are found in the assessment and resources chapter at the end of the unit.

Note: An asterisk (*) following a facility or equipment listing indicates that preparation is required before the lesson.

Social Skills and Etiquette

Social skills and etiquette should be emphasized throughout this unit. The game of floor hockey can become very competitive and rough if the proper atmosphere is not created and then maintained. Discussions about good sporting behavior, fair play, and teamwork are helpful in setting the proper tone.

In addition, students who are more aggressive in their play should be continually encouraged and reminded to involve teammates who are less assertive. This will not only help balance game play but also enhance the self-image and self-confidence of these and less-skilled students.

Lesson Modifications

Floor hockey can be a high-exertion game, particularly for students of lower fitness levels. It involves a lot of running as well as quick maneuvering of equipment. The following modifications are suggested to increase enjoyment levels for all and to include students with physical impairments in the game.

▶ Reduce the size of the playing area.

▶ Shorten playing time: use rotation systems or shorter periods.

▶ Use pucks; a puck produces slower play than a ball.

▶ Cover pucks with tape to weight them down; this enables easier control.

▶ Assign disabled or immobile students to play the goalie position.

▶ When assigning teams, consider students' skill levels, matching those with lesser abilities to play together and those with higher abilities to play together. This enables success for students with lower skill levels and provides challenge for students with more advanced skills.

Safety

Several safety factors should be observed in unit instruction.

▶ Do not allow students to raise their sticks above the waist (called *high sticking*) and strictly enforce this rule during game play.

▶ Enforce penalties for any body contact (e.g., elbowing, butt ending, interference and charging, tripping and hooking, checking and slashing). If not curtailed, these infractions can result in serious injury.

▶ Another means of reducing potential injuries is teaming up players of similar ability. This will also eliminate passive players being physically intimidated.

Rules

The object of the game is to hit the puck into the opponent's goal. A game consists of three 8-minute periods, with a 5-minute break between each period. At the end of the game, the team with the most points wins.

A typical team has 6 players:

▶ 1 goalie
▶ 1 center
▶ 2 forwards
▶ 2 guards

Play

The game begins with a face-off at the middle of the centerline; a face-off also begins play after a goal is scored. In a face-off, two opposing centers face each other, holding their sticks on the floor. As the puck is dropped between them, each player tries to gain control of the puck and advance it toward the opponent's goal (by passing it to an offensive player to take down the court). From there, play is continuous; players will be moving almost constantly. The offense and defense battle for control of the puck, trying to advance it to the opponent's goal to score.

The basic rules of floor hockey are as follows:

▶ When a puck goes out-of-bounds, the last team that contacted it loses possession.

▶ Players may advance the puck with their feet but may not kick it into the goal to score. If a team kicks the puck into the goal, they lose possession of it.

▶ All players may stop the puck with their hands but may not hold, pass, or throw it.

▶ The goalie is the only player permitted to catch or throw the puck. Goalies must throw it to the side of the goal box, not toward the opponent's goal.

▶ The puck must precede offensive players across the centerline.

▶ Players must keep their sticks below the waist.

▶ Players must avoid all body contact with opponents.

Penalties

The following penalties result in removing the offending player from the game. An unintentional violation results in a 2-minute penalty, and an intentional violation results in a 4-minute penalty. Players being penalized must sit in a penalty box or some area outside the court.

▶ Interference and charging
▶ Elbowing
▶ Cross-checking and slashing
▶ Butt ending (jabbing a player with the shaft of the stick)
▶ High sticking
▶ Tripping and hooking
▶ Guards or forwards playing over the centerline

Lesson 1

Dribbling and Passing

Purpose

In this lesson students develop dribbling and passing skills needed to play floor hockey, and learn how to grip and stick maneuver the hockey stick.

Facility and Equipment

- ◆ Gym or outdoor area with a smooth surface
- ◆ 1 plastic hockey stick per student
- ◆ 1 plastic puck (or ball) per 2 students
- ◆ 5 cones per obstacle course

Warm-Ups (6-8 Minutes)

1. Scissors
2. Horizontal run
3. Hip stretch
4. Arm support lifts

Skill Cues

Grip

1. Place the left hand (the right hand for left-handed students) on the top of the stick, as if shaking hands with it.
2. Position the right hand (usually the left hand for left-handed students) 10 to 12 inches (25.4-30.5 centimeters) below the left hand.
3. Point the thumbs toward the blade.

Dribbling

1. Use short, quick, controlled taps, keeping the puck 18 to 24 inches (45.7-61 centimeters) out in front.
2. Alternate contacting the puck with both sides of the stick (forehand or backhand).
3. Keep the stick low to be ready to receive the puck.

Passing

1. Use a pushing motion to pass short distances.
2. Avoid a backswing; instead push the puck with a sweeping action.
3. Pass using wrist action for greater control. This can be best achieved with a flicking motion.
4. Send the puck ahead of the teammate receiving the pass.

Receiving

1. Trap the puck by tilting the blade over the puck.
2. Let the stick give as the puck hits the blade; this will prevent it from rebounding away.

Teaching Cues

1. Students should thinking about *passing* or *pushing,* not hitting, the puck.
2. Remind students to keep their eyes on the puck.

Activities (30-40 Minutes)

Grip and handling position

1. Introduce dribbling and passing, emphasizing the skill and teaching cues. Introduce and demonstrate how to grip and handle the stick. (6-8 minutes)
2. Divide students into groups of 4; then position 2 students (students A and C) on one side of the gym and 2 students (students B and D) opposite them on the other side of the gym. Student A dribbles the puck across the gym. Within 5 feet (1.52 meters) of the other side, student A passes the puck to student B and remains on that side of the gym. Student B then dribbles the puck across the gym, passing to student C, who dribbles the puck across the gym, and so on. (6 minutes)
3. Zigzag accuracy dribble. Create a zigzag obstacle course using cones. Divide students into groups of 4 and have each group line up at the start of a course. Each student must dribble through the cones, and back again, without touching them. The object of this drill is accuracy. (5 minutes)
4. Zigzag speed dribble. Using the same groups and courses as in activity 3, have students dribble through the cones, and back again, as quickly as possible. Have students try to beat a certain time, set appropriately for the length of the course (e.g., 12 seconds). (5 minutes)
5. Square pass drill. Divide students into groups of 5: 4 students stand in a square and the fifth stands in the center. The outside students attempt to pass the puck to one another while the center student tries to intercept. If the center intercepts the pass, the student who made the pass switches places with the center. The purpose of this drill is that students learn how to get a defensive player out of position to set up successful passes. (8-16 minutes)

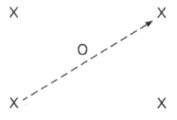

Square pass drill formation

Optional Activity

Hockey Dribble Escape (0-10 Minutes)

Designate two students to be chasers, the rest will be players. At the signal to start, players dribble their pucks around the gym. The chasers, without pucks, move around the players and attempt to push the pucks away. When successful, players surrender their pucks and become chasers. Continue until all players become chasers.

Closure (3-5 Minutes)

Review the lesson with students. Use the following ideas to reinforce learning, check understanding, and provide feedback.

1. Discuss the factors to consider when passing to a teammate (e.g., speed of the teammate, speed of the puck, direction of the teammate, and so on).

2. Discuss offensive strategies that are important in floor hockey (e.g., follow the path of all shots, use short and quick passes to prevent interceptions).

Shooting and Goaltending

Purpose

In this lesson students develop shooting and goaltending skills. Two types of shooting, the slap shot and the wrist shot, are introduced.

Facility and Equipment

- Gym or outdoor area with a smooth surface
- 1 plastic hockey puck (or ball) per student
- 1 plastic hockey stick per student
- 2 cones per 3 students

Warm-Ups (6-8 Minutes)

1. Sprint-jog intervals
2. Hip lifts
3. Mad cat
4. Hamstring straight-leg stretch

Skill Cues

Shooting

1. Use a slap or wrist shot.
2. Keep both the backswing and the follow-through short.
3. Do not raise the stick above the waist on the hit.
4. Slap shots are used for shooting a longer distance from the net.
5. For the slap shot, do not flex the wrist; instead, push the puck toward the goal by taking a swing behind and then swinging quickly forward.
6. Wrist shots are used when shooting close to the net.
7. For the wrist shot, the blade and the puck should touch before shooting; then snap the wrist for added speed during propulsion.

Goaltending

1. Use the crouch position and move from side to side to block the puck.
2. Grip the stick by placing one hand in the middle of the shaft.
3. Use the other hand to catch and pass the puck quickly out to a teammate on the side of the goal. (Holding the puck or throwing it toward the opponent's net is not permitted.)
4. Block shots with the hand, body, foot, or stick; do not use the body (i.e., lie down) to block ground shots.

Teaching Cues

1. Remind students to look at the target before shooting.
2. Emphasize that accuracy is more important than speed.
3. Remind students to transfer weight to the front foot when shooting.

Activities (30-40 Minutes)

1. Present the techniques for shooting and goaltending, emphasizing the skill and teaching cues. Introduce the slap shot and wrist shot as two shooting techniques. (6-8 minutes)

2. Shooting challenge. Set up mini goals around the perimeter of the gym using cones. Divide students into groups of three and line up each group 20 feet (6.1 meters) away from a goal. Each student shoots a puck into the goal. After every student has taken a shot, all students in the group should retrieve their pucks at the same time and then repeat the drill. For more challenge, place a tire or other obstacle in the center of the goal. This will force students to hit the puck in from the side or increase the distance of the shot. (8 minutes)

3. Goalie challenge. Using the same goals around the perimeter of the gym, add a goalie to the mix. Divide students into groups of 4: 3 shooters and 1 goalie. The goalie stands between the cones and attempts to block the shots taken by shooters, then returns the puck to the shooters after each shot. Have students rotate positions so that everyone gets the chance to be a goalie. (8 minutes)

4. Goaltending drill. Divide the class into 4 groups and distribute 3 pucks to 2 of the groups. Groups 1 and 4 stand at either end of the gym; they are goalies. Groups 2 and 3 shoot pucks over the end line; they are shooters and try to shoot over the end line past the goalies. Group 2 shoots only toward group 1 goalies; group 3 shoots only toward group 4 goalies. After 4 minutes of play, goalies and shooters should switch positions. (8-16 minutes)

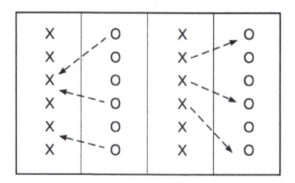

Goaltending drill

Optional Activity

Square Hockey (0-12 Minutes)

Divide the class into two teams and distribute a hockey stick and Wiffle ball to each player. One team stands behind a line opposite the other team's line. Place a large, lightweight, rubber or plastic ball in the center area between the two teams. At the signal to start, both teams shoot at the large ball, attempting to move it toward the opposite team's line. (At various times throughout the game, have students use specific shots: the slap shot or the wrist shot.) If the ball passes the other team's line or is touched by a player's body or stick, the other team gets 1 point. The team with the most points wins the game.

Closure (3-5 Minutes)

Review the lesson with students. Use the following ideas to reinforce learning, check understanding, and provide feedback.

1. Discuss the skills and strategies needed for goaltending (e.g., block shots with the hand, body, or stick; hold the stick in one hand and use the other hand to catch and pass the puck; use a crouch position).
2. Ask students to identify the positions on a floor hockey team, including the names and responsibilities of each. These will be discussed in the next lesson.

Lesson 3

Positioning and Modified Game Play

Purpose

In this lesson students further develop their floor hockey skills and learn about strategy and positioning.

Warm-Ups (6-8 Minutes)

1. Running in place
2. Inverted hurdler's stretch
3. Shoulder shrugs
4. Seated hamstring stretch

Skill Cues

Facility and Equipment

◆ Basketball court or other area with a smooth surface
◆ 1 plastic hockey stick per student
◆ 1 plastic puck (or ball) per game
◆ 1 colored pinnie per 2 students
◆ 20 to 25 cones (or floor tape)
◆ 1 floor hockey rules handout* per student
Note: The playing area should be twice as long as it is wide, with a centerline and outside boundary lines.

Positions

1. The center moves the entire length of the court, playing offense and defense depending on which team has possession of the puck. Each team typically has only one center.

2. Forwards, typically two per team, play offense from the centerline forward. When the opponent has the puck, forwards can assist guards in defensive play and in getting possession of the puck.

3. Guards, typically two per team, play defense from the centerline backward. Guards should always face the puck, never their own goal, and never have their backs toward the action. Guards try to pass to the center, who gets the puck back into offensive play.

4. The goalie, one per team, stands in or near the goal. Goalies should always remain between the goal and the puck and be ready to defend against a shot. The goalie clears the puck away from the front of the goal (i.e., passes it to the side) so that the guards or the center can move the puck back into offensive play.

Strategy

1. Follow the path of all shots, including rebounds.
2. Pass to teammates who are in a more favorable position to score.
3. Shoot for the goal when the goalie is out of position.
4. Use short, quick passes to advance the puck and prevent interception by the opposite team.
5. Pass the puck ahead of receivers so that they can continue to run.

Teaching Cues

1. Emphasize that teamwork is essential for effective play. Players should pass as much as possible and try to catch the other team off guard.

2. Have students change positions periodically throughout the activities.

3. All games in this lesson require knowledge of floor hockey rules. Be sure students understand the rules before proceeding to the games.

Activities (30-40 Minutes)

1. Present floor hockey strategy and positioning using the appropriate skill and teaching cues. (3-4 minutes)

2. Explain the rules of floor hockey (see the unit introduction on page 431). (3-4 minutes)

Optional Activity: Alley Floor Hockey

3. Divide students into 2 teams, and designate 7 active players on each team; the remaining players are sideline players. Explain the rules and play a game of sideline floor hockey. (12-16 minutes)

Sideline Floor Hockey

Active players play the regular floor hockey positions. Sideline players play at the sidelines, keeping the puck from going out-of-bounds and returning it to active teammates. Sideline players may advance the puck down the sideline or the floor, but they cannot score. Sideline and active players should switch positions after 3 minutes or after each goal. Play this game with one team occupying each sideline or with sideline players from both teams on each sideline.

4. Divide the class into two teams and assign each team member a number. Explain the rules and play a game of end zone floor hockey. (12-16 minutes)

End Zone Floor Hockey

To begin the game, players 1 through 5 from each team play as 2 forwards, 1 center, and 2 guards. The remaining players from each team play the goalie position. All floor hockey rules apply. After 3 minutes or after each goal, the 5 players rotate to the end zone to play as goalies and the next 5 players take their places.

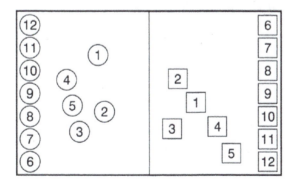

End zone floor hockey formation

Optional Activity: Win the Puck

Optional Activities

Alley Floor Hockey (0-15 Minutes)

Divide the court into five alleys using cones or floor tape. A player from each team plays in each alley; the remaining team players are goalies. All floor hockey rules apply, with one addition: when players leave their alley, their team loses possession of the puck. After 3 minutes or after each goal, alley players switch positions with goalies.

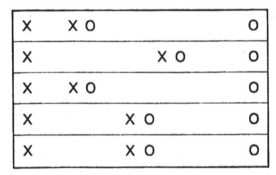

Alley floor hockey formation

Win the Puck (0-15 Minutes)

Divide the class into teams of 4 or 5 and have each team stand behind a line, across from another team. Center a puck between the two teams and assign each team player a number, 1 through 4 or 5. When their number is called, players move to the middle and try to take possession of the puck and score a goal by shooting it through the opposite team's line. After each score, a new number is called and those players move to the middle to take possession of the puck.

Closure (3-5 Minutes)

Review the lesson with students. Use the following ideas to reinforce learning, check understanding, and provide feedback.

1. Review the responsibilities of various player positions.
2. Distribute the rules handouts and tell students to be sure they know all the rules before the next class period.

Regulation Game

Purpose

In this lesson students learn the rules and play a regulation game of floor hockey.

Warm-Ups (6-8 Minutes)

1. Sprint-jog intervals
2. Push-ups
3. High jumper
4. Floor touches

Facility and Equipment

- Basketball court or outdoor area with a smooth surface
- 1 plastic hockey stick per student
- 1 plastic puck (or ball) per game
- 1 colored pinnie per 2 students
- 4 cones or 2 hockey nets

Note: The playing area should be twice as long as it is wide, with a centerline and outside boundary lines.

Skill Cues

1. Stay in position at all times.
2. Focus on the puck.
3. Use continuous movement during play.
4. Anticipate rebounds from other players.
5. Pass the puck so that the receiver does not have to stop or slow down.
6. Try to score when the goalie is out of position.

Teaching Cues

1. To keep teams balanced and maximize participation, assign teams rather than let students choose teammates.
2. Remind students of the importance of fair play and the rules of etiquette (see the unit introduction on page 431).
3. If class size is too large for normal play, increase the team sizes or set up more than one game for simultaneous play.

Activities (30-40 Minutes)

1. Review the rules of floor hockey and review the skills needed for game play. (5-8 minutes)
2. Assign students to teams and play a game of regulation floor hockey. (25-32 minutes)

Closure (3-5 Minutes)

Review the lesson with students. Use the following ideas to reinforce learning, check understanding, and provide feedback.

1. Discuss ways students could improve team play (e.g., pass more to teammates who are in a better position to score, play more to the sides of the court than to the center, anticipate the movement of the puck).

2. Discuss various strategies that can be used in floor hockey (e.g., get the goalie out of position by causing him or her to block another shot, use many passes so the opponent's defense has difficulty anticipating the path of the puck).

Assessment and Resources

Skill tests and game play assessment can be formal or informal in this unit. Formal testing can be conducted on such things as floor hockey rules, proper grip, goaltending position, and position responsibilities. You can also use many of the lesson activities for testing or give separate skill tests. In general, testing students on passing, shooting, and dribbling is sufficient.

The following lesson activities could be adapted for testing purposes:

- Zigzag accuracy dribble (see lesson 1, activity 3)
- Zigzag speed dribble (see lesson 1, activity 4)
- Shooting challenge (see lesson 2, activity 2)
- Goalie challenge (see lesson 2, activity 3)

In addition, the following tests may be used for assessment purposes in this unit. Assessment protocol is listed with each.

- Speed dribble. Time students as they dribble around a cone placed 20 feet (6.1 meters) away. Count the best of three trials.

- Target shoot. Tape one edge of several cardboard boxes to the floor as targets. Each student must shoot three pucks at a box from a starting line 20 feet (6.1 meters) away. Students get 1 point for each successful shot in the target.

- Passing for time. In partners standing 20 feet (6.1 meters) apart, students complete as many passes to their partners as possible within 3 minutes. Students may not touch the puck with their hands.

Resources

Bailey, G. 2000. *The ultimate sport lead-up games book.* Camas, WA: Educators Press.

Fronske, H. 2001. *Teaching cues for sport skills.* 2nd ed. Needham Heights, MA: Allyn & Bacon.

Mood, D., F. Musker, and J. Rink. 1991. *Sports and recreational activities for men and women.* 10th ed. St. Louis: Mosby.

Pangrazi, R., and P. Darst. 1997. *Dynamic physical education for secondary school students: Curriculum and instruction.* 3rd ed. Needham Heights, MA: Allyn & Bacon.

Other Resources

Companies selling floor hockey equipment are:

Shield Manufacturing
425 Fillmore Ave., Tonawanda, NY 14150
Phone 800-828-7669

DOM Sporting and Games (Cosom)
957 Roselawn Ave., Toronto, Ontario, Canada M6B IB6
Phone 416-781-2338

Golf

Golf is one of many games that originated from field hockey. (In fact, field hockey is the forerunner of all games played with a stick and ball.) Golf can be traced to the late 14th century, and interest in the game grew slowly over the next 40 years. From about the mid-15th century until the present, however, interest in golf has grown steadily. The game has become especially popular in the United States. Golf is a sport attractive to many, allowing rewarding participation for players of any age.

As physical education programs place greater emphasis on lifetime leisure pursuits, hobbies, and activities—not to mention total wellness throughout life—educators face an increasing demand to include golf in their curricula. For that reason, this "game of a lifetime" is included in this text.

Equipment

Golf equipment consists of a set of golf clubs, golf balls, and a carrying bag. A set of golf clubs includes woods and irons (both names reflect the material originally used in making the club heads) as well as a putter. Woods and irons are numbered: the 1 wood is a driver often used to hit the ball off the tee; the 2, 3, 4, and 5 woods, which are more lofted, are generally used for shots off the fairway. Irons are also numbered. The full range of irons, which vary in length and blade angle, goes from a 2 iron through a 9 iron and also includes a pitching wedge. The angle (or loft) of the blade (i.e.,

the iron's striking surface; also called its *face*) helps to determine the ball's trajectory, or deflection angle. The higher the iron number, the higher the properly struck ball will go. Conversely, the lower the number, the lower the ball will travel and, thus, the longer the distance it will travel. The pitching wedge, or 9 iron, gives more loft than any other iron and is usually used close to the green. Use of authentic woods and irons are recommended in this unit.

Golf balls are uniform in size and weight throughout the world. They have a compressed rubber center that is wound by cord and covered with synthetic material. In this unit, however, Wiffle golf balls may be used for every lesson except lesson 1, which develops putting skills. (A true feel for the skill of putting cannot be obtained with a lightweight Wiffle ball.)

Golf is usually played on a golf course, although in this unit a gym or outdoor field can be used (use carpeting for putting greens). If possible, however, try to gain access to a golf course. Particularly for the putting lesson (lesson 1), during which students will need to experience the feel of a green, authentic play would significantly enhance the quality of instruction.

Unit Organization

This unit may be expanded to provide more opportunities for practice. Because distance and shot accuracy will vary (sometimes widely) among students, expanding the unit or extending individual lessons may be advisable to build students' self-confidence.

Following is a brief description of each lesson in this unit.

- Lesson 1 presents the skill of putting and includes a number of putting practice activities.
- Two approach shots, the pitch and the chip, are detailed in lessons 2 and 3.
- Lessons 4 and 5 focus on developing the swing, breaking it down into the grip, stance, takeaway, backswing, downswing, and follow-through.
- In lesson 6 students use their acquired skills in a modified game of golf.

Selected resources and assessment ideas are found in the assessment and resources chapter at the end of the unit.

Note: An asterisk (*) following a facility or equipment listing indicates that preparation is required before the lesson.

Social Skills and Etiquette

Social skills are easily incorporated into the game of golf. An excellent way to promote socialization is by allowing students to work in partners or small groups, particularly while participating in the modified game (see lesson 6).

Etiquette is especially important in the game of golf. Discuss the following rules with students at the start of each lesson:

- One player hits or putts at a time.
- Other players should stand well out of the way, be quiet, and watch.
- Any interruptions or distractions are frowned upon in golf; players take the game seriously and concentration in silence is usually preferred.
- The game of golf is not a loud one; encourage students to remain quiet during play, especially when other players are hitting or putting.

Lesson Modifications

Golf is not all that strenuous, but it does take some coordination and, thus, may be difficult for many students—especially students new to the sport and those with developmental problems. In particular, executing the swing and contacting the ball can be difficult. Some modifications that may make the unit easier, and thus more enjoyable, for all players include the following:

- Use Wiffle balls instead of regulation golf balls. Wiffle balls are lighter and safer. They don't travel very far and cannot seriously injure a classmate if contact is made.
- Shorten a club by cutting the length of its shaft; this makes the club easier to control.
- Challenge less-skilled students at their own level by modifying the target areas and the size of the putting cup.

Safety

The game of golf can be hazardous if players are not watching out for balls, other players, or swinging clubs. To ensure safety in class instruction, the following precautions are recommended:

- Students must not swing the golf club until instructed to do so.
- Allocate enough space between students that they can swing without endangering others.
- Allow adequate distance for hitting practice and have students hit in the same direction. (If using real golf balls, students should never be in the path of hit golf balls.)
- Perform frequent equipment checks to make sure that golf clubs are properly maintained. There should be no cracks or loose parts on a club.
- Students must not retrieve hit golf balls until instructed to do so.

Rules

The object of golf is to get the ball into the hole in the fewest number of strokes. Thus, most golf rules are devoted to regulating the number of strokes taken or allowed. Three of the most basic rules of golf are that

- the ball must be played where it lies,
- the ball must be motionless before being struck, and
- the player farthest from the hole must hit first.

These rules should be utilized for this golf unit.

Most other golf rules are not applicable to class instruction because the likelihood of teaching this unit on a golf course is remote. Feel free to invent or modify rules to fit your particular teaching situation. If complete and official golf rules are desired for class instruction or by students, the most current official golf rules are available from the U.S. Golf Association, the governing body for golf in this country (www.usga.com).

Lesson 1

Putting

Purpose

In this lesson students develop the fundamental skills of putting, including grip, stance, body position, and stroke.

Warm-Ups (6-8 Minutes)

1. Arm rotators
2. Shoulder stretch
3. Waist twists
4. Knee lifts
5. Run continuously for 3 minutes

Facility and Equipment

◆ Putting green or large carpeted space
◆ 1 putter per student
◆ 3 regulation golf balls per student
◆ 2 yardsticks per student
◆ 5 putting cups
◆ String
◆ Markers and poster board

Skill Cues

1. Stand with the feet shoulder-width apart in a comfortable position that provides a solid foundation.
2. Flex the knees to slightly relax the legs.
3. Keep the eyes directly over the ball.
4. Grip the club using the reverse overlap grip: the index finger of the top hand overlaps between the pinky and ring finger of the bottom hand; the palm of the bottom hand covers the thumb of the top hand on the shaft.
5. Play the ball forward in the putting stance, that is near the foot that is closer to the hole and aligned with the front foot.
6. Keep the head and torso stationary throughout the swing.
7. Take the putter backward smoothly and keep it low to the ground.
8. Accelerate the putter blade through the ball (i.e., increase stroke speed as the ball is contacted).
9. Make the stroke with the shoulders. Just the arms move, not the wrists.
10. Keep the front hand and wrist (i.e., closest to the target) firm while stroking the putt.

Reverse overlap grip

Teaching Cues

1. Call out the skill cues as students perform each phase of the putt.
2. Be sure to demonstrate the putting grip and stance.
3. Check students' top and bottom hand positions for the putting grip.

Activities (30-40 Minutes)

1. Present the reverse overlapping grip, stance, body position, and stroke, emphasizing the appropriate skill and teaching cues. It is extremely important to check students' stance and grip at this point in the unit; if students learn and then use the wrong stance or grip, their shots and performance will be negatively affected. Allow each student ample time to practice the alignment, setup, and grip using a putter. If time allows, have students begin to practice the stroke without actually hitting a ball. (5-6 minutes)

2. Place a yardstick or an extra club on the ground in the direction of the putt and have students practice the full putting stroke. They should check their stroke alignments by swinging the putter along the top of the yardstick, concentrating on keeping the path of the putter straight. Once students can swing straight, place a ball at the end of the yardstick and have them putt, still concentrating on keeping the club along the target (i.e., straight) line. (3-5 minutes)

3. Lay two yardsticks parallel to each other about 3 inches (7.6 centimeters) apart: just far enough to fit the putter blade between the yardsticks. Have students practice the stroke first without a ball, trying not to hit either yardstick as they swing; then add a ball and a target. (5-7 minutes)

4. Have students putt three balls from varying distances (e.g., 3, 5, 10, and 15 feet [.91, 1.52, 3.05, and 4.57 meters]) into a circle target (3-foot [.91-meter] diameter) made of string. Award different point values for balls that stop at each distance within the target circle. (5-6 minutes)

5. Divide students into five groups and have a student from each group putt at the same time to cups placed 2, 3, 4, and 5 feet (.61, .91, 1.22, and 1.52 meters) away. Students should make three consecutive putts from each distance before moving to the next distance. (5-6 minutes)

6. Using string and numbered poster board, create several clock faces, each with a hole in the center. Divide students into groups and position each group at a clock face. Explain and play a game of clock golf. (7-10 minutes)

Clock Golf

Students take turns putting toward the cup from each hour on the clock, counting the total number of strokes necessary to hole out from all 12 positions. The student with the lowest number of strokes wins.

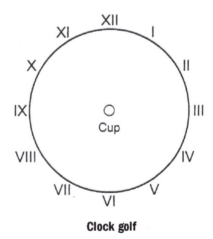

Clock golf

Closure (3-5 Minutes)

Review the lesson with students. Use the following ideas to reinforce learning, check understanding, and provide feedback.

1. Review the manner in which the club face must contact the ball to propel it in the intended direction (i.e., squarely and perpendicular to the target line).
2. Make sure students understand that putting is a crucial part of the game; it accounts for half the strokes allowed on each hole.
3. Review the putting stroke, emphasizing accelerating the putter through the ball during the follow-through portion of the stroke.

Approach Shots I

Purpose

In this lesson students learn the chip and run approach shot, which is commonly used when golfers are within approximately 50 feet (15.24 meters) of the green.

Warm-Ups (6-8 Minutes)

1. Arm pumps
2. Waist twists
3. Hip stretch
4. Push-ups
5. Arm circles

Facility and Equipment

- Gym or large outdoor space
- Medium-lofted clubs (i.e., 5, 6, and 7 irons) per student
- 3 Wiffle balls per student
- String
- 9 hula hoops
- Wooden post (2-3 inches [5.1-7.6 centimeters] high and 10 feet [3.05 meters] long)

Skill Cues

1. Use a medium-lofted club (i.e., a 5, 6, or 7 iron).
2. Assume an open stance with the feet close together.
3. Keep the head down.
4. Keep the body as stationary as possible.
5. Use a shortened full-finger grip: keep all fingers and thumbs on the club (as in a baseball grip).
6. Flex the knees to lower the body.
7. Use a short backstroke.
8. Keep the club head low on the backstroke and square to the target.
9. Form a triangle with the head, arms, and shoulders; do not break the triangle on the swing.
10. Produce a smooth, pendulum stroke.
11. Stand so that the ball is back in the stance, in line parallel with the rear foot.
12. Keep the wrists and elbows firm, and swing with the shoulders.
13. Follow through with the stroke after contact.

Teaching Cues

1. Emphasize that students should not compromise (bend) the triangle they form with the head, arms, and shoulders during the stroke.
2. Check students to make sure the lower part of the body does not move during the stroke.

Activities (30-40 Minutes)

1. Introduce the stance, setup, and stroke using the skill and teaching cues. Have students practice each part of the sequence as you explain and demonstrate it. Check that students form a triangle with shoulders, arms, and head, and remind them to keep this triangle intact. Also check for firm wrists and elbows. (4-6 minutes)

2. Have students practice the chip and run shot 15 to 20 feet (4.57-6.1 meters) from a selected target. Have them use a real ball and various clubs (i.e., 5, 6, and 7 irons). The shot should get the ball far enough airborne that it travels about a third of the total distance in the air. (Wiffle balls should travel at least two-thirds of the total distance to the target.) (7-9 minutes)

3. Place a wooden post 4 to 5 feet (1.22-1.52 meters) in front of students standing in a line. Have students practice chipping over the post to a selected target 10 to 40 feet (3.05-12.19 meters) away (10-20 feet [3.05-6.1 meters] if Wiffle balls are used). (6-8 minutes)

4. Create three-ring targets (using concentric string circles) and have students practice the chip and run shot from various distances. The rings should have diameters of 10, 15, and 20 feet (3.05, 4.57, and 6.1 meters). Score 3 points for shots that land within the smallest ring, 2 points for shots within the medium ring, and 1 point for shots within the largest ring. (6-8 minutes)

5. Set up nine holes, each 25 feet (7.62 meters) in length with a hula hoop as the hole. Divide students into nine teams and position each team at a hole. Explain the rules and have students play the chip and run golf game. (7-9 minutes)

Chip and Run Golf Game

Students proceed through each hole using only the chip and run shot. Score each hole by counting the number of shots it takes to stop the ball inside the hoop. The par for each hole is 2 strokes. The student with the lowest total score wins.

Closure (3-5 Minutes)

Review the lesson with students. Use the following ideas to reinforce learning, check understanding, and provide feedback.

1. Review the elements of the chip and run shot (e.g., it is used within 50 feet [15.24 meters] of the green, it requires the use of a medium-lofted club).

2. Make sure students understand that they must take an open stance and utilize a shoulder swing, keeping firm wrists and elbows.

3. Discuss what must happen to get the ball airborne in the direction of the target (e.g., extend follow-through toward the target or intended direction of flight).

Lesson 3

Approach Shots II

Purpose

In this lesson learn the pitch approach shot, a highly difficult shot used to get to the green.

Warm-Ups (6-8 Minutes)

1. Arm pumps
2. Waist twists
3. Arm rotators
4. Sprint five 20-yard (18.28-meter) distances.
5. Triceps dips

Facility and Equipment

- Gym or large outdoor field
- 1 high-lofted club (i.e., 8 or 9 iron, or wedge) per student
- 3 regulation golf balls per student
- Rope
- 9 hula hoops
- 3 to 6 benches

Note: Use Wiffle balls if conducting this lesson inside.

Skill Cues

1. Use a high-lofted club (i.e., 8 or 9 iron, or wedge).
2. Use an open stance with the feet close together.
3. Keep the head down.
4. Keep the body as stationary as possible.
5. Use a shortened overlapping grip: the pinky finger of the bottom hand overlaps between the index and middle fingers of the top hand; the palm of the bottom hand covers the thumb of the top hand on the shaft.
6. Lower the body by flexing the knees.
7. Sole the club (i.e., put the bottom of the club on the ground).
8. Use an easy swing; let the club do the work without guiding it.
9. Strike the ball with a descending blow.
10. Use a smooth, pendulum stroke.
11. Keep the left arm as straight as possible.
12. Follow through after contacting the ball.

Teaching Cues

1. The setup forms the basis of the swing; make sure students use the proper setup.
2. Emphasize a smooth, rhythmic swing.
3. Check that students develop a sharp descending blow to the ball and complete a high follow-through.
4. The pitch shot should get the ball airborne so that it travels airborne about two-thirds of the total distance to the target.

Activities (30-40 Minutes)

1. Introduce the setup, stance, and stroke of the pitch approach shot using the skill and teaching cues. Have students practice each phase of the shot as you explain and demonstrate the proper motion and technique. (4-5 minutes)

2. Have students practice the pitch shot from 15 to 20 feet (4.57-6.1 meters) away from a selected target. Have them use one club or try several clubs (i.e., 8 or 9 iron, or wedge). (5-6 minutes)

3. Place a bench as an obstruction 5 to 10 feet (1.52-3.05 meters) in front of the target. Have students practice the pitch shot from 10 to 40 feet (3.05-12.19 meters) away from the target. Make sure students get the ball airborne over the obstruction. (6-8 minutes)

4. Have students practice the pitch shot from various distances (10 to 50 yards [9.14-45.72 meters]) to a circle target made of rope with a diameter of at least 30 feet (9.14 meters). Score points for stopping the ball in the target area from the various distances. (5-6 minutes)

5. Set up nine holes 10 to 50 yards (9.14-45.72 meters) in length with a hula hoop as the hole. Set up obstructions near several of the holes. Divide students into 9 teams and position each team at a hole. Explain the rules and have students play the pitch and chip golf game. (10 to 15 minutes)

Pitch and Chip Golf Game

Students score each hole by counting the number of shots it takes to stop the ball inside the hoop. The par for each hole is 3. After completing all nine holes, the student with the lowest overall score (i.e., the fewest strokes) wins.

Closure (3-5 Minutes)

Review the lesson with students. Use the following ideas to reinforce learning, check understanding, and provide feedback.

1. Make sure students understand that a pitch shot is used within 10 to 50 yards (9.14-45.72 meters) of the green and requires the use of a high-lofted club (i.e., 8 or 9 iron, or wedge).

2. Have students demonstrate the pitch shot while others assess whether they are able to take an open stance while using an easy swing, letting the club do the work.

3. Discuss the mechanics of the swing and have students describe exactly what must happen to get the ball airborne (e.g., allow the face of the club to do the work, perform a smooth swing, and follow-through).

4. Ask students if they had difficulty getting the ball airborne in the direction of the target.

Lesson 4

Full Swing I

Purpose

In this lesson, the first of two lessons on the full swing, students learn the preswing elements, including grip, stance, and sequence.

Warm-Ups (6-8 Minutes)

1. Arm circles
2. Waist twists
3. Arm rotators
4. Imaginary jump rope
5. Push-ups

Facility and Equipment

- Gym or a large outdoor space
- 1 medium-lofted club (i.e., 5, 6, or 7 iron) per student
- 1 medium-sized towel per student
- 1 yardstick per student

Skill Cues

1. For the full-finger grip, keep all fingers and thumbs on the club.
2. For the interlocking grip, interlock the index finger of the top hand with the pinky of the bottom hand and keep the thumbs straight down the shaft; the palm of the bottom hand covers the thumb of the top hand on the shaft.
3. For the overlap grip, the pinky of the bottom hand overlaps between the index and middle fingers of the top hand; the palm of the bottom hand covers the thumb of the top hand on the shaft.
4. Keep the feet shoulder-width apart.
5. Use a square stance.
6. Play the ball off the forward heel in the stance.
7. Sole the club (i.e., put the bottom of the club on the ground).
8. Relax the arms; they should be hanging from the body, not extended.
9. Flex the body at the hips and knees.

Teaching Cues

1. Allow students to swing the club while trying each of the grips.
2. Be sure to spread out students when they swing the club.

Activities (30-40 Minutes)

1. Present the grips, stance, and technique of the golf swing using the skill and teaching cues. Have students practice each grip several times. Encourage students to use the overlap grip in the following activities; this grip provides the best control and feel for the club. (7-10 minutes)

2. Pair up students or have them select partners. Each partner practices the various grips while the other checks for proper position. (4-5 minutes)

Overlap grip

Interlocking grip

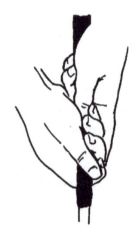

Full-finger grip

3. Cane activity. Have students assume a proper stance and invert a club (an upside down club resembles a cane), placing the top hand on the sole of the club. The bottom hand is right under the top hand, and the grip (i.e., handle) of the club on the ground is in line with the forward heel where the ball would normally be. Students should swing the club backward with the top hand and pull it through with a strong follow-through to a high finish. Have students repeat several times, reminding them to shift weight from the back to the front foot and follow through with a high finish. (4-5 minutes)

4. Towel activity. Have students grasp a large twisted towel at each end with the palm of the front hand down and the palm of the rear hand up. They should extend both arms about shoulder-width apart and swing backward and through, swinging the arms, shoulders, and body away from and toward an imaginary target. Just as students begin the forward downswing, they release the rear hand from the towel and continue with the front hand and arm to fling the towel forcefully out toward the target with a high finish. Proper timing and body action should cause the towel to snap. (6-8 minutes)

5. Wrist rolling. Have students assume a proper stance, invert the club, and grasp the sole of the club with the hand nearest the target. Students should swing the front (i.e., target side) arm backward, then pull through by strongly rolling the wrists from just after the bottom of the swing to a high finish in the follow-through. If done correctly, the club should make a swooshing sound as the wrists roll. (6-8 minutes)

6. Yardstick swinging. Have students grasp a yardstick at one end, as if it were a club, using the proper stance and grip. Students should swing the yardstick backward and through, as they would swing a club to hit a ball, emphasizing rolling the wrists as they swing. If they roll their wrists properly, they should feel a change of resistance as they swing. (3-4 minutes)

Closure (3-5 Minutes)

Review the lesson with students. Use the following ideas to reinforce learning, check understanding, and provide feedback.

1. Check that students understand the interlocking, full-finger, and both overlap grips.
2. Make certain students realize that the overlap grip is considered the best of all possible grips.
3. Ask students to properly demonstrate the address routine.
4. Have students explain the entire body action of the golf swing.

Lesson 5

Full Swing II

Purpose

In this lesson, the second of two lessons on the full swing, students learn the takeaway, backswing, downswing, and follow-through components of the actual golf swing.

Facility and Equipment

◆ Gym or large outdoor space
◆ 4 clubs (irons and woods)
◆ 3 Wiffle balls per student
◆ 3 tees per student

Warm-Ups (6-8 Minutes)

1. Arm circles
2. Waist twists
3. Arm rotators
4. Neck stretches
5. Knee lifts

Skill Cues

1. Move the hands, arms, and shoulders in one motion for the takeaway sequence.
2. Extend the target-side arm and bend the rear arm for the backswing.
3. Keep the back to the target at the top of the backswing.
4. Cock the wrists when the hands are parallel to the ground about waist high during the backswing.
5. Shift weight to the rear leg as the club comes backward.
6. Start the downswing by shifting the weight of the lower legs forward.
7. Roll the wrists after contacting the ball.
8. Finish with a high follow-through.
9. End the swing with the chest toward the target.
10. Keep the head stationary throughout the swing.

Teaching Cues

1. Demonstrate each component part of the swing several times; then demonstrate the entire swing.
2. Be sure to allow plenty of space between students as they swing.

Activities (30-40 Minutes)

1. Present the full swing, including takeaway, backswing, downswing, and follow-through, emphasizing the skill and teaching cues. Demonstrate first while students watch; then follow along several times as you cover each segment. (5-7 minutes)

2. Have students hit Wiffle balls swinging with a medium-lofted iron (i.e., 5, 6, or 7 iron) and using just a half swing. Students should take the club backward until their arms are parallel to the ground and the wrists are cocked (the clubs should be pointing almost straight up). Remind students to swing through the ball, concentrating on weight shift, solid ball contact, and a high finish. (7-9 minutes)

3. Pair up students or have them select partners. Partners continue to utilize the half swing to hit Wiffle balls with differently lofted clubs. First give them the middle irons (i.e., 5, 6, and 7 irons), then the low irons (i.e., 2, 3, and 4 irons), and then the high-lofted irons (i.e., 8 and 9 irons, and wedge). Partners should check each other for cocked wrists and a straight target arm. (7-9 minutes)

4. Have students progress to a full swing using a middle iron (i.e., 5, 6, or 7 iron). Check at the top of the backswing that the target arm is extended, the rear arm is tucked in against the body, and the wrists are flat and in line with the lower arms at the top of the backswing. (4-6 minutes)

5. Have students practice the swing using the woods. Start with a 3 or 5 wood, then progress to the driver. When using the driver, students should use a tee for the ball. (7-9 minutes)

Closure (3-5 Minutes)

Review the lesson with students. Use the following ideas to reinforce learning, check understanding, and provide feedback.

1. Ask students to describe the full swing (i.e., a smooth, unified movement consisting of the takeaway, backswing, downswing, and follow-through).

2. Discuss whether students have been able to develop a tempo or rhythm for the swing.

3. Explain that the ball gets hit only because it gets in the way of the swing, not because students hit it.

Lesson 6

Modified Game Play

Purpose

In this lesson students get to play a modified game of golf using previously presented skills.

Warm-Ups (6-8 Minutes)

1. Practice various swings using a selected iron or wood 15 times.
2. Waist twists
3. Arm rotators
4. Jump rope for 2 minutes.
5. Side squats

Teaching Cues

1. Before starting game play, quickly review all of the golf skills learned in this unit and introduce the basic rules of golf (see the unit introduction on page 447).
2. Before class, set up a circuit with 4 teeing areas using the cones to mark various distances and boundaries, as shown in the figure (see activity 2). In the center of the circuit, set up 1 practice green with a hole (delineated with the rope and obstructed by the benches) and 1 putting mat (using the carpet and cup). Set up a separate tee area for the green.

Facility and Equipment

- Large outdoor area or gym
- 6 clubs (a wood, 3 iron, 5 iron, 7 iron, wedge, and putter)
- 1 Wiffle ball per student
- 1 regulation golf ball per student (for putting)
- Cones
- Rope
- 1 putting green (e.g., carpet)
- 1 cup
- 2 benches
- 1 yardstick
- 1 score sheet per 4 students
- 1 jump rope per student

Activities (30-40 Minutes)

1. Review the skills learned in this unit, emphasizing the skill cues in lessons 1 through 6. (7-10 minutes)
2. Divide students into groups of four and position each group at a tee area. (If necessary, two groups can be at each tee area.) Explain the rules; then have students play a game of modified golf. (23-30 minutes)

Modified Golf

The game consists of 5 hitting stations: 1 using a wood, 1 using a 3 iron, 1 using a 5 iron, and 1 using a 7 iron. The last station involves using a wedge and putter. Students play 3 rounds (5 stations = 1 round), moving in order from one station to another and recording their scores at each station. At the end of the circuit, the student with the highest score wins. (For more challenge, have foursomes compete against one another; the foursome with the highest score wins.)

As students progress through the first four hitting stations—hitting a Wiffle ball with a wood, 3 iron, 5 iron, and 7 iron—points are awarded for accuracy and distance.

▶ Score 1, 2, or 3 points for marked distances.

▶ Deduct 1 point for hitting the ball outside the cones.

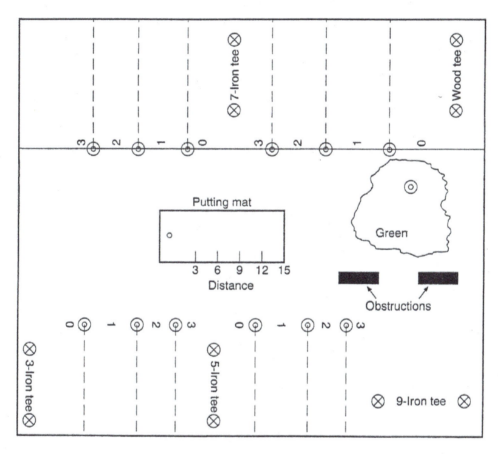

Modified golf game setup

At the wedge tee, students hit the Wiffle ball from the tee area to the green. If the ball lands on the green, students measure the distance to the hole using the yardstick, then move to the putting mat and putt a regulation ball from the measured distance. If the ball does not land on the green, students must putt from the maximum distance (15 feet [4.57 meters]). Points are awarded for the number of putts it takes to hole out:

1 putt	5 points
2 putts	4 points
3 putts	3 points
4 putts	2 points
5 putts	1 point
6 or more putts	0 points

Closure (3-5 Minutes)

Review the lesson with students. Use the following ideas to reinforce learning, check understanding, and provide feedback.

1. Ask students to answer the following questions:
   - ▸ Can a minimum of 7 points be scored per round in the modified golf game?
   - ▸ What critical aspects of performance led to success in performing the full swing, chip and run, pitch, and putt shots required in the modified golf game?
2. Discuss whether students understand each stroke well enough to perform at each station.

Assessment
and Resources

Skills and game play can be assessed formally or informally throughout this unit. The last lesson lends itself well as an informal summative evaluation of all presented skills. Use students' scores to determine the effectiveness of their shots.

Alternatively, separate skill stations could be set up to assess driving, putting, and iron technique. For example, require students to chip into a plastic wading pool or pitch over a badminton net. Skill analysis should involve determining each student's ability to get the ball airborne and to move it in a straight path.

Resources

Collins, R. 2001. *A comprehensive guide to sports skills tests and measurement.* Metuchen, NJ: Scarecrow Press.

Griffin, L., S. Mitchell, and J. Oslin. 1997. *Teaching sport concepts and skills.* Champaign, IL: Human Kinetics.

Mood, D., F. Musker, and J. Rink. 1999. *Sports and recreational activities.* 12th ed. New York: McGraw-Hill.

White, J.R., ed. 1990. *Sports rules encyclopedia.* Champaign, IL: Leisure Press.

In-Line Skating

In-line skating originally evolved out of the sport of roller-skating. Roller skates can be traced to the 1700s when Hans Brinker designed a pair by buckling wood spoons under a pair of boots. It was not until 1981 that Scott Olson, an avid ice hockey player from Minnesota, developed a skate with a single row of wheels to play ice hockey year round. His original product, based on a 1966 patent by Morris "Maury" Silver called *Super Sport Skate,* was marketed as Rollerblade. The sport of in-line skating became more popular after the inception of the International In-line Skating Association (IISA) in 1991. The IISA helped to promote the sport and provide safety guidelines and rules of the road.

Equipment

In-line skating equipment consists of a pair of skates as well as the following safety equipment: wrist guards, knee pads, elbow pads, and a helmet. In-line skates vary in frame size, wheel diameter, and durometer (i.e., wheel hardness). Beginners should choose skates with a shorter frame for a shorter stride, smaller-diameter wheels (65-72 millimeters) for more maneuverability, and a higher durometer rating (82-88A) for less grip and a more solid ride. Speed skaters prefer longer frames for longer strides, larger wheel diameter (76-80 millimeter) for faster travel, and a lower durometer rating (74-78A) for more grip and a softer ride.

Maintenance is particularly important when it comes to keeping in-line skates balanced and safe. The wheels should be repositioned and rotated periodically. Repositioning involves reversing the wheels so that the newer edge replaces the worn edge. Rotation is as follows:

▶ On a four-wheel skate, switch wheels 1 and 3, and wheels 2 and 4.

▶ On a five-wheel skate, wheel 2 becomes wheel 4, and wheel 3 becomes wheel 2, wheel 4 becomes wheel 5, wheel 5 becomes 3, and wheel 1 is not moved.

Unit Organization

This unit focuses mainly on developing skating skills. Following is a brief summary of each lesson in this unit:

▶ Lesson 1 introduces stroking, gliding, and stopping skills with an emphasis on balance, falling properly, and other safety factors.

▶ Swizzling, turning, and skating backward are developed in lesson 2. The crossover is specifically introduced in this lesson.

▶ Lesson 3 presents side surfing but focuses particularly on the technique of increasing speed.

▶ The rules, equipment, and game skills for in-line hockey are introduced in lesson 4. Stick and puck handling are an integral part of this lesson.

In lesson 5 various in-line skating activities and games are introduced to increase students' fitness levels and skills, and to have fun.

Selected resources and assessment ideas are found in the assessment and resources chapter at the end of the unit.

Social Skills and Etiquette

Social skills and etiquette are straightforward in in-line skating. First, students must learn the "rules of the road," which include basic courtesy. Because in-line skaters often share the skating trail with walkers, joggers, and bikers, students must learn to stay right and pass on the left, announcing their intention to pass. In this unit students will be participating in a group setting, necessitating keeping an eye out for and being careful not to endanger other skaters.

Lesson Modifications

In-line skating requires balance and coordination. The skates can be difficult to master, as can stopping and turning motions. Following are suggested modifications for students with disabilities and lower skills levels:

▸ Use shorter and level courses.
▸ Use roller skates instead of in-line skates; maintaining balance on roller skates is much easier.
▸ In the game of in-line hockey, assign students with disabilities to the position of goalie. Also, use a puck rather than a ball; a puck allows for much slower play and it can be further weighted with tape to make control easier.
▸ If a large class size necessitates a rotation system, match the skill levels of students when assigning teams. Those with limited abilities should play together and those with higher skill levels should play together. Likewise, partners of similar ability levels can be paired for skill practice.

Safety

Several safety factors should be observed in class organization and instruction. Students should be required to wear all in-line skating safety equipment, including wrist guards, knee pads, elbow pads, and helmets. Rules of the road should be taught and continually reviewed.

The following IISA safety guidelines and rules of the road should be emphasized in the first few lessons of this unit:

▸ Wear protective gear.
▸ Skate on the right side of all streets, paths, or trails.
▸ Pass left and announce when passing.
▸ Watch for potholes, wet spots, and debris.
▸ Control speed so that stopping is manageable.
▸ Always allow pedestrians the right-of-way.
▸ Use hand signals to cue traffic.

In the game of in-line hockey, the following safety precautions are recommended:

▸ Prohibit high sticking to avoid face, hand, or arm injuries.
▸ Enforce penalties for body contact such as elbowing, butt ending, interference and charging, tripping and hooking, and checking and slashing. These infractions can result in serious injury if not curtailed.
▸ Match up players of similar abilities to play against one another. This helps to prevent less aggressive players from being physically intimidated.

Terms

A-frame turn—A slow turn in which weight is placed on the inside edge of the outside skate.

crossover—A method of turning that involves bringing one skate in front of the other in a crossover pattern.

glide—Coasting or rolling with one skate in front of the other without pushing off.

parallel turn—A turn in which the skates are parallel; the inside foot staggers toward the direction of the new turn.

side surfing—While gliding, the toes are away from each other and the heels are slightly together, about 12 inches (30.5 centimeters) apart. Side surfing allows skaters to glide in a circle.

stroke—Pushing off with one skate by turning one foot outward and propelling forward.

swizzle—An hourglass pattern; while keeping the wheels on the ground, the skates move in and out (side by side), alternating glides on the inside and outside edges of the wheels.

T-stop—Stopping by bringing one skate at a right angle and dragging it behind the other skate.

Lesson 1

Stroking, Gliding, and Stopping

Purpose

In this lesson students develop basic in-line skating skills, including stroking, gliding, stopping, balancing, and falling.

Facility and Equipment

◆ Gym or outdoor area with a smooth surface
◆ 1 pair of in-line skates per student
◆ Cones

Warm-Ups (6-8 Minutes)

1. Running in place
2. Quadriceps stretch
3. Hip extenders
4. Achilles tendon stretch

Skill Cues

Stroking

1. Bend at the knees, keeping the center of gravity over the skates.
2. Keep the ankles flexed, the back straight, and the head up.
3. Turn one foot outward at a 45-degree angle and push off using the full row of wheels, not just the front wheels.
4. Shift weight and repeat with the opposite foot.

Gliding

1. Push off with the stroking leg in a sideward direction and allow the supporting or gliding leg to coast or roll for as long as possible.
2. Bend the supporting or gliding leg at the knee and ankle.
3. Bring the stroking leg to its original position to become the supporting leg.
4. Coast or roll on the support leg for as long as possible to avoid a short, choppy motion.
5. Shift weight from side to side while gliding.
6. Sway the arms from side to side in front of the hips when gliding.

Stopping

The two common stops used on in-line skates are the brake stop and the T-stop.

1. Brake stopping involves using the brake pad at the back (i.e., on the heel) of the skate.
   ▸ Keep the knees and ankles bent and the body in an upright position.
   ▸ Move the braking skate forward, but shift weight to the back skate.

▸ Raise the toe of the forward skate (the one with the brake attachment) and press the brake into the ground.

▸ Straighten the braking leg and balance weight on the back skate.

2. The T-stop is used to stop without the skate brake.

▸ Move one skate in front of the other while gliding.

▸ Put weight on the front skate and continue to glide with a bent knee.

▸ Lift the back skate and place it at a 90-degree angle, perpendicular to the front skate.

▸ Start dragging the wheels of the back skate until the two skates touch and are perpendicular.

▸ Place pressure on the rear skate while holding it at a right angle, continuing to drag it until a full stop is achieved.

Falling

1. Lower the center of gravity by bending the knees.
2. Fall forward to the knees.
3. Avoid falling backward.

Teaching Cues

1. Explain how to achieve a proper skate fit. The fit should be snug but still allow toe movement.

2. Discuss wheel differences in various in-line skates. For example, smaller wheels are slower but more maneuverable than larger wheels. Harder wheels (85A) have a more solid ride but are not as smooth as softer wheels (74A).

3. Teach the IISA rules of the road (see page 467).

4. Check that students are wearing all safety gear (e.g., knee pads, elbow pads).

Activities (30-40 Minutes)

1. Introduce stroking and gliding, emphasizing the skill cues. Introduce both methods of stopping as well as how to fall safely. (8-10 minutes)

2. Line up students side by side to practice stroking and gliding. Tell them to stroke, or push off, with one leg and glide with the opposite leg. Students should concentrate on achieving smooth strokes and then alternate stroking and gliding legs until they can balance equally well on both. (4-6 minutes)

3. Continue gliding practice, this time challenging students to glide with their skates together and then apart. Have students try gliding with the right skate only and then the left skate only. (3 minutes)

4. Align students side by side to practice the brake stop. They should glide a short distance and then stop at your signal. (4-6 minutes)

5. Repeat activity 4, this time practicing the T-stop. (4-6 minutes)

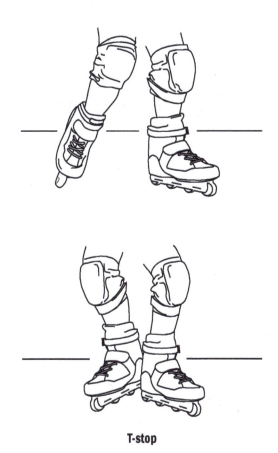

T-stop

6. Stop-and-go drill. Line up students behind a set of cones and turn your back away from them. At the signal, students should stroke and glide forward (toward you) until they hear you say, "Brake stop" or "T-stop" (request a distinct stop each time). Then turn around to face students. By the time you turn around, all students should be motionless. (7-9 minutes)

Closure (3-5 Minutes)

Review the lesson with students using the following ideas to reinforce learning, check understanding, and provide feedback.

1. Select students to demonstrate the brake stop and T-stop, and have other students analyze the skill.
2. Discuss the mechanical principles involved in balancing on in-line skates (e.g., skates should be shoulder-width apart to create a wider base of support, the skater's center of gravity should be over the skates for greater stability, and so on).

Lesson 2

Turning, Swizzling, and Skating Backward

Purpose

In this lesson students learn to turn, swizzle, and skate backward.

Warm-Ups (6-8 Minutes)

1. Jump rope or jump rope laps
2. Squat holds
3. Back stretch
4. Heel lifts
5. Toe lifts

Facility and Equipment

- Gym or outdoor playing area with a smooth surface
- 1 pair of in-line skates per student
- 1 jump rope per student
- Cones
- Chalk or marking tape

Skill Cues

Turning

Two types of turns are presented in this lesson: the A-frame turn and the parallel turn.

1. The A-frame turn is used only for slow turns.
   - ▸ Place the feet shoulder-width apart before starting the turn.
   - ▸ At the turn, shift weight on the inside edge of the outside (i.e., outside of the intended turn) skate.
   - ▸ The body will turn in the direction of the outside skate.
2. The parallel turn may be used for slow or fast turns.
   - ▸ Place the skates parallel to each other before starting the turn.
   - ▸ Stagger the inside (i.e., inside of the intended turn) skate in the direction of the turn.
   - ▸ Gradually move both skates in the same direction.

Crossovers

1. Start with the ankles side by side.
2. Shift weight and balance on the left skate; then lift the right skate and cross it over and in front of the left skate (skates are crossed).
3. Bring the left skate under and place it beside the right skate.

4. Repeat the pattern until the turn is complete (i.e., lift right skate, cross it over and in front of the left skate, bring the left skate under and place it beside the right skate).

5. Be sure to shift weight before each crossover and always look in the direction of the turn.

Swizzling

1. Start with the heels of the skates together, the toes out and the knees bent slightly.

2. Keep the wheels on the ground; never lift them.

3. While propelling forward, push the skates about shoulder-width apart, toes first; then toe inward to bring the skates together.

4. As the skates move in an hourglass pattern, alternate the inside and outside edges of the wheels.

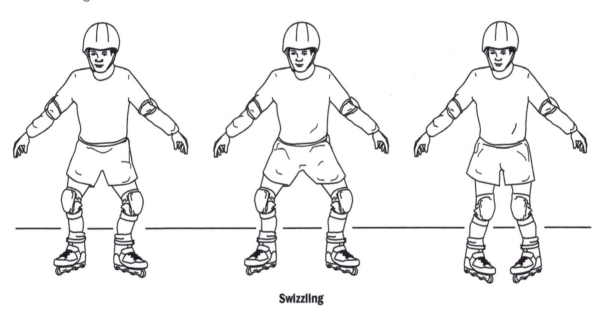

Swizzling

Skating Backward

1. Keep the knees and ankles bent forward.

2. Shift weight to one skate, pushing off from the inside wheels. Then glide on the other skate. Skating backwards requires that one skate push off first.

3. Always look behind when skating backward.

Teaching Cues

1. Because it is used on slow turns, the A-frame turn should be learned and practiced first.

2. If their ankles seem unstable when turning, have students tighten their skate buckles.

3. Have students practice the crossover pattern in place, without a glide, before trying it on a curve.

4. Remind them to place pressure on the edge of the skates and to keep the knees and ankles bent when turning.

5. Check students' skates to be sure they're pointing in the proper direction before and during turns.

Activities (30-40 Minutes)

1. Introduce crossovers and swizzling using the skill cues. Then introduce both methods of turning as well as skating backward. Demonstrate each movement. (8-10 minutes)

2. Set up cones in an oval formation. Have students practice A-frame turning, parallel turning, and crossovers in a counterclockwise direction around the cones. Then have them repeat the practice in a clockwise direction. (4-6 minutes)

3. Scatter students around the gym and have them practice swizzling. (4-6 minutes)

4. Using the same formation, have students practice skating backward. (3 minutes)

5. Set up an obstacle course as diagrammed in the figure using cones and chalk or marking tape. The course should have a segment for each type of stop, strokes, glides, both types of turns, stops and starts, and crossovers. Have students complete the course in a forward direction. For more challenge, have students try to complete the course within a designated time. (Be sure students use the parallel turn when turning quickly.) (6-8 minutes)

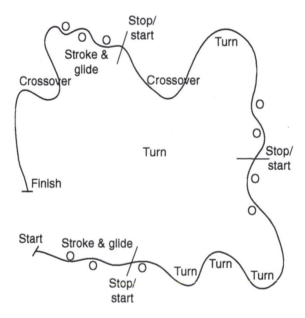

Obstacle course setup

6. Using the same obstacle course, have students execute the same skills but move in a backward direction on the glides, strokes, and turns. More advanced students may also move backward on the crossovers. (5-7 minutes)

Closure (3-5 Minutes)

Review the lesson with students. Use the following questions and ideas to reinforce learning, check understanding, and provide feedback.

1. Review in-line skating turns, asking the following questions:
   - Which turn should be used at slower speeds (i.e., A-frame turn)?
   - Which turn can be used while skating faster (i.e., parallel turn)?
   - Which turn is more stable (i.e., A-frame turn)?
2. Ask students to identify problems they had in turning, crossovers, swizzling, or skating backward.

Lesson 3

Speed Skating and Side Surfing

Purpose

In this lesson students learn how to speed skate and side surf.

Warm-Ups (6-8 Minutes)

1. Agility run
2. Squat holds
3. Gluteal stretch
4. Step and calf taps
5. Knee lifts

Skill Cues

Side Surfing

Side surfing is used to glide in a circle.

1. Begin with a glide, gradually shifting weight on the inside edge of the right skate.
2. Turn the body so that the right shoulder leads.
3. Pick up and turn the left skate so that its heel is next to, but about 12 inches (30.5 centimeters) away from, the right skate's heel.
4. Balance on the inside edge of both skates and glide in a circle, toes out and heels together.

Speed Skating

1. Bend forward from the waist.
2. Keep the wheels on the ground as long as possible while taking long strides.
3. When skating on level surfaces, place the hands behind the back to minimize unnecessary motion and conserve energy.
4. When skating on uneven surfaces, keep the arms out to the side for balance.
5. When skating on an uphill surface, pump the arms (straight) back and forth—never cross the arms in front when pumping. Also use shorter strokes.
6. Use drafting (i.e., skating fairly close behind another skater) to reduce the amount of energy used while skating.

Teaching Cues

1. Emphasize safety when attempting to race against other skaters.
2. Keep a safe distance between skaters to avoid hooking skates.
3. Tell students that they should always warm up and stretch the muscles before speed skating.
4. Make sure students' skates fit properly before speed skating; proper fit will help them maintain control.
5. Explain the advantages of drafting on in-line skates: a vacuum is formed between the front skater and the rear skater, which reduces the workload of the rear skater.

Activities (30-40 Minutes)

Side surfing

1. Introduce speed skating and side surfing, emphasizing the appropriate skill and teaching cues. Point out the differences between skating on a level and an uphill surface. (8-10 minutes)
2. Scatter students around the gym and have them practice side surfing. (4-5 minutes)
3. Line up students side by side to practice the technique of speed skating. Students may also skate side by side with a partner, trying to duplicate each other's stroke rate and stride, but they should avoid looking at each other. (4-6 minutes)
4. Set up several relay teams and position each team at a starting cone. Student teams race between the starting and turning cones using the proper speed-skating techniques. (4-6 minutes)
5. Set up an oval course and have students complete four laps. Time them. (6-7 minutes)
6. Select one or more students to be "it." Scatter students around the gym and have them play freeze tag. (4-6 minutes)

Freeze Tag

Students designated "it" skate around and try to tag other students. Once tagged, skaters must side surf until they are freed by another skater with a handshake.

Closure (3-5 Minutes)

Review the lesson with students using the following ideas to reinforce learning, check understanding, and provide feedback.

1. Discuss the mechanical differences between speed skating and skating at moderate speeds.
2. Ask students to name other sports in which participants use drafting (e.g., track, bicycling).

Lesson 4

In-Line Hockey

Purpose

In this lesson students use acquired in-line skating skills in a game of in-line hockey.

Warm-Ups (6-8 Minutes)

1. Running in place
2. Sit and stretch
3. V-sit toe taps
4. Shoulder stretch
5. Arm pumps

Skill Cues

Facility and Equipment

- Gym or outdoor area with a smooth surface
- 2 floor hockey goals
- 1 pair of in-line skates per student
- 1 hockey stick per student
- 1 hockey puck per 2 students
- 2 cones per 2 students

  Note: The area should be large enough to accommodate one or more courts 180 by 80 feet (54.86 by 24.38 meters). It is recommended that students use plastic sticks and pucks in this lesson. If regulation sticks and pucks are used, mouth guards, face guards, and shin guards are necessary for each student.

Stick Handling

1. Right-handed players should place the left hand on the top of the stick, just below the end of the stick. Place the right hand about 18 inches (45.7 centimeters) below the left hand on the stick. (Hands are reversed for left-handed players.)
2. Form a **V** with the thumb and index finger.
3. Hold the stick in front of the body.
4. Use the wrists to push the puck.

Puck Handling

1. Keep each backswing quick and short.
2. Do not slap the puck; only push and pull it.
3. Keep the puck close to prevent it from being stolen.

Dribbling

1. Dribble side to side or front to back.
   - Use side-to-side dribbling to move the puck back and forth in front of the body.
   - Use front-to-back dribbling (the puck moves back and forth at the side of the body) to move the puck near an opposing player.
2. Avoid looking at the puck while dribbling.

Passing

1. Use a sweeping motion when passing.

2. Bring the lower hand closer to the top hand (approximately 12 inches [30.5 centimeters] apart) when passing.

3. Look in the direction of the target.

4. Anticipate the contact point of the receiver before passing and remember, the puck will always travel faster than the other team can skate.

5. When receiving the puck, cushion or give with it so that it does not rebound away.

Shooting

1. Bring the puck behind the rear foot and to the side.

2. Follow through in the direction of the shot.

3. Point the front of the stick in the direction of intended travel.

4. Look in the direction of the goal during the shot.

5. Two different methods of shooting are used: the slap shot and the wrist shot. A front-hand or forearm (dominant arm) motion or a backhand (nondominant arm) motion may be used for both.

    ▸ Slap shot: the blade contacts the floor before it strikes the puck, causing a flex of the stick and a very powerful shot.

    ▸ Wrist shot: the blade and puck touch before shooting; then the wrist is snapped for added speed during propulsion.

Goaltending

1. In a standing or kneeling position, stop the puck with the glove, the stick, the skate, the body, or the leg(s).

2. Watch the puck at all times, even if bending over is required to see it.

3. Never lunge at the puck; lunging causes the loss of balance.

4. Watch for opposing team signals that may indicate they are getting ready to shoot (e.g., opposing players with the puck looking at the goal, opposing team's defensive players moving closer to the goal, many quick passes to other forwards near the goal).

Teaching Cues

1. Although students will be using their in-line skating skills in this lesson, effective game play requires that they know the rules and skills of the game. Game skills include stick handling, puck handling, dribbling, passing, and shooting. Students should practice these skills before putting on skates; their focus should be on hockey skill development, not on skating. See the floor hockey unit starting on page 431 for more information on game skills such as stick and puck handling.

2. If students are having difficulty with puck control, have them increase the width of their grips.

3. Teach students to cup the puck with their sticks. Cupping involves tilting the blade over the puck to cradle or grasp it.

4. Remind goaltenders to stretch before playing.

5. Since actual in-line hockey playing time will be minimal during this lesson, it is suggested that students play the game at least one additional class period to develop their game skills and strategies.

Activities (30-40 Minutes)

1. Introduce the skills of in-line hockey and have students practice each, first without and then with skates. (8-10 minutes)

2. Pair up students or have them select partners and scatter student pairs around the gym. Have them practice passing and receiving the puck. (4-6 minutes)

3. Using the same partners, have 1 partner set up 2 cones to form a goal and then stand in front of them as the goalie. The other partner dribbles the puck toward the goal, trying to shoot and score when the opportunity presents itself, while the goalie attempts to block the shot. After five attempts on goal, partners should switch roles. (6-8 minutes)

4. Divide the class into teams of 5 or 6. (To increase playing time, have 2 or more games running simultaneously.) Explain the rules and positions, and have students play a game of in-line hockey. (12-16 minutes)

In-Line Hockey

The game of in-line hockey is essentially floor hockey played on in-line skates. In a typical game, the clock runs continuously for 22 minutes per half, with a 5-minute rest at halftime. As noted earlier (see teaching cue 5), the game played in this class period will have to be shorter.

Each team consists of 6 players:

- ▶ 1 center
- ▶ 1 goalie
- ▶ 2 forwards (right and left wings)
- ▶ 2 defensive players (right and left defenders)

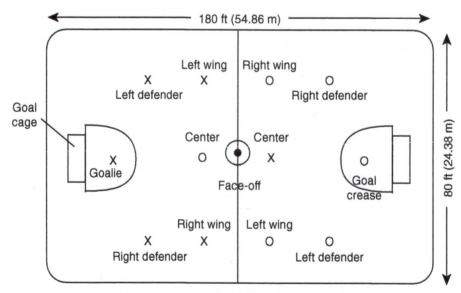

In-line hockey court dimensions and starting positions

The game begins with a face-off. From there, players try to advance the puck down the court using various passing, dribbling, and other techniques to move the puck toward the opponent's goal and score. Each goal is worth 1 point. At the end of the game, the team with the most points wins.

The rules of floor hockey apply to in-line hockey (see the rules section of the floor hockey unit on page 433), with a few exceptions.

1. Players may use one of three checking techniques:
   ▸ Poke checking: knocking the puck by extending the stick toward an opponent
   ▸ Lift checking: using the stick to lift an opponent's stick into the air and then steal the puck
   ▸ Sweep checking: using a sweep shot (low on the floor) to knock the puck away from an opponent

2. Fouls include the following:
   ▸ Holding
   ▸ Trapping
   ▸ Charging
   ▸ Slashing
   ▸ Hitting from behind
   ▸ Kneeing
   ▸ Elbowing
   ▸ Tripping
   ▸ Interference or other obstruction
   ▸ Cross-checking
   ▸ Spearing (poking another player with the blade tip of the stick), hooking, and boarding (checking another player into the boards [wall] with great force)
   ▸ Roughing
   ▸ Butt-ending (jabbing a player with the shaft of the stick)
   ▸ High sticking
   ▸ Other rough play, obscene language, misconduct, and violence

3. When a foul is committed, the offending player is sent off the rink for a designated period of time (2 minutes for unintentional violations or 4 minutes for intentional violations).
   ▸ Penalty shots are awarded when a player tosses a stick at the puck, illegally prevents the attacking player from scoring, and smothers the puck (when a player other than the goalie falls on the puck).
   ▸ A penalty shot is taken from the center circle, and the player who was offended gets to shoot directly (i.e., unguarded) at the goalie.

Closure (3-5 Minutes)

Review the lesson with students using the following ideas to reinforce learning, check understanding, and provide feedback.

1. Review the three types of checking (i.e., poke, lift, and sweep).
2. Review what constitutes a foul.
3. If this lesson will be extended to another class period, let students know they will be playing a full game of in-line hockey (i.e., 22-minute halves) during the next class.

Lesson 5

Fitness Skating, Dancing, and Game Play

Purpose

In this lesson students use in-line skating as a means of increasing fitness and learn some dances and sports that can be done on in-line skates.

Facility and Equipment

- Gym or outdoor area with a smooth surface
- 1 pair of in-line skates per student
- Cones
- Music and player (CD or audiocassette)
- 2 Wiffle bats
- 2 Wiffle balls
- 16 bases
- Stopwatch

Warm-Ups (6-8 Minutes)

1. Scissors
2. Single-leg crossovers
3. Elbow-knee touches (supine)
4. Facedown flank
5. Floor touches

Skill Cues

1. Bend further at the waist for speed skating (e.g., in interval training) than for distance skating.
2. Use the snow plow to slow down or stop in game situations. Bend the knees, point the toes slightly inward, and place pressure on the inside edges of the skate.
3. Drafting is necessary in interval training. Stay fairly close to the skater in front to reduce the amount of energy expended.
4. Remember to use the wheel edges and transfer weight when swizzling.

Bleking Step

1. Start with weight on the right skate.
2. Hop to the left skate and extend the right heel out, at the same time pushing the right arm forward to an extended position and drawing the left elbow backward, twisting the body slightly to the left.
3. Jump, reversing the feet and arms (i.e., hop to the right skate and extend the left skate forward, pushing the left arm forward, drawing the right elbow backward, and twisting the body slightly to the right).
4. Repeat steps 2 and 3 three times in quick succession.

Teaching Cues

1. Explain how to use heart rate to determine peak aerobic exertion (see lessons 3 and 4 in the aerobic conditioning unit on pages 26 and 28).

2. When students are working in partners, be sure they maintain enough distance to avoid hooking skates.

3. Always warm up and stretch before speed skating.

4. Make sure students' skates fit properly before speed skating. A proper fit will help them maintain control.

5. Challenge students to use in-line skating as a cross-training sport in their outside fitness regimen.

6. The activities presented in this lesson are too numerous to fit within a single class period. Choose a few that are best suited for students and the intended focus of the lesson, or extend this lesson to one or more class periods to give students a chance to try each activity.

Activities (45- 60 Minutes)

1. Introduce partner interval training on in-line skates as a fitness activity. Because of its aerobic demands, interval training should be used only for short periods of time. (8-10 minutes)

Partner Interval Training

In pairs, students skate together, one skater passing the other and then the trailing skater catching up and passing the first skater. Repeat the cycle every minute or so.

2. Skate for distance. Using the same partners, or reassigning partners, have student pairs skate around the gym. Partners should compete to see who can skate the farthest in 2 minutes. (3-5 minutes)

3. Set up a 1-mile (1.6-kilometer) course for in-line skating. The course should be relatively smooth with no sharp turns. Time students to determine their skating fitness level. Males with moderate fitness levels should be able to complete the course in 4.5 minutes, females with moderate fitness levels should be able to complete the course in 5.5 minutes. (7-9 minutes)

4. Have students form a large circle, all facing the center, and perform the hockey pokey, an in-line skating version of the hokey pokey. (5-8 minutes)

Hockey Pokey

Suggested music: Hokey pokey music or have students sing (use the following calls)

"You put your right skate in [into the circle],

You put your right skate out [back and away from the circle],

You put your right skate in, and you shake it all about [in the circle and shake].

You do the hockey pokey and you turn yourself around [shake hands overhead while turning once around in place],

That's what it's all about" [clap hands 4 times].

Repeat the sequence using the left skate, the right arm, the left arm, the right knee, the left knee, the right hip, the left hip, the head, the back, and the whole body.

"You do the hockey pokey, you do the hockey pokey; you do the hockey pokey [raise arms above head; lower arms and head in a bowing motion];

That's what it's all about" [clap 6 times].

5. Position students in a large circle, all facing the center. Introduce the *la raspa*, a Mexican folk dance, and have students perform it. (6-8 minutes)

La Raspa

Skills: bleking step
Perform the bleking step 4 times.
Glide clockwise around the circle for 16 counts.
Shuffle toward the center of the circle for 8 counts.
Shuffle backward, out of the circle, for 8 counts.
Glide clockwise around the circle for 8 counts.
Repeat the entire sequence as many times as desired.

6. Set up the play area by placing eight bases in a diamond formation (i.e., place a base in the normal first, second, third, and home plate areas, with additional bases between home and first, first and second, second and third, and third and home). Divide the class into 4 teams (for 2 simultaneous games). Explain the rules and have students play a game of eight-base skate ball. (16-20 minutes)

Eight-Base Skate Ball

The game is played like baseball using a Wiffle ball and bat. Skaters bat a ball thrown by a pitcher. Once they get a legal hit, they skate around the bases, trying to score runs. At the end of the game, the team with the most runs wins.

The rules of baseball apply, with a few exceptions:

▸ The pitcher must stay in a designated area (i.e., around the pitching mound).
▸ After a successful hit, skaters "run" as many bases as possible without being caught between bases.
▸ The pitcher is the only player who can get "runners" out. Fielders retrieve the batted ball and then throw it to the pitcher, who yells, "Freeze!" All runners must stop.
▸ All runners not on a base when "freeze" is yelled must return to the previous base.
▸ Fielders can tag runners. If any runner is tagged, all runners (on any base) return to first base.
▸ Batters may hit after one bounce.
▸ Rather than three-out innings, teams switch places after a few minutes of play.
▸ Pitchers may rotate after each new batter.

Optional Activity (0-18 Minutes)

Try other sports on in-line skates—for example, basketball or ultimate Frisbee (see pages 128 and 581).

Closure (3-5 Minutes)

Review the lesson with students using the following ideas to reinforce learning, check understanding, and provide feedback.

1. Ask students to calculate how many miles (kilometers) per hour they were traveling during activity 3. (It should be between 11 and 13 miles [17.7-20.9 kilometers] per hour.)

2. Discuss the most effective body position for traveling at fast speeds (i.e., bend further at the waist, hands behind the back on level surfaces, pump arms back and forth on hills).

Assessment and Resources

Skill tests and game play assessment can be formal or informal in this unit. The following activities could be adapted for assessment purposes:

- ▶ Lesson 2, activity 5
- ▶ Lesson 2, activity 6
- ▶ Lesson 3, activity 5
- ▶ Lesson 5, activity 2
- ▶ Lesson 5, activity 3

You can also conduct separate skill tests or assess skill development during game play. Following are some testing suggestions for in-line hockey skills. Assessment protocol is listed with each.

▶ Passing for time. Pair up students and position partners 20 feet (6.1 meters) apart, each with a hockey stick and 1 puck per pair. Student partners complete as many passes as possible in 3 minutes. Students may not touch the puck with their hands.

▶ Speed dribble. Time each student as she or he dribbles around a cone 20 feet (6.1 meters) away. Count the best of three time trials.

Resources

Broido, B. 1997. *Book of rules.* Indianapolis, IN: Masters Press.

Joyner, S. 1995. *In-line roller hockey.* Chicago: Contemporary Books.

Nottinghan, S., and F. Fedel. 1997. *Fitness in-line skating.* Champaign, IL: Human Kinetics.

Powell, M., and J. Svensson. 1998. *In-line skating.* Champaign, IL: Human Kinetics.

Publow, B. 1999. *Speed on skates.* Champaign, IL: Human Kinetics.

Sullivan, G. 1993. *In-line skating: A complete guide for beginners.* New York: Puffin Group.

Jumping Rope

The activity of jumping rope goes as far back as ancient Greece, where men used the stems of hop plants, which are vine-like, for skipping to celebrate the beginning of spring. In other ancient traditions, people believed crops would grow only as high as a person could jump. As this myth was perpetuated, jumping rope was eventually added to the farming ritual.

Jump ropes also have a long history. Cherokee Indians made jump ropes from grapevines and Swedish children jumped using stiff wicker. In the 19th century children used long ropes with turners and recited rhymes as they jumped in popular games.

Today, jumping rope is used throughout the world as a means of exercise and recreation. The activity provides cardiovascular fitness by improving circulation, increasing muscular endurance, and reducing stress. A bit more involved than simple childhood rope-jumping maneuvers and rhythms, formal rope jumping is primarily done to music. It has become a challenging sport using foot stunts and novelty equipment such as pogo sticks, hippity hop balls, and hula hoops. Double Dutch, with its two-rope rhythm and timing, is another exciting activity that elicits both creativity and competitive interest.

Equipment

Jump ropes are made of various materials, including the following:

- ▸ Plastic speed rope
- ▸ Beaded rope
- ▸ Sash cord
- ▸ Polypropylene fiber
- ▸ Ball bearing swivels (i.e., metal bearings used in some jump ropes to make the handles turn freely).

Different materials offer various benefits, including increased speed, improved durability, less noise, cheaper cost, and more visibility. Choose the rope material based on lesson focus, equipment inventory, and available budget.

Jump ropes vary in size and composition. The most commonly recommended length for senior high (grades 10 through 12) is 9 to 10 feet (2.74-3.05 meters), but rope length should be sized on an individual basis. The best way to determine the proper length is to stand on the center of the rope with both feet. If it is the proper length, the handles should reach the underarms. Middle school students (grades 7 through 9) would most likely use ropes 8 to 9 feet (2.44-2.74 meters) long. For specialty rope-jumping activities (e.g., double Dutch), one or two longer ropes are used. These usually range from 12 to 14 feet (3.66-4.27 meters) in length.

Unit Organization

Each lesson in this unit contains more activities than typical class times will allow. Expand the lessons to more than one class period, or select the most appropriate tasks for each class based on students' skills and interest. This unit is based on the assumption that students have had rope-jumping experience during the lower grades.

Following is a brief description of each lesson in this unit.

▸ Lesson 1 presents the basic technique of jumping rope and such beginner stunts as the jog step, crossover, side swing, double under, skier, rocker, and straddle.

▸ Intermediate individual and partner stunts are introduced in lesson 2.

▸ The use of single long ropes and double Dutch ropes (two long ropes) is taught in lesson 3. Some of the challenges include 360-degree turns, straddles, and scissors jumps.

▸ Lesson 4 presents advanced stunts using single long ropes and other equipment.

Selected resources and assessment ideas are found in the assessment and resources chapter at the end of the unit.

Note: An asterisk (*) following a facility or equipment listing indicates that preparation is required before the lesson.

Social Skills and Etiquette

Jumping rope provides an excellent opportunity for developing social skills. The activities in this unit require group and partner cooperation as well as encourage collaboration and creativity. Encourage students to give their peers positive reinforcement. It is also suggested that skilled jumpers be encouraged to help their classmates through reciprocal teaching.

Lesson Modifications

Jumping rope takes some coordination. Thus, students with disabilities may have difficulty performing some of the tasks. To enable these students to participate in class instruction and activities, the following lesson modifications are recommended:

▸ Have students try each skill without a rope until they achieve some level of comfort.

▸ Place the ropes on the ground and jump over them as they lie stationary.

▸ Use skip-it balls in place of jump ropes. A skip-it ball has a ball at the end of a rope and is swung in a circular direction.

Students new to jumping rope may also have some difficulty performing the skills taught in these lessons. Have these students begin by learning the steps without the rope; then have them develop basic jumping technique with the following methods:

▸ Hold the rope and jump over it forward and backward.

▸ Swing the rope gently and jump over it forward and backward.

▸ Model the rhythm of other jumpers nearby.

Another lead-up skill for beginners would be to swing the rope overhead, stopping it in front of the toes, and then begin the next jump.

Safety

Jumping rope is a safe activity, given that certain safety precautions are explained and enforced.

▸ Ensure that there is enough room between students so they do not hit each other when swinging ropes.

▸ Do not allow students to snap or swing ropes at or toward others.

▸ Never allow students to wrap the ropes around themselves or others.

▸ Ascertain students' ability levels before assigning stunts that involve the use of other equipment.

Lesson 1

Basic Technique and Beginner Jumps

Purpose

In this lesson students develop the basic technique of jumping rope, learning such beginner stunts as the jog step, crossover, side swing, double under, skier, rocker, and straddle.

Warm-Ups (6-8 Minutes)

1. Side slides
2. Scissors
3. High jumper
4. Arm circles
5. Hamstring straight-leg stretch

Facility and Equipment

◆ Gym or outdoor area with a resilient surface (e.g., asphalt, cement)
◆ 1 jump rope per student
◆ Stopwatch
◆ Music and player (CD or audiocassette)
   Note: Any music with a medium tempo may be used in this lesson.

Skill Cues

1. For the basic jump,
   ▶ jump on both feet,
   ▶ land on the balls of the feet,
   ▶ keep the feet together and the elbows close to the body, and
   ▶ swing the rope with the wrists and forearms.
2. For the jog step, alternate feet with each jump, bending the knee lifted upward.
3. For the crossover,
   ▶ cross the right arm over the left,
   ▶ jump continuously with the arms crossed,
   ▶ keep the hands low,
   ▶ bend the body slightly forward from the waist, and
   ▶ use a lot of wrist motion.
4. For the side swing,
   ▶ twirl the rope to one side,
   ▶ jump in time with the rope,
   ▶ keep both hands together on the twirl, and
   ▶ jump over the rope;
   ▶ then twirl the rope on the same side again.

Crossover sequence

5. For the double under, pass the rope under the feet twice for every jump. Gradually increase speed and jump higher than normal.

6. For the skier, jump to one side and then the other, keeping the feet together. Move the feet 4 to 6 inches (10.2-15.2 centimeters) from side to side.

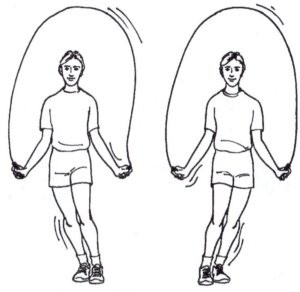

Skier sequence

7. For the rocker, place one foot forward and the other foot back, 8 to 12 inches (20.3-30.5 centimeters) apart. Alternate placing the weight on the front foot and then the back foot each time the rope comes around.

8. For the straddle, jump with the feet shoulder-width apart (this is the straddle part of the jump) and then bring them together.

9. The straddle cross starts like the straddle: Jump with the feet apart and then bring them together, but they should be crossed (the right foot in front of the left, or vice versa) on the landing. On the second jump, bring the feet back together in the reversed crossed position (the left foot in front of the right, or vice versa).

Teaching Cues

1. Have students select the proper length of rope by standing on the center of the rope and ensuring that the handles reach the underarms.

2. Make sure students practice the more difficult steps first without and then with a rope.

3. Give students verbal cues to help them perform the jumping skills.

Activities (30-40 Minutes)

1. Have students select a jump rope of an appropriate size. Demonstrate the basic jump and introduce the basic techniques for all jumps using the appropriate skill and teaching cues. (6-8 minutes)

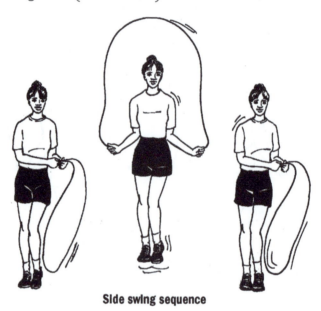

Side swing sequence

2. Scatter students around the gym 6 to 8 feet (1.83-2.44 meters) apart. Have them practice the basic jump and then try the jog step, crossover, side swing, double under, skier, rocker, straddle jump, and straddle cross. Encourage students to work at their own pace and play music during this practice time. (12-16 minutes)

3. Partner jump. Pair up students or have them select partners. One partner performs a short jumping sequence using various jumps; then the other tries to perform it. In addition to varying jumps in the sequence, students may also change levels (e.g., jump low and then high), body direction (e.g., pivot on each jump), and rope direction (i.e., backward and forward). Partners should alternate creating sequences for the other to imitate. (6-8 minutes)

4. Consistency test. Scatter students around the gym 6 to 8 feet (1.83-2.44 meters) apart. Have students count the number of jumps they can make without missing (i.e., tripping, stopping, or faltering on the rope rotation) in 3 minutes. (6-8 minutes)

Closure (3-5 Minutes)

Review the lesson with students. Use the following ideas to reinforce learning, check understanding, and provide feedback.

1. Discuss additional rope-jumping stunts students may know or have tried.
2. Give students the assignment of creating a jump rope routine using at least five jumps learned in today's lesson. Students may also add other stunts to the routine.

Lesson 2

Intermediate Stunts

Purpose

In this lesson students develop intermediate rope-jumping skills individually and with partners.

Warm-Ups (6-8 Minutes)

1. Slapping jacks
2. Shoulder shrugs
3. Hamstring straight-leg stretch
4. Single-leg curls

Facility and Equipment

◆ Gym or outdoor area with a resilient surface (e.g., asphalt, cement)
◆ 1 jump rope per student
◆ 1 long rope (10-12 feet [3.05-3.66 meters]) per student
◆ Poster board and markers
◆ Music and player (CD or audiocassette)
Note: Any music with a medium tempo may be used in this lesson.

Skill Cues

1. For the switch, jump and cross the legs (right over left) and then switch, crossing left over right. Change the position of the feet with each rope rotation.

2. Toe touches are performed forward, backward, and sideways using the following sequence.

   ▸ Hop on the right foot and touch the left toe forward to the ground.

   ▸ Hop on the left foot and touch the right toe forward to the ground.

   ▸ Hop on the right foot and touch the left toe, to the side, to the ground.

   ▸ Hop on the left foot and touch the right toe, to the side, to the ground.

   ▸ Hop on the right foot and touch the left toe backward to the ground.

   ▸ Hop on the left foot and touch the right toe backward to the ground.

   ▸ Repeat forward, forward; sideways, sideways; backward, backward; sideways, sideways; and so on.

3. For the heel click, step over the rope on the right foot and hop. Click the heels to the left and land on the right foot. Repeat on the other side.

4. The leg over is performed by hopping on the right foot and raising the left leg while reaching under the left leg with the left arm.

   ▸ Reach the arm beyond the leg as far as possible.

   ▸ Bring the rope out to a right side swing.

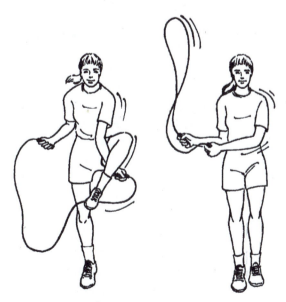

Leg over sequence

493

5. For the cancan,
   ▸ hop on the right foot and lift the left knee up high, then
   ▸ hop on the right foot and touch the left toe to the floor;
   ▸ hop on the right foot and kick the left leg up waist high, then
   ▸ land on both feet.
   ▸ Repeat the sequence, reversing the legs.

6. For the twist, rotate the hips from side to side while jumping.

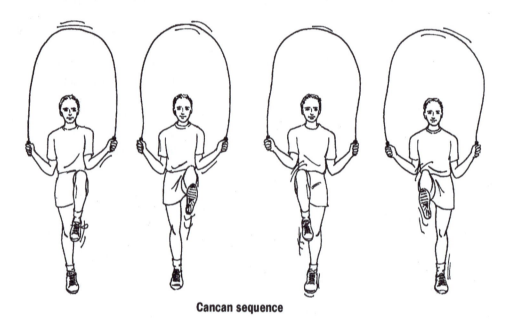

Cancan sequence

Teaching Cues

1. Demonstrate each stunt to visually reinforce the skills. A demonstration is especially helpful when calling out each skill as it is performed.
2. Clap to help students establish a jumping tempo.

Activities (30-40 Minutes)

1. Introduce the intermediate rope-jumping stunts using the skill and teaching cues. (4-6 minutes)
2. Create a stunt card for each stunt in this lesson using poster board and markers. Have students select jump ropes of the proper size. Divide the class into 6 groups (assign at least 1 student with greater skill to each group) and position each group at a different station to practice the stunt posted. Advanced jumpers should help students who are having difficulty. After 3 minutes, groups should rotate to the next station. Play music during this practice time. (14-16 minutes)

Optional Activity: Jump Rope Relays

3. Pair up students or have them select partners and give a long rope (10 to 12 feet [3.05-3.66 meters]) to each pair. One partner swings the rope and both partners jump together. Partners without the ropes may jump facing or with their backs turned to the partners, or they may pivot on each jump to complete a circle. (4-6 minutes)

4. Using the same partners as in activity 3, give each pair two long ropes (10 to 12 feet [3.05-3.66 meters]) and position partners standing side by side. Each partner takes one end of each rope and then both perform the wheel. Call out verbal cues for each part of the sequence. (4-6 minutes)

Wheel

This is a partner jumping stunt. The sequence is as follows:

 ▶ Begin by turning the left arm first (verbal cue: "turn").
 ▶ When it is overhead, turn the right arm (verbal cue: "turn").
 ▶ Jump over the first rope (verbal cue: "jump").
 ▶ Jump over the second rope (verbal cue: "jump").

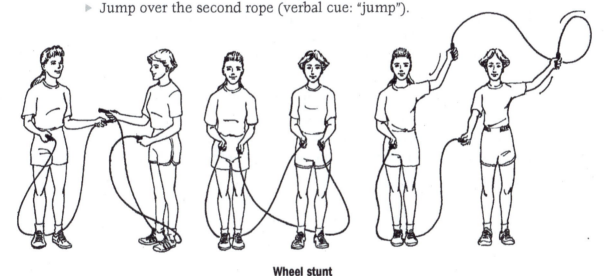

Wheel stunt

5. Group stunts. Divide students into groups of 5 or 6 and position each group side by side in a line. The end student begins jumping rope while moving sideways down the line. As the jumper passes, each group member jumps. Once at the end of the line, the jumper reverses direction and goes back to take the second position in line. Then the new student on the end proceeds. Continue until all students have been the traveling jumper. (4-6 minutes)

Optional Activity: Speed Jump

Optional Activities

Jump Rope Relays (0-8 Minutes)

Divide the class into groups of 4 or 5. Each team member must jump rope from the starting line to another point, and then back again, using a specified stunt or skill. Skills that can be used in the relay include the following:

 ▶ Skipping
 ▶ Using a jog step
 ▶ Hopping on one foot (switching to the other foot on the way back)

To make the relay more challenging, require changes in direction.

Speed Jump (0-4 Minutes)

Scatter students around the gym 6 to 8 feet (1.83-2.44 meters) apart. Have students count how many times they can jump rope in 2 minutes.

Closure (3-5 Minutes)

Review the lesson with students. Use the following ideas to reinforce learning, check understanding, and provide feedback.

1. Ask for volunteers to demonstrate a stunt learned in today's lesson.
2. Have students watch a jump rope video to improve their skill. The following titles are suggested (all from the American Heart Association; see the assessment and resources chapter at the end of this unit for ordering information):
   - *Just Jump '97* (Beginning Jump Rope Skills)
   - *Just Jump '98* (Intermediate Jump Rope Skills)
   - *Just Jump '99* (Advanced Jump Rope Skills)

Another good choice is *The Jump Rope Primer Video*, available from Human Kinetics (see the assessment and resources chapter for ordering information).

Lesson 3

Single Long Rope and Double Dutch Activities

Purpose

In this lesson students develop various rope-jumping skills using single long ropes.

Warm-Ups (6-8 Minutes)

1. Step touches
2. Shoulder pushes
3. Sit and stretch
4. Body circles

Facility and Equipment

- Gym or outdoor area with a resilient surface (e.g., asphalt, cement)
- 1 long rope (12-14 feet [3.66-4.27 meters]) per 3 or 4 students
- 1 ball per 3 or 4 students
- Music and player (CD or audiocassette)

Note: Any music with a medium tempo may be used in this lesson.

Skill Cues

Single Long Rope

1. Rotate the rope with the shoulder, keeping the wrist locked.
2. Rotate the elbow and keep the thumbs up while turning the rope.
3. Swing the rope toward the jumper before the run in. (Swinging the rope away from the jumper is much more difficult.)
4. Stand next to the rope turner and run in as the rope hits the ground.
5. Jump toward the rope turner and exit before the next jump.

Double Dutch

1. Turn two ropes toward each other, one counterclockwise and the other clockwise, keeping the ropes waist high as they are turned.
2. Keep the thumbs up and the elbows close to the body while rotating the ropes.
3. Stand next to either turner and run in when the farthest rope touches the ground.
4. Jump immediately after running in.
5. Jump twice as fast as with a single long rope.
6. Face either turner while jumping.
7. Exit by running out close to a turner's shoulder.

Teaching Cues

1. Group students of similar ability to enable them to work at their own pace and skill level.
2. Circulate around the gym to provide feedback and assistance.

Activities (30-40 Minutes)

1. Introduce the single rope and double Dutch skills. (4-6 minutes)

2. Divide students into groups of 3 or 4 and distribute a long rope to each group. Position the groups far enough apart that they have ample room to swing the rope. Two students swing the rope while the other student(s) run in and begin jumping. Remind jumpers to use a double bounce. After 1 minute, have students switch roles so that all have an opportunity to jump. (8 minutes)

3. Divide the class into groups of 3 or 4 and give each student a long rope. Have students try the following variations of single long rope jumping. Play music during this activity. (8-12 minutes)

   ▶ 360-degree turning: complete a 360-degree turn while jumping

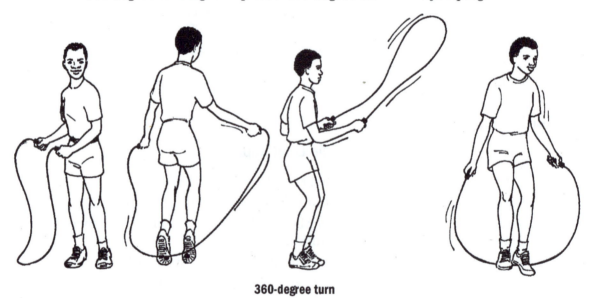

360-degree turn

   ▶ Straddle: jump to a straddle position and then bring the legs back together

   ▶ Scissors: jump with the legs in a stride position (i.e., 1 leg forward, 1 leg backward) and then reverse the legs on the next jump

   ▶ Individual ball toss: toss a ball in the air and catch it while jumping

   ▶ Partner ball toss: toss a ball to a partner (who is not jumping) and catch the return while jumping

   ▶ Ball dribble: dribble the ball while jumping

4. Distribute two long ropes to each group of 3 or 4 students and scatter groups around the gym. Have the rope turners practice the technique and rhythm of double Dutch turning before jumpers step in. To practice timing, jumpers should run through the ropes without jumping. After a few minutes of practice, two students swing the rope while the other student(s) step in and jump. The jumper(s) should step in and jump once and exit, then step in and jump for 30 seconds. Have students rotate positions periodically so that everyone gets an opportunity to jump. (10-14 minutes)

Optional Activity

Double Dutch Routines (0-10 minutes)

Divide the class into groups of 3 or 4 students and give 2 ropes to each group. Have students create a routine to music using various double Dutch skills. Suggested skills include

- ▶ turns,
- ▶ straddles, and
- ▶ scissors.

Closure (3-5 Minutes)

Review the lesson with students. Use the following ideas to reinforce learning, check understanding, and provide feedback.

1. Discuss techniques that students found helpful in double Dutch activities. (This is a good time to review some of the skill and teaching cues.)
2. Select a skilled double Dutch team to demonstrate skills in front of the class.

Lesson 4

Advanced Technique and Stunts

Purpose

In this lesson students develop advanced long rope and double Dutch skills using additional equipment and different types of challenges.

Warm-Ups (6-8 Minutes)

1. Reverse run
2. Side stretch
3. Arm pumps
4. Floor touches

Facility and Equipment

- Gym or outdoor area with a resilient surface (e.g., asphalt, cement)
- 2 long ropes (12-14 feet [3.66-4.27 meters]) per 3 or 4 students
- 2 hula hoops per 3 or 4 students
- 2 hippity-hop balls per 3 or 4 students
- 1 pogo stick per 3 or 4 students
- 2 basketballs per 3 or 4 students
- 1 medium rope (8-10 feet [2.44-3.05 meters]) per 3 or 4 students

Teaching Cues

1. Not all students will be able to perform at this level of difficulty. If necessary, allow students to continue working on activities from previous lessons.
2. Have students work with each piece of equipment without jumping rope before combining the equipment and the ropes.

Activities (30-40 Minutes)

1. Review the skills for jumping single long ropes and for double Dutch (see lesson 3). (4-6 minutes)
2. Divide the class into groups of 3 or 4 students and distribute 1 or 2 long ropes to each group. Have students perform the following challenges. (8-12 minutes)
    - ▸ Catch hula hoops while jumping.
    - ▸ Bounce and catch hippity-hop balls while jumping.
    - ▸ Jump on pogo sticks between ropes.
    - ▸ Dribble or catch basketballs while jumping.
3. Using the same group formation as in activity 2, challenge students to jump (a short) rope while jumping the long or double Dutch ropes. Jumpers should enter the long rope or double Dutch ropes holding the short rope and then, after facing either rope turner, begin to jump the short rope in time to the rhythm of the long rope or double Dutch ropes. (8-12 minutes)
4. Divide students into groups of 5 or 6 and distribute 2 long ropes to each group. Position 4 turners in a square so that the 2 ropes cross in the center. Turners swing both ropes at the same time and in the same direction while the jumper runs in and jumps using a double bounce. (10 minutes)

Closure (3-5 Minutes)

Review the lesson with students. Use the following ideas to reinforce learning, check understanding, and provide feedback.

1. Challenge students to create other rope-jumping variations using a single long rope or double Dutch ropes.

2. Select the skilled groups to demonstrate their best stunts, using various equipment (e.g., basketballs, pogo sticks, hula hoops) or short ropes.

Assessment and Resources

Skill in jumping rope can be assessed formally or informally. In general, testing the basic jump, the jog step, the crossover, and the skier is sufficient. More advanced techniques and stunts may also be tested, however. Following are suggestions for specific skill tests. Assessment protocol is listed with each.

▶ Endurance test. Time how long students can jump continuously. This measures both cardiovascular endurance and rope-jumping skill.

▶ Stunt test. Create a list of stunts from lessons 1 and 2. Have students demonstrate as many as they are able. Rate each student's performance using the following point scale:

Excellent	3
Good	2
Satisfactory	1
Unsatisfactory	0

The following activities described in this unit could also be adapted for assessment purposes:

▶ Consistency test (see lesson 1, activity 4)

▶ Speed jump (see lesson 2, optional activities)

Resources

American Alliance for Health, Physical Education, Recreation, and Dance and The American Heart Association. 1999. *Just jump '99: Jump rope skills guide.* Dallas, TX: American Heart Association.

Lavay, B., and M. Horvat. 1991. Jump rope for heart for special populations. *Journal of Physical Education, Recreation and Dance* 62 (3): 74-78.

Melson, B., and V. Worrell. 1986. *Rope skipping for fun and fitness.* Wichita, KS: Woodlawn.

Pangrazi, R., and P. Darst. 1997. *Dynamic physical education for secondary school students: Curriculum and instruction.* 3rd ed. Needham Heights, MA: Allyn & Bacon.

Solis, K., and B. Budris. 1991. *The jump rope primer.* Champaign, IL: Human Kinetics.

Additional Resources

The following companies sell the videotapes recommended in lesson 2 (see page 496).

American Heart Association
7272 Greenville Ave.
Dallas, TX 75231-4596
Phone 214-706-1324

Human Kinetics
P.O. Box 5076
Champaign, IL 61825-5076
Phone 800-747-4457

Lacrosse

The oldest sport in North America, lacrosse was originally played by Native Americans in what is now northern New York and Canada. The sport is rooted in the Native American religious ceremony called *baggataway*, meaning "little brother of war." French missionaries gave the game its name because the shape of the stick used resembled a crosier (*la crosse* in French), a staff resembling a shepherd's crook carried by bishops as a symbol of office.

The tribal lacrosse game was not only played for recreation but was also a method of training warriors. It was played on a much larger scale than the game today: it was played with hundreds of players and the distance between goals ranged from 500 yards (457.2 meters) to several miles (kilometers) apart. In addition, Native American lacrosse games typically lasted for several hours, if not days.

French pioneers started playing the game regularly in the early 1800s. The first lacrosse club was founded in Montreal in 1842, and institutionalized rules were formed by 1860. In 1867 lacrosse was declared Canada's national sport. And in 1867 Canadian Indians introduced it in the United States, in New York. Lacrosse clubs were formed throughout the Midwest and 1882 saw the formation of the Intercollegiate Lacrosse Association, an organization that today sponsors a world lacrosse championship series every four years.

Equipment

The game of lacrosse is played using a lacrosse stick (crosse) and ball, but players are required to wear gloves and helmet with a face mask. Goalies are also required to wear a throat protector. Official equipment is as follows:

▶ The crosse is made of laminated wood, plastic, or synthetic material with a net pocket at the head. The pocket is somewhat triangular in shape and is between 6 and 10 inches (15.2 and 25.4 centimeters) wide. (Newer plastic sticks have a catch guard installed, which drastically improves the ability to cradle effectively.) The length of the crosse ranges from 40 to 72 inches (101.6-182.9 centimeters).

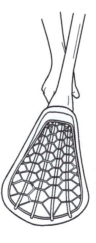

Crosse

▶ The lacrosse ball is made of solid rubber, is 7.5 to 8 inches (19.1-20.3 centimeters) in circumference, and weighs 5 to 5.25 ounces (141.7-148.8 grams).

The equipment typically used in physical education lacrosse curricula includes plastic crosse sticks and soft, rubber lacrosse balls, tennis balls, or baseball-sized Wiffle balls. (Tennis balls are suitable for the scooping lesson, but use Wiffle or rubber balls for all other lessons.) Any sort of goals (e.g., floor hockey goals) can be used in a lacrosse physical education curriculum.

Lacrosse field equipment consists of two goals, formed by two vertical posts and a top crossbar 6 feet (1.83 meters) above the ground. Pyramidal cord netting is attached to each goal post and is fastened to the ground 7 feet (2.13 meters) behind the goal line. The playing area itself is a field 110 yards (100.58 meters) long and 53.3 to 60 yards (48.74-54.86 meters) wide. For the purpose of this unit instruction, however, lacrosse may be played in a gym or on an outdoor field 50 yards [45.72 meters] or longer.

Unit Organization

Because many students will not be familiar with lacrosse, and thus their skill levels will vary greatly, this unit stresses basic lacrosse skills and includes numerous opportunities for practice. If learned correctly and mastered, these skills will give students a measure of playing success. If students are familiar with the game or are skilled at using the crosse, alternate skills and higher standards may be researched and then emphasized throughout the unit (see the assessment and resources chapter at the end of this unit for additional sources of information about lacrosse).

Following is a brief description of each lesson in this unit.

▶ Lesson 1 presents the skills of cradling and scooping, and includes a number of practice activities.

▶ Throwing and catching combined with throwing and running are detailed in lesson 2.

▶ Shooting is covered in lesson 3. Students may need two lessons for shooting skills depending on age and type of equipment used.

▶ In lessons 4 and 5, modified games using smaller groups are introduced, moving from no-resistance games to passive-resistance games. Basic offensive and defensive strategies are also introduced.

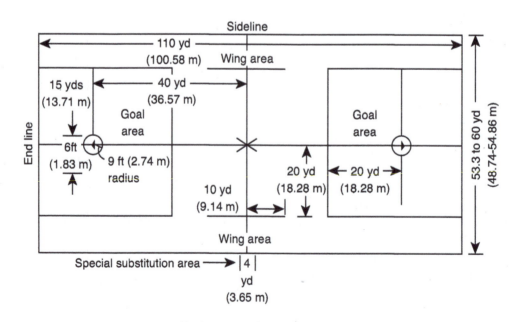

Men's lacrosse field dimensions

In lesson 6 students are able to utilize all previously learned skills in a regulation game of lacrosse.

Selected resources and assessment ideas are found in the assessment and resources chapter at the end of the unit.

Note: An asterisk (*) following a facility or equipment listing indicates that preparation is required before the lesson.

Social Skills and Etiquette

Because it is a team game, social skills are easily incorporated into the game of lacrosse. As other team sports, lacrosse demands teamwork, including sharing responsibilities for playing positions.

In addition to the usual rules of etiquette in team sports (e.g., acknowledging good plays, encouraging teammates), players should be inspired to work closely with one another. Emphasize partner and small-group work throughout the lessons, urging mutual cooperation, idea sharing, and strategic discussion. Two heads are better than one in most cases, but when it comes to lacrosse—a sport that will likely be new to most students in class—group collaboration can make up for lack of understanding and game knowledge.

Lesson Modifications

Lacrosse involves a lot of running and uses specialized equipment, both of which may be difficult for students with certain disabilities. Suggested modifications for the lessons in this unit include the following:

- Use a shorter, plastic crosse.
- Use a soft rubber ball or a Wiffle ball for better control and to avoid injury.
- Reduce the size of the playing field.

Safety

Because the equipment is distinct and because lacrosse is a fast-moving game, activities in this unit can be dangerous. Observe the following safety precautions in class organization and instruction:

- Do not allow students to swing, or check, with the crosse.
- Allocate adequate space for students when practicing throwing and catching off the wall.
- Have students throw in one direction.
- Be strict about the handling of the crosse: it should not be swung or used to impede another player while catching or throwing the ball.
- Goalies should wear helmets, throat protectors, and chest protectors when blocking incoming shots.

Rules

The object of the game is to score points by shooting the ball into the opponent's goal. Each goal is worth 1 point (as in hockey and soccer). The team with the most points at the end of the game wins.

A lacrosse team has 10 players:

- 1 goalkeeper,
- 3 defenders,
- 3 midfielders, or wings
- 3 offensive players, called attackers.

Each team must keep at least 4 players (including the goalkeeper) in its defending half of the field and 3 in the offensive half.

Center face-offs are used to start the game and after each goal. Players shoot and pass the ball to their teammate using the crosse, trying to score a goal by throwing (shooting) the ball into the opponent's goal. The strategy of lacrosse is very similar to soccer. Teams are to pass the ball toward the opponent's goal, ultimately trying to shoot the ball into the opponent's goal. The ball can be caught or "scooped" off the ground by any player for either team. Each team tries to control the ball and score into the opponent's goal.

Generally, the attackers are the players who score and are placed near the opponent's goal.

Midfielders roam on each side of the field but generally stay in the center. The defenders help their goalie stop attackers from the other team.

The following general rules govern game play:

- ▶ Shots on goal must be made from outside the goal area (also called the *crease*).

- ▶ Attacking or offensive players may not enter the crease but may reach into the crease with the crosse to catch or retrieve a ball.

- ▶ If a ball or a player with the ball goes out-of-bounds, the other team gets a free play. Free play is an unobstructed throw in at the point where the ball went out-of-bounds.

- ▶ Opposing team players must stay 5 yards (4.57 meters) away during a free play.

- ▶ Goalies are the only players allowed to touch the ball with their hands.

Cradling and Scooping

Purpose

In this lesson students become familiar with the crosse and learn how to cradle and scoop the ball, among the most fundamental and important skills in the game of lacrosse.

Facility and Equipment

◆ Gym or large outdoor field
◆ Cones or markers
◆ 1 crosse per student
◆ 1 rubber (or tennis) ball per student

Warm-Ups (6-8 Minutes)

1. Elbow squeezes
2. Shoulder stretch
3. Waist twists
4. Knee lifts
5. Arm circles

Skill Cues

Holding the Crosse

The following grip is for right-handed throwers. The hand position described is the basic position for catching, throwing, scooping, and shooting.

1. Grasp the crosse with the left lower hand, palm down, at the end of the handle.
2. Place the right hand, with the palm up, on the handle approximately 10 inches (25.4 centimeters) above the left hand.
3. Both hands are in front of the hips and slightly to the side of the body.
4. Do not grasp the stick near the head; although this position enables more control, leverage and power is lost during throwing.
5. The crosse should be angled approximately 45 degrees from the body, with the head of the crosse well outside the right side of the body.
6. The fingers should grip the stick firmly but not so tight as to lose the feel of the stick. This is particularly important when catching the ball: players must be able to give with the ball to keep it in the pocket.

Crosse grip (right handed)

Cradling the Ball

Cradling, which is the most difficult skill to learn but is key to success in lacrosse, is being able to run with the ball in the stick and not have it fall out, either when running or when being hit by an opponent or the opponent's crosse.

1. Keep a loose grip with the upper hand.
2. Keep the ball from jiggling and falling out when running.
3. Twist (rock) the crosse back and forth with a smooth motion using both hands and arms. When running with the ball, keep the crosse turning back and forth in the hands and moving from side to side, keeping the ball in the pocket.

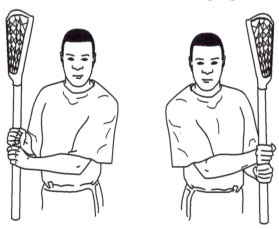

Cradling the ball

Scooping the Ball

The following sequence is for right-handed players. Left-handed players use the opposite feet and arms.

1. Bend the knees to crouch the upper body.
2. The right foot should be forward on the scoop to give an unrestricted motion with the arms.
3. Bend the left (i.e., lower) arm slightly, making an approximate 30-degree angle with the stick to scoop up the ball. If the angle of the stick is too high, it will be more difficult to scoop and control the ball.
4. The end of the handle must be to the side of the body so that it will not jab the midsection if the crosse jams into the ground when scooping.
5. Contact the ground with the head of the crosse 1 to 2 inches (2.5-5.1 centimeters) in front of the ball.
6. Scoop the ball into the pocket with a shoveling motion while continuing to move downfield.

Scooping the ball

Teaching Cues

1. Call out the skill cues as students perform each activity.

2. Demonstrate each skill as you explain it.

3. Be sure to check students' top and bottom hand positions for proper grip.

4. Remind students to bend at the knees when scooping and to keep the butt end of the stick (i.e., the end of the handle) at the side of the body.

5. The skills presented in this lesson are crucial and should be practiced throughout the lacrosse unit. You may want to expand this lesson to two class periods to ensure later success during modified and regulation games.

Activities (30-50 Minutes)

1. Introduce the grip using the skill and teaching cues. Have students practice the grip with a crosse, and check their hand position. (3-6 minutes)

2. Introduce and demonstrate cradling, first in a standing position and then while running. Tell students that cradling the ball while running is the basic mode of advancing the ball. Have students practice cradling a ball in a standing position. (3-5 minutes)

3. Have students form 3 or 4 lines and run slowly while cradling the ball a distance of 30 to 40 yards (27.43-36.57 meters). At your signal, they should stop quickly and return to their original spot while cradling. At first, students may look at the ball while running but should progress to looking downfield as they run. Once students are proficient at cradling during a slow run, have them run back and forth at a faster pace. (4-7 minutes)

4. Divide students into groups of 10 and line up groups about 4 yards (3.65 meters) apart. The first student in each line should weave in and out of the other students in line, cradling the ball from one side to another. If the students are dodging someone on their left, they should cradle to the right, and vice versa. After weaving and cradling through the line, students stop at the end of the line, turn around, and stand in position. Then the next student goes. (5-8 minutes)

5. Pivot points. Pivoting is a critical skill in lacrosse, involving stopping quickly and pivoting on one foot (180 degrees) to "shake" a defender, all the while cradling the ball. Have students run 15 yards (13.71 meters), then stop and pivot; then run another 15 yards (13.71 meters), stop, and pivot. Students should concentrate on effective cradling to maintain possession of the ball. (5-8 minutes)

6. Introduce and demonstrate the proper technique for scooping. Pair up students or have them select partners. One partner rolls the ball toward the other partner, who uses the crosse to scoop the ball. Have students practice scooping from various distances, starting with 5 yards (4.57 meters), then switch roles. (5-6 minutes)

7. Scoop relay. Divide students into teams of 4 and have each team form a line. Place 4 balls per team on the ground, about 1 foot (.3 meters) apart, 25 yards (22.86 meters) down the field. The first player in line sprints for the ball, scoops it up, and cradles it back to the starting line. Once the first player crosses the line, the next player sprints for the ball, picks it up and brings it back to the starting line. This relay continues until the last ball has been brought back. The first team who returns all 4 balls to its starting line wins. (5-10 minutes)

Closure (3-5 Minutes)

Review the lesson with students. Use the following ideas to reinforce learning, check understanding, and provide feedback.

1. Review proper gripping, cradling, and scooping techniques, and have students demonstrate each skill.

2. Make sure students understand that cradling and running with the ball is key to the game of lacrosse; it is the primary method of advancing the ball toward the opponent's goal.

3. Review safety issues relating to carrying and swinging the lacrosse stick.

Lesson 2

Catching and Throwing

Purpose

In this lesson students develop the fundamental skills of catching and throwing, also among the most important skills in the game of lacrosse.

Facility and Equipment

◆ Gym or large outdoor area with walls
◆ Cones or markers
◆ 1 crosse and ball per student
Note: Soft, rubber balls are preferable for this lesson.

Warm-Ups (6-8 Minutes)

1. Abdominal crunches
2. Shoulder stretch
3. Waist twists
4. Knee lifts
5. Hip stretch

Skill Cues

Catching the Ball

1. The upper body must face (i.e., be square to) the incoming ball.
2. The crosse is held in an upward position with the pocket wide open to the ball.
3. The catch should be made in front of the body.
4. Reach out for the ball with the head of the crosse.
5. Like catching a baseball, give with the ball at contact to cushion the force and increase the likelihood of keeping the ball in the pocket. If the crosse does not give, the ball will rebound out of the pocket.
6. Start cradling the ball immediately after catching it.

Catching sequence

Throwing the Ball

1. Shift weight from the back leg to the front leg.

2. Turn the upper body to face the front (a motion similar to throwing a ball with the hand). The quick turn of the shoulders adds power to the throw.

3. Draw the upper hand backward several inches and then follow through with a snapping motion of the wrist. This wrist snap is the key to throwing.

4. Pull the handle downward with the lower hand, making a small arc.

5. Produce more force by widening the grip (i.e., increasing the distance between the hands on the handle of the stick); this increases the leverage from the crosse.

6. After the release, the crosse should be pointing at the target (i.e., the direction of intended flight) in a nearly horizontal position.

Throwing sequence

Teaching Cues

1. Call out the skill cues as students perform each activity.

2. Demonstrate the catching and throwing technique from both a standing and a moving position.

3. Be sure to check students' hand positions (top and bottom) on the grip for the throw and catch.

4. Make sure students give with the ball as they catch it.

5. The skills in this lesson are crucial in lacrosse and, thus, should be practiced throughout the unit. You may want to repeat this lesson or expand it to two class periods to ensure later success in game play.

Activities (35-50 Minutes)

1. Check students for proper grip and review if necessary. Review the cradling and scooping techniques from lesson 1. (2-4 minutes)

2. Introduce and demonstrate catching using the skill cues, first from a standing position and then while moving. Emphasize the importance of giving with the ball as it enters the pocket. (2-4 minutes)

3. Pair up students or have them select partners. One partner has a crosse and the other has the ball. The partner with the ball tosses it to the partner with the crosse, who catches and cradles it. Students should start out 5 yards (4.57 meters) apart and then progressively spread further apart with each successful catch. The thrower should toss the ball high and low, and to the left and right of the catcher. After 10 successful catches, have partners switch roles. (6-8 minutes)

4. Using the same partner configuration, the throwing partner stands still and the other partner catches the ball while moving. Progressively increase the speed and distance with each successful catch. After 10 successful catches, partners should switch roles. (6-8 minutes)

5. Divide students into groups of 3: 1 thrower, 1 catcher, and 1 defender. The thrower and catcher toss the ball (using the hand) back and forth while the defender attempts to intercept the pass with a crosse. Have students switch roles every few minutes so that each student gets a chance to catch (intercept). (5-8 minutes)

6. Introduce and demonstrate throwing using the skill cues. Emphasize the importance of throwing accuracy, including direction and force. Show students how to produce more force (i.e., widen the grip to increase the leverage from the crosse). (3-4 minutes)

7. Have students practice throwing individually. Mark targets on the wall and have students throw the ball against the wall. As they become proficient, students should back further away from the wall. Start at a distance of 20 feet (6.1 meters) and gradually increase to a maximum distance of 40 feet (12.19 meters). (5-6 minutes)

8. Pair up students or have them select partners. One partner (without a crosse) throws the ball to the other (with the crosse), who catches the ball and attempts to throw it back. Repeat from various distances; then partners should switch roles. (6-8 minutes)

Closure (3-5 Minutes)

Review the lesson with students. Use the following ideas to reinforce learning, check understanding, and provide feedback.

1. Review the technique of giving with the ball as it is being caught (see lesson 2).

2. Make sure students understand that throwing and catching are crucial parts of the game; they are used to advance the ball downfield.

3. Select students to demonstrate the catching and throwing technique.

Lesson 3

Throwing and Shooting

Purpose

In this lesson students continue to develop their throwing skills and learn how to shoot for a goal.

Warm-Ups (6-8 Minutes)

1. Arm and leg lifts
2. Shoulder stretch
3. Waist twists
4. Lateral hops
5. Push-offs

Skill Cues

Throwing

1. Shift weight from the back leg to the front leg.
2. Turn the upper body to face the front (a motion similar to throwing a ball with the hand). The quick turn of the shoulders adds power to the throw.
3. Draw the upper hand backward several inches and then follow through with a snapping motion of the wrist. This wrist snap is the key to throwing.
4. Pull the handle downward with the lower hand, making a small arc.
5. Produce more force by widening the grip (i.e., increasing the distance between the hands on the handle of the stick); this increases the leverage from the crosse.
6. After the release, the crosse should be pointing at the target (i.e., the direction of intended flight) in a nearly horizontal position.

Facility and Equipment

◆ Gym or large outdoor area
◆ Goals
◆ 1 crosse and ball per student

Note: Baseball-sized Wiffle balls are preferable for the shooting activities in this lesson.

Starting position

Wrist snap and shoulder turn

Throwing arc

Throwing phases

Shooting

Power and accuracy are two major components of any shot. Shots can be classified in two general categories: outside shots and inside shots. Outside shots are normally taken 10 to 15 yards (9.14-13.71 meters) from the goal (shots beyond this distance are ineffective); any shot from 10 yards (9.14 meters) or less (up to the goal crease [3 yards (2.74 meters) from the goal]) is considered an inside shot.

1. Shots count if they go into the goal either airborne or after bouncing.
2. The upper hand should be over the top of the shoulder, much like the motion of pitching a baseball or throwing a football.
3. Thrust the upper hand forcefully forward with a wrist snap while pulling the lower hand downward and backward, toward the body. Shift weight from the back leg to the front leg during the throwing motion.
4. The head of the crosse should be pointing toward the target on the follow-through.

Teaching Cues

1. Call out the skill cues as students perform each activity.
2. Demonstrate the throwing and shooting technique from standing and moving positions.
3. Be sure to check students' hand positions.
4. The number of goals scored determines the outcome of the game; therefore, shooting is an important skill and should be covered in detail.
5. Shooting is 75 percent accuracy and 25 percent power. Have students concentrate on making accurate shots.
6. Discourage students from shooting further than 15 or 20 yards (13.71 or 18.28 meters) from the goal.
7. Goalies (in activity 7) should wear protective equipment such as a helmet, throat protector, and a chest protector. If Wiffle balls are used for the activity, this equipment is not necessary but is nevertheless recommended.

Activities (35-50 Minutes)

1. Review throwing (see lesson 2). Emphasize the importance of accuracy, including direction and force, and demonstrate how to produce more force by widening the grip to increase leverage. (3-4 minutes)
2. Pair up students or have them select partners. Partners should play catch (using the crosse and ball) with each other from varying distances; one partner moves and the other remains stationary. Then have both partners moving while playing catch. In both phases of this activity, partners should start a short distance apart and then spread further apart after each successful catch. (6-8 minutes)
3. Weave activity. Position students in three lines (A, B, and C), all facing the same direction and about 15 feet (4.57 meters) apart. Students in the middle line (B) get balls, and all students get a crosse. The first players in each line start down the field, player B cradling the ball while running. Player B passes

the ball to player A (or C) and then runs behind player A (or C) to take his or her place in the formation. Upon catching the ball, player A (or C) crosses the field, passes it to player C (or A), and then runs behind to take player C's (or A's) place in the formation. This weave continues for the length of the field. (6-8 minutes)

4. Divide students into groups of 3 or 4: 2 passers and 1 or 2 defenders. Have students play a keep-away game, passers passing and scooping back and forth while defenders try to intercept the ball. Limit the playing area to make this game more challenging. (6-8 minutes)

5. Introduce and demonstrate shooting using the skill cues. Describe the difference between inside and outside shots, and explain the rules of shooting (see the unit introduction on page 503). (3-4 minutes)

6. Have students practice shooting at goals (with no goalies) from varying distances. If possible, place an obstruction (e.g., cone) or a dummy goalie (e.g., foam pad standing on end) in the goal. (6-8 minutes)

7. Have students work in groups of three. Player A passes the ball to player B, who then shoots it at a goal defended by player C. Have players vary the angle and distances from which shots are taken and rotate positions, making sure that everyone gets a chance to shoot on goal. (5-10 minutes)

Closure (3-5 Minutes)

Review the lesson with students. Use the following ideas to reinforce learning, check understanding, and provide feedback.

1. Remind students that shooting on goal is a key skill in the game of lacrosse.

2. Select students to demonstrate the throwing and shooting techniques while other students identify and analyze each skill.

Individual Offense, Defense, and Goaltending

Purpose

In this lesson students continue to develop the fundamental skills in lacrosse, including throwing, shooting, catching, cradling, and scooping. They also learn individual offense, defense, and goaltending skills.

Facility and Equipment

◆ Gym or large outdoor area
◆ 1 crosse and ball per student
◆ Cones

Warm-Ups (6-8 Minutes)

1. Arm and leg lifts
2. Jog for 2 minutes
3. Waist twists
4. Abdominal crunches
5. Push-offs

Skill Cues

Individual Offensive Skills

Three basic dodges are used in lacrosse: the face dodge, the roll dodge, and the bull dodge. Dodges enable players carrying the ball to advance it further downfield.

1. Face dodge. The ball carrier feints a pass to a teammate and then moves the crosse across the body and in front of the face (hence the name), with both the pocket and the ball toward the face.

   ▶ Have two hands on the stick when faking the pass, twist the stick to the closed position in front of the face and run downfield.

   ▶ After the fake pass and in one motion, push off with the right foot, sidestep the defender with the left foot, and pull the stick across the face; then move downfield.

Face dodge

2. Roll dodge. This dodge is the most frequently used dodge in the game of lacrosse. It is effective when the defender is very aggressive.

   ▶ After making body contact with the defender, execute a pivot roll (much like the pick and roll in basketball; see lesson 7 in the basketball unit on page 149).

   ▶ Pivot away from the defender while keeping the crosse tight to the body so the ball can't be knocked away.

   ▶ Pivot on the lead foot, then push off with that leg and take a pivot step with the other leg in the opposite direction of the original path. This step must be a large step to get around the defender.

3. Bull dodge. This dodge simply involves a change of pace or a stop and go, allowing an offensive player to blast (or *bull*) past a defender.

   ▶ Slow down until a defender closes in; then bull past the defender with a burst of speed.

   ▶ Feint before the speed burst to increase the effectiveness of the bull dodge.

Individual Defensive Skills

The techniques for playing 1-on-1 (i.e., person-to-person) defense in lacrosse are identical to those used in basketball, the goal being to neutralize the opponent in possession of the ball. Skills in basic body and stick checking are also required for an effective defense. (Only the basic stick-checking technique of poke checking is presented because it is the safest.)

1. Poke checking. The poke check is one of the most effective stick checks because the opportunities to dislodge the ball are numerous throughout the course of the game.

   ▶ Thrust the crosse toward the opponent using the upper and lower hands. (This movement is much like shooting the cue ball in the game of pool.)

   ▶ Keep the upper hand in contact with the handle as it slides through the fingers. Both hands must remain on the stick.

   ▶ Poke the head of the stick at the offensive player's stick handle or pocket, attempting to dislodge the ball.

   ▶ Never contact the offensive player's body.

2. Body checking. When playing against an offensive player with the ball, that player's forward movement should be stopped. This move is called *body checking,* but no body or crosse contact is permitted.

   ▶ Position the body about a crosse's length away from the opponent and move with that player in an attempt to force him or her to slow down, stop, or change directions.

   ▶ The body check is much like 1-on-1 (i.e., person-to-person) defense in basketball. This positioning will also enable a defender to use the poke check to dislodge the ball.

   ▶ Double team an opponent with body checking, maneuvering an opponent into a position in which another defensive player has an opportunity to poke check and dislodge the ball.

Lacrosse

Goaltending

The main duties of the goalie are to

- stop the ball,
- direct the defense, and
- start the offense by rolling or throwing the ball to the side or downfield.

1. Get into position by standing with the feet shoulder-width apart and bending the knees.
2. Decrease the shooting angle by moving in an arc (about 3 feet [.91 meters]) from the front of the goal; use short shuffle steps.
3. When the ball is behind the goal, the goalie should operate in the same arc but watch the ball side first.
4. Try to block all incoming shots with the body and goalie crosse.
5. Pass or roll caught shots back to teammates.

Teaching Cues

1. This lesson is key because it presents the acceptable individual offensive and defensive skills that can be used in a game. Particularly important are the acceptable body checks and stick checks that can be used by defenders. Although stick checking is allowed in the official game, only the poke check is presented because of safety reasons.
2. Although skill cues are presented for goaltending, no activities for practice are presented in this lesson. Students will get the chance to practice goaltending in the next two lessons.
3. Call out the skill cues as students perform each activity, especially when teaching the defensive skills.
4. Demonstrate the offensive and defensive skills, being sure to detail the proper technique in poke checking.
5. Be sure to check students' hand movement during the poke check.
6. Spend time explaining the defensive skills of body checking. Present the techniques using the analogy of basketball.
7. Emphasize that students should not swing the crosse when poke checking.

Activities (35-50 Minutes)

1. Demonstrate the individual offensive techniques to students using the skill cues. Emphasize the importance of developing good dodges to use during the offensive play. (2-4 minutes)
2. Divide students into groups of 8: 4 offensive players who play with a crosse and ball, and 4 defensive players who use a crosse only. Offensive players attempt to carry the ball 30 yards (27.43 meters) downfield using different dodges to elude the defensive players. Defensive players may not touch or poke the offensive players but may force them to move in different directions (i.e., use the body check). After 2 to 3 minutes, have players switch roles. (6-9 minutes)

519

3. Repeat activity 2, this time adding a goal at the end of the field. Encourage students to use dodges to get a good shot at the goal. (6-9 minutes)

4. Introduce and demonstrate the individual defensive skills using the skill cues. Emphasize that the poke is a quick jab with the crosse at the opponent's stick, not the body, the purpose being to dislodge the ball. Also emphasize that body checking does not involve any body contact whatsoever. (3-4 minutes)

5. Repeat activity 3, this time allowing defenders to body and poke check offensive players. Offensive players should try to advance the ball downfield and score. (6-8 minutes)

6. Divide students into groups of 3: 1 offensive player (A) and 2 defensive players (B and C). Defensive players attempt to double team the offensive player, one using the body check and the other using the poke check to dislodge the ball before the offensive player can move 30 yards (27.43 meters) downfield. Have players switch positions every few minutes to make sure that everyone gets a chance to play both offense and defense. (6-8 minutes)

7. Divide students into groups of 5: 3 offensive players and 2 defensive players. Offensive players attempt to score on the defensive players (no goalies) by passing, cradling, and scooping the ball. Play continues until the offensive team scores or the defensive team gains possession of the ball; then players switch positions. (6-8 minutes)

Closure (3-5 Minutes)

Review the lesson with students. Use the following ideas to reinforce learning, check understanding, and provide feedback.

1. Review the basic individual defensive strategies.

2. Have students verbally describe the poke check.

3. Select students to demonstrate the three basic dodges and have other students analyze the skills.

Modified Games

Purpose

In this lesson students play modified lacrosse games that lead up to regulation play in the next lesson.

Warm-Ups (6-8 Minutes)

1. Faceup flank
2. Lateral hops
3. Waist twists
4. Side arm push-ups
5. Jog for 2 minutes

Facility and Equipment

- Gym or large outdoor area with walls
- 1 crosse and ball per student
- Cones
- 1 colored pinnie per 2 students
- 1 lacrosse rules handout* per student

Teaching Cues

1. Design a quick method to assign teams as you change activities; students should play on different teams for each activity.
2. Make sure students rotate to different positions during game play.
3. Possession and end zone lacrosse may be played indoors or outdoors.

Activities (30-40 Minutes)

1. Divide students into teams of 4 or 5, depending on available wall space, and line up each team 10 yards (9.14 meters) from a wall. Explain the sequence and have students perform the fly-back relay. (For more challenge, increase the starting distance to the wall.) (10-13 minutes)

Fly-Back Relay

Team members throw the lacrosse ball onto the wall and the next player either catches it on the fly or scoops it up off the ground. On the signal, the first team member throws the lacrosse ball against the wall and then immediately goes to the back of the line. The second team member catches or scoops it, then returns to the starting point and throws the ball back against the wall for the next player. Repeat the sequence until the first team member is back in front of the line. The first team to complete the relay wins.

2. Divide students into teams, give a ball to each team, and position players as shown in the figure. (Depending on the space available, 2 or 4 teams may be assigned; this game can be played with 3 or more balls as well). Explain the rules and have students play end zone lacrosse. (10-14 minutes)

End Zone Lacrosse

The object of the game is to successfully pass the ball to an end zone player, scoring 1 point. At the end of the game, the team with the most points wins. The game starts with a fielding player for each team in possession of a ball. The rules are as follows:

▸ All players may catch the ball on the fly or scoop it from the ground.

▸ Fielding players may knock down or intercept attempted passes into the end zone.

▸ All players must stay in their designated areas.

▸ Fielding players are not allowed in the end zones and they are not allowed to cross midfield.

A variation of this game, royal lacrosse, permits fielding players to cross midfield (but not in the end zones) and pass to their teammates in the end zone.

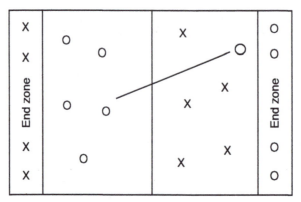

End zone lacrosse formation

3. Set up the playing area using cones to delineate boundaries. Divide students into 2 or 4 teams, depending on the space available. Explain the rules and have students play possession lacrosse. (10-13 minutes)

Possession Lacrosse

The object of the game is to pass and catch or scoop the ball more times than the opposing team. Each successful pass or scoop counts as 1 point. At the end of the game, the team with the most points wins.

Play starts with two opposing players in the middle of the playing area. An official tosses the ball onto the ground and the two center players attempt to gain possession of the ball and pass it to a teammate without being intercepted. The following rules govern play:

▸ A player with the ball has only 10 seconds to run and throw it. If a player takes too much time, the ball is awarded to the other team.

▸ Defensive players may not touch or interfere with the passer. Rather, they must try to knock down (poke check) or intercept the pass.

Closure (3-5 Minutes)

Review the lesson with students. Use the following ideas to reinforce learning, check understanding, and provide feedback.

1. Review basic individual defensive strategies (see lesson 4).

2. Distribute the rules handouts and tell students to study them before the next class period, when they will play a regulation game of lacrosse.

3. Ask students to share the defensive and offensive strategies they used during the modified games.

Lesson 6

Regulation Game

Purpose

In this lesson students review the rules and play a regulation game of lacrosse.

Warm-Ups (6-8 Minutes)

1. Facedown flank
2. Play catch with a partner
3. Waist twists
4. Upper body rotations
5 Jog for 2 minutes

Facility and Equipment

- Large outdoor field
- 1 crosse per student
- Cones
- 1 colored pinnie per 2 students
- 1 goalie helmet per team
- 2 goals per game

Note: Throat protectors and chest protectors may also be needed for goalies, depending on the type of ball used. Use the cones to delineate field boundaries.

Teaching Cues

1. Emphasize the proper safety elements before the game—in particular, that no body contact is allowed between players and the proper elements of poke checking (see lesson 4).
2. Create a team roster, including assigned positions, before class.
3. Have students rotate positions on a regular basis.

Activities (30-40 Minutes)

1. Review the skills as well as the individual offensive and defensive strategies used in lacrosse. Ask students if they have any questions about the regulation rules. (7-10 minutes)
2. Assign teams, explain position rotation to be used during the game, and have students play a regulation game of lacrosse. (23-30 minutes)

Closure (3-5 Minutes)

Review the lesson with students. Use the following ideas to reinforce learning, check understanding, and provide feedback.

1. Review the basic individual defensive strategies used in lacrosse.
2. Ask students to identify ways they could improve game play (e.g., stay spread out, guard opponents more closely, get close to the goal before shooting).
3. Ask students to identify general defensive and offensive strategies they used effectively (and not so effectively) during game play.

Assessment and Resources

As with most team-oriented sports, formative, authentic assessment is the preferred way to assess students. Using checklists, self-appraisals, and peer evaluations are great avenues for assessing students' performances and game understanding. It is also recommended that students be formatively assessed during the earlier lessons that stress psychomotor skill development (e.g., peer evaluation of shooting and passing skills, cradling the ball while running on a timed basis). This provides students with important feedback and may help to refocus their learning to improve skills.

More traditional forms of skill testing are provided here to complete the assessment process. Assessment protocol is listed with each.

▶ Throwing evaluation. Have students throw for accuracy at a target. Give 10 trials and award points based on the size of the target.

▶ Scooping evaluation. Roll 5 ground balls toward and 5 ground balls away from students. Award points for each successful scoop, checking for proper sequence and technique.

▶ Shooting evaluation. Require students to shoot five balls on goal from varying distances. Award points for each time they score.

▶ Cradling. Students must control the ball while weaving in and out of cones for a distance of 25 yards (22.86 meters). Cones are to be placed every 3 yards (2.74 meters).

Resources

Bailey, G. 2000. *The ultimate sport lead-up game book.* Camas, WA: Educators Press.

Collins, R. 2001. *A comprehensive guide to sports skills tests and measurement.* Metuchen, NJ: Scarecrow Press.

Mood, D., F. Musker, and J. Rink. 1999. *Sports and recreational activities.* 12th ed. New York: McGraw-Hill.

Pangrazi, R., and P. Darst. 1997. *Dynamic physical education for secondary school students.* 3rd ed. Needham Heights, MA: Allyn & Bacon.

Orienteering

Orienteering is a unique and exciting sport. It combines compass and map reading with walking and running in a cross-country race in which participants navigate an unfamiliar course. The sport can be traced to Sweden, where Ernest Killander is credited with introducing it in 1917. Because the Swedish people enjoy outdoor activities, it is understandable that they would combine the basic skills of compass and map reading with hiking to form a vigorous leisure pursuit. In the 1940s orienteering became a compulsory activity in Swedish physical education classes. Today it is not unusual for large Scandinavian meets to draw thousands of participants.

Although compass and map reading have been used for centuries in land and sea navigation, it was mainly through the scouting movement that orienteering skills were first introduced in North America. With the advent of wilderness education, survival courses, and Outward Bound programs in the United States as well as the ever-growing popularity of orienteering in Scandinavian countries, the sport is gaining acceptance. Orienteering is now taught in many U.S. university physical education programs and some secondary schools, and it is practiced in clubs across the nation.

Orienteering offers a challenging and inexpensive way of exploring the outdoors. Many different types of orienteering activities can be adapted to meet the interests of all people, regardless of age or gender. It can be a family or group activity, a fun and cooperative game, or a highly competitive sport. Orienteering can easily be combined with a number of other outdoor activities, such as hiking, camping, backpacking, bicycling, fishing, hunting, cross-country skiing, and nature study.

Equipment

Knowing how to use a compass and how to read a map constitute the skills involved in orienteering. In other words, the skills involved in the sport are mainly cognitive. Competitive events combine these skills with decision making and running. Thus, the equipment required is simple—a compass and either topographical maps or hand-drawn maps showing important navigational features.

Most orienteering programs use a protractor compass or the Silva compass, which can be purchased for less than $10. In class instruction, 1 compass for every 2 students is recommended. Topographical maps, the other required equipment for this sport, can be drawn by hand. If students will be practicing at a local area, maps can be obtained from sporting goods stores, bookstores, camping stores, or governmental agencies. Although not required, an instructional videotape would be helpful to introduce this unit.

Unit Organization

Following is a brief description of the lessons in this unit:

▶ Lesson 1 emphasizes map reading skills and teaches students about compass bearings.

▶ In lesson 2 students learn about the orienteering compass and how to use it.

▶ Lessons 3 and 4 provide several drills and activities to strengthen compass-reading skills. Extra orienteering activities are also suggested for additional class days or as substitutes for activities listed in previous lessons.

Selected resources and assessment ideas are found in the assessment and resources chapter at the end of the unit.

Note: An asterisk (*) following a facility or equipment listing indicates that preparation is required before the lesson.

Social Skills and Etiquette

The social value of orienteering comes from its partner or small-group structure. Working in small groups enables each student to become involved in problem solving and teamwork. It also requires each student to take responsibility for the success of his or her team. At the outset, inform students that decision making is a group process and that learning is maximized when all are involved. If you plan to conduct orienteering activities on private property, always seek permission first and then make sure that students respect the land, buildings, and other surroundings.

Lesson Modifications

Physically impaired students will not be able to participate in orienteering drills that require walking or running. It is suggested that paper-and-pencil map and compass activities be offered to these students. Many games and activities available for purchase may also be used for special-needs students (see the resource listings at the end of the assessment and resources chapter in this unit).

Safety

Normally, orienteering activities within the confines of the school or on school grounds are considered quite safe. If conducting orienteering classes off campus, however, safety considerations may be an issue. Off-site events will require forethought about where to get assistance in case of an emergency as well as the following potential safety risks:

▶ Hazardous terrain

▶ Busy roads and traffic

▶ Fences

▶ Streams or other water

▶ Animals

Terms

angle of declination—The angle representing the difference between magnetic north and true (or geographical) north. True north is a fixed location—the North Pole—whereas the magnetic north pole is a shifting location in the eastern Arctic, usually identified in the Hudson Bay area of Canada. This spot is where the earth's lines of magnetic force converge and where the magnetic needle of a compass points. The Canadian government periodically gives an average location of magnetic north. On topographical maps, the angle of declination increases as the distance increases east or west of a north-northwest line through the Hudson Bay area. The only area in which magnetic north and true north are approximately the same are those regions aligned vertically with Indiana, Georgia, and Florida. See the table for compass variations for each state, although there may also be differences in degrees between the east and west side of the same state. Eastern Kentucky, for example, has a 2-degree declination west and western Kentucky has a 2-degree declination east.

State	Declination	State	Declination
Alabama	2° east	Montana	16° east
Alaska	24° east	Nebraska	10° east
Arizona	14° east	Nevada	16° east
Arkansas	6° east	New Hampshire	15° west
California	16° east	New Jersey	11° west
Colorado	13° east	New Mexico	12° east
Connecticut	13° west	New York	11° west
Delaware	9° west	North Carolina	3° west
Florida	0°	North Dakota	11° east
Georgia	0°	Ohio	4° west
Hawaii	11° east	Oklahoma	9° east
Idaho	19° east	Oregon	19° east
Illinois	3° east	Pennsylvania	7° west
Indiana	0°	Rhode Island	14° west
Iowa	6° east	South Carolina	3° west
Kansas	10° east	South Dakota	11° east
Kentucky	0°	Tennessee	2° east
Louisiana	6° east	Texas	9° east
Maine	18° west	Utah	15° east
Maryland	8° west	Vermont	15° west
Massachusetts	14° west	Virginia	4° west
Michigan	3° west	Washington	21° east
Minnesota	6° east	West Virginia	4° west
Mississippi	4° east	Wisconsin	2° east
Missouri	6° east	Wyoming	15° east

Adapted from maps found in *Basic Essentials of Map and Compass* by C. Jacobson, 1988, Merrillville, IN: ICS Books, Inc., p. 46; and *The Expert With Map and Compass* by B. Kjellstrom, 1976, New York: Scribner and Sons, p. 112.

attack point—An identifiable feature that serves as a guide in navigating to the control point.

base point—The place where one stands to navigate toward the control point. The base point can be the control point or an attack point used to sight the next control point.

bearing—A direction of a given point measured in degrees (from 1 to 360°) from north going in a clockwise direction.

beeline—A straight line.

control point—An object or place to be located, designated by a marker on the object itself and a symbol on the map.

declination lines—Slanted parallel vertical lines drawn on a map indicating the discrepancy or the degrees between true and magnetic north.

geographical map—A map that shows a one-dimensional portion of the earth's surface using conventional signs, degrees of longitude and latitude, and true north or geographical north. Compare *topographical map.*

leapfrogging—Using a person as the attack point (i.e., when there is no visible landmark to use as an attack point).

magnetic north—See *angle of declination.*

map quadrants—Four equal parts, as marked by vertical and horizontal lines intersecting at the center point of a map. (Quadrants are NE, SE, SW, NW.)

shoot a bearing—The act of determining the direction of travel (in degrees from north) using a compass and visible landmarks or control points.

Silva system—A means devised by a Swedish orienteer and refined to the present day to combine the use of the Silva compass with a map (showing declination lines) to quickly identify the route to get from one point on the map to another.

topographical map—A three-dimensional map that shows a portion of the earth's surface featuring both man-made (e.g., roads, bridges, buildings) and natural (e.g., lakes, streams, cliffs, woods, fields) features plotted according to a distance scale. Elevation is shown by variously contoured concentric rings; the center ring is the highest elevation and each outer ring represents a progressively lower elevation moving downward. The top of the map faces north and usually the angle of declination is given. A legend defines the various symbols that denote the features.

true north or **geographical north**—See *angle of declination.*

walk a bearing—The act of following a specific degree setting by aligning the setting over the direction arrow on the compass,

Silva Compass Parts

A Silva compass is somewhat different from a regular compass. The following terms describe the features of the Silva compass shown in the figure.

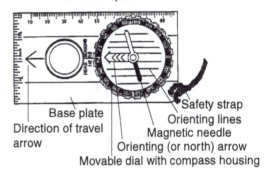

Silva compass

Base plate
Direction of travel arrow
Safety strap
Orienting lines
Magnetic needle
Orienting (or north) arrow
Movable dial with compass housing

Silva compass

Base plate or **protractor**—A Plexiglas base under the compass that shows centimeters, millimeters, and inches to match map scales.

Direction of travel arrow—An arrow indicating the direction of intended travel.

Magnetic needle—A floating needle suspended in the compass; the red end points to magnetic north. (Note: if objects made of iron are nearby, the reading could be inaccurate.)

Movable dial with compass housing—A movable dial mounted on the base plate that rotates freely, changing the position of lines and the arrow at the bottom of the dial. The numbers and hash marks around the dial indicate degrees, with each hash mark representing 2 degrees.

Orienting (or north) arrow—An arrow painted or drawn on the bottom of the compass housing that moves in the direction of rotation when the movable dial is rotated. The user aligns this arrow, which is flanked by parallel orienting lines, with the red end of the magnetic needle.

Orienting lines—Lines painted or drawn on the compass housing that are parallel with the north arrow. The user aligns them parallel to the declination lines on an orienteering map.

Safety strap—A string or strap that the user attaches to his or her wrist to prevent losing the compass. A whistle is usually attached to the safety string for use as a distress signal in case of an accident or emergency.

Lesson 1

Introduction and Map Reading

Purpose

In this lesson students learn some basic orienteering information, terms, and map-reading skills.

Warm-Ups (6-8 Minutes)

1. Horizontal run
2. Curl-ups
3. Hip rolls
4. Push-ups
5. Sprint-jog intervals

Skill Cues

1. The number of compass directions is 16, starting at the top and moving clockwise:
   - **N**—North
   - **ENE**—East-northeast
   - **NE**—Northeast
   - **E**—East
   - **ESE**—East-southeast
   - **SE**—Southeast
   - **SSE**—South-southeast
   - **S**—South
   - **SSW**—South-southwest
   - **SW**—Southwest
   - **WSW**—West-southwest
   - **W**—West
   - **WNW**—West-northwest
   - **NW**—Northwest
   - **NNW**—North-northwest

2. Keep the top of the map pointing north.
3. Measure distance with pace.

Facility and Equipment

- Gym or multipurpose area
- 5 cones
- Tape
- Transparencies* of topographical maps, geographical maps, and compass points
- Overhead projector
- 1 geographical map per 2 students
- 1 set of questions* and pencil per 2 students

  Note: Mark off a 100-foot (30.48-meter) line with tape and place cones (marked A, B, C, D, and E) at predetermined distances along the line. Note the distances between the cones for activity 6.

Teaching Cues

1. Differentiate between topographical and geographical maps, and use the terms correctly to avoid confusion.

2. Be sure students understand the terms *true north, magnetic north,* and *angle of declination.*

3. Progress slowly, allowing time for all students to develop their map-reading skills.

4. Group students in pairs to complete paper-and-pencil activities.

5. Try to instill a feeling of interest and a spirit of adventure by relating map reading to world travel.

6. To make the blank compass drawing, photocopy the figure shown in activity 3, using liquid paper to erase the compass points and bearings.

Activities (30-40 Minutes)

1. Introduce the unit by giving a brief history and description of orienteering, explaining why skills in map reading and compass reading are important, and stressing the worldwide interest in the sport of orienteering. Ask if any students have been involved with orienteering (e.g., in Scouts, at camp). (4-6 minutes)

2. Use a transparency to show a geographical map (or part of one). Try to use a familiar area such as your city, region, or state. Point out and explain the following. (3-4 minutes)

    ▶ Directions (e.g., north, east, south, west, northwest, northeast, and so on)

    ▶ Map quadrants

    ▶ Map legend

    ▶ Features (e.g., airports, rivers, national forests)

    ▶ North is called *geographical north* or *true north* and is always aligned with the top of the map.

3. Show another transparency of the 16 compass bearings and directions. These are used for finding map directions and bearings quickly, but students should also become familiar with how the 360 degrees of the compass coincide with map directions. Pass out a blank compass drawing and have students work in pairs to fill in the 16 different bearings and directions. (3-4 minutes)

4. Use the same student pairings as in activity 3 or have students select new partners. Distribute a copy of a geographical map (purchased or hand drawn) and a list of questions to each set of students. After all students have finished, review their answers. (6-8 minutes)

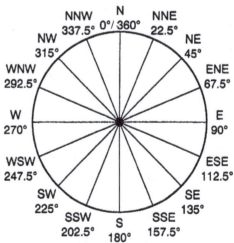

Compass bearings and directions

Some suggested questions include the following:

- ▶ Which direction is town X from town Y?
- ▶ If you went west at town X, which lake would you see first?
- ▶ How many and which directions does river X flow?
- ▶ What direction is the airport from city X?
- ▶ How many miles separate city X from city Y?
- ▶ What are the largest cities in the northeast and southwest quadrants?

5. Show an overhead of a topographical map from the local area. (If declination lines are not already marked, add them to the map.) Point out the differences between this map and the geographical map. Note the map symbols and features. Topographical maps usually display lines showing the angle of difference between geographical (true) north and magnetic north near the map legend. Explain the difference between true north and magnetic north. (6-8 minutes)

6. Have students walk 100 feet (30.48 meters) using their natural gait. They should start with the right heel at the start of the line and count each time the right foot strikes the surface. After students repeat this distance three times, have them average their pace distance, rounding off to the nearest 6 inches (15.24 centimeters). A pace is equal to two steps. If a student's pace is 4 feet (1.22 meters), then 10 paces would equal 40 feet (12.19 meters). (4-5 minutes)

7. Pace drill. Students walk along the cones set up on the 100-foot (30.48-meter) line, using their pace (from activity 6) to estimate the distance between the cones. When students have recorded their estimates, tell them the distance between each set of cones so they can see how close they came to the right distance. (4-5 minutes)

Closure (3-5 Minutes)

Review the lesson with students. Use the following questions and ideas to reinforce learning, check understanding, and provide feedback.

1. Review the difference between true north and magnetic north.
2. Have students
   - ▶ name some of the differences between a geographical and topographical map.
   - ▶ identify where magnetic north is on a map.
   - ▶ identify compass bearings and directions for 16 locations on a map.
3. Ask students to determine the distance of their pace. Then ask the following questions:
   - ▶ How many paces would it take to cover 100 feet (30.48 meters)?
   - ▶ How many paces would it take to cover 1,000 feet (304.8 meters)?
   - ▶ If 1 inch (2.54 centimeters) equals 10,000 feet (3,048 meters) on a map, about how many paces would it take to cover the distance?

Lesson 2

Compass Reading

Purpose

In this lesson students learn some basic compass-reading skills.

Warm-Ups (6-8 Minutes)

1. Inverted hurdler's stretch
2. High jumper
3. Scissors
4. Abdominal crunches
5. Step and calf taps

Skill Cues

1. Hold the compass next to the center of the body at the lower chest. The hand that cradles the compass should rest against the body at all times; moving it will alter the course of travel.
2. Read a compass by looking down at the dial and turning the body until the red end of the magnetic needle is directly over the orienting arrow. The bearing is read where the direction of travel arrow passes through the top of the movable dial.

Facility and Equipment

- Gym or multipurpose area
- 28 sheets of colored paper (2 sheets of 14 colors)*
- Tape
- 1 Silva compass per 2 students
- Silva compass transparency*
- Overhead projector
- 1 recording sheet* and pencil per student

Note: Tape the sheets of colored paper to various locations around the gym or area: the first sheet on the floor and the second sheet of the same color on the walls or bleachers. Note the compass bearings between the sheets of each color. (Pairs of numbers, geographical figures, animals, and so on could also be used.)

Teaching Cues

1. Predetermine the compass readings for activity 4.
2. Progress slowly and make sure that all students know how to read the Silva compass before moving to activities dependent on this skill.
3. If two students will be sharing a compass, make sure that each becomes proficient in using it.
4. In activity 2, all students should be facing the same direction (bearing). Watch students carefully to identify who is having difficulty using the compass.

Activities (30-40 Minutes)

1. Explain the Silva compass parts by showing an overhead transparency (use that shown in the unit introduction on page 529). Make sure that students can identify each part before you pass out the compasses. (3-5 minutes)

2. Using the overhead from activity 1, review each part of the compass by name while students examine their compasses. Explain and demonstrate how to hold the compass. In partners spaced in a scatter formation, have one partner demonstrate how to find a bearing; then call out a series of bearings (e.g., 20°, 150°, 80°, 310°, and so on). For each bearing, students with compasses should rotate the movable dial to the bearing, turn the body until the magnetic needle is directly over the orienting arrow, look over the direction of travel arrow, and sight an object or marking that aligns with the travel arrow. If two students are sharing a compass, have partners alternate, each holding the compass to find every other bearing. (5-6 minutes)

3. Walking a bearing. Pair up students or have them select partners. Partners stand next to each other about 5 to 6 feet (1.52-1.83 meters) apart, all students facing the same direction. Have students find magnetic north: One partner holds the compass in the left hand and cradled next to the body about chest height, leaving the compass in this position while turning the body until the magnetic needle is over the orienting arrow; this is magnetic north. Then the other partner does the same.

   Next students rotate the movable dial to 40 degrees. They should note the direction of travel arrow and sight some object or landmark in the distance that is aligned with this arrow. Students walk 10 paces, following the direction of travel arrow, then stop and add 180 degrees (i.e., take a setting of 220°). Students turn until the magnetic needle is over the orienting arrow and sight their landmarks over the direction of travel arrow. They walk another 10 paces, at which point they should be back where they started. Partners repeat the activity using settings of 70 and 250 degrees. (10-15 minutes)

4. Shooting a bearing. Point out the colored paper (or numbers, geographical figures, or animals) on the floor and walls. Assign one partner half of the colors; the other should work with the remaining half. Students start by standing on a colored sheet, holding the compass against the lower chest, pointing the direction of travel arrow at the same colored sheet on the wall. Without moving the compass, students then find magnetic north by rotating the dial until the red end of the magnetic needle is over the orienting arrow. Students should read the bearing at the top where the line continues through the direction of travel arrow, write down the bearing, and give the compass to their partners. Students alternate taking bearings until they have completed all 14 colors. When all are finished, students should check their results for accuracy while you read the correct bearings. (12-14 minutes)

Closure (3-5 Minutes)

Review the lesson with students. Use the following ideas to reinforce learning, check for understanding, and provide feedback.

1. Review the parts of a compass, having students point to each part.

2. Review how to find magnetic north.

3. Discuss the difference between shooting a bearing and walking (or running) a bearing (i.e., both involve reading the compass correctly and finding magnetic north, but when walking a bearing students must also count pace and move with accuracy).

4. Remind students that you will work on compass skills outside during the next class meeting.

Lesson 3

Outdoor Compass Drills

Purpose

In this lesson students learn and practice control point techniques and strengthen their compass-reading skills.

Warm-Ups (6-8 Minutes)

1. Squat holds
2. Elbow-knee touches (standing)
3. Slapping jacks
4. V-sit toe taps
5. Running in place

Facility and Equipment

- School grounds or large field with 2 control point courses*
- 1 Silva compass per 2 students
- 1 golf tee per 2 students
- 16 cones
- 1 recording sheet and pencil per 2 students

Skill Cues

1. A control point is a marker (e.g., an orange card tied to a bush) located at a destination noted on a map.
2. In orienteering events, control points are numbered in a specific order. By using a map and compass, individuals or teams decide on the best route to reach each control point in the prescribed sequence.

Teaching Cues

1. Review the parts of the Silva compass before starting the activities, being sure all students are proficient before moving on to activity 2.
2. Review shooting a bearing and walking (or running) a bearing (see activities 3 and 4 in lesson 2).
3. Explain the skill cues: a control point is a marker (or the object to navigate toward) and is generally used in orienteering competition. Each control point has an identification tool (e.g., a crayon of a particular color); students use this tool to mark their scorecard to prove they made it to that control point.
4. The goal of orienteering competitions is to reach all control points quickly; the team (or individual) with the fastest time wins.
5. Set up the control point courses for activity 3 before class. Using cones marked 1 to 8 (or to any number you choose), set up the cones around the field. The angles and distances between cones should be the same, but they should be arranged differently so that each task will be unique (and students will not be able to copy one another's movements). Note the bearings and distances.
6. Activity 3 can be conducted as a competition between teams, or between groups of teams (i.e., pair up two or more teams). The winner is the team or group with the most correct bearings and the most correctly recorded distances between control points.

Activities (30-40 Minutes)

1. Quickly review the parts of the Silva compass, and shooting and walking a bearing. (4-6 minutes)
2. Partner drills. Pair up students or have them select partners. Explain that one will participate in the square drill while the other participates in the T drill, students watching their partners while they perform the drill. For each of the following drills, students scatter around the field. Once in position, they drop a golf tee, straddle it, and find magnetic north. (11-14 minutes)

Square Drill (5-7 Minutes)

After finding magnetic north, students perform the following movements:

▶ Set a 60-degree bearing; sight a landmark over the travel arrow and walk 20 paces.
▶ Stop and set a 150-degree bearing and walk 20 paces.
▶ Stop and set a 240-degree bearing and walk 20 paces.
▶ Stop and set a 330-degree bearing and walk 20 paces.

Students should now be back at their golf tees.

T Drill (6-7 minutes)

The second set of partners performs the following movements:

▶ Sight a landmark over the travel arrow and walk 30 paces north.
▶ Stop and set a 90-degree bearing (east) and walk 15 paces.
▶ Stop and set a 270-degree bearing (west) and walk 30 paces.
▶ Stop and set a 90-degree bearing (east) and walk 15 paces.
▶ Stop and set a 180-degree bearing (south) and walk 30 paces.

Students should be back to their golf tees.

3. Explain that the control point drill is a simulated activity because students cannot leave school grounds and it does not include time, which a genuine orienteering competition would. Position student partners so that each pair has a compass and recording sheet to note the bearing and distance between cones. Explain the control point course, specifying that students should proceed from one control point (cone) to the next, in order. Then have them perform the control point drill. (15-20 minutes)

Control Point Drill

One partner establishes the bearing of cone 1, and the other paces the distance between cones 1 and 2. When the first team leaves the control point (cone 2), the next team starts on the course. Partners should switch roles halfway through the drill or alternate control points.

Optional Activities: Point-to-Point Orienteering or Score Orienteering

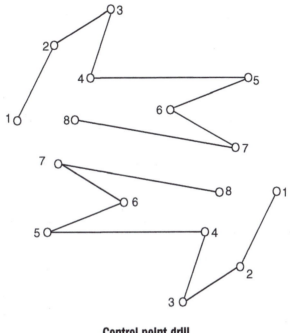

Control point drill

Optional Activities

Point-to-Point Orienteering (0-20 Minutes)

Set up 15 control points around the school grounds in such a way that some of the points are blocked by buildings, trees, parked cars, and other obstacles. Draw a map of the area with numbered control points and declination lines. In partners (or groups, or as individuals) students are given a map with only five of the control points on it. Three pairs, then, each with different control points, can start the course every 60 seconds. The objective is to navigate the course, record all bearings and distances between control points, and use the identification tool at each control point (e.g., crayons of different colors, a code word or letter to write down, and so on) to prove that the object was reached.

Score Orienteering (0-20 Minutes)

Design a course with a number of control points and give each a point value depending on its difficulty and distance from the starting line. The objective is to score as many points as possible within a set amount of time. Students are free to determine which control points to visit. Control points can be located only from the starting area, which forces students to go out and back (providing more cardiorespiratory conditioning), or they can be located by using control points on a map. Set a time limit. Give each pair (or individual or group) a map, explain the penalty for being late back to the starting area (e.g., subtract points for each minute over the set limit), and require proof of reaching each control point.

Closure (3-5 Minutes)

Review the lesson with students. Use the following ideas to reinforce learning, check understanding, and provide feedback.

1. Check students' recorded bearings and distances in activity 4.

2. Discuss the partner drills in activity 2. Ask students to recall the bearings used to arrive back at their starting point. Then ask them how they would determine the bearing to get back to their starting point in an actual orienteering event (i.e., for bearings greater than 180°, subtract 180; for bearings less than 180°, add 180).

3. Explain the following about competitive orienteering:
   - Control points are noted numerically on a map and cover several miles.
   - Contestants try to figure out the best and fastest route to each control point, which is fairly visible by its distinguishing marker.
   - The person or team with the fastest time through all control points wins the competition.
   - Sometimes maps are partial, or sectioned. Contestants find the next section of the map and the next control point at each control point.

Orienteering Activities

Purpose

In this lesson students learn attack point and leapfrogging skills that are used in control point orienteering.

Warm-Ups (6-8 Minutes)

1. Abdominal tighteners
2. Sprint-jog intervals
3. Body circles
4. Upper body rotations
5. Reverse run

Skill Cues

1. Study the map and visualize the course area. Look for the quickest and best route to each control point.
2. Keep the top of the map pointing north.
3. Be sure that the direction of travel arrow on the compass is always pointing from the current location (base point) to the destination (control point, or intermediate attack point[s]).

Teaching Cues

1. Set up the course for activity 2 before class, noting the bearings of each control point. The course should have 7 or 8 control points: use numbered cones to show the control points and use ropes, hoops, hoops connected by ropes, hurdles, or other equipment to represent ponds, streams, buildings, or other obstacles that block a straight-line sighting and approach to the next control point.
2. Attack points are easily identifiable features or landmarks that are used as aids (or even new base points) in reaching a control point. Attack points are used when a control point cannot be seen from the starting base point. Depending on the terrain, more than one attack point may be needed to reach a single control point.
3. Leapfrogging is using a person as the attack point when there is no visible landmark to use as an attack point.

Facility and Equipment

- Outdoor field with preset course*
- 1 Silva compass per 2 students
- 2 note cards and pencils per 2 students
- Obstacle maps*
- School grounds maps
- Cones
- Ropes
- Hoops
- Wands
- Pencils and crayons

Note: Course setup will dictate how many of these materials are needed; use what you have available.

Activities (30-40 Minutes)

1. Introduce the terms *attack point* and *leapfrogging* using the appropriate teaching cues. Explain that terrain features (e.g., trees, buildings) as well as distance often obstruct the view of control points in orienteering, and that this lesson focuses on moving from control point to control point in such situations. (3-5 minutes)

2. Attack point drill. Pair up students or have them select partners. Give each team a map that shows the course control points and obstacles. Two teams can start at each of the 7 or 8 control points, with the second team starting shortly after the first team leaves. Teammates study the map and find the shortest route to each control point, working around the obstacles by sighting an attack point, moving to that attack point, sighting another attack point (if the control point is still out of sight) and moving to that attack point, and so on until they reach the control point. Teams should start by shooting a bearing at each control point (see activity 4 in lesson 2). Students should write down all bearings between control points, working their way around the entire course. (12-15 minutes)

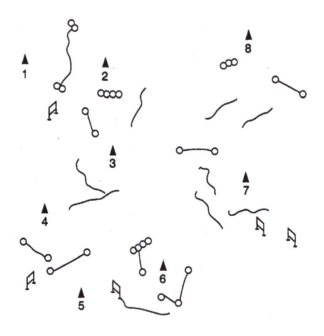

Attack point drill course

3. Leapfrogging drill. Use the course and map from activity 2, but this time teammates must act as attack points between control points, and two attack points are required for each control point. One teammate from each team goes out to act as the attack point. Then the second teammate goes out from the first teammate to act as the second attack point. Partners alternate attack point positions until they are able to shoot a bearing at the control point. (3-5 minutes)

4. Exchange orienteering drill. Use partners or small teams. Give a rope, 2 note cards, pencil, and compass, along with a map of the school grounds, to each team. These maps should show any distributed equipment pieces (e.g., cones,

hoops, clubs) and landmarks (e.g., trees, bushes, fence and goal posts). Have teams find a location somewhere on the map and mark their base or starting point with a rope. Teams select four items on the map as control points and mark them 1, 2, 3, and 4. They determine and record on one note card the bearings and distance between each and back to the base point. Each team exchanges their map with another team, which determines and records the bearing and distance between the control points and base point, starting with number 1. Encourage students to make the distances between control points at least 75 feet (22.86 meters). When finished, the two teams check each other's cards for accuracy. (12-15 minutes)

Optional Activity

Treasure Hunt (0-20 Minutes)

Design a course with a buried or hidden treasure. Provide students (or teams) with a listing of all bearings and distances on the course (or leave the next bearing and distance at each control point). You could also provide the bearing but give only a clue to the distance (e.g., the number of states, the number of days in April plus hours in a day). The objective is to reach the treasure first.

Closure (3-5 Minutes)

Discuss and review the lesson with students. Use the following questions and ideas to reinforce learning, check understanding, and provide feedback.

1. Review the terms *attack point, base point,* and *control point.*
2. Review the leapfrogging technique and have students identify situations when it is useful.
3. Ask students how many finished the exchange orienteering (activity 4). How many teams had at least four bearings and distances about right? Did anyone get them all right?

Assessment and Resources

It will be fairly obvious whether or not students understand basic orienteering by the third lesson in this unit, the activities in which demand that students apply their knowledge and understanding in simulated orienteering events. Paper-and-pencil tests administered during lessons 2, 3, and 4 can also serve as an objective measure of basic map- and compass-reading skills as well as knowledge of orienteering terms and parts of a compass.

Any of the optional activities noted in lesson 3 could also serve as skill tests. Such assessment can be conducted individually or in partners. Another option for skill testing is giving a take-home assignment, although this might require additional equipment (each student will need a compass to take home). For example, the following tests can be given as take-home assignments:

▶ Shoot a bearing. Students shoot a bearing with a parent, sibling, or friend, demonstrating how to navigate from point A to point B, then back to point A. Students should bring in an explanatory note of what they did, signed by the person they instructed.

▶ Compass reading. Students show someone (e.g., friend, parent, sibling) how to use a Silva compass, bringing in an explanatory note of what they did, signed by the person they instructed.

▶ Control points. Students can complete this take-home assessment with a partner (e.g., sibling, parent, friend) or individually. Start at a familiar base point (e.g. barn, street corner) and select a distant landmark that can't be reached by walking a beeline (straight line). Establish at least two attack points en route to the control point. After reaching the control point, determine the bearing to get back to the base point using the same attack points and bearing by adding or subtracting 180° to bearings less than or more than 180°. Students should bring in an explanation of what they did (signed and dated by their partner), including responses to the following questions:

- Describe your experience in terms of who went with you.
- What area did you choose?
- What were your starting point (base point) and destination (control point)?

- What attack points did you use to reach your control point?
- What bearings did you set?
- How close did you come to your original starting point (base point)?
- Describe any problems you encountered.

Resources

Darst, P.W., and G.P. Armstrong. 1980. *Outdoor adventure activities for school and recreation programs.* Minneapolis: Burgess.

Darst, P.W., and R.P. Pangrazi. 1985. *Dynamic physical education curriculum and instruction.* Minneapolis: Burgess.

Hodgson, M. 1997. *Compass & map navigator.* Rev. ed. Guilford, CT: Globe Pequot Press.

Mood, D., F.F. Musker, and J.E. Rink. 1991. *Sports and recreational activities for men and women.* 10th ed. St. Louis: Mosby.

Renfrew, T. 1997. *Orienteering.* Champaign, IL: Human Kinetics.

Sweeney, J. 1986. *Ohio State outdoor adventure program.* Unpublished manual.

White, J.R., ed. 1990. *Sports rules encyclopedia.* Champaign: IL: Leisure Press.

Additional Resources

Boy Scouts of America
  Supply and equipment stores sell handbooks on orienteering, which include many map, compass, and orienteering activities. Check your local listings for the location of the store nearest you.

National Cartographic Information Center/USGS
507 National Center
Reston, VA 22092
  Offers topographical maps.

Silva Orienteering Services USA
P.O. Box 1604
Binghamton, NY 13902
Phone 607-779-2264
  Sells teaching aids, videotapes, films, slides, map and compass games, books, posters, and equipment.

U.S. Geological Survey Denver Federal Center
6 Kipling, Bldg. 810
Denver, CO 80225
Phone 888-247-8747
  Offers topographical maps.

Pickleball

Pickleball originated in 1965 at the home of Joel Pritchard, located near Seattle, Washington. The game began as a family activity when Pritchard and his house guest, Bill Bell, discovered that there was not enough good badminton equipment for the two families to play. After modifying rules and replacing rackets with wooden paddles, they developed the game of pickleball, which got its name from the Pritchard's cocker spaniel, Pickles, who kept running off with the ball whenever it landed off the court. Slowly pickleball spread throughout the neighborhood and to friends. In 1972 a corporation was formed and the rules were copyrighted to protect the new game.

During the 1970s the popularity of the game grew in the Seattle area, where it was used in high school and college physical education programs as well as parks and other recreational settings. Thanks to targeted and widespread promotion of the game by its creators, and eventually the U.S. Pickleball Association as well as state and national physical education conventions, today pickleball is played throughout the United States and Canada and in a few other countries.

Pickleball is easy to learn and all players experience quick success, regardless of size and strength. It is a good family sport, is inexpensive, can be played on driveways, is exciting and entertaining, and promotes fitness.

Equipment

Pickleball is a racket sport (even though a paddle is used) and is closely aligned with badminton and tennis in terms of rules, strategies, and general play. The game is played on a court or hard surface of the same dimensions as a badminton doubles court (there are no doubles and singles lines, however), but in pickleball the service courts are in backcourt and a nonvolley zone is located on either side of the net.

Pickleball players use a square-faced wooden paddle, slightly larger than a table tennis paddle, and a plastic perforated ball about the size of a tennis ball. For safety reasons and to secure the paddle, the butt of the pickleball racket is equipped with a short cord worn around the wrist.

Unit Organization

This unit is based on the assumption that students have not been introduced to pickleball but have had some skill development in racket sports. Following is a brief summary of each lesson in this unit:

▶ Lesson 1 teaches the basic game skills of drop hitting and making forehand and backhand shots.

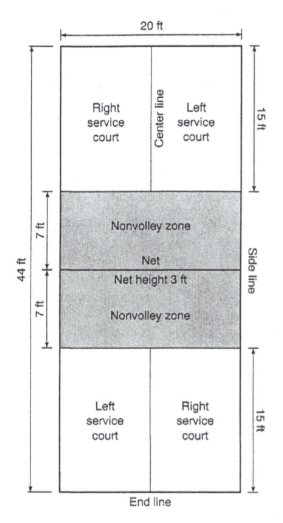

20 ft

Right service court

Center line

Left service court

15 ft

Nonvolley zone

Net

Net height 3 ft

Side line

Nonvolley zone

7 ft

7 ft

44 ft

Left service court

Right service court

15 ft

End line

Pickleball court dimensions

- Lesson 2 presents the lob, volley, and serve and continues to develop basic skills.

- Ball spin and skill combinations are reviewed and practiced in lesson 3.

- Lesson 4 introduces doubles play and game rules. Only doubles play is covered because of the ratio of students and courts.

Selected resources and assessment ideas are found in the assessment and resources chapter at the end of the unit.

This unit will likely be popular with students. Additional days may be added to con-

tinue to extend game play and refine students' playing skills.

Social Skills and Etiquette

Students should be encouraged to practice basic courtesies of the game, which are similar to those of other racket sports. These courtesies include the following:

- Do not walk behind courts or retrieve balls from adjacent courts while a point is in progress.

- Be sure opponents are ready before serving.

- Call out the score before serving.

- Acknowledge good shots made by partners and opponents.

- Abide by the rules.

Lesson Modifications

The lessons in this unit can be adapted to suit students with special needs. Suggested modifications include the following:

- For students who have problems with tracking regular ball speeds, hand-eye coordination, or mobility, substitute Nerf balls for pickleballs.

- To increase the success rate for beginners or for less-skilled students, allow the ball to bounce more than once on returning the serve or during play.

- Use brightly colored balls to help students with vision problems.

- For other disabilities or problems with the game, modify the playing rules accordingly.

Safety

Pickleball is a safe game. Be sure that students wear the wrist strap of the paddle, which prevents it from flying off during play and hitting someone. Also, encourage students to call their shots when the ball is between players and could be played by either.

Rules

Pickleball is closely aligned with badminton rules and with both badminton and tennis in terms of strategies and general play. The rules are most like those of badminton, including the following similarities:

- A game consists of 11 points, but a team must win by 2 points.
- Serving begins in the right-hand court.
- Doubles serving system is the same.
- Only the serving team can score.

The rules and playing sequence of pickleball are explained in the following sections. Unless otherwise noted, the rules for singles and doubles play are the same.

Serving

Servers must stand, with at least one foot behind the end line of their serving court, and serve diagonally crosscourt, clearing the nonvolley zone. Following are rules governing the serve:

- If the server attempts to serve but misses the ball completely, it counts as a serve.
- One serve attempt is allowed unless the ball touches the net and falls into the proper court (a let serve), in which case the serve is replayed.
- Servers must serve underhand, dropping the ball and hitting it below the waist in the air; it cannot be served from a drop bounce.
- Both the receiving and serving teams must let the ball bounce once before returning it on the opening play following the serve (double bounce rule); thereafter both sides may volley the ball or hit it after one bounce.

- The ball bouncing out-of-bounds on the serve constitutes a serving fault; the opponent gets the serve.
- As play continues, servers alternate courts until a fault is made.
- In doubles, the first serving team gets only one fault before both opponents serve; thereafter each partner on a side serves until faulting.
- In doubles play, if the serving team faults (on the serve or during the rally), the players remain in the same court and the serve goes to the opposing team. If the receiving team faults, the serving team scores a point and the server rotates to the left service court to serve.
- In singles play, the server begins in the right service court. After the first serve, however, the server's score dictates which service court is used. The server serves from the right service court when the score is even (i.e., 2, 4, 6, 8, and 10) and from the left service court when the score is odd (i.e., 1, 3, 5, 7, 9, and 11). This is the only rule difference between singles and doubles play.

Play

After the serve, the receiving side returns the ball across the net; then the players hit the ball back and forth (i.e., called *rallying*) until one side fails to return it over the net. Play ends when one player makes a fault (e.g., hitting the ball out-of-bounds). If the serving side stops play, the opposing side gets the serve. If the receiving side stops play, the serving side scores a point.

The following rules govern game play:

- Except for the opening play, when the ball must bounce once on each side before it is returned, players may either volley the ball or return it after one bounce.
- All volleying must be done with the player's feet completely behind the nonvolley zone, although a ball may be played off a bounce in the nonvolley

zone. It is a fault if a player steps over the nonvolley zone line on the follow-through of a shot taken outside the nonvolley zone line.

- All lines are in play; if a ball lands on a line, it is in play.
- The hand is considered a part of the paddle; no fault occurs if the ball is played off the hand holding the paddle.
- The ball may touch the net during a rally. If it falls inbounds, it is in play.
- A player may step into the nonvolley zone when playing a bounce inside the nonvolley zone.

Scoring

Only the serving team or player scores points. If the serving side loses the rally, the opponent gets the serve. Thus, keeping the service privilege (keeping the serve) is an important part of the game. Points are scored when the opponent

- fails to return the ball,
- hits it out-of-bounds, or
- faults.

Faults

Like in badminton, two types of faults can occur in pickleball: serving faults and playing faults. During the serve, faults include the server

- serving overhand;
- contacting the ball above the waist;
- stepping over the end line;
- not keeping the feet stationary at the time of contact; and
- failing to hit the ball to the proper opposing service court.

The receiver can be faulted for

- not being within the service court;
- not having both feet on the floor when receiving; and
- moving before the serve is made (i.e., before the ball is contacted).

During play, faults include

- hitting the ball out-of-bounds;
- hitting the ball into the ceiling, wall, lights, standards, or other players;
- double-hitting a shot (i.e., hitting the ball more than once on a side);
- stepping into the nonvolley zone when volleying the ball or on the follow-through (however, stepping into the nonvolley zone is allowed when playing a bounce inside the nonvolley zone);
- contacting the ball with any part of the body other than the paddle hand;
- "carrying" the ball on the paddle; and
- demonstrating nonsporting behavior (e.g., intentionally distracting or obstructing an opponent).

Lesson 1

Forehand and Backhand Drive

Purpose

In this lesson students develop basic paddle skills, including drop hitting, the forehand drive, and the backhand drive.

Warm-Ups (6-8 Minutes)

1. Elbow-knee touches (standing)
2. Arm rotations
3. Side slides
4. Wrist rotation and flexion
5. Running in place

Skill Cues

Grips

1. Eastern forehand. The forefinger is extended up and behind the shaft of the grip with three fingers and the thumb wrapped around the grip, forming a V on top. This grip is like a handshake.
2. Eastern backhand. Start with a forehand grip and rotate the paddle a quarter turn counterclockwise with the thumb either diagonal across the back of the handle or, for better support, extended up and behind the shaft of the grip.
3. Continental. Grip the handle midway between the forehand and backhand.

Forehand Drive

1. Take a forehand or continental grip.
2. Pivot toward the sideline while rotating the body away from the net and draw the paddle backward, waist high.
3. Shift weight forward and step into contact, tightening the grip.
4. Contact the ball with a flat paddle face in front of the forward foot. Swing the paddle upward slightly with a firm wrist.
5. Use a short follow-through in the direction of the intended flight (this is similar to all racket sports).

Backhand Drive

The mechanics of the backhand drive are similar to the forehand but taken from the opposite side of the body.

1. Take a backhand grip.
2. Pivot to the sideline (rotating further back than the forehand), drawing the paddle backward, waist high.
3. Sight the ball over the paddle shoulder.
4. Shift the weight forward.
5. Contact the ball with a flat face in front of the forward foot and closer to the hip than the forehand. Swing the paddle slightly upward with a firm wrist.
6. Use a short follow-through in the direction of the intended flight.

Teaching Cues

1. To help students keep their eyes on the ball, show them how to slide to the side while getting into position to hit the ball. Tell them to keep their eyes on the oncoming ball while sliding from side to side to get into position to hit the ball.
2. Tell students that many returns do not come at a perfect level. They will need to open the paddle face slightly when hitting low (underhand) shots and close the face slightly when hitting high (overhand) shots.

Activities (30-40 Minutes)

1. Introduce the game of pickleball, including the equipment used, and demonstrate the grips using the skill cues. (4-5 minutes)

| Eastern forehand grip | Eastern backhand grip | Continental grip |

2. Position students in a scattered formation and have them bounce the ball upward with the paddle, trying to control the ball without letting it drop to the floor. Repeat until they are able to bounce it 10 consecutive times without moving more than a step or two. Have them try dropping the ball with one hand, picking it up on the bounce with the paddle, and continuing to bounce it upward five times. (4-5 minutes)
3. Drop-hitting drill. Position students standing sideways about 15 to 20 feet (4.57-6.1 meters) from a wall, with the knees flexed and the paddle hand extended behind the back hip. They should drop the ball and hit it toward the wall before

it hits the floor. Continue practice until students can coordinate the drop and hit smoothly. After mastering the technique, increase the distance from the wall by 5 to 10 feet (1.52-3.05 meters). (4-6 minutes)

4. One-bounce partner drill. With partners and standing about 30 feet (9.14 meters) apart, students drop hit the ball to their partners, who let it bounce once before returning it (using both forehand and backhand drives). Students continue the rally and count consecutive hits, trying to reach 10. Each time someone misses, the rally starts again with a drop hit. Have students switch partners and repeat the drill. (6-8 minutes)

5. Partner rally drill. With partners and standing about 20 feet (6.1 meters) apart, students drop hit and try to keep the ball going back and forth without letting it touch the floor, using both forehand and backhand shots. After they achieve some success, students can try hitting 10 consecutive times with different partners. (4-6 minutes)

6. One-bounce and no-bounce partner drill. With partners and standing about 30 feet (9.14 meters) apart, students mix their one-bounce and no-bounce shots, using forehand, backhand, underhand, and overhand hits. (8-10 minutes)

Closure (3-5 Minutes)

Review the lesson with students. Use the following questions and ideas to reinforce learning, check understanding, and provide feedback.

1. Discuss whether students were able to coordinate dropping the ball with one hand and hitting it before it hit the floor.

2. How many student pairs were able to reach 10 consecutive one-bounce and no-bounce shots with a partner?

3. Share your observations about students' forehand and backhand shots, body position, ball control, moving into position, and other pickleball skills.

4. Review the forehand and backhand drives by demonstrating good form through the entire sequence of each (see the skill cues).

Lesson 2

Volley, Lob, and Serve

Purpose

In this lesson students develop lob, volley, and serve skills as well as refine forehand and backhand shots.

Warm-Ups (6-8 Minutes)

1. Step and calf taps
2. Arm rotations
3. Faceup flank
4. Wrist rotation and flexion
5. Reverse run

Facility and Equipment

- Gym
- 1 paddle and ball per student

  Note: Set up as many marked courts (with nets) as possible.

Skill Cues

Lob

1. Use same stroke mechanics as for the forehand and backhand drives (see lesson 1).
2. Open the paddle face on contact and follow through high.
3. Direct the ball upward with the paddle.
4. Open the paddle face to get height and distance.
5. Use the lob when opponents rush the net.

Volley

1. Step to meet the ball in front and to the side of the body.
2. Transfer weight to the forward foot.
3. Squeeze the grip just before contact, and contact the ball in the center of the paddle before the bounce.
4. Meet the ball above net level, block or direct the shot downward (using very little backswing) and angle it to an open space.
5. When forced to hit below net level, get under the ball and lift it low over the net.
6. Follow through slightly.

Serve

1. Take a forward stride position with the knees flexed and weight on the back foot.
2. Take the paddle arm backward behind the waist, cocking the wrist.

3. Hold the ball in the other hand, in front of the forward foot and waist high.

4. Drop the ball, shift weight, and rotate the body forward.

5. Contact the ball below the waist, and follow through upward.

6. Concentrate first on dropping the ball and then on swinging the paddle.

7. Learn to mix serves (e.g., high and deep, hard driven and flat) to keep opponents off balance and in backcourt on the defense.

Activities (30-40 Minutes)

1. Review the skill cues of the forehand and backhand shots (see lesson 1). Pair up students and position partners on courts to rally. They may hit the ball before it bounces or let it bounce once. Each rally should be started with a drop hit. (5-6 minutes)

2. Explain and demonstrate the lob using the skill cues. (1-2 minutes)

3. Lob drill. One partner drop hits two balls from midcourt to backcourt, concentrating on contacting the ball with an open paddle face and lifting the ball to the opposite backcourt. The other partners retrieve the balls and return them by drop hitting a lob. After a few trials, students rally and alternate drives and lobs. (3-4 minutes)

4. Explain and demonstrate the volley using the skill cues. (2-3 minutes)

5. Volley drill. Position students in partners and on opposite sides of the net. Partner 1 stands in midcourt and drop hits to partner 2, who stands two steps behind the nonvolley zone and volleys back, directing the ball downward. After five trials, students switch roles. If the ball is below the net line, the ball should be volleyed upward (a defensive shot). (6-8 minutes)

6. Present the serving sequence and explain the rules governing the serve (see the unit introduction). (2-3 minutes)

7. Serve drill. Students stand behind the four ends of the court. The first students in the first 2 lines (A and B in the figure) serve 3 balls diagonally across the net and rotate to the end of the line. Students in the last 2 lines (C and D in the figure) retrieve balls. Then the first students in lines C and D serve 3 balls to lines B and A. Continue serving and rotating positions. (6-8 minutes)

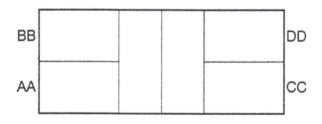

Serve drill formation

8. Keeping the same formation, have students play a game of serve and return. (5-6 minutes)

Serve and Return

The receiver stands inside the service court diagonal from the server and returns the serve after the ball bounces once. Teams score 1 point for every legal serve and 1 point for every legal return, meaning that the ball must fall within court boundaries. Players rotate after each serve and return. Players not engaged in serving and returning can retrieve balls. Play to 7 points or 5 to 6 minutes, whichever occurs first.

Closure (3-5 Minutes)

Review the lesson with students. Use the following ideas to reinforce learning, check understanding, and provide feedback.

1. Have students list five rules governing the serve.
2. Discuss the differences and similarities between the serve and the lob (i.e., a serve is always hit without a bounce, but a lob can be hit after one bounce; both are hit with an open paddle face, contact the ball at a low level, and have an upward follow-through).
3. Discuss the difference between the follow-through for the lob and volley (i.e., the lob follow-through is upward; the volley follow-through is short and downward) .

Lesson 3

Ball Spin and Skill Drills

Purpose

In this lesson students learn to use topspin and backspin and to refine other pickleball skills.

Warm-Ups (6-8 Minutes)

1. Side pattern jumps
2. Push-ups
3. Grapevine step
4. Arm circles
5. Jog-sprint intervals

Skill Cues

Topspin

With a correctly executed topspin, the ball will rise, drop sharply, and then bounce forward.

1. Keep paddle face flat or slightly closed on contact.
2. Lift the paddle face upward and across the top of the ball on contact.
3. Finish the stroke high, in front of the body, and with the paddle face closed.

Backspin

With a correctly executed backspin, the ball will rise slightly, lose momentum, and die or bounce sharply upward.

1. Open the paddle face slightly on contact.
2. Drop the paddle face downward through the ball on contact.

Teaching Cues

Emphasize the following paddle mechanics:

1. A paddle coming into a ball with a flat face will produce little spin.
2. A paddle coming upward and across or downward and across the ball will produce topspin or backspin.

Activities (30-40 Minutes)

1. Explain and demonstrate the mechanics and dynamics of topspin and backspin. Scatter students around the gym and lead them through topspin and backspin motions using only their paddles. (4-5 minutes)

2. Have students rally in partners, incorporating both kinds of ball spin. (4-5 minutes)

3. Down-the-line and crosscourt drill. Divide the class into groups of four and position each group on a court. Student A hits down the line to B, who hits crosscourt to C, who hits down the line to D, who hits crosscourt back to A. After every five rounds (i.e., each student hits the ball once) rotate positions clockwise. Encourage students B and C to use backhand shots. If courts are limited, have students hit every other round, retrieving stray balls while they wait. (5-7 minutes)

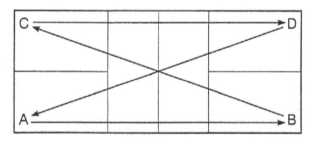

Down-the-line and crosscourt drill formation

4. Drive and volley drill. Two pairs of students to a court, partners A and C stand just behind the nonvolley zone, and partners B and D stand in the backcourt. Partners B and D drive the ball, then A and C return it with a volley. Students change positions after every five trials. (5-7 minutes)

5. Serve and lob drill. Position two sets of partners diagonally across the court from each other. Partners A and C serve to partners B and D, who return each serve with a lob (after one bounce). Each student should serve 2 or 3 balls before switching roles. (4-6 minutes)

6. Serve and rally game. Position two players on each side of the net outside the nonvolley zone. One player puts the ball in play with a legal serve. Players return the serve after one bounce. Thereafter they may volley the ball (except inside the nonvolley zone) or return it after one bounce. Play continues until either a serving fault occurs or one team fails to return the ball legally. Alternate serving side when a fault occurs. A team may score only when serving. Play to 11 points or a set time. (8-10 minutes)

Closure (3-5 Minutes)

Review the lesson with students. Use the following questions and ideas to reinforce learning, check understanding, and provide feedback.

1. Review the difference between topspin and backspin.

2. Discuss which situations are advantageous for topspin shots and which call for backspin shots (i.e., use topspin for drives down the line or when the opponent is in center or forward court; use backspin when the opponent is backcourt).

3. Ask students which skill they think is their strongest. Their weakest? Why?

Lesson 4

Regulation Game

Purpose

In this lesson students play a regulation game of pickleball using overhand offensive strategies, game tactics, and skills and rules learned in previous lessons.

Warm-Ups (6-8 Minutes)

1. Lateral hops
2. Upper body rotations
3. Curl-ups
4. Side slides
5. Jump rope or jump rope laps

Facility and Equipment

◆ Gym or outdoor area
◆ 1 jump rope per student
◆ 1 paddle and ball per student
  Note: Set up as many courts (with nets) as possible.

Skill Cues

Serving Side

1. Play deep until after the serve and opponent's first return.
2. Both partners may play behind the nonvolley zone or play one up and one back after double bounce rule.

Receiving Side

1. On the serve, the receiver should play deep (i.e., backcourt); the receiving partner should play up (i.e., front court, near the nonvolley zone).
2. After the serve, both partners may play behind the nonvolley zone or play one up and one back.

Teaching Cues

Explain the following basic strategies of pickleball before starting the game.

1. Lob the ball over opponents' heads if they are positioned close to the nonvolley zone.
2. Hit drop shots or dink shots (i.e., shots that barely clear the net) if opponents are playing deep.
3. Keep opponents off balance by mixing shots, including volleys and smashes.
4. Hit to open spaces.

Activities (30-40 Minutes)

1. Explain and demonstrate the smash and drop shots. Overhand offensive strategies, these shots use a powerful wrist snap and follow-through (smash) or a weak snap and follow-through (drop) to keep the opponents off balance. Those on the receiving end of the smash and drop shots have difficulty defending against them because preparation for both is the same, making it difficult to know which to expect. (2 minutes)

2. Position students in partners 30 feet (9.14 meters) apart. One tosses high balls and the other alternates smashes and drops. Students switch roles after five tosses and returns. (3-5 minutes)

3. Demonstration doubles game. Select four students to demonstrate a doubles game while the rest of the class is seated around the court. Explain the rules, the positions for serving and receiving, and the nonvolley zone. Then describe some simple strategies for doubles play. (5-8 minutes)

The following is an example of strategic positioning in a doubles game. In this example players A and B make up the serving team and players B and C make up the receiving team.

   ▶ Player A serves to the receiver (player C),
   ▶ who plays deep in the service court (receiving side) to allow for the bounce and return the serve.
   ▶ Players A and B remain back because their first return must be after one bounce.
   ▶ Player D plays up allowing for a quick volley if the return from A and B is shallow.
   ▶ After the opening serve, both players on each team may want to move up to volley positions, or they may play the game with 1 up and 1 back.

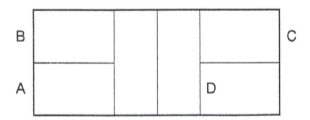

Doubles serve and receive positions

4. Doubles play. Assign doubles teams and position students on the courts to play pickleball. After a team scores 11 points or in 10 minutes, whichever occurs first, rotate the teams to a different court to play against another team. If courts are limited, reduce the time (e.g., 7-8 minutes) and have students practice their serving skills, or rally with partners in other areas or individually against walls. (20-25 minutes)

Closure (3-5 Minutes)

Review the lesson with students. Use the following ideas to reinforce learning, check understanding, and provide feedback.

1. Review scoring and doubles rotation.

2. Share your observations about students' etiquette during game play (e.g., calling faults, praising good play, calling the score before serving, changing partners when asked, and so on).

3. Ask students how well they like the sport of pickleball. If student interest and enthusiasm are high, consider expanding this unit to include a class session or two for tournament play. (Be sure to assess whether students' playing skills and knowledge of the rules are adequate; do not rush into tournaments prematurely.)

Assessment and Resources

Skill tests and game play assessment can be formal (e.g., written tests on rules) or informal (e.g., observation during drills and game play). In addition, the following skill tests can be used as presented or modified to accommodate your situation.

▶ Serve test. Divide the receiving court into four equal parts (running horizontally, i.e., parallel to the net) and assign point values of 1 to 4 to each division: 1 point for the division closest to the nonvolley zone, 4 points to the deepest division of the receiving court; if the serve is legal and lands on the line between two serving targets, use the higher of the two point values. Students serve 15 times (repeating let serves) and accumulate points. To save time and involve all students in the process, divide the class into groups of 4: 1 student serves, 1 records the score, 1 officiates (i.e., calls lines and legal serves), and 1 retrieves. Rotate roles until all students have been tested.

▶ 30-second drive test. Mark a 3-foot (.91-meter) net line on a wall and a 12-foot (3.66-meter) restraining line on the floor in front of the wall. Students drive the ball to the wall above the net line and continue to drive the ball from behind the restraining line after one bounce for 30 seconds. (Keep spare balls near the restraining line so that students being tested can get another ball if a ball goes astray.) Count the number of hits above and on the line. Drives do not count as a hit if the student steps on or over the restraining line, or hits the ball before it bounces. (A ball may bounce more than once before the student hits it.) To save time and involve all students in the process, divide the class into groups of 4: 1 student hits, 1 counts legal hits, 1 officiates (e.g., calls out foot faults or hits that occur before a bounce), and 1 retrieves. Rotate roles until all students have been tested. Give a second and third trial if there is time; average all trial scores together.

▶ 30-second volley test. Mark a 3-foot (.91-meter) net line on a wall and a 7.5-foot (2.29-meter) restraining line on the floor in front of the wall. Students volley the ball above the net line from behind the restraining line for 30 seconds. (Keep spare balls near the restraining line so that students being tested can get another ball if a ball goes astray.) The ball must be volleyed (no bounces). Count the number of shots that hit above or on the line. Call a fault (i.e., the volley shot does not count) if the student goes over the line, but the ball is still in play. To save time and involve all students in the process, divide the class into groups of 4: 1 student hits, 1 counts legal hits, 1 officiates (e.g., calls out faults), and 1 retrieves. If more time is available after all players have been tested, give 2 or 3 trials and average the scores.

Resources

Curtis, J.M. 1985. *Pickle-ball for player and teacher*. 2nd ed. Englewood, CO: Morton.

Pickle-ball, Inc. 1972. *Play pickle-ball*. Seattle, WA: Pickle-ball, Inc.

(Order from Pickle-ball, Inc., 900 N. 34th St., Seattle, WA 98103; phone 206-632-0119.)

Team Handball

Team handball originated in the Scandinavian countries in the early 1900s as a field sport using 11 players per team. Because of severe winters, the game was modified to become an indoor sport in the late 1920s. In the indoor game, teams comprise seven players.

It was not until the 1950s that team handball gained much attention in the United States. In 1959 clubs in New York and New Jersey gave official sanction to the sport by founding the U.S. Team Handball Federation. The game gained in popularity as competition extended to other parts of the country and Canada, although the East Coast continues to give more enthusiastic support to the game. The inclusion of team handball in the Olympic Games for men in 1972 and for women in 1976 gave an added boost to the sport's popularity.

Today team handball is played in more than 140 nations and more than 12 million players are affiliated with the International Handball Federation. U.S.A. Team Handball continues to act as the governing body for the Olympic sport and all U.S. competitive team handball events. It also promotes women's, men's, and juniors' team handball. Currently U.S.A. Team Handball is working to develop interest in team handball through the Boys and Girls Clubs of America, elementary and secondary schools, and colleges and universities.

Team handball is a relatively simple game, which makes it possible to enjoy playing almost immediately. The game combines the fundamental skills of running, jumping, catching, and throwing into a continuous, fast-moving sport, making it a good activity to promote cardiorespiratory health. Skill elements are borrowed from soccer, basketball, hockey, and water polo. Unlike many sports, beginners can achieve success early on.

Equipment

Equipment and court needs for team handball are minimal. Balls and goals are the major pieces of equipment, but these can be devised or substitutes may be used. Rubber playground balls (appropriately sized), for example, work just fine in team handball. Likewise, goals can be made (e.g., volleyball standards with old netting strung across at the right height), or colored tape on the wall can serve as goal outlines. In many European school gyms, goals are simply painted on the end walls.

Standard goals with netting cost about $750 a pair. Regulation balls can be purchased through most sporting goods stores or equipment catalogs for about $50 for all leather and about $25 for good synthetic leather. The men's regulation ball weighs 15 to 17 ounces (425.2-481.9 grams) and has a circumference of 23 to 24 inches (58.4-61 centimeters); the ball used by women and juniors weighs 12 to 14 ounces (340.2-396.9 grams) and has a circumference of 21 to 22 inches (53.3-55.9 centimeters). For coed physical education, the smaller ball is better, and a mini-team handball (weighing 10 to 11 ounces [283.5-311.8 grams] with a circumference of 19-20 inches [48.3-50.8 centimeters]) is best for upper elementary school students. Eye protection should be standard equipment for every goalie, as well as for those who wear glasses. Goalies should also wear a lightweight plastic helmet.

Generally team handball is played indoors, but an outside area with a firm surface for dribbling can work quite well. Team handball court dimensions are shown in the first figure; the second figure shows how to modify a basketball court for team handball.

Unit Organization

Because the skills of handball are relatively simple (i.e., throwing, catching, running, jumping, and guarding) and because the elements of play follow other well-known activities (e.g., basketball, soccer, and hockey), the game can be played successfully without great

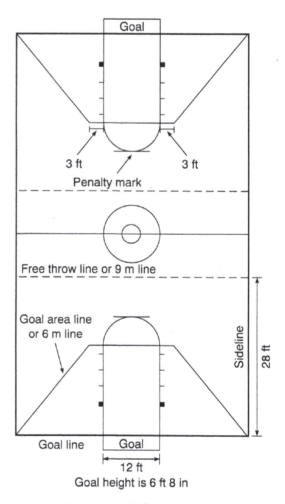

Basketball court modified for team handball

attention to practicing isolated skills. Offensive and defensive strategies can be adapted from basketball and soccer quite easily (see the basketball and soccer units starting on pages 127 and 220).

Following is a brief summary of the lessons in this unit:

▶ Lessons 1 and 2 present lead-up games that emphasize passing, catching, shooting, and interception skills. Students will practice these skills in challenging, vigorous activities that simulate actual game play in a controlled environment.

▶ In lessons 3 and 4 students will refine their team handball skills, concentrate on teamwork, and learn many of the playing rules through closely related games.

▶ In lesson 5 students play a regulation game of team handball.

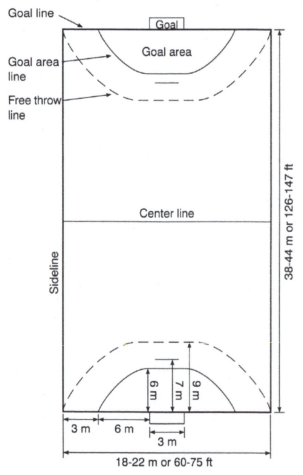

Team handball court dimensions

Selected resources and assessment ideas are found in the assessment and resources chapter at the end of the unit.

As in other units, lessons can be expanded or new lessons added for game play, depending on desired skill development or student interest. To maximize participation and skill development, the authors recommend separating teams by gender (i.e., boys play against boys and girls play against girls).

Social Skills and Etiquette

No specific rules of etiquette apply in team handball. Instead, stress the development of social skills when students are interacting in a group. For example, collective effort toward a common goal should be emphasized over individual effort. Set an atmosphere for fair and fun play by discussing the importance of good sporting behavior. This includes accepting officials' decisions and treating opponents with respect. Likewise, encourage cooperation and teamwork by rotating positions throughout each activity.

Lesson Modifications

Because team handball is fast paced and vigorous in nature, it may be difficult for students with mobility impairments or those with coordination problems. Consider adapting the court or equipment for these students—for example, use larger goals or a smaller playing area. Using additional players on a team can also help. Students with severe physical problems should be added as stationary sideline players responsible for all throw-ins.

Safety

Safety considerations primarily stem from physical contact. Collisions are almost inevitable, given that two fast-moving teams use the same space. To reduce the risk of injury, immediately call intentional roughness, grabbing, and pushing. Doing so will also discourage such behavior. As already mentioned, goalies should wear a lightweight plastic helmet as well as eye protection. Dividing teams by physical characteristics (e.g., size, weight) or gender may also be necessary.

Rules

The objective of team handball is to score a goal by passing the ball quickly and throwing the ball past the defense and goalie and into the goal. A regulation game consists of two 30-minute halves with a 10-minute intermission. The only timeouts occur when an injury occurs; other major interruptions are determined by officials.

A team consists of a goalie and six court players:

- left wing,
- circle runner,
- right wing,
- left backcourt,
- center, and
- right backcourt.

Both wings move quickly down court and usually feed the ball to the center and backcourt players (also called *backs*). The circle runner needs to be energetic and usually sets picks (i.e., closely dribbling around a teammate that the guard can't follow without fouling) or screens (i.e., moving between a teammate and the teammate's guard so the guard can't block a shot or stop a dribble; players cannot use their arms to screen) for the wings and backs. The center and backs need to be strong throwers and usually do most of the scoring, although all court players are shooters. The goalkeeper should be quick, should not be afraid of the ball, should have good coordination, and should be able to throw the ball quickly for the fast break.

Play

The game begins with a center throw-off (sometimes called a *throw-on*) by one team determined by a coin toss. The throw-off is a

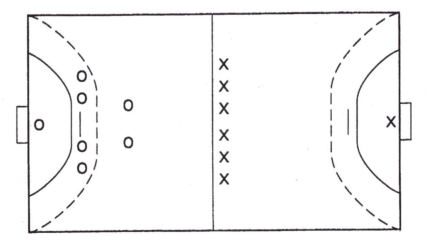

Throw-off positions

pass to a teammate within 3 seconds after the referee's whistle. Both teams must begin on their own half of the court. The offensive team lines up along and behind the centerline, and the defense usually takes a position similar to that noted in the figure. Regardless of the defensive positioning, no defender can be within 10 feet (3.05 meters) of an offensive player.

On the throw-off, offensive players advance the ball down court to score while the defense moves to adjust to the oncoming opponents. A goal, worth 1 point, is scored when the entire ball crosses the goal line and goes into the goal. After a goal is scored a center throw-off is awarded to the opposing team.

In advancing the ball down the court, different rules and privileges apply to court players (defense and offense) and goalies. The goal area also has distinct rules. These rules and privileges are listed in the following sections. First, however, some general rules and strategies follow:

▶ Sidelines are in play.
▶ Goal lines (between the goal area line and the sidelines) are in play.
▶ Basic 1-on-1 (i.e., person-to-person) and zone defenses are used in the game. Beginning and lower-skilled players will have more success with a 1-on-1 defense. Better players tend to use a zone defense with each player responsible for an area or zone. They move as a unit and try to

force the opponents into longer shots by blocking out areas of the front court (i.e. closest to the goal area).

Court Players

Court players serve as both offense and defense during a game, and possession can change quickly. Offensive players may use the body—not the arms—to obstruct or screen an opponent with or without the ball. As in basketball, defensive players may use the arms to guard and may place a hand on the shoulder or waist of an opponent and move with that person while defending the attack. All court players may do the following:

▶ Hold the ball up to 3 seconds
▶ Run three steps with the ball
▶ Dribble as many times as desired
▶ Pass or shoot
▶ Run three steps before and after a dribble.

Court players may not do the following:

▶ Use the arms or legs to obstruct, push, grab, tackle, kick, hit, or hold an opponent (The first occurrence of these actions results in a free throw for the opponent and a warning; if the violation is repeated, flagrant, or could result in an injury, the player can be disqualified or suspended for 2 minutes, during which time his or her team plays short.)

- Kick the ball
- Make contact with the ball below the knees
- Double dribble (i.e., dribble, walk three steps, and dribble again)
- Dive to play the ball on the floor
- Step on or across the goal area line (but see the rules for the goal area)
- Air dribble (i.e., toss the ball into the air with the intention of catching it)
- Charge (i.e., run into) a defender

An infraction results in an immediate free throw taken (without referee handling) at the point where the violation occurred.

Goal Area

As noted earlier, only the goalkeeper is allowed in the goal area (sometimes called the *crease*). Offensive players who begin their jump shot from outside the goal line and release the ball before landing may fall into the goal area but must quickly exit the area. The following rules apply to the goal area:

- If an offensive player is on the goal area line or within the goal area, with or without the ball, the defense gets a free throw from their own free throw line.
- If an offensive player scores a goal while a teammate is on the line or within the goal area, the goal does not count.
- If a defensive player gains an advantage by being within the goal area, a penalty throw is awarded to the offense.
- A ball within the goal area belongs to the goalie unless it is in the air.
- The 3-second and 3-step restrictions do not apply in the goal area, for the goalie.

Goalies

Goalkeepers may

- defend their goals in any manner using hands, feet, and body;
- move outside the goal area and throw for a goal (goal throw), but then must abide by the rules for court players;

- take more than 3 steps when carrying the ball; and
- hold the ball longer than 3 seconds.

Goalies may not

- leave the goal area while in possession of the ball; and
- pick up a ball outside the goal area and carry it back.

The penalty for infractions is a penalty throw against the infringing goalie.

Warnings

The referee gives only one warning to a player for a rule violation after which a 2-minute suspension results. However, warnings are not required before issuing a 2-minute suspension; if the violation is flagrant, the official waives the warning and gives the suspension. If the referee feels that an injury may have resulted from a personal foul, the infringing player should be disqualified. After a total of three warnings to a team, the team is disqualified and forfeits the game.

Throws

There are several types of throws in team handball:

- Throw-off
- Free throw
- Throw-in
- Penalty throw
- Goal-throw
- Throw-out

A goal may be scored from any throw except the throw-out. These are explained in the following sections.

Throw-Off

As noted, a throw-off starts the game and follows each goal. The rules governing the throw-off follow:

- The thrower must keep one foot stationary.

▶ Each team must be in its own half of the court, and opposing players must be 10 feet (3.05 meters) away.

▶ The ball must be passed within 3 seconds after the whistle.

▶ The ball may be thrown with one or both hands

Free Throws

Free throws are awarded for rule infractions by goalies and court players (see previous rules governing goalies and court players). The opposing team takes the free throw from a spot nearest where the infraction occurred. If the infringement occurred between the goal area and free throw line, the free throw is taken from the free throw line directly in front of the point of the violation (all offensive players must be outside the free throw line). As noted, a goal may be scored directly from a free throw.

When the free throw is taken,

▶ defensive players must be 10 feet (3.05) meters away,

▶ the thrower must have one foot in contact with the floor, and

▶ the thrower must throw or pass within 3 seconds.

Throw-Ins

Throw-ins are taken from either the sidelines or the corner, sometimes called a *sideline throw* and *corner throw*. If the ball crosses the goal line outside the goal and was last touched by a defensive player other than the goalie, the offensive team is awarded a corner throw at the junction of the goal and sideline. If a ball goes out-of-bounds over a sideline, a sideline throw is taken at the spot where it crossed the line. The following rules apply to throw-ins:

▶ Throw-ins must be taken within 3 seconds.

▶ In the sideline throw, throwers must keep one foot stationary on the sideline.

▶ In the corner throw, throwers must keep one foot on the corner line.

▶ The ball can be thrown in with one or both hands.

Penalty Throw

A penalty throw is taken by one player from the penalty line, keeping one foot stationary. All other players must be outside the free throw line except the defending goalie. The player taking the penalty throw has 3 seconds after the referee whistle to shoot. Goalies can defend a free throw from anywhere within 10 feet (3.05 meters) of the shooter.

A penalty throw is awarded when

▶ a foul destroys a clear chance to score a goal,

▶ a player displays unsportsmanlike behavior (discretion of referee)

▶ the goalie carries the ball back into the goal area,

▶ a court player intentionally plays the ball to his or her own goalie in the goal area and the goalie touches the ball, and

▶ a defensive player enters the goal area to gain advantage over an attacking offensive player with the ball.

No penalty throw is awarded if the player did not lose control of the shot, even if a foul occurred (this is a judgment call by the referee).

Goal-Throw

A goal-throw is made by the goalie from outside the goal area upon retrieving a loose ball outside the goal area.

Throw-Out

A throw-out is made by the goalie from within the goal area. The following actions result in a throw-out:

▶ A ball is caught or blocked inside the goal area before crossing the goal line.

▶ The ball is thrown or deflected over the goal line outside the goal by the offensive team.

▶ An offensive shot that is deflected or blocked by the goalie before going over the goal line outside the goal.

Referee's Throw

Another type of throw in team handball is the referee's throw, which is like a jump ball in basketball. The official tosses the ball up into the air and two opposing players try to grab or tap it to a teammate. A referee's throw is taken at the point of infraction. Any court player may participate in the referee's throw (i.e., center, wings, backs, and circle runners); all other players must be 10 feet (3.05) meters away.

A referee's throw results when

- the ball touches anything above the court (e.g., ceiling, lights),
- two opposing players make a rule infringement simultaneously, and
- two or more players possess the ball.

Lesson 1

Passing Drills and Games

Purpose

In this lesson students develop passing skills and defensive moves, within the rules of team handball play.

Warm-Ups (6-8 Minutes)

1. Horizontal run
2. High jumper
3. Extended body leg drops
4. Arm pumps
5. Agility run

Facility and Equipment

◆ Gym or outdoor area
◆ 1 handball per 8 to 10 students
◆ 1 pinnie per 2 students
◆ Cones

Skill Cues

Passing

1. Let the ball rest in the hand, on the fingertips; do not grip the handball like a softball.
2. Fling the ball by snapping the wrist when passing or shooting.
3. Make short, crisp passes.
4. Pass quickly and frequently.

Defending

1. Use the body to block or screen players with or without the ball. Keep a hand on and move with but do not push or hold an opponent.
2. Use raised arms and jumps to guard and block shots and passes.
3. Play 1-on-1 (i.e., person-to-person) defense.
4. Try to maintain a position between the attacker and the goal.

Teaching Cues

1. Use short, active games that simulate elements of game play.
2. Teach rules as each element of the game is introduced.
3. Use a ball that will fit the hand of most students.
4. Divide play areas to allow more practice time for each student. Playing more games with fewer players is preferable to playing fewer games (or one game) with many players.

5. Have students alternate between chest, bounce, overhead, underhand, baseball, and hook passes (see the basketball unit starting on page 127 for passing techniques).

Activities (30-40 Minutes)

1. Introduce team handball by presenting a short history of the game, discussing the game's similarities with soccer and basketball, and showing the types of balls used. (3-5 minutes)

2. Basic keep-away. Position students in an equal number of teams (4-5 players per team) and assign each set of 2 teams to a designated playing area with 1 ball. Use 1 ball for every 2 teams. Offensive players remain stationary, trying to pass the ball, while defensive players move around trying to intercept it. Players must pass within 3 seconds or the ball goes to the defense for a free pass. When a defensive player gets the ball or deflects it to a defensive teammate, the defense becomes the offense. Encourage students to use a variety of passes. (3-5 minutes)

3. Keep-away. Switch teams and use cones or tape to delimit the playing area for each pair of teams. In this activity, the 3-step rule (i.e., students may take up to 3 steps before passing), free throw, and boundaries are added. Opponents get a free throw if the offense holds the ball more than 3 seconds, takes more than 3 steps with the ball, or allows the ball to go out of the designated area. Encourage students to use bounce passes, pass to open spaces, and defend with body blocks and screens. (5-6 minutes)

4. Scored keep-away. This is like keep-away (see activity 3) but has the additional elements of dribbling and scoring. Switch teams and remind students that excessive dribbling slows the game down (you may want to limit the number of dribbles). Score 1 point each time the passing team completes 5 consecutive passes. Score 2 points each time the defensive team intercepts a pass. Award a free throw for rule infractions or hitting the ball out-of-bounds. (6-7 minutes)

5. Ten passes. Switch teams and have students play scored keep-away with one alteration: offensive teammates must throw 10 consecutive passes and the ball may not be returned to the person from whom it was passed. Score 3 points for each sequence of 10 passes and 2 points for defensive intercepts. (6-7 minutes)

6. End-line handball. Divide students into two teams and position them on the court. Starting with a throw-off at the centerline, and again after each score, players attempt to pass and move the ball toward their own end line, and then pass (i.e., throw or bounce) the ball to their own goalie who stands behind the end line. To score, the goalie must catch the ball either in the air or on the first bounce. The defense tries to intercept or prevent forward progress of the ball. A free throw is awarded to the opponents for taking more then three steps with the ball, grabbing or striking the ball, and pushing, holding, or running into an opponent. All players must keep 10 feet (3.05 meters) away from the free throw taker. Encourage players to spread out and not crowd around the ball. Change goalies often. (7-10 minutes)

Closure (3-5 Minutes)

Review the lesson with students. Use the following topics to reinforce learning, check understanding, and provide feedback.

1. Ask students which strategies they used to pass the ball to teammates or get into position to receive it.
2. Discuss the strategies teams used to intercept the ball.
3. Review only those basic rules of team handball that were used in the games (e.g., how many seconds players can hold the ball, how many steps can be taken with the ball).
4. Explain legal and illegal combinations of steps and dribbling (e.g., air and double dribbling).

Lesson 2

Shooting Drills and Games

Purpose

In this lesson students learn to shoot for and defend the goal, and some basic game skills.

Warm-Ups (6-8 Minutes)

1. Toe lifts
2. Arm support lifts
3. High jumper
4. Push-ups
5. Reverse run

Facility and Equipment

◆ Gym or outdoor playing area
◆ 1 handball per 4 to 5 students
◆ 1 colored pinnie per 2 students
◆ Tape
◆ Hula hoops
◆ 4 cones or bowling pins

Skill Cues

1. The shooting sequence is as follows:
   ▶ Grip the ball so that it rests in the palm.
   ▶ Reach back and above the shoulder.
   ▶ Initiate the end of the softball throw by snapping the wrist and gathering power from the lower arm.
   ▶ Jump into the air and release the shot for a goal.
2. Rebound shots off the floor and into the goal.
3. Do not shoot with a defender directly in front.
4. Apply force to make all shots quick and powerful.
5. Take shots on the move.
6. Aim shots at open spaces.

Teaching Cues

1. Caution students against forcing a shot that is not open.
2. Explain some guarding techniques for handball (see the basketball unit starting on page 127 for these techniques).
3. Before starting activity 2, tape a hula hoop (or other target; the size of the target is not as important as having something to aim at) to opposite walls of the gym (near goal lines).
4. For pin handball (activity 5), play 2 side-by-side games across the gym or 1 game using the whole gym. Before starting the activity, set up a target (cone or bowling pin) at each end of the court to designate the goal areas. Mark the court with a restricted goal area or use basketball lines and designate the key as the restricted area.

Activities (30-40 Minutes)

1. Introduce throwing or shooting for a goal. Explain shooting techniques from set and jumping positions, and a bounce shot according to the skill cues. Because the defense is usually between the shooter and the goal, most throws for goal are taken from a jump. Explain that the technique of shooting is very different than in basketball, the target being a large open floor area rising about 7.5 feet (a much larger target). Remind students that good players try to get as close to the goal area line as possible before shooting, throw quickly while on the move, and keep their shots simple. Another good tactic is to rebound the ball off the floor and into the goal. (4-6 minutes)

2. Shooting drill. Divide the class in groups of 4 or 5 players and give a ball to each group. Position the groups so that half are directed toward the target on one end of the gym and the other half toward the target on the opposite end. One player holds the ball, takes three steps, and throws the ball at the target within 3 seconds. After everyone has taken five shots, students repeat the drill, this time jumping into the air on the third step and releasing the ball before landing (i.e., no dribbling). Continue the drill until students can coordinate the jump and throw smoothly. (6-8 minutes)

3. Repeat activity 2, but this time have one group member defend the shot by standing at the goal line in a guarding position. Group members should rotate so that all get the chance to shoot and guard. (6-8 minutes)

4. Pass, shoot, and defend. In groups of 5, 2 players defend and 3 attack the goal. After passing 3 or 4 times, an offensive player shoots by jumping and releasing the ball at the wall target. (6-8 minutes)

5. Pin handball. Play two side-by-side games across the gym or one game using the whole gym. Divide into equal teams and scatter players throughout their own half of the court. Set up a target (cone or bowling pin) at each end in a goal area that players cannot enter. Mark the court with a restricted goal area or use basketball lines and designate the key as the restricted area. The objective is to play by handball rules and to score by hitting the pin. The rules can be modified to fit the experience and playing level of the students, including an extra pin. Start with a throw-off; use the out-of-bounds, 3-seconds, 3 steps, and guarding violations; and award free throws and throw-ins. If dribbling impedes the progress of play, eliminate it. (8-10 minutes)

Closure (3-5 Minutes)

Review the lesson with students. Use the following ideas to reinforce learning, check understanding, and provide feedback.

1. Review the major elements and strategies of shooting for a goal (see the skill cues).

2. Discuss why players should spread out, playing all areas of the court rather than simply following the ball.

3. Review the rules for the throw-off, throw-in, and free throw.

Lesson 3

Skill Games

Purpose

In this lesson students learn about the goal area play, the goalie position, and further refine their playing skills and knowledge of the game rules.

Warm-Ups (6-8 Minutes)

1. Triceps dips
2. Step and calf taps
3. Hip rolls
4. Inverted hurdler's stretch
5. Side slides

Facility and Equipment

- Gym or outdoor playing field with goals and line markings
- 2 handballs
- 1 pinnie per 2 students
- 4 cones
- 1 coin

Skill Cues

1. Goalies block and deflect shots by hitting the ball to the side or across the goal line, or knocking the ball down and quickly throwing it to teammates.
2. Pass to open spaces, and spread out to seek open spaces; do not cluster around the ball.
3. Defensive players should stay between the opponent and their goals.

Teaching Cues

1. Remind students that they will play both offensive and defensive roles.
2. Encourage students to pass rather than dribble; dribbling slows the game.
3. Explain the goalie position and area as well as the rules governing the goalie.

Activities (30-40 Minutes)

1. Explain the boundaries and rules governing the goal area, sometimes referred to as the *crease*. (5 minutes)
2. Pin handball. Organize two pin handball games (see lesson 2, activity 5). Add a goalie to defend the pin. The goalie assumes all the privileges of the position in regular team handball. Enforce all player violations, except penalty and corner throws. Change goalies often. If dribbling interferes with good play, eliminate it. (10-15 minutes)
3. Half-court handball. Position 2 teams of equal numbers on each half of the court (each team could have 2 goalies). Determine starting possession with a coin toss and position offensive players a step behind the centerline for the

throw-off. Thereafter, throw-offs occur after every goal. Use all markings for regulation team handball, including a regulation goal. Goalie and court players should abide by all game rules. (15-20 minutes)

Closure (3-5 Minutes)

Review the lesson with students. Use the following ideas to reinforce learning, check understanding, and provide feedback.

1. Discuss why players should pass to open spaces and constantly move around trying to get to open spaces.
2. Explain why crowding or clustering around the ball is not effective; discuss the advantages of playing an area rather than following the ball.
3. Discuss the rules governing the goalie.
4. Point out your observations about good playing skills or good strategies used in class.

Penalty Drills and Modified Game Play

Purpose

In this lesson students learn the penalty and corner throws, and apply offensive and defensive skills as well as team handball rules in a modified game.

Warm-Ups (6-8 Minutes)

1. Mad cat
2. Push-ups
3. Forward lunges
4. Sit and stretch
5. Agility run

Facility and Equipment

- Gym or outdoor playing field with line markings
- 2 goals
- 4 handballs
- 1 pinnie per 2 students
- Cones

Skill Cues

1. Move toward the goal when receiving a teammate's pass.
2. Be alert to change quickly from offense to defense, or vice versa.
3. Aim for high and low corners when shooting for the goal.
4. In a penalty throw, keep one foot in contact with the floor behind the penalty line and aim for the low or high corners.
5. Goalies try to block penalty throws from any point at least 10 feet (3.05 meters) away from the thrower.

Teaching Cues

1. Explain that a corner throw is awarded to the offense when the ball goes out-of-bounds over the goal line and was last touched by a defensive player other than the goalie. It is taken at the intersection of the goal line and sideline closest to where it went out. The thrower must have one foot on the corner sideline during the throw-in.
2. Before students start the activities, teach the six court positions: left and right wing, left and right backcourt, circle runner, and center.
3. Remind students that all players except the circle runner should stay in their own areas. Circle runners move around the free throw line areas (semi-circle) according to where the ball is and mostly set screens for teammates.

Activities (30-40 Minutes)

1. Explain the penalty throw (see the unit introduction) and strategies for aiming and defending. Throwers should quickly look for less-protected spaces and throw forcefully. The faster the release, the less time for the goalie to block the shot. Low and high corners typically offer the best target. The goalie takes a center position 2 to 3 feet (.61-.91 meters) in front of the goal line, arms out about shoulder height, knees slightly flexed and ready to move or jump to block the shot. Both the thrower and the goalie try to anticipate the other's plan of attack. (1-2 minutes)

2. Penalty shot drill. Divide students into two groups and position each at one end of the court. Line up half the players in each group at the penalty line to shoot penalty throws and the other half behind the goal to play goalie. After three penalty shots, the shooter and goalie switch places; then the next set of students moves into the shooter and goalie positions. (5-6 minutes)

3. Corner throw drill. Explain and demonstrate the corner throw. Divide students into two groups for drill practice at each end of the court. One team takes the corner throw while six other players and a goalie defend. Rotate positions after every three throw-ins so that all play offense and defense. (4-6 minutes)

4. Half-court handball. Divide the drill groups from activity 3 into two teams and play half-court handball. Award penalty and corner throws for infractions. (10-12 minutes)

5. Positions play. Describe each position and the duties of each for a regulation game of team handball (see the unit introduction starting on page 561); then have students play a half-court game using regulation teams and concentrating on playing their positions, especially during an attack. (10-14 minutes)

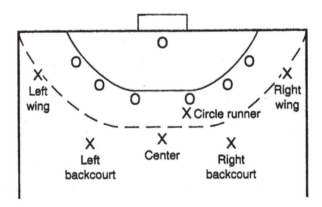

Basic attack positions

Closure (3-5 Minutes)

Review the lesson with students. Use the following ideas to reinforce learning, check understanding, and provide feedback.

1. Review the infractions that result in a penalty throw and discuss rules governing a penalty throw (for both the defender and the shooter).

2. Explain the difference between a corner throw and a throw-out.

3. Have students name the positions on a regulation team.

4. Share your observations about good playing techniques and strategies.

Lesson 5

Regulation Game

Purpose

In this lesson students practice their playing skills and knowledge of the rules in a game of team handball.

Warm-Ups (6-8 Minutes)

1. Arm rotators
2. Arm and leg lifts
3. High jumper
4. Back stretch
5. Side slides

Facility and Equipment

◆ Gym or outdoor playing field with line markings
◆ 2 goals
◆ 2 handballs
◆ 1 pinnie per 2 students

Skill Cues

1. Focus offensively on total team movement, moving the ball quickly, and staying in an attack (offensive) mode. Use picks and screens to assist teammates in passing and shooting. Take all throw-ins, free throws, and corner throws quickly without a whistle.
2. Focus defensively on shifting as a total team, staying between the opponent and the goal, forcing longer shots, and being ready to shift quickly to offensive play. Be alert to intercepting the ball during play, free throws, throw-ins and corner throws.

Teaching Cues

1. Use a 1-on-1 (i.e., person-to-person) defense unless students are advanced enough to play zone defense.
2. Emphasize staying in positions and moving the ball quickly downcourt.
3. If students have to sit out during the full-court game (see activity 2), assign them tasks while waiting to rotate into the game. For example, students can do the following:
   ▶ Note 3 good offensive plays and 3 good defensive plays.
   ▶ Come up with three ways to improve team play (including goalie strategy).
   ▶ Complete a rules quiz.
   ▶ Chart a specific player's performance.

Activities (30-40 Minutes)

1. Remind students about good offensive and defensive play using the skill and teaching cues; then review all playing rules. (5 minutes)
2. Full-court game. Position students in teams of 7 players and use a 1-on-1 defense. Have teams play 5-minute games, keeping the same positions for one game. If additional courts are available, play 10-minute games and rotate teams for new games. (25-35 minutes)

Closure (3-5 Minutes)

Review the lesson with students. Use the following questions and ideas to reinforce learning, check understanding, and provide feedback.

1. How many students scored at least one goal? (If score totals vary widely between students, discuss the importance of teamwork.)
2. Ask students which rules gave them the most problems. Do any rules need clarification?
3. Have students identify the offensive or defensive strategies they used. Which were the most effective? Which were ineffective? Describe some playing situations that could be improved.

Assessment and Resources

A written rules quiz is recommended before additional days of game play. This will help students solidify their understanding of team handball and may also improve their overall playing skill and make for smoother transitions after rule infractions.

Playing skills can also be evaluated. A subjective assessment could be made during game play (e.g., looking for effective teamwork; offensive and defensive positioning; individual skills such as shots, passes, and blocks). This has merit especially if there are more game-playing days.

Note: assessment should focus on skill development, not competition.

Resources

Manitoba Team Handball Federation, Inc. 1991. *Team handball rules and lead-up games*. Winnipeg, Manitoba: Manitoba Team Handball Federation, Inc.

Mood, D., F.F. Musker, and J.E. Rink. 1991. *Sports and recreational activities for men and women*. 10th ed. St. Louis: Mosby.

U.S. Team Handball Federation. 1991. *Team handball*. Colorado Springs, CO: U.S. Team Handball Federation.

White, J.R., ed. 1990. *Sports rules encyclopedia*. Champaign, IL: Leisure Press.

Additional Resources

U.S.A. Team Handball
One Olympic Plaza
Colorado Springs, CO 80909
Phone 719-575-4036
Offers curricular guides, videotapes, and other information.

Ultimate Frisbee

Ultimate Frisbee is a competitive, action-packed sport that can be played on any field or in any gym. Devised in 1967 by students at Columbia High School in Maplewood, New Jersey, ultimate Frisbee quickly grew in popularity. Today it is played around the country on both the high school and college levels and national championships are held annually among various universities.

Ultimate Frisbee is unique in that it relies greatly on high competition with the "spirit of the game." Unlike other sports where players often foul or attempt other infractions until a referee tells them their action is illegal, ultimate Frisbee calls for players to demonstrate honesty and fair play without the presence of referees.

The game of ultimate Frisbee has some elements found in other sports, such as soccer (defensive/offensive play), football (throwing, catching, and intercepting), and basketball (guarding and pivoting). The game is generally played with two teams of seven players, but larger or smaller sized teams may be used for class instruction.

Equipment

Ultimate Frisbee is played on a field 120 yards (109.72 meters) long and 40 yards (36.57 meters) wide. It consists of the infield (60 yards [54.86 meters] long) and two end zones (30 yards [27.43 meters] deep). Although ultimate Frisbee is best played outdoors on a field, the lessons and games in this unit can be adapted for both indoor and outdoor use.

The official ultimate game Frisbee weighs 6.2 ounces (175 grams), but any plastic disc is suitable for the lesson games and activities. Gloves or helmets may be worn, as may shoes with cleats.

Unit Organization

Some of the lessons in this unit may contain more material than can be utilized in a single class session. Be selective in your choice of activities. The activities are based on the assumption that students will have had some experience with Frisbees during the lower

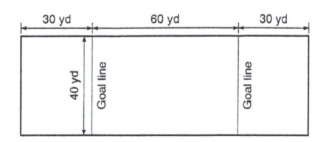

Ultimate Frisbee field dimensions

grades; some additional time may be needed to review basic skills.

Following is a description of each lesson in this unit. The first three lessons are devoted to the actual sport of ultimate Frisbee:

- ▶ Lesson 1 presents Frisbee throwing and catching.
- ▶ Guarding, pivoting, and interception techniques are introduced in lesson 2.
- ▶ Lesson 3 presents strategy and rules for actual game play, which may be extended for as many days as desired.

The final two lessons in this unit present other Frisbee games.

- ▶ The games in lesson 4 involve throwing and catching.
- ▶ In lesson 5 throwing accuracy is further improved with target games.

Although they involve the same skills, these lessons stand on their own and do not have to be linked to ultimate Frisbee. (They should, however, be conducted after unit instruction.) Use them as an extension of the ultimate Frisbee unit or spread them out during the year and use them as single-day lessons.

Selected resources and assessment ideas are found in the assessment and resources chapter at the end of the unit.

Social Skills and Etiquette

Social skills and etiquette are an important part of any sport or game, but they are particularly significant in ultimate Frisbee. Because the sport traditionally has not used officials or referees, players must call their own plays and take responsibility for following the rules. This requires that players demonstrate fair play and good sporting conduct, perhaps to a greater extent than in other sports.

Throughout the unit, remind students to support, acknowledge, and encourage one another. Hold class discussions about complimenting teammates and opponents to instill an environment of cooperative learning.

Lesson Modifications

Ultimate Frisbee involves a lot of running and, thus, may be difficult for students with limited mobility. The following modifications are recommended to make the game more enjoyable and enable success for students with lower fitness levels:

- ▶ Use a foam Frisbee.
- ▶ Reduce the size of the playing area.
- ▶ Enlarge the goal area.
- ▶ Allow more players per team.

Safety

The following safety precautions should be applied to the lessons in this unit:

- ▶ Encourage players to keep their eyes on the Frisbee at all times.
- ▶ Discourage pushing and shoving or other body contact.
- ▶ Encourage players to be aware of their surroundings and the players around them.
- ▶ When assigning teams, be careful to balance them in terms of players' skill level and size.

Rules

Ultimate Frisbee basically involves throwing, running, and receiving. Offensive players advance the Frisbee downfield to score a goal, each worth 1 point. Defensive players try to prevent the offense from scoring. The games consists of two 24-minute halves; at the end of the game, the team with the most points wins.

As mentioned, there are usually seven players per team:

- ▶ 3 handlers (or quarterbacks) who start the Frisbee off (these players should be the most accurate throwers);

▶ 2 middle receivers (also called *mids*) who advance the Frisbee downfield (these players should have solid maneuvering skills); and

▶ 2 long receivers (also called *longs*) who head into the end zone to receive (these players should be the fastest runners).

The game begins with a throw-off by one team, determined by a coin toss. A throw-off is used to restart play after every point is scored, at the beginning of the second half, and whenever the disc goes out-of-bounds. All players must stand on or behind their own goal line until the disc is thrown. If the receiving team catches the throw-off or lets it fall to the ground without touching it, it has possession of the disc at that point. If the receiving team touches the disc and fails to catch it, the throwing team gains possession at that place. After the throw-off, the team with possession of the disc attempts to pass by throwing the disc from player to player (it cannot be handed to another player) in order to ultimately make a successful pass to a teammate in the end zone and score.

Following are the rules governing ultimate Frisbee:

▶ A goal is scored when a player passes the Frisbee to a teammate in the end zone.

▶ Players may move the Frisbee downfield only by passing; running with the Frisbee is not permitted.

▶ A player in possession of the disc cannot run or move more than a pivot before passing the disc.

▶ Players in possession of the Frisbee may pivot only on one foot to change the direction of the throw.

▶ Defensive players may intercept throws, but no body contact is permitted.

▶ When a defensive player intercepts a throw or knocks the Frisbee to the ground, the defense begins offensive play at the point where the interception occurred.

▶ A Frisbee that lands out-of-bounds must be returned to the point on the edge of the field where it went out.

▶ A pass completed out-of-bounds is considered incomplete and is turned over to the defense. The other team then throws the disc from the out-of-bounds line where it went out.

▶ If a player calls "foul" (e.g., to pushing, impeding, or forceful impact) he or she is given possession of the disc at the point where the foul occurred.

Fouls

When a foul occurs, the Frisbee is immediately turned over to the other (i.e., nonfouling) team. The following actions constitute a foul:

▶ Walking while holding the Frisbee

▶ Running while holding the Frisbee

▶ Taking steps while holding the Frisbee

▶ Changing the pivot foot (after establishing one foot as the pivot)

▶ Making any body contact with an opposing player

Lesson 1

Throwing and Catching

Purpose

In this lesson students develop the throwing and catching skills needed to play ultimate Frisbee. These skills include the backhand, side-arm (forehand), and underhand throws as well as the one-handed and two-handed (sandwich) catches.

Facility and Equipment

◆ Outdoor playing area or gym
◆ 1 Frisbee per 2 students
◆ 24 cones

Warm-Ups (6-8 Minutes)

1. Sprint-jog intervals
2. Arm isometrics
3. Arm circles
4. Wrist rotation and flexion

Skill Cues

Throwing

1. Grip the Frisbee with the thumb on top and the fingers below the rim.

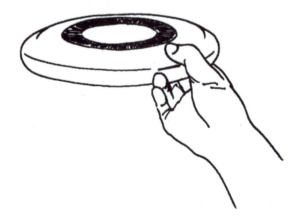

Throwing grip

2. Stand with the throwing-side shoulder in the direction of intended flight.
3. For a backhand throw, bring the Frisbee across to the other side of the body and then propel it forward.
4. For a sidearm (or forehand) throw, swing the arm backward and then rotate it forward along the same side of the body. The Frisbee should roll off the middle finger.
5. For an underhand throw, bring the Frisbee backward in an underhand motion and then release it at waist height on the upward swing.

6. Cock or snap the wrist on release, and follow through with the body and back leg.

7. Point the fingers toward the target on the follow-through.

Catching

1. For a one-handed catch,
   - position the hand with the thumb up if the Frisbee falls below the chest.
   - position the hand with the thumb down if the Frisbee approaches above the chest.
2. For a two-handed (or sandwich) catch,
   - place one hand on top and the other on the bottom of the Frisbee;
   - alternatively, bring both hands together to grasp the outside rim of the Frisbee.

Two-handed (sandwich) catch

Teaching Cues

1. Students should not try to throw too fast or too far when beginning to work on their throws. Rather, they should concentrate on developing a smooth motion and putting the proper spin on the Frisbee.

2. Explain the importance of utilizing body power—not just the force of the arms—when developing distance in throwing.

Activities (30-40 Minutes)

1. Present the Frisbee throw and catch, emphasizing the skill and teaching cues. Introduce the 3 types of throws (i.e., backhand, sidearm [forehand], and underhand) and the 2 types of catches (i.e., one-handed and two-handed). (6-8 minutes)

Backhand throw

Sidearm (forehand) throw

2. Frisbee passing drill. Form two lines of equal numbers of students 10 yards (9.14 meters) apart at one end of the field. Two students run side by side downfield, tossing the Frisbee back and forth diagonally while moving. When the first 2 students are a quarter of the distance downfield, the next 2 begin. After completing the drill, students should return to the end of the line by running along the sidelines. Repeat four times. (6-8 minutes)

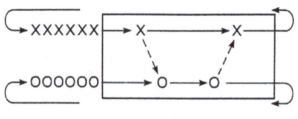

Frisbee passing drill

3. Divide students into groups of three and position them in an area on the field approximately 15 by 15 yards (13.71 by 13.71 meters). (Use cones to mark off these areas.) Explain and play the game of keep away. (6-8 minutes)

Keep Away

Two students pass a Frisbee back and forth while the third student attempts to intercept the pass. Every completed pass is worth 1 point. When a pass is intercepted, the student that threw the pass switches places with the one who intercepted it.

4. Speed flow drill. Pair up students or have them select partners and position each pair in an area on the field (use the same area squares as in activity 3). At the signal, partners try to make as many catches as possible in 1 minute. After 3 minutes, students should change partners. (6-8 minutes)

5. Back-off drill. Use the same partners as in activity 4 or have students choose new partners. Position each pair on the field approximately 16 yards (14.63 meters) apart. Partners then throw the Frisbee back and forth, taking a step backward every time a catch is made. The purpose of this activity is to help students develop accuracy in their throws. (6-8 minutes)

Closure (3-5 Minutes)

Review the lesson with students. Use the following ideas to reinforce learning, check understanding, and provide feedback.

1. Discuss the factors students must take into account when throwing to a teammate who is moving downfield (i.e., speed that the teammate is traveling and distance of the throw).

2. Give students the assignment of spending at least 20 minutes throwing and catching a Frisbee with a classmate before the next class session.

Lesson 2

Guarding, Pivoting, and Intercepting

Purpose

In this lesson students learn how to guard, pivot, and intercept for the game of ultimate Frisbee.

Facility and Equipment

- Outdoor playing area or indoor gym
- 1 Frisbee per 4 students
- 1 colored pinnie per 2 students
- 24 cones

Warm-Ups (6-8 Minutes)

1. Agility run
2. Wrist rotation and flexion
3. Shoulder shrugs
4. Phalange flings

Skill Cues

Guarding

1. Stand with a wide base of support keeping the knees bent.
2. Stay in front of the thrower and keep the arms out to the side at all times.

Guarding position

Intercepting

1. Catch the Frisbee, do not just knock it down.
2. No body contact is allowed.

Pivoting

1. Keep one foot in place, rotating on the ball of the foot.
2. Fake the opponent by pivoting another direction quickly, then throwing.

Teaching Cues

1. In the 1-on-1 (i.e., person-to-person) defense, each player guards a specific opponent.

2. In zone defense, each player covers an area of the field.

3. Explain the following offensive strategies against guarding and intercepting:
   ▶ Prevent interceptions by avoiding long, cross-field, and hanging passes.
   ▶ Show students how to disguise their intentions from their opponents (e.g., not looking directly at the intended receiver, pivoting another direction quickly, then throwing).

4. Emphasize the importance of always guarding the thrower. This may require switching from 1-on-1 to zone defense, and vice versa, throughout the game.

Activities (30-40 Minutes)

1. Introduce guarding, pivoting, and intercepting, emphasizing the skill and teaching cues. (5-6 minutes)

2. Divide students into groups of 4: 2 passers and 2 interceptors. Position each group in an area 15 by 15 yards (13.71 by 13.71 meters) on the field (use cones to mark off these areas). Two students throw the Frisbee back and forth while the other 2 students attempt to intercept each pass. At each successful interception, throwers and interceptors switch roles. Have students change partners after 4 minutes. (8-12 minutes)

3. Divide students into groups of 6, 2 teams of 3 each. In an area 20 by 20 yards (18.28 by 18.28 meters), teammates attempt to pass the Frisbee as many times as possible without being intercepted by the other team. Each successful pass is worth 1 point; if the pass is intercepted, teams switch roles. At the end of the game, the team with the most points (i.e., successful passes) wins. (8-12 minutes)

4. Pass and run. Use the same teams as in activity 3 or have students form new teams and mark off (using cones) an area of the field 20 by 30 yards (18.28 by 27.43 meters). Each group (6 students, 3 per team) moves across the field. The team with the Frisbee attempts to pass (while running) and the other team attempts to intercept the passes (using zone or 1-on-1 defense). At each interception, teams switch roles. (9-10 minutes)

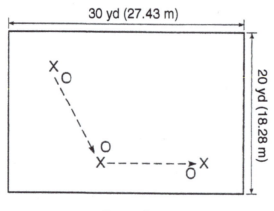

Pass-and-run

Closure (3-5 Minutes)

Review the lesson with students. Use the following ideas to reinforce learning, check understanding, and provide feedback.

1. Review the key points of guarding in ultimate Frisbee (e.g., 1-on-1 or zone defense may be used, the arms should be kept out to the side).

2. Select 3 students to demonstrate an interception: 2 students pass back and forth while the other student attempts to intercept. Have them demonstrate how pivoting can be used to fake out an opponent.

Lesson 3

Regulation Game

Purpose

In this lesson students learn the rules and play a regulation game of ultimate Frisbee.

Warm-Ups (6-8 Minutes)

1. Running in place
2. Waist twists
3. Shoulder pushes
4. Inverted hurdler's stretch

Facility and Equipment

◆ Outdoor playing area or gym
◆ 1 Frisbee per game
◆ 1 colored pinnie per 2 students
◆ 4 cones

Skill Cues

Offensive Throwers

1. Use pivots and fakes to avoid interception of passes.
2. Make fast passes.
3. Time throws properly so that teammates can receive the Frisbee.

Offensive Receivers

1. Catch the Frisbee as soon as possible (i.e., avoid letting it float); run toward and snatch it to prevent the opponent's opportunity to intercept.
2. Move around the field to remain open for a pass.

Defensive Players

1. Guard receivers and throwers by moving forward, backward, and sideways.
2. Focus on the thrower and receiver.

Teaching Cues

1. Emphasize the importance of fair play in the game of ultimate Frisbee. Ask students to call the plays themselves rather than try to violate the rules without being caught.
2. To avoid accidental hits and collisions, point out the importance of staying aware of other players and flying Frisbees.
3. Discourage pushing, shoving, and other body contact.

Activities (30-40 Minutes)

1. Present the skill cues to instruct players how to play their positions, emphasizing the teaching cues. Review the mechanics of 1-on-1 (i.e., person-to-person) defense and zone defense. (4-5 minutes)

2. Discuss offensive strategies, including explaining the following positions, and present the rules of ultimate Frisbee (see the unit introduction on page 581). (6-7 minutes)

   ▸ Quarterbacks or handlers (throw passes)
   ▸ Middle receivers, or mids (receive medium-length passes)
   ▸ Long receivers, or longs (receive long passes)

3. Divide students into 2 teams of up to 12 players each. (If class size is too large, divide students into 4 teams and play 2 games simultaneously.) Play a game of ultimate Frisbee. (20-28 minutes)

Optional Activity

Four-Team Ultimate Frisbee (0-25 Minutes)

This game is just like ultimate Frisbee, except 4 teams play at 4 goals on a square field (i.e., 1 goal and end zone on the north, east, south, and west ends). Divide the class into four teams. Each team attempts to score in their own end zone while defending the other three end zones. For more challenge, use more than one Frisbee in the game.

Closure (3-5 Minutes)

Review the lesson with students. Use the following ideas to reinforce learning, check understanding, and provide feedback.

1. Discuss ways to improve team play (e.g., move to the sides of the field to be in an open receiving position, anticipate the flight path and direction of the Frisbee, catch passes quickly without much float, and so on).

2. Have students describe the purpose of each player position.

Lesson 4

Games of Accuracy

Purpose

The first of two lessons in which students get to play other games using a Frisbee, this lesson concentrates on improving throwing and catching accuracy.

Warm-Ups (6-8 Minutes)

1. Jump rope or jump rope laps
2. Side stretch
3. Arm rotators
4. Side slides
5. Achilles tendon stretch

Facility and Equipment

◆ Outdoor playing field (at least 15 by 50 yards [13.71 by 45.72 meters]) or large gym
◆ Frisbees
◆ 4 cones
◆ 2 ropes (52 yards [47.55 meters] long)
◆ 1 jump rope per student
Note: The following number of Frisbees are required:

  Guts: 1 per game
  Double disc court: 2 per game
  Twobee: 2 (of different sizes) per game

Skill Cues

1. To make the Frisbee move quickly, use a fast wrist motion when throwing.
2. Point the fingers in the direction of the throw to improve accuracy.
3. If a catch is missed, the player can attempt to recover by hitting the Frisbee upward to keep it in the air.
4. Control Frisbee velocity (i.e., the rate of forward motion); if velocity overpowers the amount of spin (i.e., the rate of rotation), the Frisbee will flip over.

Teaching Cues

1. Review the skill cues for throwing and catching (see lesson 1).
2. Tell students to concentrate on accuracy when throwing.
3. Explain the importance of utilizing body power—not just the force of the arms—when throwing for distance.
4. Nail the ropes into the ground to form double disc courts (see activity 2).
5. Extra playing areas will be needed to accommodate more than one game of double disc court and twobee.

Activities (30-40 Minutes)

1. Present the technique for throwing accuracy, emphasizing the appropriate skill and teaching cues. (3-4 minutes)
2. For a class size of 24, divide the class into 14 teams: 2 teams of 4 each for one game of guts, 4 teams of 2 each for two games of double disc court, and 8 teams of 1 each for four games of twobee. Explain the rules for the following games

and have the group of teams at each game rotate to a different game every 9-12 minutes. Rotation could be as follows: The 8 (1-student) twobee teams rotate to double disc and form 4 (2-student) teams. The 4 (2-student) double disc teams rotate to guts and form 2 (4-student) teams. The 2 (4-student) guts teams rotate to twobee and form 8 (1-person) teams. (27-36 minutes)

Guts

Each team of four players lines up an arm's length apart along parallel goal lines 15 yards (13.71 meters) apart. The team with the Frisbee throws a hard, fast pass through the opposing team's line. The offense scores 1 point when the thrower gets a playable throw through the line. If the throw is unplayable, the opposing team gets 1 point.

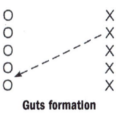

Guts formation

A playable throw

- ▷ does not strike the ground before the catch,
- ▷ does not travel higher than the height of the shortest opponent's outstretched arm (have all players stretch their arms overhead at the beginning of the game),
- ▷ does not travel outside the reach of the outside players (i.e., the players on the end of each line), and
- ▷ is not thrown at a vertical angle greater than 90 degrees.

The receiving team tries to catch the Frisbee (with one hand; the Frisbee cannot be trapped by the body or caught with two hands) to prevent it from crossing through the line. If the receiving team does not make a one-handed catch, the throwing team scores 1 point. If the receiving team makes a good catch, no points are awarded. The first team to reach 21 points with at least a 2-point lead wins the game.

Double Disc Court

This game is played on two courts 13 by 13 yards (11.88 by 11.88 meters) separated at a distance of 16 yards (14.63 meters). Each 2-player team starts on its own court with 1 Frisbee. On the signal to start, both teams throw their Frisbees at the same time into each other's court. The objective is to throw the Frisbee within the boundaries of the opponent's court while catching the opponent's throw.

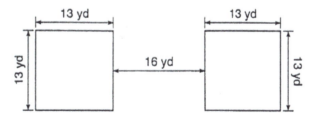

Double disc court dimensions

Rules and scoring are as follows:

- ▷ Each team must toss its own Frisbee before catching the opponent's thrown Frisbee.
- ▷ When a team drops a Frisbee or throws a Frisbee outside the court boundaries, the opposing team scores 1 point.
- ▷ When both Frisbees are in a team's court at the same time, the opposing team scores 2 points.

The first team to score 15 points with at least a 2-point lead wins the game.

Twobee

Two players stand 10 to 15 yards (9.14-13.71 meters) from each other. The object of the game is to score points by catching two different-sized Frisbees. One player throws both Frisbees, one after the other. The receiver attempts to catch both Frisbees, then becomes the thrower.

Rules and scoring are as follows:

- ▷ Catching both throws is worth 2 points.
- ▷ No points are scored if only one Frisbee is caught.
- ▷ Receivers score 1 point for each illegal throw (i.e., outside of the receiver's reach or out-of-bounds).

The first player to reach 15 points with at least a 2-point lead wins the game.

Closure (3-5 Minutes)

Review the lesson with students. Use the following questions to reinforce learning, check understanding, and provide feedback.

1. Which game required the most speed in throwing?
2. Which game was the most challenging?
3. How could these games be modified for future play?

Lesson 5

Target Games

Purpose

The second lesson in which students get to play other games using a Frisbee, this lesson focuses on improving throwing accuracy by introducing a target.

Warm-Ups (6-8 Minutes)

1. Scissors
2. Elbow-knee touches (standing)
3. Body circles
4. Arm pumps

Skill Cues

1. When throwing for accuracy, grip the Frisbee firmly.
2. A throw's direction depends on the angle of the Frisbee upon release.
3. For precise flight trajectory toward a target, increase the amount of spin on the toss.

Teaching Cues

1. Review the skill cues for throwing (see lesson 1).
2. Continually remind students to concentrate on throwing accuracy.
3. Explain the importance of utilizing body power—not just the force of the arms—when throwing for distance.

Activities (30-40 Minutes)

1. Present the skill and teaching cues, explaining how each is important to the target games in this lesson. (3-4 minutes)
2. Position students in groups of 4 or 5 players to play 3 of the following Frisbee target games. Each game should last 9 to 12 minutes. (27-36 minutes)

Floating Frisbee

In groups of three, one player holds a hula hoop. Another player stands 5 feet (1.52 meters) away and tosses the Frisbee through the hoop to be caught on the other side by the third player. The group travels down the field by switching

Facility and Equipment

- Outdoor playing area or large gym
- Poster board and markers
- 2 cones
- 1 target (or cone)
- 1 hula hoop per 3 players
- 14 wood pins or bowling pins
- Frisbees

Note: The following number of Frisbees are required:

F-R-I-S-B-E-E: 1 per player
Discathon: 2 per player
Mobile accuracy: 1 per game and 2 per player
Floating Frisbee: 1 per 3 players
Disc pin: 1 per 3 players

positions: the thrower holds the hoop, the hoop holder becomes the new catcher, and the catcher becomes the thrower. To add a competitive element to the game, have two or more groups race down the field. If the Frisbee fails to travel through the hoop, the group cannot travel.

Discathon

Players are in constant motion from start to finish in this game. The object is to throw and retrieve Frisbees along a course in the least amount of time. Each player has two Frisbees to start. Playing on a winding course of several hundred yards or meters, players throw their first Frisbee and then run to where it lies. When within 1 yard (.91 meters) of the first Frisbee, that player throws the second Frisbee and retrieves the first, then runs to the second Frisbee, and so on. The first player to get a Frisbee across the finish line wins.

Mobile Accuracy

Divide students into groups of 4 or 5 players (each gets 2 Frisbees) and place 1 Frisbee on the ground (this is the target). Players take turns throwing their own Frisbees at the target. The player whose Frisbee lands closest to the target scores 1 point. If the Frisbee actually touches the target, the player scores 2 points. The winner of the round throws the target Frisbee to the next target position and play continues. The first player to score 11 points wins.

F-R-I-S-B-E-E

This is like the basketball shooting game of H-O-R-S-E, except players throw Frisbees at a target (or cone). Divide students into groups of 2 or more players. The first player throws the Frisbee at a target. If the player makes the shot (i.e., hits the target), the second player must throw the same shot from the same place. If the first player misses, the second player gets to try a different shot, and so on. When players miss, they get a letter—F, then R, then I, and so on. Once players receive all the letters (i.e., F-R-I-S-B-E-E), they are out of the game. The last remaining player (i.e., without all the letters) wins.

Disc Pin

Divide the class into two teams and position them along two lines 20 to 30 yards (18.28-27.43 meters) apart. Place 7 pins on each team's line. The object of the game is to knock down the other team's pins. The first team to knock down all of the opponent's pins wins the game.

The rules of disc pin are as follows:

▶ Players must throw from behind their end line.

▶ Players may move forward to retrieve any Frisbee that lands on their half of the playing area (but must move back to their end line to throw).

▶ All throws must be aimed at the opponent's pins, not at players.

Closure (3-5 Minutes)

Review the lesson with students. Use the following ideas to reinforce learning, check understanding, and provide feedback.

1. Discuss the factors or skills most important in playing each game.
2. Ask students to come up with game variations for future play.

Assessment and Resources

Skill tests and game play assessment can be formal or informal in this unit. Formal testing can be conducted on such things as the rules of ultimate Frisbee and certain throwing and catching skills. You can also use many of the lesson drills for testing or give separate skill tests. In general, testing students on throwing and catching is sufficient.

The following lesson activities could be adapted for testing purposes:

- ▶ Speed flow drill (see lesson 1, activity 4)
- ▶ Pass and run (see lesson 2, activity 4)
- ▶ Double disc court (see lesson 4, activity 2)
- ▶ Mobile accuracy (see lesson 5, activity 2)

In addition, the following testing may be used for assessment purposes in this unit. Assessment protocol is listed with each.

▶ Hoop target throw. Place a hoop in a vertical position, preferably on a stand. From a distance of 20 feet (6.1 meters), each student tries to throw the Frisbee through the hoop. Total the number of successful throws from that distance; if desired, increase the distance to 25, 30, and 35 feet (7.62, 9.14, and 10.67 meters).

▶ Hit the cone. Place four cones on the ground at 5-foot (1.52-meter) intervals, each cone labeled with the following point values:

Cone 1	1 point
Cone 2	2 points
Cone 3	3 points
Cone 4	4 points

From a starting line 10 feet (3.05 meters) from the first cone, each student throws five Frisbees, attempting to hit the cones with the highest point values. Total each student's score (the maximum score is 20).

Resources

Fronske, H. 2001. *Teaching cues for sport skills*. 2nd ed. Needham Heights, MA: Allyn & Bacon.

Horowitz, J., and B. Bloom. 1983. *Frisbee: More than a game of catch*. New York: Leisure Press.

Pangrazi, R., and P. Darst. 1997. *Dynamic physical education for secondary school students: Curriculum and instruction*. 3rd ed. Needham Heights, MA: Allyn & Bacon.

Roddick, D. 1980. *Frisbee disc basics*. Englewood Cliffs, NJ: Prentice Hall.

Single-Day Lessons

Designed to be taught in a single day (hence the title of this section), the 30 lessons in this section provide an alternative teaching plan for those days when students need some variety. Indeed, a break in class routine often spurs interest and improves motivation among students. These lessons can also be used when teachers do not wish to begin a new unit—for example, before term changes, school vacations, and holidays.

This section differs from the previous sections inasmuch as each lesson is not part of a unit. That is, these 30 lessons are not connected to a particular sport, game, or activity. Because each lesson stands alone, the following sections of introduction apply to all lessons contained herein.

Social Skills and Etiquette

Before introducing each activity, it is best to emphasize the following:

- Cooperation
- Respect for others
- Group cohesiveness
- Fair play
- Adherence to rules
- Acceptance of decisions

Perseverance and patience should also be encouraged, particularly to less-skilled students trying an activity for the first time and to skilled students who may find other students' low skill levels frustrating (e.g., during group games and activities). Set the atmosphere for these behaviors by holding preliminary discussions with students or by stopping the activity for discussion if an inappropriate behavior occurs.

Lesson Modifications

Like unit lessons in sections II through IV, these lessons can be adapted for special-needs students. Such modifications usually involve the following:

- Changing the size of the playing area
- Substituting larger or different types of balls or playing implements
- Increasing the number of players
- Eliminating or altering some of the rules
- Setting different levels of performance expectations

When appropriate, such modifications are suggested in the activity description.

Rules

Rules, special terminology, and playing surfaces are provided in the lessons where appropriate.

Section Structure

The single-day lessons offer a potpourri of physical activities and skills that are both challenging and fun. Structured around rhythms, folk dance, games, self-testing tasks, and fitness activities for individual, small-group, and full-class participation, the lessons in this section focus more on learning by doing than on teaching by skill analysis. Most of the activities encompass skills that were previously learned, so no specialized instruction is necessary. Some of the activities stress cooperation and team building, while others are based on competition with self or others. A sampling of the activities in this unit include bocce ball, climbing rope, climbing wall, continuous cricket, crackle ball, hand hockey, jump bands, mat ball, modified hocker, scatter club bowls, and wall ball.

Each lesson in this section has the same structure, explained in the following listing.

▶ Lesson title. Rather than specific skills, each lesson is appropriately titled according to the games or activities. Lessons are not numbered but are arranged alphabetically in this section.

▶ Purpose. As in all previous lessons in this book, the primary objectives of each lesson are listed.

▶ Facility and Equipment. This listing provides an overview of materials needed to deliver the lesson as well as where the lesson should be conducted. Most of the single-day lessons involve activities that do not require additional or expensive equipment. Equipment for some of the activities may not be a part of the typical inventory, however, so adjustments, substitutions, or purchase may be necessary. Note: an asterisk (*) following a facility or equipment listing indicates that preparation is required before the lesson.

▶ Warm-Ups. The warm-ups found in each lesson are both general and specific, general to engage the entire body in motion and specific to prepare the muscles that will be used most frequently in the lesson activities. If suggested warm-ups do not meet the needs of students, they can be modified accordingly.

Note: Cool-down activities are not listed in this section. Nevertheless, it is advisable to allow some time for cooling down at the end of each lesson or during the lesson closure.

▶ Skill Cues. Skill cues are listed to help identify the critical psychomotor elements of each major skill. Present these elements during the lesson, generally in the first activity.

▶ Teaching Cues. These are pedagogical suggestions for setting up the learning environment to accommodate the instructional process more effectively.

▶ Safety Tips. Because each lesson stands on its own, safety considerations differ from lesson to lesson. In addition to those listed, the authors recommend staying alert to situations in the physical environment, in the activity, and in the interaction of students that could increase the risk of injury.

▶ Activities. As noted earlier, a potpourri of challenging and fun physical activities and skills are presented in the activities listing. Like every lesson in this book, single-day lesson activities are a progressive series of tasks, from the simplest to the most complex. They can be expanded to cover two class periods or shortened to accommodate shorter class times.

▶ Optional Activities. As in other lessons in this book, some of the single-day lessons suggest optional activities that can be used if more skill practice is needed before moving to the next activity or to replace a regular activity.

▶ Closure. This part of the lesson serves as a review, suggesting ways to reinforce lesson instruction and keep students thinking about the activities they did during class. As noted earlier, cool-down activities can be incorporated into each lesson closure. For example, students can sit or stand and slowly stretch various muscles while participating in class discussion.

▶ Variations. This heading is unique to the single-day lessons. Variations offer ways to change one or more activities to make it more or less challenging, more fun, and so on. Primarily intended to stimulate more challenge and interest for students, to increase class participation, and to promote safety when moving the activity from indoors to outdoors, or vice versa, variations can significantly improve a game or activity for players who are at a beginning skill level. Although these lessons are intended for a single class period, adding variations can also extend the lessons over more days. This may be appropriate if student interest is high or skill mastery requires more time.

▶ Resources. The assessment component of the assessment and resources chapters in sections II through IV units has been dropped from single-day lessons. Instead, resources listings simply provide sources of additional information or equipment for some of the lesson activities. Assessing student performance is neither necessary nor useful in single-day lessons because

- they are taught in one day and are not intended to span several days or weeks, as were the instructional units in sections II through IV; and
- the majority would fall under subjective measures of attitude, cooperation, and participation, although a few single-day lessons lend themselves well to quantifying performance (e.g., balance and flexibility stunts, climbing rope, and kickball golf).

Balance and Flexibility Stunts

These stunts have been modified from the Iowa-Brace Test, first published in the 1927 book *Measuring Motor Ability*, by D.K. Brace (New York: A.S. Barnes).

Purpose

In this lesson students learn to control their bodies through different balance activities. Students are also required to listen to directions and practice their responses mentally before performing physically.

Facility and Equipment

◆ Gym or grassy outdoor area
◆ 1 score sheet* and pencil per student

Warm-Ups (6-8 Minutes)

1. Scissors
2. Extended body leg drops
3. Mad cat
4. Hip lifts
5. Reverse run

Skill Cues

1. Listen carefully and form a mental image of the stunt before beginning.
2. Concentrate on using the eyes and muscles to maintain balance.
3. Count in seconds.

Teaching Cues

1. Stress that these stunts are not tests; rather, they offer the opportunity to check balance and flexibility.
2. State the instructions for each stunt twice.
3. Do not allow students to try the stunt until you have repeated the instructions.
4. Allow three trials for each stunt. Each attempt, however limited, counts as a trial.
5. Create a score sheet template before class. The scoring system is as follows:

Safety Tip

◆ It may be advisable to use mats for each stunt. If mats are available, have two students share a mat.

Successful on the first trial	3 points
Successful on the second trial	2 points
Success on the third trial	1 point
Unsuccessful after three trials	0 points

6. Partners should alternate starting roles after each two stunts so that neither student has the advantage of seeing all the stunts performed by one partner before attempting them.

7. Have students count the number of seconds using "one thousand" spacers between each count (i.e., "1, one thousand; 2, one thousand; 3, one thousand," and so on).

Activities (30-40 Minutes)

1. Present the purpose of the lesson and the instructions for participation using the appropriate skill and teaching cues. Pass out scorecards and have students write their name at the top of their cards. (3-4 minutes)

2. Position students in partners in two lines, facing each other and about 6 feet (1.83 meters) apart. Direct partners to watch each other closely, count the seconds aloud, and record scores on their partner's score sheets. Partner A tries the first 2 stunts (i.e., hop backward and one-knee balance), partner B tries the next 2 stunts (i.e., stork stand and half left turn), partner A tries the next 2 (i.e., crossed-leg squat and side leaning rest), partner B the next 2 (i.e., grapevine and the top), and partner A the next 2 (i.e., one-knee head to floor and single squat balance). Then partner B tries the first 2 stunts (i.e., hop backward and one-knee balance), partner A the next 2 (i.e., stork stand and half left turn), and so on. (24-30 minutes)

Partner stunt formation

The stunts are as follows (be sure to have students visualize performing each stunt as you read them—twice):

▸ Hop backward. Stand on either foot and, with closed eyes, take one hop backward; then hold the position for 5 seconds. The attempt is unsuccessful if students open their eyes, drop the raised foot, or do not hold the position for a full 5 seconds.

▸ One-knee balance. Kneeling on one knee, raise the other leg off the floor with the arms outstretched to the sides; balance and hold for 5 seconds. The attempt is unsuccessful if students touch the floor with any other body part (i.e., besides the knee) or do not hold the position for a full 5 seconds.

▸ Stork stand. Standing on the left foot, place the bottom of the right foot against the inside of the left knee. Place the hands on the hips and close both eyes; then hold this position for 10 seconds without shifting the left foot. The attempt is unsuccessful if students withdraw the right foot, move the left foot, or do not hold the position for a full 10 seconds.

▸ Half left turn. Stand with the feet together, jump into the air, make a half turn to the left, and land facing the opposite direction. Maintain balance and do not move the feet after landing. The attempt is unsuccessful if students move either foot after landing or do not complete a full half turn.

▶ Crossed-leg squat. Stand, fold the arms across the chest, cross the feet, and sit down cross-legged; then get up without unfolding the arms or moving the feet. The attempt is unsuccessful if students uncross their arms, rock forward more than once to rise to a stand, or move their feet.

▶ Side leaning rest. Sit in a pike position (i.e., legs out straight with feet together); then put the right hand on the floor behind the back. Turn to the right and take a side-leaning rest position, resting only on the right hand and the right foot. Raise the left arm and hold this position for 5 seconds. The attempt is unsuccessful if students do not take the proper position or do not hold it for a full 5 seconds.

▶ Grapevine. Stand with both heels tightly together; then bend down and extend both arms down between the knees and around the back of the ankles. Hold the fingers together in front of the ankles without losing balance for 5 seconds. The attempt is unsuccessful if students fall over, do not hold the fingers of both hands together, do not hold the position for a full 5 seconds, or do not keep the feet flat on the floor.

▶ The top. Sit down with the arms between the legs (under and behind the knees) and grasp the ankles. Roll rapidly around to the right, weight first over the right knee, then the right shoulder, then the back, then the left shoulder, and finally the left knee. Sit up facing the opposite direction. Repeat from this position, finishing the top by facing in the same direction as at the start. The entire sequence should be one continuous action until sitting in the starting position. The attempt is unsuccessful if students stop before reaching the starting position, let go of their ankles, or do not make a complete circle.

▶ One-knee head to floor. Kneel on one knee with the other leg outstretched behind the back and not touching the floor. Extend the arms out at the sides, parallel to the floor, bend forward and touch the head to the floor; then raise the head from the floor without losing balance. The attempt is unsuccessful if students touch the floor with the raised leg or with any other body part before completing the stunt, do not touch the head to the floor, or touch the floor with either hand.

▶ Single squat balance. Squat down as far as possible on either foot. Stretch the other leg forward and off the floor, and place the hands on the hips; then hold this position for 5 seconds. The attempt is unsuccessful if students remove the hands from the hips, touch the floor with the extended foot, or do not hold the position for a full 5 seconds.

3. Have students total the scores, sign their own names, and return the score sheets to their partners. (3-6 minutes)

Closure (3-5 Minutes)

Review the lesson with students. Use the following questions and ideas to reinforce learning, check understanding, and provide feedback.

1. Discuss the role of the eyes and muscles in maintaining good balance.
2. Ask students which stunts were the easiest. The hardest?

3. Inform students of the following score results:

20 or above	Very good balance and flexibility
Between 10 and 19	Good balance and flexibility
Below 10	Poor balance and flexibility

Variation

Give students a handout of the stunts and let the partners read and evaluate the performance of the other or use 10 stations and let students work independently (reading, performing, and recording).

Resources

Brace, D.K. 1927. *Measuring motor ability.* New York: A.S. Barnes.

Batting Options

Purpose

In this lesson students learn the rules for and play batting options.

Warm-Ups (6-8 Minutes)

1. Sprint-jog intervals
2. Push-offs
3. Side stretch
4. Hip stretch

Skill Cues

1. Use a backswing to increase force and momentum on the ball.
2. Follow through in the direction of intended travel.
3. Producing a backspin or forward spin on the ball makes the ball more difficult to catch.
4. Use a trajectory of 45 degrees when striking the ball to maximize the distance traveled.
5. Use both hands to catch the ball.

Teaching Cues

1. Organize two separate games to maximize participation.
2. To increase understanding and speed up learning time, demonstrate the game while explaining the rules.
3. Review striking, throwing, and catching skills (see softball lessons 1 and 5 on pages 312 and 321).
4. Emphasize that fielders must not throw the ball at runners to get them out; the way to stop a runner's progress is to throw the ball to the pitcher.
5. Do not play a certain number of outs. Teams should switch positions after everyone on a team has batted once.

Facility and Equipment

◆ Gym or large outdoor area with a baseball diamond
◆ Batting equipment
Note: A variety of batting equipment should be used—for example, tennis racket and tennis ball, pickleball paddle and ball, hockey stick and small ball, Wiffle bat and ball, cricket bat and ball, and so on. If students will bat by kicking, throwing, or serving the ball, a kickball, Nerf soccer ball, Nerf volleyball, and Nerf football can be used.

Safety Tips

◆ Do not allow students to purposely throw the ball at another player. Any dodge ball activity should result in time out from the game.
◆ A softer ball (e.g., foam ball) can be used if safety becomes a factor in the game.
◆ Space the playing fields far enough apart so that players in one game do not collide with players in another.

Activities (30-40 Minutes)

1. Introduce the game using the appropriate skill and teaching cues. (3-4 minutes)
2. Divide students into two teams, fielders and batters. Explain the rules of the game; then play batting options. (27-36 minutes)

Batting Options

The basic sequence is as follows: The game begins with one team up to bat. Each batter steps up to home plate and chooses one of the batting implements available. Batters toss and then strike the ball, then run as many bases as possible until the pitcher receives the ball. Fielders retrieve the ball and either tag the runner or throw it to the pitcher. The inning continues until all players on a team have batted once. Then teams switch positions (i.e., batters become fielders and vice versa) and play continues. The team with the most runs wins the game.

The following rules apply:

▶ Once the pitcher has possession of the ball, all runners must stay on their bases. Runners who move after the pitcher has the ball are out.

▶ Fielders get runners out by catching the batted ball on the fly or tagging the runner with the ball.

▶ Players may not throw the ball at runners or other players.

▶ Batters may not use the same equipment as the two previous batters.

▶ No batter is allowed to use the same equipment twice during the game.

Closure (3-5 Minutes)

Review the lesson with students. Use the following questions and ideas to reinforce learning, check understanding, and provide feedback.

1. Discuss which batting implements produced the best hits. Why?
2. Ask students to think of game strategies that would strengthen the offense.
3. Ask students to think of strategies that would assist the defense.

Bocce Ball

Purpose

In this lesson students learn the rules and play the game of bocce ball.

Warm-Ups (6-8 Minutes)

1. Arm rotators
2. Arm pumps
3. Upper body rotations
4. Knee lifts
5. Jog around the perimeter of the gym for 3 minutes

Skill Cues

1. Use an underhand motion when throwing the bocce ball toward the target ball (pallina).
2. Release the ball with the throwing hand either
   - ▸ with the palm up, using wrist flexion, which imparts a forward spin on the ball, or
   - ▸ with the palm down, extending the wrist, which imparts a backspin on the ball.
3. The backspin throw will cause the ball to have more height and to travel a shorter ground distance.
4. The forward spin throw will cause the ball to roll farther on the ground.

Teaching Cues

1. Encourage students to try both the backspin and forward spin throwing methods.
2. Before class, mark the play area with court markings of 12 by 60 feet (3.66 by 18.29 meters), or modify the dimensions to fit the facility.
3. If students will be playing without court markings, emphasize not to toss the pallina more than 20 to 30 feet (6.1-9.14 meters).
4. Regulation bocce balls, including the pallina, are made of solid wood. If necessary, substitute softballs for the bocce (throwing) balls and tennis balls for the target (pallina) balls.

Safety Tips

- Tell players not to approach the pallina (target ball) until all players have completed their tosses.
- To avoid accidental collisions between students and with balls, provide ample space for each team to play.

Activities (30-40 Minutes)

1. Explain the skills needed to play bocce ball using the appropriate skill and teaching cues. (2-3 minutes)
2. Divide the class into groups of 4. Give 2 bocce balls to each student and 2 pallina balls to each group of 4. Explain the rules of bocce ball. (5-6 minutes)
3. Play a regulation game of bocce ball. (23-31 minutes)

Bocce Ball

The object of the game is to roll the bocce balls closest to the pallina (smaller ball). Every bocce ball that lands closer to the pallina than the bocce balls of the opposing team is worth 1 point at the end of the frame. The first team to score 12 points is the winner.

Standing anywhere inside the court, the starting team tosses the pallina within the court boundaries and tosses the first bocce ball to establish the point (or in) ball. The opposing teams then throw their bocce balls until the point is taken (i.e., another ball falls closer to the pallina) or until all bocce balls are thrown. The team or person whose ball is in steps aside and allows the "out" teams to deliver their bocce balls. This continues until all bocce balls are played.

The rules are as follows:

▸ Players may hit any other balls, including the pallina, to change their position.

▸ Any bocce ball thrown or knocked out-of-bounds is disqualified and out of play.

▸ If the pallina is knocked out-of-bounds, the frame ends (no points are awarded) and the pallina is put back into play by the same team or person who threw it in the previous frame.

▸ To start a new frame, the team that scored in the previous frame tosses the pallina and the first bocce ball.

▸ Any member of a team can toss the pallina, and this task can be rotated among team members.

Closure (3-5 Minutes)

Review the lesson with students. Use the following ideas to reinforce learning, check understanding, and provide feedback.

1. Discuss the difference between the backspin and forward spin (i.e., with a backspin the ball is thrown higher and doesn't travel much after hitting the ground; with a forward spin the ball is thrown low and rolls on the ground most of the distance toward the target).
2. Ask students to identify strategies that can be used in playing bocce ball.
3. Give examples of scoring situations to determine if students can properly keep score.

Variations

1. Bocce ball can be played without any limitations on court boundaries. Students could continue to move through the playing area by throwing the pallina in any direction or distance.

2. The rotation sequence can also be changed to require each person or team to toss one ball at a time at the pallina. In other words, teams can alternate throws at the pallina.

Resources

American Shuffleboard Company. 1988. *How to play American custom deluxe shuffleboard with instructions for shuffleboard, bowling, five spot, horse collar, baseball, grand slam, bocce, and poker.* Union City, NJ: American Shuffleboard Company.

Brisket Ball

Purpose

In this lesson students learn the rules and play the game of brisket ball.

Warm-Ups (6-8 Minutes)

1. Leg stretch
2. Lateral hops
3. Arm rotators
4. Hip lifts
5. Arm circles

Skill Cues

1. The skills used in this game are running, passing, catching, and guarding.
2. Use either a forward overhand pass or an underhand lateral pass to pass the ball.

Teaching Cues

1. Review running, passing, catching, and guarding skills.
2. If the class is not divisible by 5, develop a rotation system to ensure that all students participate. Students can practice the skills of catching and passing while waiting to get into the game.

Activities (30-40 Minutes)

1. Divide the class into teams of five players. Present and review the skill and teaching cues for the game of brisket ball. (4-6 minutes)
2. Explain the rules and then play brisket ball. (26-34 minutes)

Brisket Ball

The object of the game is to run the ball across the goal line and into the opposing team's end zone (between the wall and goal line) for a touchdown. At the end of the game, the team with the most points wins.

Five players per team are on the court at a time. The game begins with a jump ball in the center circle. Play is continuous until a team scores a goal or the ball goes out-of-bounds. A goal is scored when a player in possession of the ball runs, without being tackled (i.e., pulling the flag), over the opposing team's goal line. This is a touchdown, worth 6 points.

(continued)

Brisket Ball

A team can also score with a free throw (worth 2 points). Free throws are awarded when the player with the ball passes to a receiver inside the opponent's key. The following rules govern the free throw:

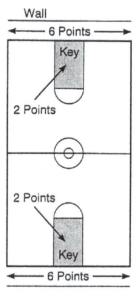

Brisket ball scoring

▶ The ball must be thrown from outside of the opponent's 3-second lane (the area identified "key" in the diagram).

▶ After a successful free throw, the other team (i.e., the team that didn't score) brings the ball back into play from behind its own end zone.

▶ If the free throw is missed, the ball is "live" and the game continues.

The following rules apply to brisket ball:

▶ Players may pick up the ball off the ground or catch it as a pass.

▶ Defensive players may not contact the offensive receiver before the receiver touches the ball.

▶ When in possession of the ball, players may run with the ball or pass to a teammate.

▶ If a player is tackled (indicated by a pulled flag) while in possession of the ball, the player stops and then passes the ball without interference to another teammate.

▶ If the ball goes out-of-bounds, the team that last touched the ball gives possession to the opposing team, which inbounds the ball from the point it went out-of-bounds.

Closure (3-5 Minutes)

Review the lesson with students. Use the following ideas to reinforce learning, check understanding, and provide feedback.

1. Discuss offensive strategies that yield success in brisket ball.
2. Highlight the defensive strategy necessary to stop opponents from scoring a free throw.
3. Have students identify the brisket ball skills used in other major sports (e.g., flag football, football, basketball).

Resources

Gustafson, M., S. Wolfe, and C. King. 1991. *Great games for young people.* Champaign, IL: Human Kinetics.

Cage Ball Games

Purpose

In this lesson students learn to play various cage ball games, including scooter soccer, parachute cage ball, and mat crash.

Warm-Ups (6-8 Minutes)

1. Slapping jacks
2. Arm circles
3. Spinal curls
4. Mad cat

Skill Cues

1. Use a striding motion with the feet to propel the scooter while sitting in an upright position.
2. Bring the foot from the floor or ground upward to kick the cage ball.
3. Use full arm motion (upward and downward) when moving the parachute.

Teaching Cues

1. To increase action and participation, use more than one cage ball for mat crash.
2. Demonstrate each game while explaining the rules to increase understanding and speed up learning time.
3. Encourage students to use teamwork. Strategy and cooperation are important in all of the activities.
4. A single class period may be inadequate for completing all of the activities in this lesson. Choose those that are best suited for your students, or expand the lesson into two or more class periods.

Facility and Equipment

- Gym or grassy outdoor field
- 1 or more cage ball(s)
- 4 cones
- 1 colored pinnie per 2 students
- 1 scooter per student
- 6 to 8 folding tumbling mats
- 1 parachute

Note: Choose an appropriately sized cage ball(s) for the grade level and age of students. For middle school students, the ball should be 2 to 3 feet [.61-.91 meters] in diameter; for high school students, 4 to 5 feet [1.22-1.52 meters] in diameter.

Safety Tips

- The following precautions should be emphasized during scooter soccer:

    Stay on the scooters at all times.

    Do not stand on the scooters.

    Do not place the hands on the floor where they might get rolled over by a scooter.

- Do not allow students to climb onto a cage ball and attempt to roll on it. This could result in an injury.

Activities (45-60 Minutes)

1. Introduce the games using the appropriate skill and teaching cues. (3-4 minutes)
2. Divide the class into two teams, explain the rules, and then play scooter soccer. (14-18 minutes)

Scooter Soccer

The object of the game is to send the cage ball over the opponent's goal line while traveling on a scooter. Students must sit on the scooters at all times. They propel the ball using only their feet, as is the case in regulation soccer. The team that scores the most points in 15 minutes wins.

To begin the game, line up each team near its own goal area. Toss the cage ball into the center. Both teams attempt to kick the ball into the opponent's goal. Each goal is worth a point. Penalty shots are awarded for the following:

- ▸ Getting off the scooter
- ▸ Advancing the ball with the hands
- ▸ Any rough play
- ▸ Holding an opponent

3. Divide the class into new teams, explain the rules, and play parachute cage ball. (12-18 minutes)

Parachute Cage Ball

The object of the game is for one team to roll the ball off a parachute over the heads of the other team. One team holds one side of the parachute while the other team holds the opposite side. The cage ball is placed in the center. Each team tries to roll or bounce the ball off the parachute so it bounces over the opposing team's heads, worth 1 point. (The momentum of moving the parachute up and down tosses the cage ball in the air.) The team that scores the most points in 10 minutes wins.

Parachute cage ball

4. Divide the class into two teams, explain the rules, and then play mat crash. (16-20 minutes)

Mat Crash

Stand the tumbling mats on end and scatter them around the gym area. Designate half of them as one team's and the other half as the opponent's by placing colored pinnies on top of the mats. Designate a crease area in front of each mat; opponents may not enter this area.

(continued)

The object of the game is to knock the opponent's mats over by kicking a cage ball into them. A team can only have one member guarding each team's mat (the goalie) and the guard must remain in a crab position. The remainder of the team is on scooters and attempts to kick the cage ball(s) into the opponent's mat(s) to knock them over. Play continues until all of one team's mats are knocked over, or for a certain amount of time (e.g., 5 minutes).

Closure (3-5 Minutes)

Review the lesson with students. Use the following ideas to reinforce learning, check understanding, and provide feedback.

1. Discuss the strategies of teamwork needed to play each cage ball game (e.g., keeping an eye on other teammates, delaying attempts to score until the optimum time).
2. Ask students to think of mat crash and scooter soccer strategies that would strengthen the offense.
3. Ask students to think of mat crash and scooter soccer strategies that would assist the defense.

Variations

1. Scooter soccer can be played without scooters by having students walk in a crab position.
2. Another variation of scooter soccer would be to divide each team into guards and forwards—forwards move full court and guards protect the goal line.
3. Parachute cage ball can be modified as follows: students roll the cage ball around the edge of the parachute as quickly as possible without allowing it to fly off. (Students need to produce a wave motion to accomplish this.) When a team's cage ball flies off the opponent's side of the parachute, the other team scores a point.

Resources

Fluegelman, A., ed. 1976. *The new games book.* New York: Doubleday.

Fluegelman, A., ed. 1981. *More new games!* New York: Doubleday.

Challenge Stunts

Purpose

In this lesson students test their strength, agility, and balance against peers of similar size.

Warm-Ups (6-8 minutes)

1. Lateral hops
2. Push-ups
3. Abdominal tighteners
4. Lower back stretch
5. Side slides

Skill Cues

1. In tug-of-war stunts, release the pull momentarily; then pull with a quick jerk.
2. For more stability in tug-of-war stunts, lower the center of gravity, use a wider stance, and flex the knees.
3. In the wand pull-up, extend the knees and straighten the legs quickly.

Teaching Cues

1. Pair or group students of similar weight and height.
2. Pair girls against girls and boys against boys.
3. Have students act as referees while waiting to perform a stunt.
4. For team challenge stunts (see activities 5, 7, 9, and 11), more points may be awarded.
5. White liquid shoe polish can be used to draw circles (activities 8 and 9) or lines (activity 11) on the floor; these markings may also be used in place of mats in activities 6 and 7.

Safety Tips

◆ Be sure to use mats for stunts that could result in injury.
◆ In pulling stunts, remind students not to let go of their opponents.

Activities (40-60 Minutes)

1. One-handed tug-of-war. Two students stand on opposite sides of a line, turn sideways, and take right hands; then they try to pull their opponents across the line. Play once or best 2 out of 3; then challenge another. (3-4 minutes)
2. Two-handed tug-of-war. Repeat activity 1, this time facing each other and using two hands. (3-4 minutes)

3. Leg wrestle. On a mat, two students lie on their backs, side by side, hips touching with each student's head next to the opponent's feet. Hook the inside arms and simultaneously raise the legs to a 90-degree angle three times. On the third time, bend the knees and hook the opponent's knee or ankle to pull the opponent over. Play best 2 out of 3; then challenge another. (3-4 minutes)

4. Tiger tail pull. Students tuck a flag or ribbon into the back of their waistbands. On a mat and on all fours, students face their opponents and try to steal each other's flag while protecting their own. A point is scored if an opponent loses the flag, does not remain on all fours, or goes off the mat. Play once or best 2 out of 3; then challenge another. (3-4 minutes)

5. Team tiger tail pull. In teams of 3 or 4 and on a large mat, repeat activity 4. When a flag is pulled, the player leaves the mat. The last team with a player on the mat wins. (4-8 minutes)

6. Rooster push. On a mat, two opponents squat down and grasp the front of their own ankles. In the squat position, each tries to shoulder push the other off the mat or force the other to let go of either ankle, scoring a point if either occurs. Play once or best 2 out of 3. (3-4 minutes)

7. Team rooster push. Repeat activity 6, this time using teams of 3 or 4 on a large mat. The last team with a player on the mat wins. (4-8 minutes)

8. Poison pin. Two opponents face each other inside a small circle, join hands, and stand at arm's length apart with a pin midway between opponents. At the signal, students start pulling or pushing, trying to force their opponents to knock over the pin. Students score a point when their opponents knock over the pin or step outside the circle. Play once or best 2 out of 3; then challenge another. (3-5 minutes)

9. Team poison pin. Repeat activity 8, this time with teams of 2 or 3 players in a larger circle. (5-7 minutes)

10. Wand pull-up. Two students sit facing each other with their knees flexed and their feet braced against their opponents'. Each takes a firm grasp of a wand, holding it between them. (If wands are not available, students may clasp hands.) At the signal, each tries to pull the other to a standing position. When one opponent stands, the other gets a point. Play once or best 2 out of 3; then challenge another. (3-5 minutes)

11. Team tug-of-war. Tie a flag in the middle of a rope and center it between two parallel lines 8 or 10 feet (2.44 or 3.05 meters) apart. At the signal, teams (of boys and girls or separated by gender, preferably of equal size or weight) pull on the rope, trying to pull the flag across their own line. Play best 2 out of 3; then challenge another. (6-7 minutes)

Closure (3-5 Minutes)

1. Review the lesson with students. Ask the following questions:
   - ▸ Which pair or team stunts were the most difficult? Why?
   - ▸ Which were the easiest? Why?
   - ▸ What role did strength, agility, and quickness play in these stunts?

2. Ask students to share their results, asking the following questions:
   - ▸ How many teams scored a victory? Two? Three? More?
   - ▸ How many students won a two-opponent match? Two? Three? More?
   - ▸ What was the key to success?

Variations

1. Rather than perform each activity in this lesson, set up a circuit, using one activity at each station. This is a good solution if sufficient equipment is not available.

2. Transform this lesson into a team contest by dividing the class into two or more teams. (Try to distribute height and weight evenly among teams.) Then students from one team challenge those of equal size from another for each contest. Keep a running team point total, scoring 1 point for each win.

Resources

Landy, J.M., and M.J. Landy. 1993. *Ready-to-use p.e. activities for grades 7-9*. West Nyack, NY: Parker.

Zakrajsek, D. 1969. Instructor notes. Unpublished manuscript.

Climbing Rope

Purpose

In this lesson students develop upper body strength while challenging themselves to focus on climbing techniques.

Warm-Ups (6-8 minutes)

1. Jump rope laps
2. Push-offs
3. Arm rotators
4. Shoulder shrugs
5. Push-up hold

Facility and Equipment

- Gym or facility with climbing ropes
- 1 mat per group
- 3 ribbons (different colors) per rope
- 1 large box or laundry basket or hoop per group
- 1 utility ball (6 or 8 inches [15.2 or 20.3 centimeters]) or beanbag per group
- 3 bowling pins per group
- 1 jump rope per student

Skill Cues

1. Climb hand over hand going up the rope.
2. Pull with the arms, letting the rope slide through the feet and knees.
3. Lock the feet around the rope after each pull, then straighten the legs and reach for another pull.
4. To lock the feet, let the rope hang on the outside of the left leg, under the left foot, and over the top of the right foot; then "stand" with the left foot on the rope to lock the feet.
5. To descend the rope, lock the feet and move the hands down the rope, hand under hand, lowering by flexing the knees and then lowering the legs.

Teaching Cues

1. When students are climbing, remind them to look up and hold the rope tightly.
2. When students are descending, caution against sliding down the rope; this can cause rope burns.
3. Team leaders or skilled climbers may be assigned as spotters or helpers.

Safety Tips

- Always place mats under the ropes.
- Do not let students stand near the ropes when others are using them.
- Do not let students climb swinging ropes.
- For swinging activities, all ropes should swing in the same direction.

Activities (44-60 Minutes)

1. Present the safety precautions and skill cues for climbing, locking the feet, and descending the rope. (2-3 minutes)

2. Divide the class into groups of equal numbers; one group for each climbing rope. Let students try to climb (to 8-12 feet [2.44-3.66 meters] above the floor) and descend the rope 2 or 3 times. Supervise practice climbs, providing feedback and encouragement, and note students' skill levels. (8-10 minutes)

3. Assign new groups and work with students who are having difficulty. For skilled climbers, encourage them to climb higher or increase their speed. (8-10 minutes)

4. Climbing game. Tie 3 colored ribbons at 3 different heights above the floor on each rope. For example, tie a yellow ribbon 6 feet (1.83 meters), a red ribbon 10 feet (3.05 meters), and a green ribbon 15 feet (4.57 meters) above the floor. (Heights can be adjusted to fit the skill level of the class.) Line up teams (of uniform skill levels) in single file behind each rope. Students get two chances to climb to a ribbon, each representing a different level of ability. (10-12 minutes)

   Use the following scoring system:

Unable to reach the first level (but try)	1 point
Reach (and touch) the lowest ribbon	2 points
Reach (and touch) the middle ribbon	3 points
Reach (and touch) the highest ribbon	4 points

5. Working with partners (optional), one student climbs to a position on the lower portion of the rope; the other pulls the rope back and releases, letting the student swing. To gain momentum, the swinger should spring with the body. Have students switch roles after two swings. (0-6 minutes)

6. Target drop. Repeat activity 5, but add a ball and retriever. Place a laundry basket or hoop (target) on the floor about 8 feet (2.44 meters) in front of the rope. (The distance and size of the target should depend on students' skill levels.) Climbers assume their positions on the lower portion of the ropes, then grip a utility ball or beanbag between their feet. Teammates pull the rope to swing the climbers forward. At the high end of the forward swing, climbers try to drop the ball in the target. Climbers get three chances to make the drop; then students switch roles. (8-10 minutes)

7. Swing and bowl. Repeat activity 6, this time setting three bowling pins in front of the rope. Rather than drop the ball into the target, students release the ball and try to knock over the pins. Bowlers get two chances to knock over the pins; then students switch roles. (8-9 minutes)

Closure (3-5 Minutes)

Review the lesson with students. Use the following questions and ideas to reinforce learning, check understanding, and provide feedback.

1. Have students explain and demonstrate locking the feet while rope climbing.
2. Ask students the following questions:
   ▸ What is the proper hand position for descending the rope?
   ▸ What is the reason for not sliding down the rope?
3. Explain which muscle groups are most used in climbing (i.e., triceps, biceps, pectorals, deltoids, quadriceps, and hamstrings).

Resources

Landy, J.M., and M.J. Landy. 1993. *Ready-to-use p.e. activities for grades 7-9*. West Nyack, NY: Parker.

Zakrajsek, D. 1984. British school notes. Unpublished manuscript.

Climbing Wall

Purpose

In this lesson students participate in climbing wall activities that build muscular strength, balance, coordination, and flexibility as well as challenge the mind with problem solving, spatial awareness, and motor planning.

Warm-Ups (6-8 Minutes)

1. Jump rope or jump rope laps
2. Shoulder shrugs
3. Hamstring straight-leg stretch
4. Single-leg curls

Facility and Equipment

- Gym or large outdoor playing area with a climbing wall
- Stopwatch
- 1 coin (e.g., penny, dime) per 2 students
- 1 jump rope per student
- Numbered pieces of tag board*

Skill Cues

1. The following grips, foot positions, and rock holds are used in wall climbing:

   ▶ Crimp. The crimp is the most common type of handgrip. The fingers bend to grasp the rock and the thumb wraps over the index finger.

   ▶ Pinch grip. In this handgrip the fingers and thumb squeeze the rock from either side. This grip can only be used on elongated rocks.

   ▶ Edging. In this foot position the edge of the shoe is placed on the rock. Various edges include the outside edge of the shoe, the inside edge of the shoe, and the forward edge of the shoe (i.e., the toe).

   ▶ Smear. This is another foot position in which the front, flat portion of the sole wedges against the wall.

Pinch grip

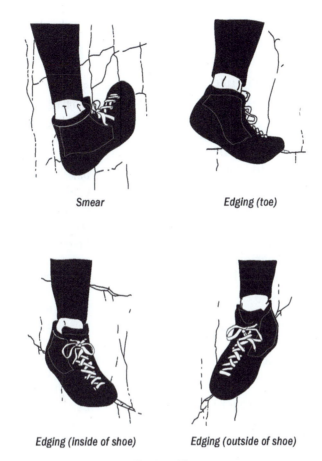

Smear   Edging (toe)

Edging (inside of shoe)   Edging (outside of shoe)

Foot positions

▸ Pocket. This is a type of rock hold that is cupped so that it provides a place to insert the finger or toe to grasp.

2. Repetitive wall climbing reinforces engrams, which are patterns of learned body movement registered in the brain. Once mastered, certain skills and movements do not require conscious thought to perform them. For example, riding a bike involves intricate skills and movement (e.g., balancing, peddling). Once children learn to ride a bike, however, it becomes automatic. It becomes an engram.

Teaching Cues

1. Emphasize the safety rules of climbing before using the wall.
2. Encourage cooperation rather than competition in climbing wall activities.
3. To increase understanding and speed up learning time, demonstrate an activity while explaining it.
4. Keep a watchful eye for signs of climbing fatigue. When muscles get tired from climbing, coordination deteriorates.
5. Attempt the more challenging individual activities when students are fresh. Save team activities for later in the class period.

6. This lesson's activities can be used on either a horizontal wall (traverse wall) or a vertical wall.

7. A single class period will likely be insufficient to complete all of the activities. Expand the lesson over several classes, or choose from among the listed activities. For example, choose from activities 3 through 6 according to students' skill and interest levels.

8. For activity 4, number small square pieces of tag board (i.e., 1, 2, 3, 4, and 5) before class. Then scatter the squares around the wall, in or under various climbing wall holds. (The squares can be placed under the edge of the holds.)

Activities (70-90 Minutes)

Note: The following activities can be used on either a horizontal (traverse) wall or a vertical wall.

1. Present the skill cues, teaching cues, and safety rules needed for climbing wall activities. (4-7 minutes)

2. Divide the class into groups of 2 or 3 so that every student has at least one spotter. Introduce wall climbing by having each climber advance only 10 feet (3.05 meters) to get accustomed to the hand and foot positions. (6-8 minutes)

3. Climbing intervals. Using proper safety and spotting procedures, have each student climb for 2 minutes and then rest. On the second round, have each student climb for 3 minutes and then rest. Continue to increase climbing time until students are able to climb for 5 minutes. (12-15 minutes)

4. Climbing for numbers. Assign each student a number; this is the sum total they must collect. During a 2-minute period, students take turns collecting the tag board squares placed on the climbing wall. The exact total must be reached. If climbers take a number that puts their total over the desired count, they must put the number back under a rock. When all students have had a turn, determine which students collected their sum total. (12-15 minutes)

5. Speed climbing. Students climb the wall twice. Time each climb and then have students compare the speeds of their first and second climbs. Note: This activity is not about competition between climbers; it is about self-challenge and personal improvement. (12-15 minutes)

6. Mystery coins. Divide students into groups of three. One student hides a coin in a rock hold while climbing. (Climbers should try to fool their teammates by faking various coin placements.) The next member of the group tries to figure out where the coin was placed, then attempts to climb to that rock hold and find the coin. Another group member hides the coin, and so on until all students have had a chance to hide and find the coin. (12-15 minutes)

Safety Tips

◆ Spotters must be used at all times for wall climbing.

◆ Students should always climb down, not jump, from the wall.

◆ Never allow students to walk or climb under other climbers.

◆ When two or more students are climbing the wall at the same time, keep several feet between climbers.

◆ Spotters should be instructed on their role, including how to support and assist a climber who is falling. On a horizontal wall, the spotter walks behind the climber with arms extended toward the climber. If the climber begins to slip or fall, a gentle support of the climber will often help him or her to regrasp and continue climbing. On a vertical wall, the climber cannot fall but the spotter's role is to hold the ropes tightly.

◆ Before each class, inspect all climbing equipment, including rock holds. If damaged or worn, equipment should be replaced.

7. One-arm climb. Note: This activity is very challenging and should only be attempted by more experienced climbers. The object is to use only one arm (but both feet) to climb the wall. Either arm may be used, but only one arm may be used per climb. (12-15 minutes)

Closure (3-5 Minutes)

Review the lesson with students. Use the following ideas to reinforce learning, check understanding, and provide feedback.

1. Discuss how students felt after completing a wall climb. Encourage students to share how they may have overcome the fear of heights, the fear of falling, or other mental barriers.

2. Ask students to compare the skills needed to climb a climbing wall with those needed for outdoor rock climbing (i.e., outdoor rock climbing does not have "rock holds" so the type of hand grip needed is not as obvious and therefore each move must be more carefully thought out; outdoor rocks may be rougher to grasp than the manufactured "rock holds" of a climbing wall; and the stretches between outdoor rock climbing maneuvers may be much more difficult depending on the natural state of the rock).

Variations

1. Speed climbing can be modified as follows:
   ▶ Set up teams of four (try to include students with various degrees of skill on each team).
   ▶ Each teammate climbs the wall and keeps track of their time.
   ▶ Have teams compare their times.

   For less-skilled climbers, have students climb a designated distance on the wall rather than climb the entire wall length.

2. The one-arm climb may be changed to a one-foot climb.

Resources

Hattingh, G. 1998. *The climber's handbook*. London: Stackpole Books.

Hyder, M. 1999. Have your students climbing the walls. *Journal of Physical Education, Recreation and Dance* 70 (9): 32-39.

Mittelstaedt, R. 1997. Indoor climbing walls: The sport of the nineties. *Journal of Physical Education, Recreation and Dance* 68 (9): 26-29.

Continuous Cricket

Purpose

In this lesson students learn the rules and play the game of continuous cricket.

Warm-Ups (6-8 Minutes)

1. Reverse run
2. Push-ups
3. Inverted hurdler's stretch
4. Side stretch

Skill Cues

1. Use an underarm motion to bowl the ball at the wicket.
2. Bowl the ball in a medium arc so that it bounces several feet in front of the batter.
3. Swing the bat in a full backward and upward motion before the downswing toward the ball.

Teaching Cues

1. Explain that runs are scored by running around one of two turning points (i.e., cones) and returning back to the crease (i.e., the line from which the batter hits).
2. Point out the importance of moving quickly so that the ball does not hit the wicket, which is behind the batter. Players are bowled out when they do not get back in time to hit the ball or they swing at a ball and miss it, allowing the ball to hit the wicket.
3. Tell students that they are not allowed to let the ball hit the leg of the batter as a means of protecting the wicket. This tactic is LBW, or leg before wicket.
4. For maximum participation, keep team size small; set up several games at a time.

Facility and Equipment

- Gym or outdoor area with a smooth surface
- 1 cricket (or softball) bat per game
- 1 cricket ball (or softball, or utility ball 6 inches [15.2-centimeter diameter]) per game
- 1 wicket per game
- 2 cones per game

   Note: A trash can, cone, or box may be used for the wicket. It should be at least 3 feet (.91 meters) high.

Safety Tips

- Set the game up so that the wicket keeper is at least 4 feet (1.22 meters) behind the batter and the batting team is well out of the batter's way.
- Never use a real cricket ball if playing indoors. (A cricket ball is much harder than a softball.) A 6-inch (15.24-centimeter) utility ball works best indoors.

Activities (30-40 Minutes)

1. Introduce continuous cricket using the skill and teaching cues. (2-3 minutes)

2. Divide the class into teams of 5 to 8 players and explain the rules of continuous cricket. (5-6 minutes)
3. Play the game of continuous cricket. Set a time limit for each game and then have the teams rotate to play a different team. (23-31 minutes)

Continuous Cricket

Two teams play per game: fielders and batters. The object of the game is for each player to take a turn at bat and score as many runs as possible without being bowled out, allowing leg before wicket (LBW), or being caught out. Each player on a team takes a turn at bat until all players have had a turn and then the other team is up to bat. As its name implies, there is continuous action in this game; batters do not rest between bowled balls.

The team bowler (similar to a pitcher, but the bowler aims for the wicket instead of sending the ball to the batter) bowls the ball at the wicket behind the bowling line. After each hit, the batter must run around 1 of 2 turning points and back to the crease (batting line). The batter scores a run with every completed run around one of the turning points.

The fielding team stops the ball as quickly as possible and throws the ball back to the bowler, who then bowls the ball immediately whether back to the crease or not. If a player is bowled out (i.e., the ball hits the wicket), an LBW occurs (i.e., the ball hits the leg of the batter), or the ball is caught by a fielder on a fly, the next batter must move quickly to the crease because the bowler is allowed to bowl again immediately.

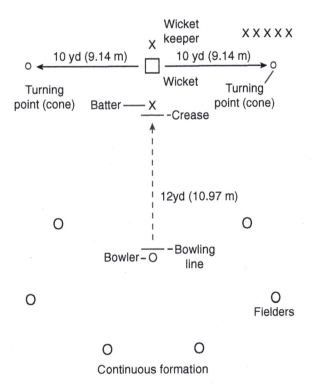

Continuous cricket field dimensions and positions

Closure (3-5 Minutes)

Review the lesson with students. Use the following ideas to reinforce learning, check understanding, and provide feedback.

1. Discuss what strategies might improve team play (e.g., directing the ball to open areas, fielding the ball more quickly).
2. For extra credit, have students find out more information about the game of cricket (e.g., its history, the countries in which it is played, necessary equipment, and so on).

Variations

Continuous cricket changes dramatically when using a different type of ball. If playing indoors, a utility ball or Nerf ball would be best. For outdoor play, a cricket ball or softball may be used. Finally, for more challenge, increase the distance to the turning points.

Resources

Australian Cricket Board. 2000. *Coaching youth cricket.* Champaign, IL: Human Kinetics.

Landry, J.M., and M.J. Landry. 1993. *Ready-to-use p.e. activities for grades 7-9.* West Nyack, NY: Parker Publishing.

Pangrazi, R., and P. Darst. 1997. *Dynamic physical education for secondary school students: Curriculum and instruction.* 3rd ed. Needham Heights, MA: Allyn & Bacon.

Werner, P., and L. Almond. 1990. Models of games education. *Journal of Physical Education, Recreation and Dance* 61 (4): 23-27.

Continuous Motion Physical Activity

Purpose

In this lesson students engage in nonstop activities that improve various aspects of fitness.

Warm-Ups (6-8 Minutes)

1. Mad cat
2. Russian floor kicks
3. Gluteal stretch
4. Push-offs
5. Upper body rotations

Skill Cues

1. Be alert and aware of nearby activity.
2. Remain in constant motion. Walk or jog between activities and while reading the task chart.
3. Select less-strenuous tasks when tired.
4. Return all equipment carefully to the area from which it was taken; do not throw or toss it.

Teaching Cues

1. Place the equipment in different areas; use hoops or boxes to contain balls.
2. Challenge students to jog rather than walk when not engaged in an activity.
3. Allow students to select the order of activities.
4. Make the charts simple (stick figures may help clarify certain activities) and be sure the words are large enough to read from 8 feet (2.44 meters) away.
5. Use floor lines to detail activities.
6. Encourage students on each task; offer positive feedback and correction when necessary.
7. Play lively music throughout the activity.
8. Use your own creativity to make up other simple activities, or enlist the help of students.

Facility and Equipment

- Gym or multipurpose area
- 6 hoops
- 6 jump ropes
- 6 scooters
- 6 paddles
- 6 beanbags
- 6 scoops
- 6 tennis balls
- 6 Wiffle balls
- 6 play balls (rubber)
- 6 volleyballs
- 2 wastebaskets
- 1 balance beam (low; use a floor line if a low balance beam is unavailable)
- 25 task charts*
- Music (CD or audiocassette) and player

Safety Tips

- Allow ample space between each activity.
- If the activity requires going around the gym, students should move in the same direction.
- Keep balls contained when not in use.
- Remind students to stay alert in high-traffic areas and to watch out for others.

Activities (30-40 Minutes)

1. Introduce the lesson as a fitness challenge that focuses on continuous body motion through a variety of stationary and moving activities. Explain the rules for participation using the skill cues, and encourage students to challenge themselves to finish each activity. Explain that students will have three trials for each activity; if unsuccessful after, they should move to another activity. Students who complete all tasks should repeat their favorite activities until the end of class. (5 minutes)

2. Have students perform the following activities. (25-35 minutes)

   ▸ Skip around the gym once with a jump rope.

   ▸ Do 25 slapping jacks and smile.

   ▸ With a partner, skip once around the gym side by side with inside hands on each other's shoulder.

   ▸ Do a partner wheelbarrow across the width of the gym; then switch roles on the way back. Students should hold their partner's knees, not the ankles, and should not push.

   ▸ Wall volley 20 times with a volleyball.

   ▸ Lie on a scooter and, using the hands only, propel around the gym once.

   ▸ Jump rope 25 times in place.

   ▸ Hula hoop 10 consecutive times (around any body part).

   ▸ Leapfrog the length of the gym with a partner.

   ▸ Hit a tennis ball up into the air with a paddle 25 consecutive times. Start over after every miss.

   ▸ Jog the perimeter of the gym three times and smile.

   ▸ Lean over; balancing a play ball or volleyball on the back, walk the width of a volleyball court. No hands are allowed. Start over if the ball falls off.

   ▸ Do a seal walk (using only hands and arms) around the basketball key.

   ▸ Holding a play ball or volleyball between the knees, jump the width of a badminton court. Start over if the ball falls.

   ▸ Toss a beanbag up in the air, turn around, and catch it five consecutive times.

   ▸ Dribble a tennis ball with a paddle around the perimeter of a volleyball court.

   ▸ "Walk" one length of a volleyball court sideline using the following sequence: place one hand on the line, then the opposite foot in front of the hand on the line, then the other hand on the line, then the opposite foot on the line, and so on.

   ▸ Do 10 push-ups.

   ▸ Standing 20 feet (6.1 meters) from a partner, throw a Wiffle ball and catch it with a scoop 10 consecutive times.

   ▸ With a partner (2 students on 1 scooter), travel the length of the gym without either partner standing. Be creative.

   ▸ Jump rope with a partner 20 consecutive jumps.

▸ With a partner, hold a ball between backs (no hands) and walk two lengths of the gym (i.e., to one end and back again). Start over if the ball falls.

▸ From the free throw line, pitch three consecutive beanbags into a wastebasket placed under the basket.

▸ Walk the length of a balance beam forward, backward, and sideways without stepping off.

▸ Lying face up, toss a play ball or volleyball and catch it 10 consecutive times.

Closure (5 Minutes)

Review the lesson with students. Use the following ideas to reinforce learning, check understanding, and provide feedback.

1. Have students point to a spot on the floor across the room, walk to it in slow motion, lie down, close their eyes, stretch their body, and relax.

2. Give students pencils and paper and ask them to express how they feel physically and emotionally. (Students will usually say that they feel tired and sweaty but alive.)

3. Collect students' responses and talk about physical conditioning. Discuss whether their bodies met the demands of continuous activity, especially if they jogged between activities.

Crackle Ball

Purpose

In this lesson students develop throwing skills that focus on accuracy and force.

Warm-Ups

1. Grapevine step
2. Facedown flank
3. Abdominal crunches
4. Triceps dips
5. Sprint-jog intervals

Skill Cues

1. Throw forcefully.
2. Sight the target before throwing.
3. Pass quickly to a teammate if it is advantageous offensively or defensively.

Teaching Cues

1. Instruct students to throw using the principles of opposition and total body assembly.
2. Remind students to focus on the target while throwing.
3. Start with fewer balls and add more as needed.
4. Remind sideline players to stay within a step of the throwing line.
5. Rotate players so that all get a chance to play sideline or end line positions.
6. If scoring is too difficult, use fewer goalies; use more goalies if scoring is too easy.
7. Use a smaller court (e.g., volleyball court) for smaller class sizes or special-needs students.

Activities (30-40 Minutes)

1. Divide students into two teams, give pinnies to one team, have players get into position, and discuss the rules of the game. Players stand around the perimeter of the court: 3 or 4 players from one team behind the end line and 3 or 4 players from the other team behind the opposite end line, both facing center court. All

Facility and Equipment

◆ Gym or playing field
◆ 1 very large utility ball (16 to 20 inches [40.6 to 50.8 centimeters]) or beach ball
◆ 1 small utility ball (4 to 6 inches [10.2 to 15.2 centimeters]) per 3 to 4 students
◆ 1 pinnie per 2 students
Note: Gym walls will restrict straying balls.

Safety Tip

◆ Tell students to stay alert; watch for oncoming balls.

other players stand along the sidelines, alternated by team (i.e., player from team 1, player from team 2, player from team 1, player from team 2, and so on). Place the large ball in the center of the court and give an equal number of small balls to opposing team sideline players. (5 minutes)

2. Play a game of crackle ball. (25-35 minutes)

Crackle Ball

The object of the game is to make the large ball roll over the opposing team's goal (i.e., end line) by throwing the small balls at the large ball. (Players will be throwing their balls in the opposite direction.) When a goal is scored, the large ball is placed back in the center and play proceeds. At the end of the game, the team with the most goals wins.

The rules of the game are simple. Players committing rule infractions must sit in a penalty area for 2 minutes. Separate rules apply to end line and sideline players.

Sideline players stand along the sidelines and try to propel the large ball down the court to the opposing team's goal. They

  ▶ may not move along the sideline to gain a throwing advantage;
  ▶ may take no more than two steps into the court to retrieve a ball; and
  ▶ must have one foot on or outside the sideline before throwing.

End line players pick up loose balls that pass over the end line or receive and throw balls passed from their teammates to block or redirect the oncoming large ball. They

  ▶ must be completely outside the court area at all times (i.e., neither foot can be on or over the end line), leaving the goal line free;
  ▶ may take no more than two steps into the court to retrieve a dead ball; and
  ▶ must be back in position (i.e., outside and not touching the end line) before throwing.

All players may retrieve loose balls that go outside the court but must be back in position before throwing.

Closure (3-5 minutes)

Review the lesson with students. Use the following questions to reinforce learning, check understanding, and provide feedback.

1. What principles of movement helped to create more force in throwing the ball (i.e., opposition, follow-through, total body assembly)?
2. What strategies helped in scoring? In defending the goal line?
3. Were any skills more important for some positions than others? If so, which skills? If not, why?

Create a Game

Purpose

In this lesson students work in small groups to create a game of their own.

Warm-Ups (6-8 Minutes)

1. Jump rope or jump rope laps
2. V-sit toe taps
3. High jumper
4. Shoulder pushes

Facility and Equipment

◆ Gym or large outdoor playing area
◆ 1 jump rope per student
◆ Paper and pencils
◆ Various game equipment

Note: Game equipment can include different types of balls, rackets, bats, bases, cones, hula hoops, jump ropes, scooters, mats, and so on.

Skill Cues

1. Use a variety of skills in each game. Skills could include catching and throwing, kicking, striking, running, jumping, and so on.
2. Work cooperatively; try to involve everyone in the decision-making process and be open to everyone's ideas.

Teaching Cues

1. Group students who can work cooperatively.
2. Discuss the principles of cooperation (e.g., giving positive feedback, being open to all ideas).
3. Provide students with guidelines for creating their games (e.g., equipment, time needed to play, appropriate ages, necessary safety precautions, and rules).

Activities (30-40 Minutes)

1. Introduce game creation using the appropriate skill and teaching cues. (2-3 minutes)
2. Divide the class into groups of 3 or 4 students. Assign each group their own area of the gym. If necessary, designate boundaries between each group using cones. (2-3 minutes)
3. Explain the following parameters of creating a game. (3-4 minutes)
    ▶ Each group is allowed 18 to 22 minutes to create a game.
    ▶ The game can use any of the equipment supplied.

Safety Tips

◆ Explain that inappropriate use of some equipment could be unsafe—for example, using a bat without assured adequate distance between players.
◆ Provide adequate space for each group to work to avoid collisions with other groups of students.

- The game should be suitable for ages to (decide on an age range before class). The greater the age, the more specific the skills and rules should be.
- Skills that could be used in each game are catching, throwing, jumping, running, kicking, striking, and so on; select certain skills before class.
- When designing a game, think about safety; specify safety rules when recording the game.
- When all group members agree on the game, come up with a game name. Then record the rules and procedures of the game on paper. This should include a written list of the rules and any diagrams necessary for understanding.

4. Allow time for each group to create a new game. (18-22 minutes)
5. Have all groups present their games to the entire class. (5-8 minutes)

Closure (3-5 Minutes)

Review the lesson with students. Use the following ideas to reinforce learning, check understanding, and provide feedback.

1. Discuss the essential elements of every game, and the rationale for these elements.
2. Have students vote on the game they like best.
3. Tally the votes and announce that the two favorite games will be played during the next class period.

Deck Tennis

Purpose

In this lesson students learn the rules and play the game of deck tennis.

Warm-Ups (6-8 Minutes)

1. Sprint-jog intervals
2. Hip lifts
3. Curl-ups
4. Mad cat

Skill Cues

1. Catch the ring with one hand.
2. Throw the ring with the same hand in which it is caught.
3. Do not use a downward motion with the ring.
4. Release the ring below the shoulder in an upward motion.

Teaching Cues

1. Demonstrate the ring pass before beginning play.
2. Explain that students may pass the ring to another player on their team; this is a good strategy to catch the other team off guard.
3. An optimal team size is 8 to 11 players, but team size can be adjusted to meet class and student needs. It would be best to use 2 nets and play 2 separate games if team sizes exceed 12.

Activities (30-40 Minutes)

1. Explain the pass and catch used in deck tennis using the appropriate skill and teaching cues. Then divide the class into teams of 8 to 11 players and explain the rules of deck tennis. (6-8 minutes)
2. Position players on the court and have them play the game. (24-32 minutes)

Facility and Equipment

- 1 or 2 volleyball courts (indoor or outdoor)
- 1 6-inch (15.2-centimeter) rubber deck tennis ring per game
- 1 volleyball net per game

Safety Tips

- To prevent accidental hits in the face or head, caution students to stay alert when the ring is thrown.
- Avoid accidental collisions when two or more students try to catch the ring simultaneously by having students watch for others.

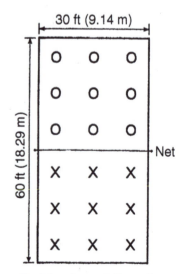

Deck tennis court dimensions and positions

Deck Tennis

The object of the game is to keep the ring traveling back and forth across the net while attempting to cause the opponent to miss. Deck tennis can be played until everyone is eliminated on one team (the other team wins) or until a certain amount of time has elapsed (the team with the most remaining players wins).

Any player on one of the teams starts the game; there are no servers. Players pass and catch the ring across the net until a miss occurs. When a miss occurs, any player on the team that has the ring continues the game by throwing it back over the net. A miss is counted when a player

- ▶ drops the ring,
- ▶ throws the ring into the net,
- ▶ fails to get the ring over the net,
- ▶ throws the ring out-of-bounds,
- ▶ catches the ring with two hands instead of one,
- ▶ does not throw the ring from the hand that caught it, or
- ▶ makes a downward motion with the ring.

When misses occur, offending players are eliminated; they must stand on the sideline until a teammate gets them back in. Teammates get players back into the game by throwing the ring over the net so that the other team does not try to catch it, called a *dead ring*. (Players often try not to catch the ring if they are concerned they will miss it and, thus, be out of the game.) Players reenter a game in the order in which they were eliminated.

At any time during the game, the ring may be passed to another teammate. Any number of passes to teammates are permitted while playing.

Closure (3-5 Minutes)

Review the lesson with students. Use the following topics to reinforce learning, check understanding, and provide feedback.

1. Discuss what students could do to improve their team strategy (e.g., throw the ring to areas of the opposing team's weakness, return the ring quickly so the other team has little time to get ready).

2. Ask students to compare deck tennis to other sports. Which skills are similar (e.g., volleyball, Frisbee, badminton, tennis, pickleball)?

Variation

Instead of the elimination rules, deck tennis can be played using volleyball rules, including server rotation and scoring. The following deck tennis rules should be added to volleyball rules in this version of the game:

- ▶ The ring must be caught in one hand.
- ▶ The ring must be caught and thrown by the same hand.
- ▶ The ring cannot be thrown in a downward motion or released above the shoulder.

Resources

AMF and VOIT. 1962. *Official rules for deck tennis.* Santa Ana, CA: AMF and VOIT, Inc.

Bailey, G. 2000. *The ultimate sport lead-up game book.* Camas, WA: Educators Press.

Pangrazi, R., and P. Darst. 1997. *Dynamic physical education for secondary school students: Curriculum and instruction.* 3rd ed. Needham Heights, MA: Allyn & Bacon.

Hacky Sack Challenge

Purpose

In this lesson students learn Hacky Sack skills and play a challenging game.

Warm-Ups (6-8 Minutes)

1. Scissors
2. Sit and stretch
3. Neck stretch
4. Squat holds

Skill Cues

1. Use the inside edge of the toe and foot to strike the Hacky Sack.
2. The Hacky Sack must always travel upward and outward, never downward.
3. When striking the Hacky Sack with the feet and other body parts (e.g., hands, arms), align the body and the Hacky Sack and follow through in the intended direction of motion.

Teaching Cues

1. Team students together by ability. This will make play more challenging and engaging.
2. Demonstrate technique while explaining the rules to increase understanding and speed up learning time.
3. Spend time developing Hacky Sack skills before introducing a game.

Activities (30-40 Minutes)

1. Explain how to strike a Hacky Sack using the appropriate skill and teaching cues. (2-3 minutes)

Facility and Equipment

- Gym or large outdoor area
- Paint or chalk
- 1 Hacky Sack per 4 or 5 students

Note: The playing area is 6 by 6 feet (1.83 by 1.83 meters), consisting of four individual squares 3 by 3 feet (.91 by .91 meters). If outdoors, paint the individual squares; if indoors, draw them with chalk.

	3 ft (.91 m)	3 ft (.91 m)
3 ft (.91 m)	Square 2	Square 1
3 ft (.91 m)	Square 3	Square 4

Hacky Sack challenge playing area

Safety Tips

- To avoid collisions, space the game squares far enough apart.
- Do not allow students to purposely aim a Hacky Sack at other students.

2. Pair up students or have them select partners. Have student pairs practice volleying the Hacky Sack. (4-5 minutes)

3. Divide the class into teams of 4 or 5 players, one team per game square. Explain and demonstrate the rules; then play a game of Hacky Sack challenge. (17-23 minutes)

Hacky Sack Challenge

The object of the game is to send the Hacky Sack to other players and cause those players to miss. The ultimate goal is to become the lead player and occupy square 1 for as long as possible.

Each of the 4 players stands in a square; in the case of 5 players, the fifth player stands outside of square 4. The player in square 1 is the lead player and starts the Hacky Sack in motion by striking it to any of the other players. The Hacky Sack must be kept in the air and volleyed from player to player. Players may use any part of the body to strike (no catching) the Hacky Sack. The volley continues until a player misses, at which point the player who missed moves to square 4 and the rest of the players move "up" a square (i.e., rotate to the next lower-numbered square) to fill any vacancies. (With 5 players, the player who misses rotates out of the game square, just outside of square 4, and player 5 rotates into the game at square 4. Other players move up a square to fill vacancies.)

A miss occurs if

▶ a player causes the Hacky Sack to fall to the ground or floor; the last player to contact it goes to square 4.

▶ the Hacky Sack goes out-of-bounds after a player contacts it; the last player to contact it goes to square 4.

▶ a player spikes the Hacky Sack; the player who spikes it goes to square 4.

▶ the Hacky Sack drops downward (rather than upward and outward) into another player's square; the last player to contact it goes to square 4.

▶ a player catches the Hacky Sack rather than strikes it; the player who caught it goes to square 4.

4. Form new teams and play another game of Hacky Sack challenge. (7-9 minutes)

Closure (3-5 Minutes)

Review the lesson with students. Use the following ideas to reinforce learning, check understanding, and provide feedback.

1. Ask students to come up with some different rules and variations for Hacky Sack challenge.

2. Have some of the skilled students demonstrate a few of their Hacky Sack techniques.

Resources

Games Kids Play

www.gameskidsplay.net

Posts rules of this and other fun games.

Hand Hockey

Purpose

In this lesson students concentrate on striking skills and teamwork.

Warm-Ups (6-8 Minutes)

1. Horizontal run
2. Mad cat
3. Hip lifts
4. Hamstring curls
5. Mule leg pushes

Facility and Equipment

- Gym or outdoor area
- 1 medium utility ball (6 to 8 inches [15.2-20.3 centimeters])
- 1 pinnie per 2 students
- 4 cones

  Note: More cones are required for an outdoor area.

Skill Cues

1. Pass quickly using either hand.
2. Keep the ball moving.
3. Maintain balance by keeping the center of gravity low.

Teaching Cues

1. Remind students not to crowd around the ball.
2. Change defenders after each goal or after a certain time period (e.g., 4 minutes).
3. Promote teamwork. If necessary, add a rule for grandstanding. For example, if certain players take over the game and shut out others, they have to sit in the penalty box for 2 minutes.
4. If teaching this lesson in a gym, use a basketball court and place a cone at each corner line. If play will be outside, use extra cones to mark end lines and sidelines.

Activities (30-40 Minutes)

1. Divide the class into two teams and distribute pinnies to one team. Each team should assign four goal defenders who will stand outside the goal line. All other teammates are offensive players. (5 minutes)
2. Scatter team players around their own half of the court and explain the rules. Play hand hockey. (25-35 minutes)

Hand Hockey

The object of the game is to score a goal by pushing, batting, or rolling the ball over the opponent's goal line. At the end of the game, the team with the most goals wins.

The game starts with a face-off in the center. The two center players tap the floor and hands twice, then bat or push the ball with their hands. After the face-off, all players may move freely around the entire court.

The rules of hand hockey are simple. Players may

- use only the hands and arms to advance (i.e., push, roll, or bat) the ball;
- not kick, throw, or loft the ball; and,
- when defending, step only one foot across the goal line to play the ball.

When a violation occurs, the opponent gets a free roll (i.e., no court players may defend) toward the goal. Players who continually violate the rules or play unnecessarily rough must sit in the penalty box for 2 minutes.

Closure (3-5 minutes)

Review and discuss the lesson with students, using the following questions to reinforce learning, check understanding, and provide feedback.

1. What strategies worked best for scoring (e.g., passing quickly, scattering throughout the playing area, faking out the opponents by pushing the ball in different directions to teammates)?
2. Which offensive plays made defending the goal difficult?

Variation

Play the same game with offensive players on scooters.

Resources

Landy, J.M., and M.J. Landy. 1993. *Ready-to-use p.e. activities for grades 7-9*. West Nyack, NY: Parker.

Initiative Activities

Purpose

This lesson focuses on activities that emphasize teamwork, trust, and group problem solving.

Warm-Ups (6-8 Minutes)

1. Lateral hops
2. Waist twists
3. Abdominal crunches
4. Arm rotators
5. Jog around the perimeter of the gym for 3 minutes

Teaching Cues

1. The primary purpose of these initiatives is to develop trust within a group.
2. Before class, give some consideration to how students will be grouped. There may be students who shouldn't be in the same group.

Facility and Equipment

- Gym or outdoor area
- 5 wooden cubes (24 by 24 by 18 inches [61 by 61 by 45.7 centimeters])
- 5 pieces of rope (10 feet [3.05 meters] long)
- 10 standards (5 to 6 feet [1.52-1.83 meters])
- 15 to 20 hula hoops
- 1 blindfold per 7 to 9 students
- Gymnastics mats

Safety Tip

- Use mats when playing faith fall (activity 2).

Activities (30-40 Minutes)

1. Introduce the initiative activities using the appropriate skill and teaching cues. (2-3 minutes)
2. Faith fall. Divide the class into groups of nine. One student, blindfolded, stands on an elevated object (e.g., a stage, balance beam, rolled mats). The rest of the group lines up in two lines facing each other and crosses arms with the wrists locked. Keeping the body straight without bending the legs and the hands folded across the chest, the blindfolded student falls backward into the arms of the rest of the group. (5-7 minutes)
3. Human circle pass. Groups of 7 or 9 students form a circle by clasping arms. One student stands in the middle of the circle, blindfolded and with the arms crossed. The student in the middle then falls backward into the arms of the group and is lifted back up and passed around the circle. (5-7 minutes)
4. Cube stand. The object of this activity is to get as many students as possible on a wooden cube. Students may grasp hands and support themselves on the side of the cube. At least one foot of all students must be on the cube; the other foot may *not* be supported by another person. Have each group hold the pose on the

cube for at least 10 seconds; then have groups challenge each other to see who can stay on the cube the longest. (6-7 minutes)

5. Prison escape. Divide students into teams of five. (This activity works best with small groups.) The rope, which is 10 feet (3.05 meters) long and 5 to 6 feet (1.52-1.83 meters) off the ground, simulates a prison wall. Using only a small base of support (such as the cube used in activity 4), teammates try to move everyone over the wall without touching it. If a student touches the wall, he or she must move back into the prison and try again. (6-8 minutes)

6. Hooper. Divide students into groups of 8 or 9 and have each group form a circle by facing inward and holding hands. Insert 3 to 4 hula hoops into the circle by having selected students place their hands and arms through the middle of the hoops and then join hands. The goal of the activity is to pass the hula hoops completely around the circle without breaking the circle (i.e., without dropping one another's hands) at any time during the process. Groups may race the clock or each other. (6-8 minutes)

Closure (3-5 Minutes)

Review the lesson with students. Use the following ideas to reinforce learning, check understanding, and provide feedback.

1. Discuss the importance of developing trust in other team members to accomplish each activity.

2. Identify different strategies each group used to climb the prison wall (activity 5).

Resources

Glover, D.R., and D.W. Midura. 1992. *Team building through physical challenges.* Champaign, IL: Human Kinetics.

Pangrazi, R., and P. Darst. 1997. *Dynamic physical education for secondary school students.* 3rd ed. Needham Heights, MA: Allyn & Bacon.

Juggling

Purpose

In this lesson students gain hand-eye coordination and improve their timing and rhythm, self-confidence, and patience while learning the skills of scarf and beanbag juggling.

Warm-Ups (6-8 Minutes)

1. Agility run
2. Sprint-jog intervals
3. Slapping jacks
4. Push-ups
5. Arm rotators

Facility and Equipment

◆ Gym or large outdoor playing area with a wall
◆ 3 juggling scarves (3 colors) per student
◆ 3 beanbags per student
◆ Stopwatch

Skill Cues

Scarf Juggling

1. Hold and catch the scarf (palm down) between the thumb, index finger, and middle finger.
2. Get height on the lift to keep the scarves floating longer.
3. Use sweeping and flowing arm movements to lift the scarf across the body, releasing at the highest point on the opposite side.

Beanbag Juggling (Cascading)

1. When catching the beanbags, hold the hands (palms up) near the waist; each toss should be approximately 2 feet (.61 meters) high.
2. Place 2 beanbags (beanbags 1 and 3) in one hand and 1 beanbag (beanbag 2) in the other hand. The juggling sequence is as follows:
   ▶ Start with the hand that has two beanbags in it, tossing beanbag 1 into the air.
   ▶ When beanbag 1 peaks (i.e., reaches the highest point of the toss), toss beanbag 2 across and underneath beanbag 1.
   ▶ Toss beanbag 3 when beanbag 2 peaks, tossing it across and underneath beanbag 2. (Beanbags 1 and 3 are now in the opposite hand.)
3. Repeat the sequence again and again for continuous juggling.
4. For continuous juggling, no more than one beanbag can be in each hand—that is, a beanbag should always be in the air.

Teaching Cues

1. Using the part-whole method, teach each skill separately; then add the next skill once students become proficient.
2. For scarf juggling use the phrase "lift and release." Also use scarf colors as verbal cues (e.g., yellow, orange, pink, or right, left, right if three colors are not available).
3. For beanbag juggling, the tosses should be made with quick wrist action, and the bags should be visible without much head motion (tosses should be 2 feet [.61 meters] in the air).
4. Two distinct peaks should mark each beanbag throw and these peaks should reach the same height.
5. Watch for frustration among students having difficulty. Work with them individually by manually moving their arms to help with the lifting rhythm.
6. Plastic grocery bags and dress netting can be substituted for scarves and will actually float longer.
7. Yarn balls may be used in place of beanbags.
8. Do not attempt ball juggling before students are proficient with beanbags. (Balls roll away too easily.)
9. The activities in this lesson can be easily extended to two or more days of instruction. Consider extending the lesson if students are not reaching a minimum level of success as they progress through the activities.

Activities (60-80 Minutes)

The first nine activities pertain to scarf juggling and are a good way to start instruction for students who have never juggled before or may lack confidence. If the class is ready for beanbag juggling, begin the lesson at activity 10.

1. Introduce scarf juggling and remind students that this is a skill that takes patience and practice. Give each student three scarves, one of each color. Scatter students around the gym and demonstrate scarf juggling using the appropriate skill and teaching cues. (3-4 minutes)
2. Basic lift, release, and catch. Use only one scarf. Demonstrate the following sequence and have students practice it five times with each hand. (2-3 minutes)
   ▶ Hold the scarf in the right hand (between the thumb, index finger, and middle finger).
   ▶ Lift the right arm as high as possible (palm down), and gently flick the wrist just before the scarf reaches the highest point.
   ▶ Release the scarf into the air.
   ▶ As the scarf floats downward, catch it at waist level with the thumb, index finger, and middle finger of the same hand (palm down).
3. One-scarf lift, release, and catch. Use one scarf. Demonstrate the following sequence and have students practice it five times with each hand. (3 minutes)
   ▶ Hold the scarf in the right hand.
   ▶ Bring the right arm across the body.

> ▸ Lift the arm and release the scarf at the highest point on the left side.

> ▸ Catch it with the left hand on the left side of the body at waist level.

4. Two-scarf lift, release, and catch. Use one scarf. Demonstrate the following sequence; then have students practice it at least five times (or until all are successful) using both hands. Call out "right hand, left hand, catch, catch" to keep students on track. (4 minutes)

> ▸ Hold two scarves, one in each hand, and both at waist level and slightly out to sides.

> ▸ Lift the right arm across the body and release the scarf on the left side.

> ▸ Lift the left arm and release the scarf on the right side.

> ▸ Catch the first scarf with the left hand at waist level, then the second scarf with the right hand at waist level.

5. Three scarves and release. Use three scarves. Have students perform the following sequence to learn how to hold and release the scarves. Repeat at least three times or until all students are proficient. (3-4 minutes)

> ▸ Take the center of one scarf (e.g., the red scarf) in the left hand and wrap the little finger and ring finger around the scarf to secure it. (Do not put the scarf between the fingers.)

First (red) scarf

> ▸ Take another scarf (e.g., the white scarf) in the left hand between the thumb, index finger, and middle finger.

> ▸ Hold the third scarf (e.g., the blue scarf) in the right hand.

> ▸ Lift and release the white scarf (i.e., the second scarf, held by the left hand between the thumb, index finger, and middle finger) and let it drop to the floor.

Both (red and white) scarves

Scarf holds

6. Three scarves and two releases. Instruct students to take the scarves in the same hands as they did in activity 5. They lift and release the white scarf (in the left hand); then they lift and release the blue scarf (in the right hand), reaching under the first throw across the body. Both scarves should fall to the floor on opposite sides of the body. Have students repeat several times, providing them with verbal cues: "white and blue" or "left and right." (3-5 minutes)

7. Three scarves and three releases. Instruct students to take the scarves in the same hands as they did in activity 5. They lift and release the white scarf (in the left hand), lift and release the blue scarf (in the right hand), then lift and release the red scarf (in the left hand). All scarves should fall to the floor on opposite sides of the body. Have students repeat several times, guiding them with verbal cues: "white, blue, red" or "left, right, left." (3-5 minutes)

8. Three scarves, 3 releases, and 3 catches. Have students perform the following sequence several times, guiding them with verbal cues: "white, blue, white, red, blue, red"; "lift, lift, catch, lift, catch, catch"; or "left, right, left, right, left, right." (4-5 minutes)

> ▸ Lift and release the white scarf with the left hand.

> ▸ Lift and release the blue scarf with the right hand.

- ▸ Catch the white scarf with the right hand.
- ▸ Lift and release the red scarf with the left hand.
- ▸ Catch the blue scarf with the left hand.
- ▸ Catch the red scarf with the right hand.

9. Juggling. This is the final progression after activity 8. Have students practice the following sequence individually. (5-7 minutes)

Start by lifting and releasing the white scarf with the left hand. Then repeat this sequence.

- ▸ Lift and release the blue scarf with the right hand.
- ▸ Catch the white scarf with the right hand.
- ▸ Lift and release the red scarf with the left hand.
- ▸ Catch the blue scarf with the left hand.
- ▸ Lift the white scarf and catch the red scarf with the right hand.
- ▸ Repeat.

10. Explain and demonstrate juggling with beanbags (cascading, reverse cascading, and showering) using the appropriate skill and teaching cues. (4-6 minutes)

11. Distribute three beanbags to each student. Tell students how to hold the beanbags (2 in the left hand and 1 in the right hand): hold a beanbag in the palm of each hand, using the fourth and third fingers; the third beanbag (in the left hand) can be held and tossed using a cradle formed by the thumb and middle finger. Remind students to catch the beanbags with the palms up; then have them practice the following sequence individually. (5-7 minutes)

- ▸ Toss the first beanbag diagonally upward to the right with the left hand, starting the infinity sign (i.e., a sideways figure 8).
- ▸ When the first beanbag reaches its peak, toss the second beanbag diagonally upward to the left with the right hand, forming a crisscross pattern.
- ▸ When the second beanbag reaches its peak, toss the third beanbag with the left hand (diagonally upward to the right); then catch the first beanbag with the right hand (palm up).
- ▸ Catch with palms up until the beanbags can be juggled continuously.
- ▸ Repeat the sequence.

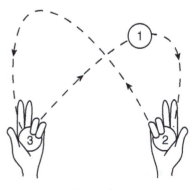

Cascading

12. Once students are proficient at activity 11, pair up students or have them select partners. One partner juggles the cascading pattern; the other partner takes one beanbag out of the juggling sequence. The partner who is juggling (with only 2 bags) maintains an "empty space" for the missing bag. Then the other partner finds the empty space and tosses or drops the beanbag back into the pattern. Partners should switch roles after a few trials. (4-6 minutes)

13. Juggling relay. Divide students into teams of 4 and have each team form a line. Students relay juggle by handing the beanbags off to the next team member in line. The first teammate juggles three beanbags while facing the second teammate

in line. The second teammate must take over the juggling from the first team-mate, catching the beanbags in a right-left-right pattern and continuing the juggle. Then the second teammate hands off to the third teammate, and so on down the line. If the bags are dropped at any time during the hand-off, the hand-off must start again. The first team to successfully complete the relay wins. (5-6 minutes)

14. Endurance juggling. Use a stopwatch to time how long a juggler can keep all the beanbags in the air. By forming teams of four students each, juggling times can be combined with other team members to determine the best juggling team. (4-5 minutes)

15. Reverse cascade. In a regular cascade, the toss is underhand from near the middle and the beanbags are caught on the outside. In a reverse cascade, the toss is from the outside, and the catch is near the middle. The infinity sign (i.e., sideways figure 8) is still the pattern. Have students practice the reverse cascade individually. (4-5 minutes)

16. Showering. Introduce showering to students using the following sequence description. Then have them practice individually. The sequence starts with holding 2 beanbags in the right hand and 1 in the left. (4-5 minutes)

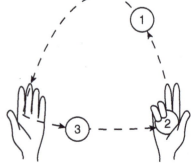

Showering

  ▸ Toss the first beanbag upward and inward and to the left with the right hand.

  ▸ Toss the second beanbag (also in the right hand) on the same upward and inward path.

  ▸ At the same time the second beanbag is tossed, toss the beanbag from the left hand horizontally to the right hand.

  ▸ Repeat the same pattern, forming a circle with the beanbags.

Closure (3-5 Minutes)

Review the lesson with students. Use the following ideas to reinforce learning, check understanding, and provide feedback.

1. Use this lesson to emphasize perseverance. Talk about the frustrations of not being able to do something and how easy it is to give up. Relate this idea to personal experiences or to what students with physical or mental disabilities experience.

2. Discuss the importance of practicing to improve performance. Tell students that 20 minutes of daily practice is recommended to make progress in juggling.

3. Have some students demonstrate their successes with various juggling skills.

Resources

Finnigan, D. 1987. *The complete juggler*. New York: Vintage Books.

Pangrazi, R., and P. Darst. 1997. *Dynamic physical education for secondary school students: Curriculum and instruction*. 3rd ed. Needham Heights, MA: Allyn & Bacon.

Additional Resources

Jugglebug
7506 J Olympic View Dr., Dept. JB
Edmonds, WA 98020
Phone 206-774-2127
> Offers juggling equipment (e.g., scarves, rings, balls, clubs) as well as an instructor's manual and videotapes on juggling.

Jump Bands

Purpose

In this lesson students will develop the following skills: jumping patterns for end jumpers, hopping, straddle jumping, and crossovers (dance steps) for the center jumpers.

Warm-Ups (6-8 minutes)

1. Reverse runs
2. Knee lifts
3. Squat holds
4. Hip lifts

Facility and Equipment

- Any smooth surface (indoor or outdoor)
- 2 jump bands per group
- Music with a 3/4 rhythm
- 1 drum

Note: Jump bands are usually 7 to 8 feet (2.13-2.44 meters) long and made of elastic. A loop at each end of the band is slipped over the ankles.

Skill Cues

1. Using 3/4 rhythm, jump with the feet together on the first count, then with the feet apart (about 24 inches [61 centimeters]) on counts 2 and 3.
2. To be ready for quick maneuvering, move on the balls of the feet.
3. Keep in rhythm with the drum or music.
4. The basic steps for the center jumpers are as follows.
   - Hop: Take a hop on the outer foot on count 1 and then hop between the jump bands (with either foot) on counts 2 and 3.
   - Straddle jump: Place the feet in a straddle position on the outside of the jump bands on count 1; then bring both feet together and jump on counts 2 and 3.
   - Crossover: Rest on count 1; on counts 2 and 3, place the right and then the left foot in the center of the jump bands. Then step with the right foot to the other side of the jump bands on count 1, and then step back into the open jump bands with the left then right foot on counts 2 and 3. (See figure on next page.)
5. For a round-off, rest on count 1 and place the hands in the center of the jump bands on counts 2 and 3; then bring both feet to the other side (outside the jump bands) on count 1.
6. Turns (180°) can be added to the hop and the straddle jump on counts 2 and 3.
7. Vary step direction by moving backward and forward instead of always sideways.

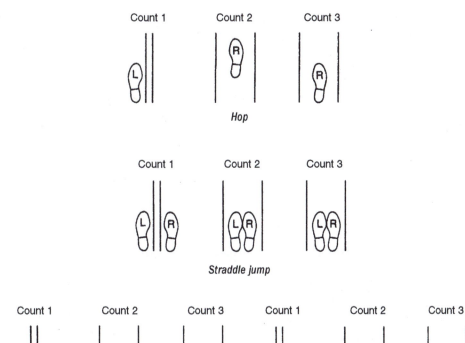

Count 1   Count 2   Count 3

Hop

Count 1   Count 2   Count 3

Straddle jump

Count 1   Count 2   Count 3   Count 1   Count 2   Count 3

Crossover

Basic steps

Teaching Cues

1. Have students practice each step with floor lines instead of jump bands. Be sure to allow ample time for students to practice each step.

2. Teach the steps at a slower tempo first; then increase the tempo.

Activities (30-40 Minutes)

1. Explain how to perform jump bands using the appropriate skill and teaching cues. (3-4 minutes)

2. Divide students into groups of 3 or 4, each with a set of jump bands, and have groups scatter around the floor. Present the first jump band rhythm for the end jumpers: count 1, feet together; counts 2 and 3, feet apart. Have students take turns as end jumpers using the jump bands in beat to the drum or music. (5 minutes)

Safety Tips

◆ Do not allow jumpers to wrap the elastic bands around their bodies or to let them go while stretched.

◆ If more than one student will be jumping at a time, tell them to be careful not to jump on each other's ankles.

3. With the same groups and positioning as in activity 2, present the three basic dance steps used by center jumpers (i.e., hop, straddle jump, and crossover) and have students practice each to the beat of a drum or music. (10-12 minutes)

Optional Activity: Jump Band Challenges

4. With students arranged in groups of 3 or 4, each with a set of jump bands, assign each group a 3-minute routine using a variety of steps and stunts. During the 3 minutes, center jumpers should exchange places with the end jumpers after every minute. This allows every student an opportunity to try the dance steps (center jumpers). (12-19 minutes)

Optional Activity: Jump Band Patterns

Optional Activities

Jump Band Challenges (0-12 Minutes)

With students arranged in groups of 3 or 4, each with a set of jump bands, present some challenges that students can try as they continue to practice various steps. Challenges could include a round-off, turn, or change in step direction.

Jump Band Patterns (0-12 Minutes)

Bring two groups (3-4 students per group) together and make a cross with two sets of jump bands (i.e., the bands should be perpendicular to each other). End jumpers jump the same pattern at the same time. Center jumpers perform in and out of both sets of jump bands simultaneously.

Closure (3-5 minutes)

Review the lesson with students, using the following ideas to reinforce learning, check understanding, and provide feedback.

1. Choose 1 or 2 groups to demonstrate part of a jump bands routine.
2. If students have come up with their own steps during class, have them demonstrate those steps in front of the class.

Resources

Sportime
One Sportime Way
Atlanta, GA 30340
Phone 800-444-5700
    Sells jump bands.

Kickball Golf

Purpose

In this lesson students develop and reinforce kicking skills while learning to develop kicking accuracy.

Warm-Ups (6-8 Minutes)

1. Side pattern jumps
2. Hamstring conditioners
3. Side holds
4. Hip stretch
5. Step and calf taps

Skill Cues

1. Swing the kicking leg back from the hip.
2. Follow through in the direction of the kick.
3. Extend the knee on the follow-through.
4. Keep the arms out and the body balanced while kicking.

Teaching Cues

1. Students may use any kicking style. Keep in mind, however, that different kicks may work better than others for distance and accuracy.
2. Before class, design a nine-hole course using the hoops, boxes, and cones. The holes should be different distances and contain fairway obstacles (e.g., equipment sheds, playground equipment) so that students must kick around them. Place a numbered cone and hoop at each tee-off area; lay the boxes on their sides for the holes (the open end acts as the hole).
3. Increase or decrease the number of holes according to class size and open space.
4. Create a grid for a nine-hole score sheet. Draw a replica of the course on the score sheet, with arrows showing the direction that the ball must travel.
5. So that students can identify their balls on the fairway, use different-colored balls in each group if possible. You might also make a distinctive mark on the balls.

Facility and Equipment

- Play field or large outdoor area
- 1 soccer ball or medium utility ball (6 to 8 inches [15.2-20.3 centimeters]) per student
- 9 hoops or ropes (numbered)
- 9 boxes or wastebaskets
- 9 cones (numbered)
- 1 score sheet* and pencil per student

Activities (30-40 Minutes)

1. Divide students into groups of 3 or 4 and assign each group to 1 of the 9 tee-off areas. Distribute the score sheets and explain the sequence and rules of kickball golf. (5-10 minutes)

2. Play kickball golf. (25-30 minutes)

Kickball Golf

The object of the game is to use as few kicks as possible to advance the ball around the course. Each hole begins with a punt kick (tee-off) taken from inside the hoop (tee-off area). Thereafter, the ball is kicked from where it lies. To hole out, the ball must enter the box. Players proceed from one hole to the next, completing the next numbered hole until they have played all holes.

The rules of kickball golf are as follows:

▶ Players must kick the ball to advance it; no hands, dribbling, or other ball-maneuvering movements are allowed.

▶ The kick is fair if the ball goes over an obstacle.

▶ When going around an obstacle, the ball must move in the direction of the arrows (on the score sheet); if it moves in the wrong direction, it must be played back around the obstacle to follow the direction of the arrows.

▶ Each kick counts as one stroke. Players keep track of the number of kicks per hole, then record them on the score sheet and add the total for each round.

Closure (3-5 Minutes)

Review the lesson with students. Use the following questions to reinforce learning, check understanding, and provide feedback.

1. How many students completed the course in less than 60 shots? Under 50? Under 40? Who had the lowest score?

2. Which types of kicks produced the most distance? The most accuracy?

3. How could the course be made more challenging?

4. Are there any suggestions for improving the design?

Variation

Kickball golf can also be played by team. Rather than keep track of their individual scores, teammates combine their scores to reach a team total for each round, and then the game. The team with the lowest overall score (i.e., fewest kicks) wins.

Mat Ball

Purpose

In this lesson students learn the rules and play the game of mat ball.

Warm-Ups (6-8 minutes)

1. Jog around the perimeter of the gym for 2 minutes
2. Step touches
3. Arm circles
4. Side stretch

Facility and Equipment

◆ Gym or large outdoor playing area
◆ 1 base
◆ 1 playground ball
◆ 3 gymnastics mats (approximately 4 by 8 feet [1.22 by 2.44 meters])

Skill Cues

1. Roll the ball to the batter; do not bounce it.
2. Hit runners below the waist with the ball to get them out.

Teaching Cues

1. Review kicking, throwing, catching, and base-running skills (see softball lessons 1 and 6 on pages 312 and 324).
2. Emphasize to students that they should not strike runners above the waist with the ball to get them out.
3. The base serves as the home plate; the gymnastics mats serve as first, second, and third bases.

Safety Tips

◆ Throwers must aim below the waist.
◆ Establish some safety rules about sliding into a base (e.g., do not slide face first).

Activities (30-40 Minutes)

1. Divide the class into two teams and explain the rules of mat ball. The game is an advanced version of kickball and is played on a diamond. (5-7 minutes)
2. Play the game of mat ball. (25-33 minutes)

Mat Ball

The object of the game is to score as many runs as possible while preventing opponents from scoring. Like softball, innings are used in mat ball. Innings are played until the offense makes three outs; then teams switch.

(continued)

Defensive players position themselves on the field as they would in softball, with players standing on each base and in the outfield. The pitcher (defense) rolls (pitches) the ball to the batter (offense) at home plate to start the game. The batter kicks the ball and runs toward first base. Fielders retrieve (or catch) the ball and throw it to get the runner out.

The runner is out if he or she:

- is hit with the ball,
- has a fly ball caught, or
- is forced out at first base.

The runner at first base may choose to run or not to run to the other bases on subsequent kicks by other team members. Any number of runners can be on a base at one time—it is not uncommon to have as many as 10 runners on a base at one time.

Each time a runner crosses home base and reaches first base again, the offense scores a run (the runner does not stop at home base). If a team runs out of batters, a player from one of the bases can come back to the plate to bat.

Closure (3-5 Minutes)

Review the lesson with students. Use the following ideas to reinforce learning, check understanding, and provide feedback.

1. Discuss with students the best possible offensive strategy when playing mat ball.

2. Have students identify how teamwork can significantly improve chances of success at this game.

Variation: California Rules

The California version of mat ball is the same, with one notable exception. When teams switch after three outs, all players on the batting team must remember their exact position in the game, such as standing on first base or third base, waiting to kick, and so on. Then, when the team comes up to bat again, all players go to the same bases they were on at the end of the last inning. If players were traveling to a new base when the third out was reached, they must return to their previous bases.

Resources

Pangrazi, R., and P. Darst. 1997. *Dynamic physical education for secondary school students: Curriculum and instruction.* 3rd ed. Needham Heights, MA: Allyn & Bacon.

Modified Hocker

Purpose

This lesson allows students to apply previously learned skills to a field game, emphasizing passing and kicking accuracy as well as motor control.

Warm-Ups (6-8 Minutes)

1. Abdominal tighteners
2. Faceup flank
3. Elbow-knee touches (supine)
4. Leg lifts
5. Horizontal run

Facility and Equipment

◆ Soccer or football field with goal posts
◆ 1 playground rubber ball (10 or 12 inches [25.4 or 30.5 centimeters])
◆ 1 pinnie per 2 students

Skill Cues

1. Advance the ball by kicking or using one or both hands to punch it, push it, slap it, or curry it (juggling the ball from hand to hand below head level).
2. Pass the ball by scooping it up with one hand, swinging it forward and releasing it in one continuous movement using a throw, roll, or bounce.
3. Pass the ball from below head level, using only one hand, and palms up. No holding the ball for even a second.

Teaching Cues

1. Encourage students to spread out and not to group around the ball.
2. Tell students to stay alert at all times.
3. Put take-offs into play quickly.

Safety Tips

◆ Continued slapping, kicking, or pushing might cause an injury. Call a square-off as soon as a ball is locked up between players.
◆ If early morning dew is present, warn students of slippery field conditions.

Activities (30-40 Minutes)

1. Introduce and explain the game of modified hocker, specifying the skills, violations, and rules. Explain and demonstrate a curry and a scoop pass. (5-8 minutes)
2. Divide students into two teams. Designate or have teammates select a center and 1 or 2 goalies per team (depending on playing ability). Divide the remaining players among offensive and defensive positions. Play the game of modified hocker. Remind students that they may use more than the kick to advance the ball. Repeat as many games as possible within the class time. (25-32 minutes)

Modified Hocker

Modified hocker is played with 2 teams of 9 or more players. The object is to advance the ball downfield and score. A game consists of 7 points. Rotate players after each game.

Opposing players are scattered throughout their half of the field. The game starts with a square-off: In a 5-yard (4.57-meter) circle in the middle of the field, two opposing players face their own goal with the instep of one foot next to the ball. On the whistle, both attempt to move the ball outside the square-off circle using only the feet and legs (no hands). After the square-off, players advance the ball to the opponent's goal and try to score. Play continues until a violation occurs, the ball goes out-of-bounds, or a team scores.

The general rules of modified hocker are as follows:

▸ Offsides is not called.

▸ Players may punch, slap-pass, push, curry, or slap the ball with one or both hands.

▸ The ball cannot be held, not even for a second.

▸ Players may kick the ball.

▸ The ball must be in continuous motion.

▸ The ball must not go above the head; no overhead passing or throwing is allowed.

▸ Players may scoop up the ball and pass or roll it with one hand. (Using two hands is holding and results in a penalty.) The hand must swing forward in a continuous movement.

▸ When the ball is lodged between two players, a square-off results.

▸ When a team commits a minor violation or sends the ball out-of-bounds, the other team puts the ball into play with a take-off.

Take-offs result when a team commits a minor violation or sends the ball out-of-bounds. The rules governing a take-off are as follows:

▸ It is played from the point nearest to where the infraction occurred (or from where the ball went out-of-bounds).

▸ All players must remain at least 5 feet (1.52 meters) from the player taking the ball off.

▸ The take-off is a two-handed overhead throw.

▸ If the violation occurred near a goal line, a goal may be attempted on the take-off.

▸ If attempting a goal on a take-off, the ball must be thrown and must go under the crossbar. During this scoring attempt, the defense can use as many players as it wants to defend the goal.

Minor violations are called for

▸ scooping up the ball with two hands

▸ picking up the ball

▸ holding or carrying the ball

▸ throwing above shoulder level, and

▸ currying above the head.

When a team commits a major violation, the opposing team gets a penalty kick. The ball is placed 10 yards (9.14 meters) in front of the goal, and two defensive goalies stand under the crossbar. The offensive player takes a step and kicks the ball, trying to score a goal under the crossbar for 2 points. Major violations that occur within 5 yards (4.57 meters) of the goal line result in a take-off.

Major violations include

- tackling,
- holding,
- pushing,
- tripping,
- charging another player, and
- engaging in unnecessarily rough or dangerous play.

Scoring is as follows:

1 point	Kicking, rolling, pushing, passing, or slapping the ball across any part of the goal line (This an optional scoring method appropriate for middle school.)
2 points	Kicking, passing, slapping, or scooping the ball over the goal line (but under the crossbar between the goal posts)
3 points	Kicking the ball above the crossbar between the goalposts
2 points	A penalty kick (for a major violation) under the crossbar between the goalposts
2 points	Throwing the ball under the crossbar between the goalposts (when attempting a goal on a take-off)

Closure (3-5 Minutes)

Review the lesson with students. Use the following questions and ideas to reinforce learning, check understanding, and provide feedback.

1. Discuss why it is important to play positions (i.e., why players should stay within their general areas on the field).
2. Because the ball may be advanced legally in so many ways, many students forget to use some of them. Review the scoop and curry; then ask how many students used them successfully.
3. Ask the following questions:
   - How many students prefer hocker to soccer? Why?
   - In terms of playing strategy, how are soccer and hocker similar?

Variation

Adaptations can be made for indoor hocker using fewer players and a slightly deflated ball.

Resources

Cunningham, C.J. 1982. *Modified hocker: Fundamental ball skills.* Sparks, NY: Arch Billmire.

Progressive Basketball

Purpose

In this lesson students use their offensive and defensive basketball skills in a modified version of the game.

Warm-Ups (6-8 Minutes)

1. Grapevine step
2. Arm circles
3. Back stretch
4. Elbow squeezes
5. Reverse run

Skill Cues

1. Play as a team.
2. Analyze offensive and defensive errors and corrections while waiting to play.
3. Move the ball quickly.

Teaching Cues

1. Urge students to use 1-on-1 defense (see basketball lesson 8, page 151).
2. In co-ed classes, try to equalize gender on teams, or assign one half court for girls and one for boys.
3. Remind students to leave and enter the court quickly.
4. Encourage students to plan their strategy when waiting on the sidelines.

Activities (30-40 Minutes)

1. Divide the class into an even number of offensive and defensive teams of 4 or 5 players each. Half of the teams start on offense and half on defense. Explain that two games are played simultaneously, each using half of the basketball court. Start with 1 offensive and 1 defensive team on each half court; the rest of the offensive teams line up on one side of the court and the rest of the defensive teams line up on the opposite side. (5-10 minutes) (See figure on next page.)
2. Explain the game and tell students that they will referee their own game. Play progressive basketball. (25-30 minutes)

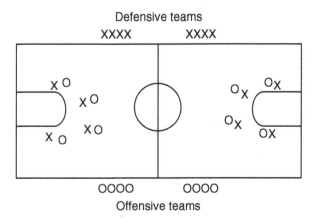

Progressive basketball positions (4-player teams)

Progressive Basketball

The object of the game is to score points and to play offense as much as possible. For the most part, regular basketball rules apply (e.g., traveling, fouls; see the basketball unit beginning on page 127), but with the following modifications:

- Each game begins with one offensive player in the center circle; the defender must be outside the circle.

- The starting offensive player dribbles or passes the ball outside the circle.

- Each offensive team gets only one shot at the basket. If successful, the team leaves the court and lines up behind the last offensive team on the sidelines. If missed, the team leaves the court and lines up behind the last defensive team on the sidelines (defensive team to offensive line). In other words, both teams leave the court as soon as a shot is taken, whether the basket is made or missed.

- If the offensive team commits a violation (e.g., traveling, fouling, staying longer than 3 seconds in the key), it leaves the court and lines up with the defensive teams on the sidelines; the defensive team leaves the court and goes to the end of the offensive sideline.

- If the defensive team steals the ball, it leaves the court and goes to the end of the offensive sideline; the offensive team leaves the court and goes to the end of the defensive sideline.

- If the defensive team fouls an offensive player, play reverts back to the center court circle.

As teams leave the court, the first offensive and defensive teams (from the sidelines) move quickly to replace them on the open court.

Closure (3-5 minutes)

Review the lesson with students, using the following questions and ideas to reinforce learning, check understanding, and provide feedback.

1. How successful was each team at remaining on the offensive?
2. Share your observations about good playing strategy, timeliness of leaving and entering the floor, sharing play action with teammates, and so on.
3. Could other rule changes make the game better?

Resources

Landy, J.M., and M.J. Landy. 1993. *Ready-to-use p.e. activities for grades 7-9*. West Nyack, NY: Parker.

Rhythmic Ribbons

Purpose

In this lesson students develop skills in creating ribbon patterns, including the arc, circle, figure 8, serpent, cobra, and spiral.

Warm-Ups (6-8 Minutes)

1. Sprint-jog intervals
2. Shoulder shrugs
3. Hamstring straight-leg stretch
4. Arm isometrics

Skill Cues

1. Keep the rod in line with the arm and hold the end in the palm (index finger is extended).
2. For most ribbon patterns, the shoulder joint is the axis of rotation; the wrist moves the ribbon.
3. Complete the entire movement (with the full length of the ribbon) before starting another movement.
4. Keep the ribbon moving continuously to prevent it from collapsing on the floor.
5. Interchange the ribbon from the right to the left hand while performing a ribbon pattern.
6. Use total body movement, not just the arm, when executing ribbon patterns. This would include using turns, rolls, hops, skips, cartwheels, leaps, and so on.

Teaching Cues

1. Tell students not to whip the ribbon because that will cause tangles, cracking, or snapping.
2. Explain how to properly care for the ribbons (e.g., how to rewrap them for storage).

Safety Tips

◆ Allow ample space between students during routines. The ribbons will become entangled if students are too close to one another.
◆ Advise students not to wrap the ribbons around their neck or other body parts.

Activities (30-40 Minutes)

1. Explain how to create ribbon patterns using the appropriate skill and teaching cues. (4-5 minutes)

2. Scatter students around the gym, allowing plenty of space between each student. Present the following rhythmic ribbon patterns and allow students to practice each. (12-15 minutes)

   ▶ Arc: swinging the ribbon from one side of the body to the other
   ▶ Circle: making a full circle with the ribbon in front of the body, to the side of the body, overhead, or under the feet while jumping
   ▶ Figure 8: moving the ribbon in the pattern of the number 8, either vertically or horizontally, in front of or beside the body
   ▶ Spiral: rotating the hand in continuous small circles in front of the body or perpendicular to the floor, also down and up
   ▶ Serpent: moving the hand and wrist in the air either horizontally or vertically
   ▶ Cobra: moving the hand and wrist on the ground either horizontally or vertically

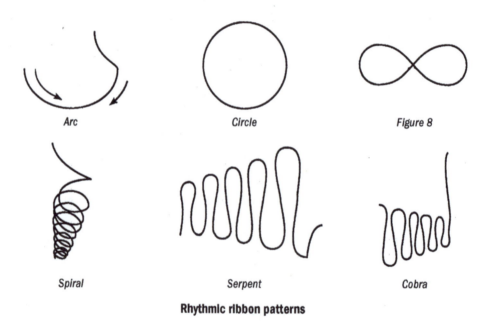

Rhythmic ribbon patterns

3. Maintaining a scattered formation, with plenty of space between each student, have students combine some of the ribbon patterns with body movements (e.g., turns, rolls, hops, skips, leaps, cartwheels) to create a 1.5-minute routine. Play background music (3/4 rhythm) to assist students in choreographing their routines. (14-20 minutes)

Closure (3-5 Minutes)

Review the lesson with students. Use the following questions and ideas to reinforce learning, check understanding, and provide feedback.

1. Ask students to demonstrate any additional patterns they may have discovered as they worked with their ribbons.

2. Encourage students to continue their work with rhythmic ribbons by giving extra credit for developing a 2-minute routine to be demonstrated during a future class period.

Resources

Bott, J. 1981. *Modern rhythmic gymnastics.* Wakefield, England: EP Publishing.

Jastrjembskaia, N., and Y. Titov. 1999. *Rhythmic gymnastics.* Champaign, IL: Human Kinetics.

Zakrajsek, D., and L. Carnes. 1986. *Individualizing physical education: Criterion materials.* Champaign, IL: Human Kinetics.

Scatter Club Bowls

Purpose

In this lesson students develop teamwork, ball skills, and defensive movements.

Facility and Equipment

◆ Gym or large outdoor play area
◆ 1 bowling pin or club per student
◆ 1 pinnie per 2 students
◆ 2 playground balls (6 to 8 inches [15.2-20.3 centimeters]) or volleyballs

Warm-Ups (6-8 minutes)

1. Side slides
2. Faceup flank
3. Abdominal curls
4. Arm and leg lifts
5. Sprint-jog intervals

Skill Cues

1. Keep the knees flexed and the arms out to the side.
2. Be alert and watch the ball(s).
3. Get rid of the ball quickly.

Teaching Cues

1. Increase or decrease the distance between players to allow for better individual and team play.
2. Tell students to move the ball quickly to a teammate if that person is in a more advantageous position.
3. Use one ball first; then add the second.
4. Remind players to remain at least 10 feet (3.05 meters) apart.
5. If players have to be repeatedly reminded to maintain the minimal distance from their pins, a penalty point can be awarded to the opposing team.

Safety Tip

◆ The ball may not be thrown at another player.

Activities (30-40 Minutes)

1. Divide students into two teams. Give one team pinnies, and give each player a bowling pin; then have players scatter throughout the area, maintaining a distance of at least 10 feet (3.05 meters) from any other player. Players should place the pin at least 2 feet (.61 meters; a stretched arm's length) away from where they are standing. Explain the rules of the game. (3-5 minutes)

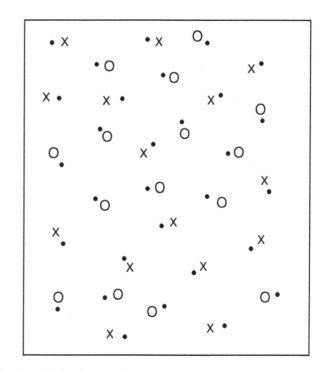

X = Red team
O = Blue team
● = Pins
Pins should be 10 feet
(3.05 meters) apart.
Players should be 2 feet
(.61 meters) away from pins.

Scatter club bowls formation

2. Play a game of scatter club bowls. If there is enough time for a second game, add a second ball and play again. (27-35 minutes)

Scatter Club Bowls

The object of the game is to knock over opposing players' pins and to protect one's own pin. When a pin is knocked over, the opposing team gets a point. (This includes players knocking over their own pins.) Pins are reset and the point is tallied. At the end of the game, the team with the most points wins.

The following play rules apply. Players

▶ must roll or bounce the ball into the pins (i.e., they must touch the floor first),

▶ may not throw the ball at an opponent's pin,

▶ may not stand over their pins to defend them,

▶ may pass the ball to a teammate, and

▶ may retrieve a loose ball that goes out of the playing area, but must go back to their pin area before resuming play.

Closure (3-5 Minutes)

Review the lesson with students. Use the following questions and ideas to reinforce learning, check understanding, and provide feedback.

1. How many players were able to topple at least one pin?

2. Discuss the (offensive) strategies that worked best for knocking over pins.

3. Discuss the (defensive) strategies that worked best for protecting pins.

4. Ask students to identify problems that might occur if they were permitted to throw the ball at opponents' pins.

Variations

1. To shorten games, set a time or point limit. For example, the first team to earn 10 points wins.

2. Games can also be sped up by adding more balls (e.g., 4 or 5 balls in play at a time) and not resetting knocked-over pins. At the end of the game (i.e., when all of one team's pins have been knocked over), the winner is the team with at least one pin left standing.

Schottische and Canadian Barn Dance

Purpose

In this lesson students learn to dance two folk dances: the schottische and the Canadian barn dance.

Warm-Up (0 Minutes)

The schottische serves as a warm-up.

Skill Cues

Facility and Equipment

- Gym or multipurpose area
- Music (CD or audiocassette) and player

Note: Suggested music includes any music with 4/4 tempo.

Schottische

The steps of the schottische are as follows:

Step, step, step, hop (left, right, left, left hop).
Step, step, step, hop (right, left, right, right hop).
Step, hop (left, left hop), step, hop (right, right hop), step, hop (left, left hop), step, hop (right, right hop).

Canadian Barn Dance

1. Drop hands to move apart during the grapevine.
2. Go from the grapevine to the open position, starting the walk on the outside foot.
3. On the open reverse, pivot inward on the third step; the boy's left arm and the girl's right arm move upward on the pivot, and both point their outside feet in the opposite direction.
4. Move from the open reverse to the couple position, the boy pulling his left (raised) arm toward him on the point, and step down.

Teaching Cues

Schottische

1. Have students walk through the steps and hop to a drumbeat; then have them convert walking to running steps followed by the hop.
2. Add music after all students have achieved coordinated movement.
3. Increase the complexity of the schottische by having students dance in open, promenade, or varsouvianna positions (see the introduction to social and square dancing on page 260).

4. The schottische originated in Scotland, Russia, and Yugoslavia. Today different versions are found in different parts of the world. Because people from these countries were used to heavy work, the dance requires stamina.

Canadian Barn Dance

1. Remind students that each sequence of steps is danced to four counts.

2. Explain that the first sequence begins with boys stepping left and girls stepping right; this is reversed on repeat sequences.

3. Demonstrate how to transition smoothly between dance positions.

4. The open reverse is like a half closed position. Instead of forward or backward, however, students face and move sideways (to the boy's right or the girl's left).

5. Teach and practice each position before adding the next.

6. The Canadian barn dance originated in England and probably came to the United States through Canada—hence its name. The dance is more popular in the western United States, although different versions are danced in many regions.

Safety Tip

◆ Students should wear shoes or go barefoot. In these fast-moving dances, dancing in socks could result in slips and falls.

Activities (40-50 Minutes)

1. Announce that two dance activities will be performed during class. Explain that the schottische will replace warm-up activities because it is a high-energy dance and tell students about the history of the dance using the teaching cues. (3-5 minutes)

2. Position students in a scatter formation around the gym. Use the appropriate skill cues to explain the sequences; then have students repeat the step, step, step, hop sequence to the beat of a drum (starting on the left foot). After students are successful, add 4 step-hop combinations after 2 sequences of step, step, step, hop. Increase the tempo and have students replace walking steps with running steps. Finally, add music and assist students in staying with the beat. (6-8 minutes)

Optional Activity: Schottische Combinations

3. Position students in partners (open or promenade position) around the room, all facing the same direction. Both partners start with the left foot and dance the schottische (i.e., step, step, step, hop; step, step, step, hop; step-hop, step-hop, step-hop, step-hop; and repeat) moving counterclockwise. Have students switch partners by moving the girls forward one place; then dance another schottische. (8-10 minutes)

Optional Activity: Schottische Patterns

4. Introduce the Canadian barn dance using the appropriate skill and teaching cues. (3 minutes)

5. Position students in a scatter formation throughout the gym. Review the following dance terms; then teach the open into the open reverse using the skill and teaching cues. (7-9 minutes)

▸ Shuffle or two-step (see the introduction to line dancing, page 190)

▸ Vine (see the introduction to line dancing, page 191)

▸ Varsouvianna position (see the introduction to social and square dancing, page 264)

▸ Open position (see the introduction to social and square dancing, page 264)

▸ Closed position (see the introduction to social and square dancing, page 263)

6. Demonstrate and have students perform the Canadian barn dance sequence, first without and then with music. (13-15 minutes)

Canadian Barn Dance

Skills: walk, vine, two-step, pivot

Positions: varsouvianna, open, open reverse, closed

Suggested music: any lively two-step music

In a varsouvianna, walk forward 3 steps and point the toe forward (boys begin with the left foot, girls with the right).

Repeat, going backward (boys start with the right foot, girls with the left).

Drop hands and part; vine.

Sidestep, cross-step behind, sidestep, and swing the foot across and in front of the other (boys sidestep left, cross-step behind right; sidestep left, and swing the right foot across; girls sidestep right, cross-step behind left; sidestep right, and swing the left foot across).

Repeat in the opposite direction with the opposite foot leading and traveling toward partner.

Come together, taking an open position.

Walk 3 steps, turning inward on the third step, and point the foot forward in the opposite direction (boys walk left, right, turn left, and point the right foot; girls walk right, left, turn right, and point the left foot).

Repeat in the open reverse, going in the opposite direction. Boys walk right, left, right, (turning on the right step into girl and taking a closed position), point left. Girls opposite.

In the closed position, take 4 shuffles or two-steps. (boys start on the left and move forward, girls on the right and move backward).

Change partners and repeat.

Open reverse

Optional Activities

Schottische Combinations (0-5 Minutes)

Encourage students to create their own versions of the schottische (keeping the same steps and rhythm) by varying their floor patterns, joining with another student, joining in small groups, or using different dance positions.

Schottische Patterns (0-7 Minutes)

In partners or small groups, students create their own schottische dance pattern using the schottische steps. Partners could separate or move in a circle on the step-hops, form a conga line, and so on.

Closure (3-5 Minutes)

Review the lesson with students. Use the following questions and ideas to reinforce learning, check understanding, and provide feedback.

1. Share your observations about students' performances, highlighting particularly graceful or creative movements.
2. Ask students why it is important to keep the fast steps short in the schottische (i.e., to maintain the art or grace of movement and to conserve energy).
3. Discuss what different couple positions add to the Canadian barn dance (i.e., they give an image of complexity and competence, and create smooth, flowing movements).

Variations

1. Dance in a circle.
2. For a mixer, use the four two-steps to get a new partner: boys go forward and girls travel in a small circle waiting for the next boy.
3. For younger students, use a facing position (see the social and square dance unit introduction on page 263) instead of a closed position, and eliminate the pivot turn by having students continue in the same direction.

Resources

Harris, J.A., A. Pittman, and M.S. Waller. 1969. *Dance a while.* 4th ed. Minneapolis: Burgess.

Additional Resources

Kimbo Educational Records
P.O. Box 477
Long Branch, NJ 07740
Phone 800-631-2187

Sideline Broomball

Purpose

In this lesson students learn the rules and play the game of sideline broomball.

Warm-Ups (6-8 Minutes)

1. Leg stretch
2. Arm rotators
3. Lateral hops
4. Push-offs
5. Jog around the perimeter of the gym for 3 minutes

Skill Cues

Sideline broom ball uses running, shooting, and stick-handling skills.

Stick Handling

1. Place the left hand at the top of the stick with the back of the hand facing forward.
2. Place the right hand approximately 6 inches (15.2 centimeters) below the left.
3. Contact the ball in front of the body and advance it with short taps.
4. Score a goal by hitting the ball with the broom into the opponent's goal.

Teaching Cue

Encourage students to use sideline players, who have the opportunity to use their hands to catch and pass the ball to teammates.

Facility and Equipment

- Gym or outdoor area with a smooth surface
- 1 volleyball-sized play or soft-skin ball per court
- 20 brooms per game
- 2 floor hockey goals or 4 cones per court

Note: Larger areas can accommodate more courts. One broomball court is normally half the size of a basketball court.

Safety Tip

- Tell students not to swing the broomstick off the floor.

Activities (30-40 Minutes)

1. Introduce sideline broomball using the skill and teaching cues. (4-6 minutes)
2. Divide the class into 2 (4 if using 2 courts) equal teams and explain the rules. (4-6 minutes)
3. Play the game of sideline broomball. (22-28 minutes)

Sideline Broomball

Each team lines up on its designated sideline with the brooms on the floor near each goal. The game begins with five players from each team running onto the court, picking up their brooms, and attempting to hit the ball, which is at midcourt, through the opponent's goal. Each goal is worth a point. After a set time period teams can rotate on and off the court, allowing all players equal time on the court. After each rotation, the ball should be placed at midcourt to start play.

The following rules and strategies apply to sideline broomball:

▶ Goalies and sideline players are the only ones allowed to touch the ball with their hands.

▶ Brooms must not be raised off the floor.

▶ A sideline player may not score a goal.

▶ Players on the floor should pass the ball to their sideline teammates, who can pick the ball up and pass it back onto the court or to another sideline teammate to help their team score.

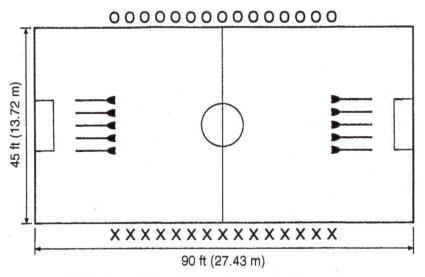

Sideline broomball court dimensions and starting positions

Closure (3-5 Minutes)

Review the lesson with students. Use the following ideas to reinforce learning, check understanding, and provide feedback.

1. Discuss the strategic advantages of using the sideline players (e.g., passing to sideline players to secure posession of the ball and then passing back to a teammate on the court).

2. Make sure students understand the importance of keeping players spread out across the court during play.

Resources

Gustafson, M., S. Wolfe, and C. King. 1991. *Great games for young people.* Champaign, IL: Human Kinetics.

Team-Building Games

Purpose

This lesson focuses on activities that require students to work together to meet a goal. Each of the activities is considered a group game.

Facility and Equipment

◆ Large open area or gym

Note: The games in this lesson do not require other equipment.

Warm-Ups (6-8 Minutes)

1. Leg stretch
2. Arm circles
3. Waist twists
4. Push-ups
5. Slapping jacks

Skill Cue

Cooperation is required to complete each task; teamwork is required in every activity.

Teaching Cue

Emphasize enjoyment and the good feeling of accomplishing a given task.

Activities (30-40 Minutes)

1. Introduce the games by emphasizing teamwork and cooperation. (2-3 minutes)
2. Mass stand-up. Two students sit back to back with their elbows locked; then they stand up. Expand the number of students to 3, 4, 5, and so on. See how many students can stand up while interlocked. When more than 2 students are trying to stand up, they should start by locking arms and sitting as close to one another as possible. Then they should stand up quickly at precisely the same moment. (5-7 minutes)
3. Centipede race. Divide the class into 4 or 6 groups of 6 and position each group in 2 lines, each line standing back to back. One line stands still while the other line takes a step to one side. Have students bend down and cross their arms between their legs, then grab one hand of the student behind them on the right and one hand from the student behind them on the left. (Everyone in both lines, except those on the ends, should be holding the hands of two different students.) In this position, the students have become a centipede. Have the centipedes race each other over short distances. (6-8 minutes)
4. Entanglement (knots). Divide the class into groups of 8 to 10 and have each group make a tight circle, students' arms pointing toward the center of the circle and clasping the hands of two different group members who are not next to them in the circle. On a signal, have each group try to untangle themselves into a circle without disconnecting hands. (Students can be facing different directions when finished.) (5-7 minutes)

5. Zipper. Divide the class into groups of 10 to 12. Group members line up in a single line, each student bending over and reaching between their legs with the left hand to grasp the right hand of the student behind. This continues down the line until all students are connected. The last student in line lies down, the next student backs over the first and lies down, and so on until all group members are lying down. After the last student lies down, he or she immediately gets back up and the process is reversed. When the activity is completed, students have zipped and unzipped the zipper. Zippers can race other zippers. (5-7 minutes)

6. Amoeba race. Divide students into groups of 10 to 12. Have two students in the middle of a circle and a third student on their shoulders. The remaining students, facing outward with linked elbows, form a circle. The nucleus (i.e., the person on top of shoulders in middle) can now guide the amoeba in racing other amoebas. (7-8 minutes)

Closure (3-5 Minutes)

Review the lesson with students. Use the following ideas to reinforce learning, check understanding, and provide feedback.

1. Discuss the role of cooperation and teamwork in completing each one of the activities.
2. Discuss the social benefits of participating in such games (e.g., working with teammates to achieve a common goal).

Resources

Glover, D.R., and D.W. Midura. 1992. *Team building through physical challenges*. Champaign, IL: Human Kinetics.

Troika Folk Dance

Purpose

In this lesson students learn a folk dance and increase cardiorespiratory fitness.

Warm-Ups (6-8 Minutes)

Prepare for the troika as a warm-up activity. (Use a drum to count out the 64 beats.)

> Take 16 short running steps forward starting with the right foot (16 counts).
>
> Take 8 short running steps in a circle to the left, then 8 short running steps in a circle to the right (16 counts).
>
> Take 12 short running steps in place; then stamp, stamp, stamp, and hold (16 counts).
>
> Take 12 short running steps in place; then clap, clap, clap, and hold (16 counts).
>
> Repeat entire sequence once.

Skill Cues

1. Take short running steps.
2. Lift the knees.
3. Hold the head and torso upright.

Teaching Cues

1. During the warm-up, beat the last count of the sequence heavily to signal the upcoming change.
2. In troika music, an 8-beat introduction precedes the 16-beat sequences.
3. Play the music and have the students listen for the changes or softly tap out the beat with the drum. Have them softly clap to the music and give a loud clap at the changes.

Safety Tips

- Dancing in socks could cause slips and falls in this fast-moving dance. Students should wear shoes or go barefoot.
- Because of the vigorous demands of the dance, a 1- or 2-minute rest between repeats is recommended.

4. Remind students not to stop during the short running steps throughout the dance.
5. *Troika* is a Russian word meaning "three horses." The dance steps are meant to resemble three prancing horses drawing a sleigh (for the Russian royal family).

Activities (30-40 Minutes)

1. Introduce the troika using the skill and teaching cues. (2-3 minutes)
2. Practice the troika without music. Using any combination of boys and girls, position students in groups of three with the tallest person in the center (creating the left, center, and right positions). Have them join inside hands; students on the outside put their outside hands on their hips. (6-8 minutes)

Troika

Skills: running step, stamp, clap, circle

Run 16 steps forward (start with the right foot).

Center and left dancers raise clasped hands to form an arch; right dancers move under the arch with 8 running steps; then center dancers follow under the arch while left dancers run in place.

Right and center dancers form an arch while left dancers move under the arch with 8 running steps; then center dancers follow under the arch while right dancers run in place.

All three dancers join hands to make a circle and run 12 steps to the left.

Stomp left, right, left; then hold.

Run 12 steps to the right, stomp right, stomp left, stomp right, and hold.

3. Have students perform the troika to music; then switch dance partners (i.e., new groups of three) and repeat. (10-12 minutes)
4. Add some variety by using the following alternative steps and combinations. (6-8 minutes)
   - The forward running steps can be 4 diagonally right, then 4 diagonally left, then 8 straight ahead.
   - After each sequence, students in the center can switch places with nearby students on the final stomp, stomp, stomp.
5. Divide students into small groups and let them create their own dance to the 64 beats using even locomotion movements (e.g., run, jump, hop, leap, step). Half of the class can demonstrate while the others watch. (6-9 minutes)

Closure (3-5 Minutes)

Review the lesson with students. Use the following questions and ideas to reinforce learning, check understanding, and provide feedback.

1. Discuss how the troika contributes to cardiorespiratory fitness, what makes it a fitness activity, and what makes it a dance.
2. Explore why dance is not perceived by most people as a demanding physical activity.
3. Discuss whether other sports require grace and efficiency of movement. Ask students the following questions: Does a baseball pitcher look awkward, or is there a flow to the pitching sequence that defines a beautiful delivery? What about the tennis serve? The football punt? The swimmer's dive? The basketball jump shot? The hurdler's stride?

Volleyball Baseball Basketball (VBB)

Purpose

This lesson uses selected volleyball, baseball, and basketball skills in a game situation.

Warm-Ups (6-8 Minutes)

1. Side slides
2. Push-ups
3. Quadriceps stretch
4. Hamstring curls
5. Step and calf taps

Skill Cues

1. Use an underhand volleyball serve (see volleyball lesson 1 on page 373).
2. Touch the inside of bases when running.

Teaching Cues

1. Position an official to see both home plate and the basketball goal.
2. To be in play, the ball should travel at least 20 feet (6.1 meters) forward.
3. Have shooters wear pinnies so that fielders can easily identify them.
4. Switch shooters each inning.
5. Alternate girls and boys in the batting order.
6. Increase or decrease the distance between bases if it is making it too easy or difficult to score.
7. Record the score where all can see it.

Facility and Equipment

- Gym or outdoor area with a hoop
- 1 volleyball
- 4 rubber bases
- 1 basketball hoop
- 3 pinnies
- Scoreboard

Safety Tips

- Place fielding students away from the bases to avoid collisions with runners.
- Keep second base away from the shooter's area.

Activities (30-40 Minutes)

1. Introduce the game of volleyball baseball basketball (VBB) and divide the class into two teams: fielders and batters. The fielding team places teammates throughout the gym area and designates three shooters who stand in the area of the basket. The batting team lines up away from the play field. (6-8 minutes)

2. Play VBB. (24-32 minutes)

Volleyball Baseball Basketball (VBB)

As its name implies, this is a combination of volleyball, baseball, and basketball. The basic game is as follows: A batter stands on home plate, serves (underhand) a volleyball, and then runs all the bases. The objective is to score a run, by making it back to home plate before the fielding team makes a basket. Once the batter serves the volleyball, fielders retrieve it and pass it to their designated shooters, who try to make a basket before the runner reaches home plate. If a basket is made, the runner is out. If a basket is not made and the runner makes it to home plate, a run is scored. After three outs, teams switch (i.e., fielders become batters and vice versa).

VBB has only a few simple rules:

▸ The batter may not stop when running the bases.

▸ Only the designated shooters (three per team) can shoot for the basket.

▸ The fielding team must make at least three passes before attempting a basket.

▸ Nothing is out-of-bounds after the ball travels 20 feet (6.1 meters).

Closure (3-5 Minutes)

Review the lesson with students. Use the following ideas to reinforce learning, check understanding, and provide feedback.

1. Discuss some tactics fielders used to increase their chance of getting a runner out.

2. Discuss some tactics hitters used to increase their chance of scoring a run.

Variations

1. Call an out for catching the ball on the fly.

2. Require students to run the bases holding hands with a partner.

Wall Ball

Purpose

In this lesson students learn the rules and play the game of wall ball.

Warm-Ups (6-8 Minutes)

1. Imaginary jump rope
2. Push-ups
3. High jumper
4. Mule leg pushes

Skill Cues

1. Throw the ball overhand.
2. A backspin or forward spin will make the ball more difficult to catch, as will using a throwing trajectory that causes the ball to bounce lower on the wall.
3. To prevent fumbles, use both hands to catch the ball.

Teaching Cues

1. Group students by ability to make play more challenging and engaging.
2. To increase understanding and speed up learning time, demonstrate skills and techniques while explaining the rules.
3. Set up court boundaries (i.e., line up cones on either side of each team's playing area) before class.

Facility and Equipment

- Gym or large outdoor playing area with a wall
- 1 tennis ball per court
- Cones

Note: Cones are used to designate court boundary lines; the number of cones will vary with the size of the playing area.

Safety Tips

- Do not allow students to purposely throw the ball at another player. Any dodge ball activity should result in a penalty or time out.
- A softer ball (e.g., a bouncy foam ball) can be used if safety becomes a factor.
- Space the mini courts far enough apart that players from one game will not collide with another.

Activities (30-40 Minutes)

1. Explain how to play wall ball using the appropriate skill and teaching cues. (2-3 minutes)
2. Divide the class into teams of 3 or 4 players and position 2 teams on a mini court against a wall. (2-3 minutes)
3. Explain the rules and play a game of wall ball. (18-24 minutes)

Wall Ball

The object is to throw the ball on the floor or ground, against the wall and away from the two opposing players within the boundaries. The ball can be caught by the thrower or another team member with one or no bounces. There are two ways that players can accumulate strikes.

- ▶ If a player throws the ball and it touches the floor or ground before it hits the wall, another team player must run to the wall before any remaining player throws the ball back to the wall. If the running player touches the wall before the ball hits the wall, he or she is safe and does not receive a strike.

- ▶ If a player drops the ball (a fumbling player) and it hits the floor or ground, the player who dropped the ball (a fumbling player) must run to the wall. If the fumbling player touches the wall before an opposing player throws the ball to the wall, he or she is safe and does not receive a strike.

In both situations, if the ball is thrown to the wall first, the running player receives one strike. When a player accumulates three strikes, he or she must trade places with another player in the group, or is out of the game for the next round.

4. After playing a full game, have students play a round-robin tournament with groups playing at other mini courts. (8-10 minutes)

Closure (3-5 Minutes)

Review the lesson with students. Use the following ideas to reinforce learning, check understanding, and provide feedback.

1. Discuss the strategies players can use to get a player out (e.g., throw the ball quickly so the other player has less time to react; throw the ball to different places on the wall—high, low, left, right—so the other player cannot anticipate where it will go).

2. Choose a skilled group to demonstrate a few minutes of wall ball.

Resources

Games Kids Play
www.gameskidsplay.net
   Posts rules of this and other fun games.

Appendix

Warm-Ups

Abdominal crunches. Lie face up with the legs extended toward the ceiling and the arms resting on the floor at the sides. Extend the arms upward while contracting the abdominal muscles to lift the head, neck, and shoulders off the floor. Reach toward the ceiling with the hands and feet.

Abdominal curls. Lie face up with the knees flexed, feet flat on the floor, and hands resting on the ears or clasped behind the head. Tilt the pelvis under to flatten the back on the floor. Using the abdominals (do not pull with the hands), lift the shoulders about 4 to 8 inches (10.2-20.3 centimeters) off the floor. Hold 3 seconds. Lower slowly; repeat several times.

Abdominal tighteners. Lie face up with the knees bent. Lower one leg and tap the toe on the floor while bringing the opposite knee toward the chest. Repeat with the other leg. Concentrate on keeping the lower back on the floor.

Achilles tendon stretch. Face a wall from about 2 feet (.61 meters) away. Rest the palms on the wall, take a step backward, and lean forward with the weight on the hands; then slowly lower one heel to the floor. Hold 15 seconds; then change legs and repeat.

Agility run. Run around cones arranged in a line (slalom) or a circle (inside or outside).

Alternate leg raises. Lie on the abdomen, the legs straight and together, one hand under the chin, and the other arm out to the side. Raise the left leg upward, keeping the knee straight. Then lower the left leg and repeat with the right leg.

Arm and leg lifts. Lie face down with the arms and legs extended. Lift the right arm and left leg 3 inches (7.6 centimeters) off the floor and hold 3 seconds; then lower the arm and leg. Repeat with the left arm and right leg.

Arm circles. Stand with the feet together, the back straight, and the arms extended upward. Bring each arm under and around in a front crawl motion. Reverse, using a back crawl motion.

Arm isometrics. Stand with the elbows bent 90 degrees at shoulder level and both palms touching. Push the hands against each other for 10 seconds; then interlock the fingers and pull the hands apart for 10 seconds.

Arm pumps. Holding the arms at shoulder level with the elbows out, punch one arm in the air, twisting the torso. Twist back, then punch with the other arm.

Arm rotators. Stand with the feet together, the back straight, and the arms extended out to the sides. Rotate the arms in forward circles. Gradually increase the size of the circles. Then reverse direction, rotating backward.

Arm support lifts. Lying face down with the forearms supporting the body, raise the hips off the floor. (Keep the knees on the floor while pushing downward with the lower arms.) Hold 15 seconds.

Back stretch. Stand tall with the right foot flat and the left leg extended slightly behind. Bend forward at the hips and extend the left leg straight back as far as possible while reaching forward with both arms. Keep the right heel and toes firmly planted and try to form a straight line from fingertips to toes of the left foot. Hold 15 seconds; then repeat, extending the right leg.

Body circles. Stand with the arms straight overhead. Move the arms clockwise, bending from the waist with the knees slightly bent. Complete a full circle using total range of movement, returning the arms to the overhead position. Repeat five circles; then reverse direction.

Crab walk. Supporting the weight on the hands and feet, and keeping the abdomen up, walk inverted on all fours.

Curl and stretch. On the hands and knees, slowly draw one knee to the chest and then extend the leg and touch the toe to the floor. Repeat with the other leg.

Curl-ups. Lie face up with the knees flexed, the feet flat on the floor and the arms folded across the chest. Curl up by bringing the head forward and pulling the upper body upward until the elbows touch the upper thighs. Uncurl back to the starting position, touching the floor first with the lower back, then the upper back, and finally the head.

Elbow-knee touches (standing). Stand with the hands clasped behind the head. Raise the left knee and touch the right elbow to it. (Stretch and reach, do not pull on the head.) Repeat with the opposite elbow and knee.

Elbow-knee touches (supine). Lie face up with the right knee flexed, the left heel on the right knee, and the hands clasped behind the head. Touch the right elbow to the left knee a few times. (Stretch and reach, do not pull on the head.) Repeat with the opposite elbow and knee.

Elbow squeezes. Stand tall with the feet together, the elbows bent, and the hands resting on each side of the back above the buttocks, the fingers pointing downward. Slowly press the elbows backward and inward, toward the spine. Hold 5 to 10 seconds.

Extended body leg drops. Lie face up with the knees pulled in toward the chest. Extend the arms straight out behind the head, palms up. Extend the right leg and lower it until the heel almost touches the floor. Draw the leg back to the starting position and perform the leg drop with the left leg.

Facedown flank. Kneel on the knees and elbows, clasping the hands in front. (The elbows should be directly below the shoulders.) Using the forearms and toes to balance, straighten the legs, one at a time. Hold 20 seconds.

Faceup flank. Sit with the legs extended in front. Rest back on the elbows, directly below the shoulders, with the palms to the sides and flat on the floor. Balancing on the heels and forearms, squeeze the hips and lift off the floor, the head dropping slightly backward. Hold 20 seconds.

Floor touches. From a standing position, step forward on the left foot and touch the fingers to the floor, keeping the back straight, the right knee down, and the head up (resembling a sprinter's starting position). Return to the upright position. Switch legs and repeat several times.

Forward lunges. From a standing position, step forward with the right foot into a forward stride position bending the right knee slightly. Keeping the weight on the right front foot and the left knee bent and parallel to but not touching the floor, hold the position for 6 seconds. Return to a standing position; then repeat with the left leg.

Gluteal stretch. Lie face up with the legs extended. Bring one knee (or both knees) to the chest and pull for a gentle stretch. Hold 5 seconds; then repeat with the opposite knee.

Grapevine step. Move sideways to the right by crossing the left leg in front of the right leg, the right behind the left; then the left behind right, the right in front of the left, and so on. (Keep the arms out for balance and rotate the body slightly with each step.) Reverse direction.

Hamstring conditioners. Lie face up with both knees bent and cross the right leg over the left leg, keeping the right leg bent at a 90-degree angle and resting above the left knee. Raise the toes of the left foot off the floor and place the weight of the leg on the heel. Crossing the arms over the chest and pushing the weight into the left heel, raise the hips so that only the shoulders and head are touching the floor. Hold 6 seconds; then repeat with the opposite leg.

Hamstring curls. Kneel on all fours. Lift the right leg, keeping it horizontal (parallel to the floor), and flex the left knee to straighten the left leg (perpendicular to the floor) and bring the hips upward. (Keep the back straight.) Repeat several times; then switch legs.

Hamstring straight-leg stretch. Lie face up with one leg flexed and the foot flat on the floor. Stretch the other leg straight up, place the hands behind the upper calf, and pull to a gentle stretch.

Heel lifts. Starting from a standing position, feet slightly apart, lift the heels from the floor and balance on the toes. (Tighten the abdominal muscles to maintain the balance.) Hold 15 seconds.

High jumper. In a crouch position with the knees flexed and the arms down and extended backward, jump as high as possible, raising the arms overhead.

Hip extenders. Lie face up with the right leg straight and the left leg bent. Hold the left leg under the knee with the right arm, and pull it toward the right shoulder for a gentle stretch in the left hip and back. Hold 5 seconds; then repeat with the opposite leg.

Hip lifts. Lie face up with the knees flexed, the feet flat on the floor, and the arms at the sides with palms down. Press the feet into the floor and slowly push the hips and back upward until the body is supported by the shoulders, head, and feet. Repeat.

Hip rolls. Lie face up with the arms down at the sides and the knees flexed and drawn up over the chest. Gently roll to the right until the right thigh touches the floor or the right forearm. (Keep the back and shoulders on the floor.) Continue rolling to the left and right.

Hip stretch. Sit with the soles of the feet together, the back straight, and the hands inside the thighs holding the toes and feet together. Slowly press the knees toward the floor. Hold 5 seconds.

Horizontal run. With knees slightly bent and hands on the floor, run quickly on all fours. Reverse direction on signal.

Imaginary jump rope. Jog while rotating the arms as if jumping rope. (Keep the arms flexed.)

Note: For a greater challenge, use different jumping patterns (e.g., hop twice on one foot and then twice on the other).

Inverted hurdler's stretch. Sit with the left leg extended forward and the right leg flexed inward with the sole of the right foot positioned against the left inner thigh. Slowly bend forward, stretching the trunk, and reach with both hands toward the left foot. After a few repetitions, perform the stretch extending the right leg.

Jump rope or jump rope laps. Jump rope in place, or skip quickly or slowly around the perimeter of the gym, field, or court.

Knee lifts. Stand with the feet together and the hands on the hips. Lift the right leg forward, flexing at the knee so that the hip and knee form a 90-degree angle. Hold 3 seconds; then lower the right foot to the floor. Repeat using the left leg.

Lateral hops. Stand with the feet together and weight on the right leg. Clasp the hands behind the buttocks. Pushing off with the right foot, hop sideways onto the left foot and bring the right foot to rest next to the left calf. Maintain balance for 5 seconds; then return to the starting position. Repeat on opposite side.

Leg lifts. Lie face down with the hands crossed under the chin. Slowly lift one leg from the hip, keeping the leg straight, and return it slowly to the floor. Repeat several times; then switch legs.

Leg stretch. Stand on the floor in front of a chair. Place one foot on the chair and straighten out the leg. Slowly stretch forward to touch the toes with both hands. Hold 15 seconds; then repeat with the other leg.

Lower back stretch. Kneel on the knees and outstretch the arms on the floor in front. Push backward and upward with the hips, raising them toward the ceiling. Push the chest downward, toward the floor, while lifting the elbows off the floor and straightening the arms. Hold 30 seconds.

Mad cat. Kneeling on all fours, stretch the back upward, holding the stretch at its highest point for 5 seconds. Return to the starting position.

Mule leg pushes. Kneel and rest the forearms on the floor. Push the right leg backward and upward until straight. (Use the forearms for support and balance.) Hold 5 seconds; then switch legs.

Neck stretch. While standing or sitting, slowly bend the neck from side to side, then from front to back. (Do not do head circles.)

Phalange flings. Stand with the arms out to the side at shoulder height and the fingers extended. Make a fist and thrust the fingers outward. Repeat with the arms extended in front, down at the sides, and overhead.

Push-offs. Stand facing a wall. Place the hands flat against the wall with the arms straight. Hold the body rigid while bending the arms fully and leaning into the wall. Push back to the starting position by straightening the arms.

Push-up hold. Lie face down in a starting push-up position with the forearms flat on the floor and the hands at the shoulders. Supporting the body with the forearms and toes, lift the torso until the body forms a straight line from shoulders to heels. Hold 6 seconds; then lower to the floor and repeat.

Push-ups. In a prone position with the hands about shoulder-width apart and the feet together, push the body upward by extending the arms, keeping the back and legs aligned and straight. (Try not to lock the elbows on the extension.) Lower to the starting position and repeat.

Note: Push-ups can also be done on the hands and knees (keep the feet lifted off the floor) or with elevated hands (e.g., place the hands on the lower step of a bleacher, or on a bench, and do a push-up).

Quadriceps stretch. Place the left hand against a wall and use the right hand to gently pull the right foot toward the buttocks, keeping the back straight. Repeat with the left leg.

Note: For greater challenge, use the right hand to pull the left foot toward the buttocks, and then the left hand to pull the right foot.

Reverse run. Run in one direction; then, at the signal, switch directions quickly.

Running in place. Keeping the upper body erect, run in place. (Push the knees upward high while running.) Increase or decrease speed as desired.

Russian floor kicks. Sit down, resting back on the elbows and forearms. Flex the knees and alternate kicking the legs upward and downward, keeping them straight.

Scissors. Start with one leg forward and one leg back, one arm outstretched in front and one arm down at the side. Simultaneously shift the front leg backward and the back leg forward while shifting the arms up to down and down to up. Continue rapidly.

Seated hamstring stretch. Sit on the floor with the back straight and the left leg extended forward. Flex the right knee and place the right hand on the knee. Extend the left arm forward and lean forward (keeping the back straight) for a gentle stretch. Repeat several times, then switch legs.

Shoulder pushes. From a standing position, extend the arms down and behind, interlocking the fingers behind the back. Push upward and backward with the shoulders.

Shoulder shrugs. From a standing position, raise the shoulders as high as possible; then lower the shoulders, stretching the neck. Pull the shoulders back; then round the shoulders forward.

Shoulder stretch. Stand with the right arm straight across the chest, holding it with the left arm. Pull the right arm slowly to the left for a gentle stretch. Hold 10 seconds; then switch arms.

Side arm push-ups. Lie on one side with the bottom arm supporting the bodyweight. Cross the top leg over the bottom leg, keeping both legs straight. Lift the hips off the floor, keeping the arm straight. Hold 5 seconds; then repeat on the opposite side.

Side lunges. Stand with the right foot diagonally forward, the left leg straight and facing forward. Slowly lunge sideways over the right foot, flexing the knee over and directly above the foot and stretching both arms in the same direction. (Keep the back straight.) Repeat using the left foot.

Side pattern jumps. Stand with the feet together. Step out with the right foot while lifting and stretching the arms outward. Step back; then step out with the left foot. Increase the pace to the speed used in jumping jacks.

Side slides. Take 5 slides to the left, then 5 slides to the right as quickly as possible.

Side stretch. Stand with the right hand on the right hip. While raising the heels to stand on tiptoes, stretch the left arm upward and over the right side of the body. (Watch the hand as it reaches toward the ceiling.) Hold 3 seconds; then repeat the stretch using the right arm.

Single-leg crossovers. Lie face up with the arms outstretched at the sides, palms down, and the legs extended. Lift the right leg straight up, pointing the toes, and slowly cross the right leg over to the left side until the right foot touches the floor. Slowly lift the right leg back up, keeping it straight; then lower the leg to the starting position. Switch legs.

Single-leg curls. Sit with the legs extended in front and the hands on the floor behind for support. Bring one knee to the chest; then bring the other knee to the chest.

Single-leg wall squat lifts. Stand with the feet together and the back pressed firmly against a wall. Walk the feet out two small steps so that the knees are above the feet and slightly lower than the hips. Exhale, tighten the abdominals, and lift one foot 6 to 8 inches (15.2-20.3 centimeters) off the floor. (Keep the abdominals tight and the head and shoulders level.) Hold 10 seconds. Lower the foot to the floor and slide back up the wall to the starting position. Repeat, lifting the other foot.

Sit and curl. Sit with the legs crossed and the arms folded across the chest. Tuck the chin and curl forward, trying to touch the forehead to the knees. Hold 4 seconds; then curl back to the starting position.

Sit and stretch. Sit with the knees bent and the soles of the feet together. Slowly lean forward as far as possible. (Keep the back straight.)

Sit-ups. Lie face up with the knees bent 90 degrees, the feet flat on the floor, and the hands over the ears. Sit up without jerking or raising the feet. Slowly curl back down; then repeat.

Note: If the sit-up is too difficult, fold the arms across the chest or stretch the arms out straight in front.

Slapping jacks. From a standing position, hop on one foot and kick the other leg outward, clapping the hands under the raised leg; then kick the other leg. (Keep the back straight and head upright.) Continue hopping on alternate legs.

Spinal curls. Lie face up with the hands under the buttocks and the knees flexed. Slowly draw both knees toward and then away from the chest. Return to the starting position and repeat.

Spinal rotations. Lie face up with the hands out to the sides. Flex and raise the left leg; then roll it over the right leg to the point of a gentle stretch. (Keep the right leg straight.) Hold the stretch for 10 seconds; then switch legs.

Sprint-jog intervals. Alternate between running at full speed for a short distance and jogging for a long distance.

Squat holds. From a squat position with the feet apart, raise both arms toward the ceiling. (Keep the knees aligned over the feet; tighten the abdominal muscles to support the back.) Hold 15 seconds.

Step and calf taps. Step quickly in place, tapping the right hand on the inside calf of the right leg as it comes up, then tapping the left hand on the inside calf of the left leg as it comes up. (Keep the back straight, the head upright, and the abdomen flat.)

Step touches. Step to the right with the right foot, bringing the left toe close to the right foot; then step with the left foot to the side, bringing the right toe close to the left foot. Increase the intensity by increasing the speed or lifting the knees higher during the steps.

Toe lifts. Starting from a standing position with the feet slightly apart, lift the toes and balance on the heels. (Tighten the glutei while balancing.) Hold 6 seconds.

Triceps dips. Sit on the edge of a bench or chair, the heels on the floor about 6 inches (15.2 centimeters) in front of the knees. Place the hands on the seat edge with the fingers pointing downward. With straight arms, shift the body forward until the hips clear the front of the seat. Exhale and bend the elbows until the upper arms are almost level with the shoulders and parallel to the floor. Pause, inhale, and press back upward. (Keep the lower back and hips close to the bench with the elbows back.) Repeat.

Triceps stretch. From a standing position, bring the right arm overhead while flexing the elbow. Use the left hand to pull the right arm behind the head to a gentle stretch.

Hold 10 seconds; then release the stretch. Repeat using the left arm.

Upper body rotations. From a standing position, clasp the hands together close to the chest at shoulder height. Rotate the upper body to the right and then to the left, trying not to rotate the hips.

V-sit toe taps. Start in a V-sit position, leaning back to support the body with the arms. Bend the knees and pull them toward the chest. Lower the right foot and tap the right toe on the floor; then bring the right knee back to the chest. Tap the right toe 12 times; then tap the left toe.

Waist twists. Stand with the arms out to the sides at shoulder height. Keeping the arms spread apart, rotate left at the waist so that the left arm is behind the back. (Do not hyperextend; keep the hips stationary and facing square to the front.) Rotate back to the front; then rotate the arms to the right.

Wrist rotation and flexion. Stand with the arms out to the sides at shoulder height, palms up. Rotate the hands forward, then backward; upward, then downward. Repeat with the arms out in front, down at the sides, and overhead.

About the Authors

Dorothy B. Zakrajsek

Dorothy Zakrajsek, PhD, is a retired educator who taught secondary physical education for 9 years, supervised student teachers for 7 years, and taught secondary physical education methods for 18 years. Zakrajsek has used her extensive experience to coauthor 6 textbooks and write more than 70 journal articles. She has also given more than 100 state, national, and international presentations, including more than a dozen keynote addresses.

Zakrajsek has received Honor Awards from the American Alliance for Health, Physical Education, Recreation and Dance (AAHPERD) University Administrators and from AAHPERD's Curriculum and Instruction Academy. She also has received an Appreciation Citation from New York AHPERD. She is a member of AAHPERD, the National Association for Sport and Physical Education (NASPE), the AAHPERD Curriculum and Instruction Academy, and the American Association for Active Lifestyles and Fitness (AAALF).

Lois A. Carnes

Lois A. Carnes, MEd, is a physical education teacher in Solon (Ohio) City Schools. Carnes has coauthored four other physical education curriculum textbooks and has written articles for numerous physical education journals. She has taught for more than 25 years at various grade levels (including the university level), and she served for 4 years on the editorial board of the journal *Teaching Elementary Physical Education.* Carnes has made numerous presentations on physical education curriculum content and methodology and is a member of AAHPERD, NASPE, and the AAHPERD Joint Projects Committee. She helped develop physical education curriculum for Solon City Schools. Among her many awards are Teacher of the Year from Ohio AHPERD, a Meritorious Award from Ohio AHPERD, and a Golden Apple Achievement Award in recognition of superior teaching.

Frank E. Pettigrew, Jr.

Frank E. Pettigrew Jr., PhD, is the dean of the college of education and a professor of sport sciences at Ashland University in Ashland, Ohio. He has taught undergraduate and graduate courses in physical and sport education. He previously directed the school of exercise, leisure and sport at Kent State University. Dr. Pettigrew is a fellow of the AAHPERD research consortium and a member of the OAHPERD state association. He also serves as a sport consultant for several school districts in Ohio.

Quality Lesson Plans for Secondary Physical Education, Second Edition CD-ROM can be used on either a Windows-based PC or a Macintosh computer.

Minimum System Requirements

Microsoft Windows

- ▶ IBM PC compatible with Pentium processor
- ▶ Windows 98/2000/XP/Vista
- ▶ Adobe Reader 8.0
- ▶ Microsoft PowerPoint
- ▶ Microsoft Word
- ▶ 4x CD-ROM drive

Macintosh

- ▶ Power Mac recommended
- ▶ System 10.4 or higher
- ▶ Adobe Reader
- ▶ Microsoft PowerPoint
- ▶ Microsoft Word
- ▶ 4x CD-ROM drive

Getting Started

Microsoft Windows

1. Insert the *Quality Lesson Plans for Secondary Physical Education CD-ROM* (Note: the CD-ROM must be present in the drive at all times.)
2. Select the "My Computer" icon from the desktop.
3. Select the CD-ROM drive.
4. Open the file you wish to view. See the "00Start.pdf" file for a list of the contents.

Macintosh

1. Insert the *Quality Lesson Plans for Secondary Physical Education CD-ROM* (Note: the CD-ROM must be present in the drive at all times.)
2. Double-click on the CD icon on the desktop.
3. Open the file you wish to view. See the "00Start" file for a list of the contents.

For product information or customer support:

E-mail: support@hkusa.com
Phone: 217-351-5076
Fax: 217-351-2674
Web site: **www.HumanKinetics.com**